AMERICAN STATES AND CITIES

Second Edition

VIRGINIA GRAY
University of Minnesota

PETER EISINGER
University of Wisconsin

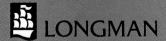
LONGMAN

An imprint of Addison Wesley Longman, Inc.

New York • Reading, Massachusetts • Menlo Park, California • Harlow, England
Don Mills, Ontario • Sydney • Mexico City • Madrid • Amsterdam

Editor in Chief: Priscilla McGeehon
Developmental Editor: Julie Martin
Project Coordination: Electronic Publishing Services Inc.
Text Design: Electronic Publishing Services Inc.
Cover Designer: Kay Petronio
Cover Photograph: Photonica Inc.
Art Studio: Electronic Publishing Services Inc.
Photo Researcher: Diane Kraut
Electronic Production Manager: Christine Pearson
Manufacturing Manager: Helene G. Landers
Electronic Page Makeup: R. R. Donnelley & Sons
Printer and Binder: R. R. Donnelley & Sons
Cover Printer: Phoenix Color Corp.

Library of Congress Cataloging-in-Publication Data

Gray, Virginia.
    American states and cities / Virgina Gray, Peter Eisinger. — 2nd
  ed.
      p. cm.
    Includes bibliographical references and index.
    ISBN 0-673-52461-2 (hc)
    1. State governments—United States.   2. Local government—United
  States.   3. Municipal government—United States.   I. Eisinger,
  Peter K.   II. Title.
  JK2408.G734   1997
  353.9—DC20   96-28150
                                                                  CIP

ISBN 0-673-52461-2

45678910—DOC—99

For Brian

and

For Jesse and Sarah

✧

CONTENTS

PART FOUR
LOCAL GOVERNMENT INSTITUTIONS   231

PART SIX
THE FUTURE   471

PREFACE

In the American political system these days, state capitals are where the action is. Perhaps it is the partisan gridlock in Washington, D.C.; perhaps it is a deeper and longer-running public disillusionment with big central government that has deprived Congress and the president of the ability to lead. Certainly some of the shift of energy in the political system lies in the large ongoing federal deficit, which diminishes the resources Washington can devote to helping states and localities. Whatever the causes, states have been taking the lead throughout the 1990s in the development of public policy in areas ranging from welfare to crime fighting to education. It is not at all unusual these days for members of Congress to sit and listen respectfully to governors instructing them on how to reform Medicaid, welfare, or some other federal program.

State governments have taken on the responsibility for policy innovation in part because federal inaction left a void. Now, however, this shift in the balance of policy responsibility is being institutionalized, as the "Devolution Express"[1] gains steam. Congress is determined to pass back or devolve authority to the states. By the century's end, it is likely that the states, not Washington, will be responsible for welfare, social services for the poor, some food assistance to the hungry, and Medicaid, among other programs. All this suggests that state governments are increasingly important institutions in the American political system, and state politics is likely to be exciting to watch and study over the next decade.

Much the same can be said about local government. Although formal devolution will probably not affect municipal governments directly, they are certainly the locus of a good deal of policy invention and activity. Local policy leadership can be observed in key areas such as economic development, education, policing, and land use regulation. Furthermore, local governments hold out real possibilities for democratic participation, an important characteristic in an age of citizen suspicion of big and distant government.

The remarkable combination of the sheer excitement of change, variety, and experimentation in state and local government with the obvious importance to our collective lives of decisions made in these arenas has sustained our respective commitments over nearly three decades of teaching and research to the study of subnational politics. Years of teaching undergraduates have helped us to refine our ideas about what is important for students to know about politics in our states and communities. These ideas led to the first edition of this book and now to this revised second edition.

---

[1]Neal Peirce, "A Bigger Bang for the Welfare Buck?," *National Journal* (February 17, 1996), 384.

The present version retains the basic framework of the first edition, but the material has been substantially revised, updated, and expanded. We have added entirely new chapters on the state bureaucracy and on community power and local economic restructuring. The two policy chapters of the first edition have been expanded to four chapters, with much more thorough coverage of various issues.

Our purpose remains to provide a sophisticated introduction to the structure of government, the patterns of politics, and the major policy issues of state and local government in a coherent framework that organizes the material and helps us to understand the dynamic forces in subnational politics.

The framework we use is drawn from Albert Hirschman's work, in which he observes that deterioration of performance in firms or other organizations (such as states or cities) may induce some members (or citizens) to leave the organization. He calls this the exit option. Others do not leave, preferring instead to "express their dissatisfaction directly to management"—*the voice option.*[2] In considering the dynamics of subnational politics, we were struck with how much could be understood in these terms.

For one thing, people and businesses move all the time, and a good deal of state and local politics is a response to or product of this movement. At least some migration of people and firms is a response to deterioration or less-than-ideal local conditions: People move or exit to suburbs to escape crime and to take advantage of better schools, firms move out of one state to another to seek lower taxes and cheaper labor, businesses move to less congested communities to gain office space and parking, unemployed factory workers migrate from depressed regions of the country to places where the economy is booming, and so on. Much public policy in states and cities, as we shall see, is designed to prevent such out-migration and induce in-migration. Places see themselves in competition with other areas for taxpayers, workers, businesses, and "good citizens." Growth is seen as good and decline as bad.

Not everyone moves or exits, of course, or even contemplates movement. But not everyone who stays is necessarily happy or satisfied. Some who do not like their current situation complain "directly to the management," as Hirschman would say, which in politics means running for office, supporting challengers, engaging in protest, writing letters to the mayor or the local state legislator, or joining reform or neighborhood organizations. Even the simple act of voting is a form of exercising voice. The state and local arenas are our great forums for democratic politics. Even though many decline to take part, the democratic possibilities are manifest. Here is a political setting of human dimensions, government on a scale that ordinary people can understand and influence. In town and city politics, people quite literally confront one another, giving voice to their opinions and concerns.

Political issues have a real immediacy at the state and local level. Fishing and hunting regulations inspire great passion in our respective states of Wisconsin and Minnesota. In other states the issues range from support for the university system to farmland preservation to affirmative action policies to relief from heavy property tax burdens to control of illegal immigration. State government is a presence in people's lives in a way that Washington is not. In local politics, real quality of daily life issues are at stake: How can

---

[2]Albert O. Hirschman, *Exit, Voice, and Loyalty: Responses to Decline in Firms, Organizations, and States* (Cambridge, Mass.: Harvard University Press, 1970), p. 5.

airport noise be stopped? Can the police really get rid of the drug traffic on the corner? Is there anything the city can do to house the homeless people who sleep in the public park? Will city or county zoning laws protect the last remaining wetlands in the area? Can the city afford to build a new public library, replacing the one with the ancient reading room, dim lights, and dusty stacks? Should children still be bused to achieve racial integration or should school attendance be based on neighborhood residence?

To speak of the democratic possibilities of state and local politics is not simply to consider the kinds of issues that people debate and the possibility for face-to-face debate and confrontation. It is also to speak of the broad possibilities for leadership. The lower the level of government, the more open it is to groups that have never traditionally wielded authority. Thus, the political careers of Christine Todd Whitman, the first female governor of New Jersey, Dennis Archer, the second black mayor of Detroit and a former justice on the Michigan Supreme Court, Michael Woo, the first Asian American to run for mayor of Los Angeles, are very much products of the state and local political opportunity structure. National politics, though more open than it once was, is still less accessible to nonwhite and female political aspirants. If the many races, ethnic groups, and social classes of the United States are to accommodate one another with respect and mutual tolerance, they will learn to do so first in the metropolitan areas and state capitols, where they can speak with one another face to face.

Our text weaves themes of geographic mobility, competition for resources among states and cities, patterns of voice or political activity, and opportunity as we trace the various aspects of state and local government, politics, and public policy. No text can be comprehensive, of course. But ours attempts a broad view, offering students a challenging and up-to-date exploration of subnational political processes and institutions.

We have received a good deal of help in writing this second edition. Some of the boxed material that appears throughout the book was written by University of Minnesota graduate students Rowzat Shipchandler, David Peterson, and Stacey Hecht. Other boxes were written by Bob Turner, a political science graduate student at the University of Wisconsin. We are grateful for their excellent and imaginative contributions. Stacey Hecht also helped to secure permissions, and Mike Solorza helped with research assistance. As with the first edition, Glen Halva-Neubauer of Furman University wrote the instructor's manual.

Various reviewers around the country provided thoughtful critiques. They have surely improved this book, and we are grateful for their help. They include: Professor William Boone, Clark-Atlanta College; Professor Carl Anthony Wege, Brunswick College; Professor Henry Carrier, Brevard Community College; Professor James Gimpel, University of Maryland; Professor John Portz, Northeastern University; and Professor Jon Baker, Wittenburg University. Finally, we wish to thank Julie Martin, our able Developmental Editor; Rob Anglin, our Production Editor; Carol Anne Peschke, for her fine copyediting; Diane Kraut, for her excellent photo research; and Leo Wiegman, our editor, for his steady encouragement and faith in this second edition and for buying us an occasional nice lunch.

VIRGINIA GRAY

PETER EISINGER

PART ONE

THE SETTING

✦

AMERICAN SUBNATIONAL GOVERNMENT IN THE 1990S

Thirty years ago many people believed that state governments in the American political system were obsolete. "It is a matter of brutal record," wrote one political scientist, "the American state is finished."[1] This conviction stemmed in part from the apparent inability or unwillingness of the states to deal with the emergence in the 1960s of a host of issues—racial disadvantage, deteriorating housing and central business districts, crime, crumbling public school systems, poverty, traffic congestion, pollution, and so on—that came to be known as "urban problems." Even state politicians doubted the capacity of the states to govern effectively. In his book *Storm Over the States*, former North Carolina governor Terry Sanford conceded that the states were antiquated, timid, ineffective, unresponsive, and unwilling to face their problems.[2]

Additional impetus for the belief that the states were no longer vital partners in the American federal arrangement was provided by the legislative whirlwind in Washington during Lyndon Johnson's presidency in the 1960s, during which the national government seemed to take responsibility for every domestic problem under the sun. Under the banner of the **Great Society,** Congress passed programs to address poverty, mass transit, community development, housing, medical care for the poor and aged, youth employment, primary education, racial discrimination, and public safety. Many of these programs provided federal grants directly to city governments, either bypassing the states altogether or minimizing their role.

This is not to suggest, however, that people thought that city governments had a vital future. Some believed that big cities in the United States had become ungovernable.[3] Others argued that Americans had better get used to the idea that cities could die: The social and physical deterioration of some old urban centers such as Newark seemed to some to be a terminal condition, leading William Baer to suggest that the most accurate metaphor for urban America was the cemetery.[4] When black Americans began to win the mayoralties of some major cities in the late 1960s and early 1970s, critics declared that city hall was a hollow prize. City governments, buffeted by great economic and demographic forces beyond their control, were powerless to affect the quality of life of their residents. Winning local office was almost pointless.

How matters had changed by the 1990s: Signs of vibrancy, activism, and innovation were the hallmarks of state and local governments. State government has emerged as the source of important domestic policy experiments in a whole range of areas. Welfare is a good example. Arguing that Washington could not reform our expensive and arguably ineffective welfare system, the states took the lead in experimenting with new programs, although, as one scholar points out, these experiments have the look of a "race to the bottom," with each state trying to be more restrictive than the others.[5] Wisconsin established a controversial reputation as a leader in trying to wean people from welfare and discourage in-migration from other states to take advantage of the state's relatively generous benefits. For example, the state implemented programs that penalize families where children are habitual truants, require welfare recipients to work at least 20 hours a week, and provide new arrivals to the state for the first 6 months with welfare checks no larger than they would have gotten in their state of origin.[6] But Wisconsin was not alone: At least 40 other states were engaged in welfare experiments that encouraged recipients to work, attend school, practice family planning, and get married.

City governments are keeping pace with the states as policy activists in a variety of areas. Long before the Clinton administration embarked on its National Performance Review to "reinvent" government, cities such as Indianapolis and Milwaukee were experimenting successfully with privatizing public services and installing quality management techniques. Other cities were winning recognition for their successful revitalization. St. Louis and Cleveland, for example, were both said to be on the verge of death in the 1970s, but urban planners now point to dramatic new development in these places, the product of effective partnerships between city government and private investors and corporations. St. Louis government and business leaders revived the core of the city—from Gateway Arch on the Mississippi River to the old railroad station—into a vibrant festival marketplace.[7] Cleveland's dramatic lakefront is the site of a new baseball stadium, a national rock and roll museum, and new business investment.

Welfare reform, reinventing government, and urban revitalization are just three examples among many of policy leadership and energy at the subnational level in the United States. It is important to acknowledge that none of these stories of vigorous innovation is meant to suggest that state and city governments have met and conquered every problem. American governments have certainly not eliminated poverty, environmental pollution, homelessness, crime, drug abuse, decaying bridges, traffic jams, and unemployment. But what we do argue in this volume is that for the most part, state and local governments have increasingly taken on major responsibility in the American system for domestic policy innovation and implementation, and in doing so they are making imaginative and important contributions to the nation's well-being. To understand the important role of states and cities in designing and implementing public policy, it is necessary to explore the context of subnational politics, the participants in the state and local political process, and the institutional framework within which political conflict and debate occur.

✧ WHY IT IS IMPORTANT TO STUDY STATE AND LOCAL GOVERNMENT

Subnational governments are worthy of study for their sheer diversity of form and approach to the governmental function. After all, there are 50 state governments and more than 86,000 local ones, and even within categories their differences are sometimes startling. These governments also command study because they have become critically important as the providers of basic services and the generators of solutions to collective problems in society. We explore these ideas in more detail by looking at six particular roles that state and local governments play: They are major crucibles of democratic politics; they are, collectively, very big government spenders and employers; they are increasingly key players in the federal system; they are perhaps the prime policy laboratories of the American political system; they are the providers of essential public services; and they are important training grounds for political leadership.

Crucibles of Democratic Politics

In what setting, a famous political scientist once asked, can opportunities for extensive political participation be maximized without trivializing the scope of the collective decisions reached?[8] Certainly not in the modern nation-state. Decisions are scarcely trivial—they deal with peace and war and environmental and economic well-being—but opportunities for individual participation in those decisions are few and indirect. Nations are simply too big. People rarely know their national leaders, nor do they have much chance of achieving a position of political influence. It is difficult in the large nation-state to hold our leaders accountable.

In contrast, towns, cities, and even city neighborhoods are ideal units for democratic politics. A recent study of neighborhood political organizations in cities such as Dayton, Ohio, and Birmingham, Alabama, concluded that such groups "clearly opened up broad avenues for ongoing citizen involvement in policymaking, extending far beyond that which is possible through electoral politics."[9]

Decisions made at the local level are important, for they bear on concerns that affect the very quality of life: land use, job opportunities, education, public health, and public safety. In contrast to the nation-state, however, it is easy to take part in politics by doing more than just casting a ritual vote every four years. Even though most places are no longer governed in the style of the New England town meeting, where the entire citizenry assembles to debate and vote on the major issues confronting the village, even in bigger cities it is not hard to find opportunities to have one's say. Indeed, it is not unusual to run for office and win (or to know people who do) or to gain a reputation as a neighborhood leader or to earn appointment to a city board, task force, or commission.

Although the city is thought by many to be the ideal setting for democratic politics, a conviction that has prevailed in Western thought from the ancient Greeks through Rousseau, much the same could be said of state politics. Of course, the physical distances separating citizens are greater than in the city, but states are nevertheless more politically intimate communities than the nation. Whereas presidential candidates are distant figures rushing by in motorcades, whose visits to places are keyed to the size of the television market, candidates for governor still drive or even bicycle across states, and they meet with citizens without the phalanx of Secret Service guardians who stand between would-be presidents and the people.

Cities and, to a somewhat lesser degree, states are important settings for the practice of political democracy. Opportunities for citizen participation and influence are higher than in the national arena, and people are more likely to know their leaders and, if they wish, achieve office.

Big Spenders and Employers

In 1993 total state and local government spending amounted to about $900 billion. This sum represented 13.9 percent of the Gross Domestic Product (GDP), up from 12.4 percent on the eve of Ronald Reagan's presidency in 1980.[10] Much of this goes for direct services such as highways, public education, welfare, corrections, policing, and public health. Although some of the costs for these functions are borne by the federal government through its system of intergovernmental grants, the major portion of the bill is footed by state and local taxpayers.

Much of the money spent by the various levels of government goes toward public employee salaries and benefits. Excluding the military services, nearly 19 million people in the United States work for some level of government. By far the largest number—over 11 million—work for local governments. (About half of these local government employees work for school districts and 2.7 million are employed by municipal governments.) Another 4.6 million people work for state governments. The federal government workforce of just over 3 million is small by comparison. State government employment grew at an average annual rate almost seven times faster than the federal workforce from 1982 to 1992, while the number of local government workers increased three times as fast as the federal workforce. In fact, in the 1990s, the size of the federal workforce actually declined, with almost 300,000 jobs cut as a result of President Clinton's National Performance Review.[11]

Clearly, state and local governments, both collectively and individually, are major economic actors, and their importance is increasing. Their spending decisions, which determine the size of their payrolls, the goods and services they purchase from the private sector, and the size of the tax levy they need to finance these expenditures, bear directly on the well-being of individuals, communities, and businesses.

Crucial Players in the Federal System

In a whole range of areas of public concern, the balance of initiative and responsibility has shifted from the shoulders of Washington to those of the states and localities. A persistent theme in the analysis of the federal system focuses on the combination of forces—particularly the federal deficit and the ideological commitment in Washington beginning in the Reagan years to a less active national government—that have led in domestic policymaking to a withdrawal of federal resources, interest, and attention, and the efforts of the subnational governments to fill the vacuum.

When President Reagan took office in 1981, for example, the U.S. Department of Justice became far less active in pursuing antitrust suits designed to maintain competition in the marketplace. As American business embarked on an era of mergers and acquisitions, state antitrust programs, almost nonexistent as recently as the 1960s, came into full force. Now the states are at the forefront in antitrust litigation.[12]

In the 1980s state supreme courts also became more important than the federal courts in extending individual rights, leading some jurists to proclaim a new era of state court activism. In a typical case, the California Supreme Court ruled that the owner of a shopping mall could not bar students from distributing pamphlets there because it violated the state's free speech guarantee. In a similar case not long before, the U.S. Supreme Court had ruled in favor of the mall owner.[13]

State and local efforts to pick up where the federal government has backed off are common in many areas of public policy. "With the federal government retrenching from a leadership role in the provision of low-income housing," write two housing policy analysts, "state and local governments and private sector interests are finding ways to fill the gap," including the establishment of state grants to rehabilitate rental housing, state and local mortgage subsidy programs, and state trust funds for housing-related activities.[14] In fact, most low-income housing these days is financed and managed by local community development corporations, nonprofit organizations that borrow money or raise it through foundations to invest in their communities.

Despite the increase in state and local responsibilities, many functions are still performed intergovernmentally. That is, federal, state, and local governments work as partners, sharing funding, planning, oversight, and implementation. Even as local a function as education is still an intergovernmental function.

However, one looks at the different roles of subnational governments—as increasingly energetic and independent actors or as important partners with Washington—it is clear that state and local governments are key players in the federal system.

Laboratories of Democracy

"It is one of the happy incidents of the federal system," U.S. Supreme Court Justice Louis Brandeis wrote during the Great Depression, "that a single courageous state may, if its citizens choose, serve as a laboratory, and try novel social and economic experiments without risk to the rest of the country."[15] Brandeis based his observation on the efforts of progressive reformers who managed to put into practice in a few states programs for unemployment compensation, old age insurance, and bank deposit insurance, among other things, before the federal government acted in these areas. These programs became models for the national programs enacted in the 1930s.

Today the states and their local governments are still policy **laboratories of democracy** in a wide array of areas. Cynics are fond of saying that government workers are just putting in their time, that they become lazy and complacent because they have no competition to worry about, and that they become wedded to outmoded ways of doing things because that represents the path of least resistance. But the fact is that state and local government bureaucrats and elected officials are inveterate tinkerers and inventors. Far from being satisfied with the old ways of doing things, they are constantly experimenting and innovating.

Over the last dozen years or so the most imaginative innovations by state and local public officials have been recognized in an annual competition run by the John F. Kennedy School at Harvard and the Ford Foundation. Each year, over 1,500 government agencies submit their innovative programs to the competition. In a rigorous process of judging, 10 are finally chosen as winners and another 20 are selected as runners-up. These programs include

✧ The St. Louis Police Department Computer Assisted Report Entry, which allows officers to phone in reports with a computer in a fraction of the time it took to do written reports

✧ The state of Michigan's Family Learning Center, which brings counseling and support services into schools for pregnant teens to help keep them in school

✧ The Pacific Northwest Economic Region's CATALIST program, which faxes carefully targeted export and domestic business leads to business firms all over the Northwest

✧ The state of Wisconsin's eight-state consortium that created a big market for recycled xerographic paper.

Some of the winners become models for other state and local governments; others do not have staying power. But all are proof that the thousands of state and local governments are constantly experimenting for better ways of doing things.[16]

BOX 1.1 WINNERS OF THE 1994 INNOVATION IN STATE AND LOCAL GOVERNMENT AWARDS

VICTOR THE CYBER LAWYER

Phoenix, Arizona, courthouses have a new advocate for justice, Victor the Cyber Lawyer. Victor is an onscreen bilingual actor in Quick Court, an interactive computer system now in three Arizona courthouses, which provides free legal information and documents to be filed in court.

In its first 12 months, the information kiosks handled more than 24,000 transactions on such issues as small claims, divorce, landlord rights and responsibilities, and how to collect money judgments. Although many states have similar kiosks, the Arizona system is unique in that it prints out completed court-ready forms that judges trust. The more accurate information thus saves courts officials valuable time and effort. More importantly, the system is easy to use. Almost 80 percent of the people who tried the system said they would use it again. Plans are now under way to expand the interactive computer system from 3 to 150 kiosks and make it accessible to more people.

MINNESOTA PARENTS' FAIR SHARE PROGRAM

In Blaine, Minnesota, as in many other communities across America, the failure of noncustodial parents to pay child support is a major reason why children end up on welfare or live in poverty. For many of these parents, their limited job prospects offer little hope of paying their financial obligations or justification for any state effort to track down the delinquent parent.

Instead of simply writing off these parents, the Minnesota Parents' Fair Share Program provides employment and training services as well as parenting education to delinquent parents. By improving these parents' future job prospects, the program also improves the prospects of their children. The program's budget is a relatively meager

Daily Service Providers

Our contact with the services of state and local government begins as we commute to work or school in the morning and does not end until we put the garbage out by the curb in the evening. In fact, even as we sleep, municipal or county police, fire fighters, and emergency medical personnel watch over most of our communities, rural and urban.

Although many state and local services, from public schools to bus systems, receive federal assistance, their character, quality, and scope are determined largely by subnational policymakers and bureaucrats. Thus, although federal money is available to most universities for scientific research and foreign language instruction, the quality of the state institutions of higher education varies considerably, in some significant measure as a function of the differing degrees of willingness by state legislatures and governors to provide the resources and freedom to hire the necessary faculty, attract good graduate students, build state-of-the-art laboratories, and establish research institutes. Similarly, although there is still federal assistance for urban mass transit systems, the particular mix of bus and rail and service for the elderly and disabled, the fares, and the service schedules are all determined at the local level.

In short, state and local decisions about public safety services, parks and swimming pools, highway construction and bus systems, streetlights and pedestrian malls, public

$900,000 a year, but its financial returns are impressive. A study of 70 of its clients showed that in the six months before entering the program, the noncustodial parents had collectively paid only 23 percent of what they owed in child support, or $16,803 out of $74,386. After completing the program, the parents had paid 84 percent, or $63,572 out of $75,443. The program saves the state money, but perhaps more importantly, it helps reestablish a link between noncustodial parents and their children.

STRETCHING NONPROFIT RESOURCES

Budgets for New York City nonprofit social service agencies are always tight. However, the rising costs for workers' mandatory insurance coverage threatened to overwhelm nonprofits' already stretched budgets. The solution was the creation of the Citywide Central Insurance Program (CCIP). The CCIP is a system of publicly managed, privately pro-

vided insurance pools to supply insurance for more than 2,000 nonprofit vendors and their 62,000 employees. The results are dramatic. The city's general liability premiums dropped from $6.4 million in 1991 to $3.1 million in 1994, despite an increase in the number of covered employees.

Moreover, the establishment of a centralized database allowed the state to identify persistent problem areas. For example, a computer analysis showed that the greatest source of on-site injury among the 73 home attendant care providers was from lifting or carrying. Using this analysis, the state was able to persuade the private insurance carriers to provide support belts to the employees and reduce the numbers of injuries and worker compensation claims. The CCIP thus saves the city money and allows nonprofits to concentrate on their mission instead of their insurance.

Source: "Government at Its Best," *Governing* (October 1994), pp. 36–45.

schools and public housing, universities, and vocational training programs all have a bearing on life opportunities and the quality of life.

Training Ground for Political Life

Many people see state or local politics as a series of stepping-stones to more and more power. At each stage they acquire a broader public reputation, greater familiarity with issues, and more skills. Thus, the neighborhood activist may eventually decide to pursue a seat on the city council or the parent involved in the PTA may decide to run for the school board. Some who serve on city councils eventually go on to compete for the mayoralty, mayors may seek to run for governor, and popular state legislators may compete for a Congressional seat. Many governors seek and some attain the presidency. Franklin Roosevelt, Jimmy Carter, Ronald Reagan, and Bill Clinton were all once governors, and so were aspirants Nelson Rockefeller, George Wallace, Michael Dukakis, Pete DuPont, Adlai Stevenson, Bruce Babbitt, Jerry Brown, Pete Wilson, and Lamar Alexander.

Local politics has been a particularly important setting for disadvantaged ethnic groups, racial minorities, and women with political aspirations. Community politics provides opportunities to gain experience and visibility for people who have historically been excluded from public affairs. Not only are there more elective jobs for people who seek political careers, but members of dominant groups are likely to have their eye on higher office, thus lessening the intensity of competition for local posts.

✧ THE DEMOGRAPHIC CONTEXT OF STATE AND LOCAL POLITICS

Much of the character of state and local politics is closely connected to the magnitude and character of population movements and demographic shifts. Poor people migrating to a state with generous welfare benefits, non-English-speaking immigrants clustering in the cities of the Southwest, young people moving from the upper plains states in search of better employment opportunities, white middle class professionals moving out of the central cities to the suburbs, and displaced workers moving from old factory towns to the New South are all examples of migrations that bear on state and local politics. In this section we shall explore the nature of these population movements and their political implications. Finally, we address the issue of whether these movements of northerners to the South, of easterners to the West, of city dwellers to the suburbs and small towns, and so on are homogenizing American politics, erasing the distinctive patterns of politics and culture that have always typified the states.

The Migratory American

Nearly one out of every eight Americans moves every year. We are a truly mobile people. Not surprisingly, this movement across the landscape has many implications, both for the places the people leave and the places to which they migrate.

Since the end of World War II there have been three major internal migration trends in the United States: the move from the Frost Belt states to the Sun Belt, the exodus of black Americans from the South, and the flight from the central cities to the suburbs. Two additional minor trends are also notable: a modest back-to-the-city movement in recent decades and the resurgence in the 1990s of rural areas. Then there is the migration from abroad, with record numbers of people immigrating to the United States in the first part of the 1990s. In a striking departure from historic patterns of immigration, these new arrivals come overwhelmingly from undeveloped nations in Central and Latin America, the Caribbean, and Asia. Each of these movements has shaped the patterns, problems, and possibilities of both national and subnational politics.

Interregional Movements   Between 1950 and 1995 the states of the Midwest and the East grew by more than 29 million people, but in the same period the states of the South and West grew by more than 81 million. To put this population shift in even more dramatic terms, consider that in 1950 the South and West contained only 43 percent of the U.S. population; today these regions account for 57 percent.[17]

Indeed, over half the entire nation's population growth since 1980 has taken place in three Sun Belt states: California, Texas, and Florida. But other Sun Belt states have experienced massive rates of growth: Since 1980 Nevada's population increased by more than 75 percent and Arizona's by about 45 percent. Compare these figures to a 4.7 percent growth rate in Massachusetts over this period, a 1.6 percent increase in Pennsylvania, and actual losses in Iowa and North Dakota.

Much of this extraordinary southern and western growth is a product of natural increase and foreign immigration, but a significant portion is the result of **interregional migration.** What makes this extraordinary is that the South was a net *exporter* of population until the late 1960s, but the flow of migrants was reversed in the next decade. Retirees heading for Arizona and Florida, people seeking work in the burgeoning aerospace industries, and northern blacks who saw new opportunities in a new South all flocked to towns and cities in Florida, Georgia, North Carolina, and Texas. When the automobile industry went sour in Michigan in the 1970s, displaced workers looking in the want ads for work in the Texas oilfields made the Houston *Chronicle* the best-selling newspaper in Detroit.

Between 1990 and 1995, every single state in the Northeast experienced net migration losses;[18] that is, more people moved out than moved in. The six New England states lost over half a million people through migration. Some of the states in the industrial heartland— Ohio, Michigan, and Illinois—lost more people than moved in during this period.

Most Sun Belt growth has occurred in metropolitan areas. Huge cities have sprung up from the desert. Phoenix, a sleepy community of 65,000 in 1940, is now the tenth largest city in the United States, with over 900,000 residents. In fact, whereas in 1950 only one

TABLE 1.1   REGIONAL GROWTH RATES, 1950–1995   More than half the entire nation's population growth since 1980 has taken place in California, Texas, and Florida.

Northeast	30%
Midwest	39
South	93
West	186

TABLE 1.2 INTERREGIONAL POPULATION DISTRIBUTION, 1950–1994

	Percentage of U.S. Population	
	1950	*1994*
Northeast	26.0%	19.7%
Midwest	29.4	23.8
South	31.2	34.8
West	13.3	21.8

Source: Statistical Abstract of the United States.

of the ten largest cities was located in the Sun Belt (Los Angeles), today the region claims six of the ten largest: Los Angeles, Houston, Dallas, San Diego, San Antonio, and Phoenix. All 50 of the fastest growing metropolitan areas since 1980 are located in the Sun Belt: They include the Texas cities Bryan, Odessa, and Midland and Florida communities Ocala, Naples, and Ft. Myers.

Black Exodus Historically, black Americans regarded the South as a place to flee. Toward the end of the nineteenth century, with the imposition of Jim Crow laws that legally segregated every aspect of life in the states of the old Confederacy, blacks began to move northward. Their departure, sometimes encouraged by local whites, was hastened by the mechanization of farming. Later in the twentieth century, wartime industrial mobilization and successful efforts by Congress to restrict foreign immigration created labor shortages that opened job opportunities in northern factories to blacks willing to migrate.

Black migrants traced three great migration streams to northern cities. People who lived in the Atlantic coastal states moved north into New Jersey, New York, and New England. Residents of Alabama, Mississippi, Arkansas, and Louisiana traveled up the Mississippi River and branched out to St. Louis, Chicago, Cincinnati, Detroit, and other cities around the Great Lakes. (A recent survey of black residents of Milwaukee found that Mississippi and Arkansas ranked second and third after Wisconsin as the most common place of birth.[19]) Blacks from Texas and Oklahoma tended to migrate westward to California. The bitter irony of this great three-pronged journey is that although blacks left the repressive society of the South in quest of better opportunities, what most found waiting for them, wherever they went, was the dark ghetto[20] of the northern cities.

Thus it is no surprise that as conditions in the South began to improve under the influence of the civil rights movement and Voting Rights Act of 1965, the influx of northerners, and the industrialization of the economy, blacks in the slums of northern cities began to move back during the 1970s. Indeed, the increase in the black population of the South in that decade was the largest single increase among blacks in any region, for any decade in history.[21]

Central City to Suburb Migration Even though the figures on interregional population flows seem enormous, most Americans who move each year are in fact short-distance movers, usually within a metropolitan area. Most of this movement is a shift from central cities to suburban communities. People began to move to suburbs in the middle of the nineteenth century when the development of rail transportation (the Philadelphia Main Line, for example) made it possible for the upper classes to escape the growing lower-class immigrant population. But the migration outward really began in earnest after World War II. Driven by pent-up demand for housing that had been on hold during the war and by Federal Housing Administration and Veterans Administration housing programs, tract developments sprang up all over the country in what were once cornfields. In the 1950s and 1960s the federal interstate highway program provided funds for the construction of high-speed limited-access arterial routes that made it possible for more and more people to live outside of central cities but commute quickly and safely by automobile to downtown areas. By 1970 the U.S. Census showed that for the first time a plurality of Americans lived in suburbs. The 1990 census suggested that the nation would soon house half its people in suburban areas: 46 percent of the entire population lived in metropolitan areas but outside the large central cities, or in other words, in suburban settlements. Within metropolitan areas (the place of residence for over 77 percent of the U.S. population), almost 60 percent lived outside the central cities.

Originally, most of those who left the city were white: upwardly mobile professionals, second-generation working-class ethnics, and young families. Motives for leaving the central city were complex. Some left for better housing, some sought green space and an escape from city streets, others moved to find better schools, and still others left because they feared crime. Some undoubtedly left to escape the growing black population of central cities, giving rise to the term **white flight.**

Today, blacks are also suburbanizing. In 1950 only 4.5 percent of the suburban population was black; by 1990 the figure had risen to 6.9 percent. Today, a little over a quarter of all blacks live in suburbs (compared to half of all whites) and the rate of black exodus from the central city to suburban locations is substantially higher than that of whites. Nevertheless, suburban housing patterns tend, as those in central cities do, to be sharply segregated by race. For example, Lawnside, located in the New Jersey part of the Philadelphia metropolitan area, was over 98 percent black in 1980. East Cleveland, Ohio, was over 86 percent black. Highland Park outside of Detroit and Markham near Chicago are other examples of predominantly black suburbs. These communities are poorer than their largely white counterparts, they are fiscally stressed, and they have higher crime rates.

Back to the City At some point in the late 1970s there was a small but discernible middle-class return migration to certain big cities. The fuel crisis of the 1970s (which drove up the price of commuting), the discovery of the joys of rehabilitating old houses in historic districts, the growth of two-career families, and delayed childbearing by professional women were among the factors behind this trend. In no city was this small migration sufficient to reverse population losses that began in the 1940s. Of all the cities in the older regions in the country, only New York has actually gained population since the 1980 census. But the impact of this middle class in-migration should not be minimized: Not only have these urban settlers often revitalized decaying residential neighborhoods or generated demands for new urban housing, but they have created a market for specialty shops, restaurants, cafés, and entertainment. If the number of these in-migrants is relatively small, their influence on the cosmopolitan character of cities is evident in neighborhoods from

Chicago's North Clark Street area to Denver's LoDo district to Washington's Capitol Hill neighborhoods.

Rural Resurgence   After a decade of rural decline, migrants began to move back to the country in droves in the 1990s.[22] Population in rural areas (technically defined as all counties not located in a Metropolitan Statistical Area) grew during the first half of the 1990s at an average annual rate of just under 1 percent. More than half this growth was due to net in-migration. Some substantial portion of this rural migration was from California, which surprisingly experienced a net loss of more than 1 million people in the migration stream. Many of these California refugees settled in rural Idaho, Oregon, Washington, and Nevada.

Many rural migrants, however, are not seeking the solitude of the western high plains or mountains. Most are moving into rural counties that border metropolitan areas. Some commute as much as 50 or 100 miles to the central cities to work each day, but many more work in the new "edge cities" that have sprung up on the periphery of major metropolitan concentrations, great concentrations of offices, corporate headquarters, shopping malls, and manufacturing facilities that often lie along the interstate ring roads that once defined the outer boundaries of metropolitan areas. The development around Chicago's O'Hare airport is one example; places such as Tempe and Scottsdale around Phoenix are examples of "edge cities" in the Sun belt.

Foreign Immigration   In 1991, 1.8 million legal immigrants arrived in the United States, a figure that surpassed even the record years at the turn of the century. The annual number of people entering the country had declined by mid-decade, but it was still running close to a million people per year. In addition to the legal immigrants, an estimated 150,000 to 250,000 people were entering the country illegally each year, bringing the total of undocumented immigrants to perhaps 4 million.[23]

Most legal immigrants flock to just a few big cities. New York and Los Angeles alone received over 400,000 of the 1.8 million immigrants in 1991. But other cities, especially in California, Texas, and Florida, are major destinations. In 1991, the metropolitan areas of Riverside and Fresno in California were the destinations for 50,000 and 33,000 legal immigrants, respectively, almost all from Mexico. Unlike the great immigration of the nineteenth and early twentieth centuries, very few of the new arrivals come from Europe. The modern immigrants come from such places as Mexico, Korea, Cambodia, the Philippines, El Salvador, Nicaragua, Jamaica, and Haiti. Although immigrants from Asia tend to have more formal education than native-born Americans, and thus are better able to adapt to a modern technology-based economy, those from Latin America and the Caribbean generally have little schooling and few skills that would enable them to cope with life in a society in which work increasingly involves the processing of information rather than the manufacture of things. Some groups, however, have made remarkable economic progress in their brief time in the United States: Korean immigrants, with their heavy presence in the small business retail sector in Los Angeles, New York, and Chicago, are a prime example.

The public burden of providing services to the new arrivals in America, both legal and illegal, falls unequally on particular states and local governments and on particular groups. The Dade County (Miami) school system, for example, counted over 8000 undocumented Central American children in its schools in 1989. Because the courts have ruled

A Korean store owner in New York City takes a telephone order. Of the approximately 1,100 fruit and vegetable stores in the city, about 900 are owned by Korean immigrants. (*Source:* M. Granitsas/The Image Works)

that all children, here legally or not, are entitled to public education, the county school system must provide for them. The cost is roughly $2,500 per child per year. For every 800 children, the county must build a new school.[24] The state of Texas is the only state that has attempted to calculate the cost/benefit ratio of illegal immigrants. Its Office of Immigration figured that although illegal workers generated almost $300 million in taxes to the state, they cost the state $456 million, mostly for education and health care.[25]

The large influx of Latin Americans has engendered ethnic tensions in certain parts of the country. Along the Gulf Coast, Vietnamese and American shrimpers coexisted for years in a virtual state of war over fishing grounds and fishing methods. In Miami, native blacks have felt particularly disadvantaged in the labor market: As Hispanic unemployment in that city was dropping in the 1980s, black unemployment was rising in the same period. In Minneapolis, blacks have complained that Hmong immigrants have virtually monopolized the available public housing.

✧ POPULATION MOVEMENTS AND POLITICS

Moving from one place to another is an activity that clearly occupies a central place in American culture. Most Americans or their ancestors came to this country from somewhere else: "Immigration . . . was America's raison d'être," Maldwyn Jones reminds us, and it "has been the most persistent and the most pervasive influence in her development."[26] But the passage from one country to another is simply the most dramatic form of migration Americans experience and cherish. Compared to many populations in the world, native-born Americans are a restless people. The open road is an important symbol of opportunity and freedom: John Steinbeck's refugees from the Oklahoma dust bowl streamed to California in search of the promised land, not so different from the westward migrants who had preceded them for nearly a century. Because mobility is so widespread and so common, it is not surprising that it has all sorts of political implications in the United States. Let us explore some of the more important of these implications.

Shifts in Political Power

The fixed number of 435 Congressional representatives is reapportioned among the states according to population after each decennial census; therefore, population shifts mean that some states gain influence in Congress while others lose it. Specifically, as population has flowed westward and southward, states in those regions have gained seats in Congress at the expense of the Frost Belt states. After the 1980 census, states in the South and West gained 17 seats. **Reapportionment** after the 1990 census produced another 19 seats for states in those regions.

The big winners in the years since World War II have been California, Texas, and Florida. When Dwight Eisenhower was first elected president in 1952, California had 32 electoral votes; today it has 54. Texas had 24 then; now it has 32. Florida, which had only 10 electoral votes in 1952, currently has 25. Those three states now control nearly one-fourth of the entire House of Representatives. On the other side of the country, New York, Michigan, Illinois, Ohio, Pennsylvania, Iowa, and West Virginia have all lost Congressional seats since World War II. New York, once the most populous state, claimed 45 seats in the House at its population peak. Today it has only 31.

All this means that certain issues of particular interest to states and cities in the North and Midwest—such as the decline of the steel industry in the Great Lakes region and federal aid for older cities—do not command the clout in Congress in the 1990s that they did in the 1960s. Conversely, the power of the South and West has risen. These are regions where water and the exploitation of natural resources are abiding issues, but such concerns are of much less interest to the urbanized states of the East or the water-rich states of the Midwest. The shift of power is true not only in Congress but also in presidential politics: It is striking that all of our recent presidents, save Gerald Ford, came from the South or West: Nixon, Reagan, Carter, Bush, and Clinton.

Growth and Decline as Political Issues

Large and persistent population movements bring issues associated with growth and decline to the top of the political agenda. For example, one ironic consequence for cities that lose population and jobs is that they receive less money from the federal government through formula programs based on population, yet their needs are as great or even greater than before. Although the population may be smaller, those left behind tend to be the poorest and least able to manage without public assistance. Furthermore, the physical structure of the city—its roads, sewers, and public buildings—remain in place. With fewer taxpayers to help support programs for people and the physical infrastructure, these cities need more, not less help as their populations decline.

Whether the federal government and the states should put money into places that are emptying out is a perennial question. Some people argue that the shift of population and firms across the country simply represents the operation of natural market processes, and should not be impeded. People seek to move to places where they will find better jobs, and firms seek to move to places where the costs of doing business are lower. Government, according to this view, should do nothing to spur the revitalization of declining areas because that would represent an effort to resist the strain toward efficiency in the market.

Others argue that it is not only immoral for government to stand by doing nothing to stem the departure of employers, but that from a national perspective, it is wasteful of the human and physical resources left behind. If government is to counter market forces and help declining areas, what sorts of programs should be put into place to encourage revitalization? Some state and local governments favor a strategy that tries to lure manufacturing plants from other places as a way to provide new jobs and increase tax revenues. Others try to grow their own new businesses.

Just as decline raises issues about how or even whether to respond, growth also raises political issues. As people and employers come to an area, they threaten its environmental quality. Austin, Texas, for example, has grown so fast in the last fifteen years that the huge aquifer that provides the city's drinking water is threatened by development in the limestone hills that abut the city. All over the country, hundreds of thousands of acres of precious wetlands and farmland are lost to development every year. Should growth be restricted and, if so, how should it be done? Some places ration building permits, setting a limit on how many they will issue each year. Others order a moratorium on sewer construction, effectively halting further development. Of course, these are controversial, stop-gap measures.

Most growing cities and states simply try to expand the services they provide for their citizens. Growing places need new streets and highways, expanded mass transit, new schools and parks, new housing subdivisions with sewers and sidewalks, more police and fire-fighting personnel, and so on. Who should pay for these and with what sort of taxes? And should these physical improvements be planned on a long-range basis or should they be built as demand warrants?

Racial and Economic Segregation

Movement within metropolitan areas in particular tends to sort people out by race and social class. The most common pattern, a result of the flight to the suburbs, is a ring of largely white, middle-class communities around a predominantly minority, poor central city. Although black suburbanization has increased sharply, we have seen that this movement has done little to break patterns of residential segregation in metropolitan areas. Massey and Denton calculate that the average Segregation Index for large northern metropolitan areas fell only from 80.1 in 1980 to 77.8 in 1990, indicating that most black urbanites live in virtually all-black communities, even though federal fair housing laws have been in place since 1968.[27]

A number of factors contribute to the persistence of segregation. Discriminatory practices in the real estate and mortgage lending industries, suburban zoning laws and building codes that make it difficult to build low-income housing, and income differences between the races are all important factors. Another barrier to racial integration in housing is violent white resistance. A 1989 national survey of hate crimes—racially or religiously motivated acts of violence or vandalism—found that nearly half of all such incidents are aimed at blacks who move into predominantly white neighborhoods.[28]

One consequence of the segregation of middle class from poor, of racial minority from white, is to divorce resources in metropolitan areas from needs. The poor are more dependent on public services than the middle class and wealthy: Poor people are less likely to send their children to private schools, to use personal transportation rather than public mass transit, and to belong to private health clubs. Their homes are more prone to fire, and they are more likely to be the victims of crime. Yet the poor cannot pay enough taxes to provide schools, mass transit, recreational facilities, and fire and police protection commensurate with their needs. Ironically, cities with high proportions of poor people must tax people at particularly high rates just to raise enough revenues to pay for minimal public services. Wealthy suburban communities, with a much richer tax base, may levy taxes at much lower rates and still raise enough money to provide first-class public services.

Another consequence of metropolitan segregation is that the poor in the central cities increasingly find that they do not have convenient access to the job market. Just as people have left the central city, so too have employers, especially industrial and retail firms. Some industries have even decentralized beyond metropolitan areas altogether. For example, whereas the automobile industry was once concentrated in Detroit and a few other large urban areas, the newest large plants are located in such places as Spring Hill, Tennessee, Bloomington, Illinois, and Lafayette, Indiana. Unlike Detroit, these communities have small minority populations. The result of the establishment of rural automobile plants has been the transformation of the racial composition of the auto industry workforce and an increase in the number of displaced black factory workers.

Competition Among Places

The movement of people across the landscape represents a redistribution of resources among states and communities. If growth causes certain sorts of problems, it also brings with it more talent and skills, more jobs, and more wealth. Places that lose people find their resource base depleted: fewer businesses, fewer able workers, and fewer taxpayers. It is not surprising, then, to find that states and communities compete with one another for people and jobs. In fact, a great deal of public policy is geared in one way or another toward attracting certain types of people and businesses from other places and keeping people and businesses already there from leaving. As Paul Peterson writes of cities (although this is equally true of states), they pursue public policies designed to "maintain or enhance the economic position, social prestige, or political power of the city."[29] Tax rates and types of taxes, welfare benefits, workers' compensation, economic development incentives, zoning laws, education financing, and infrastructure programs are all examples of public policies that states and communities believe have a bearing on whether they will grow and prosper, stay even, or lose population and decline. The particular form these policies take is thought to attract particular sorts of people and to discourage others. Thus, good schools paid for with high taxes may attract middle-class families, whereas low welfare benefits may, some politicians hope, prevent the state from becoming a "welfare magnet" for poor people.

Designing policies to attract or retain resources assumes that people and businesses have a high degree of choice in deciding where to settle and that at some level they take such matters into consideration when they make their decisions.

Of course, people do not have unfettered choice in deciding where to live: They are constrained by income, race, and the availability of employment at the very least. But people do have a certain degree of freedom to live where they wish. State and municipal boundaries are permeable; that is, they are easy to cross over. Unlike nations, states and cities cannot easily control the flow of people and businesses back and forth across their borders.

Not everyone makes a conscious decision about where to live. Some simply live where they have always lived, or they live where their spouse or family takes them, or they live where their employer sends them. There is a good deal of pure chance in where people end up, but when they do consciously consider their living situation, they generally have several options. In exercising these options we assume that they make some sort of comparison between the quality of life in the place they currently live with the quality of life in the range of places to which they might reasonably hope to migrate.

Economist Albert O. Hirschman has suggested that these options fall into three categories that he calls exit, voice, and loyalty.[30] Exit is the option to leave a place that one believes offers inferior opportunities or quality of life for a place that offers better conditions. Unemployed auto workers who migrated from Michigan to Texas during the oil boom of the early 1980s were exercising their exit option. People who leave the central city to get away from urban problems are also using exit as a solution. States and localities work hard to keep their most productive citizens from exiting; they try to make life so attractive that they cause people elsewhere to exercise the exit option and relocate to their jurisdiction.

Voice is an option that involves staying where one is, but actively seeking to make things better. Hirschman defines voice as "any attempt at all to change, rather than to escape from, an objectionable state of affairs."[31] This option may be understood literally as voicing one's opinions or giving voice to one's preferences. The voting booth is a form of voice (though a minimal one); it may be distinguished from exit, which some people refer to as voting with one's feet. Organizing a neighborhood group to protest the lack of drug enforcement or deciding to run for the city council or joining a business group that works for the improvement of the downtown area are all forms of voice.

Finally, loyalty suggests a degree of satisfaction with one's place of residence. Life is good enough, at least enough so that one wishes neither to leave nor to work to make things better. Of course, such inaction may result not only from satisfaction but also from apathy or resignation. One problem with Hirschman's framework is that it is often difficult to distinguish between the consequences of loyalty and apathy. On the surface the two quite different states of mind produce similar outcomes: In neither case does action result. Presumably, the loyal citizen possesses a reservoir of civic commitment that could in some extraordinary circumstances be called on, whereas the apathetic citizen would be far more difficult to arouse to action. Furthermore, whereas loyalty may be a sign of satisfaction, apathy may be an indicator of alienation, a sense that one does not belong and that no one cares.

✧ POLITICAL CULTURES

Much of state and local politics is really about the distribution among citizens of impulses toward exit, voice, and loyalty. Who leaves and who stays? What makes people and firms decide to locate in a different place, and how in fact do they choose a new place? Who expresses voice and with what effect? Who are the loyalists, the silent citizens, and what role do they play for those who govern? Perhaps most importantly, what sorts of things do governments do to keep people and businesses, to attract additional ones, and even to discourage "undesirable" migrants?

Not surprisingly, the choices state and local governments make about what sorts of policies to pursue both derive from and help to shape and reinforce differences among places. These differences are products of state **political cultures,** that is, the distinctive sets of attitudes and beliefs about government and politics that citizens of different states hold.

The foremost student of state political cultures, Daniel Elazar, has attempted to map state political cultures.[32] In his view, the distribution of political cultures in the United States (see Figure 1.1) is in large measure a function of the different ethnic and social groups that settled the various parts of the country. For example, Puritans and their Yankee descendants migrated from New England to the states of the Great Lakes and upper Midwest, carrying with them a view that government is a force for collective good. This *moralistic* culture was shared by Scandinavian immigrants who settled Wisconsin, Iowa, and Minnesota in the latter part of the nineteenth century.

The Yankees who settled Oregon and the Mormons who immigrated to Utah also maintain moralistic cultures. Political reform, professional government, and strong social welfare programs are hallmarks of the political life of moralistic states.

Traditionalistic cultures are common in the South, where people are more likely than in other places to view government as the domain of small elite groups drawn from old

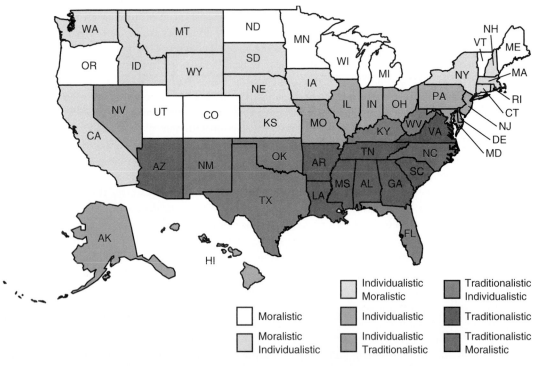

FIGURE 1.1 A Map of American Political Cultures

Source: Daniel J. Elazar, *American Federalism: A View from the States,* 3rd ed., New York: Harper & Row, 1984, p. 135.

families and favored social classes. In the settlement period, the South was dominated by the planter class, dependent on slave labor. Government is viewed as an instrument for maintaining social order, not as a means to advance the public interest. Taxes tend to be low because the array of public services is meager.

In the eastern states, settled particularly by Irish immigrants, an *individualistic* culture is dominant. These states have been dominated by adherents of the view that politics is a vehicle for economic gain for those who win office, a far different notion from using government for the common good or the public interest. Awarding patronage jobs in government, financing public works (which provide jobs and construction contracts), and social welfare are typical political features in individualistic states.

These portraits of political culture are oversimplified. They represent ideal types. Most states exhibit a mix of tendencies. But there remain in all states distinctive cultural threads. Issues such as school prayer are more intensely felt in traditionalistic states; the impulse to experiment with social policy is still more common in the moralistic states around the Great Lakes. Real political differences among the states do exist, despite our common national experiences.

Not every student of state political cultures shares Elazar's ethnic and social group explanation of the origins of these differences. Erikson and his colleagues, for example, believe that states' histories and their differential processes of development are more important than the characteristics of their populations in determining the nature of the local political culture. But beyond this observation, they find that differences in political culture are difficult to account for. They conclude that states seem to develop relatively liberal or relatively conservative political cultures "without any patterns that we can yet discern."[33]

A good deal of empirical evidence now exists to support the view that cultural differences, whatever their origin, do make a political difference. Erikson and his colleagues, for example, find strong correlations between the state of residence and people's partisan and ideological (liberal or conservative) orientation, even when all the relevant social and economic factors are held constant. Another study, one that uses Elazar's categories, finds that moralistic states are more likely to have strong patterns of political party competition than traditionalistic or individualistic states, and the content of political debate in campaigns is more likely in those moralistic states to focus on policy rather than personality issues. Furthermore, moralistic states tend to make greater use of merit systems in hiring public employees, they tend to be more willing to embrace policy innovations, and they exhibit greater economic equality among their citizens.[34] Moralistic states also have more liberal voter registration laws and higher voting turnout than states with other dominant political cultures.[35]

Finally, Russell Hanson shows that feelings of civic duty (whether people feel an obligation to become involved in politics), political efficacy (whether people feel their participation makes a difference), and actual involvement in political campaigns vary by state political culture.[36] What is especially interesting about Hanson's study from our perspective is that he shows that in certain cases migrants who move from one political culture to a different one adapt to the new norms. Earlier we posed the question of whether all of the migratory activity we have described would eventually homogenize American politics. But Hanson's work suggests that state political cultures are fairly durable. This seems particularly true in cases where migrants move from traditionalistic cultures to moralistic ones. In these cases the migrants pick up the norms of the moralistic culture, becoming more active and feeling a stronger sense of obligation to take part in politics. People who move from moralistic or individualistic cultures to traditionalistic states become less active in politics.

The idea of political culture is valuable finally because it provides a way to unite history and the distinctive demography of a state with prevailing attitudes, styles of politics, and actual policy choices. It offers a shorthand way of understanding that state boundaries are not simply arbitrary lines on a map but demarcate real differences in the ways people view and use government. Perhaps most important of all, the variety of state political cultures suggests that state (and local) politics is not simply a smaller version of national politics.

✧ CONCLUSION

We have argued in this chapter that state and local governments are important to understand because they play a major role in the American system of government. They are important settings for democratic participation, laboratories for policy experimentation, the dominant providers of public services and employers of public servants, and key training grounds for people embarking on careers in politics.

A useful way to begin the study of subnational politics is to explore the patterns of population and employment mobility among the various units. With their permeable boundaries, states and localities cannot easily control the flow of people and firms into or out of their jurisdiction. Yet this mobility has a crucial bearing on the vitality of states and cities: Population gains and in-migration of new employers may bring prosperity in the form of new jobs, new taxes, and new consumers. Population losses bring decline.

Many policy choices that states and cities make are designed in some measure to keep people and firms in the state or community, to enhance their well-being or prosperity, to attract other productive citizens and firms, and to discourage those who might pose a public burden from migrating to the area.

✧ KEY TERMS

Great Society (p. 3)   political cultures (p. 20)
interregional migration (p. 11)   reapportionment (p. 16)
laboratories of democracy (p. 7)   white flight (p. 13)

✧ FOR FURTHER READING

Richard Bernard, ed., *Snow Belt Cities* (Bloomington: Indiana University Press, 1990). The other side of the story of the growth of the Sun Belt cities, with essays on Milwaukee, Chicago, Boston, Baltimore, and several other big cities.

Richard Bernard and Bradley Rice, eds., *Sunbelt Cities* (Austin: University of Texas Press, 1983). A collection of chapters on the rise of cities in the South and Southwest, ranging from Houston, "the Golden Buckle of the Sun Belt," to Phoenix, the desert metropolis.

Paul Peterson, *City Limits* (Chicago: University of Chicago Press, 1981). A tightly argued discussion of city efforts to enhance their economic interests and how these efforts affect the sorts of policies they pursue.

◇ NOTES

1. Luther Gulick quoted in Ann O. Bowman and Richard Kearney, *The Resurgence of the States* (Englewood Cliffs, N.J.: Prentice-Hall, 1986), p. 53.

2. Terry Sanford, *Storm Over the States* (New York: McGraw-Hill, 1967), Chapter 1.

3. Douglas Yates, *The Ungovernable City* (Cambridge, Mass: MIT Press, 1977).

4. William Baer, "On the Death of Cities," *The Public Interest* (Fall 1976), 3–19.

5. Paul Peterson, *The Price of Federalism* (Washington, D.C.: Brookings, 1995), p. 108.

6. See Michael Wiseman, "State Strategies for Welfare Reform: The Wisconsin Story," Institute for Research on Poverty discussion paper, University of Wisconsin-Madison, June 1995.

7. Richard Ward, Robert Lewis, and S. Jerome Pratter, "St Louis: A City Reborn," *Urban Land*, 46 (May 1987), 14–19.

8. Robert Dahl, "The City in the Future of Democracy," *American Political Science Review*, 61 (December 1967), 953–970.

9. Jeffrey Berry, Kent Portney, and Ken Thomson, *The Rebirth of Urban Democracy* (Washington, D.C.: Brookings, 1993), p. 189.

10. ACIR, *Significant Features of Fiscal Federalism, 1994 Edition, Vol. 2* (Washington, D.C.: Government Printing Office, 1994), p. 27.

11. Donald Kettl, "Assessing the National Performance Review," Testimony before the Subcommittee on Government Management, Information, and Technology, Committee on Government Reform and Oversight, U.S. House of Representatives, Washington, D.C., May 2, 1995.

12. Charles Brown and Daniel Huck, "Watching the Nation's Business," *The Journal of State Government*, 61 (May/June 1988), 115–117.

13. Elder Witt, "State Supreme Courts: Tilting the Balance Toward Change," *Governing*, 1 (August 1988), 35.

14. J. David Hadden and Susan Giles, "Financing Low-Income Housing in the Absence of a Federal Presence," *Urban Land*, 47 (June 1988), 21–25.

15. *New York State Ice Co. v. Liebmann*, 285 U.S. 262 (1932).

16. Many of these winning programs are described in Martin Levin and Mary Bryna Sanger, *Making Government Work* (San Francisco: Jossey-Bass, 1994).

17. Peter Francese, "America at Mid-Decade," *American Demographics*, 17 (February 1995), p. 28.

18. *Ibid.*

19. Sammis White, "Black Public Opinion in Milwaukee," *Wisconsin Policy Research Institute Report*, 8 (February 1995), 6.

20. The phrase is the title of Kenneth Clark's classic analysis of ghetto life and conditions, *Dark Ghetto* (New York: Harper & Row, 1965).

21. Joint Center for Political Studies, *Blacks on the Move: A Decade of Demographic Change* (Washington, D.C.: Joint Center for Political Studies, 1982), p. 11.

22. Kenneth Johnson and Calvin Beale, "The Rural Rebound Revisited," *American Demographics*, 17 (July 1995), 46–54.

23. Elizabeth Rolph, *Immigration Policies* (Santa Monica, Calif.: Rand, 1991), p. 38.

24. Lisa Belkin, "Waves of Immigrant Children Strain Schools and Housing," *New York Times,* Jan. 29, 1989.

25. Sam Verhoevek, "Stop Benefits for Aliens? It Wouldn't Be That Easy," *New York Times,* June 8, 1994.

26. Maldwyn Allen Jones, *American Immigration* (Chicago: University of Chicago Press, 1960), p. 1.

27. Douglas Massey and Nancy Denton, *American Apartheid* (Cambridge, Mass: Harvard University Press, 1993), p. 222. The Segregation Index may be read as the percentage of blacks who would have to move from their present home to other places in the city in order for the population on each city block to reflect the racial composition of the city. An index above 60 is considered high. Among the 30 metropolitan areas with the largest black populations, only one—Norfolk-Virginia Beach—fell below 60 in 1990.

28. Ronald Smothers, "Hate Crimes Found Aimed at Blacks in White Areas," *New York Times,* April 28, 1990.

29. Paul Peterson, *City Limits* (Chicago: University of Chicago Press, 1981), p. 20.

30. Albert Hirschman, *Exit, Voice, and Loyalty* (Cambridge, Mass.: Harvard University Press, 1970).

31. *Ibid.,* p. 30.

32. Daniel Elazar, *American Federalism: A View from the States,* 3rd ed. (New York: Harper & Row, 1984).

33. Robert Erikson, John McIver, and Gerald Wright, Jr., "State Political Culture and Public Opinion," *American Political Science Review,* 81 (September 1987), 797–814.

34. Jody Fitzpatrick and Rodney Hero, "Political Culture and Political Characteristics of the American States: A Consideration of Some Old and New Questions," *Western Political Quarterly,* 41 (March 1988), 145–153.

35. James King, "Political Culture, Registration Laws, and Voter Turnout Among the American States," *Publius,* 24 (Fall 1994), 115–127.

36. Russell Hanson, "The Political Acculturation of Migrants in the American States," *Western Political Quarterly,* 45 (June 1992), 355–383.

SUBNATIONAL GOVERNMENTS IN THE FEDERAL SYSTEM

One reason that the mobility of people and firms across the landscape is so important in American politics is that much of this movement crosses political boundaries. State lines are not frontiers that divide nations, of course, but these boundaries are meaningful divisions nevertheless. For one thing, the states that they divide—and the local jurisdictions—depend heavily on the resources within their domains to finance their various government activities. This means that the quality and quantity of public services offered from state to state may vary sharply. Thus, Alabama, one of the poorest states with a per capita income in 1992 of $16,520, could manage to spend only about $585 per capita for elementary and secondary education. Connecticut, with one of the highest per capita incomes at $27,151, was able to spend $1,125.[1] It is obviously in a state's interest to keep and attract people and businesses that pay taxes. The movement of people and firms across boundaries may mean that one jurisdiction's gain is another's loss.

Another reason that state and local boundaries are important is that they demarcate jurisdictions that pursue different solutions to the same public problem. One dramatic example is the death penalty. In 1995, 38 states maintained a death penalty; the remaining states punished the same crimes with prison sentences of varying lengths. Another example from the criminal justice area involves the increasingly popular "Three strikes and you're out" laws: Through the end of 1994, 21 states, beginning with Washington in 1993, had passed or had pending laws requiring life imprisonment without parole for three-time serious offenders. Even among states with such laws, provisions vary. Most require mandatory life sentences, but Connecticut and Maryland provide for some judicial discretion. And Georgia's law is not a three-strike law, but a two-strike one. Thus, the same criminal act may be punished in quite different ways, depending on the state in which it was committed.

State differences in the approach to public issues extend beyond criminal law: States differ in how they seek to encourage economic development, promote higher education, help the economically disadvantaged, regulate business, protect consumers, and maintain environmental quality. For example, California has the toughest automobile emission standards in the country. Fewer than a dozen states have been willing to follow California's lead. Another pioneer in the environmental field is New Jersey, with the most comprehensive air pollution prevention law on the books. But 20 states had no such law at all in 1995.[2]

What gives state boundaries their importance and their strength, but also imposes certain limits, is that they are part of the American federal arrangement. American federalism is deceptively simple. Samuel Beer defines it as "a territorial allocation of authority secured by constitutional guarantees,"[3] but to leave the matter here is to mask the historic conflict over the scope of the authority of the national government in Washington and the limits of the authority of the states. What is the nature of the relationship between state and nation? What are the responsibilities and powers of the respective levels of government? Is the balance the proper one? Where do local governments enter the equation?

Turning to the Constitution for guidance is only a starting point: Neither federalism nor local government is even mentioned in that document, although the Framers in Philadelphia undeniably created a government structure in which both a strong national government and strong states coexisted. But as we shall see, the Constitution in the end supplies only clues. Neither history or practice helps to resolve the nature of federalism definitively, for this has been a matter of continuous argument from the beginning. Did the Framers create a system in which each state was a separate sovereign community, as John Calhoun contended in the 1830s, or was it "an indissoluble union," as President Andrew Jackson argued in rejoinder?[4] In the 1860s, the Civil War established the indivisibility of the union, but Americans have continued to debate the proper allocation of powers between states and nation.

✧ DEFINING FEDERALISM

One scholar has identified 267 different, though obviously overlapping, definitions of federalism.[5] What these definitions share is the notion that federalism is a structural arrangement designed to accommodate simultaneously a strong national government and strong subnational governments in the form of states. To implement this structure in practice in the eighteenth century took a real leap of imagination. David Walker has argued that this "territorial principle of divided powers was and is the prime gift of the United States to the art and science of government."[6]

Both levels of government share jurisdiction over the same land and same people. Thus, a citizen of Missouri or Arizona is also a citizen of the United States and subject to the laws of both levels of government. Both state and national governments derive their authority from the same source, the people. Therefore, the existence and authority of one is not dependent on the other. This aspect of the arrangement differentiates the U.S. federal system from unitary governments such as those of France, Britain, and Sweden. Constituent units in those countries have little autonomy; their responsibilities and even their existence are subject to the control of the central government. For example, the Swedish national parliament eliminated 90 percent of all local governments between 1952 and 1975, an occurrence unimaginable in the United States.[7]

Although both the state and national governments exercise certain identical powers (both may punish criminal behavior, both may levy taxes, and both may acquire land for various public uses, for example), the federal arrangement does divide primary responsibility for certain areas of public policy between the levels. National defense is primarily a national responsibility (although the states maintain a national guard); so are the conduct of diplomacy and the management of the money system and foreign trade. But what Harvey Mansfield once called "matters of homely concern," that is, "the provision and modification of the general legal fabric of rights and duties within which individuals, families, associations, and business firms go about their affairs," are all primarily state responsibilities.[8] Specifically, this legal fabric applies to the regulation of marriage, divorce, adoption, and custody, the enforcement of business contracts, the licensing of occupations, the chartering of corporations, the prosecution of most criminal acts, and the regulation of public morals pertaining to such matters as drinking, gambling, and prostitution. In these and other areas the states may act autonomously, that is, without securing the approval of the government in Washington.

However, it is important to understand that the national government may nevertheless influence how the states manage these matters. A good example is the drinking age. Setting the age at which young people may drink and buy liquor is a state prerogative, but in 1983 President Reagan's Commission on Drunk Driving called for the states to adopt 21 as the legal drinking age. The commission then went on to recommend that Congress pass a law that would allow the federal Department of Transportation to penalize states that did not change their drinking age by withholding federal highway funds. In 1986 Congress passed such a law, and states with lower drinking ages, although theoretically free to do as they wished, grudgingly made the change.[9]

One should not make too much of the idea that American federalism divides responsibilities between the levels of government. There are no well-established principles in constitutional law or practice that provide unambiguous guidance for such a division of powers. Patterns of division of responsibilities have changed throughout history. In practice there is often a good deal of sharing of responsibility for a particular function by both the national and the various subnational governments, rather than a sharp division of authority between them. Take the case of public primary and secondary education: In the typical state 50 percent of the funding for schools comes from the state, 44 percent from the local school district, and 6 percent from Washington. Some decisions concerning curriculum and standards are made at the local level and others are made by state education officials. Federal aid to education provides Washington with some leverage too: For example, it has required local school districts to offer bilingual education. In short, the line separating state functions and responsibilities from national ones is blurred and the subject of constant debate and change.

✦ THE CONSTITUTIONAL BASIS OF AMERICAN FEDERALISM

The Constitution recognizes two levels of government and makes some modest, although occasionally ambiguous, efforts to distribute power between them. For example, Article I, Section 8 provides that Congress shall have the power to coin money, to regulate commerce among the states and foreign nations, and to declare war. We know that these are exclusive national powers because Article I, Section 10 explicitly denies these to the states: No state shall enter into a treaty with a foreign country, coin money, lay duties on imports or exports, or engage in war.

Besides enumerating specific powers that Congress may exercise, the Constitution also gives the legislative body broad power to levy taxes and spend "for the general welfare of the United States." Combined with the provision in Article I, Section 8 that gives Congress the power to "make all laws which shall be necessary and proper" to carry out its specifically enumerated responsibilities, these **implied powers** give the national government great freedom to expand its authority by undertaking whatever programs and policies it deems to be in the national interest.

What about the powers of the states? These are never spelled out in the Constitution. The **Tenth Amendment** reserves to the states all powers (unspecified) "not delegated to the United States" nor prohibited by the Constitution to the states or the people. What this amendment really means (particularly in light of the ability of the national government to expand its authority on the basis of the taxing and spending power and the "necessary and proper" clause) has been a matter of argument that is still very much alive today.

If the states' specific powers are never spelled out, the states are nevertheless protected in other ways. Article IV promises that state boundaries will be inviolate, and it guarantees each state a "republican [that is, elected representative] form of government." Furthermore, Congress is made up of representatives of the respective states, and state interests are very much an issue in deliberations in Congress.

⬦ STATE CONSTITUTIONS

One power reserved to the states that is universally agreed on and beyond debate is the power to prescribe the basic framework and limits of state government by the writing and adoption of a state constitution. A state constitution is the fundamental law of the state in that it is superior to statutory law, that is, the bills passed in the legislature. State constitutions are subordinate, however, to the U.S. Constitution.

When Americans think of constitutional law, it is the national Constitution that normally comes to mind. In a recent national poll, an extraordinary 56 percent of adults surveyed did not even know that their state had its own constitution.[10] Yet state constitution writing and reform have been constant and important activities in state political life since the beginning of the republic.

Since 1775, the states have written and ratified 146 constitutions (Louisiana has had 11 constitutions since that time); these have been amended, usually by a popular referendum, no fewer than 5,300 times.[11] Compare this to the single national Constitution, amended only 26 times.

The contrast between state and national constitutions does not end here. State constitutions tend on average to be about three times longer: The federal document contains only 8,700 words, compared to the state mean of 26,000 words. State constitutions are also marked by excessive detail and occasionally ridiculous triviality. Perhaps one of the most blatant examples of excessive detail is Article XIC of the Maryland Constitution, devoted entirely to establishing the conditions of off-street parking in Baltimore. For triviality, few provisions better illustrate this disease of state constitution writers than South Dakota's constitutional authorization of the establishment of a twine and cordage plant in the state penitentiary, except perhaps Oklahoma's constitutional injunction that "stock feeding" techniques be taught in the state's public schools.[12]

One other contrast with the U.S. Constitution is important: Whereas the U.S. Constitution may be amended only by a constitutional convention or, more commonly, by the combined action of two-thirds of the members of both houses of Congress and a ratification vote by three-quarters of the state legislatures, the states involve ordinary voters in the process. The most common procedure, available in all 50 states, is for the legislature to propose an amendment that must then be ratified by the electorate. Of 239 total state constitutional amendments proposed in the 1992–1993 biennium, 201 originated as legislative proposals. Voters approved two-thirds of these.[13]

The second procedure for amending state constitutions is less common, but it is growing rapidly in popularity. This is the constitutional initiative, a process that allows citizens to petition (by gathering signatures) to propose amendments directly to the electorate. In the 1992–1993 biennium, the use of the initiative reached an all-time high: 34 initiatives appeared on state ballots in that two-year period, and voters approved 61 percent of them.

The initiative was an Oregon invention from 1902, part of the progressive movement's effort to wrest control of government from party bosses and backroom elites. Eighteen states, most of them west of the Mississippi, now permit some form of initiative process to amend the state constitution.

The state of Oregon has continued to experiment with democratizing the political process. In 1996, the state conducted a special election for the U.S. Senate by mail ballot, which Congressperson Ron Wyden won narrowly. The use of the mail ballot increased voter participation substantially.
(Source: © Terry Ashe/Gamma Liaison)

Although the initiative offers real possibilities for popular democracy, it also raises the specter of the old tyranny of the majority decried by James Madison in *The Federalist Papers*. One recent case illustrates the issue. In 1992, Colorado voters, by a margin of 53 percent to 47 percent, approved a constitutional amendment that prohibited local governments from barring discrimination in employment and housing against gays and lesbians. Passage of the amendment forced the repeal of gay rights statutes in three Colorado cities. Colorado courts subsequently held the initiative to be unconstitutional in the eyes of the national constitution. The decision was upheld by the U.S. Supreme Court in *Romer v. Evans* (1996).

Although state constitutions all perform in slightly different ways the necessary functions of establishing the framework of their respective state governments—the structure of the legislature, the nature of the judicial system, the length of the governor's term, the nature of local government authority, qualifications for office-holding, and so on—as well as providing a bill of rights, they have also served to limit the possibilities for government activism by providing long lists of "thou shalt nots." In his book *Storm Over the States*, former North Carolina governor Terry Sanford called state constitutions "the drag anchors of state progress."[14]

BOX 2.1 RUNAWAY REFERENDUMS IN COLORADO?

Colorado is one of the most ardent users of the ballot initiative process to amend the state constitution. Potential constitutional amendments are placed on the ballot either as referendums by a two-thirds vote of the state legislature or as initiatives by citizens who have gathered a number of signatures equal to 5 percent of the total number of votes cast for the Secretary of State in the previous general election. In the 1994 election, Colorado voters had twelve opportunities (three ballot referendums and nine ballot initiatives) to amend their state constitution on the following issues.

REFERENDUMS

Ballot Proposal A to require any constitutional amendment proposed by initiative or referendum to be confined to a single subject (passed).

Ballot Proposal B to require the nonpartisan research staff of the general assembly to prepare a ballot information booklet, available at no charge to the public, before any statewide election on any initiated or referred constitutional amendment or legislation (passed).

Ballot Proposal C to deny bail to people convicted of violent felonies and specifying the conditions under which bail shall be denied after conviction for other felonies (passed).

INITIATIVES

Ballot Proposal #1 to increase state tobacco taxes 50 cents per standard pack of 20 cigarettes and require the General Assembly to appropriate revenues: 50 percent for health care for the indigent, 30 percent for school/community cessation programs, 10 percent research on tobacco-related illnesses and prevention of tobacco use, 5 percent for economic development including health-related business activities, 4 percent for municipalities and counties, and 1 percent for administration (did not pass).

Ballot Proposal #11 to specify that workers' compensation benefits include all reasonable and necessary treatment, allow injured workers to choose health care providers, and subject provider fees to state regulation (did not pass).

Ballot Proposal #12 to make a series of changes in electoral laws including freezing

Concern over outmoded, overly detailed, and excessively restrictive constitutions led, after the mid-1960s, to a flurry of state constitutional reform. Between 1965 and 1995, eight states adopted entirely new constitutions. A number of other states attempted to put new constitutions into place, but voters rejected these at the polls. In many of these latter instances, however, a significant number of the new provisions have been successfully submitted piecemeal to the voters or the legislature. The Advisory Commission on Intergovernmental Relations summarized the results of this reform activity:

> *Most of the completely revised constitutions are significantly better than their predecessors. As a whole they are shorter, more clearly written, modernized, less encumbered with restrictions, more basic in content and have more reasonable amending processes.*[15]

Besides the substantial efforts to reform state constitutions in recent decades, one other development is important to note: the tendency in state constitutional law to afford greater individual rights protection than the U.S. Supreme Court has been willing to grant under the U.S. Constitution. This has come to be known as the new judicial federalism, and it seems to have emerged during the early 1970s when U.S. Supreme Court

state and local elected officials' compensation (salary, fringe benefits, pensions, and expenses) at 1988 levels as well as terminating elected officials' participation in state or local government pension plans (did not pass).

Ballot Proposal #13 to legalize limited gaming in Manitou Springs without a local vote and to give certain government entities the option to place slot machines in public airports without a local vote (did not pass).

Ballot Proposal #14 to permit limited gaming in the town of Trinidad (did not pass).

Ballot Proposal #15 to limit campaign contributions in statewide and legislative races by capping contribution limits per election at $100 to legislative candidates, $250 to lesser statewide candidates, and $500 to candidates for governor, and requiring candidates to raise at least 60 percent of their contributions from individuals (did not pass).

Ballot Proposal #16 to provide that the state, city or town, city and county, or county may control the promotion of obscenity to the extent provided by the First Amendment of the U.S. Constitution (did not pass).

Ballot Proposal #17 to reduce from six to three the number of consecutive terms a United States Representative from Colorado may serve and to establish a new limit for nonjudicial elected officials of two consecutive terms of office for local officials (passed).

Ballot Proposal #18 to make underage parents financially responsible to repay the state for medical assistance payments including prenatal, birth delivery, and postpartum care (did not pass).

Interestingly, Colorado voters rejected all of the nine statewide ballot initiatives proposed by voters except for Ballot Proposal 17, the term-limitation measure for members of Congress and various state and local officials. Meanwhile, all three constitutional amendments referred to voters by the legislature, including the Ballot Proposals A and B, which placed limits on the referendum process, were successful.

Sources: Jeffrey A. Roberts, "Last Word on Amendments: No," *The Denver Post* (November 10, 1994), A-15; League of Women Voters of Colorado Education Fund (Denver).

Chief Justice Earl Warren, a liberal jurist, was succeeded by the conservative Warren Burger.[16]

State supreme courts, in more than 400 decisions since 1970, have enunciated broad interpretations of their own constitutional protections, especially with respect to the rights of defendants and the right to privacy. Many of these decisions have been based not on federal civil rights but on broader state guarantees. Indiana's constitution, for example, has a more careful prohibition against cruel and unusual punishment than the national Constitution. The court in that state recently ruled, in the words of the Indiana Chief Justice, that Indiana's provision "affords criminal defendants a more searching review of extremely long jail terms than the federal constitution" provides.[17] California's supreme court gives individuals greater protection from police searches than the federal Constitution's Fourth Amendment.

✧ DUAL FEDERALISM AND COOPERATIVE FEDERALISM BEFORE THE NEW DEAL

Within the general, often ambiguous, and occasionally conflicting constitutional framework, states and nation have sought over the course of American history to define their respective roles. Participants in this process of definition have included the Congress, state and federal courts, and an assortment of governors, presidents, and political thinkers. Early in the nineteenth century Thomas Jefferson was an important figure in articulating the states' rights position, that is, the idea that states retain control over their internal affairs and that the national government cannot intrude on this domain. "The true theory of our constitution," Jefferson wrote, "is that the states are independent as to everything within themselves and united as to everything respecting foreign nations."

Opposed to this view was the nationalist—or federalist—perspective, which saw the national government as preeminent. Rather than relying on the Tenth Amendment to undergird its position, the nationalist view took as its text Article VI, the Supremacy Clause of the Constitution, which states that "This Constitution, and the laws of the United States which shall be made in pursuance thereof . . . shall be the supreme law of the land; and the judges in every state shall be bound thereby, any thing in the constitution or laws of any state to the contrary notwithstanding." Federalists, represented in the early years by such people as Alexander Hamilton, believed in addition that the "necessary and proper" clause of the Constitution gave Congress broad powers to adopt means not necessarily explicitly mentioned in the Constitution in order to carry out its responsibilities, even if this meant that Congressional action touched on areas reserved to the states. From this point of view the Tenth Amendment represented no limit on the national government.

How did this doctrinal conflict play out in practice? A good example is the Missouri Compromise of 1820. When Missouri applied for statehood, there were 11 free states and 11 slave states. The practical question at stake was whether to admit Missouri as a free or slave state, but the constitutional question was whether the national government could determine Missouri's status at all. Southern members of Congress took the states' rights position: Congress had no power to decide whether a state should permit slavery or not. This was a right reserved to the states. Northern members, however, insisted on placing an antislavery restriction on Missouri's admission. The result was the compromise, which prohibited slavery forever in the western territories but allowed Missouri in as a slave state. The states' rights position had prevailed for the moment, but John Quincy Adams wrote in his diary: "I take it for granted that the present question is mere preamble, a title page to a great tragic volume."

States' rights proponents understood the relationship between states and nation in terms of what came to be called **dual federalism,** the idea that there was a clearly delineated division of responsibility between the two levels of government. But as antagonists were struggling to determine this delineation, there also emerged a very different notion embodied in the idea of **cooperative federalism.** Where the states' rights doctrine saw a competitive relationship between the two levels of government, each seeking to protect its respective domains from encroachment by the other, cooperative federalism involved a pattern of shared responsibility for particular functions.

The most common example in the nineteenth century was the development of transportation infrastructure, the network of roads, canals, levees, and harbor facilities in the young nation. Often, all levels of government were involved in these projects. Federal participation in such undertakings as the dredging of the Dismal Swamp Canal in Virginia, part of the intracoastal waterway, took the form of providing technical assistance to the state through the Army Corps of Engineers and financial assistance through the purchase of stock in the canal company.[18] In other cases—the canal-building projects in Ohio and Indiana, for example—the federal government gave land to the states, which in turn sold the land and used the proceeds to finance their canal projects. The device of federal land grants to states was used later in the century in the Morrill Act of 1862 to provide resources to states to establish or build up their state universities, hence the term *land grant universities*.

Early in this century federal assistance to the states began to take the form with which we are familiar: direct cash grants for specific purposes, called **categorical grants-in-aid.** The first major grant of this sort came in 1916 with the passage of the Highway Act. Congress was able to provide money to the states because the new national income tax implemented after ratification of the Sixteenth Amendment in 1913 generated large cash flows into the national treasury. The Highway Act provided funds to state highway departments to pave rural roads to "get the farmers out of the mud" as they hauled their crops to market.

In transportation, education, and some other areas, states and the federal government were hardly in competition but rather sought to support and further common policy goals. Nevertheless, in the period after the Civil War and before the Great Depression of the 1930s, dual federal doctrines held sway, particularly in the courts. One of the Supreme Court cases that best exemplifies this thinking was *Hammer v. Dagenhart*, decided in 1918. The U.S. Congress had been concerned about the exploitation of children as a source of cheap labor in mines and mills. In 1916 Congress passed a law barring goods that had been produced by manufacturers employing children under the age of 14 from interstate commerce. Ronald Dagenhart, whose children worked in a cotton mill, challenged the law. The suit made its way to the Supreme Court, which declared the law unconstitutional. Congress, said the court, may regulate the interstate *transportation* of goods, but the *production* of things intended for interstate commerce is a matter of state regulation. Here the court was delineating the boundary between state and national functions and in the process barring the national government from regulating child labor involved in the production process.

✧ THE RISE OF NATIONAL POWER: 1930–1970

The idea that the national government was limited by states' rights was eclipsed by the emergency of the Great Depression. Following the stock market crash in 1929, millions of people lost their jobs. Official government estimates placed unemployment at 12.8 million workers in 1933, about 25 percent of the entire labor force.[19] Unable to pay their mortgage loans, many lost their homes. When people could not repay their bank loans, banks began to fail, and people's savings were lost. Businesses whose customers could not afford to buy what they made or sold collapsed, putting more people out of work. Welfare programs, unemployment insurance, Social Security pensions, Food Stamps, and federally insured bank deposits did not yet exist. There were local relief programs that provided small sums of money to the most destitute for short periods of time, but these were quickly exhausted.

One major consequence of this vast economic distress was that state and local tax revenues dried up: No one had any money with which to pay taxes. State and local governments could not engage in deficit spending—that is, spend more than they took in—because most of them operated (and still do) under provisions in their own state constitutions that require balanced budgets. Furthermore, their ability to borrow money—both the amount and the purposes for which it is to be spent—is greatly limited by constitutional restrictions. States and cities then turned, naturally enough, to the national government, whose borrowing capacity is unlimited and whose budgets need not be balanced.

When we speak of the explosion of national power during and after the Depression, we mean that the government in Washington began to get involved in a wide range of domestic activities to which it had rarely paid attention before. This involvement took the form of new programs, new levels of regulation of state and local activities, and, above all, the transfer of huge sums of federal money to be spent for specific purposes mandated by Congress, although the actual applications to local situations were often planned and administered by states or localities.

In 1927, just two years before the onset of the Depression, the federal government provided a total of $123 million in assistance to states and localities. Almost all of this—$83 million—was for highway construction. By the end of the Depression in 1939, federal intergovernmental fiscal assistance had risen to about $1 billion per year.

The first major indication that the federal role was on the verge of great expansion was the Federal Emergency Relief Act of 1933, the first federal grant-in-aid to states for the purpose of providing public relief. It allocated nearly $3 billion to the states between 1933 and 1936. But this was simply the first of many programs that constituted President Franklin Roosevelt's New Deal: In 1935 Congress passed the Social Security Act, which established welfare assistance to families with dependent children, the system of old-age pensions to which all workers and employers contribute, and the survivor's insurance program, which provides payments to children when their wage-earning parent dies. Two years later Congress passed the Wagner Housing Act, providing funds for the first sustained national program to build public housing for the poor.

From the end of the Depression (around 1940) to the beginning years of President Lyndon Johnson's Great Society (1964), federal grants to state and local governments grew slowly but steadily from approximately $1 billion a year to about $10.1 billion. (See Table 2.1.) In the 1940s and 1950s the federal government established only three major intergovernmental aid programs: aid for airport construction (1946), housing and urban renewal (1949 and 1954), and the interstate highway program (1956). Congress passed many smaller programs in these years, however, so that by the time President John F. Kennedy was assassinated in 1963, there were about 180 categorical grant-in-aid programs.

The Great Society years (1964–1968) saw an enormous increase in federal activity. By 1968 Washington was passing back $18.6 billion to state and local governments and the number of programs had more than doubled to 379. The Great Society was President Johnson's slogan for his domestic agenda. One element of this agenda was an effort to revitalize the cities, to make them places where, as Johnson said, people would want to come to live the good life. Another element of the Great Society were the initiatives aimed at combating poverty, a condition in which at least 33 million Americans lived in the early 1960s.

The legislative record in the Johnson years is astonishing: Leaving aside the great Civil Rights and Voting Rights Acts of 1964 and 1965 (neither involved grants-in-aid), Congress passed the Economic Opportunity Act of 1964 (the opening shot in the War on Poverty); the Medicaid and Medicare health programs for the indigent and the elderly, respectively; federal aid to elementary and secondary education; the Model Cities planning grant program for urban poverty areas; aid to urban mass transit; aid to local police and criminal justice systems; Food Stamps; Head Start for early childhood education and preventive health care; and a public housing bill that called for 6 million new units of low-income housing by the late 1970s.[20] Suddenly, the federal government was involved in the most intimate details of local administration. Federal dollars paid for street benches and planters in front of neighborhood shopping strips, for school breakfasts in poor neighborhoods, for meals for the housebound elderly, for new buses for city transit systems, and for teaching job skills to young people from poor backgrounds.

Most of these programs involved transfers of money from Washington to state or local governments to be used for purposes spelled out by Congress. Many, but not all, of these programs survive today. The main features of these categorical grant-in-aid programs are as follows:

TABLE 2.1 FEDERAL AID TO STATE AND LOCAL GOVERNMENTS

	Dollars	*Constant 1987 Dollars*	*Percentage of GNP*	*Percentage Passed on to Individuals*	*Number of Programs*
1960	$ 7.0 billion	$ 29.1 billion	1.4%	35.7%	132
1963	8.6	34.0	1.5	38.0	—
1968	18.6	64.3	2.2	32.7	397
1975	49.8	105.4	3.3	33.7	442
1978	77.9	131.4	3.6	31.8	492
1982	88.2	106.5	2.8	44.0	404
1989	122.0	112.2	2.4	55.2	492
1995 (est.)	228.0	174.7	3.2	63.9	600

Source: Advisory Commission on Intergovernmental Relations, *Significant Features of Fiscal Federalism, 1994 Edition, Vol. 2* (Washington, D.C.: Government Printing Office, 1994), p. 30.

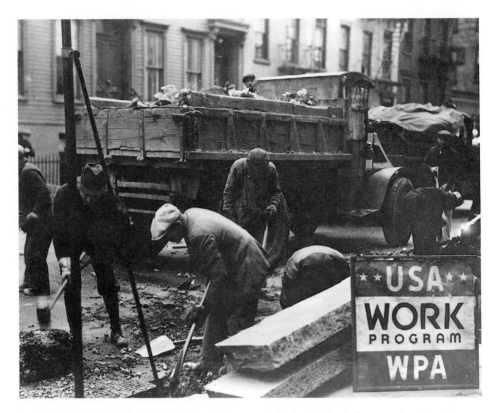

Men working under the federal Works Progress Administration widen a city street, 1935. At its peak, this Depression-era program employed about one third of the 10 million unemployed people, the vast majority of whom lived in the nation's big cities. (*Source:* The Bettmann Archive)

- ◆ The uses of the grants are carefully spelled out by Congress.
- ◆ Most are competitive, requiring that cities or states submit applications. This puts a high premium on "grantsmanship," the ability to write convincing grant applications and win supporters in the federal agency responsible for choosing recipients.
- ◆ Most require recipients to submit careful plans showing how the funds are to be used and how the project relates to other federally and locally funded projects. Despite federal program guidelines, state or local officials have a good deal of discretion over how the program is to be applied to their particular needs.
- ◆ Most require a matching grant from state or local sources. The federal government rarely supplies 100 percent of the project costs, requiring instead that the recipient jurisdiction provide between 10 percent and 50 percent of the necessary funds.
- ◆ All programs are governed by provisions of the 1964 Civil Rights Act, which bar the use of federal funds in any program that discriminates against individuals on the basis of race, religion, or national origin.

Although state and local officials welcomed this profusion of money in the 1960s, some complained that all of this federal activity, accompanied as it was by regulations, audits, and program requirements, represented an encroachment on state and local powers. Others argued that the growth of federal programs enlarged the powers of all levels of government. This latter view is not difficult to sustain if we assume that increased functions and increased resources are indications of expanded power.

Consider the following effects of increased federal aid to states and localities. The growth of federal programs, most of which required some state or local matching funds, meant first that state and local spending increased sharply in the 1960s. Between 1965 and 1970 total state and local spending per capita rose from $385 to $646.[21] This meant, among other things, that state and local governments were doing more for people than they had been before the Great Society years.

Increased responsibilities meant that the number of state and local public employees per 10,000 in population rose in the Great Society years from 358 to 420.[22] The explosion of federal programs created all sorts of new jobs in state and local government: program planners, economists, social workers, community organizers, antipoverty program workers, and grant coordinators. State and local governments could not only do more than they had before, but their workforces were better trained and more professional. Because they had to raise money to match federal grants, many states found that they had to expand and modernize antiquated and inadequate tax-collection systems. Whereas in 1950 only 17 states had both a sales tax and an individual income tax, by 1980, 37 states had both kinds. This meant that state tax systems became both more efficient at raising revenue and more equitable in distributing tax burdens on individuals and businesses.

Finally, and perhaps most important of all, the states and localities that received federal money were the ones that actually planned the specific uses to which the money would be put. Local planners had broad discretion. Consider the ways school districts use funds allocated to them under the Elementary and Secondary Education Act of 1965. Designed to help districts with high proportions of poor children, the act permits local officials to spend on virtually anything they wish: books, remedial classroom instruction, school lunches, medical exams, school crossing guards, standardized testing, teachers' salaries, libraries, transportation, and even winter coats for children who cannot afford them.

In certain respects the Great Society years represent the high point in the American experiment with big government, the last moment at which people believed that we could solve our problems through government action. Although additional federal programs were passed in the 1970s and federal aid to state and local governments increased, a reaction had set in by the end of the 1960s. For many people the promise of the Great Society simply fell far short in reality. It is true that poverty rates fell from about 19 percent of the population in 1964 to 12.1 percent in 1969. It is also true that the nation now had a program to provide medical insurance to all the elderly, half of whom had had no coverage at all before Medicare. A majority of young children were now attending preschool programs, whereas before federal aid to education and the Head Start program, only a third had done so.

But the war in Vietnam was absorbing our resources, and on the home front welfare rates, teenage pregnancy, and the incidence of single-parent families had all begun to rise. During the peak years of the Great Society, the nation's inner cities were wracked by riots. Certain groups, particularly white working and middle-class people, struggling to maintain their standard of living in a suddenly stagnant economy, began to resent what they thought was the preferential treatment accorded the poor and minorities. Others lost faith in the efficacy of the federal government in the face of apparently intractable social problems. It is striking that in the roughly three decades since the end of the Great Society much of domestic politics may still be seen as a reaction to the disappointments and perceived shortcomings of the Great Society.

✧ NEW FEDERALISM: THE NIXON REFORMS

By the end of the 1960s public officials at all levels of government had become seriously worried about the proliferation of federal programs, the lack of coordination among them, and the high degree of overlap in certain areas. For example, by 1970 there were 17 separate federal programs for employment and training, and they were administered by 13 different agencies and bureaus.[23] State and local officials contemplating applying for federal grants found the whole system increasingly bewildering. Not only did the system of federal programs seem chaotic but it also seemed to be growing out of control. Between 1964 (the first year of Johnson's Great Society) and 1969 the average annual increase in aid to state and local governments was over 15 percent and the dollar outlay had doubled from $10 to $20 billion. Public officials began to call for reform of the federal grant system.

President Nixon, elected first in 1968, was receptive to the reformers and took up their cause. In part he was interested in making the system of federal grants more efficient, but he was also committed to devolving power back to state and local governments and reducing the influence of Washington. He called his effort to stem the growth of big government and reform the grant system the **New Federalism.**

Central elements of the New Federalism were two forms of federal aid to subnational governments: **block grants** and **revenue sharing,** which differed sharply from the categorical grants. Block grants are broad-purpose grants designed to increase the flexibility of recipient jurisdictions. In 1971 President Nixon proposed consolidating 129 categorical grant-in-aid programs into six broad block grants in the general areas of law enforcement, urban community development, rural development, job training, education, and transportation. Only two of these were eventually passed by Congress—the 1973 Comprehensive Employment and Training Act (CETA) and the 1974 Community Development Block Grant (CDBG)—and only the latter survives today.

A popular program at the local level, CDBG provides an annual sum, called an **entitlement,** to cities with populations of over 50,000, to heavily urbanized counties, and to states, which in turn distribute their funds to small communities. Distribution by entitlement is based on a formula taking into account population size, the incidence of poverty, and other such factors. By using formula-based entitlements, the federal government eliminated the need of communities to apply competitively for development funds, thus simplifying and streamlining the federal grant system in this particular area. CDBG, which consolidated seven categorical grant programs, may be spent on a wide variety of community development uses determined at the local level, including land purchase and clearance, sidewalk and street improvements, and loans to private businesses that promise to create jobs.

The second grant innovation of the Nixon New Federalism period was general revenue sharing. Although the idea had been discussed for several decades, it was not until 1972 that Congress passed such a program. Revenue sharing was simple in concept: Each state and every single general-purpose local government in the United States received an entitlement every year from Washington to be spent on virtually anything the recipient wished. The idea behind the program was to take advantage of the superior revenue-raising capacity of the federal government's progressive income tax in a period during which states and cities were having fiscal difficulties, and at the same time to provide a high degree of local discretion in spending the money. Revenue sharing, though popular at the state and local level, only lasted 14 years. It was eliminated under the Reagan administration in 1986.

Nixon's New Federalism could scarcely be regarded as a success, at least in the terms in which he had proposed the reforms. It is true that states and localities had somewhat more freedom to spend the federal funds that came to them in the form of block grants and revenue sharing, but such funds accounted for only about 25 percent of federal aid to state and local governments in 1975 and less than that thereafter.[24]

More important, if the aim was to reduce the influence of big government in Washington, then the New Federalism was a stunning failure. Federal aid to state and local government rose more sharply during the Nixon-Ford years, measured in current dollar terms or as a percentage of total federal spending or as a percentage of GNP, than it had during the Great Society in the 1960s. (See Table 2.1.) Indeed, between 1968 and 1975 Congress added another 45 categorical grant programs.

In addition, the Nixon administration presided over what one scholar has called "the greatest expansion of federal regulation of state and local governments in American history."[25] Twenty-three major enactments were passed in the Nixon-Ford years. In truth, these regulatory initiatives were less the product of the Republican White House than of the Democratic Congress.

What was novel about this **regulatory federalism** was that whereas most prior regulation had affected the private sector, the new laws subjected state and local government to federal controls. As the Advisory Commission on Intergovernmental Relations observed, "Federal mandates and regulations began to rival grants and subsidies in importance as federal tools for influencing the behavior of state and local governments."[26]

These regulations took various forms. One common type was the direct order, exemplified by the Equal Employment Opportunity Act of 1972, which barred discrimination in employment by state and local governments. Failure to take adequate steps to make sure their workforces were open to women and minority groups could subject these subnational governments to civil penalties. In the Clean Air Act of 1970 Congress imposed regulations by partial preemption, acting under the Supremacy Clause of the Constitution to replace state air quality standards with federal ones. Then there were cross-cutting regulations, which applied to many subnational government activities if they were assisted with federal money. The law prohibiting discrimination by state and local governments on the basis of age (the Age Discrimination Act of 1975) is a good example. Finally, there were regulations called crossover sanctions, federal fiscal sanctions on one program for failure to comply with federal regulations pertaining to another. For example, the Emergency Highway Energy Conservation Act of 1974 permitted the federal government to withhold highway aid from states that failed to set a 55-mph speed limit.[27]

As Timothy Conlan concludes, the huge increases in federal spending and the vast expansion of federal regulation of state and local government activities "left no room for doubt over which level of government was now the senior partner in virtually all areas of intergovernmental collaboration."[28]

Perhaps this is an overstatement, however, for it turns out that not all parties to the federal arrangement have been convinced that national dominance was the natural order of things. In 1976, after decades of federal government growth, the Supreme Court suddenly and unexpectedly acted to place new limits on national power. In the case *National League of Cities v. Usery* (426 U.S. 833), the Court overturned an act of Congress that extended the provisions of the Fair Labor Standards Act, such as the minimum wage and overtime provisions, to employees of state and local governments. Control over the conditions of employment of their own civil servants, the Court said, was a "traditional function" of state and local governments, granted to them by the Tenth Amendment, on which the national government could not intrude.

The Court declined to define what it meant by "traditional function," however, an omission that opened the way to a constant flow of litigation. What was traditional and what was nontraditional? Where was the line that limited national power to regulate state and local activities? The courts were not sure: Some held that regulating ambulance services and licensing automobile drivers were traditional functions but regulating traffic on public roads and the provision of services to the disabled were nontraditional.[29] The distinctions between what the national government could regulate and what it had to leave entirely to the states and localities made little sense. At one point the Supreme Court gave up the attempt: In a case decided in 1985—*Garcia v. San Antonio Metropolitan Transit Authority* (105 S. Ct. 1005)—a majority of the justices overruled *NLC v. Usery.* "We find it difficult, if not impossible," Justice Blackmun wrote, "to identify an organizing principle" that places functions in traditional and nontraditional categories. Blackmun wrote that the idea of what functions ought to be entirely reserved to the states has changed over history. A constitutional distinction between functions immune to federal regulation and those liable to such regulation is "elusive at best." In the end, the only limitation on national power to regulate state and local activities or to become involved in some particular area of public concern is a political, not a constitutional, constraint.

But this conclusion had scarcely been reached when two elderly Missouri state judges launched a challenge in the federal courts to their state's mandatory age 70 retirement law on the grounds that it violated the federal Age Discrimination in Employment Act (1974). The U.S. Supreme Court found in favor of Missouri. The federal law did not apply to the judges, the Court argued in *Gregory v. Ashcroft* (111 S. Ct. 2395, 1991): The Tenth Amendment reserved to the people of the states the right to establish public officials' qualifications and Congress could not interfere.

The Supreme Court of the mid-1990s seemed more solidly committed to this states' rights position than the court of a decade earlier. In 1995, for example, a slim majority of the justices struck down a federal law (the Gun Free School Zone Act of 1990) that barred the possession of guns near schools.[30] It was the first time in 60 years that the Court had limited the power of Congress under the Commerce Clause of the Constitution (Congress shall have the power "to regulate commerce . . . among the several states," Article I, Section 8).

✧ NEW FEDERALISM: THE REAGAN VERSION

Despite what appeared to be a return to dual federalism doctrines on the shoulders of *NLC v. Usery,* the latter half of the 1970s saw a steady growth of national power. It was as if the Nixon reforms had been entirely forgotten. Between 1975 and 1980 no new block grant consolidations took place, but Congress passed 92 new categorical aid programs and 5 new intergovernmental regulatory acts. Federal spending for state and local government assistance reached an all-time high in 1978. When Ronald Reagan was elected, there were a record 539 categorical grant programs administered by Washington.

Reagan came to office arguing that in dealing with America's social and economic difficulties big government was a problem, not a solution. "It is my intention," he declared in his first inaugural address, "to curb the size and influence of the Federal establishment and to demand recognition of the distinction between the powers granted to the Federal government and those reserved to the states or to the people." Like President Nixon before him, Ronald Reagan called his reform agenda the New Federalism.

The New Federalism program of the 1980s had at least four elements. One was a huge tax cut, amounting to $162 billion in 1981, which dwarfed the second largest cut in history of roughly $23 billion in 1975.[31] Part of the point of the cut was to reduce the size of the federal government by denying it constantly growing revenues. Accompanying the tax cut were sharp reductions in the federal budget for domestic programs. The effects were immediate and dramatic: Intergovernmental aid (in constant dollars) fell from $127.6 billion in 1980 to $106.5 billion in 1982.

Another way of looking at the impact of reduced federal aid over the course of the Reagan presidency is to note that federal revenues as a percentage of local government revenue fell from 9 percent in 1978 to 4.2 percent in 1987. For states, the drop in federal aid over the same period went from 22.3 percent to 18.5 percent of state revenues.[32]

A second element of Reagan's New Federalism was the consolidation of categorical grants into block grants and the elimination of many categoricals altogether. The object was to strip Congress of the power inherent in categoricals and devolve it to the states and communities through discretionary block grants. Ten new block grants were passed by Congress, mostly in the areas of public health and education. Combined with those that were eliminated altogether, the effect of these efforts was to reduce the number of separate categorical grants from 539 when Carter left office to 492 when George Bush assumed the presidency. However, the percentage of federal aid that went to states and localities in the form of block grants remained virtually unchanged in the 1980s, declining only from 10.6 percent to 10.4 percent over the Reagan years. Categoricals still account for more than 88 percent of intergovernmental aid.[33]

If the Reagan era changes did not shift the balance of federal aid to block grants, they did make administration much easier than under the old categorical programs they replaced. In the seven block grants administered by the Department of Health and Human Services, over 600 pages of program regulations were eliminated and replaced by a mere seven pages of requirements.[34] State and local reporting requirements were greatly reduced, easing the paperwork burdens on state and local governments.

A third but quite unsuccessful part of the New Federalism agenda was deregulation of state and local government. Although the effort produced some relief from a growing paperwork burden connected with the administration of federal grants, President Reagan was unable to persuade Congress to roll back any of its major intergovernmental regulations. Then, in Reagan's second term there was a burst of new federal regulatory action in areas such as trucking, communications, coastal zone management, workfare, and the drinking age. Indeed, between 1981 and 1990 Congress enacted 27 new or expanded regulatory statutes that bore on state and local governments, surpassing even the record of regulatory zeal of the 1970s.[35]

Not all of this new regulatory activity was the product of a Democratic Congress forcing its will on the Republican President. New Federalism objectives became secondary to the Reagan administration in cases in which new federal regulation of state and local governments promised to enhance the operation of the free market. Thus, for example, Reagan supported a bill prohibiting local governments from regulating rates charged by cable television companies. In the field of transportation the federal government now forces states to permit the operation of twin-trailer trucks on certain highways from which they had previously been barred by state highway departments.

Finally, the fourth element was what came to be known as "the great swap." President Reagan proposed that the federal government would assume full responsibility for the Medicaid program of medical assistance for the poor in return for turning over entirely to the states Aid to Families of Dependent Children (welfare) and Food Stamps. In addition, Reagan suggested that an additional 44 programs in education, transportation, and community development be "turned back" to the states along with sufficient, although greatly reduced, federal revenues to fund them. The nation's governors, fearing that these proposals had far less to do with reforming the federal system than with reducing the national government's responsibility for social programs at the expense of the states, strongly opposed the swap and turnback. Neither the Congress nor the public showed much interest in this arrangement either. The proposals were abandoned in 1982.

The record of the Reagan New Federalism is a mixed one in the end. If the efforts to consolidate categorical grants or deregulate state and local government met with only partial success, the change in federal spending priorities and patterns must rank as a major accomplishment. No longer able to count on a steady expansion of federal aid for domestic programs, states and localities entered a new era of fiscal self-reliance at the beginning of the 1980s, what some call fend-for-yourself federalism.[36] Part of this situation, which continues today, is a result of extremely high federal budget deficits, which have made Congress reluctant to initiate new spending programs, but much of it is due to self-conscious efforts to reduce domestic federal spending through budget cuts and the elimination of programs.

Interestingly, during the Bush presidency federal intergovernmental grants began to increase sharply. By 1991 the amount of aid finally regained the level of the 1978 high point, and the amount has continued to increase since then to all-time highs. But there is a big difference in the federal aid system of today and that of the 1970s: Whereas in the earlier period about two-thirds of federal intergovernmental aid was going to state and local governments for programs such as education and highways and one-third to individuals in the form of Medicaid, welfare, and other assistance, by the 1990s the proportions were reversed. About two-thirds of all federal grants-in-aid now goes to individuals, not governments. Medicaid spending (health insurance for poor people), which more than doubled from 1989 to 1993, is the primary reason for the change.

The decline in aid for states and localities has meant that they have had to face the issue of whether to take up the program slack. For the most part they have chosen to do so, but to do so they have had to generate more revenues. Between 1985 and 1991 states increased their taxes by over 44 percent; local governments hit taxpayers even harder, increasing taxes by nearly 60 percent.[37] The states have also engaged in a frenzy of policy experimentation in economic development, designed not only to create jobs but to broaden and enlarge the tax base to generate more tax revenues. The Reagan revolution not only had fiscal effects; it also stimulated state experimentation in a whole range of domestic policy areas, particularly welfare and education reforms.

In short, the changes Reagan wrought in the federal system have greatly reduced Washington's role as a source of fiscal assistance and an initiator of domestic policy. The federal system is far more decentralized than when Ronald Reagan arrived in the White House in 1981.

✧ CONTEMPORARY FEDERALISM

Decentralization seems to accord with American tastes these days: The public has little desire for a strong central government. In a national survey conducted in 1995, only 12 percent of the respondents agreed with the statement "The federal government should not shift responsibilities for programs back to the states, but should continue to manage such programs at the federal level."[38] A solid majority agreed that the "states know what they need better than the federal government does."

President Clinton, a former governor himself, came into office committed to a federal system in which the states enjoyed maximum flexibility to experiment and to design their own approaches to solving problems.[39] With cutting the federal budget and reducing the deficit high White House priorities, Clinton's approach to federalism was closer to the devolution of authority favored by his Republican predecessors than it was to the Democratic preference for a strong central government in the Roosevelt-Truman-Johnson tradition.

But the real boost for decentralizing the federal system came with the off-year elections of 1994, when Republicans captured control of both houses of Congress for the first time in 40 years. Many Republicans ran for office on the premise that the federal government had gotten too burdensome, too big, and too intrusive. One of the first things the new majority set out to do was to control the growth of unfunded federal mandates.

Mandates are orders or requirements that a higher level of government imposes on a lower level. The various forms of federal regulation that grew so precipitously in the 1970s and 1980s—direct orders, cross-cutting regulations, and so on—are mandates. The growth of regulatory federalism in those decades greatly constrained state government freedom. When Governor Ben Nelson took office in Nebraska in 1990, he commented, "I honestly wondered if I was actually elected governor or just branch manager of the state of Nebraska for the federal government."[40] State governments had to meet federal environmental standards, comply with the federal fair labor and occupational safety and health standards, obey regulations that provide for access to public facilities for people with disabilities, meet asbestos removal requirements, and so on. Many state and local officials not only complained that federal mandates did not apply to their particular situation (Governor Nelson wondered why Nebraska had to test drinking water for pesticides used on pineapple plantations when the nearest such plantation was in Hawaii), but they objected to the fiscal burdens the federal government imposed on the states. Federal mandates often require state governments to take certain actions, but Congress rarely provides the money to pay for those actions. The cost of meeting federal standards—say, for clean drinking water or wheelchair access to public buildings—can be expensive. Complying with federal mandates cost the state of Ohio nearly $2 billion in the period between 1992 and 1995.[41]

In 1995 a sympathetic Congress passed and the president signed the Unfunded Mandates Reform Act. Although it is not retroactive, the law requires the Congressional Budget Office to provide detailed cost estimates of any new proposed mandates, and it prohibits Congress from imposing mandates on the states that cost more than $50 million unless funding is provided.

The Republican 104th Congress moved not only to provide mandate relief but also to consolidate (once again) the burgeoning number of categorical programs (one count put the number at an all-time high of 618 in 1995) into block grants. Block grants to the states for welfare, medical insurance for the poor, job training, education, housing, and food assistance programs are seen by many as the cutting edge of federalism for the next century. Others voice a classic concern about a highly decentralized federal system: Will the 50 different states develop such sharply different program standards and coverage that regional inequalities will widen in years to come?[42]

✧ THE DISTRIBUTION OF FEDERAL AID

The approximately $228 billion that Washington expended as federal grants in 1995 is a large sum. States and local governments are certainly interested in getting what they consider to be their share. What are the patterns of federal aid distribution among the states and their localities?

Depending on how one measures distribution, some obvious differences among the states leap out. One common way of measuring the distribution of federal grants is to look at the ratio of federal taxes paid by the people and businesses of a state to the amount the state gets back in federal aid. States in the deep South and upper plains region have the most favorable balance of payments: In fiscal year 1993, Mississippians received $2,184 per capita more than they paid out in federal taxes. Other states that got much more back than they sent to Washington include Alabama, Louisiana, Arkansas, South Carolina, West Virginia, New Mexico, the Dakotas, and Montana.[43]

States that paid more than they got back include the states of the upper Midwest, New York, New Jersey, Connecticut, and Nevada. Residents of Connecticut send in over $1,800 per capita more than they receive from the federal government. Senator Daniel Patrick Moynihan (D-NY) concludes that these patterns reflect a long-standing federal policy of "systematically [transferring] resources from the Northeast quadrant of the nation to the South and West. . . . [I]t reflects the fact that the older, industrial and commercial states have higher incomes."[44] As a rule, then, poor states, which generate fewer tax dollars than better-off states, do relatively better in the competition for federal grants. (see Figure 2.1)

But there are other ways of looking at the distribution of federal grants. If we take per capita receipts as our measure of distribution, we find that the top-ranked states include those with poorer populations and those that are big and sparsely settled. Among the 10 states with the highest per capita revenues from the federal government are Wyoming, Alaska, Montana, and the Dakotas. Big empty states have voracious appetites for highways but a small tax base on which to raise money for very expensive construction projects. Federal highway grants fill the need. Those big western and plains states rank among the top six states in per capita receipts for highway construction and maintenance. Other states in the top 10 include New York,

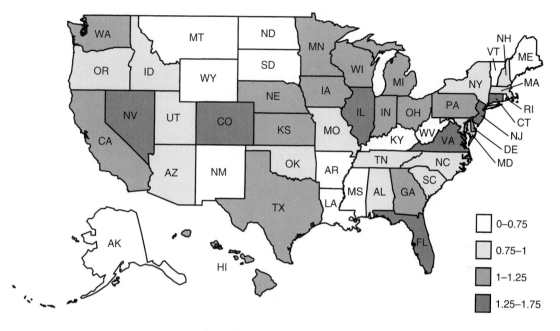

FIGURE 2.1 Ratio of Tax Burden to Grants, 1992

Source: Russell L. Hanson, "Intergovernmental Relations," in Virginia Gray and Herbert Jacob, eds., *Politics in the American States,* 6th ed. Washington, D.C.: CQ Press, 1996, p. 56.

Louisiana, and West Virginia, which are among the states with the highest numbers of poor people.

A third way of looking at distribution is by taking the actual dollar receipts into account. Here we find that states with the largest populations tend to receive the most. California, New York, Texas, Illinois, Pennsylvania, Michigan, Ohio, Florida, and Massachusetts are the big winners in total dollars.

These different ways of looking at the distribution of federal aid suggest that the determinants of allocation patterns probably vary according to the program in question. Paul Peterson has found that the 10 richest states tend to get the most federal aid for developmental purposes (including highways, education, transportation), whereas the 20 poorest states generally receive the most aid for redistributive programs (welfare, medical insurance, and housing assistance).[45] Michael Rich has found that the federal government has tended to distribute community and economic development funds over time to cities that exhibited the highest levels of distress.[46]

Another explanation, however, is that the desire of the local recipients for federal aid has a significant impact on the likelihood that they will receive funds. Peterson argues that one systematic way of assessing state demand for federal aid is to look at a state's willingness to tax its citizens in order to raise enough money to provide the matching funds required by federal categorical grants. In fact, there is a strong relationship between a state's tax effort and the amount of federal aid it receives per capita.[47]

Some states and cities demonstrate their lack of interest in receiving federal aid by failing to apply for categorical grants. By not receiving federal money, the state or community need not submit to federal requirements or influence. For a long time the state of Mississippi did not want its local governments to take part in the federal Head Start preschool program, and Louisiana refused for years to allow its cities to apply for urban renewal grants. Conversely, Rich found in his study not only that the likelihood of receiving federal grants depended to some degree on whether and how often a community applied but that the size of federal allocations was related to the number of applications for aid that the city made.[48] Many communities, particularly smaller and poorer ones, may be interested in receiving federal money but do not have enough professional staff to plan, apply for, and administer federal grants.

Other explanations of patterns of federal aid distribution include the extent of political influence of the state or city in Washington (do they have representation on the key Congressional committees that establish distribution guidelines for certain programs?), population size (Community Development Block Grants take population into account), and the objectives of the president in office. Democratic presidents, for example, sought to allocate urban renewal funds to cities where their major electoral constituencies (organized labor, particular ethnic groups, or blacks) lived.[49]

One lesson that is clear from this review of distributional issues is that the federal grant system is sensitive to differences among places, differences mainly of size, need, influence, and capacity. To some degree these differences are a function of population flows in and out of states and communities. These in- and out-migrations are important not only in terms of numbers of people involved but also in terms of their socioeconomic status. As for the latter, one can see that an influx of poor people is likely to bring with it an increase in federal aid for welfare programs, but because public officials are not free to use these funds flexibly or use them to foster prosperity (in contrast to aid for education or economic development), these are not the sort of resources that states or cities are most happy to have.

High population growth in general increases a state's representation in Congress and, thus, potentially enlarges its influence in the legislative process. Population loss diminishes political influence and decreases the capacity of a state or locality to offer public services by reducing the tax base. Growth and decline also affect the flow of federal monies tied to population size. In this context it is easy to understand why public officials were so concerned that huge numbers of people refused to participate in the 1990 census: Uncounted people have no influence on aid allocation formulas or in determining Congressional representation.

✧ STATES AND THEIR LOCAL GOVERNMENTS

We have been exploring the shifts and turns over history in the relationship between the national government in Washington and subnational governments, particularly the states. When we think in formal constitutional terms about the federal system, we think of it as a two-tier system. In reality, of course, there is a third tier made up of roughly 87,000 local governments of various sorts. These governments—municipalities, counties, school districts, and special districts such as port authorities—are players in the larger federal system. They receive federal grants, many maintain lobbyists in Washington, and their problems in particular have often fueled federal action, as during the Great Society years. Thus, we can speak of intergovernmental relations between local jurisdictions and Washington.

Localities are also involved in a set of intergovernmental relations with the state in which they are located. In certain respects the mix of tension, cooperation, and dependence that characterizes the relationship between states and nation also characterizes that between states and their localities.

One major difference between state-local relations and state-national relations is that whereas in the latter neither level of government derives its authority from the other, municipalities and other forms of local government depend entirely on the state for their existence and powers. The states themselves are not little federal systems; local governments have no autonomous existence. Local governments are literally creatures of the state. The state may create a municipality or a special authority, establish its form of government, and determine its powers. In fact, in law at least, the power of the state over a local government is absolute. As the nineteenth century jurist John Dillon wrote,

> *Municipal corporations owe their origin to, and derive their powers and rights wholly from, the legislature. It breathes into them the breath of life, without which they cannot exist. As it creates, so it may destroy. If it may destroy, it may abridge and control.*[50]

Dillon, a justice of the Iowa Supreme Court, was a student of municipal law. We refer still to his characterization of the state-local relationships as Dillon's Rule, which states that local governments may exercise only the powers expressly granted to them by the state or those necessarily or fairly implied. But any doubts as to whether a local government has the power to act or take on a new function is resolved negatively. Thus, a city cannot simply decide on its own that it will set up a housing authority to build dwellings for the homeless or that it will levy a new tax on gas-powered lawn mowers or that it will regulate plumbers. The state must first have enabled the city to act in these areas, either by a specific or general grant of power.

A general grant of power often takes the form of home rule. The most common form of home rule allows a municipality instead of the state to write its city charter. A charter is the basic law of a local government, its constitution in effect. Should the city executive be a mayor or city manager? Should the city council be elected from wards or at large? How should the city finance its activities? Some states permit their home rule cities to write charters that specify not only the basic form of the city government but also its powers. Should the city run a public housing authority? May it provide training for its police and fire cadets? May it issue bonds to build a civic center?

Whether a state grants its communities broad home rule powers or not (only about 20 states do), every state maintains a substantial degree of influence over the practice of local government. The state of New York, which grants its cities home rule, nevertheless maintains 19 volumes of law, running 6,000 pages, that deal with the powers and structure of local government.[51]

The ultimately subordinate status of cities, even where they enjoy home rule, was reaffirmed in a case decided in 1982 before the U.S. Supreme Court called *Community Communications Co. v. Boulder.*[52] The issue in the case was whether local governments (in this case, the city of Boulder) have immunity from antitrust suits filed under the Sherman Antitrust Act. An antitrust suit seeks to break up a monopoly or challenge a restraint of trade. States, as sovereign entities, are immune from such suits.

The city of Boulder had passed an ordinance that sought to regulate cable TV within its borders. Community Communications, a cable company, challenged this regulation as a restraint of trade. The Supreme Court ruled that even though Boulder had been granted home rule by the state of Colorado, it was not itself a sovereign entity entitled to antitrust immunity. It could not, therefore, enjoy sovereign immunity, unless the state had specifically granted it to the city with respect to antitrust suits. The significance of the case is that even if a state gives its cities home rule powers, those local governments may still exercise only those powers that the state deems appropriate.

One area that every state regulates is the taxing and spending power of its communities, including the types of taxes they may levy, taxing and spending limits, borrowing limits, and budget procedures. Some states even require their municipalities to submit their local budgets for state review.

Most local governments learn to live with state supervision of their spending and taxing. This is so in part because localities are fiscally dependent on their states. States provide over $200 billion a year in aid to local governments, a figure that has risen on average about 8 percent per year since 1980, much faster than the national inflation rate. State aid to local government represents about one-third of all local revenues, 10 times more than federal aid. In fact, state aid accounts for a larger share of local revenues than property tax receipts, the major local tax.

With the rise in state fiscal assistance has come tighter state control of local activities in many areas. Just as the federal government imposes mandates on state governments, state governments impose mandates on their local governments. These mandates, imposed by the legislature or by administrative agencies, are designed to ensure uniformity of services or standards from place to place within a state or to make sure that local governments perform certain functions. The most common mandates pertain to methods of solid waste disposal and special education programs. States may stipulate, for example, that school boards establish programs for the education of children with disabilities or, further, that they be "mainstreamed" in regular classrooms. Other sorts of mandates, for example, relate to the payment of workers' compensation for local government personnel, requirements for offering certain sorts of public health programs, and limits on increases in the property tax levy. It is rare that the states provide the funds to carry out these mandates, forcing local taxpayers to pick up the entire costs of these state orders.

Local government officials are, not surprisingly, just as bitter about unfunded state mandates as their counterparts in the state capital are about unfunded federal mandates. Long before the Congress sought to curb unfunded mandates, however, state lawmakers were experimenting with a variety of ways to ease the burden of state mandates on local governments.

The first state mandate relief dates from the Alaska constitution of 1959, which requires any state law that requires local funding to be approved by the voters of the state. By 1994 at least 28 states had laws in effect designed to limit or regulate unfunded mandates in some way.[53] The most common sort of limitation is a prohibition against a new mandate unless it is accompanied by state funding. But even in states with such a law, the effect is negligible: In Illinois, for example, the state legislature regularly imposed mandates anyway and then exempted itself from its own law! The annual cost of these unfunded mandates to Illinois local governments amounted to more than $100 million a year.[54] Even though more and more states are moving to halt the imposition of unfunded mandates, they remain nevertheless a source of tension between state and local officials.

BOX 2.2 UNFUNDED MANDATES IN WISCONSIN

Although states have been loudly complaining about the impact of unfunded federal mandates on their budgets, they have been guilty of imposing their own unfunded mandates on local governments. The following is a list of Wisconsin state mandates that were identified by a gubernatorial task force as overly burdensome for local governments.

◇ The Department of Transportation mandated new accident reporting forms that required the reprogramming of all county computers.

◇ Local governments are required to publish legal notices in newspapers with paid circulation.

◇ Any money remaining in the dog license fund after all claims are settled must be paid to a county humane society instead of to the municipalities.

◇ Counties are required to log long-distance telephone calls for the state Department of Health and Human Services.

◇ Participants in court-ordered community service work are considered county employees and thus eligible for worker's compensation at the county's expense if injured.

◇ Counties are required to provide and pay for treatment services for indigent cocaine possession offenders.

◇ Counties are required to house state prisoners who have violated the conditions of state probation or parole in county jails, but do not receive full reimbursement for this service.

◇ Counties and municipalities are required to zone and map floodplains and shorelands and have the maps approved by the Department of Natural Resources.

◇ Counties are required to pay the cost of federally required interpreter services for court cases.

◇ County staff must verify that a landowner is complying with soil erosion practices in order for the landowner to participate in the farmland preservation program to control soil erosion.

◇ Counties are required to initiate an investigation of a child abuse or neglect case within 24 hours of the report.

◇ Counties are required to provide at least one staff person, 24 hours a day, to oversee juveniles detained in county jails.

◇ Child care and nursing home facilities must be certified annually.

Source: Jonathan Barry, "Report of the Task Force on County and Local Mandates," Madison, Wisconsin, 1986.

Nevertheless, state-local relations should not be characterized as perpetual warfare. There are certainly tensions that naturally arise whenever one entity has ultimate control over another, but often the relationship is a cooperative one, not only in the fiscal realm but also through the state provision of technical and administrative assistance to local governments. It is probably more accurate these days to portray state-local relations as a partnership rather than an adversarial relationship.

◇ CONCLUSION

A federal arrangement is a way of institutionalizing diversity in the practice of subnational government. States and their localities are able in such a system to do many things pretty much their own way, as long as they have the resources. But there is a built-in tension in any federal system between the desires of subnational units to maximize their autonomy and the impulse of the national government in certain areas to effect uniformity and consistency.

The national government is not always determined to impose uniform standards of government on the 50 states. Washington does not insist on state death penalties or common divorce law, but in other areas the national government has regarded uniformity as an important goal—eligibility for food stamps, maintenance of clean water, and nondiscrimination in the hiring of public employees are all examples. In such cases the national government uses its great fiscal strength to coerce compliance (as when Washington tells the states to establish a drinking age of 21 or lose highway funds) or it falls back on the ultimate authority of the Constitution, invoking the Fourteenth Amendment, the Commerce Clause, or the Supremacy Clause. Thus a delicate balance is struck between national and subnational power, and it is always being adjusted and fine-tuned.

It should not be lost in this discussion that the ability of states and localities to do things the way they wish is not only a function of whether the federal government seeks to exercise influence. It is also a function of state and local resources, and these in turn are determined in part by the ability of a jurisdiction to attract and retain taxpayers and discourage those who would impose great burdens on the treasury. It is for this reason that boundaries and the flow across them matter so much in the American polity.

✧ KEY TERMS

block grants (p. 38)	implied powers (p. 28)
categorical grants-in-aid (p. 33)	New Federalism (p. 38)
cooperative federalism (p. 33)	regulatory federalism (p. 39)
dual federalism (p. 33)	revenue sharing (p. 38)
entitlement (p. 38)	Tenth Amendment (p. 28)

✧ FOR FURTHER READING

Paul Peterson, *The Price of Federalism* (Washington, D.C.: Brookings, 1995). An analysis of the evolving division of labor in the federal system between states and Washington.

Alice Rivlin, *Reviving the American Dream* (Washington, D.C.: Brookings, 1992). An essay on reallocating functions among governments in the federal system.

David Walker, *The Rebirth of Federalism* (Chatham, N.J.: Chatham House, 1995). A comprehensive account of the development of the federal arrangement from the beginning of the Republic to the Clinton presidency.

✧ NOTES

1. Advisory Commission on Intergovernmental Relations, *Signficant Features of Fiscal Federalism, 1994 Edition, Vol. 2* (Washington, D.C.: Government Printing Office, December 1994), pp. 191, 198.
2. George Hagevik, "Pollution Prevention," *NCSL Legisbrief*, 3 (January 1995).

3. The definition is contained in Beer's introduction to Timothy Conlan's *New Federalism: Intergovernmental Reform from Nixon to Reagan* (Washington, D.C.: Brookings, 1988), p. xii.

4. Quoted in Advisory Commission on Intergovernmental Relations, *The Federal Role in the Federal System: The Dynamics of Growth* (Washington, D.C.: Government Printing Office, 1981), pp. 44–45.

5. William Stewart, *Concepts of Federalism* (Lanham, Md.: Center for the Study of Federalism and the University Press of America, 1984).

6. David Walker, *The Rebirth of Federalism* (Chatham, N.J.: Chatham House, 1995), p. 20.

7. Thomas Anton, *American Federalism and Public Policy* (New York: Random House, 1989), p. 3.

8. Harvey Mansfield, "The Functions of State and Local Governments," in James Fesler, ed., *The 50 States and Their Local Governments* (New York: Knopf, 1967), p. 20.

9. James Gosling, "Transportation Policy and the Ironies of Intergovernmental Relations," in Peter Eisinger and William Gormley, eds., *The Midwest Response to the New Federalism* (Madison: University of Wisconsin Press, 1988), p. 245.

10. Advisory Commission on Intergovernmental Relations, *State Constitutions in the Federal System* (Washington, D.C.: Government Printing Office, 1989), p. 7.

11. John Kincaid, "State Constitutions in the Federal System," *Annals*, 496 (March 1988), 13–14.

12. These examples all come from Advisory Commission on Intergovernmental Relations, *The Question of State Government Capability* (Washington, D.C.: Government Printing Office, 1985), pp. 36, 38.

13. Janice May, "State Constitutions and Constitutional Revision, 1992–93," *Book of the States, 1994–95, Vol. 30* (Lexington, Ky.: Council of State Governments, 1994), pp. 2–16.

14. Terry Sanford, *Storm Over the States* (New York: McGraw-Hill, 1967), p. 189.

15. Advisory Commission on Intergovernmental Relations, *The Question of State Government Capability*, p. 60.

16. G. Alan Tarr, "The Past and Future of the New Judicial Federalism," *Publius*, 24 (Spring 1994), 63–79.

17. Randall Shepard, "State Constitutions: State Sovereignty," *Intergovernmental Perspective*, 15 (Summer 1989), 22.

18. Daniel Elazar, *The American Partnership* (Chicago: University of Chicago Press, 1962).

19. James Patterson, *America's Struggle Against Poverty, 1900–1985* (Cambridge, Mass.: Harvard University Press, 1986), p. 42.

20. For discussion of the Great Society programs, see John Schwarz, *America's Hidden Success* (New York: Norton, 1983); and John Morton Blum, *Years of Discord, 1961–1974* (New York: Norton, 1991).

21. Advisory Commission on Intergovernmental Relations, *Significant Features of Fiscal Federalism*, p. 128.

22. *Ibid.*, p. 158.

23. Conlan, *New Federalism*, p. 89.

24. Advisory Commission on Intergovernmental Relations, *Categorical Grants: Their Role and Design* (Washington, D.C.: Government Printing Office, 1977), p. 44.

25. Conlan, *New Federalism*, p. 84.

26. Advisory Commission on Intergovernmental Relations, *Federal Regulation of State and Local Government: The Mixed Record of the 1980s* (Washington, D.C.: Government Printing Office, 1993), p. 1.

27. The classification of forms of regulatory federalism comes from Advisory Commission on Intergovernmental Relations, *Regulatory Federalism: Policy, Process, Impact, and Reform* (Washington, D.C.: Government Printing Office, 1984), Chapter 1.

28. Conlan, *New Federalism*, p. 89.

29. Anton, *American Federalism and Public Policy*, pp. 14–15.

30. *United States v. Lopez*, 115 S. Ct. 1624 (1995).

31. Paul Peterson and Mark Rom, "Lower Taxes, More Spending and Budget Deficits," in Charles Jones, ed., *The Reagan Legacy* (Chatham, N.J.: Chatham House, 1988), p. 218.

32. John Kincaid, "Currents of Change in the Federal System," *Intergovernmental Perspective*, 15 (Fall 1989), 22.

33. Advisory Commission on Intergovernmental Relations, *Characteristics of Federal Grant in Aid Programs to State and Local Governments: Grants Funded FY 1993* (Washington, DC: Government Printing Office, 1994), p. 7.

34. Advisory Commission on Intergovernmental Relations, *Regulatory Federalism: Policy, Process, Impact, and Reform*, p. 232.

35. Advisory Commission on International Relations, *Federal Regulation of State and Local Government*, p. 2.

36. Steven Gold, "Local Taxes Outpace State Taxes," *State Fiscal Brief*, 11 (June 1993).

37. *Ibid.*

38. "The Dimming American Dream," *State Legislatures*, 21 (July/August 1995), 7.

39. William Galston and Geoffrey Tibbetts, "Reinventing Federalism: The Clinton/Gore Program for a New Partnership Among the Federal, State, Local, and Tribal Governments," *Publius*, 24 (Summer 1994), 24.

40. Quoted in Susan Bush, "Mandate Relief: Reality or Rhetoric?" *State Government News*, 38 (May 1995), 6.

41. *Ibid.*, p. 7.

42. Eliza Newlin Carney, "Taking Over," *National Journal*, 27 (June 10, 1995), 1382–1387.

43. "Winners and Losers in the Federal System," *Taubman Center Annual Report, 1994–1995*, John F. Kennedy School, Harvard University.

44. *Ibid.*

45. Paul Peterson, *The Price of Federalism* (Washington, D.C.: Brookings, 1995), p. 135.

46. Michael Rich, *Federal Policymaking and the Poor* (Princeton, NJ: Princeton University Press, 1993).

47. Paul Peterson, *The Price of Federalism*, pp. 144–145.

48. Michael Rich, "Distributive Politics and the Allocation of Federal Grants," *American Political Science Review*, 83 (March 1989), 206.

49. John Mollenkopf, *The Contested City* (Princeton, N.J.: Princeton University Press, 1983).

50. *City of Clinton v. Cedar Rapids and Missouri River R.R. Co.*, 24 Iowa 455 (1868).

51. Advisory Commission on Intergovernmental Relations, *The Question of State Government Capability*, p. 287.

52. 102 S. Ct. 835 (1982).

53. "States Take Lead in Mandate Relief," *State Trends Bulletin*, 1 (Feb./March 1995), 8.

54. David Hosansky, "The Other War Over Mandates," *Governing* (April 1995), 28.

PART TWO

POLITICAL ORGANIZATIONS

PEOPLE AND GROUPS IN STATE POLITICS

C itizens can participate in the governing of their state through individual acts such as voting and collective actions such as interest group activity. Indeed, as indicated in Chapter 1, cities and states are ideal units for the practice of democratic politics; they offer meaningful chances to participate in making important decisions. People differ in the kinds of participation they emphasize: Voting is more popular than contributing money to campaigns, for example. Styles of participation form a nationwide pattern but the political cultures of states modify these patterns. In the first section of this chapter we consider **political participation** by individuals.

✧ POLITICAL PARTICIPATION: WHAT IT IS AND WHY IT'S IMPORTANT

Political participation encompasses the activities of citizens aimed at influencing government, including the election of leaders and the policies they pursue.[1] Participation is central to the functioning of a democracy; it is the means by which citizens communicate with their leaders. Participation can be rewarding in itself; people derive a sense of satisfaction and self-worth from such activity. A low level or unequal distribution of participation poses potential problems for democratic governance. Government officials listen to citizens who exercise their voices and their votes. The voices of active participants may send a different set of messages than the inactives would send. Hence, equality in participation is a goal of democracies, a goal never fully achieved.

Purposes of Participation

As discussed in Chapter 1, political participation might be an act of voice, loyalty, or exit. Voting might be viewed as an expression of opinion (voice) about the direction of government or as an expression of support (loyalty) for the political system. Nonvoting can be viewed as alienation from the political system, an alienation that might conceivably lead to exit to another state. So the same act may serve different purposes for different citizens. Most of the time, however, political participation has voice as its purpose.

Types of Political Participation

In 1989 Sidney Verba and his colleagues asked a national sample of 15,000 citizens about their level of participation in eight different political activities.[2] Their study is valuable because it asks about community activities as well as presidential voting (see Table 3.1). The activity most frequently reported was voting in a national election (note that at 70 percent the self-report is inflated). The next most frequently reported activity was being a member of or a donor to a voluntary organization that takes stands in politics (48 percent). In the middle of the scale were contacting public officials (34 percent), working with others on community problems (25 percent), and giving money to a campaign (24 percent). At the bottom of the list were working on a campaign (8 percent), joining in a protest, march, or demonstration (6 percent), and serving on or regularly attending meetings of a local governing board (4 percent).

From this list it is clear that most citizens participate in ways that take the fewest resources. Voting, for example, is a low-cost action. They neglect acts that take more time and energy: working on a political campaign or serving on a community board. Another reason that voting heads the list is because it combines both voice and loyalty, whereas the other acts involve only voice. Most of us feel that voting is our duty, whereas few of us feel that contributing money to a politician is our duty. Loyal citizens vote but do not necessarily contribute money.

Modes of Participation at the State Level

People are more likely to participate in politics if they are of high socioeconomic status: Those who have an above-average income, have a higher-status occupation, and are middle-aged and well educated participate more often. However, the patterns for different modes of participation vary, and must be discussed separately.

TABLE 3.1 PERCENTAGE ENGAGING IN PARTICIPATORY ACTS More people vote than participate in any other way, according to national surveys.

Voted in 1988 presidential election	70%
Member of/donor to voluntary organization	48
Contacted government official within past year	34
Worked with others on community problem within past year	25
Made campaign contribution in 1988	24
Worked on a campaign in 1988	8
Attended protest/march/demonstration within past two years	6
Served on or attended meeting of local governing board within past two years	4
Average number of political acts	= 2.13

Source: 1989 national survey reported in Sidney Verba, Kay Lehman Schlozman, Henry Brady, and Norman H. Nie, "Race, Ethnicity and Political Resources: Participation in the United States," *British Journal of Political Science*, 23 (October 1993), 460.

Voting   Of all the modes of political participation, the act of voting is best documented. First of all, we know that the likelihood of voting varies according to one's socioeconomic status, with the effect of education being the strongest of all. However, some changes are occurring. In the past those active in politics tended to be males rather than females, and whites rather than blacks. In recent years the voting gap between men and women has narrowed: Since 1980 women and men have voted in nearly equal proportions. Similarly, the gap between black and white voter participation has narrowed over the years; indeed, if one controls for education and income, blacks' voting percentage equals or exceeds that of whites.[3] Latinos' voting rate is still lower than that of white Anglos, in part because a substantial fraction of Latinos are not citizens. The effect of age on voting, on the other hand, increased during the 1980s. One study found age to be the strongest predictor of voter turnout: 60-year-olds were two-and-a-half times more likely to vote than 26-year-olds.[4]

Second, voter participation levels vary by state. The residents of some states regularly turn out to vote at high rates whereas those in other states are less apt to vote. Table 3.2 charts this information for several different races—presidential, gubernatorial, Congressional, and all races combined—from 1989 to 1994. Montana ranks first overall with nearly two-thirds of the population showing up at the polls, followed by the Dakotas, Maine, and Minnesota (obviously weather is not a deterrent). Georgia ranks last, with only a little over one-third of its citizens voting. These rankings are based solely on the general election. Historically, in some southern states turnout for primaries has been better than that for general elections. Thus, southern states would not lag so far behind if the index included both elections.

Why are there such differences among states? Several factors—demography, political mobilization, and context—help to explain state variations in overall voter turnout. First are the differences in the socioeconomic or demographic makeup of each state's population, especially differences in average levels of education and income. One study found that socioeconomic composition explained about half of the differences among states' turnout rates.[5]

A second factor affecting interstate differences in voter turnout is the degree of political mobilization resulting from each state's electoral situation. States that have high interparty competition tend to have high turnout rates because party organizations get people out to vote. A close election often involves an advertising blitz that stimulates public interest. Other scholars have found that campaign spending, up to a point, increases turnout because it heightens voter interest.[6] The most recent research, however, shows that these mobilization factors pale in comparison to individual demographic factors.[7]

A third factor conditioning turnout is context, factors such as legal structure, culture, and region. Where state laws make it easy to vote, citizens turn out in higher numbers. Maine (ranked third in voter turnout), Minnesota (ranked fifth), and Wisconsin (ranked fifteenth) have same-day registration; North Dakota (ranked second) has no registration; most states require voter registration 30 days ahead. Studies have estimated that if all states switched to same-day registration, voter turnout would increase by 5–10 percent. Beginning in January 1995, the U.S. Congress required the 46 states not listed above to allow citizens to register to vote when they obtained or renewed their drivers' licenses. This "motor voter" law applies to federal, not state, elections. Several states, including California, Illinois, and Pennsylvania, initially refused to comply with the new law on the grounds that it is another unfunded federal mandate. Nonetheless, it is safe to assume that the federal law will be implemented everywhere; studies of previous motor voter programs in the states are encouraging as to the likely effect.[8] Such programs raised registration levels by about 10 percent and turnout levels by nearly 4 percent as compared to states without such programs.

TABLE 3.2 AVERAGE RATES OF VOTER TURNOUT RANKED BY STATE 1989–1994
Rates of voter turnout vary widely among the states, with citizens in the top states voting at about twice the rate of citizens in the bottom states. Turnout in presidential elections is almost always higher than in gubernatorial elections.

Rank	State	Total	President	Governor	U.S. Senate	U.S. House
1	Montana	63.9%	70.1%	69.6%	55.7%	60.1%
2	North Dakota	62.0	67.3	66.6	58.5	55.4
3	Maine	60.7	72.0	55.1	55.6	60.3
4	South Dakota	60.2	67.0	55.6	59.3	58.8
5	Minnesota	59.7	71.6	53.8	54.4	58.9
6	Utah	58.5	65.1	66.8	54.0	48.1
7	Vermont	57.2	67.5	48.5	58.0	54.9
8	Wyoming	56.7	62.3	54.2	54.2	56.0
9	Oregon	55.8	65.7	46.6	56.6	54.4
10	Missouri	55.8	62.0	60.8	53.3	47.2
11	Alaska	55.4	65.4	47.7	55.2	53.1
12	Idaho	55.2	65.2	48.3	54.7	52.5
13	Nebraska	53.9	63.2	49.3	50.1	53.3
14	Iowa	53.9	65.3	47.0	55.0	48.2
15	Washington	53.8	59.9	59.5	50.3	45.5
16	Wisconsin	52.3	69.0	39.8	54.2	46.2
17	Kansas	51.9	63.0	43.2	52.3	49.2
18	Connecticut	51.9	63.8	45.4	51.3	46.8
19	Massachusetts	51.5	60.2	48.7	48.8	48.1
20	Colorado	50.5	62.7	41.2	51.9	46.3
21	Ohio	49.6	60.6	41.6	50.1	46.1
22	Rhode Island	49.3	58.4	45.8	46.1	47.0
23	Indiana	48.1	55.2	53.4	41.8	42.0
24	New Hampshire	47.7	63.1	36.0	47.8	43.8
25	Oklahoma	47.1	59.7	39.7	45.0	44.2

Political culture is another contextual factor that affects turnout. Moralistic states have the highest turnout, traditionalistic the least, with individualistic in the middle.[9] Finally, we should note that the South has low turnout even after controlling for all three of these factors. Thus, there is a distinct regional component to voter turnout. Overall, since 1970 the magnitude of the interstate differences has declined: Voter turnout is becoming more similar across states and more tied to individual demographic factors.

The frequency of voting also varies according to the electoral cycle. In presidential election years turnout is about 10 percent higher than in off years. Because most states elect their governors in non–presidential election years, fewer people vote for governors than vote for presidents. The effect of insulating state elections from national electoral tides has been a reduction in the number voting for governors.

The Consequences of Low Voter Turnout   The decline in voter turnout and the strong socioeconomic basis to turnout means that the effective electorate is increasingly biased toward the upper classes. This bias is more pronounced in off-year gubernatorial

TABLE 3.2 (CONTINUED)

Rank	State	Total	President	Governor	U.S. Senate	U.S. House
26	Michigan	47.0%	61.7%	40.8%	40.5%	44.9%
27	Illinois	46.6	58.9	36.8	48.0	42.5
28	Delaware	46.3	55.2	52.8	36.1	41.1
29	Louisiana	46.2	59.8	57.8	37.4	29.7
30	North Carolina	46.1	50.1	49.7	45.2	39.3
31	Alabama	45.2	55.2	39.3	45.6	40.6
32	Arkansas	44.1	53.8	39.8	40.3	42.5
33	Arizona	44.0	54.1	36.1	44.3	41.6
34	Pennsylvania	43.2	54.3	36.3	42.6	39.4
35	New Mexico	42.5	51.6	38.6	38.8	41.1
36	Maryland	42.0	53.4	33.4	43.0	38.2
37	New Jersey	41.9	56.3	39.7	33.5	38.2
38	Nevada	41.3	50.0	34.3	42.2	38.9
39	Hawaii	41.1	41.9	40.7	41.7	40.1
40	California	41.0	49.1	34.3	42.2	38.4
41	West Virginia	40.6	50.6	48.7	30.1	32.9
42	Florida	40.3	50.2	36.6	42.3	32.0
43	New York	40.1	50.9	33.4	41.3	34.7
44	Virginia	40.0	52.8	37.9	32.2	37.3
45	Kentucky	39.9	53.7	30.5	40.7	34.8
46	Mississippi	37.5	52.8	38.8	23.4	34.8
47	Texas	37.0	49.1	32.6	31.9	34.3
48	South Carolina	36.6	45.0	31.7	36.6	33.1
49	Tennessee	36.3	52.4	29.6	29.3	33.8
50	Georgia	36.2	46.9	30.1	33.5	34.3

Source: John F. Bibby and Thomas M. Holbrook, "Parties and Elections," in Virginia Gray and Herbert Jacob, eds., *Politics in the American States,* 6th ed. (Washington, D.C.: CQ Press, 1996), p. 110.

elections, when fewer voters go to the polls, resulting in an even more unrepresentative electorate. In very interesting research Kim Hill and Jan Leighley have calculated the extent of the class bias in each state's gubernatorial elections.[10] Their index, presented in Table 3.3, assumes a value of 100 when the wealthy and the poor are equally represented in the electorate. Values above 100 indicate bias favoring the upper classes, and values below 100 indicate bias toward the poor.

Note that all states score over 100, indicating an upper-class bias in every state. But one can see in Table 3.3 that the states range considerably in their degree of upper-class bias, with New Jersey, Minnesota Louisiana, Illinois, and Nebraska having the most balanced representation and Kentucky, New Mexico, Texas, and Georgia having the least balanced representation. Note that this ranking bears some correspondence to the turnout ranking presented in Table 3.2 but the two are not the same. In fact, the correlation is a modest −.41, indicating that other factors besides low turnout contribute to class bias.

Hill and Leighley demonstrate that the class bias in the gubernatorial electorate has an effect on public policy. Using four measures of welfare spending, they show that the

TABLE 3.3 CLASS BIAS FOR STATE ELECTORATES, RANKED FROM LEAST TO MOST BIASED The class bias score reflects the degree to which rich people are overrepresented in the electorate and poor people are underrepresented. All states over-represent the rich but New Jersey does it least, and Kentucky the most, according to this study.

Rank	State	Class Bias Score
1	New Jersey	107
2	Minnesota	115
3	Louisiana	118
4	Illinois	122
5	Nebraska	122
6	Connecticut	126
7	South Dakota	126
8	Massachusetts	127
9	Pennsylvania	128
10	Utah	131
11	Maryland	133
12	Washington	133
13	Montana	134
14	North Dakota	136
15	Colorado	138
16	Alabama	139
17	Indiana	140
18	Wyoming	140
19	New York	141
20	Rhode Island	141
21	Wisconsin	142
22	Mississippi	144
23	Kansas	146
24	California	153
25	New Hampshire	153

class bias index is strongly related to generosity of benefits (the less the lower classes are represented in the electorate, the lower the benefits). Thus, voter turnout patterns have important consequences for states' public policies.

Because achieving higher and more equal participation is so important, states are experimenting with new ways of stimulating voter turnout. The "motor voter" law is one such method. Another is allowing people to vote by mail instead of in person. In 1995 the state of Oregon conducted a U.S. Senate election entirely by mail. Other states allow more generous use of the absentee ballot, including faxing the ballot.

Direct Democracy Casting a vote for a particular candidate expresses both voice and loyalty. At the state level, however, there is another type of voting that is a purer expression of voice: voting for **initiatives** and referenda. In about half the states, voters may sign a petition to force a proposed statute onto the ballot. In such states, public policy

TABLE 3.3   (CONTINUED)

Rank	State	Class Bias Score
26	Vermont	156
27	Alaska	157
28	Missouri	157
29	Oregon	159
30	Arizona	163
31	Iowa	163
32	Oklahoma	166
33	West Virginia	169
34	Michigan	171
35	Delaware	172
36	Maine	172
37	Tennessee	173
38	Idaho	175
39	Hawaii	176
40	Ohio	176
41	Florida	180
42	Nevada	180
43	South Carolina	180
44	Virginia	187
45	North Carolina	190
46	Arkansas	198
47	Georgia	200
48	Texas	206
49	New Mexico	207
50	Kentucky	245

Source: Kim Quaile Hill and Jan E. Leighley, "The Policy Consequences of Class Bias in State Electorates," *American Journal of Political Science,* 36 (May 1992), 355. Reprinted by permission of The University of Wisconsin Press.

initiatives are decided by the voters directly. Hence, the term **direct democracy** is used to describe such mechanisms.

Although most public policy is not made this way, some propositions enacted through initiative are very significant. For example, California's Proposition 13 accomplished a property tax revolution after the legislature had failed to act. Property owners led by activist Howard Jarvis voiced opposition to high taxes; their cap on taxes meant less funding for many programs, especially social programs. Scholars analyzing voters' attitudes toward Proposition 13 found that this tax revolt had an important symbolic component. The availability of the initiative allowed Californians who were "mad as hell and not going to take it anymore" a way to express their anger.[11] The initiative furnishes a direct expression of people's voice. It has been used most often in western states, especially Oregon and California (see Box 3.1 for examples of recent ballot initiatives in California).

Because initiatives follow candidate races on the ballot, some voters may tire of decisionmaking and stop voting before they reach the end of the ballot. The voter drop-off on issues is estimated at 5–15 percent, and it is most pronounced among lower-class voters.[12]

BOX 3.1 THE INITIATIVE IN CALIFORNIA

When Progressive reformers proposed the initiative near the turn of the century, they hoped it would give citizens a way to directly influence government. The initiative, however, has come with consequences the Progressives may not have intended. In places such as California, the initiative has become fertile ground for special interests and those with big bucks.

The number of initiatives reaching the ballot in the states has skyrocketed recently, and California has been the leader in the number of these measures appearing before voters. In 1990 alone, 13 initiatives appeared on California's November ballot.

California voters have voiced their opinions on wide-ranging and often controversial issues from term limits for state legislators to environmental policy. In 1994, California voters approved Proposition 187, prohibiting illegal immigrants from receiving government benefits except for emergency health care.[1]

These initiative contests have come with a high price tag. In 1988, more than $129 million was spent on initiative contests in California. This amount was more than what was spent on the presidential campaign in California and more than what was spent on lobbying in the state that year.[2]

The effects of these high-priced campaigns are not clear. For example, five competing auto insurance proposals appeared on the ballot in 1988. Insurance companies spent a lot on a few of the measures, but voters rejected all proposals except one that was not well funded.[3] California has not been able to effectively limit expenditures or contributions in initiative campaigns. The United States Supreme Court has overturned attempts in California and other states to impose ceilings.

These recent developments in initiative campaigns have prompted some to express skepticism about the initiative's potential for democratic participation. Eugene Lee, a political scientist at the University of California at Berkeley, said, "The initiative has become a political monster. It is meant to serve as a safety valve, a way to augment the legislative process, but instead it has become a way to circumvent our lawmaking process altogether."[4]

---

[1] Karen Foerstel, "Voters Favor Terms Limits, Reject Tax Restrictions," *CQ* (November 12, 1994), 3251.

[2] David Kehler and Robert M. Stern, "Initiatives in the 1980s and 1990s," *Book of the States, 1994–95, Vol. 30* (Lexington, Ky.: Council of State Governments, 1994), p. 281.

[3] *Ibid.* p. 283.

[4] Susan Biemesderfer, "Grass Roots Politics or Reform Run Amuck?" *State Legislatures* (October 1990), 24.

However, sometimes initiatives and referenda work to stir up voter interest. Particularly controversial issues on the ballot may attract more voters to turn out on election day than can political parties or candidates. For example, setting limits on legislative terms was a hot issue in many states in the early 1990s: Citizens in 20 states voted to require limited terms.

Other Typical Modes of Participation Although Americans lag behind citizens of other industrialized democracies in voting, when it comes to other political activities Americans are more active than citizens elsewhere.[13] Other common modes of participation identified in the Verba study were contacting public officials, working on community problems, and giving money to candidates. They estimated that 34 percent of the population (contacting) down to 24 percent (giving money) engages in these acts. These acts of participation are aimed more at state and local officials than at national officeholders. They went on to determine what types of people are underrepresented or overrepresented in each group of activists. Poor people are underrepresented among the contactors and community workers, and especially among the campaign contributors.[14] Other research shows that campaign contributors at the state level, like contributors at the national level, form an elite group. According to a study in Arizona and Tennessee, the average financial contributor is a conservative, married white male with a median family income over $50,000 and a college degree who is engaged in a business or profession.[15] Campaign contributors represent the elite, not the masses. Thus, the socioeconomic patterns of nonvoting participation mirror the patterns of voting participation.

At the bottom of Table 3.1 are listed the less common modes of participation: Working on a campaign, attending a protest, and serving on a governing board each attract less than 10 percent of the population. Once again, the poor are underrepresented among the ranks of the activists. Hence, their interests may not be conveyed to decisionmakers. Of particular relevance to state and local politics is the act of **protest.**

Protest activities express voice and/or a lack of exit possibilities. Protest activities include riots, demonstrations, marches, and acts of civil disobedience; in the Verba study only 6 percent of the sample had engaged in these acts. During the 1960s both violent and nonviolent actions were common in many large cities. Overt protest activity waned in the 1970s but returned in the 1980s and 1990s, focusing on different issues. The abortion issue, for example, has attracted protesters on both sides. State legislatures have witnessed marches, sit-ins, and disruption of their legislative hearings. Abortion clinics have been the focus of everything from silent vigils to fire bombings; over 30,000 protesters have been arrested since 1977.[16] In the 1990s abortion protests turned increasingly violent as doctors and other staff members were subjected to hate mail, stalking and other forms of harassment, and even murder.

Most protest activity is motivated by a particular issue—abortion or nuclear war, for example—so participants on one issue may have little in common with those on another. Generally protest is said to be a tactic of the powerless, not the powerful. However, the Verba study found in their sample that even among protesters the disadvantaged were greatly underrepresented. Perhaps protest is an activity one does on behalf of others.

Acts of Loyalty

In addition to exercising voice, citizens also display loyalty to their state's political system by voting, expressing confidence and pride in their state and its government, complying with government decisions, and remaining residents of the state (that is, not exiting). Most theorizing about loyalty to one's political system has been directed at the nation, not the state. David Easton has written about the necessity of **citizen support** to keep a political system running.[17] There are two kinds of citizen support: tangible, overt actions such as voting, and supportive orientations such as loyalty, attachment, and compliance. According to Easton, most political systems generate support by providing policy outputs that meet citizen demands and by socializing people to political life. Together, long-term socialization and day-to-day policy benefits create the legitimacy a government must have in order to survive.

At the subnational level, we would argue that short-term policy outputs are more important than socialization in generating support for a government. Socialization to state governments is relatively weak compared to attachment to one's country.

Therefore, matching policy outputs with demand is especially important for securing citizen support at the state level. There is some long-term loyalty to one's state, some attachment to place, but it can be eroded by too many unsatisfactory policy outputs. One study conducted at the local level provides support for our perspective. William Lyons, David Lowery, and Ruth DeHoog surveyed residents of two Kentucky urban areas. They found that citizen satisfaction with local government was higher where local services were better and where citizens felt efficacious about and psychologically invested in the community.[18] Thus, the quality of services is important in maintaining loyalty at the subnational level.

In this section we examine the ways citizens demonstrate support or lack of support for their state governments. First, interest in political affairs may indicate citizen support. Citizens nearly everywhere express less interest in state politics than in national politics. Still, there is considerable state-by-state variation in citizens' interest. Iowa is one state whose citizens are keenly interested in state government. One study found that twice as many Iowans were interested in state politics as in national or local politics.[19]

Secondly, citizens differ in the degree of attachment they have to their state. Texas is a state noted for having intense state pride. Texans are legendary for bragging about their state. At the other end of the scale is New Jersey, a state of low public consciousness. Bordered by New York and Pennsylvania, New Jersey tends to lack identity as a state and to have a negative image based on its ugly turnpikes and industrial sprawl. Its citizens rate the quality of state government as fair to poor (about two-thirds gave this response in 1980) and express little interest in state politics.[20] The degree of attachment and pride is quite different in Texas and New Jersey.

The reasons for these differences are, in part, complex historical ones but also more episodic and contemporary ones. A state university with a winning football team may temporarily increase state identity. The Texas Longhorns do a lot more for state pride than do the Scarlet Knights of Rutgers. Another factor that conditions citizens' reactions to state government is media coverage. New Jersey did not have a single commercial television station until 1984 (and even that has an entertainment rather than a news orientation) and its major newspaper is rivaled by the New York City and Philadelphia papers. The out-of-state TV stations give almost no coverage to New Jersey state government even during the legislative session; the in-state station has no Trenton correspondent.[21] Thus, it is difficult for New Jerseyites to learn much about what their public officials are doing in Trenton.

The media blackout extends beyond New Jersey. Many citizens have difficulty learning about state government because it is not a major topic for mass media. Television, in particular, finds state government too dull and too expensive to cover in an era when ratings of local newscasts depend on blood and gore. Doris Graber discovered that state news was extremely sparse, spotlighted a few states, and lacked political substance.[22] William Gormley found that newspapers devoted 18 percent of their stories to state government news and TV stations devoted even less.[23] This inattention to state government, he argues, shapes citizens' perceptions about the insignificance of state affairs.

A third dimension of loyalty to state government is support for the basic structures of the political system: the degree to which citizens are committed to the institutions of state government and are willing to comply with the decisions of these institutions. Political participation and involvement tend to increase citizen support for the legislature, and socioeconomic factors have a significant impact in enhancing that support. In the long run, then, basic support for a state's political system depends on having an involved and educated citizenry.

Exit

At some point citizen loyalty may decline so much that people seek greener pastures. The prospect of a better job, a warmer climate, or better schools may cause people to move elsewhere. Or voice may not pay off, and citizens may give up and move elsewhere. The option of exit is more likely to be exercised at the state and local levels than at the national level. Relatively few people, except during the Vietnam War, leave the United States to protest government actions. Many more people pull up stakes and move within the United States. Most move locally, perhaps crossing city or county lines; a smaller number move across state lines. Internal migration to other states is primarily for economic betterment and secondarily for political purposes.[24] The Kentucky survey specifically analyzed whether people are "voting with their feet," moving to other communities for political or policy reasons. They found little of this behavior; rather, exit or moving was a response exercised by those with very low levels of psychological attachment to their communities.[25]

These migration flows have political and economic effects both on the state left behind and on the new community or state. Chapter 1 documented some of these macro impacts: shifts in political power between regions, the policy problems of growing and declining states, and so on. It also described how various migration streams throughout our history have affected our political values through the establishment of different political subcultures in different parts of the country. Here we want to examine some of the micro (individual level) aspects of migration.

Migration affects citizens' political beliefs and behaviors. Migrants take some time to adjust, politically speaking, to their new environment. Recent migrants are less psychologically involved in politics, are less likely to have a partisan identification, and are less apt to vote.[26] Over time they become socialized, and most adapt to their new political environment. In a very interesting survey analysis Russell Hanson found that one's political subcultural background affects one's adjustment to a new political subculture.[27] Those raised in a moralistic culture remained dutiful wherever they lived; people from traditionalist or individualistic cultures conformed to their new environments, becoming more or less dutiful depending on where they moved to.

Even the threat of exit can have far-reaching effects on the balance of political forces in a community. Elaine Sharp has studied people who say they are likely to move because of their dissatisfaction with local government. She found that better-educated people used exit as a last resort after they had complained, whereas less educated people moved without complaining first.[28] This means that local government leaders will pay more attention to the needs of higher-status people because they hear their complaints in time to respond. They learn too late of lower-status people's discontents. Sharp provides a persuasive argument for why local (and probably state) governments could be biased in favor of higher-status groups.

Summary

Individual citizens exercise voice by participating in politics: voting, contributing money, contacting officials, and protesting, for example. The amount of participation varies by state and by political subculture. Citizens show loyalty to their state political systems by ritualistic voting, by compliance with state laws, and by expressing pride and interest.

Support of state government generally is lower than support for the national government, although there is variation from state to state. Finally, citizens can also exercise the option of exit and move to another state or city. Millions of Americans move every year, and these relocations have political consequences.

✧ POLITICAL PARTICIPATION THROUGH COLLECTIVE ACTION

Citizens also band together with others to pursue common goals. Nearly one-half of the population belongs to organizations that can be construed as having political goals (see Table 3.1). Such an organization is called an **interest group:** "an organized body of individuals who share some goals and who try to influence public policy."[29] Interest groups are important linkage mechanisms between citizens and their government. They offer a way to express voice collectively instead of individually. Like the other forms of participation, interest group activity overrepresents the upper classes, and it varies by state.

Types of Organized Interests

The term *interest group* is usually applied to membership associations that people join voluntarily (such as the Sierra Club) or even involuntarily (such as labor unions). But the range of organizations trying to influence public policy is broader than just membership groups. It also includes associations of organizations. For example, the American Federation of Labor–Congress of Industrial Organizations (AFL-CIO), which is composed of unions, has organizations, not individuals, as members. Moreover, there are many politically active organized interests that do not have members at all: Corporations, universities, and law firms are all examples of institutions that pursue some goals through political action. Today the term **organized interests** is used to refer to this broader set of organizations: interest groups that people join, associations that organizations join, and institutions that lobby.

At the state level we can analyze the mix of organized interests by reference to the list of organizations registered to lobby in each state legislature. Virginia Gray and David Lowery studied these lists in 1990 and discovered that 28 percent were membership groups, 23 percent were associations, and 49 percent were institutions.[30] Thus, although in this section we emphasize interest groups as a way citizens participate, we must keep in mind that they are a minority of the interest organizations lobbying in the state capitals.

Another way—the traditional way—of describing the range of organized interests is in terms of the sector or interest they represent. By far, the most well-represented sector is business. In 1990 business organizations constituted 60.2 percent of all state lobbying groups.[31] The business category includes individual firms that lobby for themselves plus trade associations that represent a number of businesses in a particular sector. The Illinois Manufacturers' Association is an example of the latter. Business lobbyists are generally reputed to have the greatest amount of influence in state legislatures. In Sarah Morehouse's widely used listing of influential interest groups, business was at the top in the early 1980s.[32] A 1994 assessment by Clive Thomas and Ronald Hrebenar, which used experts in each state, showed that the business sector retained its traditional clout.[33]

Another sizable category is citizens' groups, which account for 12.3 percent of the registered lobbyists. This category includes the traditional service organizations such as the League of Women Voters, hobby or sports clubs such as the National Rifle Association, public interest groups such as Common Cause, and single-issue groups such as Operation Rescue. This category grew rapidly in the 1970s and is alleged to have become very influential. However, their reputation for influence at the state level is exaggerated. Such groups tend to be sporadically active on a narrow range of issues and do not loom large on Thomas and Hrebenar's rating of powerful groups.

Still another noticeable category at the state level is governmental: representatives of local governments, school districts, and so on. They constituted 8.5 percent of registered groups in 1990. Their effectiveness, which increased in the 1990s, is enhanced by professional lobbying and a lack of opposition. Some of their increased numbers come from the fragmentation of umbrella associations into more narrowly focused organizations. In Minnesota, for example, the School Boards Association has been joined by the Association of Metropolitan School Districts, the Association of Rural School Districts, and the Association of Stable and Growing School Districts. Can the Association of Stagnant and Declining School Districts be far behind?

The next largest category of groups registered to lobby is that of professional and employee associations. They constitute 8.3 percent of registered lobbyists. This category includes state education associations, now rated as powerful as business, and state medical societies, a rising group in the 1990s, as well as newer groups of professional employees.[34] In some states, even the lobbyists have their own professional association. The professionals' clout comes from their cohesiveness, their extensive financial resources, and their geographic spread.

The next category in terms of size is that of labor unions, which account for 4.1 percent of the registered lobbyists. Unions represent large numbers of workers, so their influence is greater than the number of lobbyists would imply. Still, union membership has been declining as a proportion of nonagricultural employment, and labor's influence has declined in most states. The only growth area for organized labor is among public employees, more than 40 percent of whom now belong to unions. Public employee unions such as the American Federation of State and Municipal Employees (AFSME) are very powerful in a few states.

Finally, it should be noted that groups representing agriculture such as the Farm Bureau appear relatively infrequently these days. Less than 1 percent of registered groups in 1990 were farm-oriented. In most states, the farm bloc has declined in influence.

Across the country, interest group politics underwent considerable change in the 1970s and 1980s. In most states there was a rapid proliferation of organized interests, paralleling the advocacy explosion at the national level. Gray and Lowery's calculations indicate that the average number of registered groups per state increased from 195 to 342 between 1975 and 1980, an increase of 75 percent in 5 years.[35] Between 1980 and 1990, the average number increased from 342 to 586, a 75 percent jump over 10 years. Thus, the dramatic increases were moderating by decade's end.

Generally, the expansion has come from public interest and citizens' groups, government groups, and public employees at the expense of traditional labor unions and agriculture. The growth in local government groups is especially noteworthy in state capitols. In most states you will find a league of cities, an association of counties, and so forth. These general associations ranked ninth on Thomas and Hrebenar's influence scale.[36] In addition, you will find representatives of individual cities. They often hire a contract lobbyist to advocate their interests directly to legislators. Finally, there are myriad special districts that hire their own lobbyists. The school districts have already been mentioned but water districts, port authorities, transit authorities, and park districts also employ numerous lobbyists.

Business representation, though still the most numerous in terms of lobbying groups, has been modified in the sense that there are almost no states in which a single dominant economic interest prevails. The Anaconda Copper Company no longer dominates Montana politics, for example. But business overall retains its power relative to that of other organized interests.

The Origins of Interest Organizations

Joiners of interest groups tend to be higher-status individuals: people with more education, more prestigious occupations, and higher incomes.[37] Some states are more conducive to the formation of organized interests than others (see Table 3.4 for the numbers of registered interests in 1990). Florida, California, Texas, Michigan, Pennsylvania, and Ohio all had more than 1,000 interests registered to lobby. Generally, population is one determinant of the number of groups, with the more populous states having more interest organizations, but there are interesting exceptions to this pattern. Minnesota, for example, has nearly 1,000 registered groups but is twentieth in population size. These anomalies lead political scientists to look for other explanatory factors.

TABLE 3.4 NUMBER OF REGISTERED ORGANIZED INTERESTS PER STATE, 1990 Florida is by far the best endowed with lobbying organizations of all kinds, although most states have plenty; Mississippi has the least.

Rank	State	Number of Groups
1	Florida	3,283
2	California	1,348
3	Texas	1,180
4	Michigan	1,171
5	Pennsylvania	1,171
6	Ohio	1,010
7	New York	986
8	Minnesota	980
9	Illinois	908
10	Georgia	906
11	Nevada	821
12	New Jersey	810
13	Washington	724
14	Massachusetts	671
15	Oregon	669
16	Maryland	637
17	Arizona	599
18	Colorado	578
19	Missouri	571
20	Iowa	560
21	Kansas	510
22	Wisconsin	504
23	Virginia	496
24	North Carolina	481
25	Connecticut	476

They have found that the nature of a state's economy plays a role, in that larger and more diversified economies tend to have more groups, and their interest group systems tend to be weaker in influence relative to other political actors.[38] A single economic interest is not likely to be dominant where the state's economy is complex. California is an example of such a state, where a complex economy breeds diversity among organized interests. Research by David Lowery and Virginia Gray investigates the interactions of the economy and the interest group system.[39] They have learned that each state seems to have a natural "carrying capacity" for interest organizations: Interest group systems do not become more and more densely packed as state economic size increases. Rather, density moderates at the upper size ranges, suggesting that groups will not grow without bound. Their findings run counter to warnings about "hyperpluralism" in the states, the idea that too many organized interests will ruin democracy.

It has long been assumed that political and governmental factors play a role in structuring the interest group system, although the research findings are mixed. For a long time political scientists thought that strong political parties and strong interest organizations could not coexist, but there are examples to the contrary such as Illinois and New York.

TABLE 3.4 (CONTINUED)

Rank	State	Number of Groups
26	New Mexico	466
27	Louisiana	453
28	Oklahoma	445
29	Indiana	443
30	Tennessee	430
31	Wyoming	424
32	Utah	376
33	Kentucky	373
34	Nebraska	363
35	Montana	344
36	North Dakota	341
37	South Dakota	327
38	Alaska	318
39	Maine	305
40	Alabama	290
41	Idaho	263
42	West Virginia	260
43	Arkansas	238
44	Vermont	237
45	Rhode Island	235
46	South Carolina	221
47	Delaware	211
48	New Hampshire	195
49	Hawaii	194
50	Mississippi	111

Source: Unpublished research by Virginia Gray and David Lowery.

Lobbying is a face-to-face activity most often conducted in the state capitol. Here, one woman lobbies another in the Massachusetts State House; however, most lobbyists and state legislators are men. (*Source:* © John Nordell/The Picture Cube, Inc.)

Also, earlier studies asserted that professionalization of the legislature and the bureaucracy deters organized interest activity and makes government less vulnerable to interest group demands. But today even professional government institutions depend on interest organizations for information, expertise, and financial contributions. Thus, the relationship between organized interests and government structure is not as simple as once thought.

Lobbying Tactics

When interest groups attempt to influence policymakers, they are engaged in lobbying. A **lobbyist** is someone who tries to persuade a decisionmaker to act in a group's interest. There are five basic types of lobbyists operating in state capitals.[40] (Examples of each are given in Box 3.2.) The largest number are in-house lobbyists who are full-time employees of the organizations they represent. They are usually experienced in the business or profession they represent. Another sizable number are legislative liaisons for government agencies. They are usually career bureaucrats who, as part of their job, represent the agency before the legislature. The most prominent category is the contract lobbyist, who works on a freelance basis for several clients. Often former legislators, some are located in political law firms, some in their own consulting firms. They tend to be the best paid and

BOX 3.2 LOBBYIST PROFILES

IN-HOUSE, ALABAMA

Paul Hubbert turned the Alabama Education Association (AEA) from a "ladies' tea-sipping organization" into a potent political force that often calls the shots in the legislature.[1] He began as a classroom teacher, then got a doctorate and became a small-town school superintendent before taking over as executive director of the AEA in 1969. Hubbert recognized that teachers represented an important pool of votes, campaign contributions, and even candidates; he was able to get a large bloc of teachers elected to the legislature.

LEGISLATIVE LIAISON, MINNESOTA

Donna Peterson is Director of State Relations for the University of Minnesota. She is a former state representative and state senator; in fact, she resigned from the Minnesota Senate to take the position. Along with two other people, she represents the university's interests before the state legislature; another person handles the U.S. Congress, and still another the local governments. Peterson explains the university's budgetary requests in terms state legislators can understand, and she also explains cold political realities to academic officials.

CONTRACT LOBBYIST, ARKANSAS

Joe Bell is a lawyer who works for Little Rock's premier political law firm, Friday, Eldredge, and Clark. His father was a longtime state senator whose office served as Bell's base of lobbying operations. Bell was rated as the best lobbyist in the state in a 1990 Associated Press poll; his clients include Missouri Pacific Railroad Company, the Little Rock School District, the Oaklawn Jockey Club, the Arkansas Bankers Association, Dow Chemical Company, and R.J. Reynolds Tobacco Company. Bell lobbies in Little Rock,

in Washington, and on numerous hunting and fishing trips.

CITIZEN LOBBYISTS, MICHIGAN

The registered lobbyist for Michigan United Conservation Clubs (MUCC) is its director, Thomas Washington, but its real power derives from its "tenacious grass-roots activists" who appear often in Lansing and orchestrate numerous visits for public officials to natural sites.[2] These activists decline to register as official lobbyists because it is unbefitting to their citizen status. MUCC is an association of local environmental organizations, conservationists, and recreational clubs that speaks as one voice for Michigan's outdoor interests.

HOBBYIST, FLORIDA

Nell Foster "Bloomer Girl" Rogers stalked the corridors in Tallahassee for 37 years, wearing knickers, a corduroy shirt, and a broad-brimmed hat.[3] She was well-respected for her in-depth knowledge of pending bills, especially those affecting ordinary people: When she spoke, legislators listened. In 1990, there were 248 citizen lobbyists (hobbyists) registered with the Florida legislature.

---

[1]Alan Ehrenhalt, "In Alabama Politics, the Teachers Are Sitting at the Head of the Class," *Governing* (December 1988), 23.

[2]William P. Browne and Kenneth VerBurg, *Michigan Politics and Government* (Lincoln: University of Nebraska Press, 1995), p. 228.

[3]Anne E. Kelley and Ella L. Taylor, "Florida: The Changing Patterns of Power," in Ronald J. Hrebenar and Clive S. Thomas, eds., *Interest Group Politics in the Southern States* (Tuscaloosa: University of Alabama Press, 1992), p. 134.

usually work for private sector interests. A smaller category is made up of citizen lobbyists who represent their organizations without pay. Most of them are women. Finally, a small number are "hobbyists," private individuals lobbying for their own pet projects. They do not represent a group or business.

The differences among these types of lobbyists are notable: They vary in style, technique, and financial resources. Indeed, one scholar of lobbying says that the differences between lobbyist types are greater than the differences between states.[41] Some appear at the capitol with laptop computer, beeper, and cellular phone in hand; others rely on personal relationships, political savvy, and exchange of information and favors. Most lobbying is directed at the state legislature, but lobbying may also be directed at bureaucrats or the governor and his or her staff. Lobbying may take place with the decisionmaker directly or may proceed indirectly when lobbyists marshal others to approach the public official.

Direct Tactics Nearly every interest organization engages in **direct lobbying** of legislators. Group representatives contact officials—by phone, by mail, or usually in person—to present their points of view on a particular piece of legislation. This is the most time-consuming activity for both paid and volunteer lobbyists. Often the contact takes the form of testifying at a legislative hearing on a particular bill; it may also be a more informal presentation in the member's office.

A second tactic interest organizations rely on is providing information to busy legislators. Organizational officials prepare research reports or gather technical information on issues of concern to their members. Particularly in state legislatures with small professional staffs, such information can be very valuable to busy legislators. Sometimes, organized interests even draft legislation for members to introduce. Expertise is a major asset of in-house and government lobbyists.

A third tactic used by lobbyists is "wining and dining"—socializing to create a favorable image or to maintain access to a legislator. Texas is one state where this style still prevails: Lobbyists often provide perks to legislators such as ski vacations, tickets to the Super Bowl, outings to the King Ranch, various hunting and fishing expeditions, "rest trips" to Las Vegas and Acapulco, and golfing privileges at country clubs.[42] In most states, however, the use of entertainment as a lobbying technique has declined as the value of information has increased. Lobbyists in many states observe that the old-boy system is gone: Who you know is no longer as important as what you know.

One reason for this change is that as society and its issues become more complex, legislators need more information, and they come to depend on those who can provide it. Another reason is that state legislatures have moved to prohibit "wining and dining" and gift-giving by lobbyists. South Carolina and Wisconsin are the toughest states: They have adopted the "no cup of coffee" provision, under which public employees are banned from accepting gifts even as small as a cup of java. California, Connecticut, Michigan, Minnesota, Iowa, Kentucky, and Georgia are other states that have bans on entertainment, although theirs are less stringent.[43] Lobbyists in many states report that their business is much "cleaner" now than it used to be.

Organized interests, especially those concerned about government regulations, have also increased their efforts in lobbying the administrative branch of government. This trend, in turn, intensifies the role of lobbyists as information purveyors. If groups can provide technical information to bureaucrats implementing policy, then they will have more policy influence. Group leaders appear at public hearings of regulatory agencies; their representatives serve on advisory committees of state agencies.

With regard to courts, the traditional tactic for organized interests is litigation: Organizations initiate suits, sponsor test cases, organize class action suits, file amicus curiae (friend of the court) briefs, and so on. Through litigation, groups set the courts' agenda and influence the direction of public policy. They provide funds and legal expertise so that litigants can appeal their cases to higher-level courts. These are important tactics because it is illegal for groups to lobby judges directly on cases before them. Most research has shown that since the mid-1980s organized interests have increased their activities aimed at the judiciary.[44]

Indirect Tactics   Interest organizations also approach their legislative, administrative, and judicial targets through **indirect lobbying.** First of all, most organizations engage in grass-roots lobbying, getting their members to put pressure on legislators. For example, a university's lobbyist might organize a dinner meeting at which faculty members talk to legislators about their research and how it contributes to the state's economic future. This is a low-key lobbying effort that may pay off in future university funding decisions. A pro-life group may flood legislative offices with constituents' phone calls the day of a key vote. This is a more immediate and high-energy effort. In these situations, lobbyists are involved in orchestrating and coordinating their constituents' activities. Some refer to such lobbying as "Astroturf" to reflect the "manufacturing" of grass-roots sentiments. Most of the time constituent pressure is seen as more legitimate than lobbyists' socializing with legislators.

Secondly, organized interests try to mold public opinion in directions favorable to their cause. They often do this through advertising and public relations campaigns. The ads may project an image (for free enterprise) or they may advocate a specific position (against a proposed environmental bill). In any case, the purpose is to draw the general public toward the group's point of view in the hope that they will lobby government officials. The New Jersey Public Interest Research Group (PIRG) is known for combining solid research studies with imaginative media-oriented events. Press conferences are held at contaminated sites; on Halloween their members went door-to-door to talk about hazardous waste while dressed as toxic avengers, and naturally they held a press conference on this "scariest" day of the year.[45]

The advent of computer technology has brought about direct-mail lobbying campaigns. Interest organizations can create mailing lists of their broad constituency and send out mailings to activate thousands of people. A person identified as pro-choice on the abortion issue might receive such a mailing even though he or she does not belong to any pro-choice organization. Fax alerts just speed up this process even more.

Another tactic that combines direct and indirect purposes is the protest or demonstration. One purpose of a protest or demonstration is to gain public attention and sympathy for one's cause, thereby indirectly influencing public officials. An abortion rally on the steps of the state capitol or a sit-in by welfare recipients is sure to make the evening news, whereas a press conference or news release containing statistical information may be greeted with yawns. At the national level, the protest tactic is of little significance for most organizations but at state and local levels, it is used more often. Protest also affects decisionmakers directly. If farmers occupy the halls of the state capitol, they have an impact on the legislators. Still, the tactic is usually one of last recourse.

Organized interests often form alliances with other groups in order to enhance their effectiveness. This is an important indirect tactic for many groups. In most states there are ad hoc coalitions that spring up to fight for or against specific pieces of legislation. These may even be long-term coalitions seeking to maximize a particular perspective. For example, in Alaska arts and environmental groups have formed coalitions, as have women's groups.

The final indirect tactic is an increasingly significant one: interest organizations' attempts to influence the selection of candidates and the outcome of elections. Historically, interest groups lobbied public officials after the election. Today, interest organizations "lobby before the election"; that is, they endorse candidates, make financial contributions to their campaigns, and publicize the voting records of incumbents. Of course, groups hope to elect candidates congenial to their cause or indebted to them for campaign assistance. In this way they hope to influence public policy indirectly.

For example, in Michigan organized interests contributed $11.7 million to 1992 legislative candidates through political action committees (PACs).[46] PACs (as will be explained in Chapter 4) are legal organizations through which like-minded people contribute money to political campaigns. They may (or may not) be linked to a parent interest group. These PAC funds were much more likely to go to incumbents than to challengers. Candidates received additional campaign contributions from individuals whose giving was orchestrated by lobbyists; this practice is called "bundling." Two Michigan scholars offered this assessment: "Quite clearly, money, and the ability to raise it for officeholders, is strongly associated with group success."[47] States are increasingly regulating these financial practices: Four states (Colorado, Kentucky, South Carolina, and Vermont) completely ban lobbyists from contributing to campaigns at any time, and 18 other states prohibit lobbyist contributions during a legislative session.[48]

Interest organizations use many of the same techniques on governors as well. They "lobby before the election" by trying to influence candidate selection. Immediately after the election, organized interests display an intense interest in gubernatorial appointments to key posts, sometimes virtually dictating the governor's choice. On policy matters they try to lobby the governors directly, although many governors have an interest group liaison on the staff to handle such contacts.

With regard to state agencies, organized interests try several indirect means of shaping policy outcomes. One way is to push for the appointment of people sympathetic to their cause to key positions in state agencies and departments. The demand that top agriculture department personnel come from a farm background is one example. Another technique is to argue for increased agency appropriations. The support of constituency groups in the budgetary process is important in acquiring more resources. Providing such support may in turn ensure agency sympathy for a group's cause.

As far as the courts are concerned, indirect tactics are especially important because of the prohibition against direct lobbying on cases. One indirect tactic is influencing the selection of judges. In most states, appellate judges are selected or retained in an election typically of little interest to the public. When organized interests become involved in financing judges' campaigns, they have the potential for significant influence, especially where campaign costs are high; there are judicial candidates viewed as the candidate of the defense lawyers or the plaintiff's lawyers, and contributions flow accordingly. Which one is elected can make a big difference to lawyers even though the general public may be unaware of the difference.

Direct Democracy: A Special Role for Organized Interests

At the state level, interest organizations play a special role, one that does not exist at the national level. They are often influential in getting initiative petitions onto the ballot and enacted into law. Some are ad hoc grass-roots social movements, ones that spring up just to ensure that a proposal gets enough signatures to attain ballot status. Other initiative efforts start from a small existing group that mushrooms into something larger and then fades away after the campaign. For example, the 1970s California tax revolt was sparked by a small band of Howard Jarvis's followers. It grew into a much larger and more professional group, Californians for Proposition 13, that ran the initiative campaign. Traditional groups with broader interests are also heavily involved in initiative campaigns, as are individual business firms such as gaming companies that support the introduction of lotteries.

Some political organization must circulate the petition, an expensive proposition in itself, publicize the pros (or cons) of the proposal, and motivate people to vote. Initiative campaigns can be terribly expensive, costing more than a statewide campaign for political office. For example, in 1992 when Michigan PACs spent $11.7 million on legislative campaigns, they spent even more—$14.5 million—on ballot proposals.[49] The price tag for the 1988 campaign for Proposition 103—a proposal to cut auto insurance rates in California—was estimated at $75 million (triple the record for a California political office).[50] Various states have tried to restrict expenditures on initiative campaigns but thus far the courts have consistently ruled against such restrictions on the grounds that they infringe freedom of speech.

Among the most successful initiative campaigns is the term limits movement: In almost every state where advocates have put the issue on the ballot it has passed (although it took two tries in Washington). Three national organizations—Americans to Limit Congressional Terms, Citizens for Congressional Reform, and Americans Back in Charge—offered guidance and research expertise but indigenous state organizations did the heavy lifting of circulating the petitions and mobilizing the vote. Groups such as Badgers Back in Charge (Wisconsin) and Let Incumbents Mosey into the Sunset (LIMITS) (Oregon) are examples of the organizations activists put together in individual states.

Overall Assessment of Interest Groups

Since the late 1970s many observers of American politics have decried the advocacy explosion. Most of the charges about the "mischiefs of faction" have been leveled at the Washington community but they apply to the state and local scene as well. The criticisms include the following: The numbers of organized interests have increased, organizations have become more active and visible, and interest organizations have become too influential. Let us take up these points in turn.

Numbers   It is undeniable that the number of interest organizations lobbying in state capitals has increased just as the number represented in Washington has climbed. By our own calculations, the number of groups per state increased by 75 percent in five years and then by another 75 percent in the next ten years. The scope of representation—the range of interests represented—has also broadened to include social groups and perspectives previously unrepresented.

Activity At the national level there is solid evidence that organized interests are more active. Although there is no systematic evidence at the state level, there is a widely shared impression that organizations have stepped up their activities. New forms of organizational activity, primarily technological in nature, exist. Many interest groups have created political action committees (PACs) for campaign finance purposes or use direct mail for solicitation of funds. (Chapter 4 examines this development in more detail.) One reason for the increased activity is that campaign techniques diffuse from one state to another. As groups form interstate networks or as national groups exert more control over their subnational affiliates, new techniques are shared, increasing group activity even more. The term limits advocates, for example, imitated successful techniques used in the early adopting states.

Other technological changes increase groups' ability to lobby legislators. Interest organizations with computers or fax machines can quickly generate responses to legislative actions. In a few states—Texas, California, and Minnesota, for example—legislative roll-call votes are tracked by private firms linked by computer to interest organizations. For a fee, interest groups can find out what bills are under consideration by which committees and how legislators voted on a particular bill. The group's lobbying response can then be speeded up. Organizations can send members a "fax alert" to mobilize them to call their legislator about an issue.

The effect of interstate linkages and computer technology means that legislators find it harder to escape interests' attention. Legislators perceive more organized interest activity now than in the past. Groups, in turn, feel they have to try harder to get a legislator's attention. The net result is an escalation of organizational activity, an "arms race" among organized interests.

Influence In light of their increased numbers and activities, is it true that organized interests have more influence? Do they have too much influence?

The conventional wisdom has been that organized interests are more powerful in state legislatures than in the U.S. Congress. The reasoning is that Congressional representatives have larger staffs and should be less dependent on lobbyists for information. By the same token, state legislatures with highly professional staffs should have less need for lobbyists than do states with less professionalized legislative staffs. Logically, over time legislators should become less vulnerable to interest organization demands because legislatures, both state and national, are becoming more professionalized. Yet most observers see just the opposite occurring: They fear legislators are becoming more, not less, vulnerable to interests' pressure.

Which perspective is correct? It is difficult to answer this question because a political organization's success depends on a whole constellation of actors: the legislature, the governor, the bureaucracy, political parties, the media, and so on. But previous research does establish the conditions under which an organized interest is more likely to succeed.

1. The impact of lobbying varies with the issue involved. On some bills, at least one-fifth, interest groups do not even take a position.[51] The areas that attract organized inter-

ests are taxation, labor, occupational regulation, and public employment. Group influence is likely to be higher on these issues than on any others.

2. Lobbying success depends on whether the group adopts a defensive or an offensive stance. Groups are more successful at defeating legislation than at passing it. This is a very consistent finding in the scholarly literature.

3. Lobbying success depends on the absence of competition and the cooperation of allies. If there are countervailing organizations, a group's actions may be blocked. If the organized interest is lobbying without the support of public opinion or without the aid of other organizations, success is unlikely.

Political scientists have also tried to assess the overall impact of the interest organization community relative to other actors in the policymaking process. The 50-state assessment coordinated by Clive Thomas and Ronald Hrebenar reports the evaluation of experts taken in 1994. Table 3.5 shows that seven states, primarily southern or those with single-industry economies, are classified in the dominant category, meaning that

TABLE 3.5 **CLASSIFICATION OF THE 50 STATES ACCORDING TO THE OVERALL IMPACT OF INTEREST GROUPS**   Scholars have classified the states according to the relative strength of interest groups as a whole. Today, fewer states are totally dominated by interest groups.

States in which the Overall Impact of Interest Groups Is				
Dominant (7)	*Dominant/ Complementary (21)*	*Complementary (17)*	*Complementary/ Subordinate (5)*	*Subordinate (0)*
Alabama	Alaska	Colorado	Delaware	
Florida	Arizona	Connecticut	Minnesota	
Louisiana	Arkansas	Indiana	Rhode Island	
Nevada	California	Maine	South Dakota	
New Mexico	Georgia	Maryland	Vermont	
South Carolina	Hawaii	Massachusetts		
West Virginia	Idaho	Michigan		
	Illinois	Missouri		
	Iowa	New Hampshire		
	Kansas	New Jersey		
	Kentucky	New York		
	Mississippi	North Carolina		
	Montana	North Dakota		
	Nebraska	Pennsylvania		
	Ohio	Utah		
	Oklahoma	Washington		
	Oregon	Wisconsin		
	Tennessee			
	Texas			
	Virginia			
	Wyoming			

Source: Clive S. Thomas and Ronald J. Hrebenar, "Interest Groups in the States," in Virginia Gray and Herbert Jacob, eds., *Politics in the American States,* 6th ed. (Washington, D.C.: CQ Press, 1996), p. 152.

organized interests as a whole are the overwhelming influence on public policy. In the dominant/complementary column are listed 21 states in which power is shifting or moving away from the interest group system. The middle category contains 17 states labeled as complementary, in which interest organizations are constrained by other elements of the political system. The next category, labeled complementary/subordinate, contains 5 states in which organized interests have the least impact on public policy. They are weaker relative to other political actors. The last category, subordinate, is an empty cell: There are no states in which interest organizations are subordinate to all other actors. This new study classifies fewer states in the dominant category than did earlier research. Compared to the past, organized interests do not dominate policymaking but more often share power with other political actors.

Summary

Like individual participation, collective participation through interest groups is structured by socioeconomic status and political context. Organized interests are more influential in states with nondiversified economies. In every state business is the most well-represented sector: More lobbyists speak for business interests than for any other. Interest organizations use a variety of direct and indirect tactics aimed at the legislature, the governor, and the bureaucracy, but the most popular tactic is still personal lobbying of policymakers. In the past decade, organized interests have proliferated and have become more active and visible; their impact on public policy is considerable.

✧ CONCLUSION

Political participation encompasses all the means by which citizens influence their government. Voting is the most typical form of participation, but calling City Hall to complain about potholes in the street, demonstrating against abortion, and joining an interest group are other ways to participate. Most of the time the purpose of participation is voice, expressing one's opinion, but sometimes people participate out of a sense of loyalty. If their demands are not heeded, people may move to another state or drop out of politics.

People with similar views can join together in interest groups, thereby increasing their effectiveness. Joiners, like other kinds of participators, tend to be from the upper socioeconomic echelons. Certain types of states seem to facilitate voting, interest group formation, and presumably other types of participation. Some people worry that organized interest activity has increased too much in the past decade while participation through voting has decreased. One reason for these changes may lie in the nature of the political party system, the subject of Chapter 4.

✧ KEY TERMS

citizen support (p. 63)   interest group (p. 66)
direct democracy (p. 61)   lobbyist (p. 70)
direct lobbying (p. 71)   organized interests (p. 66)
indirect lobbying (p. 73)   political participation (p. 55)
initiative (p. 60)   protest (p. 63)

✧ FOR FURTHER READING

Virginia Gray and David Lowery, *The Population Ecology of Interest Representation: Lobbying Communities in the American States* (Ann Arbor: University of Michigan Press, 1996). Using an approach borrowed from population biology, this study focuses on variations in the number of interest groups across the 50 states and the impact of those variations, based on aggregate data from the 50 states and mail and telephone surveys in 6 states.

Kim Quaile Hill, *Democracy in the Fifty States* (Lincoln: University of Nebraska Press, 1994). A summary of research on voter participation in the 50 states, including empirical and normative perspectives.

Ronald J. Hrebenar and Clive S. Thomas, eds., *Interest Group Politics in the American West* (Salt Lake City: University of Utah Press, 1987). The first in a series of regional reports on interest groups in each state. Others volumes cover the rest of the geographic regions.

Alan Rosenthal, *The Third House: Lobbyists and Lobbying in the States* (Washington, D.C.: CQ Press, 1993). A lively and engaging portrait of the lives of state lobbyists, based on observations in six states.

Sidney Verba, Kay Lehman Schlozman, and Henry E. Brady, *Voice and Equality* (Cambridge, Mass.: Harvard University Press, 1995). A major recent study of citizen participation in its many forms. Based on a massive national survey, it is particularly valuable in its analysis of participation patterns among African Americans, Latinos, and Anglo whites.

✧ NOTES

1. Sidney Verba and Norman H. Nie, *Participation in America* (New York: Harper & Row, 1972), p. 2.

2. Sidney Verba, Kay Lehman Schlozman, Henry Brady, and Norman H. Nie, "Race, Ethnicity and Political Resources: Participation in the United States," *British Journal of Political Science,* 23 (October 1993), 453–497.

3. Verba, Schlozman, Brady, and Nie, "Race, Ethnicity and Political Resources," p. 459.

4. Lee Sigelman, Philip W. Roeder, Malcolm E. Jewell, and Michael Baer, "Voting and Nonvoting: A Multi-Election Perspective," *American Journal of Political Science,* 29 (November 1985), 749–765.

5. Jae-On Kim, John R. Petrocik, and Stephen N. Enokson, "Voter Turnout Among the American States," *American Political Science Review,* 69 (March 1975), 114.

6. Gregory Caldeira and Samuel C. Patterson, "Contextual Influences on Participation in U. S. State Legislative Elections," *Legislative Studies Quarterly,* 7 (August 1982), 359–381.

7. Jan E. Leighley and Jonathan Nagler, "Individual and Systemic Influences on Turnout: Who Votes? 1984," *Journal of Politics,* 54 (August 1992), 718–740.

8. Stephen Knack, "Does 'Motor Voter' Work? Evidence from State-Level Data," *Journal of Politics,* 57 (August 1995), 796–811; Staci L. Rhine, "Registration Reform and Turnout Change in the American States," *American Politics Quarterly,* 23 (October 1995), 409–426.

9. Daniel J. Elazar, *American Federalism: A View from the States,* 3rd ed. (New York: Harper & Row, 1984), pp. 152–156.

10. Kim Quaile Hill and Jan E. Leighley, "The Policy Consequences of Class Bias in State Electorates," *American Journal of Political Science,* 36 (May 1992), 351–365.

11. David O. Sears and Jack Citrin, *Tax Revolt: Something for Nothing in California* (Cambridge, Mass.: Harvard University Press, 1982), pp. 214–216.

12. Thomas Cronin, *Direct Democracy: The Politics of Initiative, Referendum, and Recall* (Cambridge, Mass.: Harvard University Press, 1989), p. 67.

13. Sidney Verba, Kay Lehman Schlozman, and Henry E. Brady, *Voice and Equality* (Cambridge, Mass.: Harvard University Press, 1995), p. 69.

14. *Ibid.* pp. 190, 194.

15. Ruth S. Jones and Anne H. Hopkins, "State Campaign Fund Raising: Targets and Response," *Journal of Politics,* 47 (May 1985), 432–434.

16. Mary Segers, "The Pro-Choice Movement Post-*Casey:* Preserving Access," in Mary C. Segers and Timothy A. Byrnes, eds., *Abortion Politics in American States* (Armonk, N.Y.: M. E. Sharpe, 1995), p. 233.

17. David Easton, "An Approach to the Analysis of Political Systems," *World Politics,* 9 (April 1957), 383–400.

18. W. E. Lyons, David Lowery, and Ruth Hoogland DeHoog, *The Politics of Dissatisfaction* (Armonk, N.Y.: M. E. Sharpe, 1992).

19. Samuel C. Patterson, Ronald D. Hedlund, and G. Robert Boynton, *Representatives and the Represented* (New York: Wiley, 1975), p. 157.

20. *Comparative State Politics Newsletter,* 1 (October 1980), 16–18.

21. William T. Gormley, Jr., "Coverage of State Government in the Mass Media," *State Government,* 52 (Spring 1979), 46–51; Barbara G. Salmore and Stephen A. Salmore, *New Jersey Politics and Government* (Lincoln: University of Nebraska Press, 1993), p. 71.

22. Doris Graber, "Flashlight Coverage: State News on National Broadcasts," *American Political Quarterly,* 17 (July 1989), 277–290.

23. Gormley, "Coverage of State Government," p. 47.

24. Thad A. Brown, *Migration and Politics* (Chapel Hill: University of North Carolina Press, 1988), p. 29.

25. Lyons, Lowery, and DeHoog, *The Politics of Dissatisfaction,* p. 177. The specific question concerned how bad one would feel if one had to move away.

26. Brown, *Migration and Politics,* p. 27.

27. Russell L. Hanson, "The Political Acculturation of Migrants in the American States," *Western Political Quarterly,* 45 (June 1992), 355–383.

28. Elaine B. Sharp, "'Exit, Voice, and Loyalty' in the Context of Local Government Problems," *Western Political Quarterly,* 37 (March 1984), 67–83.

29. Jeffrey M. Berry, *The Interest Group Society* (Boston: Little, Brown, 1984), p. 5.

30. Virginia Gray and David Lowery, "The Demography of Interest Organization Communities: Institutions, Associations, and Membership Groups," *American Politics Quarterly,* 23 (January 1995), 3–32.

31. Unpublished research by Virginia Gray and David Lowery.

32. Sarah McCally Morehouse, *State Politics, Parties and Policy* (New York: Holt, Rinehart & Winston, 1981), pp. 108–112.

33. Clive S. Thomas and Ronald J. Hrebenar, "Understanding Interest Group Power: Lessons from Developments in the American States Since the Mid-1980s," paper presented at the annual meeting of the Midwest Political Science Association, Chicago, April 6–8, 1995.

34. Thomas and Hrebenar, "Understanding Interest Group Power," p. 6.

35. Virginia Gray and David Lowery, "Stability and Change in State Interest Group Systems, 1975–1990," *State and Local Government Review,* 25 (Spring 1993), 89.

36. Clive S. Thomas and Ronald J. Hrebenar, "Government as an Interest and Lobbying Force in the American States," paper presented at the annual meeting of the Western Political Science Association, San Francisco, March 1992.

37. Kay Lehman Schlozman and John T. Tierney, *Organized Interests and American Democracy* (New York: Harper & Row, 1986), p. 60.

38. Morehouse, *State Politics,* pp. 112–113.

39. David Lowery and Virginia Gray, "Nationalization of State Interest Group System Density and Diversity," *Social Science Quarterly,* 75 (June 1994), 368–377.

40. Our discussion relies on Clive Thomas and Ronald Hrebenar, "Interest Groups in the States," in Virginia Gray and Herbert Jacob, eds., *Politics in the American States,* 6th ed. (Washington, D. C.: CQ Press, 1996), Figure 4.2.

41. Alan Rosenthal, *The Third House* (Washington, D.C.: CQ Press, 1993), p. 23.

42. *New York Times,* July 23, 1989; Rosenthal, *The Third House,* p. 98.

43. Joyce Bullock, "State Lobby Laws in the 1990s," *The Book of the States, 1994–95, Vol. 30* (Lexington, Ky.: Council of State Governments, 1994), p. 486.

44. For one example involving amicus briefs, see Lee Epstein, "Exploring the Participation of Organized Interests in State Court Litigation," *Political Research Quarterly,* 47 (June 1994), 335–351.

45. Rosenthal, *The Third House,* p. 170.

46. William P. Browne and Kenneth VerBurg, *Michigan Politics and Government* (Lincoln: University of Nebraska Press, 1995), p. 228.

47. *Ibid.,* p. 230.

48. Bullock, "State Lobby Laws," p. 487.

49. Browne and VerBurg, *Michigan Politics and Government,* p. 228.

50. *National Journal,* September 17, 1988.

51. Charles W. Wiggins, Keith E. Hamm, and Charles G. Bell, "Interest-Group and Party Influence Agents in the Legislative Process: A Comparative State Analysis," *Journal of Politics,* 54 (February 1991), 91.

POLITICAL PARTIES, CAMPAIGNS, AND ELECTIONS

Like interest groups, parties are political organizations linking citizens to their leaders. Political parties perform some of the same functions as interest groups: Both provide a way to express voice, for example. The major difference is that political parties contest elections and manage government. Successful parties, therefore, have to make broad appeals to many citizens and concentrate fully on political action; as a consequence they endure over many years. The party label furnishes an important cue to voters and organizes the activities of elected officials. Thus, their success and endurance give political parties a special status in our political system.

In this chapter we first consider parties as organizations: How are parties structured in order to carry out their tasks? Then, we consider parties in relation to the electorate: how they link citizens and leaders, how they organize elections, and how they participate in electoral campaigns. Finally, we consider parties in government: how they function as managers and policymakers once in office.

While looking at political parties, we will need to keep two points in mind. One is that political parties no longer have sole control of most political activity. Instead they must compete with interest groups and individual candidates for control over political campaigns. Several sections of this chapter consider the implications of these changes in the environment of political parties. A second point to keep in mind is the federal nature of political parties. In reality, there are 100 political parties: 50 state Democratic parties and 50 state Republican parties. The organization and structure of the parties differ from one state to another, the socioeconomic composition of the electorate and the patterns of party competition vary from state to state, and the degree to which parties affect policy outcomes differs across states. This decentralization (and hence possibility for diversity) is a significant feature differentiating our political parties from the more disciplined and hierarchical European political parties.

Our theme of exit, voice, and loyalty is also pertinent to this chapter. The exit or migration of residents to new states has changed the political parties of numerous states, particularly in the South, which is evolving from a solidly Democratic system to a two-party competitive system. The exercise of voice, as explained in Chapter 3, is primarily through voting in elections. In this chapter we consider elections and campaigning for them in some detail. Loyalty is also important to political parties as they seek to retain their core supporters through the policies they offer. All three elements are woven into the discussion of this chapter.

✧ PARTY ORGANIZATIONS

The most notorious party organizations were the city machines, which flourished in the second half of the nineteenth century and the first decades of this century. They were organized in a hierarchical structure with a boss at the top. The late Richard J. Daley, mayor of Chicago from 1955 to 1976, was the best-known boss of recent years. The boss was surrounded by lieutenants, who in turn controlled precinct leaders through the use of **patronage.** Precinct captains delivered votes on election day; bosses offered city jobs to their captains in return and gave small amounts of aid (such as turkeys at Christmas) to voters. The patronage system ran city government because there were many government positions to distribute and because jobs, not issues, were the focus of politics. The machine depended on close personal loyalty to the boss, his lieutenants, and the party: "Who you know" was the crucial factor in getting a job. As Mayor Daley put it, "I don't want nobody, nobody sent." He meant he wanted employees whose loyalty to his machine had already been proven.

Contemporary Party Organization

Partly in reaction to the corruption of machine politics, today's parties are tightly regulated. In fact, the United States is unique among Western democracies in the degree to which political parties are regulated. In most countries, political parties are private associations permitted to conduct their business in private. In our country parties are quasi-public agencies under the control of the state, not national, government. Each state defines what legally constitutes a political party, what determines membership in a party, the formal structure of the party organization, how candidates get on the ballot, methods of nomination, and campaign finance regulations. Naturally, the states vary in their legal definitions and regulations.

The statutes of each state spell out the organizational form parties must adopt. This format is congruent with the voting districts within each state. A typical organization chart would have at the bottom a party functionary representing the smallest voting unit in a state, usually a precinct. These local committee people are usually elected by their peers and work to ensure that their precinct votes for the party's nominees on election day. If you want to get involved in politics, being a precinct chair is a good place to begin. There are abundant opportunities: Nationwide, there are about 200,000 local positions to fill.[1]

The intermediate rung is typically a county-level committee. There are over 7,000 county (or county-equivalent) committees.[2] Membership on these committees generally consists of the local chairs and others selected at the lower level. These organizations are busy with coordinating and organizing campaign activities: distributing campaign literature, organizing rallies and fund-raisers, and canvassing door-to-door.

At the top of the organizational ladder is the state central committee. This committee varies in size from 50 to 500 members, who are chosen in a variety of ways but usually represent the county-level units. Their duties include campaigning, fund-raising, writing party platforms, and organizing state conventions. Their specific powers vary, depending on the functions of the state convention, the role of the state party chair, and the governor's role within the party.

The state convention is a gathering, usually biennial, for the purpose of adopting a platform and, in some states, nominating statewide candidates. In presidential election years state conventions may also select delegates to the national presidential nominating conventions, particularly in caucus states. The state convention, then, is an important part of the national party apparatus, one that is increasingly being affected by national party mandates. Since 1972 the national Democratic Party has required that state party delegations to the national convention meet certain requirements of socioeconomic balance regarding race, sex, and age. The Republican Party has instituted similar practices, but they are not actually mandated. National requirements are a major force for centralization within party organizations.

Each state party also has a chair, usually elected by the state central committee or sometimes by the state convention. Sometimes these elections simply ratify the governor's choice for the job. This job is increasingly a full-time one: Nearly all state party organizations have either a full-time salaried chair or an executive director. The chairs (or executive directors) head professional staffs that attempt to build the party organizations through two types of programs. The first is institutional support: fund-raising for the state party, "get out the vote" campaigns, public opinion polling, publishing newsletters, and developing issues. Their second set of activities is more candidate-centered: providing money and services for the party's candidates, recruiting new candidates (especially for state legislative races), and, in some states, endorsing candidates or influencing their nomination.

Parties as Service Agencies

In the 1990s the parties' provision of services to candidates has become the more important of the two roles, in line with the general trend toward a more candidate-centered politics. The parties now function more as service agencies to candidates than as patronage machines. The service agency function requires the ability to raise large sums of money, an ability the parties seem to possess. According to Federal Election Commission (FEC) reports, in 1992 the state Democratic parties collectively raised $89 million and the state Republican parties raised $85 million.[3] Because state parties do not have to report all of their money to the FEC, it is estimated that their actual resources were at least 25 percent higher.

It is noteworthy that the two sets of state parties raised roughly the same amounts of money in 1992. Research in the 1980s showed that the Republican state parties usually had larger budgets and more staff than did the Democratic parties. In the 1990s many of these differences in Republican organizational advantage were erased: The two parties are more similar in their budgets and staffs.

What sorts of campaign activities do these party monies buy? A recent survey of county level party leaders in eight states shows the range of services the local parties offer (see Table 4.1).[4] Distributing campaign literature and lawn signs were the most popular activities, with over 85 percent of local party organizations participating. Fewer than 10 percent purchased billboard space or coordinated PAC activity. The two parties emphasize slightly different activities (the Republicans are more involved in getting out the vote than are the Democrats, for example), but on average the Republican state parties were more active in 1994. This discrepancy was a change from 1992, when the two sets of parties reported relatively equal activity levels.

Organizational strength is not, of course, the same as success at the polls; in fact, scholars have spent time in trying to establish a firm link between the two. Just because a state party develops itself into a sophisticated service agency does not automatically mean that it will win the next election. Often it takes several years of building the organization before a payoff is realized; sometimes the payoff never comes. Perhaps the clearest case of a positive connection between organizational buildup and electoral success is that of the southern Republicans. A minority party in nearly all southern states for many years, in the 1960s and 1970s the Republican party began to build up its infrastructure and recruit better candidates. As the political climate changed in the 1980s and especially the 1990s, the strategy began to pay off, with the Republicans capturing more offices. In 1994 the Republicans picked up 669 legislative seats in Dixie, nearly 200 more than they had controlled in 1990. In this instance, party organization bore fruit.

TABLE 4.1 CAMPAIGN ACTIVITY LEVELS OF LOCAL PARTY ORGANIZATIONS IN EIGHT STATES, 1994 **Both political parties have increased their organizational activities according to a survey of local party organizations in eight states.**

Direct Campaign Activity	Republican	Democrat
Distributes campaign literature	88%	88%
Arranges fundraising events	75	72
Organizes campaign events	82	78
Contributes money to candidates	78	67
Organizes telephone campaigns	65	58
Buys newspaper ads for party and candidates	67	61
Distributes posters or lawn signs	90	86
Coordinates county-level campaigns	57	59
Prepares press releases for party and candidates	64	60
Sends mailings to voters	59	52
Conducts registration drives	37	37
Organizes door-to-door canvassing	57	54
Buys radio/TV time for party and candidates	24	25
Uses public opinion surveys	20	12
Purchases billboard space	9	5
Coordinates PAC activity	8	8
Conducts get-out-the-vote effort	71	64

Source: Adapted from Table 1 of John Frendreis and Alan R. Gitelson, "Parties, Candidates, and State Electoral Politics," paper presented at the annual meeting of the American Political Science Association, Chicago, August 1995.

The scale of campaigning for state and local offices varies around the country. Most candidates still use lawn signs, such as those outside this Austin, Texas, polling place. (*Source:* © B. Daemmrich/The Image Works)

The state central committee and the state chair direct the ongoing activities of state parties together. The state convention and the governor may interject influence from time to time on some matters. Given the decentralized and fragmented nature of most state parties, real power does not reside at the top; rather, the county is probably the most influential level. The entire party organization from top to bottom competes with (as well as cooperates with) its elected government officials for control of the party. Also, the formal organization competes against interest groups for the support of the electorate.

⬦ THE PARTY AND THE ELECTORATE

Most of the time U.S. political parties are stable and enduring organizations seeking to build broad electoral coalitions centered in the middle of the ideological spectrum; that is, they try to minimize exit of voters and maximize voter loyalty. Occasionally there are upheavals in society sufficient to pressure parties to change, to stake out new policy positions, and to accentuate their differences. The upheavals and the parties' new issue positions may lead groups of voters to desert their party and join a new one. This process of **realignment** results in a new majority party composed of new coalitions of voters.

The trauma of the Civil War turned the American electorate from Democratic to Republican. The Republican Party became the new majority party, with Democrats strong only in the South. Later, after Reconstruction ended and southern Democrats returned to full participation, the electoral forces were relatively close. The next realignment occurred in the 1890s, as a result of economic upheavals, especially on the farms, and of the populist movement splitting the Democratic Party. The election of 1896 was the realigning election that strengthened the Republican Party, especially in northern cities, and left it the dominant party outside the South.

The third party realignment was in the 1930s, precipitated by the Great Depression, when the Democrats became the majority party. Importantly, Democrats now controlled northern as well as southern states. The parties' responses to the economic crisis appealed to different groups of voters: urban, working-class, black, and ethnic voters found a new home in the Democratic Party. The basic party positions of the New Deal and the resulting voter coalitions remained intact for a long time.

It is important to note that realignment does not refer only to which party wins but also to how it wins, specifically how party cleavages change as a result of the election: Which groups of voters adhere to which party? When one looks beyond the national level to party cleavages in individual states, the New Deal party cleavage described above exists today in nineteen states, according to Robert Brown.[5] In these states, ranging from Vermont to Minnesota to Washington, the Democratic party is composed of Catholics, lower-income people, and union members, whereas the Republican party is composed of Protestants, upper-income people, and college-educated groups. Politics is class-based in these states.

In southern and border states, race seems to be the single most important factor differentiating the two parties, with the Democratic Party attracting blacks and the Republican Party the whites. A third set of 14 states exhibits a hybrid type of party cleavage, combining class and racial factors. These tend to be the industrial states with large concentrations of minorities such as Illinois, New York, Michigan, and Missouri. The Democratic party has both lower classes and blacks and the Republican party has both whites and upper classes. Hence, politics is fought over different issues in the New Deal states than in the southern states and in the hybrid states. This recent analysis by Brown shows that the New Deal cleavage structure is still very relevant today but it has been joined by another significant cleavage—race—which may offer the basis for a realignment of the parties. The Republican takeover of Congress in 1994 as well as their success in gubernatorial and state legislative races suggest that Democratic dominance is coming to an end.

Pollsters have detected a decline in allegiance to either of the two major parties, leaving many voters ripe for new appeals such as those posed by presidential candidate Ross Perot in 1992. This indifference to parties is called **dealignment.** Scholars are in disagreement over whether we are undergoing another realignment of the parties or whether further dealignment is more likely.

Patterns in Contemporary Party Identification

Part of the difficulty in analyzing party loyalty as an indicator of possible party realignment has to do with the concept of party membership itself. Most organizations, political or otherwise, impose a membership test: paying dues, signing a form, or taking an oath. American political parties are exceptions: You do not have to do anything to join. The members of our Democratic and Republican parties are simply people who say they are members. More precisely, they are the people who respond to pollsters' questions about partisan identification by answering "Republican" or "Democrat" rather than "independent" or "other" or "it's none of your business."

TABLE 4.2 PARTISAN IDENTIFICATION IN THE UNITED STATES RANKED BY PERCENTAGE DEMOCRAT, 1976–1988 Little information is available on the party identification of citizens in each state because comparable surveys are rarely carried out in all states at the same time. This survey combined exit polls conducted over several years in all states to produce the estimates shown here.

Rank	State	Democrat	Independent	Republican
1	Louisiana	55.3%	24.7%	20.0%
2	Oklahoma	50.8	19.2	29.9
3	Kentucky	49.8	24.8	25.5
4	West Virginia	48.7	22.7	28.6
5	Georgia	48.0	31.0	21.0
6	Arkansas	46.8	32.8	20.3
7	North Carolina	46.6	25.8	27.6
8	Maryland	46.4	29.4	24.2
9	Alabama	44.4	32.2	23.4
10	Mississippi	43.8	29.2	27.0
11	New Mexico	42.0	31.7	26.3
12	South Dakota	40.3	21.3	38.4
13	California	39.4	27.3	33.3
14	Texas	39.4	34.5	26.1
15	Florida	39.3	27.9	32.7
16	Tennessee	39.3	34.2	26.5
17	South Carolina	39.2	33.2	27.5
18	Oregon	38.6	30.2	31.2
19	Pennsylvania	38.4	26.8	34.8
20	New York	37.7	32.6	29.7
21	Nevada	37.0	31.2	31.8
22	Minnesota	36.8	35.8	27.3
23	Arizona	35.4	29.9	34.7
24	Ohio	35.4	33.6	31.0

Party identification is important because it structures how people vote. The party with the most identifiers has an initial advantage in the election because it has a core of supporters on whom to count. Also, partisan identity structures how people think about politics, how they receive political information, and how they process that information. About two-thirds of the electorate at any one time profess to have a party affiliation, and about one-third say they are independent. Independents, of course, ultimately end up voting for one party or another.

The distribution of partisan identification varies across states. Modern polling techniques allow a rough estimate of the proportion of citizens in each state who identify with each of the two major parties. Table 4.2 ranks 48 of the 50 states (Alaska and Hawaii are excluded) by the proportion of Democratic identifiers in the period 1976–1988. The states of Oklahoma and Louisiana had more than 50 percent of their citizens claiming to be Democrats. New Hampshire had the smallest proportion of Democrats: 21.8 percent. Thus, the two major parties have varying levels of "natural" advantage in the states. The proportion of independents also varies a lot between states, except in the South where there are few. More people are independents where it is easy

TABLE 4.2 (CONTINUED)

Rank	State	Democrat	Independent	Republican
25	Illinois	34.8%	36.5%	28.7%
26	Missouri	34.6	38.6	26.8
27	Massachusetts	34.2	50.0	15.8
28	Wisconsin	34.2	38.7	27.1
29	Virginia	32.7	37.9	29.4
30	New Jersey	32.6	39.9	27.5
31	Connecticut	32.3	43.2	24.5
32	Montana	32.2	40.4	27.4
33	Michigan	31.9	38.3	29.8
34	Washington	31.9	44.1	24.0
35	Indiana	31.2	36.0	32.9
36	Nebraska	30.9	28.9	40.2
37	Delaware	30.7	40.6	28.7
38	Wyoming	30.3	35.1	34.5
39	Iowa	29.6	38.1	32.4
40	Maine	29.5	43.5	27.0
41	Kansas	29.0	32.7	38.3
42	Colorado	28.6	38.8	32.6
43	Rhode Island	28.2	56.4	15.5
44	North Dakota	27.3	36.6	36.2
45	Utah	24.5	33.5	41.9
46	Idaho	23.8	39.0	37.3
47	Vermont	23.4	48.0	28.6
48	New Hampshire	21.8	46.3	31.8

Source: Robert S. Erickson, Gerald C. Wright, and John P. McIver, *Statehouse Democracy: Public Opinion and Policy in the American States* (Cambridge, Mass.: Cambridge University Press, 1993), p. 15.

to register and vote (for example, in open primary states) and where the parties are organizationally weaker.[6]

Differences in party identification are largely due to individuals' differences in socialization to politics, socioeconomic (class) differences, and stands on issues. Among the socioeconomic factors, education, income, occupation, race, and religion all show some difference between parties. That is, the Democratic Party has proportionately more blacks, people with less-prestigious occupations, Catholics and Jews, uneducated people, and lower-income people, whereas the Republican Party has proportionately more whites, professionals, Protestants (outside the South), highly educated people, and higher-income people. These party differences are only loose tendencies as compared to the more rigidly class-based party systems in Europe.

In addition to individuals' differences, there are also state-level differences in partisanship. Erikson, Wright, and McIver recently demonstrated that these state-level effects are a product of state political culture or context, and they have roughly as much impact on party identification as do the individual-level factors.[7] They found interstate differences in partisanship (between New Hampshire and Arkansas, for example) that were as big as partisan differences between Jews and Protestants or between blacks and whites. Where you live, they argue, is as important in determining your political party identification as who you are.

Differences in partisanship are also sectional: The southern states historically have been much more Democratic in orientation than the non-South. Indeed, this difference is observable in Table 4.2, where almost all the states with more than 40 percent Democratic identifiers are either southern or border states. But these interstate differences are much smaller than 25 years ago, when southerners first began to vote in large numbers for Republican presidential candidates.

Anomalies in Contemporary Party Identification

Amid these clear general patterns of party identification, several anomalies stand out. One is that as Southerners began to vote for Republicans at the national level and Democrats at the subnational level, the phenomenon of **dual partisan identification** emerged: holding one partisan identity at the national level and another at the state or local level. Over time we would expect many dual identifiers to convert to the other party. Indeed, this conversion process—where lifelong Democrats become Republicans—is underway throughout the South. The other source of partisan change is interstate migration, as when northern Republicans move to the South. These two processes—conversion and migration—have long been thought to be the basis for a party realignment in which the South becomes Republican instead of Democratic.

The long-awaited realignment seemed to have arrived in November 1994, when Republicans extended their Congressional victories to subnational offices. Following the 1994 election, Republicans controlled at least one state legislative chamber in North Carolina, Florida, and South Carolina, and they held the governorship in Alabama, Mississippi, South Carolina, and Virginia. But in 1995 the electoral outcomes were less definitive: Democrats won one governor's seat (Kentucky) and the Republicans two (Mississippi and Louisiana). No additional legislative chambers came under Republican control. Hence, the judgment that 1994 was a realigning election has to remain tentative until further elections take place.

Another nuance in the general pattern of party identification is how state parties vary in ideology. Although Republican identifiers tend to be conservative and Democratic identifiers liberal, the meaning of liberal ideology and conservative ideology varies by state. In some states the liberals are far to the left of the ideological spectrum and the conservatives are far to the right, resulting in a polarized party system. California (illustrated in Figure 4.1), Colorado, Connecticut, and New Hampshire are examples of extremely polarized party systems.[8] In these states, when you identify with the Republican party you are getting something quite different from the Democratic party.

In other states both parties are closer to the center of the ideological spectrum: New York is an example (as Figure 4.1 shows). Republican identifiers are not that different from Democratic identifiers. In still other states, adherents of both parties are quite conservative: Louisiana (as illustrated in Figure 4.1), Alabama, Arkansas, Idaho, Mississippi, North Carolina, North Dakota, and Oklahoma are examples of nonpolarized party systems. In no state are adherents of both parties liberal. The mean ideological differences among partisans indicate that parties in states such as Louisiana compete for votes on the conservative end of the ideological spectrum, the parties in New York compete in a relatively narrow band around the center of the spectrum, and each party in California looks for voters at its end of the spectrum and ignores the middle.

Finally, a significant change in strength of partisan identification—one that signals a possible change in the importance of both political parties—has occurred in the past few decades. The proportion of people identifying with either major party has declined and the proportion classifying themselves as independents has increased. In 1992, 38.7

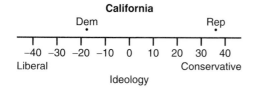

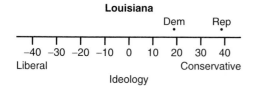

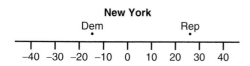

FIGURE 4.1 Three Examples of Ideological Polarization in State Political Parties.   Although all fifty states have a Republican party and a Democratic party, the ideological center of each party can vary by state as shown here.

Source: Data adapted from Robert S. Erikson, Gerald C. Wright, and John P. McIver, *Statehouse Democracy: Public Opinion and Policy in the United States.* Cambridge, Mass.: Cambridge University Press, 1993.

percent said they were independents, 25.5 percent said they were Republicans, and 35.8 percent professed to be Democrats.[9] Many scholars and political observers view this development with alarm. Frank Sorauf writes:

Since the stability of the two major American parties has been grounded in the party as a symbol or a cognitive image, the decline of that symbolic strength within the American voter poses the most serious threat imaginable to the parties and to their traditionally central position in American politics.[10]

Another aspect of the declining impact of party loyalty is that party identification is less tightly linked to a person's actual vote, at least in presidential elections. Democrats do not always vote for Democratic candidates, nor do Republican adherents always vote for Republican candidates. In 1992, an independent presidential candidate ran fairly well: Ross Perot received 19 percent of the vote, drawing voters equally from Clinton and Bush. In the 1990s a few states elected independents as governors: Lowell Weicker in Connecticut, Walter Hickel in Alaska, and Angus King in Maine. Together these signs point to an erosion in the loyalty of voters to parties and to the possibility that other organizations—interest groups, for example—may replace parties as cue-givers in voting.

Interparty Competition

Scholars of state politics have long recognized the critical significance of political competition. States with close competition between the two parties generally have higher rates of voter turnout. Competitive states are also more generous with welfare and other policy benefits. Thus, the close analysis of levels and patterns of party competition is warranted.

Given the changing nature of party loyalty and its looser relation to voting behavior, we would expect that **interparty competition** between the two major parties might increase. This is exactly what has happened; the development was first apparent at the national level. The New Deal realignment of the 1930s destroyed the sectional basis of American politics and replaced it with a system in which both parties compete for all states in presidential elections. In the 1980s the Republican Party became a dominant electoral force at the presidential level. Moreover, interparty competition increased modestly at the state level as well. In the 1990s the Republicans broke through, capturing control of both the U.S. House of Representatives and the U.S. Senate for the first time in 40 years. Their success was reinforced at the state level in 1994, when their control of state legislatures went from 8 to 19 and their control of governorships increased from 19 to 30.

Table 4.3 displays interparty competition for the period 1989–1994 using the standard index invented by Austin Ranney. Ranney's index includes four dimensions: the percentage of seats won by the Democrats in each house of the legislature, the percentage of votes won by Democrats in gubernatorial elections, and the proportion of all terms in which the Democrats had control of both legislative houses and the governorship. On the Ranney index, a perfectly competitive state would score .5000; that is, the two parties would be evenly balanced electorally. Scores approaching zero indicate Republican control, and scores approaching one indicate Democratic control. Ranney established certain cut-off points for each category of control, and we still use those categories today.

Since World War II there has been a strong correlation between states' rankings on the Ranney index from one time period to the next, suggesting a high degree of stability in the level of competitiveness, but still change occurs. Table 4.3 shows no one-party

TABLE 4.3 STATES CLASSIFIED ACCORDING TO DEGREE OF INTERPARTY COMPETITION, 1989–1994
States have become more politically competitive over time, producing movement from the two ends of the party spectrum to the center as shown here.

One-Party Democratic	Modified One-Party Democratic	Two-Party	Modified One-Party Republican	One-Party Republican
(none)	Arkansas (.831)	Tennessee (.649)	Idaho (.338)	(none)
	Louisiana (.828)	New Mexico (.645)	South Dakota (.322)	
	Hawaii (.814)	North Carolina (.636)	Arizona (.316)	
	West Virginia (.798)	Missouri (.633)	Wyoming (.313)	
	Rhode Island (.776)	Texas (.618)	New Hampshire (.259)	
	Maryland (.776)	Virginia (.617)	Utah (.232)	
	Kentucky (.741)	Minnesota (.608)		
	Georgia (.739)	Florida (.594)		
	Mississippi (.709)	Washington (.568)		
	Alabama (.666)	Vermont (.568)		
	Nebraska (.660)	South Carolina (.550)		
	Oklahoma (.659)	Nevada (.548)		
	Massachusetts (.658)	California (.537)		
		Oregon (.534)		
		New York (.530)		
		Maine (.528)		
		Delaware (.519)		
		Indiana (.518)		
		Connecticut (.518)		
		Wisconsin (.496)		
		Pennsylvania (.496)		
		Iowa (.481)		
		Alaska (.467)		
		Illinois (.462)		
		Montana (.453)		
		Colorado (.438)		
		Michigan (.421)		
		New Jersey (.410)		
		North Dakota (.394)		
		Ohio (.384)		
		Kansas (.359)		

Source: John F. Bibby and Thomas M. Holbrook, "Parties and Elections," in Virginia Gray and Herbert Jacob, eds. *Politics in the American States,* 6th ed. (Washington, D.C.: CQ Press, 1996), Table 3.5.

Democratic states, whereas in the 1981–1988 period there was one: Mississippi. Similarly, there are many fewer modified one-party Democratic states: There are now 13, whereas in the 1980s there were 21. The growth has occurred in the middle category: There are now 31 states in the two-party competitive category, compared to 22 in the 1980s. The Republican end of the scale remains the same: Six states are in the modified Republican category, and none are in the one-party Republican status. So there was quite a bit of movement between categories in the 1980s and early 1990s, mostly in the direction of more evenly balanced competition. Note, however, that the Democrats still retained an advantage in state government between 1989 and 1994: There are 13 modified Democratic states and only 6 modified Republican states. Also note the regional cast to party competition: The Democratic party is still strongest in the South and the Republican party is strongest in the mountain west and plains states.

Until the 1980s Democrats dominated at the state level, even though Republicans did well in contests for the presidency. By the end of the 1980s, a decade in which the Republicans captured the White House three times, they began to extend their strength at the state level as well. In the 1990s, as already indicated, the Republicans cemented their hold by gaining the U.S. Congress, state legislative houses, and governorships in 1994, even as they lost the presidency in 1992. One measure of the shift to Republicanism is the mean of the Ranney index, which moved in the Republican direction in the 1990s.[11] Much of the increase in Republican strength came in the South, where they made inroads in statewide offices. The states as a whole are now more competitive than at any time since the 1940s, when the Ranney index began to be recorded.

What can explain the patterns observed in Table 4.3? Why is Pennsylvania more competitive (.496) than Alabama (.666)? Among the many scholars who have tried to answer this query, Samuel Patterson and Gregory Caldeira have provided a particularly persuasive explanation.[12] They found education, the degree of owner occupancy of homes, population size, parties' organizational strength, and region to be especially important. The states that witnessed the most interparty competition tended to be large nonsouthern states with highly educated citizens, high levels of homeowner occupancy, and strong party organizations. Other scholars have discovered that incumbency suppresses competition, as does small district size.[13] The introduction of term limits might increase competition because it reduces incumbency; reducing the size of legislative bodies would increase district size and thereby increase competition. These findings are important because they indicate that interparty competition can be enhanced by active organized efforts on the part of party leaders. We can make politics more competitive, a condition most people think is healthy for democracy.

✧ THE PARTY IN THE ELECTORAL PROCESS

In the nineteenth century, party bosses recruited candidates and controlled their selection, first at party caucuses and later at party conventions. The convention system of nomination came under attack by the century's end because party bosses could easily control the convention delegates and thus the nomination of candidates. Since the first (1860) and second (1896) realignments had produced sectional parties, most localities were dominated by one party. Nomination was tantamount to election, and elite control of nominations effectively denied voters a choice in the election.

The leaders of the Progressive movement, especially Robert LaFollette, advocated the direct primary in order to democratize the selection of candidates. A **direct primary** is an election in which the party's voters, rather than its leaders, choose candidates to run in the general election. During the **general election** the entire electorate makes the final choice from the set of party nominees. By introducing the primary system the reformers hoped to break the bosses' hold over nominations and the machines' control over government.

Wisconsin voters adopted the direct primary by referendum in 1904, and by 1917 it had been adopted in most states. Although firmly entrenched as a nomination system, the direct primary today is criticized on two grounds. First, by removing an important responsibility of parties—nomination—it has led to party decline. Secondly, the reformers' ideal of democratization has not been fully achieved because voter participation is not very high. There is still some degree of elite control. We examine these criticisms in the following sections.

Contemporary Recruitment

The nation's 100 political parties organize elections: They recruit candidates, select party nominees, and contest general elections. In doing so, they compete with other nonparty organizations for influence over the outcome of elections. This increasing competition with other organizations gives rise to speculation that "the party's over." In this section we examine the role of the political party in the recruitment of candidates, as well as the roles of other participants. Later sections examine the nomination and general election phases of the electoral process.

A party's ability to recruit candidates to run under its banner is a significant measure of its strength. Indeed, Malcolm Jewell and David Olson call recruitment "an important litmus test of the existence and activity of party organizations."[14] Where parties are dominant or at least competitive, they are able to attract candidates to wear their label. Many of these candidates are self-starters, people who decide on their own to seek public office because they believe they can win. Others are talked into running by party leaders, interest groups, or other individuals who want the party to field a viable candidate. Minority parties, on the other hand, find it difficult to field candidates in hopeless situations. Few are self-starters; most have to be persuaded by party leaders. Sometimes no one can be found to run.

Some analysis has been done on the extent of party recruitment efforts at the state legislative level, the most important base (entry-level) office in our political system. One method of analysis is to ask party leaders their degree of involvement. Using this method, various scholars have determined that between 80 and 90 percent of county-level party leaders are involved in recruiting state legislative candidates. Another method of analysis is to ask legislative candidates who influenced their decision to run. Family and friends were ranked ahead of various party organizations by the candidates themselves; nonparty organizations were ranked last.[15]

In general, the party's role in recruitment varies according to its overall strength. Where parties are very strong, as in Pennsylvania, the party leadership is a major source of initial recruitment; where parties are moderately strong, as in Iowa, parties share the recruitment function with nonparty organizations such as interest groups; where parties are fragmented, as in Oregon, self-sponsorship by candidates is the norm.[16]

More limited analysis of gubernatorial recruitment has been conducted. Reichley's 1985 survey of state party chairs indicates that 71 percent of them reported involvement in recruitment, with this activity being far more common in the Republican Party than in the Democratic Party.[17] For an important office such as governor, parties do not usually need to recruit candidates; candidates present themselves. Other nonparty organizations are involved as well. However, even though parties may not initiate many gubernatorial candidacies, they can greatly influence electoral outcomes in other ways.

Nomination

Another important way in which parties can influence electoral outcomes is through their control over the nomination phase, during which party nominees are chosen to run in the general election. As explained earlier, the direct primary was adopted to democratize the selection process. All states now use some form of the direct primary to make their choices. States also allow political parties to have a role in nominations by authorizing a preprimary endorsement on either a formal or informal basis. There are several types of direct primaries, as noted in Table 4.4. These can be grouped into three categories: closed, open, and nonpartisan.

Types of Primaries   Some version of the **closed primary**—which requires that voters declare their party affiliation and vote only in their party's primary—is found in 27 states. In most of these states this declaration is made at the time of initial voter registration, well in advance of the primary. New York and Kentucky are particularly restrictive, requiring the decision to be made as much as ten months ahead of the primary. In other states there is more flexibility for new voters or party switchers to enroll later or even change on primary day.

Some type of **open primary** is found in 22 states. In some of these, voters request one party's ballot at the polling place. In others, the voter receives the ballots of both parties and in the privacy of the voting booth decides which ballot to use. The voter can vote in only one party's primary, however. Two states—Alaska and Washington—use an open, **blanket primary.** In these primaries voters can "mix and match": They do not have to indicate a party affiliation, and they can vote for a Democrat for one office and a Republican for another office. Alaska's situation is slightly more complicated because in 1992 their Republican Party passed new rules that conflict with the laws of the state: Participation in the Alaska GOP primary is now restricted to registered Republicans and independents. Box 4.1 explains how this situation came about.

Louisiana's **nonpartisan primary** is unique: All candidates of all parties are on the primary ballot. The general election is simply a runoff between the top two vote-getters in the primary.

Party leaders clearly prefer the closed primary situation because only their own party's members can participate. In the open primaries party leaders fear that members of the opposition party will cross over into their own primary and sway its outcome. It is unclear how much of this **crossover voting** does occur and to what extent crossover voters seek the weakest candidate.

Primaries in nine southern or border states are unusual in another way. The Democratic primary in the South has historically decided the winner because most voters were Democrats. The Democratic primary accordingly attracted many candidates. In order to ensure that the winner has majority support within the party, a runoff (or second) primary is held between the top two candidates if no candidate receives a majority. The winner of this second primary then faces the Republican candidate in the general election. Run-offs are required in about 10 percent of the races.[18]

Traditionally, states have regulated party primaries but a series of U.S. Supreme Court decisions has modified this power. These decisions have extended to political parties the

TABLE 4.4 **STATE PRIMARIES WITH VARYING VOTER QUALIFICATIONS** State political parties conduct primary elections under varying conditions, from primaries that are closed to all but party members, to those where everyone can vote.

Completely Closed	Closed, but May Enroll or Change on Primary Day	Closed, but Independents May Shift	Open, but Selection of Party Required	Completely Open	Open, Blanket Primary	Nonpartisan
Arizona	Colorado	Massachusetts	Alabama	Hawaii	Alaska	Louisiana
California	Iowa	New Hampshire	Arkansas	Idaho	Washington	
Connecticut	Kansas		Georgia	Michigan		
Delaware	Maine		Illinois	Minnesota		
Florida	New Jersey		Indiana	Montana		
Kentucky	Ohio		Mississippi	North Dakota		
Maryland	Rhode Island		Missouri	Utah		
Nebraska	Wyoming		South Carolina	Vermont		
Nevada			Tennessee	Wisconsin		
New Mexico			Texas			
New York			Virginia			
North Carolina						
Oklahoma						
Oregon						
Pennsylvania						
South Dakota						
West Virginia						

Source: Adapted from Malcolm E. Jewell and David M. Olson, *Political Parties and Elections in American States*, 3rd ed. (Chicago: Dorsey Press, 1988), p. 90. © 1988 Wadsworth Publishing.

BOX 4.1 ALASKA'S PRIMARY SYSTEM

In the United States, the major political parties function more like public utilities than private organizations. The state governments hold primary elections and have a hand in regulating the parties. But state party organizations, such as those in Alaska, have not always been happy with the lack of control over their own affairs.

Until 1992, Alaska was one of three states to hold blanket primaries in which voters could choose candidates from any party. The blanket primary did little for party unity. Thirty years ago Senator Robert Blodgett said, "The Democratic party is a hollow shell. The Republican party is a hollow shell. How many people actually are active workers in the two parties? Darned few." Blodgett's comments still hold true today.[1]

At different times, both Republican and Democratic activists have opposed the blanket primary. Alaska's Republicans saw an opportunity to do away with it after the United States Supreme Court handed down its 1986 decision in *Tashjian v. Republican Party of Connecticut*. The Supreme Court ruled that the state of Connecticut could not stop independent electoral registrants from voting in the Republican primary if the Republican party wanted independent voters to participate in their primaries. The case was a move away from government regulation of the political parties.[2]

In 1990, the Republican party of Alaska filed suit against the state. Party activists believed that many Democratic voters "crossed-over" to vote for weak Republicans. They argued that the doctrine established in *Tashjian* allowed the Republican party to close its primary to Democrats.[3]

The 1992 election was the first closed primary in nearly three decades. Only those registered as Republicans, undeclared, or nonpartisan voters could participate in the Republican primary. Alaska Republicans expected the Democrats to close off their primary, but the Democrats declined to follow suit. Fewer voters cast their ballots in the Republican primary than the other primary, which included Democrats and third-party voters. The closed primary seemed to have some of the effects Republicans desired. A few candidates supported by Republican activists won seats to the state legislature.[4]

Although the closed Republican primary has given some control back to the party, it has not appealed to the majority of Alaskan voters who support the blanket primary. Native Americans voiced concerns that a closed primary could hurt their representation in the state. The Alaskan Federation of Natives filed an amicus curiae brief in court on behalf of the blanket primary. It read:

Any election procedure which abridges the opportunity for Native voters to enhance their political influence through bipartisan coalitions fundamentally impairs voting prerogatives. . . . Indeed, AFN suspects that the Party Rule is specifically intended to frustrate the formation of bipartisan coalitions and, in turn, to impair the influential role of legislators who represent Native voters.[5]

---

[1]Gerald A. McBeath and Thomas A. Morehouse, *Alaska Politics and Government* (Lincoln: University of Nebraska Press), p. 216.

[2]Leon D. Epstein, "Will American Political Parties Be Privatized," *Journal of Law and Politics*, 5 (Winter 1989), 239.

[3]McBeath and Morehouse, *Alaska Politics and Government*, pp. 215–216.

[4]*Ibid.*, pp. 215–216.

[5]*Ibid.*, pp. 215–216.

freedom of association right inherent in the First Amendment and have struck down states' restrictions on parties in the process. The first decision was in *Tashjian v. Connecticut* (479 U.S. 20, 1986) where the Court held that if the state Republican party wanted independents to vote in its primary, Connecticut could not prevent them. This case potentially affects the closed primary system but thus far only a few parties, such as Alaska's Republican Party, have used this power to open up their primaries (see discussion in Box 4.1). The second decision was in *Eu v. San Francisco County Democratic Central Committee* (49 U.S. 214, 1989), where the Court threw out a California law that prevented parties from endorsing candidates in primaries. Both of these decisions indicate the Court's willingness to deregulate political parties, but other more recent decisions in the lower federal courts have discovered a compelling state interest in regulating parties. Continuing litigation over the legal status of parties seems guaranteed.

Endorsement Practices In some states, before the primary election party organizations make endorsements. The purpose of endorsement is to give party leaders some influence over the choice of candidates even though ultimate control remains in the hands of party members. Such endorsements range from requiring a formal endorsement from a party convention before being listed on a primary ballot to other legal advantages (for example, being listed first on the ballot) to simply an informal convention endorsement carrying no legal weight.

In the mid-1980s Jewell and Olson studied the effects of such endorsements on winning the nomination.[19] They found that endorsements are most effective when they are required by law and accompanied by resources. Connecticut is an example of a state with an effective endorsement system. Its system, established by law, applies to both parties and the endorsed candidate has preferential access to the ballot. Opponents tend to drop out and party activists coalesce behind the official candidate in this situation. The official candidate accrues the advantages of money, campaign workers, and other resources supplied by the party. In states where the endorsement is not a legal requirement but merely an informal custom, endorsements are more often challenged and beaten. Minnesota is such a state. Its system is set by party rules; candidates gain no legal advantage of ballot access or position, only party backing. In 1994, incumbent governor Arne Carlson failed to be endorsed by his party, but he went on to win the Republican primary and later the general election.

Overall, however, the value of the party endorsement in determining the outcome of the primary election is waning. One bit of evidence is that even in Connecticut in 1994, the endorsed Democratic candidate failed to win nomination in his party's primary. Party endorsement is apparently not highly salient to many primary voters.

So far, we have described the practices for statewide candidates. In some states political parties also endorse candidates within legislative districts. The extent and effectiveness of this practice have not been well documented. Most scholars conclude that party endorsement of legislative candidates is more likely to take place where parties are strong, where primaries are closed, where two-party competition is high, and within urban areas.[20]

Competition in Primaries Political parties' influence over candidate selection is also a function of the degree of interest potential candidates display and the degree of interest potential voters manifest by their willingness to vote. When few candidates choose to run in the primary election and few people bother to vote, then the choice remains largely in the hands of party elites. In such a situation, the reformers' purpose of democratization is thwarted. Lack of interest occurs far more often than the progressive reformers intended.

The amount of primary competition for the office of governor is critical in evaluating party influence over nomination. Jewell and Olson, examining the period 1960–1986, found that 75 percent of the gubernatorial primaries were contested; that is, about three-fourths of the time primary voters had a choice of candidates for whom to vote.[21] They found that a primary race was more likely to be contested if it was an open seat (that is, there was no incumbent), the state was in the South or West, the state was Democratic-dominated or balanced between the two parties, or if the state did not require a formal party endorsement. Basically, more candidates are willing to run if there is a decent chance of winning.

There is much less competition in party primaries for state legislative seats. Craig Grau, in a study of 14 states in the 1970s, found contests in 47 percent of Democratic primaries but in only 17 percent of Republican primaries.[22] Grau found that the absence of an incumbent increases competition, as does the prospect of a safe district. Most of the time primary voters do not have a choice of candidates because potential candidates do not perceive electoral conditions to be favorable to them. For these reasons, the direct primary has not fulfilled its promise at the state legislative level either. The political party continues to be influential in structuring the outcome of the nomination process, regardless of the reformers' intent to introduce democracy.

Voter Turnout in Primary Elections   Democratization of the nomination process also depends on voter interest. If few people bother to vote in primary elections, then the outcome can still be determined by party activists or party elites. This is often what happens. About one-fourth of the population voted in gubernatorial primaries held between 1962 and 1994.[23] Outside the South, turnout is increased by the open primary option and by a tradition of competitive primaries. In southern states, turnout in the Democratic primary usually exceeds turnout in the general election because historically the Democratic primary *was* the election.

If the small number of primary voters represented the entire electorate, there would be less concern regarding the meager turnout. However, this is not the case. Primary election voters are even less representative of the whole population than are general election voters. Voters in primaries tend to be older and more educated, and their degree of partisan identification is stronger than that of general election voters. In one-party states, turnout patterns are somewhat different. A Republican identifier in a predominantly Democratic state might vote in the Democratic primary because that is where local issues are decided. Thus, it is difficult to know just whom the few primary voters do represent.

Outcomes in Primary Elections   The purpose of any party's primary is to choose the strongest candidate to represent the party in the upcoming general election. Unfortunately, several factors reduce the likelihood of the strongest person being picked. Two already discussed are the lack of candidates and the lack of voters. This may lead to the nomination of candidates who are not attractive to voters. Another factor influencing the outcome is how primary voters make up their minds. Very little research has been done on this process but we can infer some things from our knowledge of voting behavior in general. When voters lack the cue of party identification and are faced with several candidates, they are more likely to be swayed by candidate image. Incumbents generally do better in this situation because their names are recognizable. Nonincumbents must develop name recognition somehow, usually through lavish spending.

Sometimes primary elections produce outcomes that are unpredictable or even odd. The 1986 Illinois Democratic primary is a classic example. The gubernatorial nominee, Adlai Stevenson III, refused to run on the same ticket with the candidates nominated for other state offices because they were followers of extremist Lyndon LaRouche. Stevenson formed a third party and later lost the general election to Republican Jim Thompson.

Another possible outcome of the primary election is that it is so divisive that the party's chances of winning in November are destroyed. In 1994, the Christian Right was a force that split Republican parties in many states as hotly contested primaries spilled over into the politics of the general election; Box 4.2 describes the outcome in three states. There are enough examples of such divisive primaries that parties and candidates certainly want to avoid them. Thus, the ultimate effect of having an interesting primary race that attracts many voters may be to lose the general election. This is not what Progressive reformers had in mind.

General Elections

General elections are contests between the candidates of the two major political parties (and sometimes the minor parties). However, nothing guarantees that the party's role will be anything more than its name on the ballot. Political parties must compete with the candidate, the media, interest groups, consultants, and others for a role in the electoral campaign. The party's role varies depending on the level of office (gubernatorial versus state legislative), the state (whether the parties are historically strong or weak), and the specific race (the needs of the candidate, the nature of the competition, and so forth). Overall, the influence of the party has declined while the candidate and nonparty groups have increased their influence. Let us examine the major elements of a campaign and the role each actor plays in statewide and legislative district campaigns.

Campaign Resources   Every campaign requires money, mass media, advanced technology, personnel (both paid experts and volunteer workers), and, ultimately, voters. Candidates furnish some of these resources themselves but they usually rely heavily on others to provide resources as well. Their need for resources varies widely. Gubernatorial races in Texas and South Dakota are quite different, legislative campaigns in New Hampshire and California are vastly different, but some patterns for statewide candidates and legislative candidates are clear.

First, the cost of campaigns is escalating rapidly at the state level. Between 1976 and 1988, spending on contests for statewide office and state legislative seats increased by 350 percent, from $120 million to $540 million.[24] This compares to an increase of 336 percent at the federal level. In 1982, gubernatorial elections averaged $5.6 million; in 1986, $7.4 million; in 1990, $10.6 million; and in 1994, $11.6 million.[25] The larger states illustrate the problem: In 1990 the candidates in California collectively spent nearly $58.8 million and in Texas they spent $55.9 million, and these are just the officially reported expenditures! Even millionaires cannot bankroll a campaign on this scale. Some of the most

BOX 4.2 THE CHRISTIAN RIGHT IN THE 1994 ELECTIONS

Among all the changes noted in the 1994 elections, perhaps most remarkable was the rise of the Christian right in many states. Spearheaded often by the Christian Coalition, televangelist Pat Robertson's political organization, these political activists altered the traditional balance of power in 1994, and appear to have the potential to do so for many years. The role Christian conservatives play in politics differs from state to state depending on the political structures and culture. An analysis of three states—Minnesota, Oklahoma, and Pennsylvania—provides insight into the current power of Christian conservatives and a glimpse into the possible futures.

Researchers have attempted to analyze what accounts for the influence of Christian conservatives in state Republican parties. The power of the Christian right is a result of the politicization of conservative religious communities and conservative opinions, especially in areas where the political environment is compatible.[1] In these situations the Christian right will be the most influential in the state Republican party.

Oklahoma is a state with both a politicized conservative religious community and a receptive political environment. Between 1992 and 1994, Oklahoma saw its congressional delegation go from being 5–3 Democratic to 7–1 Republican, while also capturing the governor's office. Five of the victorious representatives and both senators have strong Christian conservative ties.[2] The issue selection, campaign style, and vocal supporters of these candidates had a strong religious flair, and most of these candidates expressed public support for the Christian right and the Christian Coalition.

However, the Christian right was not monolithic in Oklahoma. There were actually two Christian rights operating in the state: one rustic and the other sophisticated.[3] The rustic Christian conservatives eschewed conventional techniques, relying instead on the "truth" of their beliefs to guide them to victory; they refused to compromise with the more moderate elements of the party, even after the primaries when the party is supposed to come together. The sophisticated religious right, in contrast, was supplied campaign managers, volunteers, and funds by the more traditional wing of the party, and used more conventional techniques to mobilize supporters. The sophisticated conservatives used these assets and coalitions to win in every instance where they conflicted with the rustics.

Minnesota provides a less successful example of Christian conservative activism. The state was shocked when its moderate incumbent governor, Republican Arne Carlson, was denied his own party's endorsement at the state convention in favor of a farmer and former state representative, Allen Quist. This was not as surprising as it may seem. Minnesota's unique caucus-based primary selection process provided a mechanism for Christian conservatives to take control of the Independent Republican party and to nominate its candidates for office. This combination of a weak Republican party and an electoral system that promoted the power of well-organized factions is precisely the type of setting that will allow for Christian conservatives' domination.

This is what happened in 1994. Although Governor Carlson was eventually able to defeat Quist for the party's endorsement in the September primary, Christian conservatives were able to make substantial gains in

expensive gubernatorial races are now in southern states where one-party Democratic dominance is dying; the new candidate-oriented campaigns requiring opinion polls, direct-mail, telephone banks, media consultants, and rapid travel are very expensive. Louisiana and Kentucky are notable example of high-cost states in the South.

At the state legislative level costs range considerably, as shown in Table 4.5. In rural states such as Idaho and Montana, an investment of a few thousand dollars can yield a legislative

the state legislature, elect a Christian conservative for Congress in the first district, and elect U.S. senator Rod Grams.

The other important lesson that can be taken from this state is how the perceptions of two Christian conservative candidates, Allen Quist and Rod Grams, differed. A content analysis of newspaper coverage found that Grams was able to win because he avoided the label of Christian conservative, which would, in this general election setting, be a detriment.[4] Because Quist appeared to be the man for Christian conservatives, he was labeled with this term, and accrued all of the negative baggage that came with it.

Pennsylvania provides the third example of Christian right activism in state parties. Although Christian conservatives attained substantial influence in the state Republican party, they do not control it as in Oklahoma and Minnesota. In the 1994 gubernatorial election, both major parties nominated candidates who were pro-choice on abortion. In response to this situation, Peg Luksik ran as an independent candidate with a staunchly pro-life/pro-family campaign, and support from the Christian Coalition. She received 13 percent of the vote.

Luksik's candidacy suggests that Christian conservatives have the potential for a third party if they cannot get what they desire from the Republican party. Although her candidacy was limited by her ineffectiveness as a candidate, one can imagine a more successful Christian conservative candidate mobilizing an upstart campaign in the future. Support patterns for Luksik suggest that a Christian conservative could pull together a winning coalition outside of the Republican party if the ground were more fertile.[5]

These three examples provide a synopsis of how the Christian right has worked within states for electoral success. Perhaps more importantly, it provides a view into the potential routes Christian conservatives may take. They may dominate the state Republican party and allow only like-minded candidates to run (Oklahoma), or they may have a loud voice in the party but work with moderate elements to run candidates amenable to both sides (Minnesota), or they may branch out on their own, taking their chances as a third party (Pennsylvania). What choices are made, and how successful they are, depends on the state's political environment, their willingness to work with moderates, and the willingness of moderates to work with them.

[1] John C. Green, James L. Guth, and Clyde Wilcox, "The Christian Right and the Republican Party: A View from the States," paper presented at the annual meeting of the Midwest Political Science Association, Chicago, 1995.

[2] Nancy L. Bednar and Allen D. Hertzke, "Oklahoma: The Christian Right and Republican Realignment," in Mark J. Rozell and Clyde Wilcox, eds., *God at the Grass Roots: The Christian Right and the 1994 Elections* (Lanham, Md.: Rowman & Littlefield, 1995), pp. 91–108.

[3] Nancy L. Bednar, "The 1994 Congressional Primaries in Oklahoma: A Window to the Christian Right Role," paper presented at the annual meeting of the American Political Science Association, Chicago, 1995.

[4] Christopher P. Gilbert and David A. M. Peterson, "Minnesota: Christians and Quistians in the GOP," in Mark J. Rozell and Clyde Wilcox, eds., *God at the Grass Roots: The Christian Right and the 1994 Elections* (Lanham, Md.: Rowman & Littlefield, 1995), pp. 169–190.

[5] Timothy R. Johnson, David A. M. Peterson, and Christopher P. Gilbert, "Religious Adherence and County Voting Patterns: Evidence from the States, 1994," paper presented at the annual meeting of the Society for the Scientific Study of Religion, St. Louis, 1995.

seat, whereas in most states a seat costs $15,000 to $25,000. California is a whole different story: Even in 1988 it cost over $370,000. The differences can be traced to factors such as varying district sizes, the expense of media markets, and the availability of public financing. As reporter Rob Gurwitt says, "It would be unthinkable, for example, to run for the California Assembly without paid staff, consultants and pollsters; in Montana, where legislative careerism has yet to take hold, you'd probably be laughed out of the state for using them."[26]

TABLE 4.5 THE COSTS OF CAMPAIGNING FOR STATE HOUSE SEATS, 1988 The costs of legislative campaigning, and therefore the type of people who can afford to run, differ a great deal from large states to small states.

State	Campaign Average
California	$370,722
Idaho	4,425
Minnesota	13,244
Missouri	9,618
Montana	2,692
New Jersey	48,033
North Carolina	12,085
Oregon	35,982
Pennsylvania	18,462
Washington	25,811
Wisconsin	14,868

Source: These spending data were collected in the course of a research project conducted by David Breaux, William Cassie, Anthony Gierzynski, Keith Hamm, Malcolm E. Jewell, Gary Moncrief, and Joel Thompson. They are reported in Rob Gurwitt, "Searching for the Cheap Seats," *Governing* (August 1992), 50. Reprinted with permission, *Governing Magazine*, copyright 1992.

Campaign funds go to purchase the essential resources of media advertising, polling, and direct mail, all elements of the new campaign technology orchestrated by consultants. Some call these "the substitute political party organizations."[27] New campaign technology can be seen in gubernatorial elections in all large states and most small ones. The media campaign is often a very expensive element, with television advertising alone typically costing 15 to 30 percent of the campaign budget. Thus far, the average state legislative campaign does not rely on electronic media or polling but that day may be coming.

Campaigns also need personnel. A campaign staff is needed to organize and direct the entire effort and to provide expertise and knowledge. In a statewide campaign these are typically paid (though short-term) positions. Some portion of these activities may be purchased from campaign management firms, some may come from the party, and some from the candidate's own personal organization. Often there is tension during the campaign over the relative influence of each. A second kind of personnel is the volunteer worker who may work the phones, canvass door-to-door, distribute literature, and put up signs. A statewide campaign requires thousands of such people. A state legislative campaign, in contrast, typically relies on volunteers to do all of the work. Paid campaign staff for legislative candidates is rare in most states.

Party Influence What can political parties offer candidates during a campaign? One resource is an attractive ticket. Candidates for state legislative office may be helped or hindered by the gubernatorial candidate at the top of the ticket. Illinois Democratic legislative candidates surely regretted the disarray at the top of their 1986 ticket. Another party resource is electoral mobilization and support: Parties offer voter identification programs, voter registration drives, poll watchers, get-out-the-vote drives, and so forth. Most state parties routinely provide such programs, aimed at increasing voter turnout, so that all their candidates will benefit. Still another party resource is direct services to candidates: Campaign seminars are quite typical; less common but increasingly available are public opinion polling, issue development, and media assistance. These are resources tailored to individual candidates. As the chair of the Colorado Democratic party said, "I see the state party organization as a sort of quartermaster corps, delivering services that achieve economies of scale. Many of the services the state party performs would cost ten times as much if the individual candidates went out and bought them on the open market."[28]

Finally, parties can help by making financial contributions to candidates. In state legislative races a primary source of party money is the legislative caucus campaign committee. This committee is composed of the incumbent party members in each chamber and is normally directed by the party leader of the chamber. This practice is found in 38 states; the most active caucus committees are found in states with substantial amounts of interparty competition, high legislative professionalization, high campaign costs, and weak state central commitees.[29] Illinois, New Jersey, New York, Ohio, Wisconsin, Indiana, Maine, and Minnesota are examples of such states. As Tom Loftus, former Democratic speaker of the Wisconsin House, explains, the caucus committee "is a mature machine with a single function: to recruit, staff, and fund candidates in marginal seats. The function is carried on for a single purpose: to retain or gain control of a house in the legislature."[30] By funding candidates in close races rather than safe incumbents, the caucus committee makes races more competitive. It also provides noncash assistance such as polling, research, campaign workers, and assistance with fund-raising. Thus legislative caucus committees act as political parties used to.

Closely allied with the legislative caucus committee is the leadership **political action committee** (PAC). Many party leaders establish a personal PAC to which individuals and interest groups contribute; for example, the speaker's birthday is often a popular occasion for a fund-raiser where lobbyists contribute. Because the speaker is usually a safe incumbent, he or she does not need the money so the funds are transferred to someone who does, often buying that candidate's loyalty to the speaker in the process. This practice exists in half of the states. Democrat Willie Brown, the legendary former speaker of the California Assembly, perfected this strategy. For example, in 1988 he gave $2.7 million to needy fellow Democrats.[31] Throughout the 1980s Brown was the largest single contributor to Assembly races, outspending the rest of the party and the largest PACs.[32] But in other states, leadership PACs are less important revenue sources.

Although the legislative caucus committee and the leadership PAC supplement other party sources, in most states the party is not the primary source of campaign funds. As of the most recent study in the mid-1980s, contributions from individuals were still the major source.[33] PAC contributions (see next section for more on PACs) from nonparty groups were typically second, and political parties usually ranked third. This ranking is probably still accurate for the smaller states, but in the larger states PACs have achieved more importance. Recent examination by Herbert Alexander indicates that PACs are now the largest campaign finance source in California, Oregon, Colorado, and Michigan, but no 50-state analysis has been done recently.[34]

Interest Groups Interest groups have become increasingly active in electoral campaigns. Groups attempt to "educate" candidates by having them appear before the group to answer questions. In addition, they often provide direct campaign services to their favored candidates in much the same way parties do: They furnish volunteer workers, telephone banks, mailing lists, and so forth. Often such services go to "endorsed" candidates, candidates whose records are judged to merit the group's support. These are all time-honored methods of interest group involvement.

Newer methods of interest group involvement in the electoral process focus on financial contributions. Many interest groups, labor unions, corporations, and other nonparty organizations have formed their own PACs for the purpose of raising and disbursing money to political candidates. A PAC is a legal organization through which like-minded people funnel their campaign contributions. For example, you might start a Student Power PAC at your university. If each student at a university of 10,000 students contributed $5, you would have a kitty of $50,000, an effective PAC in many state legislatures. If everyone contributed $10, the war chest of $100,000 might put you among the fat cats. PAC leaders would then figure out how to allocate the money to elect candidates supportive of students' interests. Probably you would end up doing what most PACs do: giving money to incumbents, especially to those on key committees concerned with higher education. You would most likely give money to both sides of the aisle—to Republicans and Democrats alike—in order to maximize your chances.

The number of PACs at the state level continues to grow. In the early 1990s, California, Pennsylvania, and Texas led the nation in the number of PACs, with over a thousand each.[35] As we saw earlier, their role in campaign finance is important: PACs are the first or second prime source of campaign dollars in most states, contributing to both gubernatorial and legislative campaigns.

It is important to note that PACs and interest groups are not the same thing. PACs are legally constituted entities that exist solely to raise and distribute campaign funds; they may or may not be associated with an interest group. Only about one-third of state interest groups even have PACs.[36] In addition, there are many "nonconnected" PACs, which do not have parent interest groups; they exist solely for campaign finance purposes.

In response to public concern about PACs' influence in campaigns, several states considered or enacted limits on their activities. Kentucky and Minnesota, for example, place a limit on the proportion of a candidate's total receipts that can come from PACs. Other states have tightened up their reporting and disclosure requirements, increased their enforcement activities, and limited the transfer of surplus funds from one campaign to another.

The Candidate Although we think of candidates as being the standard-bearers of the party, sometimes candidates are distant, even estranged from the party. Some candidates rely on their own private funds to finance the campaign: Clayton Williams's expenditure of $9 million in the 1990 Texas governor's race (which he lost) is illustrative.[37] Self-financing on this scale is rare in statewide races, although in state legislative races some degree of self-financing is common.

Some candidates also run their own campaign organizations, relying on their friends, acquaintances in nonparty organizations, and the new campaign technologies instead of the party. The use of mass media allows communication with voters without going through the political party. It encourages an emphasis on the candidate's image, his or her personal qualities, or charisma. Of course, it costs money. Particularly at the state legislative level, candidates are likely to run their own campaigns with little dependence on the party organization. They do not wait for the party to organize the race for them. A 1994 survey of state legislative candidates found that family and friends were rated as the primary source of help in all aspects of campaigns except for registering voters; for that activity the local party ranked highest.[38]

State Governments In about half the states electoral campaigns benefit from direct or indirect public financial assistance. Some states allow tax deductions or credits for private contributions to candidates or political parties or allow taxpayers to donate some amount of money at tax time. Twelve states provide public funding for campaigns or political parties through tax checkoffs, a more popular option that raises more money than a donation. A few states (such as, Hawaii, Minnesota, and Wisconsin) provide public funds for both state legislative races and the governorship but more states fund only the governor's race.

Due to the 1976 Supreme Court decision in *Buckley v. Valeo*, a candidate cannot be forced to accept an expenditure limit, but he or she may voluntarily do so in return for accepting public financing. In practical terms, this means that public funding programs must offer a candidate enough money to make it worthwhile to accept the expenditure limit; otherwise, expenditure limits are not viable. The only states where sufficient public money has been raised to attract the participation of most candidates are Michigan, New Jersey, Minnesota, and until recently, Wisconsin.[39] Due to its paltry sums, public funding has not lived up to its promise of offering a clean source of campaign funds.

The intent of public funding and other reforms is to bolster interparty competition, help new candidates, put a cap on total spending, reduce dependence on interest groups and fat cats, and in general clean up campaign financing. Other reforms include prohibiting anonymous donations, limiting certain kinds of contributions, and requiring candidates to account for their contributions and expenditures. Experience in the 20 years since campaign finance reforms began has been sobering. The worst ethical breaches have been cleaned up, but every year new problems crop up that state legislatures attempt to deal with. In the mid-1990s a second generation of reform legislation was enacted; it remains to be seen whether it works better than the first generation.

In sum, general election campaigns are an amalgam of political party resources, the candidate's own personal resources, and the resources of nonparty organizations, including PACs and public funds. The political party must compete with other contributors in order to exert control over electoral campaigns. In some parts of the country party organizations are strong, and candidates run as a partisan team. In other instances parties have been able to play a strong role because they adapted to new campaign technologies, formed legislative caucus and leadership PACs, or formed alliances with existing PACs.

They took the attitude "if you can't beat 'em, join 'em." In other states the parties are relatively weak and moribund. In the end, parties' aggressiveness determines their influence.

Party Loyalty and Voting The parties' influence over general elections also depends on the degree of party loyalty displayed by voters. If voters continue to vote along party lines, then campaign involvement by others may not matter much. However, if voters pay less allegiance to their self-professed party identification, then the party loses influence. Research by various authors has determined that party identification is often the strongest predictor of a person's vote for governor.[40] However, what has changed is that there are fewer partisans today and more independents than there were in the 1950s. Hence, gubernatorial voting is less structured by party allegiance today.

Another way to examine this question is to look at the incidence of ticket-splitting in state and local elections. How often do voters vote a straight ticket and how often do they split their ticket between the parties? Scholars have found that at least 25 percent of the electorate engages in **split-ticket voting** between presidential and congressional races; when one looks across all races on the ballots, it may be higher than 50 percent of the electorate.[41] Probably nearly everyone has split a ticket in some election. The party team concept has weakened, so gubernatorial elections are considerably more volatile than in the past. No gubernatorial candidate can afford to rely on the party alone to win an election.

Another factor that might affect state voters is national voting patterns. Perhaps one's vote choice for president affects one's gubernatorial choice. If so, when a presidential candidate wins the election, his or her party might sweep state elections too. In reaction, states have attempted to isolate themselves from this coattail phenomenon. Five states have gubernatorial races in odd-numbered years, totally separating themselves from national elections. Thirty-six states hold gubernatorial elections during the off-year Congressional elections, thereby partially isolating themselves. Nine states choose governors during presidential years, and two states elect governors every two years. These eleven states (the nine plus the two) then are the only ones susceptible to direct presidential coattails, but much evidence indicates that gubernatorial elections in off-years can still be influenced indirectly by national factors such as presidential popularity and national economic performance.[42] As the authors of the most recent study summarize, "we can say that factors at the national level influence state-level voting, though the extent to which those factors involve the economy or revolve around the president more generally remains somewhat ambiguous."[43]

The elections in 1994 are only one example: As the Republicans swept the national Congress, they also swept the state legislatures. Of the new legislators, 472 were Republican and 11 were Democrats. A recent interpretation of the Republican landslide in state legislatures traces the results in the lower houses to President Bill Clinton's unpopularity in 1994: "It is clear that if the Democrats had a more popular president in the White House, their electoral wounds would not have been so severe."[44] Interestingly, however, the results in the upper houses were tied more to state economic performance than to national coattails.

✧ THE PARTY IN GOVERNMENT

After the election is over, interest groups, campaign consultants, journalists, and the public turn their attention elsewhere. It is up to the winning candidate and his or her party to govern. This duty of managing government and the possibility of being thrown out of office are the key characteristics distinguishing parties from interest groups. Interest groups are not held responsible for how government runs, nor can voters get rid of group leaders. How a party behaves once in office is, in contrast, very important to its continued existence. If a party does not perform, we can "throw the rascals out." One important standard by which party behavior in government is measured is the enactment of public policies and programs. In Europe, significant shifts in public policies often occur when the government changes hands. In the United States such dramatic shifts are less typical. Still, we retain the idea that parties should make a difference in policymaking.

The idea that parties matter in policymaking is called the **responsible party model.** Some years ago a committee of the American Political Science Association issued a report criticizing our political parties for failing to achieve responsible party government.[45] The report argued that each party should have an ideology, each party should offer a clear and distinct party platform, and, once in office, the party should carry out its promises. Political scientists have since used these criteria to judge whether parties are behaving responsibly, that is, whether parties are doing what they promised to do.

Notice that the responsible party model also requires that voters be responsible, that is, that they examine the party's ideology, platform, and performance, and vote accordingly. The model assumes that people cast their votes on the basis of issues and performance, not on the basis of the candidate's looks, charisma, or hometown. The model assumes that voters will desert a political party if it is not responsible in its performance.

Do state political parties behave as responsible parties? Many political scientists have tried to produce a positive response to this question, presumably because they believe responsible party government is a good thing. But few scholars have found dramatic policy differences between Republican and Democratic parties once they hold state offices. Particular attention has been focused on differences in welfare policies between the states, following V. O. Key's notion that politics revolves around the struggle between the haves and the have-nots.[46]

Recent work by Thomas Dye, Robert Brown, and James Garand is more encouraging about the prospects for party responsibility in state government.[47] They found that the party in control has an impact on the policies enacted under two conditions: when there is a high degree of competition between the parties, presumably because the competition forces parties to stick to their promises; and when the parties are ideological, cohesive, and focused on issues. Under these conditions the competition between the two parties is policy-relevant, to use Dye's term. In other words, interparty competition must focus on issues and policies for party responsibility to occur. Some examples of states with policy-relevant parties are California, Hawaii, Iowa, Maine, Michigan, Minnesota, Nebraska, North Dakota, Oregon, Wisconsin, Wyoming, New Jersey, Ohio, and Pennsylvania. Most of the non-policy-relevant states are southern, where party competition, historically, has been practically nonexistent. It is no surprise that the party in control does not change policy outputs in these states; this situation may be changing, however, as party competition intensifies in the South.

Another team of researchers tried to find out why state electoral politics does not have more policy relevance. Their findings are intriguing, if a bit complicated. Erikson, Wright, and McIver found that liberal states elect liberal Democrats to the legislature and conservative states elect conservative Republicans.[48] But once in office, both sets of legislators respond to public opinion and move toward the middle of the policy spectrum in order to get reelected. The Democratic legislators trim to the right and the Republican officeholders trim to the left. Because the individual legislators behave similarly once in office, the result is that party control has little correlation with the policies enacted, yet their findings mean that parties are responsive to voice. The electorate is in control after all.

Divided Party Control

Several factors make it difficult for parties to fulfill the ideal of responsible party government at the state level. One is **divided party control.** Separation of powers makes it possible for one political party to control the executive branch and the other party to control the legislative branch. In addition, there may be divided party control within the executive branch; that is, the governor's party does not necessarily control the other elected offices (such as auditor, secretary of state, and attorney general). Also, there may be divided control within the legislative branch because the Democrats may control one house and the Republicans the other. If the same party does not control all the institutions of government, it is hard for the party to carry out a coherent program.

Unified party control, whereby the same party controls the governorship and both houses of the legislature, is not an empirical reality in most states. In the early 1950s, 34 percent of states had divided control.[49] By 1989, 64 percent of the states had divided control. Following the 1994 elections, however, divided party control was reduced to 53.1 percent. Still, about half the time it is impossible for a party to achieve responsible party government because it does not control the institutions of government.

The increase in divided control since mid-century is linked to the increase in ticket-splitting and to growing party competition. It is also traced to a fall in unified Republican control brought about by a decline in Republican legislative control.[50] From the 1950s to the 1990s, the Republican party was able to elect governors but not legislators. The reversal in these trends in 1994 was due to the Republicans picking up 472 legislative seats and adding a net 10 new governors. The term limitations now adopted in 20 states will probably increase the number of Republican legislators and bring about more unified Republican government.

The effect of divided control is to reduce parties' ability to manage the government responsibly. The party controlling one branch of state government can always blame the party controlling the other branch for a bad situation. In such a situation it is hard for voters to know which "rascals" to throw out. In the long run the stalemate between government institutions may erode voters' confidence in parties and in democratic government.

Legislative Cohesion

Another requirement of the responsible parties notion is that legislators must vote together in party blocs once in office, demonstrating **legislative cohesion;** that is, Democratic legislators must behave differently from Republican legislators. This requirement is difficult to fulfill in part because legislators do not always place party above constituency, interest groups, and their own beliefs. Legislators vote with their own party on some issues and not on others; election law, for example, is normally a very partisan issue, as are labor legislation and appropriations bills.[51] In some states legislators are cohesive in their voting patterns; these tend to be the states with strong party traditions, such as New York, Massachusetts, and Connecticut. In one-party states—Arkansas and Georgia, for example—party affiliation does not structure voting. In general, the political party is of some importance in structuring legislative voting patterns but by no means do the states' parties fulfill the cohesion test of the responsible party model.

Just like our national parties, states' parties do not meet the severe tests of the responsible party model. However, the parties do structure government in the sense that legislators organize their work and their committees along party lines. In some states and on some issues the legislative parties actually do function as cohesive voting blocs. However, state parties face one important constraint that is missing at the national level: Not only can voters leave one party and go to another, but they can leave the state altogether.

✧ CONCLUSION

In this chapter we have examined the role of political parties in state politics and government, with particular emphasis on the changing role of political parties. With respect to party organization, research shows that both parties have become stronger. They now provide more and different services than in the past and have larger budgets and more staff; in short, they are more professionalized. Second, with respect to the party in the electorate, partisan identification has declined in terms of both the level of attachment to party and the extent to which partisan identity structures voting. Interparty competition has remained more or less stable, with some tendency toward more competition.

The party's role in the electoral process has changed the most. The party's control over nominations was loosened first; next the party's dominance in campaigns was diminished. Parties now must compete with many well-funded actors, including PACs and ancilliary party organizations, to get a share of the action in electoral campaigns. Finally, the responsible party model was an ideal that could never be realized fully due to the lack of unified party control of government. Recently the degree of party unification has improved but is far from complete. In these ways, then, parties have been transformed, a transformation that some people call decline.

Two points should be kept in mind about party decline, however. The decline argument implies that parties have fallen from some glorious heights they once occupied. In fact, the past history of strong parties at the state and local level brings back different memories: memories of city machines and bosses such as the late Mayor Daley in Chicago, or tales of patronage and corruption in governors' offices from Massachusetts to Illinois to California. If these are the glamorous parties that have died, then so be it. One could hardly miss such party shenanigans. The second point to remember about party change is that few of the changes are inevitable and irreversible. Political leaders can learn new campaign techniques, they can raise funds from new sources, and they can recruit attractive candidates. There is no reason for interest groups and outside consultants to have a monopoly on innovative campaign technology. Parties that have adapted to the changed electoral environment have achieved success.

◇ KEY TERMS

blanket primary (p. 96)
closed primary (p. 96)
crossover voting (p. 96)
dealignment (p. 88)
direct primary (p. 94)
divided party control (p. 110)
dual partisan identification (p. 90)
general election (p. 95)
interparty competition (p. 92)

legislative cohesion (p. 110)
nonpartisan primary (p. 96)
open primary (p. 96)
party identification (p. 89)
patronage (p. 83)
political action committee (p. 105)
realignment (p. 87)
responsible party model (p. 109)
split-ticket voting (p. 108)

◇ FOR FURTHER READING

Cornelius P. Cotter, James L. Gibson, John F. Bibby, and Robert J. Huckshorn, *Party Organizations in American Politics* (New York: Praeger, 1984). A report of a major study of state-level party organizations, based on interviews with the party chairs in each state.

Anthony Gierzynski, *Legislative Party Campaign Committees in the American States* (Lexington: University Press of Kentucky, 1992). A definitive study of legislative caucus committees and leadership PACs in selected states, including an analysis of their finances, structure, and allocations.

V. O. Key, Jr., *Southern Politics in State and Nation* (New York: Random House, 1949). The classic statement about political parties in the South, focusing on the negative effect of one-party politics.

Maureen Moakley, ed., *Party Realignment and State Politics* (Columbus: Ohio State University Press, 1992). An examination of party realignment and change in 14 states.

Mark J. Rozell and Clyde Wilcox, eds., *God at the Grassroots: The Christian Right in the 1994 Elections* (Lanham, Md.: Rowman & Littlefield, 1995). Case studies of the effect of the Christian Right in 11 states in the 1994 elections.

◇ NOTES

1. Frank J. Sorauf and Paul Allen Beck, *Party Politics in America*, 5th ed. (Glenview, Ill.: Scott, Foresman/Little, Brown, 1988), p. 78.

2. Cornelius P. Cotter, James L. Gibson, John F. Bibby, and Robert J. Huckshorn, *Party Organizations in American Politics* (New York: Praeger, 1984), p. 182.

3. Robert Biersack, "Hard Facts and Soft Money: State Party Finance in the 1992 Federal Elections," in Daniel M. Shea and John C. Green, eds., *The State of the Parties: The Changing Role of Contemporary American Parties* (Lanham, Md.: Rowman & Littlefield, 1994), p. 119.

4. John Frendreis and Alan R. Gitelson, "Parties, Candidates, and State Electoral Politics," paper presented at the annual meeting of the American Political Science Association, Chicago, August 1995.

5. Robert D. Brown, "Party Cleavages and Welfare Effort in the American States," *American Political Science Review*, 89 (March 1995), 23–33.

6. Malcolm E. Jewell and David M. Olson, *Political Parties and Elections in American States*, 3rd ed. (Chicago: Dorsey, 1988), p. 43; Barbara Norrander, "Explaining Cross-State Variation in Independent Identification," *American Journal of Political Science*, 33 (May 1989), 516–536.

7. Robert S. Erikson, Gerald C. Wright, and John P. McIver, *Statehouse Democracy: Public Opinion and Policy in the American States* (Cambridge: Cambridge University Press, 1993), p. 55.

8. *Ibid.*, pp. 40–41.

9. National Election Study data reported in Robert L. Lineberry, George C. Edwards III, and Martin P. Wattenberg, *Government in America*, 6th ed. (New York: HarperCollins, 1994), p. 256.

10. Frank J. Sorauf, *Party Politics in America*, 4th ed. (Boston: Little, Brown, 1984), p. 159.

11. John F. Bibby and Thomas M. Holbrook, "Parties and Elections," in Virginia Gray and Herbert Jacob, eds., *Politics in the American States*, 6th ed. (Washington, D.C.: CQ Press, 1996), Table 3.6.

12. Samuel C. Patterson and Gregory A. Caldeira, "The Etiology of Partisan Competition," *American Political Science Review*, 78 (September 1984), 691–707.

13. Thomas M. Holbrook, Maurice Mangum, and James Garand, "Sources of Electoral Competition in the American States," paper presented at the annual meeting of the American Political Science Association, New York, September 1994.

14. Jewell and Olson, *Political Parties*, p. 100.

15. Frendreis and Gitelson, "Parties, Candidates, and State Electoral Politics," Table 3.

16. Samuel C. Patterson, "Legislative Politics in the States," in Virginia Gray and Herbert Jacob, eds., *Politics in the American States*, 6th ed. (Washington, D.C.: CQ Press, 1996), p. 166.

17. A. James Reichley, *The Life of the Parties* (New York: The Free Press, 1992), p. 390.

18. Bibby and Holbrook, "Parties and Elections," p. 101.

19. Jewell and Olson, *Political Parties*, p. 96.

20. Richard J. Tobin and Edward Keynes, "Institutional Differences in the Recruitment Process: A Four-State Study," *American Journal of Political Science*, 19 (November 1975), 667–682.

21. Jewell and Olson, *Political Parties*, p. 105.

22. Craig H. Grau, "Competition in State Legislative Primaries," *Legislative Studies Quarterly*, 6 (February 1981), 39.

23. Bibby and Holbrook, "Parties and Elections," p. 103.

24. Herbert Alexander, *Reform and Reality* (New York: The Twentieth Century Fund Press, 1991), p. 7.

25. Thad Beyle, "Governors," in Virginia Gray and Herbert Jacob, eds., *Politics in the American States*, 6th ed. (Washington, D.C.: CQ Press, 1996), p. 214. The 1990 figures are in 1993 constant dollars. The 1994 figures are calculated from unpublished data compiled by Beyle.

26. Rob Gurwitt, "The Mirage of Campaign Reform," *Governing* (August 1992), 50.

27. Larry Sabato, "Gubernatorial Politics and the New Campaign Technology," *State Government*, 53 (Summer 1980), 148–152.

28. Reichley, *The Life of the Parties*, p. 387.

29. Bibby and Holbrook, "Parties and Elections," p. 89; Anthony Gierzynski, *Legislative Party Campaign Committees in the American States* (Lexington: University Press of Kentucky, 1992); Cindy Simon Rosenthal, "New Party or Campaign Bank Account? Explaining the Rise of State Legislative Campaign Committees," *Legislative Studies Quarterly*, 20 (May 1995), 249–268.

30. Tom Loftus, *The Art of Legislative Politics* (Washington, D.C.: CQ Press, 1994), p. 37.

31. Frank J. Sorauf, *Inside Campaign Finance* (New Haven: Yale University Press, 1992), p. 119.

32. Patterson, "Legislative Politics in the States," p. 170.

33. Ruth S. Jones, "Financing State Elections," in Michael J. Malbin, ed., *Money and Politics in the United States* (Chatham, N.J.: Chatham House and American Enterprise Institute, 1984), p. 183. Frank Sorauf speculates that campaign finance sources at the state level break down as they do on the national level, where the order is individuals, PACs, candidates themselves, and political parties. See Sorauf, *Inside Campaign Finance*, p. 32.

34. Alexander, *Reform and Reality*, p. 19.

35. Clive S. Thomas and Ronald J. Hrebenar, "Political Action Committees in the States: Some Preliminary Findings," paper presented at the annual meeting of the American Political Science Association, Washington, D.C., August 29–September 1, 1991, Table 4.

36. Virginia Gray and David Lowery, *The Population Ecology of Interest Representation* (Ann Arbor: University of Michigan Press, 1996), p. 7.

37. Alexander, *Reform and Reality*, p. 10.

38. Frendreis and Gitelson, "Parties, Candidates, and State Electoral Politics," Table 4A.

39. Alexander, *Reform and Reality*, p. 44; Gurwitt, "The Mirage of Campaign Reform," p. 51.

40. Craig J. Svoboda, "Retrospective Voting in Gubernatorial Elections: 1982 and 1986," *Political Research Quarterly*, 48 (March 1995), 135–150.

41. Estimated from figures in Ohio reported in Paul Allen Beck, Lawrence Baum, Aage R. Clausen, and Charles E. Smith, Jr., "Patterns and Sources of Ticket Splitting in Subpresidential Voting," *American Political Science Review*, 86 (December 1992), 916–928.

42. Svoboda, "Retrospective Voting"; Thomas M. Holbrook-Provow, "National Factors in Gubernatorial Elections," *American Politics Quarterly*, 15 (October 1987), 471–483; Dennis M. Simon, "Presidents, Governors, and Electoral Accountability," *Journal of Politics*, 51 (May 1989), 286–304.

43. Richard G. Niemi, Harold W. Stanley, and Ronald J. Vogel, "State Economies and State Taxes: Do Voters Hold Governors Accountable?," *American Journal of Political Science*, 39 (November 1995), 948.

44. Paul Brace and Laura Langer, "Interpreting the 1994 State Legislative Elections," *Spectrum*, 68 (Spring 1995), 12.

45. American Political Science Association, *Toward a More Responsible Two-Party System* (Washington, D.C.: American Political Science Association, 1950).

46. V. O. Key, Jr., *Southern Politics in State and Nation* (New York: Random House, 1949).

47. Thomas R. Dye, "Party and Policy in the States," *Journal of Politics*, 46 (November 1984), 1098–1116; James C. Garand, "Partisan Change and Shifting Expenditure Priorities in the American States, 1945–1978," *American Politics Quarterly*, 13 (October 1985), 355–391; Brown, "Party Cleavages and Welfare Effort in the American States."

48. Erikson, Wright, and McIver, *Statehouse Democracy*.

49. William H. Flanigan and Nancy H. Zingale, "Ticket-Splitting and the Vote for Governor," *State Government*, 53 (Summer 1980), 157–160.

50. Morris Fiorina, *Divided Government* (New York: Macmillan, 1992), pp. 36–37.

51. Patterson, "Legislative Politics in the States," p. 193.

PART THREE

STATE GOVERNMENT INSTITUTIONS

STATE LEGISLATURES

egislatures are at the heart of democratic government. Because it is impossible for all citizens to gather and make laws together, a representative assembly takes on the task. The great advantage of representative democracy over direct democracy is that the representatives can discuss and debate public affairs and learn from one another. Their deliberations then improve public policy. According to prevailing political theory at the time the U.S. Constitution was written, the legislature, not the executive, should have the supreme power to make laws.

The early colonies had representative bodies called general assemblies, general courts, or houses of delegates, which were advisory to the King of England. These evolved into legislatures with full lawmaking powers as the states were constituted. Reacting against the power of the king, the new state constitutions carefully separated powers among the three branches, keeping the governor's power in check and vesting much power in legislative bodies. From these heady days, state legislatures began a gradual decline in power and respect that has been arrested only in recent decades. Myriad examples of corruption in state legislatures occurred, especially in the decades following the Civil War, when special interests seemingly owned individual lawmakers. Negative public reaction to corruption and excess spending led to constitutional restrictions on legislative power. State legislatures had to limit the length of their sessions and were no longer responsible for selecting U.S. senators.

Since mid-century state legislatures have gradually regained their prominence, restored their credibility, and modernized their operations. Today's representative assemblies are the product of a nationwide reform movement that began in the 1960s; this movement and the current backlash against legislative incumbents are described in more detail shortly.

Today state legislatures are perhaps the most improved branch of state government. Historically the object of scorn, they are now much more capable. They have become more professionalized and modernized than the citizen legislatures of the past. Some state legislatures such as California's handle state budgets the size of some nations' budgets. California legislators represent districts with populations as large as others states' Congressional districts. Other state legislatures, such as New Hampshire's, deal with tiny budgets and are populated by part-timers.

Legislatures are important institutions in state government. More stable in composition than the governorship and more visible than the courts, legislatures provide a focus for citizen support and evaluation of state government overall. Satisfaction with the legislature and its performance can increase citizen loyalty; dissatisfaction can give rise to voice or eventual exit. Hence, legislative capability is an important bulwark of states' ability to control their futures.

We first examine the people serving in the legislature. Then we discuss the institution itself, and how its work is organized. Finally, we analyze the legislative process: how laws are passed, how money is appropriated, and how oversight is conducted.

Throughout this discussion students may want to keep in mind the U.S. Congress. Both national and subnational legislatures are bicameral; that is, they have two houses (except in Nebraska). The U.S. Senate represents the states equally, but state senates do not represent counties or any other geographic units. State senate districts are apportioned on the same population basis as lower house districts; they are just larger. State legislative bodies are smaller than the U.S. Congress, with the largest state senate having 67 members and the largest state house having 400 members. As a result, state assemblies tend to be less formal and hierarchical.

The central organizational features are the same: committee and party. The committee system is less important at the state level than in the larger U.S. Congress and the role of party varies by state. In some it is stronger than in the U.S. Congress (Connecticut is usually cited as an example) and in other states party is weaker (Nebraska, with its nonpartisan body, is an extreme case). We explore reasons for these variations later on. Staff is more crucial in Congress than in state legislatures, although a few of the larger states approach the Congressional staff-intensive model. Both national and subnational legislatures enact laws and appropriate funds but the U.S. Congress also conducts foreign policy. Thus, both similarities and differences abound between the national and state legislatures.

✧ THE PEOPLE

There are 7,461 men and women serving in the 50 state legislatures. They arrive there by winning an election. Some campaign in very populous districts: For example, a California Assembly member represents about 400,000 people; his or her campaign would probably involve extensive use of television and mass mailings and would have cost an average of $370,000 in 1988.[1] Others campaign in very large districts: Alaskan candidates often use private planes to fly into remote areas. Still others campaign in small, compact districts: For example, New Hampshire House districts average only 3,000 voters. Their campaigns can be conducted door-to-door and cost relatively little.

Electoral Conditions

Most would-be legislators conduct their campaigns in single-member districts, where the voters of a district may cast a vote for only one person. For some the election takes place in a **multimember district,** where the voters elect several members to the state legislature. As of 1986, multimember districts constituted less than 15 percent of all districts.[2] Multimember districts are disappearing, especially in the South, where they have been challenged in court as discriminatory against blacks.[3]

Most legislators run in primary and general elections that are not highly competitive. A minimal condition for competition is that at least two parties provide a candidate so

State legislative campaigns in most states are people-intensive. Candidates try to meet as many voters as possible. Here, a state senator in Connecticut campaigns at a local fire station. (*Source:* © Gale Zucker/Stock, Boston)

that the seat is contested: This happened 65 percent of the time during the period 1968–1991.[4] The rest of the time potential candidates were scared off, perhaps by an entrenched incumbent or by a long tradition of not being in the majority. A more stringent condition for competitiveness is that each party receive at least 40 percent of the two-party vote: This happened about one-third of the time in the same period. Most of the time, then, legislative contests have lopsided victory margins; they are not very competitive.

One reason for the lack of competition is the so-called incumbency advantage: About three-quarters of incumbents run again; of those over 90 percent win.[5] Evidence is mixed about whether incumbency advantage has grown over time. But in any case it is a significant deterrent to challengers, and public perception is negative about careerists (people who make a career of legislative service). To counter the incumbency advantage, 20 states have now adopted limits on legislative terms; this reform is described later in the chapter. As a result of these electoral patterns, the composition of a legislative body is relatively stable from session to session. There is less stability, however, following the decennial census, when district boundaries change in line with population shifts.

Who the Legislators Are

Who survives the process of election and goes to state capitols to legislate? Traditionally, state legislators have been white, male, middle-aged attorneys, with higher income and education levels. This homogeneous picture has changed a great deal in the past decade, particularly outside the South. By 1995, there were more than 800 minorities and more than 1,500 women among the 7,461 legislators.[6] Clearly women have made more progress than have blacks and other minorities: Women now constitute 20.7 percent of all legislators. Table 5.1 displays the proportion of women who served in each state legislature in 1995. In southern states female legislators are still a rarity: Louisiana, Kentucky, and Alabama have fewer than 10 percent women in their legislative chambers. Nevada and Washington each have more than one-third women and are the states with the highest

TABLE 5.1 PERCENTAGE OF WOMEN SERVING IN STATE LEGISLATURES, 1995

The percentage of women serving in the state legislatures has grown over time, although in no state does it approach fifty percent. The western states tend to have the highest female percentages, and the southern states the lowest.

Rank	State	Percentage of Women Overall
1	Washington	39.5%
2	Nevada	34.9
3	Colorado	31.0
4	Arizona	30.0
4	Vermont	30.0
4	New Hampshire	30.0
7	Oregon	28.9
8	Maryland	28.7
9	Idaho	28.6
10	Kansas	27.9
11	Connecticut	26.7
12	Maine	26.3
13	Michigan	24.9
14	Nebraska	24.5
15	Ohio	24.2
15	Wisconsin	24.2
17	Massachusetts	24.0
17	Montana	24.0
17	Rhode Island	24.0
20	Illinois	23.7
21	Alaska	23.3
22	Minnesota	22.3
23	Indiana	22.0
24	South Carolina	21.4

female proportion.[7] Western states traditionally have had high proportions of women serving: Colorado, Arizona, Oregon, and Idaho are among the top ten states. Smaller states with many legislative seats have also attracted more women to their legislative ranks: Vermont and New Hampshire illustrate this tendency.

The numbers of minority representatives are somewhat more difficult to track, especially when speaking of Hispanics, Asians, and Native Americans. Hispanics, who numbered 155 in state legislatures in 1995, tend to be elected in the states with larger Hispanic populations: the New Mexico legislature had 37.5 percent Hispanic legislators and Texas had 18.2 percent, for example.[8] Asian Americans, who numbered 53 in state legislatures in 1995, are present in significant numbers only in Hawaii (61.8 percent); Native Americans, who numbered 44 in state legislatures in 1995, are noticeable only in Alaska, Arizona, and Hawaii, where they constitute around 10 percent. Blacks have been increasing

TABLE 5.1   (CONTINUED)

Rank	State	Percentage of Women Overall
25	Wyoming	21.1%
26	Delaware	21.0
27	California	20.8
28	New Mexico	20.5
29	Missouri	19.8
30	Hawaii	19.7
31	Florida	19.4
32	Georgia	18.2
32	Texas	18.2
34	South Dakota	18.1
35	New York	18.0
35	Iowa	18.0
37	North Carolina	16.5
38	North Dakota	15.5
39	West Virginia	14.9
40	Utah	14.4
41	Tennessee	13.6
42	New Jersey	13.3
43	Arkansas	12.6
44	Pennsylvania	11.9
45	Mississippi	11.5
46	Virginia	11.4
47	Oklahoma	10.7
48	Louisiana	9.7
49	Kentucky	8.0
50	Alabama	3.6

Source: CAWP Fact Sheet on Women in State Legislatures, Center for the American Woman and Politics, Eagleton Institute of Politics, Rutgers University, 1995.

their percentage nationwide, with the most marked legislative gains coming in southern states. By 1995, they totaled 557, holding over a fourth of the seats in the Mississippi legislature and more than 15 percent in Alabama, Georgia, Louisiana, Maryland, and South Carolina.[9]

Practically everywhere the average age of legislators is declining. The number of legislators who are lawyers is also declining, especially outside the South. According to a survey of legislators serving in 1993 (reported in Table 5.2), attorneys now constitute only 16.5 percent of all legislators. People with a business background—owner, employee, real estate, or insurance—are the largest category at 27.7 percent. Professionals other than attorneys constitute 10.6 percent and educators total 8.2 percent. Few blue-collar workers serve in the legislature, few people of limited education serve, and fewer from agricultural backgrounds serve than in the past. The change in composition has occurred primarily within a professional and managerial elite.

Perhaps the most telling change has been the increase in the number of people who say their full-time occupation is that of legislator, which is now 14.9 percent overall. In some states this trend is more pronounced than in others: In New York, Pennsylvania, and Wisconsin, for example, more than two-thirds of the lawmakers are full-timers.[10] This self-identification as a full-time legislator is indicative of the **professionalization** of the legislative career. Fewer legislators are part-time amateurs who serve for a few years and then resume their primary careers. Today's legislators are more likely to serve in the legislature as a "first job" and to stay in politics as a career. Because most legislatures, especially in the large states, now meet annually and some in lengthy sessions, it is difficult for today's legislators to maintain or to begin another career. It is even more difficult to hold down an outside job and a legislative job and raise a family. More and more people are choosing to combine only two of these roles.

Although professionalization has meant an end to most corruption and to the backward ways of state legislatures, this development brings its own concerns. A legislative professional who has no other job to return to will be very concerned about the possibility of defeat. He or she may be especially vulnerable to pressure from interest groups or from constituents. Many observers see professionalization and the passing of the "citizen legislature" as a negative development; this judgment fuels the term limitations movement.

The composition of the legislature in terms of age, gender, race, and occupation is important because the state legislature is the most common entry-level office for national political leaders. Perhaps as many as half of those who leave the state legislature do so in order to run for higher office.[11] Serving in the legislature is an important rung on the career ladder of ambitious politicians. In the 101st Congress (1989–1990), over 50 percent of House members had served previously in their state legislature.[12] Apprenticeship at the state level prepares them for Congressional service because the two legislative bodies employ similar processes, demand similar skills, and face many of the same issues. Of the governors serving between 1970 and 1994, nearly half had been state legislators.[13] Prior service facilitates the governor's ability to interact with legislators while in office. Thus, the state legislature is a schoolhouse for ambitious politicians. Its attractions entice some to make it their life's work, it trains others for higher office, and it screens out still others and returns them to private life.

Legislative composition is also important because it has an impact on how legislators respond to issues and ultimately on what the legislature does. Box 5.1 illustrates how

TABLE 5.2   OCCUPATIONS OF STATE
LEGISLATORS   The occupational makeup of state
legislators has grown more diversified over time,
with business people of various types now being the
most numerous.

Occupation	1993 Overall Percentage
Business owner, business executive, business, real estate, insurance	27.7%
Attorney	16.5
Full-time	14.9
Other professionals[a]	10.6
Retired, homemaker, student	8.8
K–12 educator, college educator	8.2
Agriculture	7.9
Local government/government employee	2.5
Labor union	0.3
Other[b]	2.7

[a] Includes those employed in the following fields or professions: consultant, professional, communications, arts, medical, engineer, scientist, architect, accountant, and clergy.

[b] Insufficient information or information not available.

Source: Diana Gordon, "Citizen Legislators: Alive and Well," *State Legislatures,* 20 (January 1994), 27. © The National Conference of State Legislatures.

background, especially occupation and ethnicity, can affect a legislator's approach to his or her job. The box also demonstrates that there are still plenty of citizen legislators around. A particularly telling example of the impact of legislative composition is the effect of female legislators. The representation of women in state legislative bodies has reached a point where scholars can observe noticeable impacts. A 1988 survey of legislators in twelve states was conducted by Sue Thomas. She found that female legislators, more than males, placed a high priority on policies relating to women, children, and the family, and women were more successful in getting family legislation passed.[14] As the percentage of female legislators increases, we can expect a shift in legislative priorities from business-related items that interest men to family legislation.

Women have also made noticeable inroads into the leadership structure of legislatures. By 1991 females held 17.7 percent of formal leadership positions in the 100 legislative chambers.[15] Female leaders tend not to be found in southern or border states; rather, they represent urban districts or hail from small states where it is easy to commute to the capital. Also, women are more likely to be elected leaders where there are more female members. Malcolm Jewell and Marcia Whicker interviewed legislative leaders around the country in an effort to discover the differences between male and female leadership styles. They found that women tended to adopt a consensus approach to leadership rather than a more traditional command approach.[16] Interestingly, they found that some men adopted the consensus style too and that modern legislative members are resisting the command style; the authors speculate that in the future the consensus style will be the norm

BOX 5.1 CITIZEN LEGISLATORS

Connecticut Representative Bob Maddox says "Staying in touch" is the reason he maintains his frantic schedule, juggling ownership of two coin shops and part-time employment at Macy's department store with his responsibilities in the General Assembly. By engaging in the day-to-day activities of business and commerce, Maddox gains information about the practical significance of the legislation he works on in the state legislature. Because he can speak to the needs of both small business owners and employees of major corporations, Maddox feels he has a special role to play in developing public policies and passing laws as he "represents the society they will affect."[1]

Citizen legislators can stay in touch in other ways. Oregon Senator Jeannette Hamby has her own, privately sponsored home page on the World Wide Web, providing information about her employment, heritage, political history, legislative involvement, and family. Hamby makes particular mention of her roots, which spread outside of the state of Oregon. The daughter of Finnish immigrants to Minnesota, Hamby feels that her childhood experiences of beginning school without speaking English and witnessing the environmental degradation of Minnesota's Iron Range have caused her to support "the common folk" and environmental causes.[2] She is currently chair of the Ways and Means subcommittee on Human Resources.

Nebraska Senator Ernie Chambers lists his occupation as "defender of the downtrodden," but such a description may belie his true vocation. Chambers is also the unofficial poet laureate for the Nebraska Legislature, drawing inspiration from pending legislation and controversies in state government, but ultimately writing his verse to "give perhaps a pinch of pleasure."[3] One of only four legislators in Nebraska's part-time, unicameral legislature who considers himself a full-time legislator, Chambers lives on the $12,000 annual salary and honoraria for speeches. On his relationship with his constituency, Chambers says, "when they have no place else to turn, they call me."[4]

Knowing "when to insist, when to bend, and when to compromise" seem crucial skills for state legislators, but Vermont Senator Cheryl Rivers has not learned these skills in the statehouse; she gained them in the training ring with her Morgans. For Rivers, the skills gained in her full-time occupation are transferable to her activities as a state legislator. Training horses also allows Rivers the flexibility necessary to serve her 6,000 constituents, who "expect to be able to call us on the phone with any personal problem they may have with state government," while still earning a living when the legislature is not in session.[5]

---

[1]Dianna Gordon, "Citizen Legislators—Alive and Well," *State Legislatures,* 20 (January 1994), 25.

[2]http://www.teleport.com/~senhamby/index.html June 27, 1995.

[3]Gordon, "Citizen Legislators—Alive and Well," p. 26.

[4]*Ibid.,* p. 27.

[5]*Ibid.,* p. 24.

for leaders of either sex. As one Oregon leader put it, the consensus style "is one that is more comfortable for women, but also for many men. It is much less confrontational and much more concerned about the other person's perception of the situation."[17]

How Legislators View Their Jobs

Political scientists have devoted a considerable amount of attention to the question of how state legislators view their jobs—in short, their role definitions. Different legislators, as you might expect, emphasize different parts of their jobs. Some practice what we might call a service orientation: They try to straighten out problems for individual constituents. This is called casework. Others are interested in controlling what state administrators are doing, or **oversight.** Most are particularly interested in proposing and sponsoring legislation, in making laws.

In this section we look at some of the different hats legislators wear and how they wear them. In the late 1970s, Richard Elling interviewed legislators in Minnesota and Kentucky about their jobs. His survey showed that most members in these two state legislatures thought legislating was the most important component of their job, with constituency service second and oversight third.[18] This ranking still seems valid today.

Legislating   Most legislators identify legislating as the most important part of their job. In order to vote on the many bills that are considered each year, legislators have to devote a great deal of time to this task. Moreover, legislators sponsor legislation themselves, which involves time spent formulating bills and obtaining additional sponsors. A number of years ago a team of researchers described legislators' roles in lawmaking.[19] John Wahlke and his associates found that representatives may act as **trustees,** people who follow their own judgment on different issues; they believe in following the dictates of their own conscience. Or they may act as **delegates,** people who follow the instructions of their constituents or other groups. Or they may act as **politicos,** people who are both, depending on the issue, its salience, or their reelection prospects. Few people adhere strictly to the delegate or trustee role all the time.

In the past 30 years, Wahlke's role concepts have been used to explain many facets of legislative behavior, especially voting on legislation. One of the more straightforward of the voting studies was that done by Eric Uslaner and Ronald Weber in 1973.[20] According to their survey, legislators tend to consult first either their friends in the legislature or legislators who specialize in the subject under consideration. Next, they consult interest groups, followed by a variety of other legislators. Relatively remote in their voting calculations are party leaders, the governor, and their constituents. For most legislators, voting decisions are arrived at by a process of consultation largely within the legislative body itself.

Legislators in different states may have different patterns of cue-taking. In some— Connecticut, New York, and Massachusetts, for example—the party plays an important role. Roll-call voting is usually divided along partisan lines in these states. In other states, interest groups play a larger role. In the more professionalized legislatures, such as that of California, the legislator's staff has a major impact on how he or she votes and on what bills he or she sponsors. In Ohio, a majority of legislators said in 1993 that they turn to their constituents first.[21] Constituent opinion tends to matter more if the issue is highly salient (e.g., abortion) and if constituent opinion is consistent and homogeneous. Finally, from time to time a strong governor will heavily influence voting among the party's members. So the state context affects the cues on which legislators rely.

Constituency Service   Because most state legislators still live and work in their districts, they necessarily spend a lot of time with their constituents. They spend weekends and many weeknights attending meetings at which they see constituents. Many schedule office hours in the district. They may write newsletters or columns in neighborhood newspapers through which they communicate with silent constituents. The typical member of a less professionalized state legislature also has many occasions for informal contact. As one New Hampshire legislator put it,

> We don't need public opinion polls to tell us what concerns are on their minds; we know firsthand about a solid-waste crisis when we stop by the dump on Saturday; we hear our children complain about the trailers they are taught in because we can't afford new schools; we hear from our elderly neighbors about a tax crisis.[22]

Such contacts often lead to requests for assistance, what is called **casework** in the professional literature. Some legislators spend a lot of their time dealing with constituent requests, whereas others get few requests. Elling's study showed that Minnesota legislators averaged 25 percent of their time and Kentucky legislators 38 percent of their time on casework. A more recent study in 1992 surveyed legislators in four states—North Carolina, Colorado, Maryland, and Ohio—and concluded that more time is devoted to casework today, with the Ohio legislature having the strongest casework orientation among the four states.[23]

The variation in emphasis on casework in different states seems to be related to whether the state has a tradition of doing casework and whether staff resources are available to do the work. Massachusetts, Texas, and Ohio have been identified as states in which political culture and a legacy of patronage made casework the norm.[24] California legislators are able to emphasize service because they have staff members to provide the assistance.

There is also variation in the devotion to casework due to the individual legislator's interest in being an ombudsman. Research shows that more experienced and ambitious legislators perform more service than beginners; representatives from poor districts do more casework, presumably because their constituents have greater needs; and women place more emphasis on casework than men do.[25] Generally, legislators get involved in casework because they enjoy it and derive a sense of satisfaction from it. For example, an Indiana legislator explained,

> Serving constituent needs is one of the big satisfactions of being a legislator. The requests may seem trivial, but they are very important to these people, and I like being in a position to help people. I get more satisfaction out of this than anything else.[26]

Oversight Casework may lead to an emphasis on oversight, the review of activities of the executive branch. When legislators intercede with administrative agencies on behalf of constituents, they are exercising oversight in a narrow sense. Over time the pattern of casework requests may furnish valuable feedback about certain agencies, or the pattern of requests may lead a legislator to make broader inquiries about a state agency's operations. For example, a legislator may decide as a result of a number of calls from frustrated taxpayers that state tax forms are needlessly complicated.

Still, Elling's study showed that oversight does not occupy much of the typical legislator's time: 18 percent in Minnesota and 13 percent in Kentucky. One reason it does not take up much time is that staff members can perform the oversight function on behalf of the legislator. In later sections of this chapter we discuss these formal mechanisms of oversight.

◆   THE INSTITUTION

Legislators serve in institutions with long traditions that shape their behavior and performance. Each body has its own informal rules about what is appropriate behavior or suitable dress on the floor. In some chambers members are not allowed on the floor without coat and tie; they cannot eat or read at their desks during a session. There are norms about how members will treat one another. They may address each other by name rather than as "the representative from district Y."

Among the most salient features of legislative organization is the fact that they are organized by political parties. Nebraska is the sole exception: It has the country's only nonpartisan legislature. From the mid-1960s to the mid-1990s, the Democrats were the dominant party in state legislatures. In well over half the states they normally had the majority in both houses; in only 13 states have the Republicans usually been in control.[27] Thus, 1994 was a watershed year when Republicans led in party control: Republicans held 19 state legislatures, Democrats 18, and split control was in effect in 12 states. After the 1995 election, Republican-controlled states stayed the same but the Democrats lost ground in two states, leading to split control in those states (see Figure 5.1 for details).

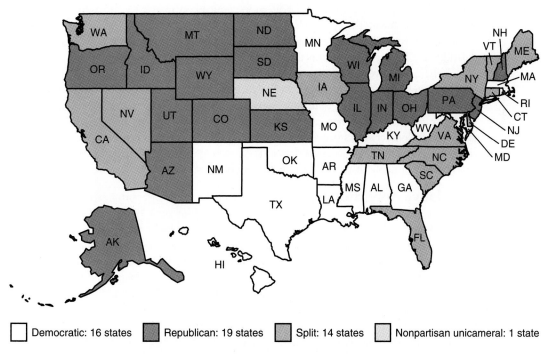

Democratic: 16 states   Republican: 19 states   Split: 14 states   Nonpartisan unicameral: 1 state

FIGURE 5.1   1996 Party Control of State Legislatures.   The Republican party made dramatic strides in gaining control of state legislatures in the mid-1990s; by 1996 the GOP controlled 19 state legislatures.

Source: National Conference of State Legislatures World Wide Web Site, http://www.ncsl.org, December 28, 1995.

Another common structural feature is that all states, save Nebraska, have a bicameral legislature. Usually the smaller upper body is called the senate and the larger lower body the house of representatives.

Still another salient feature of legislatures is their size. Minnesota has the largest senate, with 67 members; proposals to reduce its size or have only one house have been advanced, but to no avail. The average state senate has about 40 members. Alaska has the smallest senate, with only 20 members. New Hampshire has the largest house, with 400 members; Alaska is again the smallest, with only 40 members. Many reform groups argue that lower houses should be no larger than 100 members to be effective and upper bodies no larger than 50. They believe that organizational effectiveness would be improved by reducing the size of many state legislatures. For example, the amount of time spent debating bills might decrease if there were fewer members talking. The contrary argument is that having more members allows representation of more constituent interests.

Institutional Changes

A thumbnail sketch of the history of state legislatures will help to place recent changes in perspective. As mentioned briefly earlier, in the early years of our country, the colonists ousted royal governors and invested great power in the legislatures of the new states. In the first half of the nineteenth century, the democratization of the legislature eroded its stature while experience with good governors reduced antipathy toward state executives. Consequently, during the century's second half governors were granted increased powers while the power of legislatures was attacked because they had become corrupt and scandal-ridden. The buying of legislation was all too common.

Early in the twentieth century, the Progressive movement succeeded in instituting many reforms of state government and in further diluting legislative power. Many states limited the frequency of legislative sessions on the theory that the less often they meet, the less harm they do. Others adopted the use of the initiative, recall, and referendum to allow direct democracy. However, by mid-century it became apparent that the society and the polity were placing increased demands on state government, demands that state legislatures were unable to meet. So a second era of legislative reform began.

Legislative Apportionment
One of the first and most important sources of change was the reapportionment revolution. Before the U.S. Supreme Court's decision in 1962 in *Baker v. Carr* (369 U.S. 186), many state legislatures were badly malapportioned. That is, some legislators represented rural districts with small populations and some represented urban districts with many more people. For example, in the California Senate, one senator represented 6 million people in Los Angeles County and another represented 14,000 people in a mountain district.[28] In Tennessee, where the *Baker* case originated, the legislature had not been reapportioned in 60 years. The district boundaries had stayed the same while the population grew and shifted.

The 1962 decision enunciated the rule of one person, one vote: Legislative districts must be equal in population, as determined by the most recent U.S. census, and it is the responsibility of the state legislature to draw boundary lines so that this principle is achieved. Subsequently, in the case of *Reynolds v. Sims* (1964), the Court said that representation in both legislative houses must be based on population; state senates are not like the U.S. Senate.

These and other Supreme Court rulings had immediate effect in every state. By the end of 1965 all but three states had redrawn their district boundaries even though a firestorm of criticism greeted these decisions.[29] The U.S. Congress came close to initiating a constitutional amendment to overturn the *Reynolds* decision, and state legislators predictably were highly critical of the Court. But the principle of one person, one vote prevailed and is now firmly embedded in our political values.

Reapportionment brought an influx of younger, better-educated legislators from urban and suburban areas, people unlikely to be elected in conservative rural areas. It especially increased minority representation and to some extent female representation. In partisan terms, reapportionment advantaged the Democratic party in the North and the Republican party in the South. State legislatures were now more responsive to the interests of urban and suburban residents. Of all the reforms described in this section, reapportionment had the greatest impact on the quality of state legislatures.

Following each U.S. census thereafter, state legislatures, often with court intervention, have redrawn their legislative district boundaries so as to follow the one person, one vote criterion. Although the principle is clear, the process is fraught with difficulty because incumbents are drawing the district lines. The majority political party may still try to draw district boundaries so as to ensure their continued success at the polls. This procedure is called *gerrymandering,* drawing district boundaries for partisan advantage, even while equalizing population among districts. But boundaries can be drawn to achieve other purposes too: When the intent is to influence the representation of minority groups, we call it racial gerrymandering. This form of gerrymandering, especially as it advantages (or disadvantages) black voters, is the major issue in the 1990s. Box 5.2 documents the tortuous course reapportionment has taken in recent years.

Legislative Reform Soon after the reapportionment revolution, a number of reform, or "good government," groups began to call for fundamental reforms of state legislatures. Notable among these groups was the Citizens' Conference on State Legislatures (CCSL), which sponsored a massive study in the late 1960s. Its report in 1973 evaluated each state's legislature on the degree to which it was FAIIR: functional, accountable, information-capable, independent, and representative.[30] Its ratings placed states such as California and New York at the top and states such as Alabama and Wyoming at the bottom. The ratings had a great impact, as did the report's specific recommendations for improvement in each legislature. In the two-and-a-half decades since the publication of this report, states have revitalized their legislatures. We will now examine some of the more important changes.

One of the chief concerns of the reformers was that legislatures allow adequate time for full consideration of bills. They argued that a single three-month session every second year was not nearly enough time to deal with a state's business. States have gradually expanded the time spent so that most legislatures have annual regular sessions, allow for special emergency sessions, and use interim periods between sessions for various committee meetings. These changes allow for fuller consideration of bills, making the legislature more functional. It also means that the job of the state legislator is very time-consuming, and at some point being a legislator becomes the primary occupation rather than a sideline.

Along with the increase in the number of legislative days has come an increase in compensation for legislators. A principal recommendation of the reformers, adequate pay

BOX 5.2 LEGISLATIVE REDISTRICTING

After each decennial census, states redraw district lines for state legislative offices and the U.S. House of Representatives to reflect population changes that have occurred since the last census. In most states redistricting is done by the state legislature, but in nine states independent nonpartisan commissions conduct redistricting, and in one state, Alaska, redistricting is done by the governor's office. After the *Baker v. Carr* decision in 1962, the principle was simple: All citizens should have an equal share of representation, so every district should contain equal numbers of people.[1]

State legislatures in the 1970s and 1980s bore the marks of *Baker v. Carr.* Redistricting after the 1970 census resulted in the election of better-educated, younger legislators from urban areas. The 1980s redistricting continued the trends of the 1970s, reflecting population changes, particularly movement to and within the Sun Belt states. Still, the 1980s redistricting was not without controversy as 43 state plans faced legal challenges.[2]

Two important changes in the reporting and processing of data occurred at the time of the 1990 census. First, the census bureau furnished the states with more accurate measures of population for the drawing of district lines. Second, the widespread use of more powerful personal computers made it possible to run software programs that drew districts that were perfectly equal in population and enabled more individuals and groups to offer redistricting plans of their own.[3]

The principal redistricting controversy of the 1990s has been over what should be done to ensure just representation of racial and ethnic minorities. In its 1986 *Thornburg v. Gingles* decision, the Supreme Court ruled that plans that have the effect of diluting minority votes are unconstitutional.[4] This new ruling, coupled with technological advances, resulted in the drawing of districts that were oddly shaped to ensure that the district would contain a majority of racial or ethnic minorities; that is, the Court encouraged racial gerrymandering to increase black representation.

These oddly shaped districts have been the subject of legal challenges. In *Miller v. Johnson* (63 USLW 4726) in 1995, the Supreme Court narrowly ruled that districts drawn with race as a "predominant factor"

is a key ingredient in attracting able people to serve. Five states' legislatures now pay more than $40,000; in six other states, salaries exceed $30,000 annually. The fact that a legislator can live on the salary enhances the legislature's attractiveness as a long-term career. There are other perks too: Legislators in all but five states receive a per diem allowance during the legislative session. In over 40 states legislators receive retirement benefits and health insurance benefits similar to other state employees.

Another concern of the reformers related to capability and functionality of the legislature: The adequacy of staff, facilities, and information sources is critical so that legislators can know something about the bills on which they vote. The growth of professional staff is perhaps the biggest change in this area. By 1988 it was estimated that more than 33,000 people worked for state legislatures.[31] Staff members may work for individual legislators, assisting in all phases of the legislator's job from lawmaking to constituency service, or they may work for standing committees or for the party leadership. The availability of professional staff is significant because it reduces the legislature's dependence on the executive branch and lobbyists for information.

were unconstitutional. This ruling makes the future of redistricting to ensure equal effect unclear, in part because race must now presumably be treated equally with factors such as geography and party preferences in drawing district lines.[5] So now the Court discouraged racial gerrymandering.

What have the effects of redistricting been? Redistricting, along with the continual decline in the number of multimember districts, has had an effect on minority membership in state legislatures, particularly in the South. The redrawing of district lines after the 1990 census resulted in substantial increases in the number of "majority-minority" districts (legislative districts where half or more of the population are minorities). This increase in majority-minority districts in turn resulted in a more than 20 percent increase in the number of African-American state legislators and a more than 35 percent increase in the number of Hispanic state legislators.[6]

Despite careful attention to the politics and process of redistricting, inequities in minority representation persist. "Packing" minorities into districts may dilute the overall effect of minorities' gains as neighboring districts gain a majority of the opposing political party. For example, Congressional redistricting in southern states in the 1990s concentrated blacks into districts that elected Democrats, many of them black, and put whites into districts that elected conservative white Republicans. White moderate Democrats were squeezed out in the process. In addition, racial gerrymandering may not have its desired effect, as many minority citizens either cannot or do not vote, or do not vote in expected ways. These realities, coupled with recent Court decisions, ensure that controversy over redistricting plans in the states will continue.

---

[1]*Baker v. Carr*, 369 U.S. 186.

[2]Rich Jones, "The State Legislatures," in *The Book of the States, 1992–93* (Lexington, Ky.: Council of State Governments, 1992), p. 128.

[3]*Ibid.*, p. 126.

[4]*Ibid.*, p. 127; *Thornburg v. Gingles*, 478 U.S. 30.

[5]Linda Greenhouse, "Justices, in 5–4 Vote, Reject Districts Drawn with Race the 'Predominant Factor,'" *The New York Times* (June 30, 1995), A1.

[6]David G. Savage, "Court Goes a-Hunting Gerrymanders," *State Legislatures*, 19 (September 1993), 14.

A number of other changes recommended by the reformers took place in state legislatures: streamlined rules and procedures to make the legislative process more efficient, "sunshine" laws (which require open meetings), lobbyist registration, improved and expanded office facilities, and expanded information systems. Some of these reforms were directed at providing greater public understanding and access; others were aimed at enhancing the capacity of legislative bodies to develop and analyze information. In sum, state legislatures have achieved many of the ideals of the reformers of the 1970s. Progress is apparent even in Alabama, the state ranking last in the old ratings. Neal Peirce and Jerry Hagstrom write about changes in Alabama: "Barefoot boys no longer passed up and down the aisles selling peanuts, members were less frequently seen relieving the monotony with nips of booze, and the general quality of legislators and committee operations did pick up."[32]

Turnover and Professionalization   Finally, it is noteworthy that membership turnover in state legislatures has declined since these reforms were initiated. As shown in Figure 5.2, turnover has gradually declined over the last 30 years despite some peaks in turnover. The peaks are a result of reapportionment, as in 1973, 1983, and 1993. Following the shuffling of district lines, many sitting legislators lost their seats or choose not to run again. The decline in turnover indicates that members perceive state houses as attractive places to be; it is also another sign of incumbent advantage, which is increasingly under attack in the 1990s.

These developments generally relate to the professionalization of the state legislature: the enhancement of its capacity to perform its policymaking role. The adoption of these reforms, and hence the degree of professionalization, varies a lot from state to state. Karl Kurtz, research director of the National Conference of State Legislators, recently classified legislative bodies into three categories of professionalism.[33] As shown in Figure 5.3, the legislatures of California, Illinois, Massachusetts, Michigan, New York, Ohio, Wisconsin, New Jersey, and Pennsylvania have moved furthest in the professional direction. They have lengthy sessions, relatively high salaries, large staffs, and many members whose primary occupation is that of legislator. These states are classified as highly professional. At the other end of the scale are sixteen smaller, rural states whose legislatures meet part-time, have small staffs, and earn low pay. Twenty-five states are classified as hybrid or in transition: They have some but not all aspects of the highly professional legislatures. These differences in legislative professionalization become relevant as the federal government turns over more responsibilities to the states.

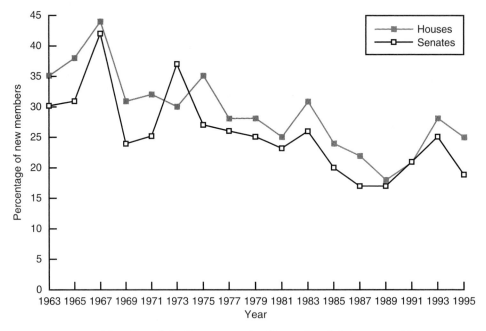

FIGURE 5.2 Membership Turnover in State Legislatures. The turnover of membership in state legislatures has declined over time as legislative bodies have become more professional. The introduction of term limits is designed to reverse this trend.
Source: Samuel Patterson, "Legislative Politics in the States," in Virginia Gray and Herbert Jacob, eds., *Politics in the American States,* 6th ed. Washington, D.C.: CQ Press, 1996, Figure 5.6.

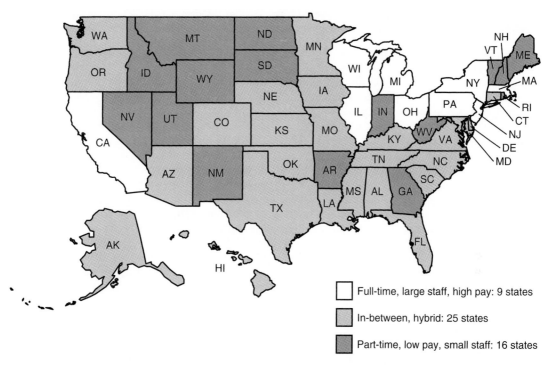

FIGURE 5.3 Professionalization of State Legislatures. State legislatures have become more professional over time, although there still remain wide variations in levels of professionalization. The small states tend to have part-time legislatures, low legislative pay, and small staff size.
Source: State Legislatures, 20, November 1994. © The National Conference of State Legislatures.

The Current Attack on Legislatures What seemed like a good idea 30 years ago no longer seems like a good idea. State legislatures, as measured in public opinion polls, have sunk to a new low of public approval because of the reforms instituted in the 1970s. Professionalism and careerism, in particular, are held in low regard: Stable and capable bodies are seen as entrenched and unresponsive, out of touch with reality. One study found that the more professional the body, the lower the approval rating by the public.[34] Perhaps nowhere is the fall in public esteem as evident as in California, the state rated the nation's best legislature in 1973. In the 1990s the California legislature was taught an object lesson by its citizenry, as outlined in Box 5.3.

A specific manifestation of the public's unhappiness with state legislatures is the adoption of term limits by 20 states. Term limits are obviously aimed at careerists in the hopes of restoring the citizen legislature. Term limits have generally been instituted through citizens' use of the initiative; understandably, legislators are loath to limit their own service (although Utah lawmakers did so).

The first successful initiative campaigns occurred in 1990 in California, Colorado, and Oklahoma. In 1992, 11 more states limited terms: Arizona, Arkansas, Florida, Michigan, Missouri, Montana, Ohio, Oregon, South Dakota, Washington, and Wyoming.

BOX 5.3 THE CALIFORNIA LEGISLATURE

In 1973 the Citizens Conference on State Legislatures judged California's full-time, professional legislature to be the best among the 50 states. In the 1990s, one commentator called this same body the "Not-So-Golden State Legislature"; a lobbyist called it a "dysfunctional family."[1] What happened in the span of two decades to so radically change the perception of this prototype of the "professional" state legislature?

In many ways, the California legislature resembles the United States Congress more than it does the other state legislatures. The California legislature meets nearly year-round and its members earn the highest salary of any state legislature ($52,500 in 1994). The General Assembly has an operating budget of nearly $73 million, and the legislature is supported by a large full-time staff of approximately 3,000 people).[2] These resources are necessary to administer the state's $83 billion annual budget. However, the professionalization of the California legislature has brought with it some unintended consequences.

Some evidence that political scientists might use to demonstrate the professionalization of the legislative career are legislators' occupations, campaign expenditures, and turnover in office. In 1965 the profession listed by the most legislators (46) was lawyer, with only 2 legislators listing their occupation as legislator. By the close of the 1980s, most legislators (25) listed their full-time occupation as legislator, with another 7 listing their legislative title along with their other occupation.[3] In 1990 the mean cost of a state senate race in California exceeded the cost of a seat in the U.S. Congress. Total expenditures on legislative campaigns were over $58 million, whereas total expenditures in 1960 were approximately $7 million.[4] Turnover in office did not decrease uniformly through this period but one particularly noteworthy legislator, 30-year veteran Speaker Willie Brown, became a lightning rod for anti-incumbent sentiment.

In 1990 two propositions concerning the state legislature were placed on the California ballot in an attempt to remedy the problems of professionalization, or, in the view of some analysts, to punish legislators such as Willie Brown (see Chapter 3 for a discussion of initiatives). The first of these, Proposition 140, was narrowly approved. The "pro" side argued that voting "yes" would reform a system "that has given a tiny elite (only 120 people out of 30 million) almost limitless power over the lives of California's taxpayers and consumers." This proposition reduced the legislative budget by 40 percent, (including a 40 percent cut in staff that began in 1991) and subjected members of the state assembly to a lifetime limit of three 2-year terms and state senators and the governor to two 4-year terms.[5]

The full effect of term limits on the California legislature will not be known until after 1996, when the representatives elected in 1990, the year the proposition passed, are prevented from running again. A survey of California legislators suggests that term limits might act as a disincentive to running for the state legislature, as 11 of 34 respondents said that if the limits had been in effect when they ran for office, they would not have run.[6] Another study shows that the number of "new" legislators—that is, the number of members starting their first term—will peak at 61 of 120 in 1996, the first year of term limits, but that the magnitude of this turnover will decrease through time.[7]

But what of the time between the enactment of Proposition 140 and 1996? The events following the 1994 election seem emblematic of the California legislature in the 1990s. After the November elections, the Republicans gained their first majority in the General Assembly in 25 years: 41 Republicans and 39 Democrats were elected.

The new Republican majority should have caused an end to Willie Brown's 14-year tenure as speaker, but a Republican to whom Brown had given a choice committee assignment switched parties before the vote for speaker, deadlocking the legislature in a 40–40 tie. Because parliamentary procedure prohibits the legislature from conducting any business at the start of a new term until the speaker is elected, the legislature was prevented from acting for seven weeks. Finally, due to the illness of the chief clerk, Brown (the senior member of the General Assembly) assumed the gavel, orchestrated the removal of a Republican member, and ensured his own reelection as speaker.[8]

But the fun didn't end there. Later in 1995, California voters punished the defecting Republican by recalling him from office. Brown decided to step aside as speaker in order to run for the major's job in San Francisco. He installed Republican Doris Allen as his successor; 39 Democrats plus Allen voted for this plan over the bitter objections of 38 Republicans. Predictably, Republican members and voters reacted with outrage; Allen was recalled from office by the voters in November 1995. Then, Assembly Democrats cut a deal with freshman Republican Brian Setencich, a former professional basketball player, and elected him speaker. Not until early 1996 did Republicans finally seize control of the Assembly and elect their own speaker.

Many observers ascribe the chaos in the California Assembly to the imposition of term limits in 1996. Republican members willing to ally with the Democrats were about to lose their seats anyway so party loyalty mattered little to them. "The legislature has, in effect, become a bus station where some people have just arrived and others are waiting to leave, and as a result the institution itself does not elicit much loyalty or devotion."[9] Californians someday hope to get their legislature back to the business of full-time lawmaking. Meanwhile, the "unsinkable Willie Brown" is the new mayor of San Francisco, dealing with "dog doo and potholes," as he quaintly puts it.

---

[1]Sherry Jeffe, "California: The Not-So Golden State Legislature," in Eugene W. Hickok, ed., *The Reform of State Legislatures and The Changing Character of Representation* (Lanham, Md.: University Press of America, 1992); Tony Quinn, quoted in B. Drummond Ayres, Jr., "California's Squabbling Legislature Just Stumbles Along," *New York Times* (July 9, 1995), A12.

[2]*The Book of the States, 1994–95* (Lexington, Ky.: Council of State Governments, 1994), p. 125; Daniel Weintraub, "The Unsinkable Willie Brown," *State Legislatures*, 20 (March 1995), 23.

[3]Jeffe, "California: The Not-So-Golden State Legislature," p. 105.

[4]*Ibid.*, p. 105.

[5]Charles M. Price, "The Guillotine Comes to California: Term-Limit Politics in the Golden State," in Gerald Benjamin and Michael J. Malbin, eds., *Limiting Legislative Terms* (Washington, D.C.: CQ Press), p. 121; Jeffe, "California: The Not-So-Golden State Legislature," p. 110.

[6]Price, "The Guillotine Comes to California: Term-Limit Politics in the Golden State," p. 126.

[7]Karl T. Kurtz, "Assessing the Potential Impacts of Term Limits," *State Legislatures*, 18 (January 1992), 32–34.

[8]Weintraub, "The Unsinkable Willie Brown," p. 23; William Schneider, "Old Politics Hangs on in California," *National Journal* (December 17, 1994), 3004.

[9]Peter Schrag, "The Populist Road to Hell," *The American Prospect*, 24 (Winter 1996), 27.

Then in 1993 Maine joined their ranks, followed by Idaho, Massachusetts, Nebraska (its 1992 adoption was invalidated), Nevada, and Utah in 1994. Each state's limit is different, ranging from 6 to 12 years; some limits are for consecutive years and others are a lifetime ban. Unlike the states' attempts to regulate Congressional terms, these limits on state service are clearly constitutional.

None of the laws affected members serving at the time; they are just now coming into effect in the first set of states. Thus, their actual impact is subject to speculation. Political scientists, who generally oppose term limitations, argue that many legislatures already have higher turnover than would be imposed arbitrarily by term limits legislation, so the new laws won't alter average tenure much. This argument seems particularly true for the citizen and hybrid legislatures listed in Figure 5.3, where less than one-third of members serve as long as 12 years.[35] But the highly professional bodies should be more affected because between 40 and 60 percent of their members serve as long as 12 years, and states that adopted 6-year limits would see more change. Political scientists fear that because legislators and their leaders will be newer to the job, more permanent figures will gain power: bureaucrats, the governor, and lobbyists. Overall, they predict a weakening of the legislative branch of government.

Term limitations are not the only reaction to legislative professionalization. There is increased public desire to limit the length of legislative sessions; a few states have reinstituted session limits. A reassessment of the need for professional staff is also under way, with many states streamlining their staff operations. California voters initiated a budget ceiling on legislative operations and a staff cut at the same time they adopted term limits. The most popular response has been to adopt more stringent ethics legislation in response to corruption problems evident in Kentucky, New Mexico, Arizona, Michigan, and South Carolina in the 1990s. States have enacted restrictions against the use of legislative office for economic gain, acceptance of gifts from lobbyists, and solicitation of campaign contributions during the legislative session. Standards of conduct for lawmakers and lobbyists have shifted, and legislators are running to catch up.

Committee Organization

The major work of the legislature is done in committees. Since the 1970s reform movement began, states have reduced the number of committees and the number of assignments per member, thereby increasing the attention each member can give to a single committee. Standing committees engage in two tasks: screening legislation and studying problems. During a legislative session, screening legislation absorbs most of the committee's attention. Committees usually meet for several hours each week, often in the morning before the regular floor sessions begin. Some active committees may have several hundred bills to consider during each session. A member's work on committee assignments consumes about half of the legislative working day; thus, the committee is an important focus of a member's attention.

Between regular legislative sessions, standing committees are working on their second task: studying problems. During these interim periods committees may meet one day a month in the state capitol, hold public hearings, make visits to field sites, and conduct oversight studies. Much of this activity depends on the availability of professional staff because many legislators return to their regular jobs during the interim periods. The states with large staffs, such as New York, are able to tackle more problems than are states with few staff members.

Although state legislative committees do not have the clout of committees of the U.S. Congress, scholars believe that state-level committees have become much more important as decisionmakers in recent years. Wayne Francis has conducted several investigations of the importance of committees and how it varies across states. He finds that the states with one-party dominant legislatures tend to place more importance on committees, whereas in two-party competitive states committees recede in importance.[36] Other research agrees that committees are especially vital where parties are not important.

Membership on committees roughly reflects the party ratio in the legislative body. If the Republicans have 60 percent of the seats and the Democrats 40 percent, then each committee would have approximately 60 percent of its seats occupied by Republicans and 40 percent held by Democrats. Limited research shows that this rough proportion is followed most of the time; departures tend to occur when the majority "stacks" important committees with its members and gives the minority greater representation on the less important committees.[37] Committee assignments are made by legislative party leaders, taking into account the members' own preferences for assignments, experience outside the legislature, and seniority. As in the U.S. Congress, certain committees are prized assignments, such as the appropriations committee. Committee chairs are significant actors in state legislatures, particularly when the committees themselves are important. We can anticipate that after term limitations take effect, the committee system will lessen in importance as members will necessarily not serve long on any committee.

Party Leadership

Besides committee structure, the other important feature of a legislature's organization is its partisan nature. Except in Nebraska, state legislatures are organized along party lines. The leadership of each house of the legislature depends on the political party in the majority. If the Democratic party holds a majority of the seats in the lower house, the speaker of the house will normally be a Democrat, as will be the majority party leader, assistant majority leaders, and majority whips. The minority party in each house elects its own leadership, including the minority party leader, assistant minority leader, minority whip, and other party leaders. Exceptions do occur, such as when Democrat Willie Brown continued as speaker in the Republican-controlled California Assembly (see Box 5.3).

In the upper house the leader is typically called the president. This office is filled by the lieutenant governor in 28 states; in the other states the president is selected by senate members, ordinarily from the majority party. In some states the lieutenant governor's role is similar to that of the vice-president in the U.S. Senate: He or she might occasionally cast the deciding vote but does not normally preside over the deliberations. In other states the lieutenant governor routinely presides over the sessions. Texas is one of the few states in which the lieutenant governor wields real power. In the Lone Star State the lieutenant governor by custom and by virtue of appointive powers is one of the three most important officials in the state, along with the governor and the speaker of the house.

Party leaders (that is, the speaker of the house and the president of the senate) exert considerable influence on what goes on in their domains. They control the committee system through their appointment of committee chairs and members. They control the agenda of the institution by referring bills to committees, scheduling consideration of bills on the floor (a crucial time-management question), and presiding over debates on the floor.

They formulate legislation for their own party, mediate policy disputes within the party, and play a major role in shaping the budget. Finally, they represent their party to the governor and ultimately to the general public.

Typically each party's leadership is selected by the party's caucus and ratified later in a party-line vote on the floor. In some states the governor traditionally has had influence in selecting the top legislative leaders for the party, but this practice is waning. Occasionally the majority party is so factionalized that a bipartisan coalition is needed to elect the leader of the majority party. In the 1980s, more instances of bipartisan (or cross-party) coalitions occurred, usually dissident Democrats and minority Republicans joining forces to oust incumbent speakers or majority leaders, illustrating the difficulty of maintaining the cohesion required for responsible party government. Sometimes the body is evenly divided between Democrats and Republicans; in this case ingenious power-sharing arrangements are hammered out between the two parties. For example, when this happened in the Indiana house in 1989, the two party leaders were named co-speakers, and each one presided on alternate days (the plan was nicknamed "speaker du jour"). In 1995 the Nevada house also had co-speakers who alternated daily in running the chamber.

Outside of the South and nonpartisan Nebraska, the **party caucus** plays a prominent role in legislative matters. In the most partisan states, party caucuses meet daily and take positions on major bills, positions that party members are bound to uphold on the floor. This is true of Connecticut and a few other states. However, in most states party caucuses discuss general policy matters in order to build cohesion and mobilize votes but do not require every member's allegiance on every bill. They may take straw votes on pending issues in order to help leadership assess member opinion. New York, Pennsylvania, Ohio, Indiana, Michigan, Iowa, Arizona, and California are states of this type.[38] In weak-party states the caucuses are more a forum for the dissemination of information than a means of policy deliberation, more of a briefing session. Southern and border states fit into this category.

As mentioned, the committee system's and the party system's influences tend to be inversely related: Committees are strong where parties are weak and vice versa. Surveys of state legislators indicate that party leaders are the most significant decisionmakers overall in state legislatures, closely followed by standing committees, then the party caucuses.[39] Thus, it can be said that the party system through its leaders and caucuses is perceived to have the most significant influence on legislative decisions.

There is general agreement among scholars that the job of legislative leaders has become more difficult, primarily because careerist members are more independent and more difficult to lead. Individual members want to have their say on a variety of matters rather than following the dictates of leaders. Also, the growing complexity of states' problems, especially their fiscal situations, places more pressure on leaders. For these and other reasons, we may see a transition from traditional command leadership to more of a consensus approach. Also, the introduction of term limitations will mean that legislative leaders necessarily will come into office with less experience and will enjoy shorter tenure in office, both of which may weaken their leadership capacity. In some term-limited states the speakership will probably rotate each term, perhaps on the basis of seniority; some less professionalized legislatures already follow this practice.[40] More professionalized legislatures may follow an apprenticeship model in which leaders are groomed and chosen well in advance. This model would preserve strong leadership.

✧ THE LEGISLATIVE PROCESS

Legislators as individuals spend their time voting on legislation, answering constituents' requests for assistance, and overseeing the bureaucracy. As already mentioned, most legislators regard legislating as their main business. Legislating consists of making policy through passing laws and appropriating funds to carry out those laws. The making of policy and the appropriation of funds are two of the important collective functions of the legislature. The oversight function is another important function carried out collectively by the legislature and individually by legislators. Helping constituents, in contrast, is an individual activity that does not require collective action by the legislative body. In this section we describe the collective actions of the legislature: making policy, appropriating funds, and overseeing the administration.

Making Policy

State legislators are presented with a mind-boggling number of bills each year, approximately 200,000 in total. The state assembly is indeed something like an assembly line in a factory where many products are manufactured in a short period of time. The overwhelming number of proposals are minor housekeeping bills to which no one voices objection. Other bills are of importance to some groups and attract their attention. Still others are important to the entire state and generate widespread interest. Nearly one-quarter of the bills introduced each session become law, a bill passage rate much higher than that of the U.S. Congress.[41] The legislative process is less of an obstacle course at the state level.

Certain states see many bills introduced each year: New York saw 32,263 and Massachusetts saw 15,020 during 1992–1993.[42] Legislators in these states, even if working full-time, can devote only a small amount of time to studying each bill. Other state legislatures—such as those in Alaska, Colorado, North Dakota, Vermont, and Wyoming—consider less than a thousand bills each session. Chambers in 11 states have deliberately limited the number of bills each lawmaker can introduce; for example, Colorado has a limit of five bills per member. What else causes some legislatures to produce many bills and others few bills? Alan Rosenthal and Rod Forth found that population, urbanization, and industrialization were important factors in explaining enactments and introductions.[43] Populous, urbanized, and industrialized states have more needs to be met by legislation. Political culture might be another reason. Legislators in moralistic climates (discussed in Chapter 1) should be more activist than those in individualistic or traditionalistic climates.

State legislatures have made a number of improvements in order to cope with their burgeoning workloads: They have imposed prefiling of bills before the session begins, established consent calendars for noncontroversial bills, and mandated deadlines and cutoff dates for the handling of bills. These time-management techniques provide a more even flow of work during the session and prevent a logjam at the end. The most severe technique, as mentioned above, is limiting the number of bills each legislator can introduce.

State legislatures have also invested in computer technology to aid in drafting bills, provide up-to-date information on the status of bills, and automate roll-call voting.

Several states provide computer terminals to legislators on the floor. For example, in North Dakota legislators can review bills, send and receive e-mail messages, and draft correspondence from their desks in the chamber. Information technology allows individual legislators more effective participation in policymaking and tends to disperse power within the legislature. These innovations have allowed state legislators to increase their collective influence in the policymaking process. As they develop institutional capacity they become more assertive. Legislatures can take on a leadership role in policymaking rather than just react to what the governor proposes.

All bills travel through a complicated procedure that is similar across the states. As outlined in Figure 5.4, the process begins with someone drafting a bill. The author may be a lobbyist, a legislator, a staff member, or the governor. However, only a legislator can introduce the bill. The bill is assigned a number and is read aloud by the clerk of the house (or senate) and is then referred by the speaker to the appropriate committee. The committee or its subcommittee may hold a public hearing or series of hearings on the proposal, may amend the bill, and eventually votes to recommend or kill it. In a hostile committee the bill may never be considered, and it dies there. Bills may be considered by more than one committee; for example, the appropriations section of a bill would be considered by an appropriations committee as well as a substantive committee.

Clearly the committee stage is a critical one for a bill. A proposal may be voted down in committee, it may be "gutted" (amended to the point of meaninglessness), or it may never be considered due to lack of time. Without favorable committee action, the bill has no chance for approval.

Once reported out of committee, the bill goes to the floor of the house (or senate), at which time the title of the bill is read a second time. At this point debate generally commences, and further amendments are taken on the floor. Debate is usually strictly limited due to the time constraints on legislative sessions. Then a third reading of the bill is given, after which a final vote is taken. In 49 states (all but Nebraska) the bill is considered in the other house in a similar manner. If the versions of the bill are different, and they usually are on important matters, then a conference committee is appointed by the leadership of both houses.

Once the differences have been ironed out, then the identical bill is voted on in each house; if approved, it goes to the governor for his or her signature. The governor either signs the bill, in which case it becomes law, or vetoes the bill. If the governor vetoes the bill, then the legislature may override the veto by an extraordinary majority (usually two-thirds). The gubernatorial veto is exercised infrequently (about 5 percent of the time), and legislative overrides are quite rare (only about 6 percent of vetoes are overridden).[44]

Legislators arrive at their votes on policy issues by consulting their own consciences and by taking cues from a variety of sources including party leaders, committee members and other legislative experts, staff, lobbyists, the governor and bureaucratic experts, and constituents. As already explained, different legislators weight differently their own views versus the views of others: Trustees vote their own conscience whereas delegates vote their constituents' preferences. But nearly every lawmaker sometimes responds to the wishes of others; these influences on voting have been the subject of considerable research.

The influence of party on legislative voting varies from state to state and issue to issue. As described in Chapter 4, partisan cohesion is substantial in a few states such as

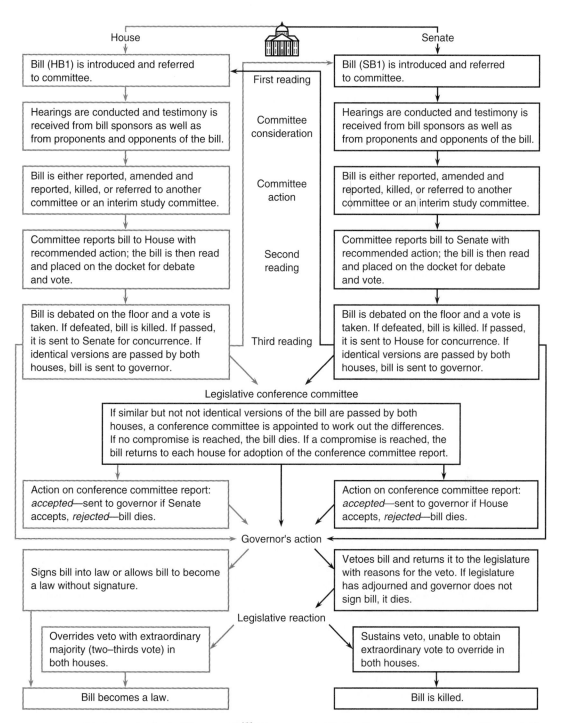

FIGURE 5.4 How a Bill Becomes State Law. The process of how a bill becomes a law is fairly similar from one state to the next. This figure shows the typical path a bill would follow to be enacted as a law.

Source: Thad L. Beyle, ed., *State Government: CQ's Guide to Current Issues and Activities, 1987–1988,* p. 247. Copyright © 1987. Reprinted by permission of *Congressional Quarterly.*

New York and Connecticut, nonexistent in southern states, and falls somewhere in between in the rest. Party line voting is most often found on electoral legislation, labor legislation, welfare, and the budget. Other issues are less likely to evoke strict party line voting. The ability of legislative leaders to forge partisan cohesiveness in their ranks is also a factor.

Lawmakers also defer to the judgment of committees, whose members are necessarily more informed about the substantive issues before their committee. If members feel that a committee has done its homework, the members are likely to vote to uphold the committee's position on the floor. Sometimes there are experts in the chamber who are not on the relevant committee, and their counsel might be sought by the average member. Thus, a doctor might be consulted about pending health care legislation or a university professor about higher education issues.

Legislative staff is also relied on a great deal in deciding how to vote. Staff are able to provide information on the extent of the problem, how other states have solved this problem, and the implications of the proposed solution for the member's constituents. They assist members in authoring legislation and in deciding how to vote on individual bills. The staff is likely to have more influence in states such as California that have many staff members per legislator than in states with smaller staffs.

Lobbyists representing interest groups can play many of the same roles as staff, but of course lobbyists present only their side of the issue. Lobbyists tend to carry more weight where the other external influences are weak. Where legislative cohesion is low (in southern states and Nebraska, for example) lobbyists have more clout. Where staff is lacking or not very competent, lobbyists will prevail.

The governor almost always plays an important role in the lawmaking process. If the legislator is a member of the governor's political party, then he or she more often will follow the governor's lead on an issue. But as already noted, party cohesion is not high in many states, and the member may be from a different faction than the governor. If the member belongs to the opposite political party from the governor, then the governor may become a negative cue-giver; that is, the member may often vote against the governor's position. Legislators also take advice from members of the governor's staff or from the bureaucracy; bureaucrats may be perceived as independent sources of information.

Finally, every legislator must pay some attention to constituents' desires in his or her voting. If the issue is highly salient, and the constituents are of one mind, then the lawmaker is very likely to vote accordingly. However, most of the time, constituents are divided in their preferences or the issue does not capture much public attention. Then the legislator is free to vote according to other cues.

Appropriating Funds

Most state constitutions specify that "no money shall be drawn from the State treasury but for appropriations made by law." This clause gives the power of the purse to the legislature. Appropriations bills are among the most important bills a state legislature considers each year. Yet in practice it is the governor and the executive branch that wield the most influence in the budgetary process. As will be explained in Chapter 6, the state budget is formulated by the executive branch. This gives the governor great power to set the budget.

The role of the legislature's appropriations committee and its subcommittees is to review and adjust the budget. Such committees are among the most important and powerful in the legislature because they deal in cold, hard cash. Committee members can exercise some discretion in allocating monies to favorite projects or districts. Many such projects are found in special appropriations bills, generically called pork barrel bills. "Pork" may be contained in separate bills on which votes are traded or it may be folded into one omnibus state special. In North Carolina, for example, approximately $10 million was available in the 1985 omnibus special, half of which was allocated by the chair of the House Appropriations Committee while the other half was doled out by the senate chair.[45] A favorite request of members was for county courthouse restoration. This bill is passed on the last day of the North Carolina session and rewards members' loyalty to the leadership.

In the regular (nonspecial) part of the budget, the legislature begins its task with a review by its fiscal staff of agency requests and gubernatorial recommendations. Next come budget hearings, during which agency heads defend their requests (explained in more detail in Chapter 12). Due to limited staff and limited committee time, the typical state legislature does not make huge changes in the governor's budget recommendations. Budget recommendations are revised but not totally rewritten. One exception occurs when one party controls the legislature and the opposition party controls the governor's office. In this instance the governor's recommendation may be pronounced dead as soon as it gets to the legislature.

Once the two houses have agreed on a budget, then the appropriations bill (or bills) goes to the governor for his or her signature. At this juncture, nearly all governors have the power of the **item veto,** a power even the president of the United States does not possess. The item veto, as explained further in Chapter 6, gives the governor the power to eliminate appropriations for specific programs or line items. Although the legislature could still override any veto, it usually does not, thus conceding even more budgetary power to the governor.

In addition to considering the entire budget, in more than half the states all policy bills with substantial fiscal impact are referred to the appropriations committee as well as to a substantive committee. Thus, the appropriations committee members have power over policymaking as well as spending. Recently, some legislatures have fused the two types of committees so that everyone has some responsibility for expenditures; Minnesota, for example, has adopted this system.

Exercising Oversight

The third function of legislatures is exercising oversight. Although historically of little significance, oversight has become increasingly important. Attention to oversight was another product of the legislative reform movement of the 1970s. With enhanced institutional capacity, legislators are able to turn their attention to overseeing administrators. Oversight includes both the informal activities of individual legislators and the formal actions instituted by the legislature collectively.

Much oversight is of the informal ad hoc variety resulting from casework done for constituents; that is, a constituent's phone call initiates a legislator's inquiry to a bureaucrat. A pattern of complaints about an agency might lead the legislator to investigate the agency's competence more fully. Or a negative newspaper article may inspire a legislator to check on an agency and ultimately to propose legislation to correct the problem. A few legislators who are willing to create a stink can have a big impact on state administration.

In addition to informal oversight, state legislatures have set up four types of formal oversight mechanisms: policy and program evaluations, legislative review of administrative rules and regulations, **sunset legislation,** and review and control of federal funds received by the state. Some of these mechanisms are explained more fully in Chapter 7, but a brief look at the legislature's role is warranted here.

The policy and program evaluation function was the first to be established in the early 1970s. Originally limited to an audit of expenditures, this function has been extended in most states to include evaluating the impact of government programs. Professionals employed by the legislative auditor conduct assessments of how well programs are achieving their objectives and then recommend changes to the legislature. Whereas the older type of studies could only point to corruption in government, the newer type can provide an objective basis for reallocation of resources from one program to another. Curiously, many of the recommendations of such studies entail increasing expenditures rather than reducing them.

The second kind of formal oversight, legislative review of rules and regulations, is newer. This involves a legislative committee's analysis of rules proposed by state agencies to see whether the rules follow legislative intent. Forty states have such committees; in half of them the legislature has the power to prevent or modify the rule.[46] In many states the legislature had a veto over the rule, but the legal status of the legislative veto is questionable because the U.S. Supreme Court ruled it unconstitutional at the federal level (*Immigration and Naturalization Service v. Chadha,* 462 U.S. 919, 1983). Its use began to decline, with few states now employing it. However, legislatures can always get back at agencies whose rules they question through the budgetary process or other means.

The third type of formal oversight is sunset legislation, which requires that state agencies be reviewed on a periodic schedule; agencies are terminated unless they pass the review. This innovation began in Colorado in 1976 and has since been adopted by 35 other states. The intent was to force government to review state agencies and to cut out redundant or inefficient ones. The experience thus far is not as successful as the reformers had hoped; in fact, a dozen states have "sunsetted" their sunset legislation.[47] Thorough reviews of all state agencies are so time-consuming and expensive that few are carried out. Without full-scale evaluations legislators are reluctant to axe entire agencies. Therefore, most agencies continue.

Finally, state legislatures also review the expenditure of funds provided by the federal government. Nearly one-fifth of state and local government expenditures is derived from the federal government. The lure of "free" federal funds is quite strong for bureaucrats and their constituency groups. Most federal programs require a state matching share, typically 10 percent, which legislatures are usually willing to put up. However, later on the Federal government may require a higher state contribution or may phase out the program entirely, leaving the state legislature little choice but to pick up the popular program. In recent decades, state legislatures have asserted their right to accept or reject these funds or at least to exercise some control over their use. Occasionally states even turn down federal funds.

In summary, oversight is a combination of individual legislators' motivation to engage in informal oversight and the collective capacity for formal control. As we saw earlier in this chapter, few legislators spend much of their own time on oversight. Much more effort comes from the various commissions and committees formally charged with oversight functions. Still, all these efforts amount to nothing if legislators do not use the results of policy evaluations in making policy and setting expenditures. Examining old programs is tedious and boring work for most legislators in comparison with allocating pork barrel funds or authoring legislation to solve new problems. It remains to be seen how much impact oversight units will have.

The Legislature at Work

The legislators of the 1990s will spend a great deal of time on the hot issues such as health care, crime, education, immigration, and the budget. Although governors may take the lead as spokespersons on such issues (as we will describe in Chapter 6), the legislators are still the people who pass the programs, fund them, and oversee their administration. Legislators' abilities to understand the problems of the 1990s and their institutions' capacity to deal with them structure how the states will respond. A few examples will illustrate legislatures in action.

Although many people think health care reform is too big a challenge for states to handle, three states—Minnesota, Washington, and Florida—in the 1990s passed comprehensive bills incorporating elements of managed competition. Oregon and Vermont based their reform legislation on different principles; Oregon rationed Medicaid benefits and Vermont contemplated a single-payer system. Although governors sometimes played important roles, in at least two states, the key policy champions were in the legislature.

In Minnesota, it was the "Gang of Seven," a bipartisan group of seven experienced legislators in positions of formal authority, who set aside partisan differences and dedicated themselves to the cause of health care reform.[48] They agreed that once the group had reached consensus on a bill, they would stand united in defending it; this cohesion was very effective in combating the barrage of criticism from health industry lobbyists. "Blitzkrieg" tactics also worked; at one critical point they moved the bill through six policy committees in five working days in order to meet chamber deadlines. By the time the opposition woke up, it was too late. The bill passed both houses, and the governor threw in his support at the end.

In Oregon, the senate president, an emergency room physician, was the dominant force in formulating the new health care policy, while the governor pursued other priorities.[49] Based on his prior legislative service, John Kitzhaber was able to lead a coalition of key legislators from both houses. His personal experience and background as a practicing physician gave him credibility with health industry groups. It is fair to say in both cases that the legislature was the driving force behind health care reform.

✧ CONCLUSION

In this chapter we have portrayed the legislature as a significant institution of state government and a much improved one. We first described the types of people attracted to legislative service and how they go about their jobs. The legislature's role as a school for young politicians should be stressed. William Muir wrote an entire book about the California legislature as a school.[50] He stated that bill sponsorship, policy specialization, and the committee system provided the curriculum, and interest groups were the tutors. The country's best legislature was able to provide a first-rate education for its politicians. The quality of the nation's politicians depends on the training they receive in the 50 state legislatures.

We also discussed the many institutional improvements in state legislatures over the past two decades, changes that have made legislatures more capable of performing their tasks. State houses are now more attractive places for members to be. These enhancements also make the legislature a more equal partner in policymaking. Legislatures no longer need to passively accept gubernatorial direction; they can now take more policy initiative. Of course, this sometimes leads to heightened tension between the two branches. The success of the 1970s reform movement has now led to a backlash against professionalization and careerism, with the public viewing legislatures with disfavor. Several reactions—shortened sessions, term limits on legislative service, and staff reductions—attempt to restore the citizen legislature but it is too soon to predict their outcome.

Finally, we described the major functions of legislatures: passing laws, appropriating money, and overseeing the administration. We should stress again that legislatures are making these policy decisions in a competitive environment in which their state's policies are continually compared to those of others. National rankings facilitate such comparisons. If a state is at the bottom of educational rankings, then there is pressure on the legislature to rectify this situation. If it is at the top of the tax scale, there is enormous pressure to lower taxes. The possibility that people will exit means that each state legislature must attempt to maintain its status among other states.

✦ KEY TERMS

Baker v. Carr (p. 128)
casework (p. 126)
delegates (p. 125)
gerrymandering (p. 129)
item veto (p. 143)
multimember district (p. 118)
oversight (p. 125)

party caucus (p. 138)
politicos (p. 125)
professionalization (p. 122)
Reynolds v. Sims (p. 128)
sunset legislation (p. 144)
trustees (p. 125)

✦ FOR FURTHER READING

Wayne L. Francis, *The Legislative Committee Game* (Columbus: Ohio State University Press, 1989). The definitive study of the committee system in state legislatures. Based on a survey of over 2,000 legislators in the 50 states.

Malcolm E. Jewell and Marcia Lynn Whicker, *Legislative Leadership in the American States* (Ann Arbor: University of Michigan Press, 1994). Based on personal interviews with legislative leaders in 22 states, the authors identify various leadership styles and their occurrence in different states.

Tom Loftus, *The Art of Legislative Politics* (Washington, D.C.: CQ Press, 1994). The former speaker of the Wisconsin Assembly gives an insider's account of legislative life.

Gary F. Moncrief and Joel A. Thompson, eds., *Changing Patterns in State Legislative Careers* (Ann Arbor: University of Michigan Press, 1992). A series of articles by some of the leading scholars of state legislatures. Emphasis on professionalization of legislatures.

John C. Wahlke, Heinz Eulau, William Buchanan, and Leroy C. Ferguson, *The Legislative System* (New York: Wiley, 1962). The classic study of legislative roles and attitudes toward the job of legislator. Based on interviews in four states.

✦ NOTES

1. Rob Gurwitt, "Searching for the Cheap Seats," *Governing*, 5 (August 1992), p. 50.

2. Richard G. Niemi, Simon Jackman, and Laura R. Winsky, "Candidacies and Competitiveness in Multimember Districts," *Legislative Studies Quarterly*, 16 (February 1991), 92. No study has

been done since the 1990 reapportionment to determine the current number of multimember districts.

3. Interestingly, the research consistently shows that blacks are less likely to be elected from multimember districts as compared to single-member districts; the opposite is true for women who are advantaged by multimember districts. See Gary Moncrief and Joel A. Thompson, "Electoral Structure and State Legislative Representation: A Research Note," *Journal of Politics,* 54 (February 1992); 246–256; Charles S. Bullock III and Ronald Keith Gaddie, "Changing from Multimember to Single-Member Districts: Partisan, Racial, and Gender Consequences," *State and Local Government Review,* 25 (Fall 1993), 155–163.

4. Keith E. Hamm and R. Bruce Anderson, "State Legislative Elections, 1968–1991: Patterns of Contestation and Competitiveness," paper presented at the annual meeting of the Southern Political Science Association, Atlanta, Georgia, November 1992.

5. Harvey J. Tucker and Ronald E. Weber, "Electoral Change in U.S. States: System Versus Constituency Competition," in Gary F. Moncrief and Joel A. Thompson, eds., *Changing Patterns in State Legislative Careers* (Ann Arbor: University of Michigan Press, 1992), pp. 91–92. These averages are based on data from 18 legislatures over the period 1978–1986.

6. National Conference of State Legislatures, February 6, 1995; Center for the American Woman and Politics, 1995.

7. The small number of female officeholders is not, however, related to differential success at the polls. A recent study by the National Women's Political Caucus shows that the reelection rates for incumbent males and females is virtually identical, and the success rate of women seeking open seats or running as challengers is as good as or better than that of men. The difference is that most incumbents are men, and most incumbents are reelected. Reported in *State Legislatures,* 20 (December 1994), p. 5.

8. National Conference of State Legislatures, February 6, 1995.

9. National Conference of State Legislatures, Joint Center for Political and Economic Studies, February 23, 1995.

10. Dianna Gordon, "Citizen Legislators—Alive and Well," *State Legislatures,* 20 (January 1994), 25.

11. Wayne L. Francis and John R. Baker, "Why Do U.S. State Legislators Vacate Their Seats?," *Legislative Studies Quarterly,* 11 (February 1986), 119–126.

12. Michael B. Berkman, "Former State Legislators in the U.S. House of Representatives: Institutional and Policy Mastery," *Legislative Studies Quarterly,* 18, (February 1993), 77.

13. Thad Beyle, "Governors," in Virginia Gray and Herbert Jacob, eds., *Politics in the American States,* 6th ed. (Washington, D.C.: CQ Press, 1996), Table 6.1.

14. Sue Thomas, *How Women Legislate* (New York: Oxford University Press, 1994).

15. Malcolm E. Jewell and Marcia Lynn Whicker, *Legislative Leadership in the American States* (Ann Arbor: University of Michigan Press, 1994), p. 169.

16. *Ibid.,* p. 178.

17. *Ibid.,* p. 183.

18. Richard C. Elling, "The Utility of State Legislative Casework as a Means of Oversight," *Legislative Studies Quarterly,* 4 (August 1979), 353–379.

19. John C. Wahlke, Heinz Eulau, William Buchanan, and Leroy C. Ferguson, *The Legislative System* (New York: Wiley, 1962).

20. Eric M. Uslaner and Ronald E. Weber, *Patterns of Decision Making in State Legislatures* (New York: Praeger, 1977).

21. Samuel Patterson, "Legislative Politics in the States," in Virginia Gray and Herbert Jacob, eds., *Politics in the American States*, 6th ed. (Washington, D.C.: CQ Press, 1996), Figure 5.8.

22. Steven R. Mavioglio, "The N.H. Legislature: Unwieldy But in Touch with the People," *Governing* (February 1990), 70.

23. Elling, "The Utility of State Legislative Casework," p. 357; Patricia K. Freeman and Lilliard E. Richardson, Jr., "Casework in State Legislatures," *State and Local Government Review*, 26 (Winter 1994), 21–26.

24. Malcolm Jewell, *Representation in State Legislatures* (Lexington: University Press of Kentucky, 1982).

25. *Ibid.*; Lilliard E. Richardson, Jr., and Patricia K. Freeman, "Gender Differences in Constituency Service Among State Legislators," *Political Research Quarterly*, 48 (March 1995), 169–179.

26. Jewell, *Representation in State Legislatures*, p. 150.

27. Malcolm E. Jewell and David M. Olson, *Political Parties and Elections in American States*, 3rd ed. (Chicago: Dorsey, 1988), pp. 226–227.

28. Wilder Crane, Jr., and Meredith W. Watts, Jr., *State Legislative Systems* (Englewood Cliffs, N.J.: Prentice Hall, 1968), p. 25.

29. *Ibid.*, p. 27.

30. Citizens Conference on State Legislatures, *The Sometimes Governments* (Kansas City, Mo.: Citizens Conference on State Legislatures, 1973).

31. Rich Jones, "State Legislatures," in *The Book of the States, 1994–95, Vol. 30* (Lexington, Ky.: Council of State Governments, 1994), p. 102.

32. Neal R. Peirce and Jerry Hagstrom, *The Book of America* (New York: Warner, 1984), p. 447.

33. "Statestats: A Second Look at the Cost of Legislatures," *State Legislatures*, 20 (November 1994), 5.

34. Peverill Squire, "Professionalization and Public Opinion of State Legislatures," *Journal of Politics*, 55 (May 1993), 479–491.

35. These figures apply to those entering office in 1979–1980; see Appendix in Moncrief and Thompson, eds., *Changing Patterns in State Legislative Careers*, p. 208.

36. Wayne L. Francis and James W. Riddlesperger, "U.S. State Legislative Committees: Structure, Procedural Efficiency, and Party Control," *Legislative Studies Quarterly*, 7 (November 1982), 453–471.

37. Keith E. Hamm and Ronald D. Hedlund, "Stacking State Legislative Committees: Does the Majority Party Always Rule?," paper presented at the annual meeting of the Western Political Science Association, San Francisco, March 1992.

38. Jewell and Whicker, *Legislative Leadership in the American States*.

39. Francis and Riddlesperger, "U.S. State Legislative Committees," p. 455.

40. Timothy Hodson, Rich Jones, Karl Kurtz, and Gary Moncrief, "Leaders and Limits: Changing Patterns of State Legislative Leadership Under Term Limits," *Spectrum* (Summer 1995), 6–15.

41. Jones, "State Legislatures," p. 102.

42. *The Book of the States, 1994–95, Vol. 30* (Lexington, Ky.: Council of State Governments, 1994), pp. 148–149.

43. Alan Rosenthal and Rod Forth, "The Assembly Line: Law Production in the American States," *Legislative Studies Quarterly*, 3 (May 1978), 265–291.

44. Charles W. Wiggins, "Executive Vetoes and Legislative Overrides in the American States," *Journal of Politics*, 42 (November 1980), 1110–1117.

45. Joel A. Thompson, "Bringing Home the Bacon: The Politics of Pork Barrel in the North Carolina Legislature," *Legislative Studies Quarterly*, 11 (February 1986), 93.

46. Ann O. Bowman and Richard C. Kearney, *The Resurgence of the States* (Englewood Cliffs, N.J.: Prentice Hall, 1986), p. 90.

47. Richard C. Kearney, "Sunset: A Survey and Analysis of the State Experience," *Public Administration Review*, 50 (January/February 1990), 49–57.

48. Details are taken from Howard M. Leichter, "Minnesota: The Trip from Acrimony to Accommodation," in Daniel M. Fox and John K. Iglehart, eds., *Five States That Could Not Wait: Lessons for Health Reform from Florida, Hawaii, Minnesota, Oregon, and Vermont* (Cambridge, Mass.: Milbank Memorial Fund, 1994), pp. 95–134.

49. Details taken from Daniel M. Fox and Howard M. Leichter, "Rationing in Oregon: The New Accountability," in Daniel M. Fox and John K. Iglehart, eds., *Five States That Could Not Wait: Lessons for Health Reform from Florida, Hawaii, Minnesota, Oregon, and Vermont* (Cambridge, Mass.: Milbank Memorial Fund, 1994), pp. 135–174.

50. William K. Muir, Jr., *Legislature: California's School for Politics* (Chicago: University of Chicago Press, 1982).

CHAPTER 6

THE GOVERNOR

The governor, more than any other figure, is the focus of the competition among states for families and firms. The governor has become the growth manager and economic entrepreneur for the state. Governors now spend a lot of their time on the road trying to attract business and industry to their states. In addition, governors retain their roles as policy leaders, budget formulators, and chief administrators. Governors also are concerned with relating to the legislature and interest groups, representing their state to the federal government, and representing their political party to the public.

But the governorship was not always an attractive job; historically the powers of the office were weak. Colonial governors were agents of the King of England and became a focal point of the rebellion against the Crown. Because of the colonists' bad experiences with governors, the original state constitutions carefully divided powers among the three branches of government, giving full lawmaking powers to the legislature and weak executive powers to the governor. Governors were basically figureheads, often selected by the legislature and limited to one term of service (usually a year). Most did not have the veto power or the ability to dissolve legislative sessions. Nor did governors have much in the way of judicial powers. The legislature clearly had the upper hand in the eighteenth century.

During the nineteenth century governors gradually acquired more power: Veto power was added, and the terms of office were lengthened. The governorship became an elective office rather than an appointive one. But alongside these augmentations in power, other reforms reduced gubernatorial power. The Jacksonian period introduced the concept of the plural executive, in which other state officials were elected separately from the governor. Because these officials might be from different political parties, independent election fragments executive power.

In the early twentieth century, the Progressive party demanded strong governors who could reform state government and end corruption. Governors such as Teddy Roosevelt of New York and Robert LaFollette of Wisconsin provided great examples of gubernatorial leadership. Still, most governors did not possess the constitutional powers needed to be strong executives. The Great Depression further revealed the structural weaknesses of government as states were unable to cope with the social problems engendered by economic collapse. People turned to Washington because the states and cities were unable to act quickly.

In the 1940s and 1950s criticism of governors was especially severe, as they were considered second-rate politicians.[1] Calls for governmental reform intensified in the 1960s, especially from commissions and foundations analyzing the organization of the executive branch. Particularly influential was *Storm Over the States* published in 1967 by Terry Sanford, former governor of North Carolina.[2] Collectively, these reform movements have wrought great changes in the office of governor since mid-century. Today the office of governor is a far cry from that in the 1780s.

In this chapter we examine first the people who become governors, their career patterns, and their campaigns. Next we review the history of the governorship and how the governors' powers have gradually expanded. We also chronicle how the rest of the executive branch has evolved. Then we describe governors' different roles on the job and how they spend their time. Finally, we look at how governors exit from the office..

✧ THE PEOPLE

Like legislatures, the governors of the 50 states have improved enormously. Indeed, one recent book about governors has the apt title *Goodbye to Good-time Charlie*. Author Larry Sabato sums up the changes:[3]

> *Once the darlings of the society pages, governors today are more concerned about the substantive work of the office than about its ceremonial aspects. Once parochial officers whose concerns rarely extended beyond the boundaries of their home states and whose responsibilities frequently were slight, governors have gained major new powers that have increased their influence in national as well as state councils. Once maligned foes of the national and local governments, governors have become skilled negotiators and, importantly, often crucial coordinators at both of those levels. Once ill prepared to govern and less prepared to lead, governors have welcomed into their ranks a new breed of vigorous, incisive, and thoroughly trained leaders.*

Examples of the "new breed" can be seen in the two accompanying profiles. Box 6.1 describes Governor Lawton Chiles, a Democrat from Florida. William Weld, a Republican of Massachusetts is profiled in Box 6.2 as a representative of the "new breed." Although of different political parties, both share some of the same views about the role of government.

Social Background

Those elected to the office of governor are an elite group in terms of socioeconomic criteria. They are above average in income and education, and about half are lawyers.[4] They are a homogeneous group with respect to race and gender: Nearly all are white males. Only one African-American has been elected to the governorship: Douglas Wilder of Virginia in 1989. At least four Hispanics were elected during the 1970s and 1980s: Bob Martinez (Florida), Jerry Apodaca and Toney Anaya (New Mexico), and Raul Castro (Arizona).

It was not until 1974 that the first woman was elected to the governorship in her own right: Ella Grasso of Connecticut. Until that time women had been chosen only to serve as surrogates for their husbands. In the first half of the 1990s, the following women served:

BOX 6.1 REINVENTING GOVERNMENT, NEW DEMOCRAT STYLE: FLORIDA GOVERNOR LAWTON CHILES

So named for his walk across Florida during his first run for the U.S. Senate in 1971, "Walkin' Lawton," has been governor of Florida since 1990. Chiles retired from a powerful position as chair of the Senate's budget committee in 1989 due to frustration and burnout, and ran against the incumbent governor, Republican Bob Martinez. Despite a campaign during which it was revealed that Chiles was taking the antidepressant drug Prozac, Chiles won the election by 14 percentage points. In 1994 Chiles was challenged by Jeb Bush, son of former president George Bush, for the governor's seat. After a hotly contested race, Chiles narrowly defeated Bush, despite low approval ratings that had plagued Chiles throughout his first term as governor.

Chiles inherited a $1 billion budget shortfall as well as the continuing problems with immigration, an older population, and a prohibition against a state income tax that are hallmarks of Florida politics.[1] Although Chiles's terms as governor have been marked by policy innovation, it has not always been the kind of innovation one might expect from a Democratic governor. Principal among Chiles's policy thrusts as governor has been his "rightsizing" initiative (also described in Chapter 7). Rightsizing involves a belief that the federal government cannot know state government needs well enough to solve state problems, and that government in general is too big.

Rightsizing is in keeping with the times, and has been called "reinventing government" by other commentators. Chiles's activities in Florida were purportedly inspired by David Osborne's *Laboratories of Democracy*, a book about state government policy innovation.[2] During his first term Chiles proposed a reorganization plan that would have abolished certain state agencies, radically redesigned others, and subjected all state agencies to a performance audit based on measurable performance standards. In addition, Chiles sought reforms in the legislative branch and governor's office, including a 72-hour "cooling off" period after the enactment of a state budget, a 5 percent special reserve fund, and a line item veto for the governor. In the end, Chiles was able to achieve legislative approval to reduce agency salaries and benefits by 5 percent, cut $700 million from agency requests to the general revenue fund, and initiate a sunset law for the state civil service system.

Rather than reinventing government in his second term, Chiles seems to want to reinvent the laws that control how government must act.[3] Chiles developed an interest in this kind of reform after witnessing citizens' hostility toward government during the 1994 campaign and after experiencing the frustrations of regulation firsthand. After estimating the cost of adding a cook shack to his hunting cabin in the northern Florida woods at $60,000 due to hurricane tie downs

---

Madeleine Kunin (Vermont), Kay Orr (Nebraska), Joan Finney (Kansas), Barbara Roberts (Oregon), Ann Richards (Texas), Rose Mofford (Arizona; she replaced an impeached governor), and Christine Todd Whitman (New Jersey). In 1996 Whitman was the lone female serving. Progress has been slow for women and minorities in attaining state government's top position.

Because there have been so few, little analysis has been done of the possible impact of women and minorities on the office, but Madeleine Kunin's reflection on being the first woman governor in Vermont is noteworthy:[5]

and new plumbing required by the building department, Chiles concluded that "the Lord gave me this problem so I could understand why people are so damn mad at government."[4] Chiles's concern over the proliferation of rules and regulations prompted him to send copies of Philip Howard's book *The Death of Common Sense* to each member of the state legislature and the cabinet, as well as President Clinton, at his own expense. Since the start of the first legislative session of Chiles's second term, a Senate Committee on Government Reform and Oversight has been established, and a bill streamlining the state's Administrative Procedures Act has been passed. In the state House, members were granted a bonus bill—that is, a bill beyond their allotted six—if they wished to remove certain government functions.[5] The current legislative session seems to bode well for Chiles as he seeks to continue his new brand of rightsizing.

Chiles has also been an innovator in a policy area important to both his state and the nation. In 1993 Florida passed a managed competition health care plan that closely resembles the plan ultimately proposed by the Clinton administration. This plan created 11 voluntary Community Health Purchasing Alliances (with a separate pool for Medicaid recipients), which are available to small businesses and individual purchasers.[6] Although Florida, under Chiles's guidance, enacted health care reform before the federal government, recently an effort to move Medicaid money to a managed competition plan that would cover 40 percent of the currently uninsured stalled in the state senate. This seems in keeping with Chiles's belief that "without a federal plan we can't get . . . to universal coverage."[7]

Lawton Chiles' role as a leader in the movement to reinvent government at the state level has ensured his continued national visibility as he deals with the troubles of the Sunshine State.

---

[1]Michael Barone and Grant Ujifusa, *The Almanac of American Politics 1994* (Washington, D.C.: National Journal, Inc., 1994), p. 273.

[2]Robert Crew, "Florida: Lawton M. Chiles, Jr., Reinventing State Government," in Thad Beyle, *Governors and Hard Times* (Washington, D.C.: CQ Press, 1992), p. 80.

[3]Bill Moss, "The Monster that Nonsense Created," *State Legislature*, 21 (June 1995), 19.

[4]*Ibid.*, p. 16.

[5]*Ibid.*, p. 19.

[6]Daniel M. Fox and John K. Iglehart, *Five States That Could Not Wait: Lessons for Health Reform from Florida, Hawaii, Minnesota, Oregon and Vermont* (Cambridge, Mass.: Blackwell Publishers, 1994), pp. 50–51.

[7]Ceci Connolly, "If Governors are Harbingers, Clinton Faces Tough Road," *Congressional Quarterly Weekly Report* (August 21, 1993), 2261.

The search for an appropriate and effective expression of my womanhood in a male-defined position of power was constant. Often I felt my feminine perspective might sabotage me, make me critical of the very system I was trying to master. Gender gave me a certain degree of political naiveté, an insider-outsider dual perspective, which at times was valuable and at other times damaging, when it impeded my wholehearted participation in the political system.

One indicator—age—suggests possible change among this elite. The average age is decreasing. Bill Clinton, elected governor of Arkansas at age 32, is an example of this

BOX 6.2 REINVENTING GOVERNMENT, LIBERTARIAN STYLE: MASSACHUSETTS GOVERNOR WILLIAM WELD

Massachusetts Governor William Weld's fiscally conservative but socially liberal political philosophy can perhaps best be summed up in a comment he made in a speech to the Republican National Convention that it was necessary to keep government out of our pocketbooks and our bedrooms.[1] Weld's libertarianism makes him unique among Republicans nationwide. Through tax reductions, privatization, and a host of bold moves constructed to reduce the size of government, Weld has radically reformed politics in Massachusetts.

Harvard and Oxford educated and from an old, wealthy family, Weld—called by his 1990 gubernatorial opponent John Silber an "orange-headed WASP"—could easily be miscast as a "Boston Brahmin," but he grew up in New York, coming to Cambridge to attend prep school.[2] Before defeating Boston University president John Silber to win the governor's seat in 1990, Weld served as a U.S. attorney for Massachusetts, and was appointed assistant attorney general by President Reagan in 1986, with responsibility for all federal criminal investigation. Weld's particular focus in the attorney general's office was on public corruption, narcotics, and white-collar crime. Weld won the governor's seat narrowly—by 3 percent—in 1990.

In part Weld's victory was due to certain missteps by Silber (nicknamed "Silber shocker") during the course of the campaign: Silber remarked that a generation of children had been "abused by women who have thought a third-rate day care center was just as good as a first-rate home." Silber's stance gave Weld needed support from baby boomers and women and helped to subtly emphasize Weld's liberal position on social issues.[3] Weld was easily reelected in 1994.

Weld is acutely aware of just who constitutes his constituency. After refusing to submit state public employment contracts negotiated by the Dukakis administration to the state legislature as part of his first budget, Weld was told that he would alienate unionized public employees. Weld replied, "They are not my people, they are not my constituents."[4] In his first year Weld's initiatives reflected this awareness as he balanced the state budget without raising taxes and made cuts in the provision of social services.

---

trend. Younger governors exhibit several socioeconomic differences from older governors, but the most important difference may be quality. A study of governors previously identified as outstanding found that age was the crucial characteristic distinguishing the outstanding from the average governors.[6]

Political Experience

Thirty years ago Joseph Schlesinger wrote an intriguing book, *Ambition and Politics*, in which he argued that a state's structure of political opportunities shapes political ambition among politicians.[7] He found that two-thirds of all national leaders had held prior office in their state. Anyone who wants to be president, senator, or congressional representative should start out by running for local or state office. The office of governor is a key position in the office hierarchy because it is the focus of ambition within the state and is a funnel to national office. Three recent presidents, Jimmy Carter, Ronald Reagan, and Bill Clinton, have been governors, imbuing the governorship with even more strategic importance.

Privatization has been a recurring theme during Weld's watch. Weld says that he has asked the question, "Why is government performing this service? Could somebody else do it better?"[5] He has privatized state hospital functions, resulting in the closing of 34 state hospitals. In addition, prison health care and mental health services have been privatized with a projected savings of $8 million per year. Even formerly state-run skating rinks have been privatized in an attempt to reduce state losses. Weld would even like to sell the Massachusetts turnpike to a private owner.

In his 1995 inaugural address, Weld seemed to signal that more of the same was in store. Weld remarked that Massachusetts was poised to "become an international capital for new technology and innovation," but that in order to achieve this goal, the state would have to "tear down industrial-age regulatory barriers."[6] Weld has been true to his inaugural promises. Recently he called for the repeal of a state law requiring employers to provide health care for their employees.

Weld's critics have argued that all Weld has done in Massachusetts is to shrink government—that his policies have not changed the way government does things, but rather have just eliminated government services and responsibilities. But what bothers some critics more is that his experimentation comes without anticipation of the risks involved. Weld has been indifferent in the face of critics, and has commented that he considers the selling off of state properties to be like a game of Monopoly, which troubles those who take a loftier view of public service.[7]

Republicans consider the young, smart, and experienced Weld a potential candidate for national office; indeed, by 1996 he was already running for the U.S. Senate.

[1]Michael Barone and Grant Ujifusa, *The Almanac of American Politics 1994* (Washington, D.C.: National Journal, Inc., 1994), p. 596.

[2]Dennis Hale, "Massachusetts: William F. Weld and the End of Business as Usual," in Thad Beyle, *Governors and Hard Times* (Washington, D.C.: CQ Press, 1992), p. 131.

[3]Barone and Ujifusa, *The Almanac of American Politics*, p. 598.

[4]Kathleen Sylvester, "The Weld Experiment," *Governing* (June 1992), 36.

[5]*Ibid.,* p. 39.

[6]William F. Weld, Inaugural Address, 1995.

[7]Sylvester, "The Weld Experiment," p. 39.

The "halfway" position of the governorship means that political careers before holding the governorship are important to understanding the people who seek the governor's office. Building on Schlesinger's pioneering work, several scholars have researched modern governors' previous office experiences. Thad Beyle's recent analysis shows that 48 percent of the governors during the period 1970–1994 had state legislative experience, 32 percent had held statewide elective office, and 25 percent had held a law-enforcement position at some point.[8] Some governors had held more than one office, of course. The "jumping off point" or penultimate office for governors is most often the state legislature or statewide elective office, most likely lieutenant governor or attorney general. This means that most governors have prepared for a major executive position by working in the legislature or by working in a lesser executive office. They have become more acquainted with the issues of state government than with higher-level management problems.

Recently, a reverse trend has developed: an increase in the number of congressional representatives interested in becoming governor. During the 1970–1994 period, 13.3 percent of governors made the transition from the halls of Congress to the statehouse.[9] Pete

The typical governor is a white, middle-aged man. Christine Todd Whitman, shown here in the New Jersey House chamber, was the nation's only female governor in 1996. (*Source:* Reuters/Bettmann)

Wilson's move from the U.S. Senate to the California governorship is only the most visible example. Observers say this development signals a shift in the action from Washington to the states and from legislatures to the executive branch.[10] Some also see the change as evidence that the governor's seat is the shortest route to the White House. Consistent with that view, Governor Wilson in 1995 initiated a short-lived campaign for the presidency.

Political career paths differ by party: Prior service in electoral office is more crucial for Democrats than for Republicans. Republican candidates may enter the governor's race on the basis of a successful business background. Ronald Reagan as governor of California is a case in point: He was an actor, never a state legislator. Also, there are regional variations, with northeastern governors using state offices as their springboards less often than governors in other parts of the country. Further, political career paths differ by gender, with female candidates having more political experience on average than male candidates.[11]

Due to its location on the national career ladder, the governorship has historically been more of a transitory office than the U.S. Senate, which has been a career office with low turnover. This fleeting quality creates problems for state government. According to Schlesinger,

The most transitory positions in the elective hierarchy are precisely those which can best provide the leadership to resolve state problems, the governor, attorney general, and lieutenant governor. It is not that the offices do not attract capable men, but that the nature of these offices forces capable men to look outside the range of the states to satisfy their political ambitions. They must move on, and the only way is up and out of the state to federal office, preferably to the Senate where a man can settle down.[12]

For this reason governors may sometimes be tempted to make the easy or popular decisions and leave the tough decisions—raising taxes, for example—to the next incumbent. The governors of the larger states are almost automatically considered "presidential timber" and are called on to travel around the country representing their party. For example, Mario Cuomo was perceived as a national spokesperson and potential presidential nominee by virtue of being governor of New York. Governors of smaller states must work much harder to be recognized outside their own states. In either case, governors' participation in the presidential sweepstakes is a time-consuming activity, one that may detract from governing the state. Certainly Michael Dukakis found it extremely difficult to govern Massachusetts while seeking the presidency in 1988.

Gubernatorial Campaigns

The nature of gubernatorial campaigning, particularly its cost, also dictates the type of people attracted to the office. As reported in Chapter 4, the cost of gubernatorial campaigns has escalated in recent years due to an emphasis on new campaign technologies. In 1994 gubernatorial elections were held in 36 states; candidates spent an average of $11.6 million per race. Money flowed most freely in California, where over $60 million was spent. Table 6.1 displays the costs for each gubernatorial race in the early 1990s. Following the megaspending California are New York and Pennsylvania. In this league gubernatorial races exceeded $30 million. Only three states had contests costing less than $1 million: Vermont, New Hampshire, and North Dakota. The necessity of raising millions of dollars can be a deterrent to potential candidates, especially to women and minorities. Millionaire candidates are formidable contenders.

Research on campaign spending's impact on electoral outcomes indicates that money is indeed essential, along with party strength. In an analysis of the 1978 gubernatorial elections, Samuel Patterson demonstrated that the amount of spending is important for both incumbents and challengers in determining the outcome.[13] Sitting governors cannot substitute incumbency for money in the same way that congressional representatives can. On the other hand, money alone cannot substitute for partisan strength among the electorate. In the 1970s and 1980s, the built-in Democratic strength among the state electorate was an electoral advantage for Democratic candidates. Republican gubernatorial candidates had to be prepared to spend a lot to overcome Democratic opponents. In the 1990s the Democratic advantage of partisan identification narrowed, and by 1996 Republicans had secured 31 of the 50 gubernatorial seats.

Some of the most dramatic increases in campaign spending have occurred in the South, where one-party Democratic control gave way to a more evenly competitive situation. Louisiana is particularly interesting because that state uses a unique primary system in which all candidates run, regardless of party. This structure encourages many candidates, usually about 20, to run. A lot of money must be spent just to gain name recognition in such a situation.

TABLE 6.1 COST OF GUBERNATORIAL CAMPAIGNS, 1991–1994 The cost of gubernatorial campaigns has escalated rapidly, although there still remain wide variations between states in the cost of a gubernatorial seat. The most populous states tend to exhibit the highest costs, as shown below for the most recent cycle of elections.

State	*Year*	*Total All Candidates*[a]
Alabama	1994	$19,485,301
Alaska	1994	4,116,586
Arizona	1994	8,170,337
Arkansas	1994	3,608,127
California	1994	60,636,241
Colorado	1994	8,659,592
Connecticut	1994	8,665,349
Delaware	1992	2,709,940
Florida	1994	21,121,103
Georgia	1994	11,950,762
Hawaii	1994	9,331,098
Idaho	1994	3,355,554
Illinois	1994	22,005,539
Indiana	1992	6,700,884
Iowa	1994	6,859,797
Kansas	1994	6,699,331
Kentucky	1991	19,595,885
Louisiana	1991	9,778,386
Maine	1994	5,334,180
Maryland	1994	13,443,783
Massachusetts	1994	6,126,316
Michigan	1994	11,047,370
Minnesota	1994	4,820,840
Mississippi	1991	5,234,205

Partisan Composition

In the 1950s and 1960s Republicans sometimes held most of the nation's governorships, but since 1970 the office has been captured most often by Democrats. As Table 6.2 shows, the party lineup has been predominantly Democratic in some years (for example, 1982 and 1984) and narrowly Democratic in others (for example, 1986). However, in the 1994 elections dominance shifted to Republicans: the lineup was 30 Republicans, 19 Democrats, and 1 independent. Republicans added one more governorship in the 1995 elections. Most striking in Figure 6.1 was that Republican gains penetrated the heart of the South (Louisiana, Mississippi, and Alabama); they also control the governorships in the industrial Northeast, the Midwest, and as usual the Mountain West. Money, name recognition, and issue development are some of the tools Republican candidates used to increase their electoral victories.

TABLE 6.1   (CONTINUED)

State	Year	Total All Candidates[a]
Missouri	1992	$13,834,134
Montana	1992	2,657,748
Nebraska	1994	2,499,719
Nevada	1994	5,662,734
New Hampshire	1994	834,880
New Jersey	1993	22,458,552
New Mexico	1994	4,910,560
New York	1994	32,323,688
North Carolina	1992	13,353,473
North Dakota	1992	762,322
Ohio	1994	6,910,137
Oklahoma	1994	5,484,887
Oregon	1994	6,427,900
Pennsylvania	1994	36,051,532
Rhode Island	1994	4,141,612
South Carolina	1994	12,322,069
South Dakota	1994	2,751,491
Tennessee	1994	27,990,695
Texas	1994	26,435,001
Utah	1992	3,908,307
Vermont	1994	345,410
Virginia	1993	13,507,697
Washington	1992	6,994,269
West Virginia	1992	3,941,775
Wisconsin	1994	6,055,956
Wyoming	1994	1,233,453

[a] Includes primaries and general elections; all figures are actual dollars for the year involved.

Source: The Book of the States, 1994–95, Vol. 30 (Lexington, Ky.: Council of the State Governments, 1994), p. 39; unpublished research by Thad Beyle.

✧ THE EVOLUTION OF THE GOVERNORSHIP

In the preceding section we described the changes in the type of people who become governors, emphasizing the overall improvement in quality. States have rewritten their constitutions and drastically overhauled the structure of state government, thereby strengthening the office of governor. Also, they have gradually accorded more formal powers to governors so that their authority more nearly matches their responsibility.

Formal Powers

The contemporary reform movement emphasizes the desirability of the governor having four **formal powers:** tenure potential, appointive power, budgetary power, and veto power. We will now look at each of these powers more closely.

TABLE 6.2 PARTY LINEUP OF GOVERNORS, 1950–1994 The Democrats dominated the office of governor from midcentury to 1994 when Republicans captured 30 gubernatorial seats.

Year[a]	Democratic	Republican
1994[b]	19	30
1992[b]	30	18
1990[b]	28	20
1988	28	22
1986	26	24
1984	34	16
1982	34	16
1980	27	23
1978	32	18
1976[b]	37	12
1974[b]	36	13
1972	31	19
1970	29	21
1968	19	31
1966	25	25
1964	33	17
1962	34	16
1960[c]	34	16
1958[d]	35	14
1956	29	19
1954	27	21
1952	18	30
1950	23	25

[a] Five states (Kentucky, Louisiana, Mississippi, New Jersey, and Virginia) hold gubernatorial elections in odd-numbered years. In the chart, results of those contests are counted in the following year (for example, the 1983 Kentucky, Louisiana, and Mississippi results are counted under 1984, and the 1981 Virginia and New Jersey results under 1982).

[b] The rows do not sum to 50 because one or more independents were elected.

[c] Hawaii held its first gubernatorial election on July 28, 1959.

[d] Alaska held its first gubernatorial election on November 25, 1958.

Source: CQ Weekly Reports (January 4, 1986), 3; and other sources.

Tenure Potential   Governors should be elected for four-year terms rather than two-year terms and should be eligible for reelection. Nearly all states have moved to four-year terms. Rhode Island made the switch in 1994, leaving only New Hampshire and Vermont with the two-year term. The longer term removes the governor from continuous campaigning and allows him or her to concentrate on governing. Twenty-eight of the states restrict the governor to serving two terms and the rest allow more terms. One state, Virginia, prohibits successive terms. Increasing the tenure potential means that the governorship may become more of a career office rather than the **transitory office** it has

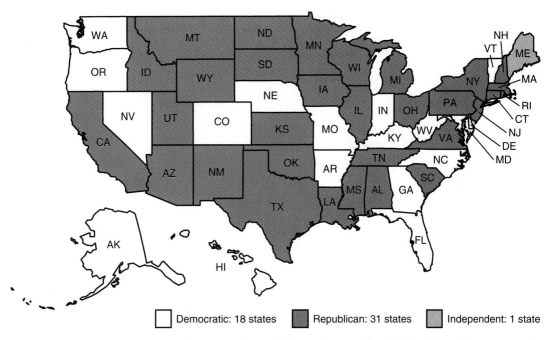

FIGURE 6.1 Gubernational Party Control, 1996.   Republicans gained control of the majority of gubernatorial seats in the 1994 election and by 1996 occupied 31 seats.
Source: Adapted from *Congressional Quarterly Weekly Report,* November 12, 1994, p. 3250, and other sources.

always been. However, a byproduct of the recent legislative term limits movement has been that several states mandated a two-term limit on the governor for the first time.

Appointive Power   Governors should have the authority to appoint other key administrative officials in the executive branch. Without **appointive power,** the governor has little control over the actions of executive agencies. Historically, governors have been hamstrung by the fact that many administrators were elected separately by the people or were appointed by boards or commissions. As a part of the reform movement begun in the 1960s, the number of elected officials was reduced and more appointment powers were granted to the governor.

Today the average state has six separately elected officials, typically the governor, lieutenant governor, secretary of state, attorney general, treasurer, and auditor. Other examples of elected officials, as shown in Table 6.3, are comptroller, superintendent of public instruction, secretary of agriculture, public utilities commissioner, insurance commissioner, and labor commissioner. The fewest number of elected officials per state is 1 (in New Hampshire, New Jersey, and Maine) and the largest number is 12 (in North Dakota).[14]

By the 1980s governors could appoint about half of top administrative officials, and the rest are appointed by someone else or are elected.[15] About two-thirds of those appointments require confirmation by a legislative body. In addition to these agency chief

TABLE 6.3 STATE ELECTED OFFICIALS, 1992
States vary in the number of officials elected statewide. All states elect the governor but only five elect the labor commissioner.

Category	Number of States
Governor	50
Lieutenant governor	42
Secretary of state	36
Attorney general	43
Treasurer	38
Auditor	25
Comptroller	16
Superintendent of public instruction	16
Secretary of agriculture	12
Public utility commissioner	11
Insurance commissioner	10
Labor commissioner	5

Source: Keon S. Chi, "Trends in Executive Reorganization," *Journal of State Government,* 65 (April/June 1992), 37. Copyright April–June 1992. The Council of State Governments. Reprinted with permission from *Journal of State Government.*

appointments, governors make hundreds, even thousands, of appointments to boards and commissions. For example, Minnesota's governor appoints members of the Board of Boxing, the Podiatry Board, and the Arts Board, among others.

Budgetary Power   Governors should prepare and submit an **executive budget** to the state legislature and should appoint the budget director. These powers allow governors to play a leading role in determining the state's revenues and expenditures. Budgets are also a means of controlling the state bureaucracy. In fact, state administrators indicate that the governor's budget authority is the most important source of control over them.[16] The budgetary process is explained more fully in Chapter 12.

In this century budgetary control has shifted from legislative committees to the governor. At present ten states require the governor to share budget formulation with other state officials. Texas is the state whose governor has the least budgetary power, as the Legislative Budget Board does most of the work. The power to formulate a budget is a substantial policy and management resource.

Veto Power   Governors should have the power to veto laws and should have **item veto** power on appropriations bills. The threat of a veto of an appropriations item is a powerful weapon for the chief executive, one that most governors but not the U.S. president have long possessed. Ronald Reagan frequently complained that he had more veto power as governor of California than he had as president. All but one state—North Carolina—allow gubernatorial veto. Vetoes tend to be used sparingly except where party control is split between the executive and legislative branches. An extreme example is New Mexico Governor Gary Johnson, who in 1995 vetoed 200 of 424 bills passed by a Democratic legislature, seemingly a national record. Johnson, a conservative, struck down laws introduced by Republicans as well as Democrats, and eliminated laws that reduced expenditures as well as laws establishing new programs. He even vetoed a bill designating "Red or green?" (as in red or green chili peppers) as the state question.[17]

On appropriations bills, nearly all states allow some form of the item veto, that is, they allow the governor to reject some individual expenditure items in the bill while accepting others. Ten states provide the governor with a more refined item veto by which he or she can reduce the amount of the item without striking it entirely.[18] Seven states allow the governor to suggest rewording or amendments before approval; this is called the partial veto. Governor Tommy Thompson of Wisconsin has made frequent and creative use of his partial veto power, issuing over 1,300 vetoes. He excised isolated digits, letters, and words from bills even to the point of creating new words, which changed legislative intent.[19] His has been called the "Vanna White veto," in reference to the *Wheel of Fortune* hostess who manipulates letters on camera.

Summary Index of Formal Powers   Scholars have summarized the formal powers of the governor in a single index. Table 6.4 reports the most recent updating of the gubernatorial power index for 1994. Thad Beyle has ranked the governors from most powerful (5) to least powerful (1) on the basis of the four formal powers just discussed plus party control. He feels that it is difficult for governors to exercise their constitutional powers unless their party also controls the legislative branch. The table shows that no state attained the top score but nine states scored four points on this scale; they tend to be the large industrial states such as Ohio, Pennsylvania, and New York, although there is a range of states in this category. Most states are clustered in the middle of the scale at either 3.5 or 3; only three states score as low as 2.5. Those low-scoring states are North Carolina (whose governor lacks the general veto power), Vermont (whose governor has a two-year term), and South Carolina (whose governor lacks budgetary power). Thus, the effect of the reform movement has been to enhance gubernatorial power generally and to reduce the discrepancies among states.

The increases in formal powers since 1965 have occurred in the areas of tenure potential, appointment power, and budget making. Veto power has increased very little in recent decades. However, state legislatures have enhanced their capabilities at the same time so that the relative balance between the two branches has changed less dramatically. The use of the governors' formal powers depends on the influence of other competing actors and on the governor's own personal attributes. In theory, the governors of New Jersey and New York should be more effective than the governors of Texas and South Carolina but it doesn't always work out that way. Informal powers also come into play.

Informal Powers

It is important to close this discussion of gubernatorial power by noting that chief executives also possess important **informal** (or personal) **powers.** These personal attributes affect the exercise of formal power. Formal powers provide the opportunity or potential for influence. However, the governor must use the power.[20] A governor may be very popular, impress the media, be a good bargaining agent with the legislature, or be a strong

TABLE 6.4 THE GOVERNORS' FORMAL POWERS BY STATE, 1994 States have gradually given their governor more formal powers; the states now cluster between 2.5 and 4 on the power scale.

5	4.5	4	3.5	3	2.5	2
		Hawaii	Alaska	Alabama	North Carolina	
		Iowa	Arizona	California	South Carolina	
		Maryland	Arkansas	Colorado	Vermont	
		New Jersey	Connecticut	Florida		
		New York	Delaware	Georgia		
		Ohio	Illinois	Idaho		
		Pennsylvania	Kansas	Indiana		
		Tennessee	Kentucky	Maine		
		West Virginia	Louisiana	Massachusetts		
			Michigan	Mississippi		
			Minnesota	Nevada		
			Missouri	New Hampshire		
			Montana	Oklahoma		
			Nebraska	Texas		
			New Mexico	Virginia		
			North Dakota	Washington		
			Oregon	Wyoming		
			Rhode Island			
			South Dakota			
			Utah			
			Wisconsin			

Source: Thad Beyle, "Governors," in Virginia Gray and Herbert Jacob, eds., *Politics in the American States,* 6th ed. (Washington, D.C.: CQ Press, 1996), Table 6.17.

party leader, all qualities that may compensate for a lack of formal powers. Or a "strong" governor on the index of formal powers may be so lacking in personal qualities that he or she accomplishes very little. Still, all governors would rather have the legal resources of the strong governors than do without such powers.

According to Alan Rosenthal, the most important informal powers a governor can have are skills at bargaining and persuading, prestige in office, popularity, political party backing, and mass media approval.[21] Informal power starts with the election. A governor elected by a wide margin whose party controls the legislature is in a favorable position to wield influence over the legislature and the administration. Governors who use the media skillfully to generate favorable publicity and who maintain positive public opinion ratings have a better chance of getting their programs enacted. As former Governor Thomas Kean of New Jersey said, "With a 75 percent rating, legislators have to be sensitive to your programmatic appeals."[22]

The governor's personal qualities—personality, energy, and charisma—are also crucial. Former Governor Richard Riley of South Carolina exemplifies these virtues. Despite possessing weak formal powers (see Table 6.4), Riley was judged by his peers as the third most effective governor in the country.[23] He was particularly praised for his leadership role in gaining legislative approval of a comprehensive package of education reforms in the 1980s. Riley marshaled public opinion behind his program, masterfully using media access, his own popularity, and the prestige of his office to his advantage. His skills in negotiating and consensus building and the energy and devotion displayed in his 18-hour workdays allowed Riley to win an uphill struggle. Riley's case shows how a weak governor can become strong.

Thad Beyle conducted a survey in 1994 asking observers in each state to rate their governor's personal powers such as margin of victory and press relations.[24] His ranking of governors on personal powers correlates −.11 with the index of formal powers, indicating that the two kinds of power are not positively related. Formal power does not equate with informal power. On personal powers Roy Romer of Colorado and Mel Carnahan of Missouri ranked highest; David Walters of Oklahoma and Bruce Sundlun of Rhode Island ranked lowest. The latter two were in their final term, lending some validity to the scale.

✧ THE EVOLUTION OF THE EXECUTIVE BRANCH

The governors' powers are not the only part of the executive branch that has undergone a major transformation in the past two decades. Structural reorganization has been pursued in an effort to streamline state administration and to make the governor a stronger chief executive. One effort already described involves reducing the number of separately elected officials so that executive power is consolidated into the governor's office.

Separately Elected State Officials

Aside from the governor, the most commonly elected officials are the lieutenant governor, attorney general, treasurer, and secretary of state.

Lieutenant Governor   The lieutenant governor is analogous to the vice president of the United States. He or she replaces the governor if the governor is unable to function due to illness or death; in about half the states the lieutenant governor also steps in when the governor is out of the state, which has produced a number of interesting situations when the two people are enemies. These tense situations can happen because in 19 states the governor and his or her lieutenant are elected independently. For example, in 1994 when Arkansas Governor Jim Guy Tucker was out of the state, his lieutenant governor issued a proclamation against his orders. Other acting governors have vetoed legislation, granted pardons, issued executive orders, made judicial appointments, called the legislature into special session, and cut the budget. To prevent such actions, increasingly states are turning to team elections in which the top two candidates run together.

Lieutenant governors have few defined responsibilities: About half preside over their senates, about half can vote to break a tie in their senate, a few make legislative committee assignments, and about half are members of the governor's cabinet.[25] But otherwise, they wait for the governor to assign them tasks such as chairing a council, attending certain ceremonies, performing liaison with particular groups; often with nothing to do they become invisible to the public. Seven states have eliminated the job altogether.

Attorney General The attorney general (A.G.) is the state's legal counsel, analogous to the U.S. attorney general. He or she issues formal legal opinions upon request of the governor or other public official. Usually the question posed is whether a statute is constitutional; these legal opinions can be challenged in court. If the state is sued by someone, the A.G. (or his or her subordinates) represents the state in court, or if the state has a beef with the federal government, the A.G. goes to court on the state's behalf.

Using their power to initiate civil and criminal proceedings, many attorneys general have gone after consumer fraud. Minnesota's A.G., Hubert H. Humphrey III, in alliance with Blue Cross/Blue Shield, is currently suing the nation's largest tobacco companies for the damage their products cause smokers. Other A.G.s have investigated the activities of their governors: In 1992, Alabama A.G. Jimmy Evans indicted Governor Guy Hunt for converting inaugural funds to personal use. Hunt was convicted by a jury and immediately removed from office.

Treasurer The state treasurer is the steward of all state funds. He or she oversees the investment of state funds, which is a big job, receives tax revenue and federal grants, and disburses state money. (You may have seen the treasurer's signature on your tax refund, for example). Sometimes their actions have major repercussions: In 1989 the West Virginia treasurer lost $279 million in bad investments.[26]

Secretary of State The secretary of state has dual responsibilities. He or she conducts elections and acts as a registrar for various functions. In his or her electoral responsibilities, the secretary receives the filings of candidates, determines who is eligible to be on the ballot, supplies ballots to local officials, and conducts and encourages voter registration. In Minnesota, the longtime secretary of state, Joan Growe, has established herself as the best predictor of voter turnout in the state. In their registrar role secretaries register corporations, publish statutes, and file agency regulations.

Most people run for these offices because they eventually want to be governor or a U.S. senator. As explained earlier, statewide elective office is usually the jumping off point for people who become governor, so serving in one of these offices is a reasonable strategy for an ambitious politician. Of course, sometimes the clash of ambitions causes a problem when one of the state officials runs against the sitting governor. This potential competition explains much of the tension between governors and other state officials.

Structural Reorganization

Structural reorganization may involve consolidating multiple agencies into superagencies in order to locate responsibility for decisions. In the past some states had as many as 300 agencies, for example. Another aspect is the abolition of boards that have purely administrative duties and the placement of these tasks into executive departments. The governor had little power over such independent boards. Still another change is that nearly all states have combined staff functions—budgeting, accounting, purchasing, and so forth—into a single department of administration. Finally, states have combined disparate but related functions into a single agency. For example, previously there might have been one agency for each type of tax collected (income, sales, and liquor, for example) and now there is a single revenue department.

About half the states have undertaken comprehensive reorganizations along these lines since the 1960s, usually initiated by the governor and approved by the legislature. Georgia is a case in point. As governor, Jimmy Carter prevailed on the Georgia legislature to reduce 300 boards and agencies to 22 superagencies. The governor was granted authority to appoint the heads of 16 of the 22 new agencies. (This accomplishment was stressed in his presidential campaign.) South Carolina followed suit in 1993 when its governor prodded the legislature to replace 75 state agencies with 13 cabinet departments and 4 revamped agencies. Gubernatorial appointment power was enhanced as well.

Many of these agency consolidations emulate the federal government's organizational structure, allowing governors to use cabinets modeled after the president's in order to encourage policy coordination. Thirty-nine states now use some variation of the cabinet model.[27] Some governors (as in Ohio) include as many as 30 officials in a weekly cabinet meeting; others (such as Vermont) limit the cabinet to 6 officers who meet at the governor's discretion. Cabinets usually include the heads of the most important departments such as health, human services, and transportation, but may also incorporate elected officials. Regular meetings of such officials can improve communication and coordination among diverse programs.

Executive branch reorganizations have made it easier for citizens to contact state agencies and for governors to exert administrative control. They have not resulted in substantial cost savings, however. Iowa's reorganization seems to be the major exception: Its streamlining in the mid-1980s resulted in savings of $40 to 60 million.[28]

Governor's Staff

Aside from structural reform, the other major change in the executive branch has been the expansion of the governor's personal staff. Originally the governor's office was staffed by a handful of political cronies and secretaries but by 1979 the average governor had a staff of 34, a number that has undoubtedly grown since then.[29] Governors typically employ a chief of staff, press secretary, intergovernmental coordinator, legislative liaison, legal counsel, budget director, and a variety of policy professionals such as a health expert, an education person, and a corrections guru. Staff members function much as the White House staff does: They provide the governor with political advice and counsel, policy analysis, and information; they communicate to the bureaucracy for the governor and are often quite influential in his or her decisionmaking.

By and large, governors now work in more streamlined and efficient administrative structures in which they can draw on the talents of professional men and women. In the next section we describe the many tasks the governor has to accomplish each day.

✦ THE ROLES OF THE GOVERNOR

The governor fulfills many roles in state government and state politics. First of all, he or she is an important political leader. Second, the governor is a significant policymaker, both in terms of placing issues on government's agenda and in proposing solutions to the state's problems. Third, the governor is the chief legislator; that is, he or she must push many programs and budgets through the legislature. Fourth, the governor manages the state bureaucracy. Fifth, the governor is the intergovernmental coordinator. Finally, governors are also people with families to consider. Every governor finds it difficult to balance multiple and diverse professional and personal goals.

The Governor as Political Leader

Traditionally the governor has been the titular head of his or her political party. Simply by virtue of the office, the governor is looked to for leadership in raising campaign funds, filling party leadership positions, finding legislative candidates, and representing the state in national party affairs. Today's governors seem to be less interested in partisan affairs and spend less time on them than in the past. Still, whether they like it or not, few governors abandon this role entirely.

Governors nurture their political parties for several reasons. One is that the governor's success in the legislature rests on party ties. Sarah Morehouse has shown that governors with strong statewide party coalitions are in the best position to receive legislative support for their policies.[30] If the governor is traditionally nominated with broad party backing, then the incumbent governor can expect more cohesion among legislators. In their own self-interest, governors must be attentive to their party's legislators and to various factions in the legislative party. They have an incentive to help their party's legislative candidates get elected or reelected; candidates whom they have campaigned for may be expected to demonstrate loyalty by voting with the governor, at least for awhile.

Another reason for the governor's attention to the party is that the U.S. Congress and the presidency are organized along party lines. The governor's success in the state is partly dependent on attracting federal dollars or large federal projects. Federal officials of the same party as the governor are more sympathetic to his or her pleas than are officials of the opposition party.

Finally, most governors want to seek reelection. They need renomination by the party in order to run, and they need a strong united party in order to win. Consequently, it is in the governor's political interest to maintain and nourish party ties. Many governors relish partisan politics, so politicking comes naturally to them. Others come to it more grudgingly. But all must invest some effort into the political game.

The Governor as Policy Formulator

Governors are the most significant policy initiators and formulators in their states. Former Governor Kunin decided that "the greatest power conferred on me by the governorship was the power to set the agenda and frame the debate."[31] In their electoral campaigns governors can highlight emerging state issues; in public addresses and statements they can focus attention on state problems; in legislative and budgetary proposals they can offer solutions to these problems. For their proposals to become laws, governors must have the support of a majority of the legislature. For the programs to work, governors must gather the support of state bureaucrats as implementers. In this section we concentrate on how governors go about putting issues on the public agenda and keeping them alive until the legislature acts.

First, governors spend a lot of time relating to the general public in an effort to command attention and build support for their priorities. The power of publicity is one of the executive's principal strengths; there is only one governor for people to focus on, but there are many legislators competing for attention. Governors make public appearances, meet groups visiting the capitol, host foreign visitors, and travel to other states and foreign countries to drum up business. The governor's staff usually handles routine contacts with the public, such as the many phone calls and letters. Governors employ press secretaries to manage their relations with the mass media. It is estimated that governors spend between 20 and 40 percent of their time in ceremonial functions, working with the media, and meeting the general public.[32] This is more time than is spent on any other single function. Governors believe that the general public's support is crucial; they use the bully pulpit they have been given.

In addition to attempting to maintain a high public profile, governors also try to focus public attention on their priorities. Successful governors undertake a few major initiatives each year and commit themselves to working on them personally. These ideas may come from the governor's own experience, from particular circumstances in the state (economic recession, for example), from other states' experiences, or from external events.

One index to a governor's policy concerns can be found in public speeches, such as the inaugural address, the state-of-the-state message, and the budget address. The inaugural address is the new governor's first speech; usually it lays out broad themes and a vision of the future. The state-of-the state address, required by most states' constitutions, is delivered to the legislature at the beginning of the legislative session; it reviews the state's condition, highlights current accomplishments, and recommends programs for the future. In most states it is followed by a budget message to the legislature, which communicates specific dollar amounts. The governor's policy priorities become clear as the resource commitments to various programs are identified.

Political scientist Eric Herzik analyzed state-of-the-state speeches in order to track changes in governors' policy agendas over the years.[33] He found that education consistently receives a lot of attention in governors' public speeches. Other areas frequently mentioned in the 1980s were economic development, the environment, and government reorganization. Other scholars examined the 1990 speeches and found that the number one topic was jobs and economic development, followed by drugs and crime (#2), education (#3), and environment (#4).[34]

The issues highlighted in the governor's formal public addresses constitute a general statement of his or her program. A series of bills that describe in more specific fashion the proposals recommended by the governor is prepared. This package is introduced in the legislature by a leader of the governor's political party. Such bills are labeled the governor's program. Governors then have to follow through: They marshal public support behind their agenda and put pressure on legislators to pass their program. Governors also lend their support to administration bills, proposals—usually noncontroversial housekeeping items—submitted by state agencies.

Perhaps the most important policy statement the governor makes is the budget submitted to the legislature. Accordingly, the authority to formulate the budget is one of the governor's prime powers. The money recommended for various programs is the real indication of the governor's priorities. In the next section we examine the resources the governor possesses in pushing the legislative program and budget through the legislature.

The Governor as Chief Legislator

A governor's relations with the legislature are critically important to the success of a legislative program and hence to overall success in policymaking. Governors view relating to the legislature as necessary but difficult. In fact, working with the legislature may be the most difficult part of the governor's job.[35] This is interesting, given that many governors formerly served in the legislature themselves.

One circumstance that makes the governor's life difficult is opposition control of the legislature. As we saw in Chapter 4, this occurs fairly often; for example, in 1994 split control was a fact of life in 26 states. The sharing of power is often difficult, and governors' programs tend to bog down when the other party gets control. Moreover, political parties sometimes split into ideological factions, some of which may give the governor as much trouble as the opposition party. As former Governor Dukakis expressed it,

> And when you've got majorities of four to one in the Legislatures—I'm sure you recognize that that is by no means an unmitigated blessing—you've got conservative Democrats, you've got liberal Democrats, you've got moderate Democrats, you've got suburban Democrats, you've got urban Democrats, you've got rural Democrats, and you don't have any Republicans.[36]

Normally though, it is to his or her own political party that the governor looks for votes in passing a program.

Governors try to get the support of legislators in many personal ways. They may be helpful in the electoral campaigns of some legislators; they may intervene in contests for legislative leadership positions so that friendly leaders are chosen. They may invite legislators to breakfasts or lunches at which the governor's legislative program can be discussed informally. Nearly every governor has at least one legislative liaison, who maintains contact with legislators and lobbies them on a daily basis. Governors with great personal charm, especially if backed by political clout, find that legislative resistance can be overcome or worn down.

Today's governors are very effective in getting their proposals through the legislature. Rosenthal cites success rates of 75 to 85 percent across the states.[37] Ultimately, if a governor cannot get his or her way with the legislature, then he or she may use, or threaten to use, the veto. The veto indicates that all other weapons have failed with the legislature; thus, it is used sparingly.

The Governor as Manager

The governorship is an executive office; that is, the governor is supposed to manage the organizations and agencies that make up the executive branch. However, state government is not neatly organized into a hierarchy of departments ultimately accountable to a chief executive officer (CEO). Rather, some state officials are elected separately from the governor and do not necessarily share his or her views about anything. Some top administrative positions are appointed by others (boards, agency heads, or the legislature). Positions below the top level are covered by the civil service merit system. As a result, the governor does not hire and fire as easily as does a CEO in the private sector; rather, he or she attempts to influence state agencies and officials to move in a certain direction.

Lynn Muchmore has described the governor's managerial role as having four layers.[38] At a minimum governors try to ensure that state agencies conduct their business in a way that cannot be called corrupt or grossly incompetent. Normally the role of the governor is to project integrity in government, a few exceptions notwithstanding.

Second, governors must be able to respond in times of crisis: snowstorms, nuclear accidents (Three Mile Island in Pennsylvania), prison violence, flooding, earthquakes (San Francisco in 1989), or an infestation of mosquitoes. The appearance of disinterest or the inability to mobilize state agencies to meet the crisis may result in defeat at the polls. Conversely, looking strong during a crisis—taking charge—can provide the winning edge in the next election. It is said that Ella Grasso owed her second term as governor of Connecticut to the fact that she took command of the highway patrol during a severe snowstorm.

Third, governors are formally charged with carrying out routine administrative duties such as extraditing criminals and signing certain documents. Fourth, more and more governors act as managers, planning, controlling, and coordinating activities of state agencies. The reorganization efforts described previously were aimed in part at increasing the governor's managerial potential.

Governors possess several managerial tools. One is the power to hire and fire, which has its limits. Another is budgetary: A governor can reduce an errant agency's expenditures or omit it from the budget entirely (of course, the legislature can always change that). As mentioned earlier, budgetary power is the most powerful resource for gubernatorial control over administration.[39] A third tool is the governor's personal efforts at coordinating activities and striving for efficiency. The power of persuasion is a critical one for the top manager.

However, several situations impose limits on the extent of gubernatorial control. One is the professionalism of state civil servants. Being professional means being responsive to the peers in one's profession (for example, to other social workers or engineers) rather than to a political boss. Professionals act autonomously, sometimes to the governor's dismay. Bureaucrats also enjoy long tenure, so they can usually outlast a governor. Hence, governors are at a disadvantage in figuring out how to run government without bureaucrats, or in spite of them.

Another factor limiting managerial control is unionization of public employees. A public sector union may set wages and working conditions to such an extent that supervision and management are constrained. Chapter 7 explores bureaucracy and unionization in more detail.

Still another constraining factor is the legislature's interest in overseeing state administration. According to a variety of surveys of administrators, control over administration seems to be equally shared between the governor and the legislature. This trend suggests potential for more conflict between governors and legislatures.

The core role of manager is one for which many governors are ill-prepared, having previously served in legislative rather than executive capacities. It is also time-consuming: About one-quarter of the governor's time is spent on managing state government.[40] In addition, executive work can be tedious and detailed, demanding day-to-day attention. Such duties pale in comparison to delivering a speech, thinking up an innovative program, or politicking with the legislature, but it is in the role of manager that modern governors have improved most. The "new breed" is a group interested in making state government work. Lawton Chiles in Box 6.1 and William Weld in Box 6.2 exemplify this trend.

The Governor as Intergovernmental Coordinator

Governors also have an important representational role: They represent their states in Washington, and they represent state government to the localities within their own borders. They are involved in interstate relations such as regional governors' associations, interstate compacts, and a variety of joint endeavors such as reciprocity in college tuition, and ongoing disputes such as boundary issues and pollution leaking from one state to another.

Federal grants-in-aid, if nothing else, command gubernatorial attention. With states receiving about one-fifth of their revenues from the federal government, governors cannot afford to ignore the financial opportunities in Washington, D.C. In addition to grants, governors are vitally affected by policies enacted by Congress and by regulations issued by federal bureaucrats. Each governor has a staff that tries to assess the impact of laws and regulations on their state. Much policy implementation—such as welfare and pollution control—is intergovernmental in nature, which often draws the governor into the picture. Especially during crises such as earthquakes and hurricanes, the governor is the point person coordinating relief efforts with federal agencies. Also, governors are interested in expanding the resources allocated to state governments in general. Toward this end governors band together to lobby for common goals.

There are several ways by which governors try to influence what goes on in the nation's capital. Many states, especially the larger ones, maintain permanent lobby offices in Washington. Through these offices governors are able to keep tabs on new federal grants, regulations, and legislation. The offices also facilitate interstate cooperation in lobbying coalitions and provide occasional assistance to private corporations. In addition, governors pursue their Washington agendas by lobbying their own state's congressional delegation, federal bureaucrats, and the White House. Depending on the political party of the people involved and whether the governor is perceived as a future opponent, such contacts may or may not be helpful. One study found that governors spent 10 to 14 percent of their time on federal affairs, allocating most of their time to federal agencies, followed by Congress, and then the president.[41] A follow-up study reasoned that governors engaged in federal lobbying as much to advance their own careers as to protect their state's interests.[42]

The nation's governors have banded together in several organizations in order to present state government's case to Washington. There are regional governors' organizations but the most important group is the **National Governors' Association** (NGA). Once just an annual conference of governors who enjoyed socializing together, today the NGA is an influential participant in national politics. With a staff of over 100, it sponsors a lobbying office, a services branch (primarily helping new governors learn their jobs), and a policy research office furnishing policy options to governors. It is housed, along with several of the individual state's offices, in the Hall of States, located a stone's throw from Capitol Hill.

About ten years ago, the NGA began a series of year-long studies of specific issues of concern to the states. The NGA's studies of education and job creation were instrumental in achieving national reforms in education and welfare policy. Other topics under study have been international trade, children's policies, health care reform, economic competitiveness, and the changing balance in the federal system. Activities within the NGA, especially television coverage of its annual meeting, provide politically ambitious governors with a highly visible national outlet. Looking good in the company of other governors is a plus in the competition for national office.

The Governor as Person

We have reviewed the major roles of the governor: political leader, policy initiator, chief legislator, manager, and intergovernmental intermediary. Yet most governors say that the hardest part of the job is not any of those tasks. Rather it is trying to maintain personal balance and find time for family and friends. Nearly half of the former governors interviewed in one study said that interference with family life was the most difficult part of the job.[43] These tensions increase the longer one serves and are one reason for stepping down. In the next section we look at how governors leave office.

✧ AFTER THE GOVERNORSHIP

In most states at the end of a gubernatorial term, a governor has several choices. One is running again. Many governors do this, and their chances of success are quite high. Another choice is to run for higher office. Obviously, few can achieve higher office but gubernatorial experience is an advantage. Still another choice is to retire from politics altogether. Most eventually make the latter choice.

Reelection

All states but Virginia allow successive gubernatorial terms, some without any limit on the number of terms. Consequently, many sitting governors can and do choose to run again. Between 1970 and 1993 the proportion of incumbents running again (when permitted by law) averaged 76 percent.[44] Most incumbents will try again because there is no higher office open, because their odds of reelection are high, or because they like being governor.

Most incumbents win their reelection bids. From 1970 to 1993 the proportion of incumbents running who were reelected averaged 72 percent.[45] Those defeated are more likely to have lost in the general election than in the primary. In 1994 all the defeated incumbents were Democrats, although the overall reelection rate was about the same as in previous years. Although reelection cannot be taken for granted, the odds are very good that an incumbent will be returned to office.

The explanation for why some incumbents win and some lose is far from clear, but there are some patterns. Beyle's analysis of the key issues involved in governors' defeats identifies taxes and scandal as two of the major reasons for defeat.[46] He estimates that taxes were a major element in over one-fifth of the defeats in the 1950–1994 period. In the 1990s the tax issue loomed even larger: It was an issue in 7 of 15 losses. Avoiding scandal continues to be a good idea, as governors Hunt of Alabama, Walters of Oklahoma, and DiPrete of Rhode Island found out in the 1990s; their financial dealings got them into legal trouble, ending any reelection prospects. In 1987, Arizona Governor Evan Mecham became the first governor in 50 years to be impeached for financial misdeeds and obstruction of justice and removed from office.

Another potentially important reason for a sitting governor's defeat is the performance of the state's economy. Scholars reasoned that if the president is held accountable for the nation's economic performance (the theory of retrospective voting), then the governor might be held similarly accountable. Initial studies could not document this effect but research published in the 1990s has rather consistently demonstrated that voters reward and punish governors for how well the state economy is doing. Craig Svoboda, for example, found that after party identification, responsibility for the state's economy was the most important determinant of vote choice in the 1982 and 1986 elections.[47]

Other studies indicate that governors of higher quality and governors who can work in hostile partisan environments are more likely to be reelected.[48] A related ability is the capacity for issue preemption: Republicans who can take stands to the left of their party fare better at the polls. Likewise, Democrats who can take the lead on economic policy and other traditionally Republican issues are more durable than other Democrats. Such pragmatic individuals tend to survive longer than do other politicians.

Seeking Higher Office

Every year some governors leave office in order to follow their dreams for national office. Since mid-century, at least one-third of former governors succeeded in moving to Washington.[49] In their quest for upward mobility governors may become senators or representatives, federal judges or administrators of cabinet rank, or presidents or vice presidents. Since 1970 there has been a decline in the number of governors moving to the senate en route to the presidency. Rather, governors have been more inclined to skip the senate and try for the presidency directly. As governors have become more capable, they have increasingly been viewed as presidential timber. Jimmy Carter, Ronald Reagan, and Bill Clinton are three successful examples.

Retirement

Eventually governors return to private life: They are constitutionally prohibited from serving another term, they are defeated, or they just retire. They return to their jobs in the private sector and to their families. They travel, write books as Madeleine Kunin did, make money, or become university presidents as Lamar Alexander and Thomas Kean did. Some tire of private life and yearn for public office again. Each year several people come out of retirement to make another bid for the governorship.

✧ GOOD GOVERNORS AND GOOD POLITICS

At present, the nation's governors are at center stage in the competition among the states. Many governors have seized on international trade as an important issue, illustrating the issue preemption strategy of successful politicians. In the 1980s the nation's governors made educational and welfare reform front-page national issues. Both Democrats and Republicans entered this fray. In the 1990s, the "reinventing government" movement found a receptive audience among the nation's governors. Governors Chiles and Weld, described in Box 6.1 and Box 6.2, are just two of the many governors who have attempted to "rightsize" their bureaucracies. No actions better demonstrate the high quality of the new breed of governors than do their accomplishments in these important areas. Let us close by looking at a few examples of gubernatorial leadership in the laboratories of democracy.

Elementary and Secondary Education

The nation's governors individually and collectively have embraced school reform as a significant issue. In the early 1980s, Lamar Alexander battled the Tennessee legislature to change the teachers' reward structure. In neighboring Arkansas, Bill Clinton also fought the teachers' unions. Governor Clinton was responsible for the first law requiring teachers to take a competency test in order to maintain their certification. His popularity on the education issue led to his election as head of the NGA and helped brought him favorable national attention.

The governors collectively have embraced the notion that education is good politics. The 1986 NGA conference was devoted almost exclusively to education. The governors released a 171-page report on educational reform, a document that cost the NGA over $400,000 to prepare. The governors formulated an action agenda of 65 proposals to improve public schools and appointed a committee to monitor implementation in the states.[50] There was general consensus among members that radical reform was needed in order to meet economic competition from abroad. In addition, interstate competition to attract business taught several governors about their schools' inadequacies. Nearly all the states adopted some elements of school reform legislation.

International Trade

Efforts to foster export to new overseas markets and to attract trade and investment from outside a state's boundaries have increased dramatically since the mid-1980s. It is estimated that the fifty states spend more on international trade promotion than does the federal government.[51] Some of this money goes to support more than a hundred trade offices maintained by 41 states in locations around the world. But the most vigorous "salespeople" for a state's firms are the governors. Most governors travel abroad every year, touting everything from costume jewelry (from Rhode Island) to procelain bathroom fixtures (from Wisconsin). They are also major recruiters of foreign companies looking for locations in the United States.

These economic interests lead governors to get involved in international affairs. For example, in 1993 governors were some of the more enthusiastic supporters of NAFTA, the North American Free Trade Agreement with Canada and Mexico. After leading a trade delegation to Mexico, Michigan Governor John Engler was convinced that lowering Mexico's trade barriers would be good for his state:

> The way to protect Michigan jobs is not by building a wall around our state and ignoring the competition. Michigan, remember, is made of peninsulas, not islands. We live in, and are connected to, the global marketplace. So the way to bolster Michigan jobs is by creating the best entrepreneurial climate possible.[52]

States' economies have become globalized, and governors' entreprenurial efforts have become worldwide.

◇ CONCLUSION

In this chapter we have stressed the historical development of the governor's office and the improvement in gubernatorial talent. More and more of the governors are impressive leaders and managers, a situation that bodes well for state and national government. Governors have acquired greater formal powers that, when combined with informal powers, are used in governing effectively. Governors' lives are busy ones, with responsibilities from politics to policymaking, including legislating, managing, and lobbying Washington. Still, most governors want to continue in public life, either as governors or as higher-level officials.

✧ KEY TERMS

appointive power (p. 161)	item veto (p. 162)
executive budget (p. 162)	National Governors' Association
formal powers (p. 159)	(p. 172)
informal powers (p. 163)	transitory office (p. 160)

✧ FOR FURTHER READING

Thad L. Beyle, ed., *Governors and Hard Times* (Washington, D.C.: CQ Press, 1992). A collection of essays about governors in ten states, emphasizing the difficulties of governing in the 1990s.

Thad L. Beyle and Lynn R. Muchmore, eds., *Being Governor: The View from the Office* (Durham, N.C.: Duke University Press, 1983). Report of a study by the National Governors' Association, based on surveys of governors and personal interviews. This report focuses on the governors' day-to-day responsibilities.

Madeleine M. Kunin, *Living a Political Life* (New York: Random House, 1994). A very literate and revealing account of Vermont's first woman governor.

Alan Rosenthal, *Governors & Legislatures: Contending Powers* (Washington, D.C.: CQ Press, 1990). A very readable book by a seasoned observer of state politics. An examination of the dynamics between governors and legislatures, showing how improvements in both have led to increased conflict between the branches.

Larry Sabato, *Goodbye to Good-time Charlie,* 2nd ed. (Washington, D.C.: CQ Press, 1983). An update of Schlesinger's classic study, this work argues that the caliber of governors has improved tremendously. Focuses on gubernatorial careers: backgrounds, electoral opportunities, and the pathway to the presidency.

✧ NOTES

1. Larry Sabato, *Goodbye to Good-time Charlie,* 2nd ed. (Washington, D.C.: CQ Press, 1983), p. 9.
2. Terry Sanford, *Storm Over the States* (New York: McGraw Hill, 1967).
3. Sabato, *Goodbye to Good-time Charlie,* p. 2.
4. *Ibid.,* p. 26.
5. Madeleine M. Kunin, *Living a Political Life* (New York: Random House, 1994), p. 11.
6. Lee Sigelman and Roland Smith, "Personal, Office and State Characteristics as Predictors of Gubernatorial Performance," *Journal of Politics,* 43 (February 1981), 169–180.
7. Joseph A. Schlesinger, *Ambition and Politics* (Chicago: Rand McNally, 1966).
8. Thad Beyle, "Governors," in Virginia Gray and Herbert Jacob, eds., *Politics in the American States,* 6th ed. (Washington, D.C.: CQ Press, 1996), Table 6.1.
9. *Ibid.*
10. Dick Kirschten, "Hillside to Stateside," *National Journal* (February 17, 1990), 372–378.

11. Peverill Squire, "Challenger Profile and Gubernatorial Elections," *Western Political Quarterly,* 45 (March 1992), 130.

12. Schlesinger, *Ambition and Politics,* pp. 48–49.

13. Samuel C. Patterson, "Campaign Spending in Contests for Governor," *Western Political Quarterly,* 35 (December 1982), 457–477.

14. Keon S. Chi, "Trends in Executive Reorganization," *Journal of State Government,* 65 (April/June 1992), 33–40.

15. Thad L. Beyle and Robert Dalton, "Appointment Power: Does It Belong to the Governor?," *State Government,* 54, no. 1 (1981), 7.

16. Nelson C. Dometrius, "Some Consequences of State Reform," *State Government,* 54, no. 3 (1981), 94.

17. Peter Eichstaedt, "No, Two Hundred Times No," *State Legislatures* (July/August 1995), 46–49.

18. Thad L. Beyle, "The Governors, 1986–87," in *The Book of the States, 1988–89* (Lexington, Ky.: Council of State Governments, 1988), p. 30.

19. *Ibid.*

20. One study demonstrates that it is the interaction of formal and informal powers that produces influence over state administrative agencies; see Lee Sigelman and Nelson C. Dometrius, "Governors as Chief Administrators: The Linkage Between Formal Powers and Informal Influence," *American Politics Quarterly,* 16 (April 1988), 157–170.

21. Alan Rosenthal, *Governors & Legislatures: Contending Powers* (Washington, D.C.: CQ Press, 1990), p. 5.

22. *Ibid.,* p. 35.

23. Richard C. Kearney, "How a 'Weak' Governor Can Be Strong: Dick Riley and Education Reform in South Carolina," *Journal of State Government,* 60 (July/August 1987), 150–156.

24. Beyle, "Governors," Table 6.10.

25. *The Book of the States 1994–95, Vol. 30* (Lexington, Ky.: Council of State Governments, 1994), p. 84; Thad L. Beyle and Nelson C. Dometrius, "Governors and Lieutenant Governors," in Thad L. Beyle and Lynn R. Muchmore, eds., *Being Governor: The View from the Office* (Durham, N.C.: Duke University Press, 1983), pp. 144–156.

26. Michael Barone and Grant Ujifusa, *The Almanac of American Politics 1994* (Washington, D.C.: National Journal, Inc., 1994), p. 1362.

27. Chi, "Trends in Executive Reorganization," p. 34.

28. James K. Conant, "Executive Branch Reorganization: Can It Be an Antidote for Fiscal Stress in the States?," *State and Local Government Review,* 24 (Winter 1992), 3–11.

29. Thad L. Beyle, "Governors' Offices: Variations on Common Themes," in Beyle and Muchmore, eds., *Being Governor,* 158–173.

30. Sarah M. Morehouse, "Legislative Party Voting for the Governor's Program," paper delivered at the annual meeting of the American Political Science Association, Chicago, September 1992.

31. Kunin, *Living a Political Life,* p. 381.

32. Thad L. Beyle and Lynn R. Muchmore, "The Governor and the Public," in Beyle and Muchmore, eds., *Being Governor,* p. 53.

33. Eric B. Herzik, "Policy Agendas and Gubernatorial Leadership," in Eric B. Herzik and Brent W. Brown, eds., *Gubernatorial Leadership and State Policy* (New York: Greenwood Press, 1991), pp. 24–37; Eric B. Herzik, "Governors and Issues: A Typology of Concerns," *State Government,* 56, no. 2 (1983), 58–64.

34. Alan D. Monroe, George C. Kiser, and Anthony J. Walesby, "Comparing the State of the States," paper delivered at the annual meeting of the Midwest Political Science Association, Chicago, April 1991, p. 6.

35. Thad L. Beyle and Robert Dalton, "The Governor and the State Legislature," in Beyle and Muchmore, eds., *Being Governor*, p. 126.

36. Beyle, "Governors," p. 241.

37. Rosenthal, *Governors & Legislatures*, 113.

38. Lynn R. Muchmore, "The Governor as Manager," in Beyle and Muchmore, eds., *Being Governor*, pp. 78–84.

39. Glenn Abney and Thomas P. Lauth, *The Politics of State and City Administration* (Albany: State University of New York Press, 1986), 47.

40. Beyle and Muchmore, "The Governor and the Public," p. 53.

41. Dennis O. Grady, "American Governors and State–Federal Relations," *State Government*, 57, no. 3 (1984), 106–112.

42. Dennis O. Grady, "Gubernatorial Behavior in State–Federal Relations," *Western Political Quarterly*, 40 (June 1987), 305–318.

43. Thad L. Beyle, "Governors' Views on Being Governor," in Beyle and Muchmore, eds., *Being Governor*, p. 24.

44. Thad L. Beyle, "The Governors, 1992–93," in *Book of the States, 1994–95, Vol. 30* (Lexington, Ky.: Council of State Governments, 1994), pp. 36–37.

45. Beyle, "The Governors, 1992–93," pp. 36–37.

46. Beyle, "Governors," pp. 248–249; other analysis shows that increases in the sales tax make more difference to the voters than do increases in the income tax; see Susan L. Kone and Richard F. Winters, "Taxes and Voting: Electoral Retribution in the American States," *Journal of Politics*, 55 (February 1993), 22–40.

47. Craig J. Svoboda, "Retrospective Voting in Gubernatorial Elections: 1982 and 1986," *Political Research Quarterly*, 48 (March 1995), 117–134. Similar results are reported by Randall W. Partin, "Economic Conditions and Gubernatorial Elections: Is the State Executive Held Accountable?," *American Politics Quarterly*, 23 (January 1995): 81–95; Susan E. Howell and James M. Vanderleeuw, "Economic Effects on State Governors," *American Politics Quarterly*, 18 (April 1990), 158–168; Richard G. Niemi, Harold W. Stanley, and Ronald J. Vogel, "State Economies and State Taxes: Do Voters Hold Governors Accountable?," *American Journal of Political Science*, 39 (November 1995), 936–957. Leyden and Borrelli found that unified party control intensifies the economic effect on voting; see Kevin M. Leyden and Stephen A. Borrelli, "The Effect of State Economic Conditions on Gubernatorial Elections: Does Unified Government Make a Difference?," *Political Research Quarterly*, 48 (June 1995), 275–290.

48. Mark E. Tompkins, "The Electoral Fortunes of Gubernatorial Incumbents: 1947–1981," *Journal of Politics*, 46 (May 1984), 520–543; William W. Lammers and David Klingman, "Durable Governors as Political Leaders: Should We Limit Tenure?," *Publius*, 16 (Spring 1986), 53–72.

49. Sabato, *Goodbye to Good-time Charlie*, p. 46.

50. Ellen Hoffman, "Reform's Second Wave," *National Journal* (September 13, 1986), 2165.

51. "News/Trends," *Fortune* (November 23, 1987), 15.

52. Douglas Seay and Wesley Smith, "Free Trade's Forgotten Amigos," *Policy Review*, 65 (Summer 1993), p. 60.

THE BUREAUCRACY

The "fourth branch" of government is the **bureaucracy;** the term *fourth* suggests that the power of the bureaucracy is comparable to that of the traditional three branches of government. In this chapter we consider the growth of state bureaucracies, challenges to the bureaucratic model, and bureaucrats' relations with other branches of government.

First, we need to define some terms. In common parlance *bureaucratic* often means impersonal and harsh, bureaucrats are lazy and incompetent government employees, and bureaucracies are the targets of attack. But these terms actually have rather precise meanings: Bureaucrats are employees of organizations organized in a bureaucratic fashion. That is, they work in organizations characterized by hierarchy of position, specialization of function, formalization of rules, and employment on the basis of merit. Bureaucratic positions are organized in a pyramid with a chain of command—there is a well-defined division of labor, processes and procedures are specified in detailed rules (known as red tape), and employees are hired on the basis of their technical expertise. Some contrasting organizational forms are familial (employees are hired because they are members of a family), nonhierarchical (everyone has an equal say in running the organization, as in Bill Clinton's presidential staff), and **patronage** (people are hired on the basis of who they know).

Bureaucratic organizations have arisen in modern times as an efficient way to structure large organizations; small organizations may continue to operate on a more freewheeling basis. Thus, bureaucracies can be found in both the private and public sectors (such as the Catholic Church, hospitals, corporations, and your universities), as well as government agencies such as the Agriculture Department and the Environmental Protection Agency. Bureaucracies have emerged in state government because states are large entities that have complex responsibilities to carry out. Because nearly every unit of state government is a bureaucracy, the term *state bureaucrat* is synonymous with *state employee* or *civil servant*. Even though state bureaucracies are subject to frequent criticism, they are and will continue to be the dominant organizational structure.

It may not be immediately apparent why bureaucracies are important enough to be considered a fourth branch of government. Legislatures and governors make the laws; bureaucrats administer them. This means that the quality of government programs depends on the caliber of the people administering the program. Whether a gun control law actually deters violent crime depends on the skill and vigor of the police. How the

State and local bureaucrats do everything from A to Z. Here, a zookeeper performs her job at the Central Park Zoo in New York City. (*Source:* © Robert Brennhan/ Photo Edit)

government service is delivered matters in another way. Citizens' perceptions of government are influenced by their interactions with bureaucrats; ultimately their satisfaction with government is affected by how bureaucrats treat them. Welfare recipients often complain that they are treated in a dehumanizing and patronizing manner by lower-level personnel, for example. Such treatment may reduce their attachment to the political system and may lower their self-esteem. The administration of policy affects what policy is delivered and how it is delivered. In addition, bureaucrats influence the formulation of policy because they possess expertise that elected officials don't have. Higher-level bureaucrats propose new policy initiatives that are adopted by state legislators; they outline new ways of delivering services. In all stages of the policy process, bureaucrats play a role that may be equivalent in importance to that of the other three branches of government.

✧ STATE GOVERNMENT EMPLOYMENT

In 1992 state governments employed nearly 4.6 million workers, or about one-quarter of all government employees in the country. The federal government (civilian only) workforce was smaller, constituting 16 percent of the total, and local government employment was larger, constituting 59 percent of the total.[1] Table 7.1 displays the states ranked with respect to the number of state government employees; the table also reports the number of employees per 10,000 residents.

Several factors should be kept in mind when reading this table. Although more populous states employ more workers, the ratio of employees to residents is lower in the larger states, reflecting economies of scale. For example, California employs the most workers, 321,860, but has the lowest ratio of employees per 10,000 residents, 104. Alaska, on the other hand, is well-endowed with bureaucrats: It has 413 employees per 10,000 citizens. The division of responsibilities between local and state governments also affects state employment patterns. In general, the poorer, smaller, and southern states rely more heavily on the state level of government, whereas in other states local government is used more extensively. So the states with centralization of services at the state level tend to have higher staffing levels. Finally, more than 40 percent of state government workers are employed in higher education. Thus, states that make more extensive use of public higher education, as in the Midwest, have proportionately more state employees than states that rely on private universities, as in the Northeast.

In the past ten years, the state government workforce has grown by a little over 2 percent each year, reflecting the expansion of state government responsibilities. The growth tends to be concentrated in certain areas of state government, notably in the corrections field. The number of correctional employees increased by nearly 90 percent in the decade from 1982–1992, reflecting the growth of correctional facilities.[2]

The pay of state government employees is periodically a topic of concern, with many citizens arguing that state workers are overpaid. But available data suggest that lower-level state employees are paid about as well as comparable private sector employees and middle and upper-level state bureaucrats lag behind the private sector by as much as 25 percent.[3] In addition to wages, state employees receive fringe benefits such as health insurance, vacation and sick leave, and pensions after retirement, all of which tend to be relatively generous, and perhaps more important, secure. Access to health insurance, for example, is not guaranteed in the private sector; also, companies that go out of business may not pay benefits to former employees. State jobs are more secure than most private sector jobs because the civil service system makes it difficult to dismiss employees. Lengthy hearings and procedures are required to fire incompetent workers, so relatively few are let go. Unlike private companies, state governments do not go out of business, although in recent years there has been downsizing of the workforce in several states. In such circumstances, senior employees can usually bump or replace less senior employees.

Finally, the demographic makeup (race, age, and gender) of the bureaucracy is a concern. Advocates of **representative bureaucracy** argue that the bureaucracy should mirror the population it serves. They believe that the social characteristics of bureaucrats affect how they deliver programs and interact with clients; therefore, the deliverers of services should be a heterogenous group of people. Social workers operating in minority communities, for example, should not be all white. Moreover, some argue that bureaucratic posi-

TABLE 7.1 THE NUMBER OF FULL-TIME STATE GOVERNMENT EMPLOYEES RANKED BY NUMBER OF EMPLOYEES, 1992 The most populous states tend to employ the largest number of bureaucrats, though their ratios of employees to citizens are relatively low compared to ratios in smaller states.

Rank	State	Number	Number per 10,000 Population
1	California	321,860	104
2	New York	267,429	148
3	Texas	239,702	136
4	Florida	164,501	122
5	Pennsylvania	143,438	119
6	Ohio	140,305	127
7	Michigan	137,853	146
8	Illinois	136,623	117
9	Virginia	115,817	182
10	New Jersey	115,770	149
11	Georgia	114,464	170
12	North Carolina	109,046	159
13	Washington	98,016	191
14	Indiana	95,157	168
15	Louisiana	88,767	207
16	Massachusetts	84,983	142
17	Maryland	82,072	167
18	Alabama	81,101	196
19	South Carolina	77,754	216
20	Kentucky	76,254	203
21	Tennessee	75,930	151
22	Missouri	74,049	143
23	Wisconsin	72,674	145
24	Minnesota	67,332	150
25	Oklahoma	67,071	209

tions can serve as an avenue for social advancement and that government has a special obligation to promote advancement. They argue that a certain proportion of positions should be set aside for members of minority or disadvantaged groups, that is, principles of affirmative action should be followed. Others argue that the merit system means just that: Merit should be the only basis on which people are hired and promoted. Any departure from merit compromises the quality of the bureaucracy, and the people deserve the best government they can get.

Available data show that the proportion of female and black state employees exceeds their percentage in the overall labor force.[4] Women constituted 49 percent of the state workforce in 1989, African Americans made up 18 percent, and other ethnic minorities made up 7 percent. However, the concentration of women and minorities shrinks as one goes higher in the job hierarchy; at the top ranks of state employment, women and minorities are underrepresented. For example, the most recent survey of state agency heads conducted in 1988 found that 17 percent of agency chiefs were female and 8.3 per-

TABLE 7.1   (CONTINUED)

Rank	State	Number	Number per 10,000 Population
26	Connecticut	54,154	165
27	Arizona	54,064	141
28	Colorado	53,004	143
29	Hawaii	50,657	437
30	Oregon	49,704	167
31	Kansas	47,882	190
32	Mississippi	47,433	181
33	Iowa	47,354	168
34	Arkansas	46,596	194
35	New Mexico	42,159	267
36	Utah	39,618	219
37	West Virginia	33,597	185
38	Nebraska	28,746	179
39	Alaska	24,246	413
40	Maine	22,006	178
41	Idaho	20,250	190
42	Delaware	20,179	293
43	Rhode Island	19,890	198
44	Nevada	19,142	144
45	Montana	17,095	207
46	North Dakota	16,468	259
47	New Hampshire	16,296	147
48	South Dakota	13,517	151
49	Vermont	12,923	227
50	Wyoming	11,274	242

Source: The Book of the States, 1994–95 (Lexington, Ky.: Council of State Governments, 1994), p. 442. Copyright 1994–95 The Council of State Governments. Reprinted with permission from *Book of the States.*

cent were minorities.[5] These percentages have increased over time but still are undesirable from the perspective of representative bureaucracy.

Female employees tend to be concentrated in certain state agencies such as libraries or social services, and in certain job classifications such as secretary. Similarly, minorities are concentrated in particular agencies such as corrections. This tendency for certain tasks to be stereotyped by gender or race is referred to as occupational segregation. Occupational segregation has been most worrisome in regard to gender because it leads to lower pay scales in agencies and job classifications dominated by women. Occupational segregation by gender is so extensive that women earn less than men on average. For example, a 1990 six-state study showed a gender difference for annual salaries of full-time employees in every state, ranging from a $1,771 gender gap in Alabama to $9,764 in California.[6] These differentials had increased since 1980.

In the early 1980s, advocates of **comparable worth** argued that equal pay (paying the same salary for employees performing identical jobs) was not enough. They argued that jobs that require comparable skill, experience, and knowledge must offer the same salary, controlling for seniority, merit, and other relevant criteria. The classic example was that nurses, a female-dominated occupation, should earn the same as tree trimmers, a male-dominated occupation, because the amount of responsibility and risk was comparable. Because state bureaucracies have a job classification scheme that describes each job in great detail, it is relatively easy to assign a score to each position, thereby establishing their equivalence.

When the state of Minnesota went through this assessment process in 1982 (see Box 7.1), it found that all female-dominated job classifications were paid less than comparable jobs dominated by males. The state set about to rectify the situation, allocating $22 million, or 3.7 percent of its salary base, to equalizing pay. In the state of Washington a study found that employees in female-dominated areas were paid about 20 percent less

BOX 7.1 PAY EQUITY IN MINNESOTA

In the early 1980s, Minnesota became the first state to adopt and implement a comparable worth policy for government employees. The state legislature passed the State Employees Pay Equity Act in 1982, which instituted a comparable worth policy for state employees. Two years later, the state extended the pay equity policy to Minnesota localities.

For advocates in Minnesota and elsewhere, the issue behind comparable worth was the income gap between men and women and, to a lesser extent, between minorities and nonminorities. During the 1970s, women as a group earned two-thirds of what men did. Receiving equal pay for equal work was not the only issue in the debate, however. Women often found themselves segregated into low-paying jobs. Census data from 1980 indicated that more than two-thirds of members of each sex worked in jobs dominated by members of the same sex.[1] This job segregation was evident in Minnesota: 97.8 percent of clerk-typist 1s were female, and 99.9 percent of senior highway maintenance workers were male. Before the state adopted its comparable worth policy, female state employees earned 20 percent less than males in similar level jobs.

In order to equalize men's and women's pay scales, Minnesota had to use a job eval-

uation system. Several years before adopting comparable worth, the state had already completed a job evaluation that facilitated instituting pay equity. The state used a point system developed by Hay Associates to rank state employee jobs. For example, correctional counselor 2 (a male job) was assigned 188 Hay points and licensed practical nurse 2 was assigned 183 points, indicating roughly comparable jobs. Unlike most other states, Minnesota used the salary levels of male-dominated jobs as a standard with which to compare the salary levels of female-dominated jobs. It then raised females' salaries to the level of the males, rather than lowering males. In our example, nurses who made $1,382 per month were raised to the level of counselors at $1,656 a month.

Although individual state employees might not have noticed large increases in their paychecks, the policy's impact on the pay scale was quite significant. By 1987, more than 8,500 employees had received pay equity raises. Most of those receiving the raises were in female-dominated health care and clerical positions.

[1]Data in this box are taken from Sara M. Evans and Barbara J. Nelson, *Wage Justice: Comparable Worth and the Paradox of Technocratic Reform* (Chicago: University of Chicago Press, 1989).

than those in male-dominated areas for doing comparable jobs.[7] At least 20 states have followed the lead of Minnesota and Washington in erasing sex-based (or race-based) pay differentials.[8] Generally, these are states where collective bargaining is strong.

✧   FROM PATRONAGE TO MERIT

In the 1800s most government positions, state and national alike, were filled through the patronage system, that is, on the basis of who you know (your patron) rather than what you know. The patronage system is also called the spoils system because those elected to office get to distribute the spoils of office such as jobs and contracts to their friends. Under such a system, government jobs are awarded on the basis of who you voted for, whose campaign you contributed to, or whose friend or relative you are. When employees are selected on the grounds of these criteria, merit and competence suffer. By the end of the Civil War, the pattern of incompetent public employees led to substantial citizen dissatisfaction with government.

Following the assassination of President James Garfield by a man seeking appointment to office, Congress passed the Pendleton Act in 1883. This act set up a Civil Service Commission, independent of elected officials and political parties, to select federal employees on the basis of merit, not patronage. In the same year New York became the first state to enact a merit system for filling its jobs; Massachusetts followed suit the next year. For about 20 years thereafter, these were the only two states to adopt merit criteria. But after 1900, the merit system gradually spread throughout state governments, gaining an important impetus in 1939 when Congress required that states receiving federal welfare funds had to staff their welfare agencies on the merit principle. In the 1940s, nine states added merit coverage.

Today about three-quarters of the states have comprehensive merit systems that include virtually all employees and the rest of the states have more limited coverage, typically in agencies where the federal government requires merit coverage. The comprehensive merit systems typically include all bureaucratic positions except the very top level jobs in a department. Generally, the governor appoints the agency head, who in turn appoints his or her immediate assistants, such as assistant commissioners or deputy directors. Then the rest of the department's positions are classified as civil service positions and appointed according to merit.

As we noted earlier in this chapter, modern bureaucracies fill their positions through the merit system. In practice, this means that a job description and salary range are drawn up for each job to be filled. Potential employees take a civil service test that assesses their skills, aptitude, and competence for the open position. The employer is obliged to pick an employee from among those scoring highest on the test, typically from among the top three applicants. In this way, the best person is chosen for each job. One compromise to this merit-based system is to provide preference to veterans (that is, to add a certain number of points to their test score). This practice, used in all 50 states, disadvantages women.[9] Once a person has passed a probationary period of service, he or she is protected from arbitrary dismissal. This civil service protection means that a new governor cannot fire a bunch of state bureaucrats and replace them with his or her friends, even if the friends score high on the civil service test.

Of course, people find ways to subvert the merit principle or to adapt it to their political desires. Some states' merit systems look better on paper than they do in practice.

Perhaps the most egregious example was in Illinois, where nearly all employees had been under a civil service system since 1955 but patronage still flourished. Particularly during the 14-year reign of Governor Jim Thompson, very little hiring took place without a political patron or a referral from a party person.[10] A dissatisfied job-seeker who did not have the approval of her county Republican chairman sued the state. The case eventually reached the U.S. Supreme Court (see Box 7.2), which ruled in 1990 that hiring and promotion decisions based on party affiliation are an impermissible infringement of First Amendment rights (*Rutan v. Republican Party of Illinois*, 497 U.S. 62). This ruling has meant a sea change in Illinois government and to a lesser extent in some other states. In Illinois they have had to learn how to hire employees because "nobody knew how to do it on merit."[11] Perhaps we will finally see an end to political patronage and a full embrace of the merit system.

Besides the shadow of the patronage system, there is another challenge to the merit system: unionization. As Bowman and Kearney put it, "Public employee unions present a potentially serious threat to the merit principle. They usually insist on seniority as the primary criterion in personnel decisions; they often seek to effect changes in merit system rules and procedures; and they regularly challenge management authority."[12] Unionization in state government developed in the 1960s and 1970s; today about three-quarters of the states allow some form of collective bargaining between workers and managers.

Although 40 percent of state employees belong to a union or other employee organization, the extent of unionization varies a lot around the country. Public sector unionization is not a factor in most southern or western mountain states, whereas in 20 states more than 70 percent of the state workforce is covered by union contracts. These tend to be states where private sector unions are also strong, such as Michigan, Minnesota, New York, and Ohio. However, the fiscal stringencies of the 1980s and 1990s have made the environment for unions less hospitable. The growth of union membership has leveled off, and no states are adding new bargaining rights for their employees.

Unions and civil service procedures coexist comfortably in some states and uncomfortably in others. Unions place more emphasis on seniority as a hiring rule whereas the civil service system stresses merit. Both are opposed to patronage hiring and political firing. Unions also contest a range of personnel issues with management and sometimes manage to get civil service procedures and rules changed. Perhaps the greatest potential impact of unions is on wages and benefits, but even there the actual effect has not been as great as predicted. Unionized employees seem to earn between 4 and 8 percent more than nonunionized peers.[13] But they have secured at the bargaining table relatively generous benefits such as health insurance and pensions. In the 1990s, however, unions have had to give up pay increases in order to save state jobs; fiscal stringency has affected unionized and nonunionized employees alike.

Despite the vestiges of the patronage system and the overlay of unionization, the civil service system remains the dominant way of hiring bureaucrats. But even people who support this system acknowledge its problems and are attempting to address them. Sometimes hiring practices are so complex and slow that competent potential employees get discouraged and go elsewhere. Moreover, civil service rules make it very difficult to fire employees who are not doing their jobs. In a recent survey of state administrators, Richard Elling found these two problems listed among the five most serious problems hindering

BOX 7.2 POLITICAL PATRONAGE IN ILLINOIS

In recent decades, many states have moved away from overt partisan considerations in hiring public employees, but in Illinois, the patronage system continued to be as strong and elaborate as ever during the 1980s. In rural areas of Illinois, many state highway trucks carried materials from the local party organizations instead of road salt. State employees in these areas would often put up campaign signs during their work day.[1] This patronage system hummed along until the *Rutan v. Republican Party of Illinois* decision issued by the U.S. Supreme Court in 1990.

One of the main architects of the Illinois patronage system was 14-year governor Jim Thompson, a Republican, who hoped to use the system to gain control of the state's bureaucracy. In 1980, Thompson instituted a hiring freeze for government offices. Although the freeze was designed to save the state money, Thompson used the freeze to his political advantage. The state could still hire and promote employees under the freeze, but the governor's personnel office had to approve the actions. For the most part, Republicans reaped the spoils of the patronage system, but because Democrats controlled the legislature, they also received some of its benefits.[2]

Although party affiliation had little to do with actual job performance, it was a major factor in hiring and promotion. During the freeze, the state hired few nonparty referrals.[3] The Republican party in Sangamon County, where the state capital is located, distributed state employee applications with Sangamon County Republican party applications attached. Many of those who applied were encouraged to work for and contribute to local Republican party organizations.

These hiring practices greatly affected many parts of the state's workforce. For example, more than 90 percent of employees at one correctional facility in Illinois had voted Republican in a recent primary.[4]

These practices continued until Cynthia Rutan, a state employee denied a promotion on the basis of her political affiliation, took the state Republican party to court and won. Before leaving office in 1990, Gov. Thompson issued an order prohibiting inquiry into a job candidate's political affiliation in order to comply with the United States Supreme Court decision. Thompson's successor, Republican Jim Edgar, lifted the hiring freeze in 1991. Although Illinois has taken steps away from overt patronage, some have expressed doubts about leaving patronage behind. Shortly after the *Rutan* decision, Sangamon Country Republican Chair Irv Smith said, "I don't think they can take the politics out of government."[5] In 1996 when a suit was filed against a Chicago suburb for practicing patronage, Governor Edgar filed an amicus curia brief asking the Supreme Court to reverse its ban on government favoritism. He argued that patronage actually helps the democratic process.[6]

---

[1]Jeffrey L. Katz, "The Slow Death of Political Patronage," *Governing* (April 1991), 60.

[2]*Ibid.*, pp. 60–61.

[3]David K. Hamilton, "The Staffing Function in Illinois State Government after *Rutan*," *Public Administration Review*, 53 (July/August 1993), 382.

[4]Katz, "The Slow Death of Political Patronage," pp. 61–62.

[5]*Ibid.*, p. 62.

[6]Dirk Johnson, "A Plea to Return to Days of Political Patronage, *New York Times* (March 13, 1996), A9.

bureaucratic performance; approximately one-third of the managers responding to the survey reported hiring and firing to be serious problems.[14]

In recent years many states have streamlined their dismissal and disciplinary procedures. Nearly every state has transferred personnel management responsibilities from an independent civil service commission to a central personnel agency, often headed by a gubernatorial appointee. Twelve states have joined the federal government in creating a senior executive service; employees in this classification earn more money, often awarded on a performance basis, but can be removed by the governor for poor performance on the job. Half of the states have increased the number of top managers, typically those involved in policymaking, who are exempt from the civil service; they are appointed by the governor. All of these reforms are aimed at improving bureaucracy's responsiveness to the public but in the wrong hands they may instead politicize the bureaucracy.

The other major reform effort is aimed at improving bureaucratic performance through reorganization. As already described in Chapter 6, about half of the states undertook significant restructuring of their state bureaucracies in the past 25 years. States reduced the number of separate agencies from 100 or so to a manageable number; this was accomplished by consolidating agencies into broad functional areas such as human services and transportation. Figure 7.1 displays the results of a recent reorganization in South Carolina. Another reform was to eliminate independent boards and commissions with separately elected heads; these administrators were made subject to gubernatorial appointment also. Most scholars believe that reorganization has made

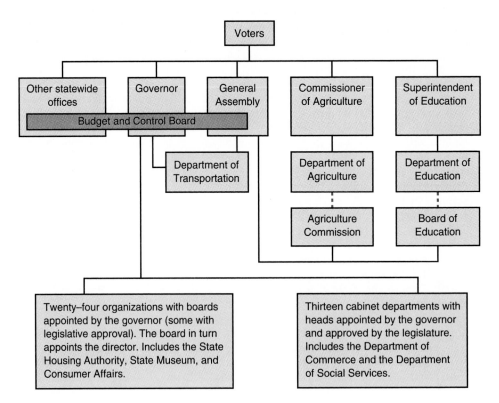

FIGURE 7.1 The South Carolina Bureaucracy. Many states have streamlined their bureaucracy; this figure shows the organization chart of South Carolina, the most recent example of restructuring.

Source: "A simpler more accountable government," *Restructuring: The players and the politics,* a special reprint of stories appearing in *The State,* (1993), 16.

agencies more accountable, especially to the governor, and more effective in performance but not less costly.

✧ THE POSTBUREAUCRATIC AGE?

Some argue that tinkering with the merit system or reorganizing state agencies is not enough. Some reformers believe that bureaucracy is outmoded and can no longer serve the public interest in a postindustrial society.[15] They advocate nothing short of a revolution in their call for **reinventing government.** The most well-known advocates of this perspective are David Osborne and Ted Gaebler, whose 1992 book *Reinventing Government* ignited a great debate over the future of bureaucracy.[16]

Osborne and Gaebler argue that government must be more entrepreneurial, more customer-focused, and more competitive. They assert that governments must separate "steering" (making policy decisions) from "rowing" (service delivery). They envision that government will determine what services will be provided and how they will be paid for but the actual work might be done by government bureaucrats or outside vendors. The work product is then evaluated by government. The state agency would have to compete against a private firm for the contract to do the work. The most cost-effective organization that provides value to the customer would get the contract. If public bureaucracies can't compete on this basis, they would go out of business. Box 7.3 summarizes the key points of their argument for entrepreneurial government.

Osborne and Gaebler have given the catchy title *reinventing government* to a **privatization** movement that has been going on in state government for 20 years. States have long used private contractors to build highways. Now they have added contracting out for building maintenance, clerical services, security services, day care, adoption and foster care, child support enforcement, drug and alcohol abuse treatment, employee training and placement, mental health services, correctional institutions, and medical claims.[17] Contracting out is usually tried when alternative providers can deliver services more cheaply or of higher quality than government bureaucracies. Contracting out often saves money because of wage differentials: Public employees are likely to be unionized and earning higher wages and fringe benefits than private employees, who are more likely to be nonunionized.[18] Contracting is also used when the job to be performed is for a limited time period; contracted employees can be let go when the job is over, whereas bureaucrats are hard to fire, for the reasons described earlier. Determining whether a contracted service is actually cheaper is difficult because you have to factor in the cost of monitoring contractor performance.

A few cities are even contracting out their public school systems: The schools in Minneapolis, Baltimore, and Hartford have been run by consulting firms. Both Connecticut and Minnesota are leaders among the states in privatization. Minnesota's journey began in 1983 when Democratic Governor Rudy Perpich unleashed significant experimentation with staff functions such as internal services, purchasing, staffing, and information systems.[19] Instead of being provided by internal monopoly suppliers, these functions were fulfilled by competing providers. Connecticut's experiments are more recent, beginning with independent Governor Lowell Weicker's election in 1990. Weicker's goal was debureaucratization, or changing the administrative culture to focus more on the customer, as well as downsizing government.[20] He introduced **Total Quality Management** (TQM) to his state, which is a private sector approach to improving the

BOX 7.3 THE PRINCIPLES OF ENTREPRENEURIAL GOVERNMENT

The bureaucratic system of government is unwieldy, inflexible, unresponsive, and wasteful according to David Osborne and Ted Gaebler. In *Reinventing Government,* the two argue that the answer is not to do away with government, but to alter it radically. They offer ten principles they believe will strengthen American communities and make American government better able to deal with issues such as education, crime, housing, and poverty. The principles of "entrepreneurial government" are:

✦ *"Catalytic Government: Steering Rather than Rowing"* Instead of simply providing services, entrepreneurial governments actively shape communities. They do not hire more employees, but ensure that other institutions function properly.

✦ *"Community-Owned Government: Empowering Rather Than Serving"* Entrepreneurial governments encourage communities to take charge of services because communities are more

committed to their members, more creative, and cheaper than service professionals.

✦ *"Competitive Government: Injecting Competition into Service Delivery"* Entrepreneurial governments foster competition between private companies who provide public services and between governmental units and agencies in order to decrease costs and encourage responsiveness and innovation.

✦ *"Mission-Driven Government: Transforming Rule-Driven Organizations"* Rather than letting budgets and rules determine actions, entrepreneurial governments first define their goals, and then their budgets. These organizations free their employees to pursue the agency's missions.

✦ *"Results-Oriented Government: Funding Outcomes, Not Inputs"* Entrepreneurial governments create ways of measuring performance and reward success. As

quality of service delivery. TQM has been introduced in numerous other government jurisdictions as well, but so recently that its payoff is uncertain.

Most people don't expect bureaucracy to wither away entirely, but these experiments are taking hold in a variety of governments from cities to states to Washington, D.C. There is a pervasive feeling that government must change because citizen dissatisfaction is so strong. Because bureaucracy *is* the government to many people, it must change or at least adapt to the new realities. One key to how reinvention will proceed is the response of public sector union leaders to the new initiatives. There are indications that union leaders around the country are taking a conciliatory posture, trying to be partners in redesigning government rather than just reacting angrily.[21]

✦ BUREAUCRATIC PERFORMANCE

Implicit in the traditional concept of the bureaucracy is a dichotomy between administration and politics. Trained professionals with job security administer policy while the elected officials set up the agencies, authorize their programs, and allocate the money for those tasks. Administration was considered to be largely a technical process involving routine decisionmaking. Today we realize that the dichotomy is a false one: Administrators' tech-

governments produce results, public support of them increases.

◇ *"Customer-Driven Government: Meeting the Needs of the Customer, Not the Bureaucracy"* In an entrepreneurial system, public services put money into the hands of consumers and let consumers decide what they need. Entrepreneurial governments conduct community surveys and hold customer training sessions for their employees.

◇ *"Government: Earning Rather than Spending"* Entrepreneurial governments make profits from services that benefit individuals such as golf courses and tennis courts by charging user fees and investing for a return.

◇ *"Anticipatory Government: Prevention Rather than Cure"* Entrepreneurial governments do not only react to problems. They create a means of decisionmaking that anticipates and addresses problems before they become crises. The governments utilize futures commissions who analyze trends and develop alternative scenarios, formulate long-term budgets, and create contingency funds.

◇ *"Decentralized Government: From Hierarchy to Participation and Teamwork"* Entrepreneurial leaders hand over decisionmaking powers to individuals, communities, and private organizations. Decentralized organizations generate higher morale and are more flexible.

◇ *"Market Oriented Government: Leveraging Change Through the Market"* Entrepreneurial governments restructure the market of the public sector by changing the incentives of customers and employees. These governments embrace communities to remedy the impersonal nature of markets.

Source: David Osborne and Ted Gaebler, *Reinventing Government: How the Entrepreneurial Spirit is Transforming the Public Sector* (New York: Penguin Books, 1993).

nical decisions have policy ramifications, their expertise puts them in a good position to formulate policy alternatives, and their style of implementation can have negative or positive effects on clients. So much of what bureaucrats do is political in one way or another. Politicians, on the other hand, were loath to surrender administration to the administrators. In earlier times they incorporated political favoritism into patronage appointment. Today they are responding to citizen dissatisfaction by trying to reengineer government. Thus, politicians have breached the dichotomy from the other side.

Bureaucrats' influence in the public policy realm comes first from their specialized knowledge, which allows them to be active in identifying problems and formulating solutions to deal with them. Bureaucrats may notice that reports of child abuse have increased, signaling a problem; they may suggest to legislators that enforcement be strengthened, new criminal penalties be assessed, or preventive social programs aimed at at-risk parents be implemented. The appropriate legislative committee may receive this report and act on it or the bureaucrats may get the ear of a sympathetic legislator who will introduce legislation. But the idea originated with the bureaucrats.

Bureaucrats' influence in shaping policy has been borne out in several studies. For example, Elling surveyed managers in ten states; 72 percent said their agency had great or very great impact in major policy or program changes. In fact, 39 percent of the managers

BOX 7.4 TQM IN THE PUBLIC SECTOR

In this time of fiscal constraints, state governments are forced to develop new ways to manage their operations if they hope to continue current services. Although each state takes a unique course to achieve these goals, the most common technique, used by 26 state governments, is called Total Quality Management (TQM).[1] TQM is a technique that attempts to bring the efficiency of the private sector to government offices. The strategy involves five elements: a commitment to customer-driven quality; participation of employees in quality improvement; use of fact, data, and analysis in decision-making; a commitment to constant improvement; and development of an integrated perspective on services, both means and ends.[2] Many of these elements depart from the normal manner in which bureaucracy operates.

This management philosophy was originally conceived by W. Edwards Deming. Deming argues that only 15 percent of all the quality problems result from the workers directly involved; the remainder result from the broader systems in which the individuals work (the budget system, the personnel system, and so on). Therefore, the entire system must be restructured.[3] The particulars of the restructuring are directed by the workers because they are the ones who best understand how it works; governments using TQM are much more responsive to the public than are most insulated bureaucracies.

States that have implemented TQM strategies cite a variety of reasons for doing so. Gubernatorial initiatives are among the most common reasons; often a newly elected governor will make TQM and reinventing government an important objective of his or her administration. Public complaints are also a common motivating factor. The public in many states is fed up with the inefficient

manner of government, most notably its lack of timeliness and responsiveness. Finally, state agencies themselves have initiated TQM to better manage the resources allocated to them.

Of the 26 states that have implemented TQM in some form, three provide a good demonstration of the complexities of implementing such a strategy: South Carolina, Connecticut, and Florida.

The first state to undergo a shift to TQM was South Carolina. Governor Carroll Campbell made the restructuring of state government the focus of his term in office. Beginning in 1988, Campbell implemented the TQM strategy to help reduce the size of the bureaucracy and save money.[4] In 1990 Campbell made TQM and the restructuring of government his main campaign issue, calling for a mandate from the people about the reforms he proposed. The 70 percent of the vote he received enabled him to carry on with the reforms.

Campbell proposed combining 59 semi-autonomous agencies into 10 state departments whose heads would make up the governor's cabinet. He planned to do away with a series of government positions, merge departments, and shift responsibilities to streamline their operation. In addition, he continued the pressure to empower the workers within the departments and focused their attention on the needs of the customers. In sum, Campbell effectively worked his electoral mandate into massive changes, both in the administrative structure and in the manner in which the agencies operated.

When Connecticut's independent Governor Lowell Weicker entered office in 1990, he faced two major problems: a government ranked 46th in management quality, and a partisan legislature that would make life as difficult as possible for him.[5] Poor management quality was addressed by TQM with a tremendous amount of assistance from the private sector. A pilot program had four of the state's main agencies (transportation, mental retardation, labor, and policy and management) work with Connecticut Fortune 500 firms in an adopt-an-agency program. The business firms acted as mentors to the agencies and provided training to their employees.[6]

Because Weicker was an independent governor, he had to take a low profile in the implementation of the policies to prevent their becoming politicized. This approach actually contributed to the success of TQM. The workers did not perceive TQM as merely a political tool to make a public splash, but realized that the governor was serious about reforming the bureaucracy.

When Lawton Chiles entered office in Florida, his disdain for the manner in which state government operated was clearly evident (recall Box 6.1). Throughout his 1990 campaign, downsizing government was a central theme. To achieve this end, he appointed the Commission for Government by the People to advise him on rightsizing the government. This commission attacked the state bureaucracy as bloated, calling for it to be revamped. Despite a potential budget shortfall, Chiles refused to raise taxes, insisting that the money should instead come from restructuring bureaucracy.

Although the battle over taxes overshadowed the administrative reforms he implemented, Chiles was able to decentralize the bureaucracies of the health and rehabilitative services department and the education system, merge two agencies into the new Department of Management Services, and experiment broadly with most of the others.[7] Overall, through TQM, Chiles was able to address most of the bloated aspects of state government.

The results from the 26 states that have initiated TQM since 1988 seem quite promising. Arizona officials estimate that TQM saved the state $43 million over two years. Although this is an extreme case, evidence from across the country suggests that TQM is an effective way to restructure state governments and save substantial amounts of money.[8] It should be noted, however, that it is too soon to determine the full impact of TQM; many agencies are only in the early stages of implementation and cannot tell how effective it is. Unless TQM is followed through, these results may prove to be short-lived. Only a commitment from the managers of the agencies will make it effective.

[1]Council of State Governments, "TQM Rings Cash Registers for States," *State Trends Bulletin* (February/March 1995), 2.

[2]Evan M. Berman, Jonathan P. West, and Michael E Milakovich, "Implementing TQM in the States," *Spectrum,* 67 (July 1994).

[3]David Osborne and Ted Gaebler, *Reinventing Government: How the Entrepreneurial Spirit Is Transforming the Public Sector* (New York: Penguin Books, 1992), p. 159.

[4]Council of State Governments, "TQM Rings Cash Registers for States," p. 2.

[5]Robert S. Kravchuk, "The 'New Connecticut': Lowell Weicker and the Process of Administrative Reform," *Public Administration Review,* 53 (July/August, 1993), 336.

[6]*Ibid.,* p. 336

[7]Dan Durning, "Governors and Administrative Reform," *State and Local Government Review,* 27 (January 1995), 47.

[8]Council of State Governments, "TQM Rings Cash Registers for States," p. 2.

said half or more of the legislation affecting their agency was initiated by their unit.[22] This was a higher proportion than originated with the governor, the legislature, or interest groups. Although it is possible that managers exaggerate their importance, it seems clear that they play an important role in policy initiation or formulation.

This policy shaping role stems from the increasing professionalism of the state bureaucracy. State governments employ people in nearly every professional category, including librarians, social workers, doctors, lawyers, engineers, teachers, and professors. An increasing number of government workers hold graduate or professional degrees. Among agency heads, 90 percent have college degrees and 60 percent hold graduate degrees.[23] The professional backgrounds of bureaucrats structure how they perceive problems and how they generate solutions. For example, state government reactions to the AIDS crisis were significantly shaped by the outlook of state health departments. They viewed the outbreak as a public health crisis, rather than a moral breakdown of society; their influence with state legislators deflected harsh restrictions on victims such as quarantine.[24]

The relevance of professionalism is demonstrated in a survey of several hundred people who had been responsible for nationally recognized innovative programs in state government. The innovators were well-educated (about half had advanced degrees), were mid-career employees with substantial experience in state government, and were slightly more likely to be permanent bureaucrats rather than appointed administrators (45.6 percent versus 38.8 percent).[25] Most had generated the innovative idea by themselves as part of their day-to-day professional responsibilities. For example, one bureaucrat said, "As we traveled the state making inspections of solid waste disposal sites, local officials kept mentioning that they had a junk vehicle problem and no funds available to solve the problem. We wrote up legislation and circulated it to the cities and counties and motor vehicle facilities for comment. During the next legislative session we had members from these groups available for testimony."[26]

Once a policy is enacted into law, state bureaucrats must interpret the language of the legislation in order to implement it. Because laws are written in very general terms, bureaucrats have a lot of discretionary authority in their interpretations. Their knowledge and expertise put them in the best position to apply the law so that its intent is achieved. They can craft the regulations with more specificity than can legislators, who are busy with many other details and who lack substantive knowledge of the topic.

Agencies follow a set process in promulgating administrative rules: They issue a tentative set of rules, there is a period for public comment and objection, and then the final rules are announced. These have the effect of law. There are checks to ensure that the agency has followed legislative intent. After this stage, agency action is relatively autonomous unless someone complains. For example, a law to limit emissions from cars in urban areas would entail the appropriate agency issuing a rule specifying the level of allowable emissions and how that is measured, a definition of *urban areas*, which motor vehicles must be tested (just old cars or new ones too), where they are to be tested (at a local service station or a state facility created for this purpose), how motorists will be notified of the process, when motorists must conform (before they can get their car licensed), and what happens if your car fails the test (you must get the repairs done within a certain time period). Then there are the inevitable questions such as what happens if you are living in another state when your car tags expire (you can get the tags issued on a provisional basis but must have the test done by a certain date).

Bureaucrats have even more influence in the implementation stage than in the formulation stage. For instance, Elling's study found that 85 percent of managers felt they had great or very great impact on the content of rules and regulations, 90 percent felt they had great impact in establishing administrative procedures, and 95 percent felt the same way about daily administrative operations.[27] This greater influence in administration than in formulation is natural because administration is the main job of the bureaucracy.

Another source of the bureaucracy's influence comes from its relations with interest groups. Most government programs have beneficiaries—welfare clients, farmers receiving price supports, listeners of public radio, and so on—who organize themselves into constituency or client groups. Such groups work with the relevant agency to increase funding for the program or to thwart cuts in tight budgetary years. They can be very influential with the legislature in expanding the agency's purview. Many professions and occupations are regulated by state government so their organizations may seek to reduce the agency's impact on their autonomy. They will try to get agency officials appointed who have a sympathetic view of them and who may wield a soft hand in regulating them.

But groups can help shore up the agency's influence. In a national survey Abney and Lauth found that 65 percent of agency heads said the groups provided valuable information, 50 percent said they aided in passage of legislative program, and 27 percent said they encouraged support by the governor.[28] Overall, agency chiefs find organized interests politically useful to them. However, many people are critical of the cozy relationships between agencies and interest groups, arguing that the agencies are "captured" by groups. But the Abney and Lauth survey reported a different view from agency chiefs: They said that groups encouraged impartiality of rule application more than they discouraged it.

For all these reasons, bureaucrats' activities are not strictly administrative but diverge into the political realm. But note that their power is delegated power: Their professional autonomy can be reined in at any minute by elected officials. The agency can be abolished, its budget can be cut, or its director can fail to be reappointed. If bureaucrats go too far, politicians will move into the administrative realm.

In fact, in recent years there has been an increased demand for bureaucrats to be accountable to elected officials. This demand is reflected in the debureaucratization movement described earlier. As a leading scholar of state bureaucracy notes,

> State bureaucracies have paid a price for their growing importance, and that price is a loss of discretion. In recent years, state bureaucracies have become more permeable, more vulnerable, and more manipulable. They are subject to a growing number of controls, as governors, state legislators, state judges, presidents, members of Congress, federal bureaucrats, interest groups, and citizens all attempt to shape administrative rule making, rate making and adjudication at the state level. Of equal significance, they are subject to tougher, more restrictive, and more coercive controls.[29]

✧ OVERSEERS OF BUREAUCRATIC INFLUENCE

In this section we examine the accountability mechanisms used by governors, legislatures, courts, and the federal government, as well as the public and interest groups. We begin with the governor.

The Governor as Chief Executive

Governors have obvious formal tools of control: They appoint (and remove) department heads, who in turn set the tone for their agency. As mentioned earlier, the central personnel agency is usually under the governor's control. In more than half the states, governors can initiate structural reorganization unless the legislature objects within a certain time period. Often there is a flurry of reorganization at the beginning of a governor's term when governors promise to cut costs and improve services.

The other major instrument of control is the governor's budgetary powers. As mentioned in Chapter 6, nearly every governor has the power to formulate the budget; thus, they can recommend an increase or a decrease in an agency's expenditures. Then the agency has to go to the legislature and fight to get it changed. In practical political terms, often the governor's recommendation sets a ceiling on the eventual appropriation so the initial step is a critical one. The power to initiate the budget is seen by agency officials as the governor's most important tool. In the Abney and Lauth survey, two-thirds of the respondents identified the executive budgetary power as a significant factor, compared to 30 percent who cited the governor's appointive power.[30]

However, the overall gubernatorial power is not as extensive as it looks. In the same survey of state agency heads, 38 percent rated the governor as the most influential actor but 43 percent chose the legislature. The governor was particularly influential in such states as Maryland, New Jersey, Kentucky, and Rhode Island, where 75 percent or more agency chiefs rated the governor as the key actor.[31] The governor was weakest in Iowa, Texas, Arizona, Virginia, Montana, Colorado, and South Carolina, where 15 percent or less rated him or her as most influential. However, the Wright, Yoo, and Cohen national survey produced the opposite finding: Governors were said to exercise the greater control by a 43 percent to 38 percent margin.[32] The conflicting results seem to stem from the fact that gubernatorial influence is more variable than legislative influence because it depends on one person's skills.

Vigorous gubernatorial direction of the bureaucracy is often lacking for several reasons. One is that governors are typically not trained as executives; they do not find directing the bureaucracy very interesting or rewarding. They have many other things to do with their time. This lack of effort makes a difference according to Elling's and other studies, where gubernatorial influence was correlated with frequency of interaction.[33] A second reason for lack of influence is that other actors are contending for custody of the bureaucracy; the legislature may block the governor's efforts to become involved. A third reason is the lack of formal powers of some states' governors. Despite the fact that formal powers have generally increased (see Chapter 6), it is still the case that some governors' powers are relatively weak, and this matters. Texas, for example, was listed in the lowest category of influence, and its governor has weak formal powers. Many boards and commissions remain beyond the governor's appointive control so that he or she has to contend with multiple centers of influence.

Faced with these obstacles, governors tend to pick their spots; that is, they concentrate on a few agencies and ignore the rest. They have to respond to particular crises such as snowstorms and hurricanes. Beyond that, they may focus on the agencies with the biggest budgets or the ones whose programs are near and dear to their hearts. The elections of 1990, however, brought to power a class of governors unusually interested in managing their state government: Campbell, Chiles, and Weicker were described in Box 7.4. If these governors' efforts have political payoffs, then other governors may place more emphasis on managing state government.

The Legislature as Overseer

The legislature rivals and often exceeds the governor in its power to control the bureaucracy. Its control mechanisms include those shared with the governor: approving budget requests, approving reorganizations of agencies, and confirming gubernatorial appointments to top positions. But its oversight is exerted through other exclusive weapons as well: reviewing proposed agency rules, performing legislative audits, passing sunset legislation, holding monitoring hearings, and doing casework (following up on constituent requests). Like the governor's impact, the legislature's impact is correlated with its intensity of interaction with administrative units. Agency chiefs, in fact, reported more frequent interaction with legislators than with governors.[34]

As indicated earlier, the power of the purse is the most powerful weapon of control, and the legislature has the final say in budgetary matters. As will be explained in more detail in Chapter 12, the governor proposes a budget and then it is up to the legislature to review and modify it. Legislators can add, subtract, or eliminate funds, programs, and projects; therefore, bureaucrats spend a great deal of time maintaining good relations with legislators so as to favorably influence their treatment of budgetary requests.

The other powerful legislative weapons, some of which were already mentioned in Chapter 5, lie in areas solely within the legislature's control such as review of administrative rules and regulations before promulgation. Legislators do not fully trust bureaucrats to act as they intended; therefore, four-fifths of the legislatures have some formal means of reviewing proposed regulations; half have the means to prevent them from going into effect.[35] Some use the legislative veto, a procedure whereby the legislature (or a part of it) can invalidate a proposed rule. The legislative veto has been ruled unconstitutional in several states on the grounds that it violates the separation of powers; thus, it may decline in its influence. In general, though, agencies have to take heed of legislative criticism and suggestions about rulemaking; failure to do so will come back to haunt them in the budgetary process.

Legislative auditors are a relatively new tool at the legislature's disposal. Such offices are found in about 40 states; they conduct reviews of ongoing policies and programs by means of performance audits or program evaluations.[36] These are objective, nonpartisan analyses of the extent to which an agency or program is meeting its goals. They can identify problems in implementation, financial malfeasance, or poor management. If the audit's results are used by legislative committees, they can result in program abolition or reorganization, replacement of top personnel, or an increase in appropriations or expansion of program authority, depending on the recommendations contained in the report.

The ultimate form of a performance audit is sunsetting, or agency termination. Since 1976, 36 states have enacted sunset laws, which place numerous agencies on a fixed cycle to be reviewed; the agency automatically terminates unless it is reauthorized by the legislature following its review.[37] The experience of most states has been that sunset laws are too blunt an instrument to be really useful. The reviews take a lot of time and money and result in very few agency terminations. For example, in 1991 the Texas Sunset Advisory Commission reviewed the performance of 30 agencies and concluded that Texas could live without the Good Neighbor Commission but it prolonged the existence of the Cosmetology Commission and the Board of Barber Examiners.[38] Other agencies previously consigned to the dustbin of history include the Pink Bollworm Commission, the Stonewall Jackson

Memorial Board, the Board of Tuberculosis Nurse Examiners, the Board of Examiners in Social Psychotherapy, and the Texas Historical Resources Development Council. None of these abolitions resulted in significant savings to the state, however. Thus, the sunset process is generally regarded as a less effective tool than the legislative audit.

Another legislative control mechanism is the oversight hearing, a hearing held for the purpose of monitoring program performance rather than enacting new legislation or appropriating funds. Crises such as prison riots may lead to an investigatory commission to review the prison system. A scandal in an agency may lead to the relevant standing committee chair calling the administrator on the carpet. Or the impetus may be a more generalized need to know: The higher education subcommittee may want a report on how student financial aid is working as a prelude to thinking about new loan programs.

Another form of oversight is more individualized and sporadic, and that is casework: legislators responding to their constituents' questions and complaints. Eventually such queries may form a pattern in the legislator's mind so that he or she decides the agency has a problem that needs fixing. For example, legislators sometimes get calls from state university students complaining that courses won't transfer, they can't get into classes, they are graded unfairly, professors are poor teachers or they don't speak English. Legislators may then decide that something is broken at the university, and they may try to fix it by regulating the university.

Such interventions can smooth the way for constituents in their dealings with complex bureaucracies; legislators can explain how the system works in simpler terms. They can alert agencies and legislators that some processes are not working as well as they should; this feedback can lead to program changes and improvements. But casework can also undermine administrative impartiality, one of the hallmarks of the bureaucracy, if constituents expect special favors or exceptions to the rules. Apparently, managers do not consider favoritism to be a significant problem: In the Elling study only 5 percent of agency chiefs said legislative favors for constituents were a serious problem.[39]

Courts as Overseers

State and federal courts from time to time exert some control over the bureaucracy, although not on as regular and sustained a basis as the governor and legislature. Courts are usually concerned with the process rather than the substance of the issue: Was the welfare client afforded due process, did the environmental impact statement include all the affected parties, are the prison conditions humane? Appalled by various conditions in state institutions, judges have seized control of state prisons and homes for the mentally ill and the mentally retarded and have substituted their managerial judgment for that of bureaucrats.

The area where federal and state judges have had the greatest impact on administration is in state prisons. They have intervened in nearly every state on issues ranging from crowding to medical care, food, sanitation, and overall prison conditions. Their intervention affects not only correctional officials but also governors and legislators, who must appropriate money to improve conditions or reduce crowding, sometimes through early release of prisoners.

The court's influence over administration is limited because it must wait until someone else has acted before it can react. If the implementer fails to do his or her job and someone sues, the court can fashion remedial action but it cannot step in from the start.

Thus, the court does not have the reach of either the legislature or the governor when it comes to overseeing the bureaucracy.

The Federal Government's Influence

Many state agencies have another boss—the federal government—because state agencies implement federal programs as well as state programs. If they receive significant amounts of money from Washington, D.C., they have to be attentive. The federal government may attach to the money various rules that govern agency conduct, such as affirmative action for federal contractors. Thus, the federal government constrains state administrative action at the same time federal funding expands programmatic activity.

The major problem for state managers seems to be the unpredictability of federal grant funding; it was listed as a serious problem by 30 percent of the agency chiefs in Elling's study.[40] Also mentioned were the paperwork, delay, and strings attached to federal grants. Many state officials chafe under the federal bit. Some of the chafing may be removed by the Federal Unfunded Mandates Reform Act that Congress passed in 1995, but it has so many exceptions that its relief may be less than hoped. Also, if Medicaid and Aid to Families with Dependent Children (AFDC) are converted to federal block grants, more flexibility in use of funds will be introduced.

Federal aid is not necessarily viewed as a negative by agency leadership, however; if they are federally funded, then they are somewhat insulated from gubernatorial and state legislative influence. So federal aid is a mixed blessing. Because state officials expect to see a loss of some of their federal aid once the 1996 federal budget is implemented, it is uncertain whether the reduction in red tape will make up for the loss in federal dollars.

Organized Interests' Influence

As stated earlier in the chapter, administrators and leaders of organized interests have extensive interaction; Wright, Yoo, and Cohen find that agency chiefs have more extensive contact with clientele groups than with any government body.[41] Some view this close relationship as negative, but administrators themselves do not see groups as harmful; rather, they view them as providing their agencies with valuable resources such as information and political support with the legislature.[42] Groups can provide feedback about how a program is working or about the magnitude of problems experienced in the industry. They can furnish data the agency does not have. Many agencies have a formal mechanism for group input, such as an advisory committee. Some agencies have more intense interactions with groups than other agencies, and such interaction is more common in some states than in others. But overall, state managers do not consider groups to have as much influence on them as do governors and legislatures.[43]

Most of the criticism of interest groups' influence on agencies centers on regulatory agencies that are alleged to be captured by interest groups. This allegation means that the regulators make decisions in favor of the regulated interest; for example, they favor the truckers over the consumers or the bankers over the customers. But in recent years the numbers of interest groups have increased, bringing more variety of perspectives to be represented (see Chapter 3 for details on this point). More means of citizen participation have been implemented so that the possibility of interest group capture is less now than in the past.

Overall, the nature of the relationship between groups and administrators is that of allies rather than opponents. Administrators want to keep their allies happy, so they cultivate these relationships just as they cultivate relationships with legislators and governors. A university, for example, would be unwise to make its alumni society, its student body president, or its faculty leadership unhappy. It depends on these constituencies to lobby for increased appropriations and expanded programs. Administrators want to be on good terms with their constituents.

The Public's Influence

The public's interest is represented to bureaucracies in various ways. One is through interest groups; however, the constituency of an agency goes beyond those organized into formal groups. Many people are directly affected by an agency's actions or use the agency's services and programs; they contact the bureau themselves if they have problems or concerns. Elling's survey shows that such client contacts are moderately influential across the board; in the case of daily administrative operations, client contacts carry more weight than any other nongovernment force.[44]

Besides the clients directly affected by an agency, many other people have an interest in what a bureaucracy is doing, such as consumers, taxpayers in general, or even opponents of the agency. In recent years, several states have attempted to represent broader interests or to represent those not in organized groups. For example, some states have established proxy advocates to represent consumer interests in public utility rate hearings, some mandated lay representation on occupational licensing boards, others required public hearings in various environmental policy decisions, and a few have established ombudsman offices.[45] More generally, sunshine requirements, open meeting laws, and freedom-of-information laws provide access to information so that citizens do not have an undue burden in acquiring such materials.

The reinventing government movement described earlier brings with it some innovations in citizen evaluation of the bureaucracy. Its advocates tout the value of a customer-driven government, one in which agencies try to please their users, not interest groups, other bureaucrats, or elected officials. Osborne and Gaebler cite a variety of ways state and local governments have used to listen to the voice of the customer: customer surveys, community surveys, putting managers into front-line offices to listen to customers, focus groups, electronic mail, toll-free telephone numbers, and suggestion boxes.[46] Of course, innovations such as school vouchers allow customers (parents) to choose which public agency will deliver schooling to their children. The reinventing government movement promises to increase the accountability of bureaucracies to citizens.

In the final analysis, perhaps none of these external controls on bureaucrats' behavior is as important as the individual bureaucrat's own norms. Each bureaucrat has his or her own conception of how to behave on the job: whether he or she works until the job is done or simply punches the time clock and how he or she responds to citizens. This internal orientation has a lot more to do with the bureaucracy's performance level than do the external controls that could be implemented by others. These norms are first inculcated by one's profession: Bureaucrats are socialized at the beginning of their professional training to a particular set of values. These internalized values tell them how social workers or doctors or teachers should behave on the job. Such socialization is often more powerful than what the legislature tells them to do. Norms are reinforced by the administrative culture on the job: What are the norms about fairness, equality, due process, service to the public, and so forth, and how is adherence to these norms rewarded by the department? Finally, the norms are individualized. Each of us has his or her own ideas about what makes a good worker. These normative controls cost nothing and can be highly effective in motivating performance.

✧ CONCLUSION

In this chapter we have examined the so-called fourth branch of government. We have seen that bureaucracies, for all their alleged faults, are an essential part of modern society. State bureaucracies in particular are a significant sector of public employment, employing about one-fourth of all government workers. We examined certain problems within the civil service, especially those affecting women such as the glass ceiling and inequitable salaries.

Historically, state employees were hired on the basis of patronage considerations, but by mid-century the merit system took hold throughout the states. Vestiges of patronage remained until the *Rutan* decision in 1990. More recent challenges to the merit system have been the spread of public sector unionization and the recent debureaucratization movement. The latter movement includes efforts to privatize or contract out many government services as well as efforts to make government more customer-driven.

Although a hallmark of the modern bureaucracy has been the dichotomy between politics and administration, we saw that in practice neither side of the dichotomy is really observed. Bureaucrats, for their part, engage in many activities besides technical administration, including policy formulation, implementation, and relations with interest groups. Their power derives from their professional expertise and their political allies. Elected officials, for their part, intervene into administration in various ways to hold bureaucrats accountable for their actions. These mechanisms include the appointment process, the budgetary process, reorganization of agency functions, review of administrative rules, performance auditing, and sunset laws. Nongovernment actors are also involved in enforcing accountability, especially interest groups, agency clients, and the general public. Recent innovations in accountability such as TQM emphasize improving citizens' ability to hold bureaucrats accountable.

✧ KEY TERMS

bureaucracy (p. 179)
comparable worth (p. 183)
patronage (p. 179)
privatization (p. 189)
reinventing government (p. 189)

representative bureaucracy (p. 181)
Rutan v. Republican Party of Illinois
(p. 186)
Total Quality Management (p. 189)

⬥ FOR FURTHER READING

Richard E. Elling, *Public Management in the States* (Westport, Conn.: Praeger Books, 1992). A leading scholar of public administration in the states reports on a survey of administrators in ten states and the management challenges they face.

Sara M. Evans and Barbara J. Nelson, *Wage Justice* (Chicago: University of Chicago Press, 1989). A case study of the first comparable worth law and its implementation in Minnesota.

David Osborne and Ted Gaebler, *Reinventing Government: How the Entrepreneurial Spirit is Transforming the Public Sector* (New York: Penguin Books, 1993). This is the bible of the reinventing government movement. It outlines the authors' argument about how governments need to change and gives examples of how state and local governments have reinvented themselves.

Frank J. Thompson, ed., *Revitalizing State and Local Public Service* (San Francisco: Jossey-Bass, 1993). Papers prepared by noted experts for the National Commission on the State and Local Public Service. The experts outline a series of reforms to improve public management.

⬥ NOTES

1. Meredith De Hart, "Government Employment in 1992," in *The Book of the States, 1994–95, Vol. 30* (Lexington, Ky.: Council of State Governments, 1994), p. 435.

2. *Ibid.*, p. 435.

3. Richard C. Elling, "Bureaucracy," in Virginia Gray and Herbert Jacob, eds., *Politics in the American States*, 6th ed. (Washington, D.C.: CQ Press, 1996), p. 300.

4. Ted F. Hebert, Deil Wright, and Jeffrey Brudney, "Challenges to State Governments: Policy and Administrative Leadership in the 1990s," *Public Productivity and Management Review*, 16 (1992); 1–21.

5. Deil S. Wright, Jae-Won Yoo, and Jennifer Cohen, "The Evolving Profile of State Administrators," *Journal of State Government*, 64 (January–March 1991), 32.

6. Mary E. Guy, ed., *Women and Men of the States* (Armonk, N.Y.: M.E. Sharpe, 1992), p. 8.

7. Keon S. Chi, "Comparable Worth in State Government: 1984–85," in *The Book of the States, Vol. 26* (Lexington, Ky.: Council of State Governments, 1990), p. 291.

8. Rita Kelly, *The Gendered Economy* (Newbury Park, Calif.: Sage Publications, 1991), p. 22.

9. Carolyn Ban and Norma Riccucci, "Personnel Systems and Labor Relations: Steps Toward a Quiet Revitalization," in Frank J. Thompson, ed., *Revitalizing State and Local Public Service* (San Francisco: Jossey-Bass, 1993), pp. 87–88.

10. David K. Hamilton, "The Staffing Function in Illinois State Government After *Rutan*," *Public Administration Review*, 53 (July/August, 1993), 382.

11. Jeffrey L. Katz, "The Slow Death of Political Patronage," *Governing* (April 1991), 60.

12. Ann O. Bowman and Richard Kearney, *State and Local Government*, 2nd ed. (Boston: Houghton Mifflin, 1993), p. 226.

13. *Ibid.*, p. 230.

14. Richard C. Elling, *Public Management in the States* (Westport, Conn.: Praeger, 1992).

15. Michael Barzelay and Babak J. Armajani, "Managing State Government Operations: Changing Visions of Staff Agencies," *Journal of Policy Analysis and Management*, 9 (1990), 307–338.

16. David Osborne and Ted Gaebler, *Reinventing Government: How the Entrepreneurial Spirit Is Transforming the Public Sector* (New York: Penguin Books, 1992).

17. Elling, "Bureaucracy," p. 295.

18. Donald F. Kettl, "The Myths, Realities, and Challenges of Privatization," in Frank J. Thompson, ed., *Revitalizing State and Local Public Service* (San Francisco: Jossey-Bass, 1993), p. 251.

19. Barzelay and Armajani, "Managing State Government Operations."

20. Robert S. Kravchuk, "The 'New Connecticut': Lowell Weicker and the Process of Administrative Reform," *Public Administration Review*, 53 (July/August 1993), 336.

21. Jonathan Walters, "The Reinvention of the Labor Leader," *Governing* (November 1994), 44.

22. Elling, *Public Management in the States*, p. 111.

23. Wright, Yoo, and Cohen, "The Evolving Profile of State Administrators," 33.

24. Leonard S. Robins and Charles H. Backstrom, "The New Politics of AIDS," in Theodore J. Litman and Leonard S. Robins, eds., *Health Politics and Policy*, 2nd ed. (Albany, N.Y.: Delmar Publishers, 1991).

25. Keon S. Chi and Dennis O. Grady, "Innovators in State Governments: Their Organizational and Professional Environment," in *The Book of the States, Vol. 28* (Lexington, Ky.: Council of State Governments, 1990).

26. Chi and Grady, "Innovators in State Governments," p. 398.

27. Elling, *Public Management in the States*, p. 111.

28. Glenn Abney and Thomas P. Lauth, *The Politics of State and City Administration* (Albany: State University of New York Press, 1986), p. 89.

29. William T. Gormley, Jr., "Accountability Battles in State Administration," in Carl E. Van Horn, ed., *The State of the States*, 2nd ed. (Washington, D.C.: CQ Press, 1993), p. 171.

30. Abney and Lauth, *The Politics of State and City Administration*, p. 47.

31. *Ibid.*, p. 42. The Elling study of ten states produced findings consistent with these; see Elling, *Public Management in the States*, p. 154.

32. Wright, Yoo, and Cohen, "The Evolving Profile of State Administrators."

33. Elling, *Public Management in the States*, p. 170.

34. *Ibid.*, p. 197.

35. Alan Rosenthal, *Governors and Legislatures: Contending Powers* (Washington, D.C.: CQ Press, 1990).

36. *Ibid.*, p. 189.

37. Charles Mahtesian, "Why the Sun Rarely Sets on State Bureaucracy," *Governing* (June 1992), 24–25.

38. *Ibid.*, p. 24.

39. Elling, *Public Management in the States*, p. 185.

40. *Ibid.*, p. 16.

41. Wright, Yoo, and Cohen, "The Evolving Profile of State Administrators," p. 35.

42. Abney and Lauth, *The Politics of State and City Administration*, p. 103.

43. Elling, "Bureaucracy," p. 310.

44. Elling, *Public Management in the States*, p. 236.

45. Gormley, "Accountability Battles in State Administration," p. 174.

46. Osborne and Gaebler, *Reinventing Government*.

CHAPTER

8

STATE COURTS

Americans know little about how their legal system operates. Nearly half of Americans do not even know that their state has its own constitution, according to a 1991 survey.[1] The workings of state courts are almost invisible to most people, yet state courts are involved in nearly every aspect of society. They determine the division of powers between state and local governments, outline relations within families and among contractors, define individual rights and liberties, and levy criminal sanctions. Their rulings affect people who never go to court. Decisions on school segregation, medical malpractice, usury limits, and product liability affect all of us.

In our political system, courts are supposed to be removed from the political process: Judges are to be protected from political pressures so that justice can be dispensed evenhandedly. However, democracy requires of its officials responsiveness to the public; various provisions, such as appointment and retention elections, build in judicial accountability. Still, citizens' lack of knowledge about judges means that democratic control is not fully exercised.

In this chapter we explore this tension as we examine the workings of state courts. We look first at the institutional structure of courts, including the division of labor between trial and appellate courts and between federal and state courts. Then we describe the people involved in the judicial process, how judges are selected, and how accountability is built into this process. Finally, we focus on the process of decisionmaking in courts: what different courts do and how judges make up their minds.

✧ INSTITUTIONAL STRUCTURE AND RELATIONS

In order to understand how courts function, we first need to understand their organizational hierarchy. Its precise nature varies from one state to another but there are certain identifiable commonalities. Also, we need to recognize how state courts fit into the federal legal system: Restricted by actions of the U.S. Supreme Court, they are also influenced by other state supreme courts. Finally, we need to understand how courts fit into state political systems—how they relate to the legislative and executive branches and how they are shaped by state political culture.

Organization of Courts

In most states there are three tiers of courts: **trial courts,** intermediate **appellate courts,** and a supreme court (Texas and Oklahoma have two supreme courts, one for civil matters and one for criminal cases). In a minority of states there are no intermediate courts. Because trial and appellate courts function quite differently, we will discuss them separately.

Trial Courts   Trial courts are where all litigation begins; they involve a formal hearing before a single judge. The trial's purpose is to assess the facts in a disputed situation and arrive at a resolution. Toward this end attorneys for each side argue their cases and present their witnesses. Sometimes they do so before a citizen jury. The jury or the judge returns a verdict. Their decisions can be, and often are, appealed to higher-level courts, the appellate courts.

The volume of business in trial courts is huge, numbering in the millions of cases every year. In 1992, for example, nearly 23 million cases were filed in courts of general jurisdiction.[2] Due to the volume of business and the relatively small stakes involved, cases are handled expeditiously and decisions are announced immediately. In their daily operations trial courts are somewhat analogous to bureaucracies; that is, they apply the law to thousands of routine situations. Their decisions typically have little policy significance, although a personal injury award or a custody decree has great significance to the parties involved. Judges also try to deflect cases from the trial stage: Roughly 90 percent of all cases are resolved before trial by either plea bargaining in criminal cases or out-of-court settlements in civil matters.[3] Still, the courts are clogged, and speedy justice is seldom achieved.

Trial courts are of two types: those of general jurisdiction (they hear all types of cases) and courts of limited jurisdiction. *Limited jurisdiction* means they hear only cases involving certain topics such as small claims, probate, or traffic cases. Forty-four states have this division; in the remaining handful of states the general jurisdiction courts handle all cases. In the past two decades a major effort of court reform has been to consolidate these diverse, fragmented courts into a more integrated system. Most states have reduced the number of different courts but only a handful have true consolidated courts handling all types of cases. Figure 8.1 illustrates the difference between consolidated and fragmented court systems.

Trial courts of general jurisdiction are the most familiar type of court; the O.J. Simpson trial, for example, was in such a court, although what went on there is not very typical of normal court proceedings. These courts handle the more serious criminal and civil cases. The criminal cases are felony cases such as burglary, rape, and murder; felony cases typically involve imprisonment of a year or more. The civil cases involve sums of money above a certain minimum amount.

Appellate Courts   Appellate (or appeals) courts operate quite differently from trial courts. There are no juries, no witnesses, and usually no litigants present at the proceedings. Often even the attorneys are not present; they argue their cases in written briefs. The purpose of the proceeding is to review a lower court's decision. This does not involve ascertaining the facts in a case but rather assessing whether the law was applied correctly.

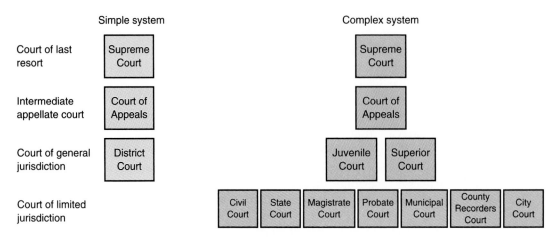

FIGURE 8.1 State Court Systems Like state bureaucracies, state court systems have been streamlined. This figure contrasts a complex system with the simple system many states have recently adopted.

There is a panel of judges, rather than just one judge. The court renders a collective written decision some time after the arguments are heard.

Appellate courts have great discretion in determining which cases to consider; consequently, their caseload is considerably lower than that of trial courts. In 1992, for example, state appellate courts decided over 250,000 cases, as compared to the millions decided by trial courts.[4] In certain circumstances the court's jurisdiction is mandatory; for example, cases involving the death penalty must usually be reviewed by the state supreme court. Appellate courts have much greater policy impact than trial courts because appellate decisions affect people other than the litigants. Appellate judges interpret the law and publish their opinions, binding future litigants by their interpretations.

Every state has a supreme court (although it may go by another name), which is the final arbiter of disputes; 37 states also have intermediate appellate courts. The intermediate courts are supposed to relieve the caseload pressure on the supreme courts. Appeals of trial court decisions go to the intermediate court first, leaving the supreme court time to focus on significant cases. Supreme courts in these 37 states tend to have more policy impact than supreme courts that have to process all routine appeals.

In addition to hearing appeals from lower courts, state supreme courts have some administrative authority over them. They make rules about court practices and procedures that lower courts must follow. In response to the court unification movement, states in recent years have moved unevenly toward centralization of court administration. Typically, centralization means that the supreme court and its chief justice hire a professional court administrator to handle budgetary and administrative matters, including the assignment of judges. Thus, a supreme court oversees some aspects of the entire judicial system in its state. On the other hand, trial courts are funded by a combination of local and state monies; their judges are mostly selected locally, not statewide, so they are not fully creatures of the state.

The Business of State Courts

Federal law outlines the jurisdiction of federal courts and leaves the rest to state courts. Generally speaking, this means that cases arising under state law are heard in state courts and cases involving federal statutes, the federal government as a party, or citizens of two or more states are heard in federal courts. The latter legal point was invoked in 1989 when Cincinnati Reds star Pete Rose sought to avoid a hearing on his betting before baseball commissioner Bart Giamatti. The case began in an Ohio county court before a friendly judge (no doubt a Reds fan) who issued a restraining order blocking the hearing. An Ohio appellate court, doubtless full of Reds fans too, refused to hear Giamatti's appeal, but his lawyers got the case transferred to federal court because Rose and Giamatti were citizens of different states. Rose was eventually found guilty and barred from baseball.

Criminal law is primarily state-based, so most ordinary crimes are tried in state court. Also, the most common kinds of civil cases, such as personal injury and contract disputes, are within the state's jurisdiction. Thus, the great bulk of litigation flows through state courts rather than through federal courts: Over 99.7 percent of all filings in 1988 were in state and local courts.[5]

Business is booming in state courts in both the criminal and civil areas. Criminal cases are a function of the crime rate and the actions of the police and prosecutors. Criminal filings have grown faster than civil cases, registering a 25 percent increase between 1985 and 1992.[6] Criminal case numbers also depend on the passage of laws designating new crimes and on society's attitude toward criminal actions. For instance, when the Connecticut legislature passed a law that required arrests in situations of family violence, it added 600 new cases per month to the courts' dockets.[7]

Civil cases, in contrast, are a function of individuals' decisions to settle their disputes in court. Many people have decried the increasing litigiousness of Americans, which has contributed to more than 4.5 million suits filed in 1992.[8] Even though states have added more judges (primarily through creating intermediate appellate courts), they have not kept up with caseloads.

Interestingly, most civil litigation is related to trends in the economy: In good economic times, more cases are filed, and during recessions filings decline. Just the opposite is true for small claims courts: They are inundated in poor economic times. Wide variations in the propensity to litigate exist in the states. For instance, in 1992 there were 65 filings per 100,000 residents of North Dakota but 1,130 filings per 100,000 Massachusetts residents in tort (injury) cases.[9] The explanations for interstate differences in litigiousness have not been developed but probably they relate to the economic structure of the state. Massachusetts, for example, contains many insurance companies, which are likely to be sued; Delaware, the legal home of many corporations, is also a source of significant amounts of litigation.

Although both trial and appellate courts handle a diverse array of criminal and civil business, there are some differences in the caseloads. Certain kinds of cases are more likely to be appealed to a higher level, such as serious criminal cases and high-stakes civil cases. In addition, appellate judges are more likely to accept certain kinds of cases for review, namely those that have a significance beyond the facts of the particular case. As a result, the caseload at the appellate level is not an exact replica of the cases heard at a lower level.

Due to the smaller caseload of appellate courts, scholars have been better able to track their substantive agenda. In a mammoth study, Kagan and colleagues categorized the agenda of supreme courts in 16 states from 1870 to 1970.[10] They found a diverse array of business: The largest category was torts (negligence, personal injury, and so forth), but that made up only 22 percent of the cases. Public law (regulation, taxes, and so forth) was the second largest category at 19.4 percent, then criminal cases at 18 percent, followed by debts and contracts at 15 percent. State courts in this period had less to do with civil liberties issues. (Their concern expanded in the 1980s; this is discussed later in this chapter.)

State Courts' Relations with Other Courts

State courts function within a federal judicial hierarchy. As already mentioned, federal law distinguishes the jurisdiction of state courts from that of federal courts. Moreover, the U.S. Constitution has certain requirements of state courts when federal matters appear before them; they must interpret such matters in line with current rulings of the U.S. Supreme Court. This requirement has had great ramifications in shaping rulings of recalcitrant state courts, such as southern states in school desegregation cases. State courts that behave in a manner inconsistent with the U.S. Supreme Court are reversed on appeal. When state supreme courts rule on cases where the legal arguments are grounded in the federal Constitution, they act as proxies for the U.S. Supreme Court.

Conversely, federal courts accept state supreme courts' interpretations of state law so that in practice the federal relationship is not strictly hierarchical. When a litigant bases his or her claim strictly on the state constitution or state law, rather than the federal Constitution, the state supreme court's interpretation is final. This gives state supreme courts considerable policymaking potential. State constitutions are usually longer and more specific than the U.S. Constitution; for example, the Alaska constitution expressly grants the right to privacy to its citizens, and on this basis it has invalidated state laws against possession of marijuana.[11] Also many state constitutions grant citizens open access to courts so that they can redress greviances more easily than in federal courts.

The horizontal relationships among state courts are also quite important. Because courts in different states face many of the same issues, judges often look to precedents established in other states. These precedents may help justify a judicial decision or solve a troubling problem of interpretation. The extent to which judges rely on other states' decisions is measured by the frequency of citations of other states' opinions. State supreme courts that are cited a lot are presumably looked to as authorities in the field, whereas state courts less often mentioned are presumably less influential. Thus, the patterns of citation (who cites whom) can be used as a measure of prestige in the legal profession.

Gregory Caldeira ranked state supreme courts on the basis of citation patterns in 1975.[12] On his index California was the most influential court in the nation, with New York and New Jersey also scoring very high. Their decisions are frequently mentioned outside the state. Other state courts tended to be borrowers: Wyoming, for example, borrowed from many others but was cited by few. States tend to borrow from nearby populous states with similar migration streams and from states in their legal reporting region. They also borrow from courts with high caseloads and ones that are professional and liberal in ideology.[13] Through this process of emulation, the judicial doctrines of the leading state courts spread to other states and influence their courts' decisions. Judges, it appears, behave much like state legislators in imitating the actions of policy leaders.

A recent example of judicial diffusion can be seen in the series of right-to-die decisions. In 1976 the New Jersey Supreme Court in the Karen Quinlan case ruled that life-support could be withdrawn. The patient Quinlan had been in a vegetative state for years; the court reasoned that the patient's right to privacy and her parents' right to act as guardians allowed them to remove the respirator that was assisting her breathing. By 1992, over 100 right-to-die decisions had been rendered by state high courts, with a remarkable degree of unanimity on this controversial issue; the New Jersey opinion was cited as a legal precedent in 80 percent of these rulings, almost as if it were a case law precedent in their own state.[14] New Jersey continues to have one of the trend-setting courts that other judges emulate.

Courts' Relations Within States

In addition to being part of a federal judicial system, state courts are also components of state political systems. Judges, as we shall see, typically come from a political background. They are products of their state's political subculture just as state legislators and governors are. Judges bring to the court ideological and partisan predispositions that structure how they view the court's role.

At the same time judges are also part of a national legal culture. This legal culture also structures how judges view their roles and their decisionmaking. Often the political and legal cultures clash. Some courts are held rather firmly in the grip of the national legal culture, which in recent decades has emphasized policy activism. Others are more responsive to the state's own political culture, whether it be individualistic, traditionalistic, or moralistic. Still other courts are somewhere in the middle of the continuum, moving from politically dominated to legally dominated.

Alan Tarr and Mary C. Porter have written an interesting book illustrating how cultural identity affects judicial behavior in three states.[15] They show how the New Jersey Supreme Court insulated itself from the prevailing political culture in the state, emphasizing instead professionalism, nonpartisanship, and collegiality as desirable judicial characteristics. Through solid consensus on its judicial norms, the New Jersey Court was able to exert strong national leadership. Box 8.1 profiles the New Jersey Court.

In marked contrast stands the Ohio Supreme Court. The Ohio Court is very partisan and reflective of the state's individualistic political culture. Partisan conflicts in the state are carried into the court and fought again, leading to one of the highest dissent rates in the country. It has rarely led in judicial innovations, and historically it paid little attention to legal developments outside the state, according to Tarr and Porter.[16] In the early 1980s its chief justice routinely made political appearances and even briefly ran for governor without resigning his judicial post.

Extreme politicization, such as that found in the Ohio Supreme Court, can damage a court's credibility and ultimately undermine legitimacy of the judicial system. As discussed in Chapter 3, people's loyalty to their states is tied to their evaluation of its institutions and the legitimacy of their decisions. Nowhere is this more important than in the judicial system: If people cannot trust their judges to be impartial in handing out justice,

BOX 8.1 THE NEW JERSEY SUPREME COURT

New Jersey is a heavily urbanized northern state with a competitive two-party political system and an individualistic political culture. Its politics has been marred by corruption, and the phrase *Jersey Justice* carried unseemly connotations in the first half of this century. Thus, the emergence of an activist, highly regarded supreme court is quite a surprise.

Since World War II the New Jersey Supreme Court has become a national leader in many fields of law, refusing to automatically defer to the rulings of the U.S. Supreme Court. In 1990, the New Jersey Court ruled, contrary to the U.S. Supreme Court, that searching an individual's trash violated the right to privacy, which is, according the Court "the right most valued by civilized man."[1] In the key area of tort law it was rated the most innovative court in the nation.[2] Its rulings resulted in reducing or eliminating institutional immunity against negligence or injury lawsuits.

The New Jersey Supreme Court's decisions on school finance, beginning in 1973, helped to begin a nationwide reform that resulted in more equitable statewide financing of public education. The court revoked local governments' power of exclusionary zoning when used to keep out the poor. In numerous other fields it has attacked controversial issues and issued novel opinions. These opinions have been the basis for other states' judicial decisions, earning New Jersey a top rating on the judicial reputation scale.

The judiciary has also had a profound effect on New Jersey state government. A number of its rulings have forced the state legislature to deal with new issues or to appropriate money for new purposes. In this way the Court has acted as an agenda-setter for the state legislature. At the same time, the court's rulings have consistently upheld the prerogatives of the executive branch, making the New Jersey governor one of the nation's most powerful. The court has also led the way in curtailing corruption and influence peddling in the county courts.[3] The court has been a positive force for change in many areas of state and local government.

whom can they trust? Such crucial considerations have led to reforms in the way judges are selected. In the next section we outline the different selection systems and how they affect judges' qualifications.

⋄ THE JUDGES

As government officials, judges share certain characteristics with governors and legislators. Usually judges have attended law school alongside future politicians and have been involved in government before ascending to the bench. However, we expect judges to advance because of their merit in the legal profession, not exclusively because of their political connections. The expertise judges bring to the job may be somewhat different from that of elected officials' and possibly even more important, because judges are protected from immediate voter retribution.

Background of Judges

There is a judicial career ladder just as there is a gubernatorial career ladder. Many judges are intimately involved in politics and government before attaining their position on the bench. Among supreme court judges, over 90 percent have held government office of some type. More than half have been elected to some office. Thus, they have been polit-

How did the New Jersey Supreme Court accomplish these feats? According to Tarr and Porter's study, a crucial role must be assigned to Arthur Vanderbilt, appointed chief justice in 1948.[4] He is credited with creating the modern New Jersey Supreme Court. Vanderbilt instituted many procedural reforms that improved the judicial system's efficiency. In an important decision (*Winberry v. Salisbury,* 1950) he was able to fend off the legislature's attempt to control rules of judicial procedure. This victory established the judiciary's independence from other institutions. Vanderbilt encouraged legal professionalism and intracourt consensus; he discouraged partisan divisions and the expression of personal antipathies toward other judges. The establishment of these norms of conduct made the recruitment of highly qualified judges much easier. Through these means Vanderbilt was able to insulate the court from New Jersey's political culture.

This prestige and autonomy stood the court in good stead as subsequent chief justices led the court into new areas and issued innovative doctrines. The New Jersey Supreme Court's landmark decisions have been widely imitated by other states, reforming legal doctrines nationwide. Achieving national stature helped to protect the court from retribution when its decisions affected powerful political forces in the state. The efforts of Justice Vanderbilt and his successors created and maintained a national judicial resource in the New Jersey Supreme Court.

[1]Barbara G. Salmore and Stephen A. Salmore, *New Jersey Politics and Government: Suburban Politics Comes of Age* (Lincoln: University of Nebraska Press, 1993), p. 191.

[2]Bradley C. Canon and Lawrence Baum, "Patterns of Adoption of Tort Law Innovations: An Application of Diffusion Theory to Judicial Doctrines," *American Political Science Review,* 75 (December 1981), 975–987.

[3]Maureen Moakley, "New Jersey," in Alan Rosenthal and Maureen Moakley, eds., *The Political Life of the American States* (New York: Praeger, 1984), pp. 219–246.

[4]G. Alan Tarr and Mary Cornelia Aldis Porter, *State Supreme Courts in State and Nation* (New Haven: Yale University Press, 1988).

ical successes before becoming judges. Among the most frequent prior positions are state legislator (20 percent), prosecutor (21.5 percent), and judge at a lower level (63 percent).[17] The number with prosecutorial experience has declined since the 1960s, suggesting that the politicization of the judicial career may be declining as more states use merit selection procedures (see next section), but political offices are still the stepping-stones to the supreme court bench.

Judges' political ties tend to be local. More than three-quarters were born in-state, and nearly as many attended law school in-state.[18] Their career advancement often depends on the contacts made in law school. Few minorities are judges but women have made more progress in attaining the supreme court bench. In 1995 there were 61 female supreme court justices, constituting 17.9 percent of all justices.[19] There were 17 African Americans on the high courts, 5 Asians, 6 Hispanics, and no Native Americans, totalling 8.2 percent of seats.

Selection Systems

The selection procedures used in different states reflect differing emphases given over the years to democratic accountability, judicial independence, and competence. In the colonial period, the states emphasized judges' independence from popular control and relied on

Most state supreme court justices are white men. The 1994 Minnesota Supreme Court was unique in that it had a female majority and an African-American justice, Alan Page, a former NFL All-Pro lineman. (*Source:* © 1995 Faye Ellman/NYC)

appointment of judges by the legislature or sometimes the governor. Gradually, states moved to popular election of judges as demand for popular control of all institutions was voiced in the Jacksonian era. Mississippi in 1832 was the first state to elect its judges. By the turn of the century, political machines were accused of controlling the selection process, and judges were alleged to be corrupt and incompetent. States began to institute nonpartisan elections as a way of enhancing democratic accountability while removing partisan politics. Modern reformers sought to instill more independence and more competence in the judiciary at the expense of democratic control. Since 1940 many states have adopted some version of a merit selection plan. A key feature of these plans is the judicial nominating commission, populated by attorneys, which screens out less qualified candidates.

Today the 50 states use various combinations of appointment, election, and merit selection. Just to make things more confusing, they use different selection procedures for trial and appellate courts in the same state. Table 8.1 classifies the states according to the system currently used to select supreme court judges.

Gubernatorial Appointment   In eight states the governor appoints the judges, usually with the senate's confirmation. Appointments tend to go to members of the

TABLE 8.1   JUDICIAL SELECTION SYSTEMS FOR STATE SUPREME COURTS
States use one of five selection systems to choose supreme court justices, the most popular system is merit selection.

Gubernatorial Appointment	Legislative Election	Partisan Election	Nonpartisan Election	Merit Selection
Delaware[b]	Connecticut[c]	Alabama	Georgia	Alaska
Hawaii[b]	Rhode Island	Arkansas	Idaho	Arizona
Maine	South Carolina[b]	Illinois	Kentucky	California[a]
Massachusetts[b]	Virginia	Mississippi	Louisiana	Colorado
New Hampshire		North Carolina	Michigan	Florida
New Jersey		Pennsylvania	Minnesota	Indiana
New York		Tennessee	Montana	Iowa
Vermont[b]		Texas	Nevada	Kansas
		West Virginia	North Dakota	Maryland
			Ohio	Missouri
			Oregon	Nebraska
			Washington	New Mexico[d]
			Wisconsin	Oklahoma
				South Dakota
				Utah
				Wyoming

[a] Appointment by governor subject to confirmation by judicial committee; retention election.
[b] Nomination by judicial commission.
[c] Nomination by governor from list submitted by judicial commission.
[d] Initial appointment by governor from list submitted by judicial commission, then partisan election followed by nonpartisan retention elections.

Source: Adapted from information in *The Book of the States, 1994–1995* (Lexington, Ky.: Council of State Governments, 1994), pp. 190–191.

governor's political party and especially to his or her political associates. In four of the states, however, the governor must use a judicial screening committee to rate the candidates' professional qualifications and then choose from those nominees, so merit considerations are built in at this point.

Legislative Election   In four states the legislature elects the judges according to its own internal procedures. In these states, justices tend—not surprisingly—to be former legislators. In two of these states they select from a list of nominees initially submitted by a judicial screening commission, again injecting merit criteria.

Partisan Election   Nine states elect their justices on a partisan ballot in the general election. Party nominees are selected through partisan primaries or caucuses, thus maximizing partisan considerations in the selection process. Judicial elections are held at the same time as presidential and gubernatorial elections; therefore, the coattails of higher-profile races may affect judicial election outcomes. A Republican presidential landslide may sweep in Republican judges at the state level, for example.

Nonpartisan Election Thirteen states elect their supreme court justices on a nonpartisan ballot; the candidates are nominated by petition or by surviving an earlier nonpartisan primary. In a few states, notably Ohio and Michigan, political parties control the nominating process, although the general election is formally nonpartisan. Nonpartisan elections are often held apart from the regular general election; therefore, few people bother to vote. Thus, nonpartisan elections are not only insulated from partisan considerations, but hidden from most voters' attention.

Merit Selection Sixteen states use some form of merit selection, often called the **Missouri Plan,** after the first state to adopt it. This procedure involves three steps. A nonpartisan commission screens candidates and produces a short list of qualified candidates. Usually the commission contains lawyers and judges appointed by the state bar association and laypeople appointed by the governor. This is the merit step of the process. In the second step the governor selects one person from the list of qualified candidates and makes the judicial appointment. The third step is a retention election after a year or two, and at periodic intervals thereafter; voters are asked whether the judge should be retained. If the judge receives a majority of votes cast, he or she retains the position. If not, the commission produces another list of qualified candidates, and the governor appoints another person. Few justices lose the retention election. In fact, voters have even retained judges accused of bank fraud and corruption in office.

Two states have unique twists on the merit plan. California's version has a slight difference, in that the first two steps are reversed: The governor makes the initial appointment, subject to confirmation by a judicial commission. New Mexico's version has a partisan twist: A judicial screening commission produces a list of qualified candidates from which the governor appoints; at the next general election, the justice runs for reelection on a partisan, contested ballot; thereafter, the justice runs for retention on a nonpartisan basis.

Table 8.1 indicates some regional pattern in the selection systems used by different states. The older, eastern states are the ones with gubernatorial or legislative appointment. Partisan election is more popular in the South. Nonpartisan election and merit selection systems dominate in the West and Midwest. The trend in recent changes has all been in the direction of the merit system.

A considerable amount of research has been conducted on the effect of different selection systems on the quality of the judiciary. Those advocating reform of the selection process believed that professional competence and independence from popular control would be improved by the merit selection process. Consequently, most research has centered on whether judges chosen by the merit system differ from judges chosen by other methods. Few differences have been uncovered in judges' background, education, or previous experience. What differences exist are mainly due to the region of the country; different characteristics are more popular in different regions.[20] Also, the general public does not hold judges in higher regard in states with merit plans than they do in other states.[21] On the basis of research thus far, it does not appear that the merit selection system picks more meritorious judges than other systems do.

A related question is whether any selection system operates to the advantage of women and minorities. Studies of this question usually include judges at both the trial and appellate levels because the numbers are so small. Alozie found no differences among selection systems in the numbers of women, blacks, and Hispanics selected.[22] Graham concurred about the lack of effect of the formal selection system but then reasoned that this null finding was due to the fact that the distinctions between selection systems blur in practice because the governor so often makes the initial appointment.[23] She found that when the selection process begins with gubernatorial or legislative appointment rather than election, more black judges are selected.

Presumably women also fare better under initial appointment rather than election, regardless of the formal selection system. One illustration is that in 1991, Minnesota became the first state to have a majority of women on its Supreme Court. Minnesota uses the merit selection system but the critical variable here was that Governor Rudy Perpich appointed three of the four women.

Additionally, minorities have argued that the structure of the electoral system matters; they assert that single-member districts, especially if drawn with minority voting strength in mind, will improve blacks' chances as compared to at-large districts or statewide districts. These lawsuits, as described in Box 8.2, raise very complicated issues of representation and apportionment.

Judicial Selection in Practice

In actual operation the different selection systems are more similar than they appear on paper. In all systems the governor is important, judges have long tenure in all systems, and political considerations are key. More generally, the processes of judicial selection do not fully achieve the ideal of democratic accountability. Several features of judicial selection in practice help to compromise its ideals.

One feature is the frequency of interim appointments. Vacancies between elections are filled by the governor, and these new incumbents almost always win reelection. As many as half the elected judges may have reached their positions through interim appointment.[24] As a result, the governor as appointing officer is very influential even in elective systems. The saying that "a judge is an attorney who knew a governor" is still true.[25]

A second feature is the power of incumbency: The electoral success rate of sitting judges is very impressive. A study of judicial retention elections for major trial courts found that only 22 of 1864 judges were defeated (about 1 percent).[26] Perhaps even more remarkable is that few challengers present themselves. As many as half the races for supreme court are uncontested.[27] This means that in practice the state supreme court is a lifetime sinecure, even though formally there are limited terms in most all states.

A third feature is the limited amount of knowledge most voters bring to judicial elections. Accountability is hard to exercise if voters do not know much about the candidates and their records. Generally, little money is spent by the candidates (although this situation is changing in some states), and the media pays little attention to them. During the campaign judges feel constrained by professional ethics not to discuss specific cases. As a result voters can uncover little relevant information even if they want to. Because potential voters are operating in a vacuum, certain cues become more salient. The name recognition afforded an incumbent is one clue for some voters. The party label—Democrat or Republican—can be significant if it is the voters' only information about the candidates. In nonpartisan elections the voters' only clue may be the candidate's name; therefore an ethnic name or affiliation with a famous family may be quite helpful. Sometimes even these clues are not enough: Many people do not bother to vote by the time they reach the end of a long ballot in a partisan general election.

BOX 8.2 JUDICIAL SELECTION AND MINORITY REPRESENTATION

The ways in which judges are selected in the states can have profound effects on the likelihood that minorities will be represented on various state courts. As the text discusses, states vary in the methods they use to select judges, and the methods through which judges are selected have come under scrutiny by those concerned about minority representation. Just as with state legislatures (see Box 5.2 in Chapter 5), state courts have faced challenges based on the Voting Rights Act of 1965 in states where selection procedures appear to dilute the voices of minorities.

In states where judges are selected in at-large elections, or from large multimember districts, minority members are less likely to be elected to the bench, as minority votes are diluted by whites in these voting situations. In response, some states have constructed remedies that either turn multimember districts into single-member districts, create smaller multimember districts, or create electoral subdistricts, that is, districts contrived solely for the purpose of elections.[1] Other remedies that have been suggested include schemes for limited voting or cumulative voting. These plans would grant all citizens more than one vote per office, thereby allowing minority voters to cast multiple votes for minority candidates for the judiciary.

In 1988 a black state representative in Georgia, Tyrone Brooks, filed a suit alleging that Georgia's system of electing judges hindered the election of black jurists. An agreement was reached to replace the system of judicial elections with gubernatorial appointment (aided by a nominating commission) of state trial court judges. But it was struck down by the federal courts on the grounds that it was an "improper usurpation of legislative power." Furthermore, the federal court ruled that the only "compelling state interest" in such a plan was that the state might avoid further litigation by enacting it. This plan would have increased the number of black state judges from 3 in 1992 to 25 in 1994.[2]

In states that use a merit selection plan, minority representation has not necessarily been better than in states that elect their judges. In part this may be due to the fact that minority members are less likely to be networked into the legal community.

One study of trial court retention elections held during general elections found that 36 percent of the voters failed to vote in the judicial races.[28] Judicial elections are not always democracy at its best.

All of these shortcomings reduce accountability and blur the distinction between systems of popular control and systems of merit selection. Even in Missouri, where the merit system has worked well for nearly 50 years, political loyalties and ideology matter in selection. One team of scholars concluded in their examination of Missouri, "politics is endemic to the process of judicial selection."[29]

Recent events suggest that the public may be ready to exert more control over the judiciary. In 1986 California Chief Justice Rose Bird and two other justices—Joseph Grodin and Cruz Reynoso—were defeated in a retention election. This was the first time a California justice had been ousted from the bench. Box 8.3 describes the bitter campaign. As is clear from this analysis, voters were reacting to decisions on the death penalty and criminal penalties more generally. California's voters did indeed hold their justices accountable.

Campaigns have been waged in other states against justices because of their voting records on abortion, school busing, and other issues. This raises the question of judicial

Recently, the governor of Maryland, Parris Glendening, signed an executive order designed to remedy the exclusion of minorities from Maryland's bench. Fewer than 10 percent of Maryland's 240 judges are minority members, so Glendening altered the process for appointing members to the selection panel, giving the governor control of nine of the thirteen members on the panel.[3] It is hoped that with the governor in charge of the majority of appointments, rather than the state bar association, minority members will be more likely to appear on the selection panel, and hence on the bench.

The ambiguity embodied in these states' attempts to better represent minorities on the bench reflects the broader ambiguity over what the states are required to do under the Voting Rights Act of 1965 to ensure adequate minority representation. Early cases dealing with judicial selection questioned whether judges should even be considered representatives under Section 2 of the Voting Rights Act. Georgia Attorney General Michael Bowers expresses the frustration of the states well: "The Justice Department says that we as states must take race into consideration in anything political and to the maximum degree beneficial to black citizens. . . . But then the courts and the Supreme Court tell us we can't do that."[4]

The U.S. Supreme Court's most recent ruling on legislative redistricting may further confuse state reformers, as race is no longer to be considered the primary factor in legislative redistricting (see Box 5.2). Controversy over state plans for judicial selection is likely to continue until the states receive a clear statement of their responsibilities for providing adequate minority representation on state courts.

---

[1]Judith Haydel, "Section 2 of the Voting Rights Act of 1965: A Challenge to State Judicial Election Systems," *Judicature*, 73 (August–September 1989), 68.

[2]Ronald Smothers, "Court Overturns Georgia Accord on New Judges," *New York Times* (March 9, 1994), A12.

[3].Charles Babington, "Maryland to Change Makeup of Judicial Selection Panels," *Washington Post*, (April 29, 1995), B3.

[4].Smothers, "Court Overturns Georgia Accord on New Judges," p. A12.

independence: Do we want justices to weigh their decisions in the same way that legislators weigh their votes? Or should we allow judges the freedom to act according to their best reading of the legal principles involved? Justice Grodin, one of those defeated in California, has his own answer:

> We need to demonstrate, to reconfirm, the value to society as a whole in having a branch of government not subject to lobbying or political pressure—the value to society of insisting upon judicial integrity, upon the right and duty of judges to decide cases on principled grounds, even when the decision meets with boos rather than cheers.[30]

✧ JUDICIAL PROCESS AND OUTCOMES

Thus far, we have discussed the organization of the courts and the role of judges. Now we are ready to consider what judges do and how they go about doing it. The major function of courts is to settle disputes. In settling these disputes, judges engage in one of two functions: **norm enforcement** and **judicial policymaking.**[31] Norm enforcement is the

BOX 8.3 THE DEFEAT OF ROSE BIRD

The following ads do not sound like the usual quiet judicial election.

"Karen Diane Green won't be celebrating Christmas this year. The man who murdered her will."[1]

"My daughter Robin never got to her ballet lesson. But the man who kidnapped and killed her is still alive. Your vote can stop them from letting other killers escape justice."[2]

"Vote three times for the death penalty; vote no on Bird, Reynoso, Grodin."[3]

"Do you want a Supreme Court that will be dominated by the extremist left-wing philosophy of Jerry Brown, Tom Hayden, and Jane Fonda?"[4]

The 1986 California retention election was anything but quiet and decorous. The $5.5 million spent by the opponents of Chief Justice Rose Bird bought a lot of ads such as these. The anti-Bird groups pursued a strategy of making her court's decisions highly visible. This was a sound strategy because some of her opinions were more liberal than the voters'. For example, public opinion polls showed that Californians strongly favored the death penalty. The Bird court overturned 95 percent of the sentences to death row; Justice Bird herself voted to overturn the sentence every time. More generally, voters felt that the Bird court was too lenient toward all kinds of criminals: In August 1986, 62 percent of citizens said that Bird had gone too far in protecting criminal defendants.[5]

An effort to defeat a sitting judge requires much more than a discrepancy between the public's views and a justice's voting record. It requires money and organization. Among the major groups opposing Bird were Crime Victims for Court Reform, agricultural associations angry at her actions when she was secretary of agriculture, a coalition of prosecutors, the Californians to Defeat Rose Bird (whose leadership included tax crusaders Howard Jarvis and Paul Gann), and business groups angry at the court's proconsumer decisions.

The California Supreme Court under Chief Justice Bird had continued its long tradition of judicial activism, supporting the underdog against corporate interests. Conservative and business interests had been trying to dislodge Bird since 1978. With the election of conservative Republican George Deukmejian as governor in 1982, they suddenly had a chance to change the court's composition drastically if Deukmejian

application of a previously defined rule to a situation; in other words, it is a routine decision, arrived at routinely. It usually affects only the parties in the lawsuit. Judicial policymaking, on the other hand, involves a departure from the routine and affects a broader set of people. For example, convicting someone of robbery and handing down a sentence is a routine decision reinforcing the norm that robbery is wrong. Deciding that illegally obtained evidence about the robbery is unconstitutional is a policy decision that affects all those accused of robbery.

Norm enforcement is mainly the province of trial courts, the courts in which civil and criminal cases originate. Trial judges find out the facts in the case, and they apply the law; they do not interpret it. Policymaking, on the other hand, is handled by appellate courts. Appellate judges interpret the law in the light of the state's constitution. They also do some routine work, such as correcting the errors of lower courts.

Appellate courts in different states vary in their emphasis on policymaking. Often the size of the caseload erodes their capacity for policymaking: The sheer volume of routine

could make several appointments. Thus, they had the incentive to attack Bird and any other liberal justices up for reelection.

The support for Bird was inadequate and disorganized. Few leading Democratic politicians publicly supported her. Relatively little money was raised: Together the three defeated justices spent about $2 million, compared to $5.5 million for their opponents. Bird's campaign organization, the Committee to Conserve the Courts, managed to put on only two television ads. At her insistence and over the objections of her campaign manager, these ads stressed judicial independence rather than defending her record. By not taking the gloves off and railing against her opponents, Bird failed to diffuse the attack effectively. Yet to have done so would have violated judicial ethics and canons of behavior; judges are not supposed to discuss past or potential cases in public.

As expected, Governor Deukmejian named a new conservative chief justice, Malcolm Lucas, known as "Maximum Mal" because of his stiff sentences. The governor also appointed two other new conservative justices. Their decisions have taken the California Supreme Court in a new direction, narrowly construing the rights of criminal

defendants, making it tougher for individuals to sue companies for damages, and in general exercising judicial restraint.[6] In death penalty cases, the change was especially dramatic: Between 1987 and 1990 the Lucas Court reversed only 22 percent of the death sentences under review as compared to a 90 percent reversal rate in the Bird Court.[7] Because of California's prestige among other state courts, their rulings may carry weight beyond the state's borders.

---

[1]John T. Wold and John H. Culver, "The Defeat of the California Justices: The Campaign, the Electorate, and the Issue of Judicial Accountability," *Judicature*, 70 (April/May 1987), 348.

[2]"A Vote on the Quality of Mercy," *Newsweek* (November 3, 1986), 63.

[3]Joseph R. Grodin, "Judicial Elections: The California Experience," *Judicature*, 70 (April/May 1987), 376.

[4]Wold and Culver, "The Defeat of the California Justices," p. 350.

[5]*Ibid.*, p. 354.

[6]Richard B. Schmitt, "Right Turn: California High Court Makes Mark on Law by Limiting Damages," *Wall Street Journal* (July 11, 1989).

[7]Craig F. Emmert and Carol Ann Traut, "The California Supreme Court and the Death Penalty," *American Politics Quarterly*, 22 (January 1994), 42–43.

cases drives out the time needed for consideration of major cases. In reaction, most states have created intermediate appellate courts whose job is to review the decisions of trial courts, thus preserving the agenda of supreme courts for more important cases. Intermediate appellate courts decide nearly three-quarters of the appeals filed.[32] They have become the draft horses of state appellate review, using a variety of shortcuts to manage their burgeoning caseloads. For example, increasing the number of judges, using three-judge panels to hear cases, deciding appeals without issuing opinions, and not publishing opinions are all options states have adopted. Now one hears the criticism that the intermediate appellate courts are becoming too bureaucratic and are devaluing the process of legal appeal.

In certain states, usually the populous ones, the percentage of cases heard at the intermediate level is quite high: In California, for instance, 99 percent of appeals are decided by the intermediate courts. This means that the California Supreme Court is free to focus on truly significant cases. In 1988 it received 4,670 petitions for appeal, granted 541 of them, and issued signed opinions in 122 cases.[33] This production rate is lower than the U.S. Supreme Court's average of 130–140 full written opinions per term. Perhaps because of their selectivity, the California court has ranked at the top of the reputational scale. Many state supreme courts are moving in the direction of the "federal" model of high-discretion, low-caseload courts.

Norm Enforcement in Trial Courts

Trial courts operate in much the same way as administrative agencies: They process a huge volume of routine cases. Traffic violations alone account for half the filings in general jurisdiction courts and three-quarters of the caseload in limited jurisdiction courts.[34] Divorce, child custody, personal injury, traffic tickets, shoplifting, landlord-tenant disputes, and similar cases are dealt with by trained personnel in specialized courts, adhering to standard operating procedures. The judicial task is to uncover the facts of the case through the adversarial process and then to administer the applicable law.

An example from the state of Minnesota illustrates the nature of assembly-line justice. In 1994 each trial court judge averaged 706 major cases and 6,000 minor cases. The judges spent an average of 11.3 minutes per drinking-while-intoxicated case, 20.5 minutes per domestic abuse case, and five minutes per juvenile traffic offense.[35] Obviously in these situations fine-tuned justice is not dispensed.

Various mechanisms are used to avoid bringing the dispute to trial. Plea bargaining is one such means; in a criminal case it may be in everyone's interest for the defendant to agree to plead guilty in exchange for a lighter sentence. The defendant receives less punishment, the prosecutor's time can be saved for pursuing more important criminals, the state is spared the expense of trial preparation and court time. In civil cases, pretrial (out-of-court) settlements accomplish the same goal. Time is saved; justice is served.

Especially in civil cases the courts are being driven to separate serious cases that deserve judicial time from other cases that can be dealt with in alternative forums. Before resorting to a court, judges may require that the contending parties try a mediation service to settle landlord-tenant problems, consumer-merchant problems, or child custody cases. Mediators may be social workers, retired judges, or other professionals whose procedures are less formal and less costly than a court's. If the mediator can help the two parties reach a voluntary settlement, then court time can be saved. If not, then they go to court. Many states also require arbitration in private disputes below a certain monetary threshold. In binding arbitration, the two sides have to accept the arbitrator's decision, which substitutes for a judicial decision. But the arbitration procedure is faster and less costly than going to court, which may be advantageous to some disputants.

Policymaking in Appellate Courts

Appellate courts, especially the supreme courts of the 50 states, exert much more influence than do trial courts. In part, their influence comes from their supervision of lower courts, but mostly it derives from their ability to interpret the law. In the act of interpreting a statute, the judges may actually make policy; that is, they may go beyond the case at hand to enunciate a general rule that applies to future cases. They may strike down a law as unconstitutional or they may declare that a government program does not fulfill legislative intent. In their policymaking role appellate courts resemble legislatures more than they do trial courts. Their decisions have broad impact, require considerable public expenditures, venture into new areas, and are highly controversial, just as legislatures' decisions are. They may lead to exit, incite voice, or increase loyalty.

Appellate courts get cases on appeal from trial courts. The appeal alleges that the trial judge misapplied the law. The higher court can construe this as a narrow question (did the judge make a mistake?) or it can pose broader questions. Was the law itself unconstitutional? Was the rule fairly applied with due process? Does the limited funding deny a fundamental right? By answering the broader questions, the appellate judges maximize their policy impact. This is called **judicial activism:** judges taking every opportunity to make policy.

Especially since mid-century, state and federal appeals courts have engaged in judicial activism. At the federal level this activism was in a liberal direction during the Warren Court of the 1960s but turned conservative during the Burger Court of the 1970s and the current Rehnquist Court. However, the federal courts' turn toward conservatism seemed to invite more activism by state courts. State judicial activism has taken several forms. One kind of activism is invalidation of a legislative or executive action on state constitutional grounds. In the first half of the 1980s the 50 state supreme courts handled about 630 constitutional challenges to state laws; they declared nearly a third of these laws unconstitutional.[36] In the 1987–1992 period Paul Kramer found more challenges, 776 of them, but a slightly lower invalidation rate, 26.5 percent.[37] State courts have not been shy about using their state constitutions to overturn state laws.

Another kind of activism is overturning past precedent; still another is issuing advisory opinions, which is allowed in ten states. Such actions tend to be controversial within the state, especially with the legislature or governor. Massachusetts is a state noted for its use of the advisory opinion.

In the more conservative 1980s, the pendulum in some states swung back toward a posture of judicial restraint, from which judges do not seek opportunities to make policy and overturn laws. Instead they try to make decisions within the context of past decisions or without overruling the actions of other branches of government. The California Supreme Court in the post-Bird era is a good example of a court exercising judicial restraint.

Trends in State Supreme Court Policymaking

The consensus among judicial scholars is that state courts in recent decades were pioneers in two areas: tort law and civil liberties. We will examine each of these areas in turn.

Tort Law   At the beginning of this century it was difficult for people to sue for damages suffered. Various immunity doctrines shielded institutions from liability; for example, government bodies could not be sued without their consent, nor could charitable institutions such as nonprofit hospitals. Manufacturers were liable for injuries their goods produced only if they sold the product directly to the injured party or if the defect could be linked to negligence by the manufacturer. Employers had little responsibility for injuries on the job. In general, such doctrines protected businesses and other large institutions from suits brought by workers or consumers.

In recent years, these shields have been removed by state courts' interpretations of the common law and state statutes and by their overturning their own precedents. This

tort law revolution has been accomplished without legislative action. Once a leading court such as California's decided to reinterpret the doctrine of liability, other states quickly followed. The speed of the changes and the sweep of the rulings were unprecedented. Courts eliminated the immunity of charitable institutions and either eliminated or greatly narrowed government immunity. Perhaps the most dramatic change was the adoption of strict liability rules for makers of defective products. This means that the manufacturer is strictly liable, whether or not negligence was proven, for damages caused by defective products. By broadening the rights of injured parties, the courts encouraged more lawsuits from more victims. Thus, the higher volume of civil litigation and the higher monetary sums awarded by juries can be traced to courts' new sympathy for victims.

Tort law is an excellent example of judicial policymaking, showing the changes state courts can bring about without any legislative assistance. But the liberalizing trend has slowed considerably in recent years, moving away from the proplaintiff position. Businesses that are typical defendants in product liability lawsuits have gotten state legislatures to enact protective legislation more favorable to their interests. Some judges have become concerned about increasing civil litigiousness and large damages collected by plaintiffs.

Civil Liberties   As the U.S. Supreme Court became less supportive of citizens' rights in the 1970s and 1980s, state courts began to take the lead in supporting civil liberties. They did so by relying on state constitutional law, not on the U.S. Constitution. States have to afford to their citizens the protections of the federal Bill of Rights, as interpreted by the U.S. Supreme Court, but they can furnish additional protections in their own constitutions. In other words, the U.S. Bill of Rights establishes a floor of protection but a state court can raise protection above that floor. A case can be decided on state constitutional grounds if they are "independent and adequate," even though that right does not exist in the federal constitution. Because the U.S. Supreme Court does not review rulings based on state constitutional law, a state court can expand civil liberties without federal interference.

Since 1970 more than 700 cases have involved civil liberties derived from state, not federal, constitutions.[38] This movement, called the new judicial federalism, began in the state of Oregon with Justice Hans Linde, who is considered the architect of this movement. Linde is described in Box 8.4.

State bills of rights have been applied in the areas of criminal procedure, zoning, sex discrimination, free speech in private shopping malls, gay rights, gun control, freedom of the press, protection of obscenity, nude dancing, and abortion funding. State bills of rights are often longer and more detailed than the federal Bill of Rights, covering areas such as privacy, women's rights (18 states have equal rights amendments to their constitutions), and environmental rights that are not specifically enumerated in the U.S. Bill of Rights. State courts may become especially important in protecting abortion rights if the U.S. Supreme Court moves away from such protection (see the discussion of the *Webster* case in Chapter 16).

Perhaps the most visible example of constitutionally based interpretation of civil liberties is in the area of school finance. In the early 1970s the U.S. Supreme Court ruled that inequalities in educational funding arising from the local property tax did not violate

BOX 8.4 HANS LINDE AND THE "NEW JUDICIAL FEDERALISM"

Since the civil rights era of the 1950s and 1960s, the phrase *states' rights* has been used as a euphemism for state policies that subjugated minority rights. In the 1980s, however, a phenomenon took place in state supreme courts that began to give the idea of states' rights new meaning. This phenomenon, the new judicial federalism, began as a response to U.S. Supreme Court decisions that, under Chief Justice Warren Burger, had begun to curtail certain individual liberties. The movement to restore individual rights at the state level owes its genesis in part to the work of former Oregon Supreme Court Justice Hans Linde.

Hans Linde immigrated to the U.S. in 1939 from Germany via Denmark. He began his judicial career in 1950, clerking for Supreme Court Justice William O. Douglas, a noted liberal justice. After serving as a law professor at the University of Oregon in the 1960s and working as a senatorial aide on Capitol Hill, Linde was appointed to the Oregon Supreme Court in 1977.[1] Linde won reelection to Oregon's high court easily in 1978, but faced challenges from two "law-and-order" candidates resulting in a runoff election in 1984. He retired from the Oregon bench in 1990.

Linde's style was "homegrown" and his sparse office accoutrements and simple lifestyle seemed in contrast to his status as the intellectual architect of judicial federalism.[2] Central to Linde's judicial philosophy was the idea that state bills of rights were of equal or greater importance than the federal Bill of Rights. Linde noted that "State bills of rights are first in two senses; first in time and first in logic."[3] He argued that the federal government's Bill of Rights mirrored existing state bills of rights, which already protected citizens from incursions on their liberties by local government. Because of this, state supreme courts need not automatically turn to the U.S. Supreme Court's rulings on the federal Bill of Rights for justifications for state-level decisions. This philosophy provided a basis for states to make rulings irrespective of decisions of the U.S. Supreme Court, provided they grounded their decisions in state constitutions, as the U.S. Supreme Court has said that it will not review state court rulings based on state constitutions.

The new judicial federalism is nicely illustrated in certain Oregon Supreme Court rulings during Linde's tenure on the bench. In one case, Oregon male state prison inmates filed suit against the state of Oregon, claiming that their privacy rights had been violated when they were body searched by female prison guards. Rather than turning to the U.S. Supreme Court's decisions on privacy cases, Linde turned instead to the Oregon constitution. Linde based his striking of the searches on the doctrine of "unnecessary rigor" in searches and seizures, thereby removing the need to resort to federal privacy rulings.[4]

Linde's activism embodied a healthy respect for the activities of the legislature, as he saw the role of the courts as keeping the process working rather than making law. This perception of the separation of legislative and judicial functions was evident in a ruling on dentist licensure issued while Linde was on the bench. In this case Linde argued against removal of licensure based on his perception that the agency responsible for licensing had not constructed rules for removing licenses, as the legislature had intended, but rather was relying on the accumulation of rulings of the Court. Linde argued that a term such as *professionalism* as a requirement for continuation of licensing had to be grounded in agency-made or legislated rules, rather than ad hoc Court decisions, thereby ensuring both legislative control and fairness.[5]

Continued

Hans Linde's new judicial federalism provided for the possibility of the extension of individual rights during an era in which such extensions were unlikely at the federal level. By taking advantage of the climate created by Ronald Reagan's "new federalism," Linde was able to liberalize individual rights at the state level in an otherwise conservative political climate. Although evidence of the persistence of judicial federalism is not conclusive, Linde's opinions are cited throughout the country, and his work provided an important line of argument to state supreme courts.

1Elder Witt, "Hans A. Linde: The Unassuming Architect of an Emerging Role for State Constitutions," Governing, (July 1989), p. 56.
2Ibid.
3Ibid.
4Ibid., p. 57.
5Ibid., p. 59.

the U.S. Constitution, but several state supreme courts, beginning with California, Michigan, and New Jersey, said that the school financing formulae violated their state constitutions. This precipitated a revolution in the financing of public education, which had been locally based. Because of state supreme courts' decisions in Arkansas, Connecticut, Washington, West Virginia, Wisconsin, and Wyoming, state legislatures had to increase their share of educational expenditures. (The consequences of the school finance revolution are traced in Chapter 17.)

The second wave of school finance reform launched in the late 1980s was also anchored in state constitutions. For example, the Texas constitution requires the state legislature to "make suitable provision for the support and maintenance of an efficient system of public education." In a unanimous ruling in 1989 the Texas Supreme Court said that the efficiency criterion was violated when the 100 wealthiest districts spent $7,233 per pupil while the 100 poorest averaged $2,978 per student.[39] The legislature had to come up with millions of dollars. Similarly, the Kentucky constitution has a provision requiring "efficient" education; the Kentucky Supreme Court in 1989 in *Rose v. Council for Better Education* construed *efficient* to mean both equal and adequate.[40] They declared the entire school system unconstitutional and said that it was the General Assembly's job to create a unified school system and to monitor student performance. The following year the legislature acted, putting in place a radical set of reforms. Courts in New Jersey, Montana, and Wisconsin have enunciated similar decisions.

The school finance cases demonstrate the impact state courts can have on other branches of government, forcing legislatures to spend millions of dollars on state aid to public schools. The civil liberties area shows how state courts can function outside the purview of the U.S. Supreme Court, crafting their own set of rights. More generally, this development offers opportunity for interstate competition in civil rights just as in economic development. As one author queries,

Will states, in effect, seek to attract or repel different kinds of residents by offering different rights protection packages? In a "public choice" fashion, will people migrate, at least in part, in search of attractive rights packages?[41]

Judicial Decisionmaking

Most appeals to higher-level courts are decided rather easily and affirm the decision of the lower court. Intermediate appellate courts' business is largely of this nature. However, at the supreme court level cases are more complex and difficult to decide. Often these cases are not unanimous, and dissenting opinions are written in response to the majority opinion. In such divided cases factors other than the law influence judges' decisions.

Research on federal appellate courts has identified three influences on judicial decisionmaking: the policy preferences of the judges themselves, group decisionmaking processes, and the political environment of courts. These sets of influences are believed to affect state appellate courts in a similar fashion, but comparative research across states has not yet confirmed this.

Judges' Policy Preferences Many cases that come before appellate courts elicit different responses from liberals and conservatives. For example, liberals tend to favor the defendant in criminal cases and the employee in labor disputes, whereas conservatives favor the prosecutor and the employer. Accordingly, judges' ideological predispositions—liberal or conservative—might affect their response to arguments of different social classes. Over a series of cases, judges' voting records may show a consistent pattern of support for liberal or conservative policy positions.

At the state level, judges' political party affiliation is often used as an indicator of ideology. In a study of judges' voting behavior in the mid-1950s, Stuart Nagel established that party affiliation before becoming a judge structured judges' voting in 15 types of cases.[42] Democratic judges took the liberal position more often than did Republican judges. This tendency was especially pronounced in states using the partisan electoral system. The tendency toward partisanship is more marked in some political cultures than in others: Voting on the Michigan Supreme Court is heavily partisan, for example.

Certain issues are more likely to elicit policy preference voting from judges: Death penalty cases are one example. Emmert and Traut examined judicial decisionmaking in 190 death penalty appeals decided by the California Supreme Court between 1977 and 1990.[43] Their measure of judicial policy preferences (or values) was a liberalism score based on newspaper accounts of judges' qualifications. Using this method of scoring ideology, liberals were more than twice as likely to vote to reverse a death sentence as were conservatives (58.6 percent versus 26 percent). The authors concluded that "judges' values are of overriding importance for explaining judicial decisions in ideologically charged cases."[44]

Small Group Processes Appellate judges are small groups of people who work closely together for long periods of time. It is well-known that in small groups certain processes work to generate consensus. In courts, the larger the majority issuing an opinion, the greater the authority it carries. For this reason, there is an incentive for judges to work together to reach consensus.

Certain chief justices are particularly skilled at persuading their colleagues to work together. Justice Vanderbilt (whose efforts on the New Jersey Supreme Court were described in Box 8.1) engendered harmonious relations among his colleagues and developed consensus on core issues. This in turn allowed the court to be more authoritative within the state and across the nation. Other courts exhibit a breakdown of consensus: The switch from a liberal to a conservative majority on the California Supreme Court was accompanied by a breakdown in interpersonal relations.

One intriguing question is how women and minorities will fit into the small, collegial work group. Few studies have been conducted as yet but Allen and Wall did analyze gender difference in decisionmaking patterns on 12 supreme courts in the 1970s and 1980s.[45] They determined that women occupied an "outsider" position; instead of moderating their behavior and conforming to group norms, they occupied either the extreme liberal or extreme conservative position on their court on criminal rights and economic liberty cases. However, where the issue was women's rights, the women consistently took a supportive position. Now that more women are judges, it would be fruitful to analyze their impact on the small group process, especially on the Minnesota Supreme Court, where women formed the majority.

Political Environment   Judges, like other public officials, are influenced by political conditions in their states. Supreme court decisions are often big news items, which generate public discussion and even controversy. In states where judges have to stand for election or retention, public opinion is registered very directly. For example, popular support for capital punishment has increased in recent years (over three-quarters of the public support the death penalty for murderers), and judges' reluctance to enforce the death penalty has become a campaign issue. California is only the most publicized case; Oregon, North Carolina, Louisiana, and Oklahoma are other states in which the death penalty was raised in judicial campaigns in the 1980s.

Melinda Hall's study of judges' voting patterns on the supreme courts of Louisiana, North Carolina, Kentucky, and Texas discovered that judges "follow the election returns"; that is, they uphold the death penalty assessed by trial courts because they fear electoral retribution.[46] Judges sustain the death penalty if they are more electorally vulnerable or in states with high murder rates. State judges seem to be becoming more responsive to the public than they were in the past.

Other important players in the political environment are interest groups. Although groups cannot directly lobby judges as they do legislators and governors, they do pursue several legitimate routes of access. One is that interest groups, often representing portions of the legal profession, express an active interest in who becomes a judge, participating in the selection process and in funding election campaigns. Interest groups also affect the agenda of the courts by their sponsorship of test cases and by their filing of amicus curiae (friend-of-the-court) briefs in cases where the organized group is not a party.

The latter tool—the amicus brief—was the subject of Lee Epstein's 16-state study between 1965 and 1990.[47] She found that the number of briefs filed has increased and that the range of groups using this technique has expanded. This finding is consistent with the general growth in the number and types of interest groups and in the activities of such groups, as described in Chapter 3.

State legislatures and governors also affect the judiciary. Legislatures fund the courts' operations, and they enact statutes that affect the courts' jurisdiction. They can pass new legislation if a court overturns a law. Mark Miller conducted personal interviews with legislators in Ohio and Massachusetts to see how they would respond to an unfavorable decision by their state's supreme court.[48] In Ohio, where the supreme court is very politicized, 88 percent of the legislators said they would file a bill or introduce a constitutional amendment to overturn a ruling they considered incorrect; in Massachusetts only 53 percent of legislators said they would do the same. In Ohio the relationship between the court and the legislature is confrontational whereas in Massachusetts the court is a passive partner in policymaking. Thus, Bay State lawmakers do not need to pay attention to their high court.

Governors play a crucial role in judicial selection and in overseeing compliance with judicial decisions. The recent example of the California Supreme Court shows the impact governors can have in their appointments: The court's position on the death penalty shifted nearly 100 percent when a new governor was able to make several appointments. Similarly, the courts need the moral support of their governors when controversial decisions are implemented. School finance reform, abortion rulings, and so forth rely on the goodwill of the governor and the executive branch to make them work. Supreme court justices cannot afford to ignore the legislative and executive branches.

✧ CONCLUSION

State courts are a vital part of state government, both in furnishing legitimacy to the political system and in policymaking. Where courts are perceived to be fair and efficient, citizens believe in their government. A sense of legitimacy increases citizen loyalty to the state and reduces the incentive for exit. In recent years more state courts have engaged in judicial activism, and thus their policymaking role has increased. This activism has engendered public reaction that may change the balance between judicial independence and democratic accountability.

The tensions among independence, popular control, and competence are apparent in several areas. The variety of judicial selection systems represents different approaches to this question. Some states maximize accountability through elections; others seek more independence and competence through merit selection procedures. No system is perfect, however. Courts' responsiveness to their immediate political culture and to the national legal culture also illustrates the tension. Some courts are distinct products of their state's political culture. Others manage to eschew their state environment and respond more to national legal trends. These courts tend to be more prestigious and to influence other courts' opinions. Thus, like other government branches, the courts are linked together through cooperation and competition.

✧ KEY TERMS

appellate courts (p. 205)
judicial activism (p. 221)
judicial policymaking (p. 217)
Missouri plan (p. 214)

norm enforcement (p. 217)
tort law revolution (p. 222)
trial courts (p. 205)

✧ FOR FURTHER READING

Joseph R. Grodin, *In Pursuit of Justice: Reflections of a State Supreme Court Justice* (Berkeley: University of California Press, 1989). The reflections of a California justice who was ousted from the bench along with Justice Rose Bird.

Harry P. Stumpf and John H. Culver, *The Politics of State Courts* (New York: Longman, 1992). One of the very few textbooks exclusively on state courts, covering trial and appellate courts and civil and criminal process.

G. Alan Tarr and Mary Cornelia Aldis Porter, *State Supreme Courts in State and Nation* (New Haven: Yale University Press, 1988). An interesting comparative analysis of three state supreme courts (Alabama, Ohio, and New Jersey). Particularly strong on how political and legal cultures influence courts.

✧ NOTES

1. 1991 Advisory Commission on Intergovernmental Relations national survey reported in John Kincaid, "The State and Federal Bills of Rights: Partners and Rivals in Liberty," *Intergovernmental Perspective* (Fall 1991), 32.

2. Brian J. Ostrom, Karen Gillions Way, Natalie B. Davis, Steven E. Hairston, and Carol R. Flango, *State Court Caseload Statistics: Annual Report 1992* (Williamsburg, Va.: National Center for State Courts, 1994), p. 6.

3. Harry P. Stumpf and John H. Culver, *The Politics of State Courts* (New York: Longman, 1992), p. 23.

4. Ostrom et al., *State Court Caseload Statistics*, p. 67.

5. Stumpf and Culver, *The Politics of State Courts*, p. 2.

6. Ostrom et al., *State Court Caseload Statistics*, p. 31.

7. Stumpf and Culver, *The Politics of State Courts*, p. 14.

8. Ostrom et al., *State Court Caseload Statistics*, p. 10. The number of civil cases constituted a 4.7 percent increase since 1985.

9. *Ibid.*, p. 18.

10. Robert A. Kagan, Bliss Cartwright, Lawrence M. Friedman, and Stanton Wheeler, "The Business of State Supreme Courts, 1870–1970," *Stanford Law Review*, 30 (November 1977), 127–156.

11. Paul Kramer, *Analyzing the Determinants of State Constitutional Activism: A Search for State Court Independence in the American Federal System*, Ph.D. dissertation (Minneapolis: University of Minnesota, 1995), p. 36.

12. Gregory A. Caldeira, "On the Reputation of State Supreme Courts," *Political Behavior*, 5, no. 1 (1983), 83–108.

13. *Ibid.*; Gregory A. Caldeira, "The Transmission of Legal Precedent: A Study of State Supreme Courts," *American Political Science Review*, 79 (March 1985), 178–193; Peter Harris, "Ecology and Culture in the Communication of Precedent Among State Supreme Courts, 1870–1970," *Law and Society Review*, 19, no. 3 (1985), 449–486.

14. James M. Hoefler, "Diffusion and Diversity: Federalism and the Right to Die in the Fifty States," *Publius*, 24 (Summer 1994), 159; Henry R. Glick, *The Right to Die* (New York: Columbia University Press, 1992), p. 147.

15. G. Alan Tarr and Mary Cornelia Aldis Porter, *State Supreme Courts in State and Nation* (New Haven: Yale University Press, 1988).

16. *Ibid.*

17. Henry R. Glick and Craig F. Emmert, "Stability and Change: Characteristics of State Supreme Court Judges," *Judicature*, 70 (August/September 1986), 107–112.

18. *Ibid.*

19. Personal communication from the Information Service, National Center for State Courts, 1995.

20. Henry R. Glick and Craig F. Emmert, "Selection Systems and Judicial Characteristics: The Recruitment of State Supreme Court Judges," *Judicature*, 70 (December/January 1987), 228–235.

21. Erik Wasmann, Nicholas P. Lovrich, Jr., and Charles H. Sheldon, "Perceptions of State and Local Courts: A Comparison Across Selection Systems," *The Justice System Journal*, 11, no. 2 (1986), 168–185.

22. Nicholas O. Alozie, "Distribution of Women and Minority Judges: The Effects of Judicial Selection Methods," *Social Science Quarterly*, 71 (June 1990), 315–325.

23. Barbara Luck Graham, "Do Judicial Selection Systems Matter? A Study of Black Representation on State Courts," *American Politics Quarterly*, 18 (July 1990), 316–336.

24. Lawrence Baum, *American Courts: Process and Policy* (Boston: Houghton Mifflin, 1986), p. 98.

25. Stumpf and Culver, *The Politics of State Courts*, p. 56.

26. William K. Hall and Larry T. Aspin, "What Twenty Years of Judicial Retention Elections Have Told Us," *Judicature*, 70 (April/May 1987), 343.

27. Baum, *American Courts*, p. 98.

28. Hall and Aspin, "What Twenty Years of Judicial Retention Elections Have Told Us," p. 347.

29. Kenyon D. Bunch and Gregory Casey, "Political Controversy on Missouri's Supreme Court: The Case of Merit vs. Politics," *State and Local Government Review*, 22 (Winter 1990), 15.

30. Joseph R. Grodin, "Judicial Elections: The California Experience," *Judicature*, 70 (April/May 1987), 369.

31. Herbert Jacob, "Courts: The Least Visible Branch," in Virginia Gray, Herbert Jacob, and Robert Albritton, eds., *Politics in the American States*, 5th ed. (Glenview, Ill.: Scott, Foresman, 1990), pp. 252–286.

32. Stumpf and Culver, *The Politics of State Courts*, p. 145.

33. *Ibid.*, p. 141.

34. *Ibid.*, p. 24.

35. *Minnesota Courts: Annual Report 1994* (St. Paul: State of Minnesota, 1995), p. 1.

36. Craig F. Emmert and Carol Ann Traut, "State Supreme Courts, State Constitutions, and Judicial Policymaking," *The Justice System Journal*, 16, no 1 (1992), 37–48.

37. Kramer, *Analyzing the Determinants of State Constitutional Activism*, p. 86.

38. John Kincaid and Robert F. Williams, "The New Judicial Federalism: The States' Lead in Rights Protection," *Journal of State Government*, (April/June 1992), 50–52. Other scholars point out that the new judicial federalism is not necessarily in a liberal direction; see Barry Latzer, "The Hidden Conservatism of the State Court 'Revolution,'" *Judicature*, 74 (December/January 1991), 190–197; Kramer, *Analyzing the Determinants of State Constitutional Activism*.

39. Robert Suro, "Courts Ordering Financing Changes in Public Schools," *New York Times*, (March 11, 1990), A1, A13.

40. Penny M. Miller, *Kentucky Politics and Government* (Lincoln: University of Nebraska Press, 1994), p. 249.

41. John Kincaid, "State Court Protections of Individual Rights Under State Constitutions: The New Judicial Federalism," *Journal of State Government*, 61 (September/October 1988), 168.

42. Stuart S. Nagel, "Political Party Affiliation and Judges' Decisions," in Frank Munger, ed., *American State Politics* (New York: Crowell, 1966), pp. 467–479.

43. Craig F. Emmert and Carol Ann Traut, "The California Supreme Court and the Death Penalty," *American Politics Quarterly*, 22 (January 1994), 41–61.

44. *Ibid.*, p. 58; another study demonstrating the effect of ideology on decisionmaking in criminal cases is John M. Scheb II, Terry Bowen, and Gary Anderson, "Ideology, Role Orientations, and Behavior in the State Courts of Last Resort," *American Politics Quarterly*, 19 (July 1991), 324–335. Still another study shows that judges' party affiliation is a significant predictor of positions in death penalty cases but it is contingent on institutional variables; see Paul Brace and Melinda Gann Hall, "Studying Courts Comparatively: The View from the American States," *Political Research Quarterly*, 48 (March 1995), 5–29.

45. David W. Allen and Diane E. Wall, "The Behavior of Women State Supreme Court Justices: Are They Tokens or Outsiders?," *The Justice System Journal*, 12, no. 2 (1987), 232–245.

46. Melinda Gann Hall, "Justices as Representatives: Elections and Judicial Politics in the American States," *American Politics Quarterly*, 23 (October 1995), 485–503.

47. Lee Epstein, "Exploring the Participation of Organized Interests in State Court Litigation," *Political Research Quarterly*, 47 (June 1994), 335–351.

48. Mark C. Miller, "Court-Legislative Relations: The Policy Role of the Courts in Three American Governmental Systems," paper delivered at the annual meeting of the Midwest Political Science Association, Chicago, April 1992.

PART FOUR

LOCAL GOVERNMENT INSTITUTIONS

✦

THE STRUCTURE OF LOCAL GOVERNMENT

Americans assign the tasks of local government to nearly 87,000 different jurisdictions, which exhibit a bewildering variety of structural and functional characteristics. In this chapter we begin by sorting through the different basic types of local governments. Then we focus in detail on structural variations in municipal government, asking whether these variations in structure make any difference. As we shall see, different structures—say, whether city council representatives are elected by ward or at-large, or whether the city's chief executive is an elected mayor or a hired manager—may help certain groups in the city and hurt others in their respective efforts to influence government. Not surprisingly, therefore, the structures of city government have been the subject of debate since the nineteenth century. Interestingly, people seldom leave the city (exit) because they do not like the structure of their city government. Instead, they tend to join reform movements seeking change, a perfect illustration of people exercising their voice option.

✧ THE BASIC TYPES OF LOCAL GOVERNMENT

There are five basic types of local government: special districts, school districts, townships, counties, and municipalities. They have in common their status as creatures of the state, their responsibility for providing one or more government services to people in territories smaller than the whole state, and their ability to tax, borrow, and spend money for public purposes. Beyond these general common features, these various types of local governments—and even examples of the same type—vary markedly in what they do and how they do it. Table 9.1 shows the change in the numbers of these types of governments between 1942 and 1992.

Special Districts

Sometimes the citizens of a particular place decide to form a unit of local government to administer a single function or a limited set of related functions. They may already live in

TABLE 9.1 NUMBER OF LOCAL GOVERNMENT UNITS BY TYPE, 1942 AND 1992

	1942	1992
Counties	3,050	3,043
Municipalities	16,220	19,296
Townships and towns	18,919	16,666
School districts	108,579	14,556
Special districts	8,299	33,131

Source: U.S. Bureau of the Census, *Statistical Abstract of the United States: 1995* (Washington, D.C.: Government Printing Office, 1995), p. 297.

a municipality with its multipurpose general government, but they may believe that a **special district** (sometimes called a special authority) will suit their purposes and needs more effectively. Not only are special districts the most numerous form of local government today, but their numbers are growing rapidly. More than 5,000 new special districts were formed in the 1980s alone.

Special districts, which are found in both urban and rural areas, are used most commonly for natural resource functions such as flood control, irrigation management, wildlife and land conservation, and parks. The second most common function is fire protection. Social services, housing, transportation and port administration, solid waste disposal, water, sewage, and planning units are other common special district functions.

The impetus for establishing a district usually comes from individual political leaders, private businesspeople or corporations, groups of homeowners, or in some states other local governments. In any case, the process is enabled (that is, authorized) and governed by the state legislature.

The motives for choosing the special district form are various: Sometimes people think it will be cheaper to finance the function through a special district, particularly if it can pay for its service not through the general tax levy but by charging fees. New York political leaders established the Triborough Bridge Authority simply to build and maintain that bridge, and the tolls the authority charges go to pay off the bonds and cover maintenance costs. People might form a special district because their municipality has exhausted its own borrowing authority and cannot finance a big urban redevelopment project or a major sewer extension. A special district has its own authority to borrow money by issuing bonds.

Sometimes people wish to serve a larger territory than is encompassed by the boundaries of their municipality or county. Several of Wisconsin's Vocational and Technical Adult Education districts, which run the vocational colleges in the state, cover large land areas, extending across county lines and encompassing several cities, towns, and rural areas. Sometimes people resort to special districts when they do not want to establish a whole complex municipal government but they nevertheless want access to the services municipalities typically provide. Many Californians who live in the hills around San Francisco Bay in quasi-rural settings do not want to support a whole city government but are willing to pay for special districts to supply sanitation services (Central Contra Costa Sanitary District), water (Contra Costa County Water District), fire protection (San

Ramon Valley Fire Protection District), and health care (Mount Diablo Hospital District).

Occasionally, the architects of special districts choose this form because it is the only type of local government that can establish jurisdiction across state lines; thus, the Port Authority of New York and New Jersey finances, builds, operates, and maintains airports, tunnels, and bridges and docks in both states.

Most special districts perform a single function, such as Metropolitan Atlanta Rapid Transit Authority (MARTA) or the 655 cemetery special districts in the state of Kansas or the rural flood control districts found in most states. About 8 percent of the special districts are multifunctional, such as the Port Authority in New York and New Jersey and the Reedy Creek Improvement District (Orlando, Florida), better known to most people as Disney World. This latter district has the power to lay sewer lines, provide police and fire protection, construct waste treatment plants, do flood control, and build an aiport.[1]

Special districts are governed in a variety of ways. Some have elected boards of commissioners, others are governed by officials appointed by the governor or mayor, and some have governing bodies made up of officials from other local governments. In most cases, the citizen role in governing special districts is not great. Few people vote in special district elections, and even fewer can name the officials who run them.

School Districts

In most—but not all—states, school systems are run not by the city government but by autonomous school district governments. These governments have their own taxing, spending, and borrowing authority. They are typically governed by an elected school board, which hires a superintendent. Their boundaries may or may not coincide with the boundaries of the community they serve. Unlike special districts, school districts have been declining in number since World War II. In 1942 there were 108,579 school districts in the United States, many of them responsible for running the proverbial one-room rural schoolhouse. Today there are only about 14,000. The little rural districts have been steadily consolidating.

Although school districts are autonomous local governments in most places, in some cities the school system is just another agency of city government. New York, Boston, Baltimore, Memphis, Norfolk, and Hartford are among the few cities that do not have independent school districts.

Townships and Towns

Another 16,666 local jurisdictions are townships, found in only 20 states in the Midwest and New England. In New England the towns, which often cover territory more the size of counties in other states, are multipurpose general governments for very small communities and their surrounding rural areas. Many New England towns are governed by periodic town meetings of all the adult residents. These are presided over by the elected town selectmen, who function like a city council. These towns offer a range of services, from running the public library to providing police, fire, and emergency medical services to paving and plowing local roads. Towns in Wisconsin, Michigan, New Jersey, and a few other states resemble the New England town in the scope of their powers.

In other states, mainly in the Great Plains, these small rural units of government, usually called townships, cover six square miles, the original unit or section laid out in surveys in the nineteenth century. They tend to perform a more limited range of functions than the multipurpose towns of New England. Some have constables and many service local rural roads. Some rural areas served by township governments have become so depopulated that the governments themselves have ceased to exist. In fact, one study found that 58 percent of all townships have no full-time employees.[2] The number of townships and towns has been slowly but steadily dropping.

Counties

Counties are general-purpose governments that function on a level between the state and the municipality. One role that counties play is to serve as an administrative arm of the state, managing such functions for the state as the state trial and sometimes intermediate appellate court system, the district attorney's office, and various health and welfare services, such as child welfare and mental institutions. In this role, the county government serves all the people of the county, whether they live in a municipality or not. Other common county functions in this category include assessing property taxes, recording deeds, and running the county jail.

In another role, counties provide services primarily for rural areas, replicating services provided for urban dwellers by municipalities within the county: Farm-to-market roads, law enforcement through the county sheriff's office, and land use management are perhaps the most common of these functions. Complicating this profusion of local governments, some township governments provide these same services on a local level in rural areas, functioning essentially as adjuncts to the county government.

Counties and municipalities have some differences, but the line between these two types of local government is fast disappearing. Historically, states have given county governments less discretion than city governments, but this has gradually changed as more and more states give their counties greater freedom to run their affairs. There are some structural differences between counties and municipalities too: Whereas nearly all cities have chief executives (mayors or city managers), counties are more likely to be "headless" commission governments. Two-thirds of the 3,043 counties are governed by small elected boards of commissioners with no single executive to coordinate and focus policymaking and administration. Only 786 counties have an administrator or manager hired by an elected commission to run the county's affairs; another 383 have an elected county executive, similar to a mayor.[3] Commission counties are far more likely to be found in rural areas; heavily urbanized counties tend to have county executives. Another difference between counties and municipalities is that counties are more likely to be responsible for health and welfare functions such as hospitals, welfare, general relief, and public health departments. Figure 9.1 shows the structure of a strong county government headed by an elected executive.

Certain of these generalizations have begun to break down in recent decades, however, blurring the distinction between county and city governments. As suburbanization has increased, with people moving into areas beyond the city limits that are not themselves organized into municipalities, counties have had to pick up more and more functions that were once thought to be municipal or urban in nature. This is particularly

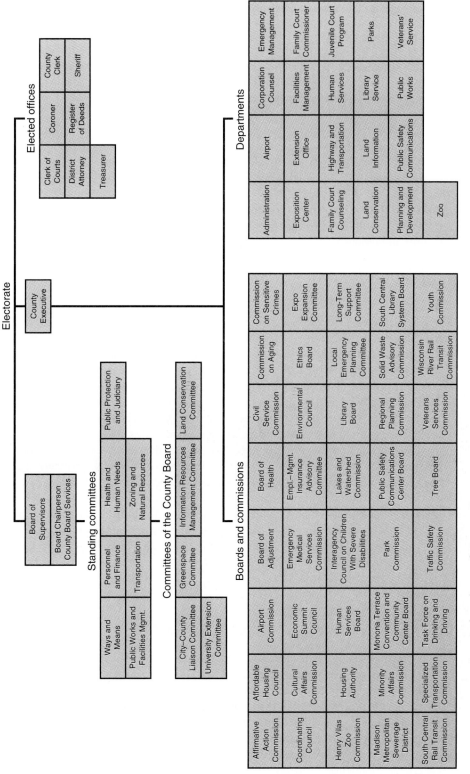

FIGURE 9.1 Organization of Dane County Government Counties are general purpose governments that function on a level between the state and the municipality.

true of the 738 counties found in metropolitan areas. Today, it is not uncommon to find these heavily urbanized counties involved in mass transit, economic development, water supply, airports, highways, zoning, housing, waste disposal, and parks. Most of them, as we have noted, have a chief executive, much like the cities within their borders.

A few counties (27 to be exact) have consolidated with the cities within them. Now their borders are the same and their governments are, for most part, meshed into one. The oldest of these consolidations is New Orleans and New Orleans Parish (counties are called parishes in Louisiana), which dates back to 1805. Others include Boston, San Francisco, and Philadelphia. New York City's five boroughs are also each counties. Nineteen of these city-county consolidations have occurred since World War II, the most notable of which include Indianapolis and Marion County and Jacksonville and Duval County in Florida.

Municipalities

The most common sort of general-purpose government is the municipality. There are nearly 19,300 of these, most of them tiny places. Only slightly more than a third of them have more than 2,500 people—technically called urban places—and they are the focus of the remainder of this chapter. Legally, these cities and villages are municipal corporations, a status that carries with it the general powers to sue and be sued, hold property, make contracts, tax, regulate commerce, and even make money in proprietary undertakings. Municipalities may also exercise police powers, defined in the law as the right to limit, regulate, or prohibit business and personal activity and property uses in order to protect the public health, safety, morals, and general welfare.

The particular powers of municipalities, as noted in Chapter 2, are set out in the charter and its amendments. So too is the particular structure of government laid out in the charter: unlike the states and national government, which adopted single elected executives and bicameral legislatures (except for Nebraska, which has only one legislative house), municipalities come in many different forms. We study these structural variations in part because we are interested in the sheer capacity for human invention. But structural variety is of more than academic interest: Structure may influence who wins power and representation in a community and how responsive its leaders are to popular opinion.

✧ WHY STRUCTURAL VARIATION IN LOCAL GOVERNMENT IS IMPORTANT

The structural features of government establish the context within which politics occurs. Politics is the struggle among interests over the allocation of public resources, and often the interests or groups in contention approach this struggle with very different chances of winning. One aspect of the political world that helps to establish these different chances is the structure of government. Structure is not neutral. Different structures tend to favor different interests in the political struggle by making it easier or more difficult to attain office and mobilize a constituency. Thus, structures not only shape and constrain political conflict; sometimes structure itself is the issue.

We are concerned with three elements of structure: the nature of the executive, the method by which city council members are elected, and the role of political parties in local elections. Let us first examine variations in the structure of the executive.

Manager or Mayor

Some cities vest all the executive power in the hands of an elected mayor; other cities hire a professional manager and relegate their mayor to mainly ceremonial duties such as ribbon-cutting and handing the key to the city to visiting personalities. (A handful—no more than 170 or so—govern by commission, much like the counties without a single executive.) The mayor form is more prevalent in big cities than in medium-sized cities, but it is also more common in smaller places, where the city budget is too small to permit hiring a full-time professional manager. The **city manager** form, or council-manager government, as it is generally called, is more common in medium-sized cities with populations between 25,000 and 250,000. Table 9.2 lists the numbers of cities with each of these types of government.

Some people believe that the mayoral executive is the more responsive, or democratic, arrangement: It allows the voters to pass judgment on an incumbent, something the mayor keeps in the back of his or her mind while in office. Officials who have to face reelection try hard to satisfy enough people and interests to make a winning electoral coalition. In contrast, a professional manager, hired by the city council, never has to defend a record during an election campaign. A manager does have to satisfy a majority on the council, of course, but that may be quite different from satisfying the electorate.

Whose interests do each of these two basic executive forms seem to favor? Proponents and analysts of the manager plan, which originated in the civic reform movement (discussed in the following section) early in the twentieth century, have long thought that it favored middle-class business interests, whereas a mayoral system favored working-class, minority, and ethnic groups that could put together an electoral majority. When the manager plan was under consideration in Dallas in the 1930s, the local newspaper asked,

> *Why not run Dallas itself on a business schedule by business methods under businessmen? . . . The city manager plan is after all only a business management plan. . . . The city manager is the executive of a corporation under a board of directors. Dallas is the corporation.*[4]

TABLE 9.2 FORMS OF MUNICIPAL GOVERNMENT, CITIES 2,500 AND OVER, 1995

Mayor-council	3,294
Council-manager	2,738
Commission	163
Town meeting	435

Source: International City Management Association, *Municipal Yearbook,* 1995 (Washington, D.C., ICMA, 1995), p. xii.

In Dallas and other manager cities, the manager, a business-trained professional, is typically drawn from a middle-class background. He or she responsive to other elites, namely, the people on the city council, and committed to efficient government.

At its inception at least, the city manager system was regarded not only as an arrangement for ensuring businesslike government but also, by some, as a way of undercutting the clout of newly powerful working-class ethnic groups—primarily the Irish, Italians, and Jews—who could win positions of influence through the ballot box. "Adoption of the [manager] plan," two political scientists wrote nearly 30 years ago, "represents a victory for those who favor the Anglo-Saxon Protestant middle-class ideal."[5]

It is important to understand that structural biases do not guarantee that certain types of people and the interests they represent will achieve positions of authority while other types are barred. Business credentials and social background may once have been primary considerations in the selection of city managers, but most managers these days have been trained at schools of public administration and worked their way up the career ladder, beginning as assistant managers in small cities and moving as opportunities open up.[6] Merit and experience are probably more important now than social or business backgrounds. City manager positions are no longer held exclusively by whites: The International City Management Association reports that in 1995 there were 29 African-American city managers and 78 Hispanic city managers. Tucson, which had a Hispanic manager for many years, and Dallas, which had an African-American manager, are two examples.[7]

Likewise, the stereotypical mayor of times past, the cigar-chomping politician, the product of his working-class ethnic neighborhood, is scarcely an accurate representation of the typical mayor today. The mayoralties of big cities are no longer mainly working-class preserves. Many mayors, such as Richard Riordan of Los Angeles, come from the middle-class world of business rather than a working-class background.

Still, it has been easier for members of disadvantaged groups to win the mayoralty than to gain positions as professional city managers. As Table 9.3 shows, blacks and women are slightly better represented among the nation's mayors than they are among its managers and chief administrative officers.

TABLE 9.3 DIVERSITY IN CITY HALL: MINORITY AND FEMALE CITY EXECUTIVES IN CITIES OVER 2,500, 1995 Blacks and women are slightly better represented among the nation's mayors than they are among its managers and chief administrative officers.

	Mayors	*Managers, Chief Administrative Officers*
Black	2.5% (106)	1.1% (53)
Hispanic	1.6 (70)	2.1 (116)
Female	14.2 (613)	11.1 (379)

Source: International City Management Association, *Municipal Yearbook,* 1995 (Washington, D.C.: ICMA, 1995).

Ward Versus District Elections

Another structural variation concerns the method by which city council members are elected. Some cities use a ward system; that is, each council member is elected from a single-member district of the city. Other places use an **at-large election,** by which each council member is elected by the entire city electorate and represents the whole city. The city as a whole functions as a multimember district. Still other communities use a combination of at-large and ward elections.

A ward system favors residentially concentrated minorities, whereas an at-large system favors the majority. An ethnic or racial group that makes up, say, only 15 percent of the city's population can nevertheless win representation on the council if it constitutes a majority in a small geographical ward. Residential concentration of particular ethnic and racial groups—white ethnic neighborhoods such as "Little Italy" and "Poletown" or the black ghetto or the Hispanic barrio—are commonplace in American cities.

Such groups are likely to be disadvantaged in an at-large system, however. In the typical at-large arrangement, each voter has as many votes as there are seats on the council. Every candidate is competing against every other candidate. Suppose there are seven seats on the council, contested by seven candidates of Yankee Protestant origins and seven of Irish-Catholic background. Now suppose that the Yankees make up 51 percent of the electorate and each Yankee voter casts his or her seven votes only for the Yankee candidates. At the same time the Irish make up 49 percent of the electorate and they cast their votes only for Irish candidates. In such a situation, the Yankees would win 100 percent of the seats with only 51 percent of the vote.

Such a situation has been common in American history. Take the case of Boston, a city that switched its electoral system back and forth several times. In the first half of the twentieth century, Yankee Protestants were the minority ethnic group in a city dominated by Irish and Italian voters. In the 25 years during which the city elected its council members by wards, the 84 Irish aldermen elected in this period shared the city council with 12 Jews, 9 Yankees, 4 Italians, and 1 black. When the city switched to at-large elections, the only people to sit on the council until the 1960s were Irish and a few Italians.[8] Not surprisingly, with the rise of black political power in contemporary cities, the issue of what sort of electoral system is used has become the subject of much debate and litigation. We shall examine this development in more detail later.

Partisan or Nonpartisan

A third structural variation deals with the role of political parties in municipal elections, specifically whether elections are held on a partisan or nonpartisan basis. Slightly over one-quarter of all municipalities with a population over 2,500 use party labels on their ballots. Thus, voters are able to identify candidates as Democrats or Republicans or as members of some other party (such as Liberals and Conservatives in New York City). In **nonpartisan elections,** only the names of the candidates appear on the ballot, and competition for office is pursued by ad hoc groups rather than ongoing political party organizations.

The absence of identifying cues means that voters must be more attentive to election issues and the contestants' respective positions. In contrast, a voter in a partisan election may use party labels as a shorthand way of "knowing" what the respective candidates stand for. Nonpartisanship, therefore, gives an advantage to people who follow local politics through the news media or through membership in organizations whose leaders provide information on candidates and endorsements. Such people are more likely to be middle-class.

People who do not read about local politics or follow it through other means have little information about election contestants in a nonpartisan system. Lack of interest in politics is associated with lack of education and income, that is, with lower-class status. Although such people might be mobilized to come to the polls by party workers in a partisan system, or might be persuaded out of party loyalty to vote for a party's candidate even if they do not know much about the candidate, there are few pressures or incentives in a nonpartisan system to bring the uninterested into the voting booth. Thus, a nonpartisan system is thought to bias local elections in favor of middle-class interests.

Because working-class and poor people tend disproportionately to be Democratic voters, whereas middle-class people are more often Republican voters, nonpartisan electoral systems are thought to bias elections in favor of Republicans and conservatives. The evidence to support this notion is mixed, however. One extensive study of city council elections finds that nonpartisanship is not a significant factor in explaining the election of Republicans.[9] Another study, of nonpartisan county supervisory elections in California, suggests that the bias against Democratic candidates does hold. Edward Lascher finds that although 59 percent of county board supervisors were Republican, Democratic voters held an edge in voter registration and expressed party preference. His explanation is that Republican candidates had better backing from business and agricultural interest groups and thus more resources with which to campaign.[10]

✧ STRUCTURAL VARIETY IN MUNICIPAL GOVERNMENT: MACHINES AND REFORM

In order to understand how such variety came about, it is necessary to know something about the **reform movement** in the late nineteenth and early twentieth century. Different municipal government structures emerged from a deep and long-lasting conflict between native middle-class reformers and working-class people of mainly immigrant stock. *Reform movement* is a broad term for a variety of primarily middle-class responses to profound changes that were occurring in American society after the Civil War. The vastly increased immigration in this period, much of it from southern and eastern Europe, seemed to threaten American values and social patterns as native-born Americans, mainly of Protestant, northern European descent, understood them.

At the same time the nation, where about three-quarters of the population had lived in small villages or on farms until the Civil War, was undergoing rapid urbanization. Chicago, for example, went from a frontier trading post in 1830 to a city of 1.5 million people in 1900. Indeed, of the 153 U.S. cities with more than 100,000 people in 1970, 65 percent were not even established until after 1850.[11] Urban growth on this scale brought large numbers of people of very different backgrounds together in dense settlements, engendering cultural and political tensions. At the same time, the establishment of cities necessitated vast expenditures of public resources to build streets, sewers, schools, jails, and water systems. To give some sense of the size of the task, Jon Teaford points out that during the late nineteenth century Chicago constructed waterworks capable of pumping

500 million gallons a day, a drainage system of more than 1,500 miles of sewers, and a paved road system totaling 1,400 miles lit by 38,000 street lamps and served by 925 miles of streetcar lines.[12] The sheer size of the task of city-building in Chicago and other places created troubling social tensions, on the one hand, and great opportunities for both honest and dishonest profit, on the other.

Along with immigration and urbanization, the country was also undergoing the strains of industrialization. The late nineteenth century saw the creation of a large industrial proletariat: poorly paid, semiskilled, and unskilled workers performing repetitive and often dangerous tasks. Many Americans yearned for a simpler and highly romanticized version of the rural society they had known in the early part of the century.

These societal transformations generated a host of severe strains. Anti-Catholicism, anti-Semitism, and racial prejudice all flourished in the decades around the turn of the century, belying the myth of the melting pot. The new industrial order was making some Americans very rich, but wealth came at the expense of a vast and increasing working class living on the edge of poverty. The United States was thought to be a classless society, but bitter labor strikes and their brutal suppression by hired "goons" and sometimes even the U.S. Army emphasized the chasm between the industrial proletariat and the middle class. In the cities, the urban boss emerged as the dominant political figure in a nation that cherished in its mythology the democratic town meeting as its preferred form of local government.

People in the broad middle class responded to these great changes and the strains they created in a variety of often contradictory ways, yet many of their responses are subsumed under the term *reform*. Some, such as Jane Addams, sought through the settlement house movement to help immigrant women in particular to adjust to American life by teaching English, helping them to adapt to American standards of housekeeping and cooking, and providing nursery and kindergarten care. The Settlement House movement, which laid the foundations for the modern social work profession, was marked by its sympathetic approach to the immigrant poor. Other reform groups sought to regulate tenement housing, notorious for its lack of sanitation and fresh air. As a contemporary magazine writer observed, "You are liable to arrest if you allow your stable to become filthy and a nuisance [but] the landlord may do pretty much what he pleases with his tenements."[13]

A different wing of the reform movement, the famous muckraker journalists, sought to expose the corruption of large corporations and the venality of urban political machines. Others sought to ban or regulate child labor in the mills and mines.

Many other reformers, however, were unsympathetic to the abuse of the poor or the plight of the immigrants. Instead, they embraced a virulent anti-immigrant "nativism," arguing that the influx of Catholic and Jewish immigrants threatened American civilization and morals. Harvard art historian Charles Eliot Norton wrote in 1897, "I fancy that there has never been a community on a higher and pleasanter level than that of New England during the first thirty years of this century, before the coming in of Jacksonian Democracy and the invasion of the Irish."[14]

Many of these strains—both the sympathetic and the nativist—combined in the civic or urban reform movement. Proponents of urban reform believed or professed to believe that politics ought to be pursued in the interests of the public good, not for private benefit, which seemed to be the motive of the urban political bosses of immigrant stock. Reform, Richard Hofstadter wrote in his classic study of this movement, was "founded upon the indigenous Yankee-Protestant political traditions, and upon middle-class life, [which] assumed and demanded the constant disinterested activity of the citizen in public affairs."[15] In contrast, it was said, immigrants saw politics as an avenue for dealing with personal economic insecurity and their generally disadvantaged status in American society, not as an activity to promote the public good. The immigrants' need for protection and help provided a rationale for the emergence of the political machine and the urban boss.

Political machines, which flourished in American cities from the period after the Civil War until perhaps the 1950s, are organizations that rely largely on material incentives to guarantee the allegiance and participation of their supporters. Machines are thus distinguished from political organizations that bring adherents together for ideological reasons or to further some policy or principle. The object of machines was to win municipal political power, specifically by controlling the mayor's office, the city council, and whatever other commissions, officers, or boards provided a locus of authority. In order to put together electoral majorities among the increasingly numerous ethnic and immigrant groups of the twentieth-century American city, machines offered material help in the form of patronage jobs (working on street crews or in the parks, running the elevator in city hall, or inspecting the city waterworks, for example), contracts to do business with the city (ranging from construction of new public buildings to the sale of office supplies), and various forms of assistance (emergency cash or food for the poor, intervention with the authorities to fix parking tickets, and the like).

Machines were led by bosses, some of immigrant stock, others native-born Americans. Some bosses, such as William Marcy Tweed, who ran New York City from 1866 to 1871, never held major municipal office, but through the adroit bestowal of favors and money managed for a time to control the mayor and the city attorney and most of the people on the council. Others ruled a city as mayor, such as Richard J. Daley, who ran Chicago from 1955 to 1976.

Some have argued that the urban machines performed many beneficial functions, ranging from centralizing power in a governmentally weak and fragmented local political system to integrating the immigrants into the political life of the nation to providing an avenue for socioeconomic mobility when other routes were closed.[16] (As the famous Boston political boss James Michael Curley once remarked, "I chose politics because prospects of ever getting anywhere elsewhere seemed remote."[17])

From the reformers' point of view, however, machines and bosses raised a number of problems. One was that by uniting and mobilizing a diverse and numerous ethnic constituency, machines were able to capture and hold political office. Yankee Protestants, increasingly a numerical minority, were rendered powerless in electoral competition. Another problem was that the idea that politics was an avenue for private benefit, combined with the assumption that loyalty could be ensured in exchange for material incentives, could lead to enormous corruption. Voters, often willing to trade their vote for free drinks in the local tavern, voted, in the famous phrase of the day, "early and often." Bosses skimmed the public till: Tweed made a fortune by exacting kickbacks from municipal contractors, who happily paid in order to win the city's business. The Tweed Ring, as his machine was called, diverted between $30 and $100 million for its own purposes.[18]

Reformers were convinced that machines flourished particularly in partisan, ward-based mayor governments. The party offered an organizational base, the wards provided a territorial base, and the mayoralty constituted a seat of authority easily captured by the growing legions of ethnic and immigrant voters. As prominent civic reformer and Cornell University president Andrew White once complained,

Boss Tweed of New York, a frequent target of cartoonist Thomas Nash, firmly believed that the city was so split into factions, ethnic groups, and interests that the only way to govern was through bribery, patronage, or corruption. (*Source:* Archive Photos)

A crowd of illiterate peasants, freshly raked in from Irish bogs, or Bohemian mines, or Italian robber nests, may exercise virtual control. . . . The vote of a single tenement house, managed by a professional politician, will neutralize the vote of an entire street of well-to-do citizens.[19]

One answer to the problem of machines, the reformers believed, was to change the structures under which such organizations and their bosses seemed to arise.

In the years around the turn of the century, reform groups, exercising their voice option, began to advocate the elimination of party labels and the establishment of at-large electoral systems in cities. The idea was to attract people committed not to party or neighborhood but rather to the general or public good. Presumably, people who could gain office without the aid of party organization (seen by many reformers as synonymous with the political machine) and who could appeal to the entire city electorate rather than just those inhabiting one small ward would be people with greater vision.

In addition, the reformers began to advocate professional management of the city in order, as they argued, to separate politics from administration. Managers, as trained administrators not beholden to an electorate, would run the city without regard to favoritism or party advantage; efficiency would be their bottom line.

Each of the variations in municipal government, then, derives from the conflict between the reformers, who sought not only clean government but a reassertion of white,

Anglo-Saxon political dominance, and the newly powerful immigrant and ethnic groups, principally the Irish, who relied on political power for economic and social advancement.

Today, much of that particular conflict has been forgotten. For one thing, there are hardly any urban machines left. The last great machines, located in Chicago and Albany, disintegrated after the deaths of their leaders, Richard J. Daley in 1976 and Erastus Corning in 1983. In addition, court rulings in Chicago eliminated much of the patronage that provided the lifeblood of the machine, opening various government jobs to people on the basis of merit rather than political connections.

More generally, local politics as a livelihood has lost much of its allure, nor is it a source of social welfare or entertainment for many. The development of civil service employment helped to reduce patronage jobs, the passage of federal welfare programs and social security legislation eliminated much of the need for people to turn to ward bosses for help, and the development of television greatly reduced the propensity to participate in politics for social or entertainment reasons. People are much less likely to go down to the party clubhouse for the evening or welcome the ward boss on their front porch when they could instead be watching their favorite sitcom on television.

As machine government has died out and as the older immigrant groups have become assimilated, certain structural arrangements that reformers pushed have become relatively noncontroversial. The city manager form, for example, is no longer regarded as a device to hold ethnic groups in political check. Nor is it thought to offer a special advantage over mayor cities in achieving efficient government, because most mayor cities now have city administrators, appointed by the mayor, who function in much the same way as city managers. Of the more than 3,000 municipalities that have a manager system, fewer than 10 per year consider changing their charter to a mayor system. Although some of these cities occasionally do change—Rochester, New York, switched from a manager to a mayor system in the mid-1970s—more than 90 percent of such proposals fail.

As for nonpartisan local elections, they have become the norm in most places. The scope and strength of partisan attachment to the major political parties in the general electorate have weakened in the last several decades and party organization at the municipal level has withered. In 1981, just under a third of all municipalities had partisan elections; now it is down to about a quarter of all cities. There is virtually no agitation to abolish nonpartisan elections, even though, as we have seen, there is evidence that they tend to have lower voter turnout than partisan elections, and they generally overrepresent high-income groups.[20]

At-large council elections, as we shall see later on in this chapter, have been under attack for more than a decade as posing barriers to minority representation. Of all the structural arrangements introduced in the civic reform era, at-large elections are the only ones that still engender controversy and conflict.

✧ CITY EXECUTIVES

Mayors

Municipal chief executives, whether mayors or managers, occupy a central place in the local policymaking system. Let us first examine mayors. They are typically the source of policy initiatives, and they are usually the ones responsible for putting together a coalition to support the development, passage, and implementation of particular programs. Mayors also seek to influence public opinion or to mobilize it in ways that support their initiatives. During the nineteenth century most cities were governed by **weak mayor** systems, an arrangement in which power is dispersed among numerous independent boards, commissions, and officeholders, where the mayor typically lacks the authority to develop the city's budget, make administrative appointments, or exercise a veto over city council legislation. The New York City of Boss Tweed's day had a weak mayor system. As one contemporary observer wrote,

> *The Mayor has been deprived of all controlling power. The Board of Aldermen, the Board of twenty-four Councilmen, and twelve Supervisors, [and] the twenty-one members of the Board of Education are so many independent legislative bodies. . . . The police are governed by four Commissioners, appointed by the Governor. The charitable and reformatory institutions of the city are in [the] charge of four Commissioners whom the City Comptroller appoints. . . . Four Commissioners, appointed by the Governor for eight years, manage the Fire Department. . . . The finances of the city are in [the] charge of the Comptroller, whom the people elect for four years. . . . Was there ever such a hodge-podge of government before in the world?*[21]

Today the weak mayor form, which exists in whole or in part in somewhat more than a third of all cities with populations over 25,000,[22] means that not only does the mayor share the ballot with other independently elected officials, but he or she also lacks veto power, does not prepare the budget for the city, and does not appoint the heads of the major city departments. San Francisco is an example of a city with certain weak mayor features. Although the mayor supervises the budget process and may veto city council (Board of Supervisor) actions, he or she shares appointment powers with other elected officials and commissions. In an unusual arrangement, the mayor appoints a chief administrative officer (CAO), who serves a 10-year term. The CAO in turn appoints the heads of the departments of Public Health, Purchasing, and Public Works. These account for roughly one-third of the city's budget. In addition, the mayor appoints a city controller, who serves for life (most mayors inherit some previous mayor's CAO and controller). The controller is responsible for the city's fiscal affairs. Other city functions are controlled by commissions, whose members are appointed by the mayor, but which in turn appoint department heads. This applies, for example, to the City Planning Department, the Housing Authority, and the Redevelopment Agency. Finally, power is shared with a number of entirely independent regional authorities such as the Bay Area Rapid Transit District, the Metropolitan Transportation Commission, and the Bay Area Sewer Services Agency. Clearly, the San Francisco mayor is only one of a large number of formal power holders in the government of the city.

Weak mayor systems are, naturally, distinguished from **strong mayor** cities. This arrangement, introduced during the reform era, is designed to centralize authority and make it easier for the chief executive to hold accountable and control the various parts of the city government. Strong mayors control the budget process, exercise a veto, and appoint the key heads of city agencies. Boston provides a good example of a strong mayor system. The mayor in that city appoints all department heads, most of them without the approval of the city council. In addition, he or she controls over 2,000 other appointments, some to full-time jobs, others to various boards and commissions. The mayor's staff is exempt from civil service rules and is not limited in size. The mayor prepares the city budget, which the council may only decrease, not increase. Although parks, roads, public transportation, and schools are all controlled by independent authorities, there are no officials independently elected on a citywide basis or appointed for long terms who share executive authority with the mayor.

These structural differences in mayor systems are important to the degree that they disperse or centralize formal authority in city government. They tend to make the job of managing and leading the city more or less difficult: The less a mayor must share authority, the easier it is to take action and to achieve high visibility as a leader. The more a mayor can appoint people to positions of authority and influence the budget, the more he or she is in control. But the formal structure of authority does not determine the quality of a mayor's political leadership: Many imaginative, vigorous leaders have operated in what are formally weak mayor systems. Mayor Richard J. Daley of Chicago (1955–1976) was a weak mayor by the terms of the city charter, but he presided over one of the most effective political organizations in modern urban history.

Henry Maier, who served as mayor of Milwaukee from 1960 to 1988, also operated for most of his years in office under a weak mayor arrangement. The mayor shared power with several independently elected officers, he could make appointments only with the city council's consent, and he did not have responsibility for drawing up the budget. Yet Maier exercised strong leadership by developing a good mayoral staff to gather information and keep an eye on the city bureaucracy. He drew up a budget even though this was formally a city council function, and he reorganized city government by consolidating a number of departments, which enabled him to monitor just a few departments rather than many. Furthermore, during his tenure he emerged on the national scene through force of personality as an articulate spokesperson for urban interests. Clearly, a determined politician can transcend many of the limitations of formal structure. As a former mayor of Minneapolis put it, "If you have a mayor with a strong personality, he can be a strong mayor."[23]

Managers

First instituted in Staunton, Virginia (1908), and Sumter, South Carolina (1912), the manager form became a major plank in the civic reform agenda. In theory, the council-manager system, as it is formally known, was designed to put policymaking authority in the hands of an elected city council and administrative responsibilities into the hands of the manager, who was hired by and accountable to the city council. Nearly all council-manager cities also have mayors, either elected by the city electorate (San Antonio, Texas, for example) or chosen by the city council from among their number (Kansas City, Missouri, and Hartford, Connecticut, for example). But such mayors typically have little formal authority. They are really ceremonial mayors, presiding over city council meetings, greeting visiting dignitaries at the airport, and cutting ribbons at the opening of new public buildings. One survey found that only about one out of ten mayors in city manager cities could exercise a veto over council actions. Only 1 percent of these ceremonial mayors prepare a budget and appoint department heads.[24] These crucial powers all belong to the professional manager.

Reformers believed that administration placed in the hands of a trained manager could be divorced from the political process. They were convinced that the development of a budget, management of personnel, implementation of legislative actions, provision of information to the council, and so on could be done in a neutral, professional way without the need to take into account the desires of differing interests in the city and without the need to bargain, persuade, and make promises.

Two problems immediately became apparent, however. One was that it is usually not practical to try to maintain a sharp distinction between political and administrative roles. The second is that it is not immediately apparent how a city manager can be made responsive to public opinion and whether he or she can be held accountable by the people of the city.

Formally, the manager's responsibilities are much like those of an elected mayor: He or she appoints department heads, supervises the administration of city agencies, attends council meetings and takes part in the debates, prepares a budget and presents it to the council, recommends programs and courses of action to the council, and generally sees to it that the laws and ordinances of the city are carried out. Naturally, each of these functions involves choices, and those choices promote certain ideas and help certain interests and not others: A budget, for example, represents a set of priorities and an agenda for action. What is left out of the budget may be as important as what is included. Some groups will believe that their interests have been promoted; others will feel that they have been ignored. Appointments, of course, are also intensely political choices: Which groups have been recognized in the appointment process and which ones have not?

Many managers work in communities in which the city council is composed of part-time amateurs with no independent staff. Through their intimate familiarity with the operations of the city government and their ability to recommend action to the council (and back up those recommendations with information and staff reports that they have commissioned), managers typically emerge as the most powerful political figures in their city government. In wielding power and participating in political debates, managers may be seen as politicians as well as professionally trained managers. Yet unlike most politicians, they never have to stand for election.

How accountable are they to the people? Managers argue that they are held accountable to the electorate by the elected city council, for they can be dismissed at any time. The average tenure of city managers is less than four years. One city manager who runs a community with a ten-person city council puts the matter of accountability this way: "I learn to count to six all over again, in a hurry, after each election."[25]

Opponents of the manager system point out that most managers are brought in from outside the city and do not immediately understand its array of interests. Furthermore, popular control of the manager through the city council is problematic to the degree that voting in council elections is very low and many people do not even know the identity of their councilperson. Under such circumstances, democratic accountability is tenuous. Finally, by their control of the information on which the council acts, managers can easily manipulate the legislative body.

✧ WHAT DIFFERENCE DOES IT MAKE WHO IS CHIEF EXECUTIVE?

One school of thought maintains that no incumbent of the chief executive's office, no matter what its form, can make much difference. Cities are beset by such severe problems that political leadership is helpless. A city's fortunes, in this view, are determined by great international economic forces, the decisions of great multinational corporations, and the hard fact of racial division. Urban executives are simply caretakers in crumbling city halls.

Yet there is evidence that this pessimistic determinism must be modified. Many would contend that mayoral leadership does make a difference, in manager cities where the mayor is a ceremonial figure as well as in mayor-council cities. We can evaluate the impact of mayoral leadership in both symbolic and substantive terms.

Symbolic leadership involves setting a tone, providing reassurance, or playing on certain fears or concerns. By their rhetoric and actions, mayors can pull communities together or divide them. When Norman Rice, mayor of Seattle, was elected president of the U.S. Conference of Mayors in 1995, the first plank in his urban agenda was a "campaign for tolerance and respect." "Mayors," he said, "need to spearhead a national movement to bring more light and less heat into our national political dialogue."[26]

Mayor Richard M. Daley of Chicago, the son of another Mayor Daley, had been trying to bring the people of his city together since he was elected in 1989. The vote in that election was sharply divided along racial lines, and many thought that the young Daley would reconstitute the old, white political machine his father had run. But Daley confounded the skeptics. Saying he was tired of the city's racial bickering, he called repeatedly for racial harmony and reconciliation. To back up his call, he appointed minorities to head seven of the nine largest city departments, and he appointed the head of the Urban League as president of the city's school board. Daley supported an affirmative action program for city contractors and pushed for more low-income housing. Mayor Daley made frequent speaking appearances in black neighborhoods, usually without extensive publicity or fanfare, "to preach unity."[27]

In contrast, former mayors such as Ed Koch of New York, Sam Yorty of Los Angeles, and Frank Rizzo of Philadelphia were widely perceived in their time as having exacerbated racial tensions in those cities, the former by his often harsh public pronouncements about black leaders such as Jesse Jackson, the latter two by their aggressive tendency to play on the fears of black crime among their white supporters. It is not always easy to show in a direct causal sense how symbolic leadership, exercised through the mayor's choice of rhetoric, the sorts of appointments he or she makes, or the issue positions taken, has a measurable impact on people's sense of well-being or confidence. Nevertheless, we can be sure that a mayor's symbolic acts and utterances help to create a climate of tolerance or tension, a sense of community or division. This climate influences everything from the likelihood that white police will use racial epithets to the priority that an issue such as homelessness or care for people with AIDS commands on the city council and in the city's newspapers.

Of course, there are more substantive demonstrations of mayoral leadership. From the 1960s to the 1980s, the mayors who caught the nation's attention were those who oversaw huge revitalization projects that transformed the downtowns of their cities.[28] William Schaefer will always be associated with Baltimore's renaissance, sparked by the development of Harborplace. William Hudnut and Richard Lugar left a legacy of downtown redevelopment in Indianapolis, and Mayor Richard Daley senior was winning a reputation for building the McCormick Place Convention Center, the Chicago Circle campus of the University of Illinois, and the modernization of O'Hare Airport.

In the 1990s the most dynamic mayors are not developers but rather the new reformers, the mayors committed to "reinventing government" by introducing competition,

BOX 9.1 THE CAREER PATHS OF FEMALE MAYORS IN AMERICA

The United States has approximately 1,100 cities with over 30,000 residents. Of these, 170 cities, or about 15 percent, have female mayors, including such cities as Ann Arbor, Berkeley, Corvallis, Durham, Eugene, Lexington, and Manhattan—all of which happen to have large public universities. The female mayors of these cities have a wide range of academic, business, volunteer, and political experiences before being elected to office.

Many of the mayors worked for either the local university or the school district before serving as mayor. Helen Berg, mayor of Corvallis, Oregon, was a statistics professor and later served as director of Oregon State University's Survey Research Center. Edith Stunkel, mayor of Manhattan, Kansas, was a gerontology professor and later assistant director of the Center for Aging at Kansas State University. Sylvia Kerckhoff, mayor of Durham, North Carolina, taught in Durham city schools as a ninth grade civics teacher and in a special program for unwed pregnant high schoolers before her election to the city council in 1981.

Several present mayors are also former entrepreneurs with private sector experience. Pam Miller, mayor of Lexington, Kentucky, was a former owner and operator of a small specialty advertising firm. Ruth Bascom, mayor of Eugene, Oregon, formed her own small publishing company called Bikeways Oregon Inc., which sold monographs about Eugene's success as a bicycling-friendly city.

All of the mayors are also active in local volunteer organizations. For example, Ingrid Sheldon, mayor of Ann Arbor, Michigan, volunteered in a number of organizations and capacities as block coordinator of the Ecology Center, board of directors of the Rotary Club and Ann Arbor Historical Foundation, co-chair of the Youth Corporate Spelling Bee, treasurer of the SOS Community Crisis Center, vice president of Huron High PTSO, and president of the Jaycee Women and the Ann Arbor Republican Women.

All of the mayors have some political experience, but Shirley Dean, mayor of Berkeley, California, has perhaps the most extensive involvement. She was elected to the Berkeley City Council in 1975 in her first attempt at citywide office and was subsequently reelected in 1979 and served as vice mayor for two years of that term. She also served as president of the Alameda County Solid Waste Management Authority, the statewide California League of Cities Revenue and Taxation Committee, and as an elected delegate to the Democratic National Convention, before being elected mayor in 1994.

As we can see from the tremendous variety in these mayors' backgrounds, there is no single career path to the mayor's office. Indeed, the only common experience shared by these seven female mayors is that they all served on the city council before being elected mayor.

management reforms, and privatization. These mayors have successfully put their cities on a stable fiscal course, held taxes steady, and increased the productivity of their city employees. Consider three examples: Ed Rendell of Philadelphia, Stephen Goldsmith of Indianapolis, and John Norquist of Milwaukee.

Rendell, a Democrat elected in 1991, inherited a city with a $208 million deficit. The tax burden on Philadelphia's citizens was the highest on the East Coast. Mayor Rendell believed that the cost of running city government was rising because of absurd work rules and unusually generous public employee salaries and benefits (city typists were being paid 50–70 percent more than typists in private companies in the city). Mayor Rendell faced down the public employee unions in wage negotiations, freezing salaries for two years and winning the right to fire unproductive workers. He also managed to eliminate work rules such as the one that said that employees did not have to perform any duty not listed in their job description, which had caused program analysts in the Department of Human Services to refuse to use computers for word-processing because using a computer was not in their job description. Mayor Rendell also initiated a series of tough management and productivity reforms, such as centralizing the maintenance operations of the city's car fleet and eliminating duplication of services by different city agencies. These changes saved the city $150 million in the first 15 months alone, the city is now fiscally stable, and Mayor Rendell's approval rating is very high.[29] Mayor Rendell is a mayor who made a difference.

Stephen Goldsmith, the Republican mayor of Indianapolis, has established a model for privatizing certain city government operations, that is, contracting out some of the city's service responsibilities to private companies. The idea is that private companies must be as efficient as possible, keeping costs low (though still meeting the standards required) in order to win the bid but still make money. Competition from other private firms interested in the same contract forces all the firms to keep their bids as low as possible. Mayor Goldsmith has privatized the city's microfilming, sewer bill collections, tree maintenance, printing, picking up trash from roadsides, and nearly 40 other city services.

But privatization is not the core of Mayor Goldsmith's reforms: Competition is. In Indianapolis, city departments are allowed to compete with private firms to offer a service, forcing the city department to think about increasing the efficiency of its operations. Sometimes the city department wins the bid, as the Street Department did when it won the right to fill potholes.[30]

Another mayor who made a difference is John Norquist of Milwaukee, elected in 1988 at the age of 38. Norquist, a Democrat elected in a nonpartisan system, is a management reformer, restructuring city departments, streamlining middle management through layoffs, and holding his department heads accountable for meeting certain goals. Mayor Norquist is also proud that he reduced the property tax rate every year that he was in office. In addition, he has experimented with a variety of ways to encourage neighborhood redevelopment by putting resources into the hands of people and organizations in the neighborhoods.

Management reforms, privatization, cost-cutting, and competition are not dramatic, eye-catching initiatives. They are rarely covered in the press. They do not attract the televison news crew as the announcement of a big downtown development deal might. (Mayor Tom Bradley of Los Angeles liked to boast that office space in that city quintupled during his years in office.)[31] But reforms such as these are making a difference in the taxes people pay and the quality of the services they enjoy.

Mayors make a difference in other aspects of city government. For example, black mayors have greatly increased the number of minority employees in city government, particularly at the managerial and professional levels. Likewise, female employment in nonclerical and professional and administrative jobs has increased in cities governed by female mayors.[32]

There is also evidence that black businesses do better in cities run by black mayors. Such businesses are more likely to expand than their counterparts in white-led cities, they are less likely to fail, and they tend to create more jobs for minorities.[33] The most likely explanation for these findings is that black mayors help minority-owned businesses gain access to city contracts, a steady and lucrative source of business.

BOX 9.2 ATLANTA'S POLICE CHIEF

Beverly Harvard took the Atlanta police department's entrance exams in response to a $100 bet that she would fail, from her husband and a family friend who were skeptical about a woman's ability to do the job. She won that $100 and has since risen to become Atlanta's chief of police at age 43, one of three women and the only black woman to head a major city police department.

After walking a beat and doing street patrols for her first 2 years on the force, Beverly Harvard spent the next 21 years supervising a variety of police operations including criminal investigations, administrative services, and liaison for a 1983 investigation of missing and murdered children, as well as getting a master's degree in public administration from Georgia State University. In the process, she built a reputation as a trained manager and supervisor, especially among the younger officers in the department. In naming Beverly Harvard police chief, Mayor Bill Campbell noted that she brought "an openness to new ideas" along with the distinction of having come up through the ranks rather than being brought in from outside.

Since becoming chief, Beverly Harvard has attempted to improve the reputation and morale of the department. She instituted a policy of nighttime sweeps of drug and prostitution markets in Atlanta. In the first sweep, 49 people were arrested and charged with 189 crimes from drug and weapons possession to public indecency and solicitation. Although some officers felt that such arrests were likely to be dropped and thus a waste of time, Chief Harvard countered that "The mission was more than arrests. It all adds to police visibility and allows people to feel safer."

Chief Harvard has also tried to improve morale within the department by creating a series of councils of officers from different squads and shifts to meet regularly with her, as well as encouraging officers to fax suggestions to her over the heads of their superiors as a way of improving department operations. These meetings have led to scrapping the requirement that officers wear uncomfortable high-gloss shoes that don't bend or breathe and that they always wear their hats, two precedents established by her predecessor.

Source: Ronald Smothers, "Atlanta's Police Chief Won More Than a Bet," *New York Times* (November 30, 1994).

No political leader or even a whole mayoral administration can solve all the problems of large cities. But each mayor comes to office with a different agenda, or set of policy problems and goals arranged in some rough priority that the mayor sets out to tackle. Each mayor comes to office with different resources and varying ideas about how to mobilize and increase those resources. Of course, each mayor also has a distinctive personality, which means differing tastes for conflict, differing abilities for convincing people to do things the mayor wants, and differing levels of energy. All these add up to variations in how a mayor governs and what he or she accomplishes. Most mayors are not simply caretakers, then. Their distinctive efforts and abilities do make a difference.

✦ CITY COUNCILS

A few cities, such as Detroit, Los Angeles, New York, and Milwaukee, have full-time city councils. But in most places, including a number of big cities such as Dallas and Cincinnati, councils are part-time institutions, poorly paid bastions of citizen politics.

The chief requirement is the ability to spend one long evening a week in council meeting. Most councils provide their members with little professional staff (only 21 percent of all cities provide such help), which means that the council members are highly dependent on whatever information and analyses the chief executive of the city, the mayor or the manager, is willing to share with them.

Councils may be amateur, but they are not unimportant. They pass budgets, they may approve mayoral or managerial appointees, they hire and evaluate managers in manager systems, they oversee the city's agencies, their members provide a first point of contact between ordinary citizens and city government, and they put the city on record on various policy issues ranging from a commitment to affirmative action to support of gun control. In some communities, city councils even declare their communities nuclear-free zones, condemn U.S. foreign policy in Central America, or declare a boycott of California grapes in municipal cafeterias.

Councils average just over 6 members, but many large cities have many more. Chicago's council has 50 members and Baltimore's has 21. In New York City's major charter revision of 1989, the council was expanded from 36 to 51 to give minority group members a better chance of getting elected. Council membership in cities all over the country has steadily become more diverse demographically.

Since the 1960s city councils have been the first battleground in the efforts by black and Hispanic Americans to gain access to positions of political authority. Two structural arrangements have been seen as impediments to fair representation. One is the small size of councils. Small councils have been the subject of litigation. A federal court ruled in 1987 that the city of Springfield, Illinois, had to increase the size of its council as part of an effort to provide more opportunities for minority representation.[34]

The second structural problem concerns whether elections are held on a district basis or at-large, a question that has been the subject of extensive litigation. A large body of research has demonstrated that as long as blacks are a minority in a city, they are more likely to win fair representation in district systems than in at-large systems. Fair representation on a council is achieved, according to this research, when the proportion of black people on the city council equals the proportion of black people in the population. Interestingly, the electoral arrangements are less important for Hispanic representation, perhaps in part because they are not as residentially segregated as blacks and thus do not dominate small wards in many cities.[35]

Beginning in the 1970s black plaintiffs argued successfully against at-large systems. One of the most famous cases concerned Mobile, Alabama, which was governed by a three-person commission whose members were elected at-large. No black had ever been elected to the commission. In 1976 the federal district court ruled that the at-large system unconstitutionally diluted the voting power of the city's blacks. On appeal in 1980, the U.S. Supreme Court overruled the decision, asserting that although the at-large system may have had discriminatory results, it was necessary to prove that the system had been designed with discriminatory intent.[36]

This ruling so angered the U.S. Congress that it amended the 1965 Voting Rights Act in 1982 to say that any electoral arrangement that "results in a denial or abridgement" of a citizen's right to vote was just as impermissible as one designed intentionally to discriminate. Since 1982 the courts have applied a results test rather than the much more difficult and elusive intent standard in evaluating local election arrangements. As a consequence, a number of at-large systems have been struck down in cities where blacks were historically underrepresented. Thus, for example, in *Derrickson v. City of Danville*, the federal court ordered Danville to change its system to election by district.[37] After the change blacks won two seats on the new council, the first representation they had ever had in that city. Since 1981 the proportion of cities using pure at-large systems has declined from 67 to 60 percent. To avoid litigation, a number of at-large cities have now adopted mixed systems in which some council members are elected by district and others are elected at-large.

✧ CONCLUSION

The structural characteristics of any city's government may easily be illustrated by an organization chart, a series of boxes and connecting lines showing the layers of authority and the division of responsibility. For most people, there are few things more boring than an organization chart, yet we have seen in this chapter that it is important to understand the various structural features of municipal government because these structural characteristics influence the political process. Structural features impose biases that groups in the political process must confront.

Variations in the form of modern municipal governments are the result of the historical conflict around the turn of the century between the urban reform movement and working-class and poor urban dwellers of immigrant stock. As the number of immigrants in the big cities grew, some middle-class people of Yankee stock fled to the newly developing suburbs, a classic exit response. But more often they stayed in the city to try to regain political control.

The aim of the middle-class reform movement was to exercise the voice option with the aim of making urban government more businesslike and thus more responsive to its interests. Reformers were fond of saying that there is no Democratic or Republican way to pave a road. Street paving, the reformers claimed, is a matter of efficient engineering, ignoring the fact that which streets are chosen for paving, which construction firm gets the bid to do the work, and how much the city council allocates for paving work are all political questions.

Under the conviction that cities were just like corporations, the reformers pushed for city manager government and the elimination of party labels. They also agitated for municipal civil service reforms so that people who worked for the city would be hired for their skills, not as a patronage reward for loyal political service. Of course, the reformers sought to do away with wards, home of the ward boss and the party club. In certain ways, reform succeeded. Most cities today hold nonpartisan elections. City managers run over 40 percent of all cities. At-large elections are under siege, but they survive in many cities in combination with district elections. Adoption of these forms is one indicator of success, but it is not clear that these changes produced more efficient, less corrupt government or that they hastened the demise of the political machine. Some machines—notably the Pendergast Machine of Kansas City—flourished equally well under mayor and manager systems.

Reform did succeed in making political participation by the working class, the poor, and minorities a more difficult and less fruitful enterprise, and for many reformers this was a key objective. At-large council elections virtually shut blacks out of the city council, even in cities in which they had large populations and the right to vote. Detroit's black community, representing about one-third of the city's population, did not elect a council representative under the at-large system until 1957. That person was not joined by a second black council member until 1968. By that time the city was almost half black, but blacks had managed to win only two of the nine council seats.[38]

City managers, as we have seen, have also been drawn traditionally from the majority group. Clearly, opportunities for racial minorities and women are greater in old-style, or unreformed, systems.

In sum, structure may not determine patterns of representation and participation, but it certainly influences them. Therefore, structure matters. To the degree that certain groups are helped or hindered in the political process by structural features, structure itself becomes an issue in urban politics.

✦ KEY TERMS

at-large election (p. 241)   special district (p. 234)
city manager (p. 239)   strong mayor (p. 247)
nonpartisan elections (p. 241)   weak mayor (p. 247)
reform movement (p. 242)

✦ FOR FURTHER READING

Nancy Burns, *The Formation of American Local Governments* (New York: Oxford, 1994). An analysis of the origins and consequences of creating new municipalities and special districts.

Alexander Callow, *The Tweed Ring* (New York: Oxford University Press, 1966). The story of Boss Tweed and his times in New York City.

Stephen Erie, *Rainbow's End* (Berkeley: University of California Press, 1988). An account of the rise and fall of Irish political machines in eight different cities.

Susan Welch and Timothy Bledsoe, *Urban Reform and Its Consequences* (Chicago: University of Chicago Press, 1988). A study of the impact of the various reform structures.

✦ NOTES

1. Nancy Burns, *The Formation of American Local Governments* (New York: Oxford University Press, 1994), p. 31.

2. G. Ross Stephens, "The Least Glorious, Most Local, Most Trivial, Homely Provincial and Most Ignored Form of Local Government," *Urban Affairs Quarterly,* 24 (June 1989), 502–503.

3. J. Edwin Benton and Donald Menzel, "County Services: The Emergence of Full-Service Government," in David Berman, ed., *County Governments in an Era of Change* (Westport, Conn.: Greenwood, 1993), p. 55.

4. Quoted in Edward Banfield and James Q. Wilson, *City Politics* (Cambridge, Mass.: Harvard University Press, 1963), p. 170.

5. *Ibid.*, p. 171.

6. One study found that 62 percent of managers have master's degrees in public administration. As for moving from one post to a better one, about half of all managers said they had switched jobs for purposes of career advancement. Craig Wheeland, "Council Evaluation of City

Managers' Performance," in *Municipal Year Book 1995* (Washington, D.C.: International City Management Association, 1995), pp. 13–20.

7. International City Management Association, personal communication.

8. Banfield and Wilson, *City Politics,* pp. 94–95.

9. Susan Welch and Timothy Bledsoe, *Urban Reform and Its Consequences* (Chicago: University of Chicago Press, 1988), p. 47.

10. Edward Lascher, Jr. "The Case of the Missing Democrats: Reexamining the 'Republican Advantage' in Nonpartisan Elections," *Western Political Quarterly,* 44 (September 1991), 656–675.

11. Eric Monkonnen, *America Becomes Urban* (Berkeley: University of California Press, 1988), p. 79.

12. Jon Teaford, *The Unheralded Triumph: City Government in America, 1870–1900* (Baltimore: Johns Hopkins University Press, 1984), p. 217.

13. Quoted in Robert Bremner, *From the Depths: The Discovery of Poverty in the United States* (New York: New York University Press, 1956), p. 204.

14. Quoted in Peter Eisinger, *The Politics of Displacement* (New York: Academic Press, 1980), p. 40.

15. Richard Hofstadter, *The Age of Reform* (New York: Knopf, 1955), p. 9.

16. The most famous proponent of this view was Robert Merton, *Social Theory and Social Structure* (London: Free Press of Glencoe, 1957). It should be pointed out, however, that many machines discriminated against other ethnic and racial groups, fostered enormous corruption, and ran roughshod over the civil liberties of those who opposed them. Frank Hague, the boss of Jersey City in the 1920 and 1930s, used to say, "I am the law."

17. Quoted in Alfred Steinberg, *The Bosses* (New York: New American Library, 1972), p. 134.

18. Alexander Callow, *The Tweed Ring* (New York: Oxford University Press, 1966).

19. White's article, "Municipal Affairs Are Not Political," was written in 1890. It is reprinted in Edward Banfield, ed., *Urban Government,* rev. ed. (New York: Free Press, 1969), pp. 271–274.

20. Welch and Bledsoe, *Urban Reform and Its Consequences,* p. 37.

21. Quoted in Seymour Mandelbaum, *Boss Tweed's New York* (New York: Wiley, 1965), pp. 50–51.

22. David Morgan and Sheilah Watson, "Mayors of American Cities: An Analysis of Powers and Responsibilities," paper presented at the annual meeting of the American Political Science Association, Washington, D.C., September 1993.

23. Arthur Naftalin is quoted in Jane Mobley, "Politician or Professional? The Debate Over Who Should Run Our Cities Continues," *Governing,* 1 (February 1988), 42.

24. Morgan and Watson, "Mayors of American Cities."

25. Mobley, "Politician or Professional?," p. 48

26. Norman Rice, "Community, Tolerance, and Opportunity," *Focus,* 23 (July/August 1995), 5.

27. Dirk Johnson, "Daley Embraces Changes, Confounding His Chicago Critics," *New York Times* (May 28, 1989); Dirk Johnson, "Mayor Still Enjoying a Honeymoon in Chicago Despite Nagging Problems," *New York Times* (May 7, 1990).

28. Jon Teaford, *The Rough Road to Renaissance* (Baltimore: Johns Hopkins University Press, 1990).

29. William D. Eggers, "City Lights: America's Boldest Mayors," *Policy Review* (Summer 1993), 67–74.

30. *Ibid;* see also Rob Gurwitt, "Indianapolis and the Republican Future," *Governing,* 7 (February 1994), 24–28.

31. Robert Reinhold, "Los Angeles Mayor, Once Challenged, Regains Willing Ways," *New York Times* (January 29, 1989).

32. Peter Eisinger, *Black Employment in City Government, 1973–1980* (Washington, D.C.: Joint Center for Political Studies, 1983); and Grace Saltzstein, "Female Mayors and Women in Municipal Jobs," *American Journal of Political Science*, 30 (February 1986), 140–164.

33. Timothy Bates, *Banking on Black Enterprise* (Washington, D.C.: Joint Center for Political and Economic Studies, 1993).

34. *McNeal v. Springfield*, U.S. District Central Illinois, 685 F Suppl. p. 1015 (1987).

35. Susan Welch, "The Impact of At-Large Elections on the Representation of Blacks and Hispanics," *Journal of Politics*, 52 (November 1990), 1050–1076.

36. *City of Mobile v. Bolden*, 48 L.W. 4436 (1980).

37. U.S. District Central Illinois, 87-2007 (1987).

38. Eisinger, *The Politics of Displacement*, p. 61.

WHAT DETERMINES THE CHARACTER OF CITIES?

very year or so the *Places Rated Almanac* and *Money* magazine rank more than 300 American cities on a livability index, taking into account the tax rate, the number of hospital beds per capita, recreational facilities, the cost and age of the housing stock, cultural opportunities, transportation, unemployment, and a host of other indicators. Although most analysts agree that the rankings are based on incomplete information and often produce unfair and even silly results,[1] they do acknowledge that the rankings make one important, if obvious, point: Cities are different from one another on a host of different dimensions.

Cities differ in size, of course, but they vary in countless other ways as well. Consider density of settlement. Boston, a compact city whose founding dates to 1630, has almost 12,000 people per square mile; Fort Worth, a much newer city with a population only slightly smaller, has a density of only 1,600 people per square mile. Nashville, the equal of Fort Worth in population, has fewer than 1,000 people per square mile. The newer cities of the West and Southwest tend to be more spread out than the older cities of the East. Density is a function of the style of housing, the geography and topography of the city, the nature of the downtown, and the location of the city's boundaries.

Cities also differ in their population makeup. Few modern cities are more ethnically heterogeneous than Los Angeles, with its high concentration of people from Mexico, Central America, and every country in Pacific Asia. Cities such as Omaha and Tulsa, however, are still dominated by Americans of Northern European stock. Not only do cities differ in their ethnic and racial mix, but they vary in their class makeup. Milwaukee is a decidedly blue-collar town, reflecting its long reliance on manufacturing, whereas Columbus, Ohio, nearly as big, is a solidly middle-class city whose residents work in state government, the university, health care, and insurance. Cities differ also in their cost of living, their physical appearance, the quality of their downtown office space, parks and recreation facilities, social services, education systems, crime rates, tax burdens, and transportation systems. They also differ in their political culture, particularly their accessibility to citizen politics, and in their business culture, especially the degree to which there is a tradition of business philanthropy and civic involvement. What accounts for all these differences? Are differences a matter of accident or are they the product of conscious choices?

No single theory fully explains the physical shape of a city, its distribution of people and functions in space, its economic base and opportunity structure, its array of amenities and quality of life, and its civic life and political character. Nevertheless, analysts tend to focus on one of two broad explanations: The city is either the product of conscious, collective decisions or the product of economic impulses and social forces beyond the influence of governments.

The first explanation, which revolves around the issue of who exercises voice and the ways in which they do it, usually asks Who governs the city? With what effects? The assumption here is that people, acting through or in league with their local government, shape the urban environment. The second explanation looks at great economic and social forces, such as the migration of people and capital, to account for the character of cities. The exercise or contemplation of the exit option by firms or individuals is a key idea here. Individuals and corporations who choose to exit the city often move in response to market and social forces that governments cannot easily control.

✦ WHO GOVERNS?

To assume that people consciously shape their urban environment is to ask who governs or runs the city. Putting aside the issue of whether anyone is capable of running the city, the question requires a search for the influential and powerful people on the local scene. Half a century ago, most people, including political scientists, thought that the answer to the question of who runs the city was obvious: The mayor and the city council, working with the powers given them by the city charter, run the city. In other words, people vested with formal government authority governed the city.

But social scientists soon came to realize that the mayor, the city council members, and the other local officeholders represented only one set of potentially influential actors. They were subject to pressures from a variety of interest groups, and it was even conceivable that they were controlled by behind-the-scenes actors. These other interests who sought to influence the shape and character of the city might include neighborhood associations, ethnic and racial groups, public employee unions, downtown developers, bankers, public utility executives, small business owners, corporate executives, and a host of other interested parties.

In seeking to discover who governed American cities, the focus shifted from describing the formal offices of local government to an examination of the conflict, competition, and coalition-building among government and nongovernment actors. To understand who governed, in other words, one had to understand the local political process.

The clash of ideas and interests and organizations that make up the political process raise issues about the distribution and use of resources in the city. Some actors may be influential because they control the resource of formal authority, as the mayor does. Other figures may be influential because they control the resource of information, as the owners of TV stations or the publishers of the daily newspaper do. Others are influential because they can get out the vote or mobilize people to protest or give money to campaigns. Still others are influential because they control capital, which they may invest either in the city (thus creating jobs and taxable property) or somewhere else. The way in which resources are distributed and used in local politics creates patterns of control, domination, subordination, and cooperation. These patterns may be described as the **structure of political power.**

In short, one school of thought argues that we can account for the character of the city by discovering the nature of the structure of political power and the way in which the political process is played out within it. Out of the clash of ideas and goals by actors and interests with varying types and amounts of resources come decisions about downtown investment, the tax rate, the style of the police department, whether to build a public swimming pool or a new light rail mass transit system, whether to subsidize public artworks, and so on. All of these decisions combined give the city a distinctive character.

✧ COMMUNITY POWER STRUCTURE

The study of the local structure of power preoccupied political scientists and sociologists mainly during the 1960s and 1970s. Although social scientists never really resolved the question of who governed American cities, the studies and the questions they raised are still of interest to students of the city today. Those investigators laid the groundwork for research on a range of contemporary problems such as the role of race in city politics, the growing partnerships between business and government in the local setting, and the power of neighborhood groups.

The origins of community power studies lie in the sociological research on social stratification in American communities in the 1920s and 1930s. Some sociologists were convinced that the United States was far from a classless society and sought to show it by studying the social, economic, and political gradations in various communities. Among the most influential of these stratification studies was an investigation of Muncie, Indiana by Helen and Robert Lynd.[2] According to the Lynds, Muncie, which they called Middletown, was dominated by the business class; indeed, ultimate power in the community lay with one family, the "X" family, whom we know today to have been the Balls, manufacturers of Ball canning jars. The Lynds showed that the Balls and the business class of Muncie dominated not only the economic life of the city but also its social life and its politics. These economic elites exercised political control by enlisting and manipulating local politicians, whom the businesspeople considered to be socially unequal and people of "meager caliber."

The notion that economic, social, and political power converged in American communities and led to business dominance was reinforced by studies of other communities. Such a situation obviously ran counter to democratic ideals. Concern about the nature of local democracy prompted sociologist Floyd Hunter to undertake a study of Atlanta's community power structure; because his book, more than the Lynds', focused mainly on political power, it marks the beginning of the intense debate over who governed American cities.

"It has been evident to the writer for some years," Hunter states "that policies on vital matters affecting community life are acted upon, but with no precise knowledge on the part of the majority of citizens as to how these policies originated or by whom they are really sponsored. . . . This situation does not square with the concepts of democracy that we have been taught to revere."[3] If the structure of power was not democratic, then who really ruled? Hunter set out to explore this question in Atlanta. First he obtained from such organizations as the Chamber of Commerce and the League of Women Voters lists of people active in community affairs, business, politics, and society. Then he asked knowledgeable insiders—newspaper people, academics, and local historians—to identify the top leaders of the community from the names on the lists. Hunter took the top 40 vote-getters (most of whom were from the business world) and claimed that they were the community's top leaders. Then he asked the 40 people on this list to pick 10 people among their number who were the very top leaders and then the single person who was the "biggest man in town." Hunter's method led to a self-fulfilling prophecy: By asking these questions he inevitably produced a pyramid-shaped roster of the apparently most powerful people in Atlanta. All those at the very top were businessmen. Well down in the pyramid were politicians, labor leaders, prominent blacks, women, and representatives of other interests. In Hunter's view, economic status implied political power as well.

Political scientists, however, were doubtful about Hunter's assertion that a small business elite ran the city. They pointed out that Hunter had not observed anyone actually exercising power; instead, he had taken people's nominations of others as evidence that those named were powerful. It was possible, political scientists thought, that a person who had a reputation for being powerful might not in fact be so.[4]

A decade after the publication of the Atlanta study, political scientist Robert Dahl offered a rejoinder to Hunter in a book titled, *Who Governs?*, a study of New Haven, Connecticut. Dahl, like Hunter, was interested in the larger issue of the paradox of democratic beliefs and forms and the inequality of resources. He set out to examine who really participated in and influenced community decisions in such areas as redevelopment, school politics, and political nominations. Power, Dahl believed, could not be a function of reputation, as it appeared to be in Hunter's study, but rather had to be observed at work in the political arena.

On the basis of his observations, Dahl believed that he had found in New Haven not a single pyramid of power but rather many centers of power and influence, each with its own set of key actors. No single small power elite, sitting atop the pyramid, ran everything. The influential actors differed from issue to issue. Many of the influential actors were politicians, and Dahl could find no evidence that they were controlled from behind the scenes by wealthy businesspeople. Although citizens certainly had different resources at their command, ordinary people with modest resources who felt strongly about an issue could counteract wealthy or socially prominent people who might have greater resources but did not feel passionate enough to use them. Dahl's understanding of the structure of political power, with its emphasis on diffused power and the high penetrability of the political system by mobilized citizens, was called **pluralism.**

Not everyone was convinced that Dahl had gotten it right, however. It was possible, some argued, that power in urban politics was exercised not only through the decision process (in a debate, for example, over whether to build a new school or to expand the city's boundaries) but also by preventing issues from ever being debated and decided at all. Very powerful people might limit the political process by keeping certain issues off the public agenda. This process was labeled nondecisionmaking, the "means by which demands for change in the existing allocation of benefits and privileges in the community can be suffocated before they are even voiced."[5]

Sometimes those in positions of political authority declined to take action because they anticipated how powerful actors *might* react if government were to do something adverse to their interests. Matthew Crenson found this to be the case in Gary, Indiana, whose political leaders refused to try to regulate the pollution caused by the city's biggest employer, U.S. Steel, for fear that the corporation would fight back or even leave the city entirely.[6]

Elitist studies (those that took Hunter as their inspiration), pluralists, and the non-decisionmaking scholars produced literally thousands of community studies. In the end they did not settle the debate over the nature of the structure of power in cities. Politics in some places, it seemed, conformed to the model of dispersed power, in others to the model of concentrated power. But what is important about the community power studies is that they explored the idea that human beings, acting collectively, determined the nature of their city. The city—its downtown form, its tax system, the quality of its political life, its housing opportunities—was a product of conscious striving and conflict and purposeful behavior.

In addition, the community power studies taught observers to be alert to the changing roster and roles of participants in the struggle to govern the city. Scholars began to ask first about the political influence of minorities, particularly black Americans. Where did they sit in the local structure of political power? Others were concerned with the manner in which business interests have adapted to the growing strength of new participants in local politics, particularly minority and grass-roots groups. A third issue is the extent to which neighborhood and other forms of citizen organization are a force in urban politics. Today, the classic question of who governs has been restated in the following terms: To what extent and under what circumstances is governance shared among groups in the city?

✧ THE RISE OF AFRICAN AMERICANS IN URBAN POLITICS

When Hunter and Dahl set the terms of the debate over the structure of community power in the 1950s and early 1960s, African Americans were not yet major participants in the political life of most cities. Hunter notes that no black leader in Atlanta was ever "called upon to contribute to top policy-making in the larger community."[7] In New Haven a decade later, Dahl found that black voters participated in city elections at a high rate, but their interests and problems were not a major concern of politicians in city hall. A massive study of pluralist politics in New York City from that era scarcely mentioned blacks or black political organizations.[8] No black leader had yet been elected to the mayoralty of a major American city.

Things changed very quickly in the 1960s. First there were the riots that broke out in the nation's black ghettos. Although several occurred in 1964, including one in Harlem, it was the 1965 violence in the Watts section of Los Angeles that caught the nation's attention. At the end of six days of rioting, 34 people were dead, thousands were injured, and at least 1,000 buildings had been damaged at a cost of more than $40 million.[9] Although there were more costly riots to come, both in human and monetary terms, including the South Central Los Angeles riot of 1992, Watts was regarded as the beginning of a new form of racial conflict in the cities. Between 1965 and the spring of 1968, when Dr. Martin Luther King was assassinated, there were more than a thousand riots, or "civil disorders," including extremely destructive ones in Detroit, Newark, Milwaukee, Rochester, Tampa, and a host of other big and small places.[10] Black urban dwellers were suddenly part of the political equation in the cities. One consequence of the riots was that black demands and black needs, though rarely fully met, nevertheless could not be ignored.

Partly in response to the riots and to the civil rights movement that had moved from the South to the North in the early 1960s, but also in response to the growing realization that poverty in general was a widespread and dangerous condition in American society, the federal government embarked on the Great Society agenda (discussed in Chapter 2). Some of its programs, particularly Community Action, stimulated and supported political organizing in the nation's urban ghettos. In addition, the Voting Rights Act of 1965, which provided federal protection for blacks seeking to register to vote in the states of the deep South, opened the political system in many places to black voters for the first time in history.

The convergence of the experience gained from the civil rights movement, the feelings of deprivation and injustice that fed the riots, and the opening of the political system

After the riot of 1967, sections of Detroit looked to many Americans like the photographs of bombed-out German cities in World War II. That summer marked the peak if the urban riots, although violence flared quickly in 1968 after the assassination of Dr. Martin Luther King. Gradually, however, the local electoral system began to open to African Americans. (*Source:* UPI/Bettmann)

all eventually stimulated political organizing in the cities. In a number of cities, black voters began to elect black mayors. Carl Stokes and Richard Hatcher led the way, winning control of city hall in Cleveland and Gary, Indiana, respectively, in 1967, the first significant urban electoral achievements by African Americans. Black mayors were elected shortly thereafter in Newark, Los Angeles, Detroit, and Atlanta. Black Americans had arrived on the urban political scene.

But having arrived, where exactly did African Americans really fit in the structures of power of American cities? Eventually, black leaders went on to win the mayoralties of New York, Chicago, Minneapolis, Baltimore, Seattle, Birmingham, Denver, and hundreds of other cities and towns. But did winning the mayoralty of big cities—particularly, the older ones—really make a difference to the black community? In cities where African Americans did not win the top office but were nevertheless active in local politics, did they share in local governance?

It quickly became evident that getting to city hall was only the first modest step for blacks in their quest to occupy a significant place in the local structure of power. Because so many of the cities that black mayors governed were losing population and industry and were seriously strapped for cash, it was possible that African American voters had simply captured control of sinking ships. A number of political scientists showed that having a black mayor did make a difference in the policies of their cities: Not only did the cities increase the number of blacks on the police force and in other municipal jobs, but they were also more attentive to black neighborhoods when money was available to build new recreation facilities, senior citizen centers, and sidewalks.[11]

Rufus Browning and his colleagues studied minority politics in ten northern California cities and found that blacks could wield real influence even if they did not capture the mayoralty. The key was not simply to gain representation but to win an influential position in the governing coalition on the city council. This **political incorporation** could produce measurable gain for minority citizens.[12] A later study of eleven different cities with large black and Latino populations also found that political incorporation, which might be understood as a favorable location in the local structure of political power, led to identifiable minority benefits, including city jobs, favorable police practices, and neighborhood development.[13]

Whereas the incorporation studies focused primarily on the role of minority representatives in relation to other actors within government, Clarence Stone's *Regime Politics* studied the relationship between a minority-dominated government and a white-dominated local business sector.[14] In Hunter's Atlanta, the white business elite had ruled unchallenged through hand-picked white mayors. By the time Stone was writing, however, the mayor and many of the city's public officials were black and had come to office with the support of an electoral base independent of business domination. Stone discovered that the two groups managed to work across the racial divide, constituting what he called a governing regime, an informal but ongoing cooperative working arrangement between private interests and government for the purpose of making and implementing authoritative decisions. The regime is held together by a mutual interest in merging resources to accomplish certain ends. Stone believes that the view of power that emerges through the study of urban regimes is different from the understanding of power by the elitists and pluralists. For the latter two schools, power is an instrument of social control; people exercise power over others mainly to get others to do things they ordinarily would not do. For

BOX 10.1 THE NEW MAYOR OF SAN FRANCISCO, WILLIE BROWN

On November 6, 1995, Willie Brown became the first African American elected as mayor of San Francisco by soundly beating incumbent mayor Frank Jordan with 57 percent of the vote. Some were surprised that a city that is only 10 percent black would elect an African American, but many more were surprised that Brown would want a job he once described as only "dog doo and potholes."[1]

Before being elected mayor, Brown had served for 15 years as speaker of the California Assembly and was the most powerful African American elected official in the country. As already described in Box 5.3, his unique combination of raw charisma and political savvy had made him the acknowledged master of state legislative wheeling and dealing. He was called the Ayatollah of the Assembly, known for his political efficacy and success—that is, until the enactment of term limits in California. Facing certain political extinction in the legislature, Brown jumped at the opportunity to run for mayor of San Francisco. Brown told San Francisco voters that his previous tenure as speaker would make him more effective in protecting financial support for the city and in gaining new aid, a potent claim in the present era of federal budgetary cutbacks. Moreover, his legacy of procuring pork for the city in state budgets had earned Brown the support and endorsements of most other city politicians.

Mayor Willie Brown of San Francisco is one of the most recent African Americans to achieve the mayoralty of a major American city. Brown had a long career in the California state legislature before term limits forced him to seek an alternative political career. (*Source:* REUTERS)

Despite his charismatic allure and potent fund-raising capabilities, a Brown mayoral candidacy faced a number of hurdles. Even before announcing his candidacy, Brown had suggested that he could not afford to give up his quarter million dollars in income from legal fees to survive on the $139,000 annual mayor's salary. "I can't expect the members of my immediate family to make that kind of sacrifice for what is essentially my hobby."[2] Many also thought that Brown was out of touch with the concerns of San Francisco after his 31 years in the California State Assembly. During the first publicized walking tour of his mayoral campaign, Brown marvelled at how much the city had changed, until a reporter noted that they were in his legislative district, to which an unfazed Brown replied, "You're right."[3] Moreover, Brown faced a number of lingering questions regarding the more than $700,000 in donations from tobacco interests and $800,000 from gambling interests he had received while speaker, especially because he had often sided with both in legislative matters.[4]

In contrast, the incumbent Democrat mayor Frank Jordan, a former police chief, was elected in 1991 as a "citizen mayor" with no outside political baggage. Moreover, he had an impressive record of balanced budgets, unraised taxes, and an effective crackdown on aggressive panhandling during his tenure. However, Jordan sabotaged his own campaign by chosing to demonstrate the differences between himself and Brown by posing nude in the shower with two radio disc jockeys to show voters he was "squeaky clean" and "had nothing to hide." Faced with a choice between an outsider with a reputation as a bumbler and an insider with a reputation as political operator, San Franciscans chose the political operator, Willie Brown.

After 4 years of the relatively dull Jordan, San Franciscans rejoiced in having a mayor with the flash and flair to match the city's colorful reputation. Indeed, his first month in office was characterized by intense civic interest in Brown's snappy wardrobe, especially after he ended the "dress down" policy for City Hall employees. The $450 snap brim fedora that he wore to his swearing in ceremony reportedly stirred a citywide run on men's dress hats.[5] Style aside, Brown also knew that the honeymoon for elected officials doesn't last long and moved quickly to implement his agenda. In his first 10 days, Brown replaced the police and fire chiefs, appointed new people to numerous municipal commissions, cancelled a controversial police crackdown on homeless people, and restarted efforts to build a new baseball park downtown.

However, many critics still question whether Brown will be able to handle the mundane mechanics of municipal government. The prospects of leading a city of 724,000 people with an annual budget of $2.9 billion and a crushing array of urban problems from deteriorating public housing, the continuing AIDS epidemic, a faltering transit system, homelessness, an unreliable 911 emergency system, and $600 million in looming federal and state budget cuts are unenviable. Many have suggested the present Brown "love-in" will founder quickly as Bown is forced to oversee a competition over declining budget resources after federal and state cutbacks.

San Franciscans have also seen that Brown has not entirely abandoned the practices that earned him the reputation in the California legislature as the original Slick Willie. One of Brown's first steps was to appoint southern Californian Paul Horcher, a former Republican assemblyman who had defected from his party and helped Brown and the Democrats retain power in the Assembly after the 1994 elections, to a $70,000-per-year job as a liaison to the Board of Supervisors. Noting Horcher's total unfamiliarity with San Francisco, a local

Continued

newspaper editorialized that the mayor might as well have handed Horcher the money in a brown paper bag.[6] Brown also found himself in hot water after suggesting that a group of "street dudes," including former gang members whom had been used as plainclothes security for his inaugural bash, could patrol a high-crime bus line. He also defended his newly appointed police chief, Fred Lau, who was found to have lied on his résumé about graduating from San Francisco State University, by proclaiming "I don't know anyone who doesn't lie on their résumé."[7]

[1]David Beiler, "How One of America's Most Controversial Politicians Got Elected Mayor of San Francisco," *Campaigns and Elections* (February 1996), 43.

[2]Ibid., p. 46.

[3]*Ibid.*, p. 48.

[4]*Ibid.*

[5]Peter H. King, "Mayor Brown: The Emperer has Clothes," *Los Angeles Times* (January 21, 1996), A3.

[6]David Frisk, "Some Folks Call It Style," *National Review*, 48(3) (February 26, 1996), 1.

[7]*Ibid.*, p. 6.

regime theorists, power is to be harnessed for what Stone calls **social production.** People exercise power with others to pursue common purposes and to realize collective benefits.

Like the elitists, Stone was convinced that business is the most important of the private interests that government actors might seek as regime partners, for business controls crucial resources, particularly the ability to invest in economic undertakings. Stone quotes one black mayor of Atlanta speaking to white business leaders in the city, encapsulating the essence of the regime idea: "I didn't get elected with your help . . . [but] I can't govern without you."[15] This is the essence of the regime idea.

◆ THE ROLE OF GRASS-ROOTS ORGANIZATIONS

The structures of local power observed in the community power debate—monolithic business domination or plural competition among largely white interests—clearly altered with the rise of black neighborhood organizations and black mayors backed by united black electorates. After 1960, racial concerns and racial conflict became central to urban politics, and leaders and organizations from the African-American community were major participants. Other interests appeared on the scene, including grass-roots organizations of poor, working class, and middle-class white and Hispanic citizens, intent on preserving the integrity of their neighborhoods.

In Dahl's study of New Haven in the 1950s, a neighborhood organization made up mainly of working-class Italian Americans had managed a successful fight against two developers who planned to build cheap (and ugly) housing in their neighborhood. The mobilized neighborhood organization in New Haven was one of several forerunners of a proliferation of such groups in the cities in the 1960s and 1970s. At first, most of these grass-roots organizations arose in working-class white communities to contest urban renewal plans that threatened to destroy their residential neighborhoods.[16] Later, black communities mobilized to fight efforts to displace residents to build schools, commercial projects, or high-income housing. Some of these groups, such as those Clarence Stone studied in Atlanta, were regarded as formidable organizations in local politics.[17]

In other cities, such as Boston, neighborhood groups fought highway plans that promised to slash through areas of low- and middle-income housing.[18] Neighborhood organizing received a boost from federal programs that required citizen participation, such as the Community Action Program and the later Community Development Block Grant program. In the 1980s and 1990s, citizen groups in poor areas began to form community development corporations to pursue economic development. These often grew out of protest organizations, but they quickly evolved into economic self-help institutions.

Today, there are approximately 2,200 community development corporations (CDCs) nationwide.[19] Their most notable achievements lie in housing development: Using federal block grant money, foundation grants, and private investments (mostly from large banks and corporations), CDCs have developed nearly 450,000 housing units in poor neighborhoods. They also raise capital for small business investment. One study estimates that the businesses formed through CDC investments have created 67,500 jobs in the inner cities.

The flowering of all these different grass-roots organizations naturally raised the question of their role in city policymaking. Where did neighborhood groups fit into the local structure of power? Were the pluralists right when they argued that local political systems are essentially open to all mobilized groups? Although some scholars suggest that neighborhood organizations are not very durable participants in local politics,[20] one recent study offers a different conclusion.[21] In the five cities chosen for study, neighborhood associations not only are well-institutionalized participants in the local politics, but they often held their own in negotiating and bargaining with business interests in the politics of development.

✧ THE UNGOVERNABLE CITY

Most studies that take questions about community power structure as their starting point assume that urban dwellers can manage to govern their city. That is, through the processes of conflict and cooperation, confrontation and negotiation, contestation and coalition, people manage to shape their urban environment in purposeful and beneficial ways. But not everyone believes that such self-conscious, collectively determined outcomes occur very often. These more pessimistic observers look at the various participants in city politics and see only chaos, not any type of discernible, stable structure of power. They see a city where little can be done, where politicians mostly react to one crisis after another.

Beginning with Douglas Yates' *The Ungovernable City*, these observers have argued that the once-ordered relationships of domination or competition and compromise have given way to extreme fragmentation or "hyperpluralism."[22] The old political machines have disappeared, and the political parties have disintegrated. Many business firms have dispersed to the suburbs or moved offshore, while a new politics of identity in which the key organizing principles revolve around race, ethnicity, sexual orientation, and gender has generated unbridgeable divisions among those who were once partners in electoral coalitions. Under such conditions, paralysis sets in. No interest—not business, minorities, or neighborhoods—can impose their will on government, nor can government act in the ensuing din. As Carolyn Adams writes of Philadelphia, under such chaotic circumstances, "the city's chief administrator finds it difficult to move the machinery of government in rational, purposive ways."[23]

BOX 10.2 CIVIC ASSOCIATIONS IN NEW YORK CITY

During his visit to America in the 1830s, French political observer Alexis de Tocqueville suggested that the most unique characteristic of the new republic was its citizens' propensity for forming civic associations. In his classic work *Democracy in America*, he noted that "Americans of all ages, all stations in life, and all types of disposition are forever forming associations. There are not only commercial and industrial associations in which all take part, but others of a thousand different types: religious, moral, serious, futile, very general and very limited, immensely large and very minute."[1] The proliferation and vitality of these associations, de Tocqueville argued, were the backbone of American democracy.

Nowhere are de Tocqueville's ideas more relevant than in New York City, which has seen a sudden resurgence in the numbers, variety, and activities of its community groups. Communities that have never organized before and groups that had lain dormant for many years are suddenly sprouting powerful new neighborhood associations. According to a survey by the Citizens Community for New York, the number of these voluntary organizations has mushroomed from only 3,500 in 1977 to over 8,000 in 1995.[2] Perhaps even more importantly, these new organizations are no longer just long-term residents of stable middle-class neighborhoods in Queens, but are

becoming more ethnically and socioeconomically diverse and representative of the city as a whole. For example, the long-dormant Hillcrest Estates Civic Association was recently restarted by a local real estate agent, George Yee, drawing heavily on the increasing Chinese American population in the community. Other organizations, such as the well-established Ozone Tudor Civic Association, are actively trying to recruit new residents by holding Halloween celebrations and Easter egg hunts as well as spearheading a drive for the neighborhood to start its own youth program.

One explanation for this increase in activity is that dwindling federal, state, and local budgets are forcing communities to unite just to preserve their share of the pie. However, this explanation overlooks the nationwide trend toward increasing public-private partnerships between community groups and government agencies. Instead of simply demanding greater resources from government, local associations are now helping government to deliver those services. In Santa Barbara, California, a neighborhood association has initiated a block-watching program in response to gang shootings. In Austin, Texas, a Parks Department health and nutrition plan for children is augmented by volunteers from local neighborhood groups. Michael Krasner, associate professor of political science in

✧ DO ECONOMIC FORCES ACCOUNT FOR THE CHARACTER OF THE CITY?

Many scholars believe that urban politics is simply a response to larger forces that local government and interests cannot control. It makes little sense, in this view, to focus on the structure of political power to understand urban outcomes; instead we must look at economic behavior.

This approach to accounting for the character of the city begins with the classic economics assumption that individuals and business firms seek to maximize their well-being (or utility, as economists call it). The sum of these utility-maximizing behaviors, aimed at individual rather than collective ends, represents a powerful influence on the nature of

Queens College, explains, "People see a sort of decline in their quality of life, institutions like the school system deteriorating around them, and they feel that they have to get involved."[3]

One of the most successful of the new partnerships in New York City is the Fort Greene Coalition in Brooklyn. Fort Greene residents had watched their neighborhood deteriorate until, according to one long-time resident, gunfire and crime had become so prevalent that at times "you couldn't even go to the grocery store and you had to be in by five p.m."[4] Residents banded together and with the help of housing police officers and the local assemblyman obtained a grant for two-way radios and started training teenagers to patrol the neighborhood and escort elderly residents to the stores. The Fort Greene Coalition is a prime example of the new civic formula where community groups cooperate with government officials and use government programs to find grant money or use neighborhood volunteers to supplement government services.

The rise of neighborhood associations and civic organizations is helping to transform the political landscape in New York City. Historically, the responsibility of fighting City Hall for the neighborhood's share of services and spending fell to political parties. However, young people are increasingly abandoning political parties, which they see as corrupt, to pursue their interests through civic associations instead. As a result, political parties are gradually losing influence to civic associations. This trend has been encouraged by a change in the New York City Charter that weakened the power of elected borough presidents over the city's budgets. Neighborhoods can no longer rely on the borough president to protect their "fair share," but must directly petition and lobby the mayor's office and agency heads.

The new-found activism of community groups is also drawing the attention of elected politicians. As City Council Speaker Peter Vallone explains, "The civic associations are the voters. The politicians are going to listen to the voters."[5] Moreover, the local nature of most community groups' concerns matches closely with New York Mayor Rudolph Giuliani's emphasis on quality-of-life issues. This combination, Deputy Mayor Fran Reiter suggests, is why such groups are "getting greater entree than they may have in the past."

---

[1] Alexis de Tocqueville, *Democracy in America.*

[2] Pam Belluck, "Neighborhood Muscle," *New York Times* (February 25, 1996), A1, 30.

[3] *Ibid.*

[4] *Ibid.*

[5] *Ibid.*

the city: This behavior ends up shaping its layout, job opportunities, tax rate, public amenities, economic profile, housing stock, downtown structures, and so on. In contrast to the community political structure model, which sees urban outcomes as the deliberate result of the political process, the outcomes of utility-maximizing behavior are, from a collective point of view, unplanned and often unintended. When over 600,000 people left the city of Detroit in the three decades after 1960 because automobile jobs were drying up, they did not intend to leave the city with an abandoned, decaying housing stock, a weak tax base, and a downtown with no major retail stores. But those were some of the unplanned consequences of this great out-migration.

It is important to note that a good deal of utility-maximizing behavior involves the use of exit. People move for better job opportunities or because they are thrown out of work, firms move to get a better tax climate or more skilled labor force or cheaper workers, and cities adjust their tax rates or provide benefits in order to keep firms and middle-class homeowners from exiting.

Some analysts who believe that utility maximization is central focus on how the interests of economic elites shape the cities, mainly through their development priorities and investment decisions. Others focus on the utility-seeking behavior of individual workers and families and firms; others seek to understand the city as a utility-maximizing entity in itself.

Economic Elites

One of the most important examinations of the impact on the city of economic elites portrays urban politics as a contest between those who would use land for profit (its exchange value) and those who seek to preserve communities or live on it (its use value).[24] Urban political conflict is driven by the clash of developers and homeowners, between corporations and neighborhood organizations, and between landlords and tenants. On one hand are "people dreaming, planning, and organizing themselves to make money from property," and on the other are those who oppose those dreams that threaten neighborhood and community.[25]

Growth is seen as so important that it succeeds in uniting elites who stand to profit and government leaders who feel responsible for expanding the local tax base. The consensus on the desirability of growth between "place entrepreneurs" and government produces what Logan and Molotch call a growth machine. Seeking to promote the exchange value of land, the growth machine is a powerful engine: It "closely determines the shape of the city, the distribution of people, and the way they live together."[26] The size and appearance of the downtown; the array of convention centers, hotels, and parking facilities; the availability of downtown housing and shopping; and the condition of outlying neighborhoods are all outcomes of growth machine efforts. Many of the city's basic forms of social organization—downtown business groups, corporations, neighborhood associations, social clubs, and parent-teacher organizations—are created to pursue use or exchange values, and government itself, through its zoning, planning, and economic development functions, is enlisted in the struggle, usually on the side of the growth machine.

Conflict between use and exchange values provides a useful framework for understanding what Logan and Molotch call the sociology of urban property relations, a process, mainly internal to the city, of entrepreneurial initiative, competition, and resistance surrounding the issue of land use and the purposes of local government. But cities are subject not only to internal conflict between economic elites and ordinary residents; they are also affected by great national and international economic forces. We refer to the influence of these great forces in terms of **economic restructuring.**

Economic restructuring processes—the spatial change in the location of investment and the processes of deindustrialization—have been set in motion in part by the mobility of capital. Corporations seek cheap labor and investors seek the highest return on their money. Since World War II, investors have shifted capital from the Northeast to the Sun-Belt states, with their lower taxes, nonunion workforces, and milder climates. But American businesses have also increasingly sought overseas locales, particularly for the basic manufacturing operations that were once done in the great industrial cities around the Great Lakes and in the Northeast. Partly as a result of the overseas migration of capital, the proportion of the American workforce engaged in manufacturing has fallen from more than one-third in 1960 to only about 16 percent today.

Economic restructuring is also a product of the growing information-processing and business service industries. The rise of the complex business corporation, the explosion of knowledge and information, and the development of instantaneous communications and data-processing technologies have created millions of new jobs in what is broadly called the service sector. Many of these jobs are located in the central cities.

The geographical movement of businesses and money and the rise of service occupations have changed social and economic patterns in American cities. Specifically, the increasing dispersion of capital from historic urban manufacturing locales has diminished the traditional role of the city as a place of economic opportunity, particularly for the unskilled. However, the various service and information-processing occupations—law, accounting, advertising, management consulting, insurance, finance, real estate, and communications—have meant new urban jobs for the educated middle class. The workers who once earned their living by making steel, rubber, chemicals, televisions, and other goods rarely have the advanced training and education to compete for these new jobs. While the educated urban middle class prospers, the blue-collar working class and the unskilled workers find few opportunities. Thus, cities are becoming more and more economically and socially polarized.[27]

Some scholars have focused on the impact of these economic transformations on the least-skilled people in the city, who have virtually no hope of climbing the economic ladder. The despair and hopeless poverty of this group give rise to a whole range of antisocial behaviors such as crime, drug trade, and teen pregnancy. Sociologist William J. Wilson speaks of this group as an underclass.[28] With their lack of schooling and job training, they are victims of an employment mismatch: Job opportunities in the city call for training in information processing and business services but the members of the underclass have no skills.[29] Thus, some cities have booming downtown economies but high unemployment: The new jobs are filled by middle-class commuters, not the unemployed inner-city residents.

Family and Worker Utility Maximizers

Another way of seeing how economic behavior affects the cities is to look at people's residential location choices. Since World War II, as we shall see in Chapter 11, millions have chosen to leave the central city for suburban communities. Their motives are varied: They have sought better housing, yards, better schools, proximity to jobs and friends, greater safety, and racial homogeneity. Economists would say that in moving, these suburban immigrants were simply trying to maximize their well-being. Instead of using voice, or local politics, to try to improve their lives in the cities, people opted to exit. They voted with their feet.

The consequences of this massive suburban migration (about half the entire U.S. population now lives in suburban communities) have been sprawling urbanization, a proliferation of local governments in metropolitan areas, high levels of racial and class segregation, and a divorce of tax resources, now heavily located in the suburbs, and inner city needs. How reformers have sought to remedy these problems is the subject of Chapter 11.

The City as Utility Maximizer

Paul Peterson has argued that it is not just individuals who try to maximize their utility; cities do so too. Cities constantly "seek to improve their market position, their attractiveness as a locale for economic activity."[30] For Peterson this insight provides a means of acounting for municipal policy choices. In response to this economic imperative, cities tend to avoid redistributive programs such as homeless shelters, public hospitals, and other sorts of programs for the poor, for fear of driving away those whose incomes would be redistributed. Instead, they favor developmental policies, designed to encourage investment. Low tax rates and good infrastructure—roads, sewer and water systems, port facilities, and airports—are thought to attract capital.

Economic imperatives felt by those who govern the city, then, account for its array of amenities, taxes, and spending priorities.

✦ CONCLUSION

Neither local politics nor economic behavior provides a complete account of the American city, yet each makes a useful contribution. By focusing on the nature of the structure of power, we can assess the city's democratic possibilities. How easy is it for citizens to take part in the governance of their community? How widely is power dispersed? How easy is it to change things in the city? An account of the structure of power is best understood as a snapshot of a city's political opportunity structure. By understanding this structure, we can gauge the relative influence of different groups and actors in the city. This in turn provides a perspective on local patterns of conflict and coalition. In addition, by observing the concerns of those situated at different places in the structure of power, we can also understand the creation of the political agenda, or the issues that come up for public debate and resolution. Finally, to understand the politics of the city is to measure patterns of loyalty, apathy, and alienation among citizens as they go about the task of local self-government. The political structure model tells us much, then, about the texture of civic life.

The perspective on the influence of economic or utility-maximizing behavior on urban life provides a different window on the city. One important product of economic thinking is that it helps us to assess the array of economic opportunities in the city. In addition, economic behavior by investors, developers, and ordinary citizens helps to account for the physical city: its housing, its neighborhoods, its infrastructure, and its downtown. Moreover, utility-maximizing behavior by firms and individuals explains the rise of metropolitan or suburban America.

If the political structure model informs us about the democratic possibilities inherent in the political opportunity structure, the economic perspective offers us a view of the possibilities of utility maximization for investors, entrepreneurs, developers, and individuals through the economic opportunity structure. Just as some cities are more democratic than others, so do some places offer greater potential for the satisfaction of economic aims. But no theory or paradigm in urban politics research adequately accounts for the structure of both economic and democratic possibilities.

✦ KEY TERMS

economic restructuring (p. 272)

pluralism (p. 262)

political incorporation (p. 265)

social production (p. 268)

structure of political power (p. 261)

✧ FOR FURTHER READING

Bernard Frieden and Lynn Sagalyn, *Downtown, Inc.* (Cambridge, Mass.: MIT Press, 1989). A lively set of case studies showing how developers, financiers, and local government interact to build new urban downtowns.

William Grimshaw, *Bitter Fruit: Black Politics and the Chicago Machine, 1931–1991* (Chicago: University of Chicago Press, 1992). A discussion of the emergence and development of black political power in Chicago, including an analysis of the rise of Mayor Harold Washington and the period after his death.

✧ NOTES

1. Jonathan Walters, "Why Nice Cities Finish Last," *Governing,* 8 (September 1995), 18–22.

2. The Lynds published two studies: *Middletown* (New York: Harcourt Brace, 1929) and *Middletown in Transition* (New York: Harcourt Brace, 1937)

3. Floyd Hunter, *Community Power Structure* (Chapel Hill: University of North Carolina Press, 1953), p. 1.

4. The major critique of Hunter and other stratification theorists is Nelson Polsby's *Community Power and Political Theory* (New Haven, Conn.: Yale University Press, 1963). A second, revised edition was published in 1980.

5. Peter Bachrach and Morton Baratz, *Power and Poverty* (New York: Oxford University Press, 1970), p. 44.

6. Matthew Crenson, *The Un-Politics of Air Pollution* (Baltimore: Johns Hopkins University Press, 1971).

7. Hunter, *Community Power Structure,* p. 148.

8. Wallace Sayre and Herbert Kaufman, *Governing New York City* (New York: Russell Sage, 1960).

9. See Mark Baldassare, ed., *The Los Angeles Riots* (Boulder, Colo.: Westview Press, 1994).

10. The most comprehensive study of the riots was the federal government's *Report of the National Advisory Commission on Civil Disorders* (Washington, D.C.: Government Printing Office, 1968). It contains the famous conclusion that "Our nation is moving toward two societies, one black, one white—separate and unequal."

11. Peter Eisinger, "Black Employment in Municipal Jobs: The Impact of Black Political Power," *American Political Science Review,* 76 (November 1982), 754–771; Rufus Browing, Dale Marshall, and William Tabb, *Protest Is Not Enough* (Berkeley: University of California Press, 1984); and Albert Karnig and Susan Welch, *Black Representation and Urban Policy* (Chicago: University of Chicago Press, 1980).

12. Browning, Marshall, and Tabb, *Protest Is Not Enough.*

13. Rufus Browning, Dale Marshall, and William Tabb, eds., *Racial Politics in America* (New York: Longman, 1990).

14. Clarence Stone, *Regime Politics* (Lawrence: University of Kansas Press, 1989); see also Peter Eisinger, *The Politics of Displacement* (New York: Academic Press, 1980).

15. Stone, *Regime Politics,* p. 110.

16. John Clayton Thomas, *Between Citizen and City* (Lawrence: University of Kansas Press, 1986).

17. Stone, *Regime Politics,* pp. 68–69.

18. Alan Lupo, Frank Colcord, and Edmund Fowler, *Rites of Way: The Politics of Transportation in Boston and the U.S.* (Boston: Little, Brown, 1971).

19. Rochelle Stanfield, "Block By Block," *National Journal* (July 8, 1995), 1763–1766.

20. Matthew Crenson, *Neighborhood Politics* (Cambridge, Mass.: Harvard University Press, 1983).

21. Jeffrey Berry, Kent Portney, and Ken Thomson, *The Rebirth of Urban Democracy* (Washington, D.C.: Brookings, 1993).

22. John Clayton Thomas and H.V. Savitch, "Introduction: Big City Politics, Then and Now," in H.V. Savitch and John Clayton Thomas, eds., *Big City Politics in Transition* (Beverly Hills, Calif.: Sage, 1991).

23. Carolyn Adams, David Bartelt, David Elesh, Ira Goldstein, Nancy Kleniewski, and William Yancey, *Philadelphia: Neighborhoods, Division and Conflict in a Postindustrial City* (Philadelphia: Temple University Press, 1991), p. 152.

24. John Logan and Harvey Molotch, *Urban Fortunes* (Berkeley: University of California Press, 1987).

25. *Ibid.*, p. 12.

26. *Ibid.*, p. 2.

27. Edward Soja, "Poles Apart: Urban Restructuring in New York and Los Angeles," in John Mollenkopf and Manuel Castells, eds., *Dual City* (New York: Russell Sage, 1991).

28. William Julius Wilson, *The Truly Disadvantaged* (Chicago: University of Chicago Press, 1987).

29. John Kasarda, "Urban Industrial Transition and the Underclass," *Annals*, 501 (January 1989).

30. Paul Peterson, *City Limits* (Chicago: University of Chicago Press, 1983), p. 22.

CHAPTER

11

THE POLITICS OF METROPOLITAN AREAS

The Great Depression of the 1930s and then the extraordinary industrial mobilization required to fight World War II forced Americans to defer new residential construction for almost two decades. Thus, by the end of the war in 1945 over half a million families were living in quonset huts or other temporary dwellings, and another 6 million were doubling up with relatives or friends.[1] The return of the GIs from Europe and Asia, anxious for a resumption of normal life, simply added to the pent-up demand for new housing.

Many European countries, devastated by the war, also faced housing crises, to which they responded by constructing new government-financed apartment buildings. But Americans did not want to live in public housing or apartments: The single-family private home surrounded by a yard was, as it always had been, a central feature of the American dream. "A man is not a whole and complete man," Walt Whitman wrote, "unless he owns a house and the ground it stands on."[2] After the war people embraced this ideal with new determination.

Before 1945, the year the war ended, the typical American building contractor could rarely put up more than five houses per year; clearly this small-scale approach was inadequate to meet the heavy demand for new housing. Abraham Levitt and his sons pioneered the solution: They transformed what had been the decentralized craft of house-building into a mass-production industrial enterprise.[3] In 1946 they purchased 4,000 acres of potato farms in the flat country of Long Island 25 miles east of New York City. Using a standard four-room design, careful planning, volume purchase of appliances, and cheap construction techniques, they built over 17,400 single-family homes on the site between 1947 and 1951. To ensure a steady supply of lumber, Levitt bought a forest in California; to guarantee enough nails, he built a nail factory on the Long Island site. In addition to the housing, Levitt built seven "village greens" with shops, nine swimming pools, and a community meeting hall. The resulting community, named Levittown, was the largest housing development ever put up by a single builder. The Levitts went on to build more large developments in the 1950s, and other builders emulated their techniques in other parts of the country. In 1950 nearly 1.7 million single-family houses were started nationwide, up from just over 100,000 per year during the war. The majority of these new houses were located outside the central cities.

Although suburbs had been part of the American landscape for at least a century, the level of growth of these settlements on the big-city fringe in the decades after the war was unprecedented. In 1950 the Census Bureau reported that about 60 percent of residents of metropolitan areas—central cities and their suburbs—lived in the central cities themselves. By 1980, however, 60 percent lived in suburbs. By 1990, 46.2 percent of the entire U.S. population could be classified as suburban, that is, as living in metropolitan areas but outside of the central cities.

Some specific examples give a better sense of the dimensions of suburban growth. Between 1940 and 1980 the city of Atlanta grew by 40.6 percent, but its suburbs grew by 1,046.2 percent. Oklahoma City grew in these years by 97.2 percent but its suburbs grew by 2,464 percent. San Diego's population increased by an impressive 330 percent, but this was dwarfed by suburban growth of 1,760 percent.[4]

Population growth on this scale on the periphery of cities gave birth almost overnight to scores of new communities and transformed others from quiet villages to substantial

The sameness of the small houses built in Levittown gave rise to jokes and cartoons about people coming home to houses that were not their own and to songs about the "ticky tacky" little boxes in a row. Nevertheless, the mass production of single-family houses made home ownership a real possibility for working people. A close inspection of the picture reveals modest efforts to individualize the houses through awnings or distinctive paint or flower boxes. (*Source:* UPI/Bettmann Newsphoto)

towns. In fact the number of new municipalities in the United States increased by a little over 10 percent between World War II and 1962, and the number of special districts in this period increased by over 120 percent.[5] Thus, an important consequence of suburban development has been the growth and creation of new local political units in metropolitan areas. The multiplication of political jurisdictions has led to the characterization of metropolitan areas as politically fragmented.

✧ METROPOLITAN POLITICAL FRAGMENTATION

Metropolitan areas are defined for statistical purposes by the U.S. Office of Management and Budget (OMB). As a general concept, a metropolitan area is a place with a large population nucleus and the surrounding population and communities, which have a high degree of social and economic integration with the core settlement. The technical definition is quite a bit more complex.

In 1993, metropolitan areas consisted of 250 Metropolitan Statistical Areas (MSAs) and 18 Consolidated Metropolitan Statistical Areas (CMSAs). Within the CMSAs there were 73 Primary Metropolitan Statistical Areas (PMSAs).

An MSA is one or more counties with a central city of at least 50,000 people *or* a densely urbanized area with 50,000 and a total metropolitan population of at least 100,000 people.[6] An MSA may include one or more adjacent counties if at least 15 percent of the labor force commutes to the central county and if the population of the adjacent county meets various urbanization criteria (for example, density per square mile and proportion of communities over 2,500 people). A typical single-county MSA is Bloomington, Indiana, located in Monroe County. Its total population in 1993 was 111,000. An example of an MSA with more than one county is Birmingham, Alabama. The city of Birmingham lies in Jefferson County, but significant proportions of the workers in the adjacent three counties of Blount, St. Clair, and Shelby commute into Jefferson County every day. The total metropolitan area population of this four-county MSA was 859,000.

When the total metropolitan area is one million or more and there are several large population centers (competing central cities), the OMB designates the area a Consolidated MSA. An example is the Denver-Greeley-Boulder area in Colorado, home to more than 2 million people. Within this CMSA, Denver County and its surrounding four counties, as well as the city of Greeley (located in Weld County), and the communities of Boulder and Longmont (in Boulder County) constitute three distinct PMSAs.

A number of metropolitan areas cross state lines: The Philadelphia metropolitan area is an example, stretching across the Pennsylvania line into southern New Jersey, Maryland, and Delaware, embracing almost 6 million people. In some states virtually the entire population lives in a metropolitan area. In New Jersey, in fact, every single county—and thus 100 percent of the population—is contained within an MSA; in California, almost 97 percent of the population is in a formally designated metropolitan area, and 93 percent of Maryland's people are metropolitan.

These figures make it clear that the use of the county as the basic unit of the metropolitan area may be somewhat misleading. Particularly in California, but even in New Jersey, large numbers of people live in what most of us would regard as rural communities. Because their county is sufficiently integrated with a central county with a substantial population core and has a high proportion of people living in towns with over 2,500 people, we count these country dwellers as part of the metropolitan population. The least metropolitanized states are Montana (24 percent of the population lives in formally designated MSAs) and Vermont (27 percent).

Each metropolitan area is characterized by a multiplicity of local governments. By one estimate the average metropolitan area contains more than 100 different local governments, including municipalities, school districts, counties, townships, and special districts. About 1 out of every 12 MSAs has 250 or more local governments. The Chicago metropolitan area is regarded as the most fragmented, with over 1,250 jurisdictions; by one recent count there were 6 counties, 261 municipalities, 113 township governments, 313 school districts, and 503 special districts and authorities.[7] Many of the municipalities found at the edge of big cities are quite small; half have fewer than 2,500 people. Only a quarter of all of these communities govern more than four square miles.[8]

Several characteristics of the fragmented metropolis are important to understand. Nearly all of these various jurisdictions have independent taxing authority. Thus, the typical metropolitan resident pays taxes to five or more different jurisdictions, such as the city, the county, the school district, the library district, the water conservation district, and the vocational education district. Furthermore, the boundaries of these various governments rarely coincide with one another. There is much overlap. People who live in different municipalities may nevertheless be served by the same school district. The vocational education district may encompass some entire counties and parts of others. The boundaries of school and special districts in particular are often drawn without reference to the existing boundaries of other jurisdictions.

✦ METROPOLITAN FRAGMENTATION: TWO VIEWS

Concerned citizens of the fragmented Philadelphia metropolitan area warned in the early 1850s that "these divisions and unseen lines and complications of powers" could "paralyze or arrest every effort to advance the common welfare and to suppress general evils."[9] Indeed, reformers are still convinced that the multiplicity of governments in the metropolis represents a sort of civic pathology and must somehow be eliminated or mitigated. David Rusk, former mayor of Albuquerque, writes that "The fragmentation of metro areas into multiple local governments is associated with the degree of residential segregation" by class and race, which he considers to be the very heart of America's urban problem.[10]

Not everyone sees metropolitan fragmentation as a problem, however. For some, the fragmented metropolis represents a way of offering a range of opportunities for citizen-consumers: The many municipalities are like so many choices in a metropolitan supermarket, each providing a different array of amenities at a different "price," or tax rate. Citizens may engage in a search for a community in which to live, choosing the one in which they achieve the best match between their ability to pay the price of taxes and the package of public services they desire. Thus, for example, some families will move from a low-tax school district with poor schools to a higher tax area with a reputation for better schools because they are willing to pay more for the better service. Conversely, retirees may seek a low-tax town, even though modest revenues cannot support an excellent school system, because the retirees do not have school-age children. Many people leave the central city for the suburbs in order to take advantage of lower taxes and what they perceive to be better services. This perspective, one should note, emphasizes the possibility of exit from communities that offer less than satisfactory services or high tax burdens. Let us look at these two views of metropolitan fragmentation in greater detail.

The Reform View of Metropolitan Fragmentation

Reformers have identified at least three different problems associated with political fragmentation of metropolitan areas: coordination, accountability, and intercommunity inequities.

Consider the problem of coordination. Most metropolitan areas may best be understood as relatively integrated urban social and economic systems without an overarching government responsible for the whole. That is to say, these areas are composed of interdependent and complementary parts: residential suburbs, industrial areas, corporate parks, shopping centers, financial districts, and recreational areas. Each needs the others to fulfill various economic and social needs. Often these are located in different political jurisdictions. Thus, it is not uncommon for residents of one community to commute to work in another, shop in a different town, and go to yet another for entertainment. Employers, too, are dependent on many different parts of the metropolis, for they draw their workforce from many surrounding communities. In addition, they may both sell to customers and subcontract with suppliers located in other parts of the metropolitan community. Social patterns may also cross jurisdictional boundaries; for example, grandparents may still live in the central city, but their married offspring may live in a suburb not far from where they grew up. Although metropolitan residents and businesses thus typically rely on more than one community for their economic and social transactions, few metro areas have a government responsible for the entire system.

The absence of an overarching government creates problems of coordination. Consider the problem of moving around the San Francisco Bay Area on public transportation. Seventeen different agencies—including Bay Area Rapid Transit (BART), CalTrain, SamTrans, and MUNI—run bus or train systems. Their different stops and stations are often blocks apart, requiring long walks or cab rides. Another example of coordination problems concerns the speed limits on Old Country Road on Long Island. The boundary between the towns of Mineola and Garden City runs down the center of the road. Going westbound, drivers may travel at 30 miles per hour, but going east they may go 40, for each town has set its own speed limits.[11]

Or take the Minneapolis–St. Paul area. In the mid-1960s the metropolitan area had more than 300 governments, each independently serving the residents within their respective borders. They were unable to deal with common problems. The situation reached crisis proportions when a state Department of Health survey found over a quarter million people drinking water from wells contaminated by septic tanks. If one town banned septic tanks and put in a sewer system, it still could not protect its residents from the septic tanks permitted in the neighboring community. There was no government body with the authority to ensure a clean water supply for the entire metropolitan region.

Water table contamination does not respect political boundaries drawn up by human beings, nor do many other problems that afflict metropolitan areas. Air pollution wafts across city and state borders, but the strict pollution laws of one city are scant protection against the smoke permitted to belch from factories in another. Traffic congestion crosses city lines, criminals flee easily from one jurisdiction to the next, the homeless cluster in some parts of the metropolis but not others, people in need of public health care may not live in communities that have decent and affordable medical facilities, and employment opportunities may be unevenly distributed across metropolitan space. Yet as political scientist Norton Long writes, "There are not institutions with sufficient power and overall responsibility to make decisions settling metropolitan issues and solving metropolitan problems."[12] In the extreme situation, every community is on its own.

Reformers are also convinced that the fragmented metropolis also makes it difficult for voters to hold elected leaders accountable. The problem is simply put: The multiplicity of overlapping governments means that there are various public officials with different functional and territorial responsibilities. Voters have a difficult time keeping track of who is responsible for what. In the Indianapolis metropolitan area before its 1969 reorganization, there was so much duplication of legislative and executive functions that the League of Women Voters titled its local government study of the area *Who's in Charge Here?*[13]

One can understand the problem of accountability more clearly by considering the typical property tax bill sent to homeowners once a year. The bottom line—what the property owner must pay—is generally the product of decisions about taxes made in the city council, the county board of supervisors, the school board, and possibly other bodies as well. If the person's taxes have gone up, which government is responsible? Although both the news media and the property tax bill may tell the taxpayer that the city raised its taxes by 5.5 percent (although it is responsible for levying only 25 percent of the total property tax), the school board 3 percent (it may account for over half the tax bill), and the county 2.2 percent on its share, most voters will be confused about what this really means in dollar terms. Which government really caused the increase? Whom should they call to complain, and what should they say?

Furthermore, it is hard to keep track of what many public officials actually do from day to day or year to year. Some officials administer relatively specialized public authorities of which the public may not even be aware. This produces voter fatigue, the symptoms of which are low voter turnout and general lack of interest in local politics. A newspaper in Florida reported that in the countywide election for the Pinellas County Soil Conservation District board of supervisors, not even the three candidates on the ballot bothered to vote. No one in the county seemed to know anything about the election except the district conservation officer responsible for holding it.[14] Some metropolitan areas have so many different governments that it is hard to find people to run, much less to vote. In the nine-county San Francisco Bay Area, home to 383 special district governments, over 180 elections for sanitary district and fire protection district supervisors were canceled in the years 1956 to 1962 because there were no contests.[15]

A third problem that reformers believe is a consequence of the fragmented metropolis is that serious intercommunity inequities occur because of differences in community resources. This is particularly so when we compare central cities with their suburbs. Per capita income in central cities, for example, is on average only about 84 percent of that of suburbs.[16] In addition, the median value of real estate—houses, businesses, and firms—is as much as 135 percent greater in suburbs than in cities for comparable property. This means that for a city to raise the same amount of tax revenue per capita as its suburbs, it must impose higher tax rates.[17] Ironically, these higher tax rates fall heavily on poor people, who are disproportionately concentrated in central cities: Roughly 18 percent of central city residents fall below the federal poverty line, compared to 8 percent of suburban dwellers.[18] Even with higher tax rates, however, cities rarely are able to raise the necessary funds to finance public services.

Cities with high concentrations of poor people must pay more for services than cities with lower poverty levels. For example, per-capita spending in cities with low poverty levels for such functions as welfare, hospitals, and housing was $124, but for the same set of services in cities with high poverty, per-capita spending was $277. High poverty levels also raise the cost of police, fire, and education.[19]

Many suburban communities were created precisely for the purpose of avoiding high central city taxes. In the nineteenth century, promoters of the Indianapolis suburb of Woodruff Place promised that "a man who lives there will not have to pay city tax . . . and the difference of taxation will amount to a sum worth considering."[20] Michael Danielson and Jameson Doig cite additional evidence of tax avoidance as a major spur to suburban incorporation, in this case in New Jersey and New York.[21]

As described in Chapters 8 and 17, intercommunity inequities in tax base led to successful court challenges to property tax-based financing of public schools in at least a dozen states by the early 1990s.[22] In a case decided by the California Supreme Court in 1971, *Serrano v. Priest,* the court agreed with the plaintiff that unequal property tax bases were unlikely to produce equally good school systems. **Fiscal disparities** in school financing constituted a denial of state-guaranteed equal educational opportunities, which the state had to address by working out a method of funding education that did not rely so heavily on the property tax. A similar case in New Jersey in 1973, *Robinson v. Cahill,* actually led the court in that state to insist that the legislature pass a state income tax, more progressive than a local property tax, to help with school financing. After the New Jersey legislature reluctantly passed an income tax in 1976 (enabling the state to redistribute revenues from better-off school districts to poor ones), the state share of school funding rose from 23.6 percent in 1975 to more than 35 percent in 1983.

Since the Serrano case, school systems in at least ten states have been challenged in the courts. One of the most recent suits occurred in Texas, where that state's supreme court ruled in 1989 that the property tax system for funding schools violated the Texas constitutional guarantee of an "efficient system" for the "general diffusion of knowledge." The court ordered the state legislature to change the way the system is financed.[23]

Unequal tax bases lead to competition among communities in the metropolitan area for tax-paying industry and residents. This competition is pursued by offering tax breaks, land write-downs (subsidies for the purchase of land), and cheap capital. Ironically, Mark Schneider finds in a study of 812 suburban communities that growth in local property wealth is inversely related to a modest degree to the property tax rate.[24] In other words, low taxes, a luxury available mainly to communities of well-to-do people, may help somewhat to spur growth.

The Metropolis as a Marketplace

Some analysts, mainly political economists, reject the notion that the fragmented metropolis encourages inefficiency, problems of overlap, and duplication. Although reformers see small units of government as creating confusion in metropolitan areas, political economists believe that they increase the possibilities for local democracy.

Recall that the political economists' view, often called the public choice position, sees the metropolitan area as giving rise to "a quasi-market choice for local residents [by] permitting them to select the particular community in the metropolitan area that most closely approximates the public service levels they desire."[25] This position makes three crucial assumptions: One is that people make decisions about where to live that maximize their own welfare. A second is that each person gathers enough information about the alternative places to live—what their tax rates are, what their public services are like, and what the housing market offers—to make the best personal decision. (Although most citizens are uninformed about what different communities offer, and thus could not in the abstract make an intelligent choice, there is evidence that the small subset of people who move do gather this information, particularly with respect to school quality and school taxes.[26]) The third assumption is that once people have made their choices, they are able to act on them.

The result of this decision process, according to the public choice theorists, is that each community is composed of individuals with similar public service needs and desires and, if not necessarily similar socioeconomic status, at least similar notions of how much they are willing to pay in taxes for those services. In such communities there is little conflict over such matters as tax rates or on which services to spend revenues. Under these conditions, local government finds it easy to be responsive to its relatively homogeneous constituency. Elinor Ostrom and Gordon Whitaker provide support for this view in their comparison of police services in Indianapolis and in small neighboring communities. Compared to their neighbors in the city, people in the suburban towns on the border of Indianapolis reported that the police were more active in following up reported crimes, quicker to respond to calls for help, and more likely to be performing at an outstanding or good level. Ostrom and Whitaker conclude that:

> The findings strongly suggest that . . . small police forces under local community control are more effective than a large, city-wide controlled police department in meeting citizen demands for neighborhood police protection.[27]

The public choice position sees small units as more democratic than large units in part because the ratio of public officials to citizens is smaller. The St. Louis metropolitan area, for example, is highly fragmented, with some 91 different municipalities. In many of these communities the ratio of elected officials to citizens is 1:1,000 and in no case is it less than 1:5,000. By contrast, in unincorporated areas, where people are served only by the county government with no intervening municipal government, the ratio of officials to citizens is 1:140,000.[28]

The assumption here is that small units encourage voice, that is, political participation in an effort to influence public policy, rather than exit to a more congenial community. There is evidence, however, that smaller communities are no more likely to encourage voice behaviors than larger ones. In a study that compared citizen political activity in communities in a fragmented metropolitan area (Louisville) with that in neighborhoods in a consolidated area (Lexington), William Lyons and David Lowery found no evidence that smaller communities encouraged more participation. For the most part, levels of voice activity were about the same in the two settings, although in a few cases they were actually higher in the consolidated neighborhoods, contrary to the public choice prediction.[29] The issue of the effects of small units is hardly resolved, however. In the view of public choice theorists, such places are not only likely to be more responsive than larger ones, but they are also often more efficient. The lack of efficiency of many small jurisdictions offering similar services is a key point in the reformers' list of concerns about the fragmented metropolis. For example, reformers argue that much money could be saved if there were just one police dispatcher for a metropolitan area (modern communications could make this possible) rather than a police dispatcher in each small community. Likewise, a single repair shop for buses servicing a metropolitan transportation system is more efficient than several garages for separate municipal bus services. In general, infrastructure services—water, sewer, mass transit, road maintenance, and communications—may be administered more efficiently by a single agency over a large area than by several agencies over smaller ones.

But contrary to the notion that increasing size always produces efficiencies of scale, public choice researchers have found that some services are more efficient when they are administered by smaller units. A good deal of research indicates that the average unit cost of public school systems, for example, is U-shaped; in other words, the cost of very small and very large systems is higher than for moderate-sized systems.[30]

The argument is that there is a large amount of information and control lost between layers of large bureaucracies. Smaller organizations find it easier to change and adapt to shifting conditions. Furthermore, public choice theorists point out, small communities compete with one another for tax-paying residents by trying to offer the best services at the lowest cost. Several smaller units create a competitive market situation in which the need to attract residents and firms creates an incentive to behave efficiently. A single large agency represents a monopoly and thus has no incentive, in this view, to strive for efficiency.

Metropolitan Residential Discrimination

The public choice model of the ideal metropolitan community assumes that citizen-consumers can move freely from one community to another until they find one that matches their service desires with their ability or willingness to pay the cost in taxes. One result of this sorting out of people, according to the public choice model, is a large number of relatively homogeneous communities, each offering a different package of services and social environment. A number of factors help to maintain socially and racially homogeneous communities in metropolitan areas. Several of these are related to purely market factors: The cost of housing in different towns is a major factor that obviously divides people by class. Only relatively wealthy people can choose to live in Oak Park, Illinois, or Grosse Pointe, Michigan, because the houses there are expensive. Although patterns of residential settlement by income create unequal governments, as we have seen, Americans tend to accept such inequalities as a justifiable outcome of the market.

Another factor that makes for a certain homogeneity is that people may choose to live with others of their religious or ethnic background. Thus, some Jews and Catholics, particularly, may cluster in certain communities out of a desire to form religious congregations. Skokie, Illinois, is a heavily Jewish community, not because the options Jews have on the housing market are necessarily limited but because some want easy access to Jewish social, commercial, and religious institutions that can flourish when there is a critical mass of potential clients. Some communities in the metropolis are heavily settled by one particular ethnic group. Hamtramck, Michigan, for example, is a city (located entirely within the boundaries of Detroit, incidentally) with a predominantly Polish-American population. The streets are lined with Polish delicatessens, bakeries, restaurants, and other shops that cater to the needs of that ethnic group.

Not all housing segregation in metropolitan areas is a product of varying abilities to pay for housing or of free choices to cluster with others who share one's ethnic background. When this is the case, the market analogy begins to break down. Some communities maintain their population makeup by their reputation for hostility toward others. Sometimes people use outright violence, as when they burn crosses on the lawns of new black neighbors. Sometimes they use less violent forms of intimidation. The city council president of Parma, Ohio, a suburb of Cleveland, once said publicly, "I do not want Negroes in the city of Parma."[31] That city also maintained its all-white status for years by requiring a public referendum on any low-income housing project and by denying building permits for federally subsidized housing on the assumption that such housing attracted minorities.

Maintaining racial homogeneity in communities and neighborhoods is usually achieved through the more subtle discriminatory efforts of the private real estate and lending industry. Real estate agents may steer African American home buyers to all-black neighborhoods or communities and away from predominantly white areas. Agents may even tell blacks seeking to buy that there are no houses on the market, even though they may be simultaneously showing houses to white buyers. As Douglas Massey and Nancy Denton write,

> Rather than encountering "white only" signs, [black home-seekers] are met by a realtor with a smiling face who, through a series of ruses, lies, and deceptions, makes it hard for them to learn about, inspect, rent, or purchase homes in white neighborhoods.[32]

Once blacks find a house they wish to buy, it is more difficult for them to get a mortgage loan. In the 50 largest metropolitan areas of the country, the average rejection rate for black mortgage applicants was almost twice as high as for whites: Whereas 12.1 percent of white applications were turned down by banks and savings and loans, 22.7 percent of black applications were rejected.[33] In some cities, such as Milwaukee, the rejection rate for blacks is higher among high-income home buyers, which suggests that the differences in racial access to mortgages is not just a function of differences in income.

Class and racial homogeneity may also be achieved through the use of **zoning laws.** Although zoning has legitimate functions as a tool for the regulation of land use, it may also be used to drive up housing prices or limit housing choices to the extent that poor people are effectively barred from a community.

Zoning is the practice of determining the permissible uses of land within a jurisdiction. It first appeared in the United States in 1916 in New York City as a device to protect residential neighborhoods in Manhattan from encroachment by garment industry

BOX 11.1 DISCRIMINATION WITH A SMILE

Although the days of "whites only" signs have ended, African-American home-seekers still encounter a formidable set of covert barriers that make it harder for them to find homes in white neighborhoods. Outright racial discrimination against minority homeseekers and prospective renters all but ended with the passage of the 1968 Fair Housing Act. Realtors who overtly refused to rent or sell to blacks could be sued and prosecuted under the Fair Housing Law.

Now, however, black homeseekers face more subtle forms of exclusion from real estate agents. Their phone calls may not be returned, they are told the advertised unit has been rented, they are not told about financing opportunities, they are treated rudely in hopes that they will leave, or they are shown units only in black or mixed residential neighborhoods. Although these individual acts are small in comparison to previous discrimination, the cumulative effect is to radically decrease the likelihood of black entry into white neighborhoods.[1]

In such instances of latent discrimination, it is unclear even to the person experiencing it that discrimination has taken place. The realtor may smile when he or she says no houses or apartments are available and clients have no way of knowing whether they are being told the truth or being discriminated against. The only way to test whether such latent discrimination has occurred is to examine the differences in the treatment of white and black homeseekers with similar social and economic characteristics expressing comparable preferences in housing. These audits reveal that discrimination against African Americans has persisted on a widespread scale despite the passage of the Fair Housing Act. In a national study of both rental and sales markets, housing was systematically more available to whites in 45 percent of the transactions in the rental market and 34 percent of those in the sales market. Whites also received more favorable credit assistance in 46 percent of sales encounters and more favorable financial terms in 17 percent of rental transactions.[2]

The same study also examined the severity of discrimination, measured in terms of the number of units shown to whites but not to blacks with similar characteristics and preferences in housing. These estimates directly measure the extent of realtor proclivity for discrimination because if an agent has additional housing units to show, he or she can discriminate by showing fewer units to black clients than to white ones. With rental units, the probability that an additional unit was shown to a white but not a black auditor was 65 percent, and the probability that another unit was recommended to whites but not to blacks was 91 percent.[3] In short, when realtors have the ability to discriminate, they usually do.

These findings prove that discrimination against African Americans in housing has continued despite the intentions of the 1968 Fair Housing Act, albeit in a more subdued fashion. The irony of such subtle forms of discrimination is that African Americans are likely to underestimate the true extent of discrimination they have experienced. In a 1977 survey, 74 percent of blacks said they had experienced discrimination in housing. However, only a quarter of blacks interviewed in a 1989 *USA Today* poll said they had experienced discrimination.[4]

---

[1]Douglass Massey and Nancy Denton, *American Apartheid: Segregation and the Making of the Underclass* (Cambridge: Harvard University Press, 1993), pp. 96–98.

[2]John Yinger, "Housing Discrimination Study: Incidence of Discrimination and Variation in Discriminatory Behavior" (Washington, D.C.: U.S. Department of Housing and Urban Development, Office of Policy Development and Research, 1991), pp. 23–43.

[3]*Ibid.,* Tables 42 and 44, pp. 39, 40.

[4]Cited in Massey and Denton, *American Apartheid,* p. 105.

workshops. All of Manhattan was divided into districts that were designated as exclusively residential, exclusively industrial, or mixed. Although zoning was clearly a restraint on the free use of private property, the Supreme Court upheld its use in 1926. By 1936, 1,322 cities had adopted zoning codes.[34]

As a legitimate tool of land-use regulation, zoning may be used to segregate noxious or dangerous industrial activities from residential or recreational areas, preserve green space, minimize population density and congestion, and separate commercial from residential activity. In recent years zoning has been used to designate whole areas of cities as historic districts in an effort to preserve distinctive neighborhoods and architecture. But zoning may also be used to maintain class and, by implication, racial exclusiveness. In suburban towns particularly, zoning boards may require such large building lots (one acre, for example) that only the wealthy can afford to build. Other towns bar apartment houses, prefabricated housing, and mobile homes, all of which make housing more accessible to low income and poor people. Other communities bar publicly subsidized housing projects or require complex approval procedures. California's law requiring prior voter approval in a referendum for the construction of public housing in a community was upheld in a Supreme Court decision (*James v. Valtierra*) in 1971. The court reached its decision on the grounds that the procedure would ensure that the people would have a voice in the expenditure of local government funds required to provide services to such projects. In subsequent years, however, zoning that has exclusionary effects has been successfully challenged in the courts. The first important breakthrough occurred in 1975 in the New Jersey Supreme Court in a case that concerned the zoning ban against mobile homes, small lots, and apartments in the town of Mount Laurel. The state court ruled in the **Mount Laurel I** decision that such zoning laws barred poor people unconstitutionally from the right to decent housing outside of central cities. The court went on to say that Mount Laurel and other communities had to make positive efforts by encouraging housing opportunities for all classes.

Very few towns complied with the court's order, however, and by 1983 the New Jersey court was angry. In what has come to be known as the 1983 **Mount Laurel II** decision, the state court followed up its earlier ruling by ordering New Jersey towns and cities not simply to eliminate exclusionary zoning laws but to take active steps to ensure housing opportunities for all income groups. Communities must now submit plans for encouraging affordable housing (through offering builder incentives, for example) to a state council set up to monitor progress. One of the first to offer a plan was the town of Bedminster, which had always required minimum five-acre lots for each house and where fox hunting and steeplechasing were the preferred sporting events. Bedminster promised to construct nearly 1,000 units of low-income housing. However, many New Jersey towns still refused to comply with the court order of *Mount Laurel II*. A similar case involving exclusionary zoning in a Long Island community was the subject of a U.S. Supreme Court case in 1988: Here the court ordered the town of Huntington to rezone 15 acres of land to permit the construction of low-income apartment units. Before the court ruling, Huntington had effectively maintained racial segregation and restricted housing opportunities in the city by limiting the construction of apartments to one predominantly black neighborhood. Despite successful legal action, progress in opening the suburbs by challenging restrictive zoning laws has been slow. Huntington, for example, planned to arrange for the construction of 162 housing units. Urban planners in the region estimate the need for low-income housing in the New York metropolitan area at over 100,000 units.

Metropolitan Residential Differentiation and Free Choice

An important element in the public choice perspective is that if people do not like the services or the tax rates of the town in which they live, they can move, or exit. A major problem with this view is that not everyone is perfectly free to move around the metropolis in search of the optimum community. Racial minority groups in particular face significant barriers in the housing market. To the extent that race restricts choice, the metropolitan marketplace does not really function as a perfect market. Sociologists calculate that nearly 80 percent of the black population in large northern metropolitan areas would have to be relocated to other parts of the city in order for each census tract to have a population that reflected proportionally the racial makeup of the area. Although segregation indexes declined slightly between 1980 and 1990, they still indicate an extreme degree of separation between the races.[35]

People who suffer discrimination or even who fear that they will suffer cannot exercise their exit option freely, nor can they perform the sort of calculation, essential to the public choice view, that results in the choice of a community in which ability and willingness to pay taxes and the desired level of public services are matched. The differences among communities in the metropolitan area are thus not entirely a matter of many individual choices about where to live.

✧ POLITICAL RESPONSES TO METROPOLITAN FRAGMENTATION

Political reformers have historically been interested in eliminating metropolitan fragmentation, whereas public choice advocates have been interested in accommodating fragmentation. Both approaches to the political organization of metropolitan areas have produced a rich variety of institutional arrangements and procedures designed to promote the efficient provision of public services in a democratic setting. Some of these arrangements call for a single metropolitan government; others at the opposite end of the spectrum are designed to maintain the autonomy of individual communities within some framework for coordinating their activities.

Annexation

At one time the simplest approach to creating a single government over an urbanized area was through the **annexation** of land adjacent to the city. By incorporating land on its fringe, the city could extend its jurisdiction over areas as they became settled. Before 1900 annexation was the principal means by which cities accommodated growth beyond their borders. The trouble with this procedure today, however, is that most land on the edge of big cities is now incorporated (that is, organized as municipalities) and it is virtually impossible in most states for cities to annex incorporated territory.

In this century only a few cities have used annexation to grow significantly. Los Angeles is one famous case. Between 1905 and 1913 the city engineered and financed an elaborate water system, a series of aqueducts and pipelines that reached over 250 miles to bring fresh water from the Sierra Nevada mountains. When the water first began to flow into the city, the supply was more than five times what the city needed. Neighboring communities in this arid region of Southern California watched in envy. But the city's Public Service Commission resolved that surplus water would be sold only to communities that allowed themselves to be annexed to the city. As the city's Annexation Commission noted in a report,

> Annexation . . . will give Los Angeles official standing as the metropolis of the Pacific Coast. Greater Los Angeles, coextensive with the territory receiving aqueduct water, will have a population, assessed valuation, bank clearings, building permits, etc., in excess of any other city on the Pacific Coast. All this has an economic value to which Los Angeles is entitled by reason of the great investment it has made and risk it has incurred in the Owens River aqueduct enterprise.[36]

Between 1915 and 1927 the city annexed huge territories. The incorporation of the San Fernando Valley alone doubled the territory of the city overnight.

Houston is another city that grew through annexation in the twentieth century. Using the most liberal annexation laws in the country, Houston grew from less than 73 square miles in 1940 to 579.6 square miles today. It covers a land area approximately the size of New York, Chicago, and Philadelphia combined.[37]

A few other cities also used annexation extensively in this century. They include Oklahoma City (its territory went from about 50 square miles in 1950 to more than 660 by 1990), Dallas, and other Texas cities, San Diego, Atlanta, and Memphis. Note that these places are all in the South and Southwest, regions of late urbanization. When cities in these areas began to grow, they were not hemmed in by incorporated suburbs, as are cities in the older regions of the Midwest and Northeast.

Cities still annex land today, but they tend to involve quite small areas. Only a handful of the annexations in any given year involve more than 5 square miles. The average annexation brings in a little over one-tenth of a square mile into the city and an additional 45 people.[38] Clearly, annexation is not an effective strategy for imposing the authority of a single government over densely settled, fragmented metropolitan areas.

Metropolitan Reform

The preferred reform solution to the problem of governmental fragmentation, with its attendant inequities and inefficiencies, has been the creation of a single metropolitan government. The idea is simple: Create a government with one mayor (or manager) and one council over the entire metropolitan area, replacing the many mayors and many city councils of all the independent municipalities. In the reform view, this would increase the ability of voters to know which public officials were responsible for what, it would permit more rational planning, and it would promote efficiency in service delivery.

There exist in practice several variants of the single-government idea, although none exactly matches the reform vision of a grand metropolitan government. The most common reform arrangement is **city-county consolidation,** found currently in 29 metropolitan areas. Consolidation involves making the boundaries of the municipality the boundaries of the existing county and eliminating individual jurisdictions within the county. In practice, consolidation seldom works exactly this way.

The first consolidations occurred early in the nineteenth century when New Orleans and Boston consolidated with their counties. Altogether, nine such consolidations occurred before World War II, all accomplished by the actions of state legislatures. Each of the New York City boroughs has also been a county since Brooklyn was added to the city in 1898. Denver, San Francisco, and Honolulu are the other major prewar consolidations.

There have been 20 city-county consolidations since World War II, beginning with Baton Rouge, Louisiana, in 1947. The most recent involved the municipality of Athens, Nevada, and Clark County in 1990.[39] Several of the more famous consolidations are interesting. In 1962 Nashville merged with surrounding Davidson County. Unlike the prewar consolidations, Nashville and Davidson County chose merger by popular referendum. In fact, 19 of the 20 consolidations accomplished in the modern period have been by referendum rather than legislative action, the only exception being the merger of Indianapolis and Marion County in 1969. Referenda on city-county mergers rarely pass, however: More than 100 such referenda since World War II have failed in other parts of the country, including ones in Cleveland, St. Louis, and Philadelphia. Suburban dwellers, who often must approve the merger, resist being subject to the city's taxing authority. City residents, particularly members of minority groups, fear that their voting strength will be diluted by the incorporation of largely white, middle-class suburbs.

But these issues did not come into play in the Nashville case. The major issue that led to consolidation in this Tennessee metropolitan area was the deterioration of public services in the growing suburbs. For example, because there were no adequate municipal sewer systems in much of the county, over 100,000 suburbanites had to rely on septic tanks, severely threatening private wells that provided most of the drinking water.[40]

The new arrangement in Nashville created a single elected council and merged the county and city school systems and public health departments, among others. The consolidation scheme created a general services district that provides everyone within the city-county boundaries with schools, police, courts, welfare, streets, libraries, and public housing services. People living in the old city of Nashville, more densely populated than suburban and rural areas, are included in an urban services zone. They pay a higher property tax for the slightly more extensive services required in their heavily urbanized neighborhoods. Service zone systems are also used in the Jacksonville-Duval (Florida) and Baton Rouge city-county consolidations.

Another notable city-county consolidation occurred in 1969 when the Indiana state legislature, without seeking the views of the citizens affected through a referendum or public hearings, merged Indianapolis and Marion County. Although proponents claimed that merger was important for efficiency reasons, many suspected that the desire to undercut growing black political power in the city was a powerful motivation as well. The consolidated government, popularly called Unigov, vaulted Indianapolis overnight from the twenty-sixth largest city in the United States to the ninth largest. The merger expanded the city territorially from 82 square miles to more than 400.

The Indianapolis arrangement is extremely complex. Although the reform created a single mayor and a single council by combining, respectively, the city and county executives and the two legislative bodies, it did not eliminate all the separate governments in Marion County. The old school districts remain independent, which distinguishes Indianapolis from other city-county consolidations such as Lexington (Kentucky),

Nashville, and Jacksonville, which created single metropolitan school systems. In addition, four previously existing suburban municipalities were left unconsolidated (although 16 small towns were consolidated), and a number of services, including police, fire, and water, are still administered by local government bodies in Marion County.

Nevertheless, some 28 separate city and county departments were merged into just 6 functional agencies. They provide a host of services on a metropolitan basis, including welfare, sewers, parks, hospitals, housing and renewal, health, planning, libraries, sanitation, and highways. As Owen and Willbern write, "The establishment of Unigov, in fact, was much less an act of geographic centralization than of administrative integration."[41] Most observers agree that the impact of Unigov has been to improve administrative efficiency, strengthen mayoral leadership, improve transportation services, and hasten and rationalize downtown development.

Another variant of the metropolitan government ideal is Miami-Dade's two-tier system. Created in 1957, the arrangement involves a greatly strengthened Dade County government responsible for a host of metropolitan functions, including expressways, mass transit, police and fire records and communications, hospitals and public health, traffic control, and air pollution abatement. One of the most important countywide functions is the preparation and enforcement of a comprehensive plan for the development of the county. Local municipal governments—some 27 in all—remain in existence and provide local services. Unincorporated areas, in which nearly half the population in the county now lives, are served only by the county. The county is governed by a county manager and a council, whose members, although elected at large, must come from separate districts. Miami-Dade government is a big operation: It provides services for about 2 million people and administers a budget of $1.5 billion per year.

As in Indianapolis, metropolitan government in Miami has managed to integrate a formerly chaotic administrative structure, and it has led to the adoption of a strong land-use plan, strong air and water pollution controls, uniform traffic laws, and the initiation of a rapid transit system.

Closely related to the Miami-Dade arrangement is the piecemeal increase in the responsibilities of county government as a way of gradually effecting some degree of coordination and service uniformity and achieving economies of scale. This is a less systematic approach than the Miami-Dade reform, but it is based on a similar principle. The growth of county government is now a well-established trend.[42] County governments in large metropolitan areas, such as DuPage near Chicago, Cobb near Atlanta, and Fairfax County in Virginia, are taking on more and more responsibilities, and they are growing at a faster rate than suburban municipal governments. Schneider and Park find that whereas suburban government expenditures between 1972 and 1982 rose by 118 percent, county government expenditures went up by 143 percent. Furthermore, they write, "compared to suburban cities, metropolitan county governments are involved in a broader range of functions."[43]

County governments not only continue to offer a full array of services to unincorporated areas, but they are now often the sole provider to residents of all parts of the county—city, suburbs, and unincorporated territories alike—of various redistributive social services such as welfare, public health, housing, and hospitals. In Tennessee's Shelby County, for example, the county now administers the entire criminal justice system. The city of Memphis, located in Shelby County, no longer runs a city jail or city courts.

Another way in which county governments have helped to achieve efficiencies in service provision in metropolitan areas is by providing services to municipalities (as opposed to individuals) on a contract basis. This arrangement was first used in Los Angeles County in 1954, and it is called the **Lakewood Plan,** after the first suburb to take part. Under the Lakewood Plan, the county offers municipalities the chance to contract for the provision of any number of a whole array of services. These services, such as law enforcement, tree planting, traffic light maintenance, animal control, ambulance service, and building inspection, would ordinarily be the responsibility of the municipal government. The Lakewood Plan permits smaller suburbs to take advantage of the economies of scale that derive from the county's ability to spread fixed capital costs among a large number of municipal contracts. Although the plan achieves greater efficiencies in service provision across the county, it actually encourages suburban fragmentation. Communities no longer must allow themselves to be annexed in order to take advantage of comparatively inexpensive, state-of-the-art services. The practice of contracting for a service between governments is now fairly widespread. One survey in the mid-1980s found that over half of all cities had entered into a service agreement with another government, most often the county.[44]

Single-county solutions to metropolitan fragmentation are not very effective in multicounty metropolitan areas. A few innovative models have been implemented to provide services in these larger urbanized territories. One of them is Portland Metro. In 1970 the Oregon legislature authorized the creation of a Metropolitan Service District, described by Secretary of Housing and Urban Development Henry Cisneros as "a flexible governmental 'box' that could be assigned as many service responsibilities as voters or legislators in the Portland area wanted."[45] In 1978, voters in the 3 county Portland metropolitan area approved a metropolitan governing structure that combined the Columbia Region Association of Governments and the Metropolitan Service District, with the new agency retaining the name Metropolitan Service District. The Portland Metropolitan Service District now covers 3 counties and 24 municipalities. It began by assuming responsibility for planning and financing a regional solid waste disposal system; later, voters approved adding responsibility for the Portland Zoo and the Oregon Convention Center. It also functions as the regional land use planning authority to manage growth in the area. It is governed by a directly elected 12-person board and chief executive.

Not all such regional institutions are directly elected. The Metropolitan Council of the Twin Cities, established in 1967, and Seattle's Metropolitan Municipal Corporation, created in 1957, are both governed by appointed boards. The former is responsible for long-range planning for highways, mass transit, airports, parks, sewers, and the administration of a metropolitan tax sharing plan discussed below. Seattle's Metro is more limited: Voters have permitted it only to manage sewage treatment facilities for the region and mass transit, although the state legislature authorized it to take on several other functions.[46]

Sometimes state governments seek to increase metropolitan uniformity and efficiency by creating new institutions such as Portland's or Seattle's Metro. But sometimes the states simply preempt local authority by imposing state standards and regulations on municipalities. A Connecticut state law, for example, permits state courts to overrule local zoning decisions when they seem inimical to regional interests. For example, the

BOX 11.2 THE METROPOLITAN SERVICE DISTRICT, PORTLAND, OREGON

In 1978, citizens of Multnomah, Clackaman, and Washington counties voted to create a new hybrid form of regional government to address the transportation and growth issues facing the greater Portland, Oregon, area. The first of its kind in the United States, the Metropolitan Service District, more commonly known as Metro, was nothing less than a dramatic leap of faith to abandon traditional geographic and political boundaries and concentrate political power at a regional level. Fifteen years later, greater Portland area voters pronounced the experiment a success by approving a referendum to transform Metro into an elected regional government, making Metro the only regional authority in the country with the right to pass legislation bearing on local governments in its jurisdiction.

In other metropolitan areas, political responsibility is divided into well-defined and compartmentalized segments among the city, suburbs, and county government. However, Metro has sole responsibility for transportation and growth issues in its jurisdiction of 3 counties, 24 cities, more than 150 service districts, and 1.2 million residents. Its regional jurisdiction allows Metro to bring together urban and suburban interests into developing common policies to address regional issues such as urban growth and transportation planning, which would overwhelm any one local government.

Nowhere is the evidence of the success of the Metro regional government more evident than in Portland's ability to avoid the problems of urban sprawl. Portland is one of the most rapidly growing regions in the United States, but it has largely avoided the problems of urban sprawl that have plagued other high-growth areas such as the nearby Seattle-Tacoma area. Whereas Seattle is suffering from rising highway construction, traffic congestion, and pollution, Portland has developed a comprehensive mass transit system. Nearly 40 percent of downtown employees travel to work on light rail or buses—one of the highest rates of public transit use in the United States.[1] Rich Carson, the planning director, notes that "part of the reason light rail works is because we addressed it on a

state may override local zoning barriers to the siting of solid waste landfills. In addition, the state may override local laws that bar the construction of low-income housing. In New Jersey, state planners may restrict access to highways at the sites of new development in order to reduce traffic congestion. Some analysts see such developments as eroding home rule. Some argue, however, that home rule (which Robert Wood calls essentially the power to say no)[47] tends to reinforce racial and class segregation in metropolitan areas and hinder the achievement of rational land-use planning and traffic circulation, and they do not mourn its withering.

For a time, the federal government also sought to encourage regional governance, primarily through requirements for comprehensive regional planning as a condition for receiving federal assistance. The Housing Act of 1961, the Urban Mass Transit Act of 1964, and a host of other programs required the development of a plan by a regional metropolitan body, such as a council of governments. By 1977 there were at least 39 federal programs with such requirements. When Ronald Reagan took office, however, he worked to eliminate federal planning mandates; by the end of his first term in office, all but one of the requirements had been terminated or weakened.[48]

regional basis. You can't make sense of transportation on a city by city basis."[2]

Similarly, Metro has been able to keep the region's rapid population growth from translating into urban sprawl by establishing a strict growth boundary for the Portland urban area. Inside the 362-square-mile area, building is encouraged. However, Metro discourages building growth outside the boundary by refusing to provide certain road improvements or new sewer service. One immediate impact of this tough regional zoning is to decrease the average size of a single-family lot from 13,200 to 8,700 square feet.[3] By increasing residential density, the region has doubled the number of houses and apartments that could have been built under previous planning and zoning. The smaller lots make government services more cost-effective to deliver, thus containing home prices and property taxes, making the region as a whole more livable.

With many regions looking to emulate the successes of the Metropolitan Service District, Rena Cusma, Metro's chief elected officer, is quick to tout the accomplishments of this unique set of governing arrangements, but cautions, "That's not to say it comes easily. It doesn't. One of things I think is true is most metropolitan areas in the country are trying to figure out how to get something similar to this place. One of the things that is clear is that the old governmental forms really aren't working very well for metropolitan areas."[4] As the scope of regional problems such as transportation, growth, and the environment continues to outgrow the fractured political authorities of metropolitan areas, the allure of new regional governing arrangements such as Metro will only increase.

---

[1]Philip Langdon and Corby Kummer, "How Portland Does It: A City That Protects Its Thriving, Civil Core," *The Atlantic* (November 1992), 134.

[2]Ron Karten, "Land Use System Still Controversial," *Oregon Business,* 14(2) (February 1991), 70.

[3]Langdon and Kummer, "How Portland Does It," p. 137.

[4]David Noack, "Crossing the Boundaries; Regional Governments," *American City & County* (September 1993), 86.

At this point the states sought to take up the slack by requiring regional review of local government applications for federal aid. This is accomplished either by a regional planning commission, established by state law, or a council of governments, a voluntary association of local governments. The regional body relays its comments to a state clearinghouse for review to make sure that local governments in a single metropolitan area do not seek competing or redundant facilities financed by federal grants. The review process has rarely resulted in state efforts to bar a local government from seeking federal aid for some particular project.

Interlocal Agreements

Achieving the reform goal of a single overarching metropolitan government is a difficult and rare event. As we have already discussed, most reform responses to metropolitan fragmentation are piecemeal; many represent major compromises with the ideal. The desire for suburban autonomy from the big city, the fear that single government solutions will raise taxes, the sense that smaller governments are more accessible and democratic than large ones, and the vested interests of public officials who would lose their jobs in a con-solidation all work against the successful implementation of single-government arrange-ments in metropolitan areas.

Nevertheless, local officials in suburbs and central cities do agree that fragmentation poses severe problems of coordination and duplication. Recently, scholars have recognized an emerging set of efforts that seeks to preserve municipal independence in metropolitan areas but achieve coordination through various interlocal or interjurisdictional agree-ments.

In the highly fragmented Pittsburgh metropolitan area, where the depressed steel towns of the Mon Valley jealously guard their autonomy, glimmerings of regional cooper-ation have begun to emerge. The Steel Valley Council of Governments is now responsi-ble for regional building code inspection and enforcement, saving the individual cities a great deal of money. Several towns in the valley have agreed to share a city manager, who works part of each week in each place.[49]

The most thorough documentation of interlocal agreements is contained in a study of St. Louis sponsored by the federal Advisory Commission on Intergovernmental Relations, which concludes that although government fragmentation does exacerbate intercommunity inequalities, it does not necessarily lead to inefficiency and lack of coor-dination.[50] Municipalities deal with problems of coordination through a variety of mutu-al agreements. For example,

✧ The separate police departments have pooled investigative resources to form a major case squad to respond to serious crimes.

✧ Police and fire recruits for each community are trained by the St. Louis County Police and Fire Training Academy.

✧ The separate fire departments are all party to various mutual aid arrangements.

✧ The various school districts jointly purchase supplies and equipment, computer hardware, software, and maintenance to take advantage of economies of scale.

✧ City and county schools are linked through a voluntary desegregation plan.[51]

The study concludes that "it is possible to have a form of metropolitan governance in the absence of a metropolitan government."[52] Governance in this view is the ability to make rules that apply on a metropolitan-wide basis. If this rulemaking is accomplished through voluntary agreements rather than the actions of an overarching government, the effect may be just the same. Whether the level of interlocal cooperation in the St. Louis metropolitan area is typical of other metropolitan areas in the United States is not clear.

As for intergovernmental inequalities, we have seen that these are a product in part of unequal tax base resources. There have been few metropolitan efforts to redress such inequalities, but one arrangement worth noting is the Minneapolis metropolitan area rev-enue-sharing plan implemented through the Minnesota Fiscal Disparities Act of 1971. Under this plan, the property tax revenues gained from new real estate development in the metropolitan area are split, with 60 percent going to the community in which the build-ing is erected and 40 percent going to a metropolitan pool, to be shared among all the municipalities in the area. This arrangement is designed to dampen intercommunity com-petition for investment and at the same time to share the benefits of new industry or com-mercial developments across the whole metropolitan community. After nearly a quarter century of operation, the tax base sharing scheme has significantly reduced interlocal fiscal inequalities in the Twin Cities region.[53] Unfortunately, even though metropolitan tax base sharing apparently does work, such arrangements have not spread to other areas.

✧ CONCLUSION

Americans have been moving out of central cities since the mid-nineteenth century, seeking space and greenery, better housing, and escape from city problems and ethnic groups who differ from them. The result of this pattern of out-migration from the central cities and municipal incorporation is a high degree of government fragmentation in the metropolis, for in order to provide certain necessary services for themselves, suburban settlers have formed municipal corporations. Incorporation, the establishment of city government, makes possible the creation of local police and fire departments, sanitation services, park departments, street departments, and so on. Each community tends to offer a slightly different package of services and tax burdens, enabling people on the move to shop for the community most congenial to their service desires and ability to bear the tax burden.

There are two prevailing views of metropolitan fragmentation. One view decries it, seeing in the hodgepodge of separate governments a highly inefficient and uncoordinated system of government. The solution in this reform view is to create some sort of overarching metropolitan government to impose a single government, a single set of rules, across the entire area. The other view sees fragmentation as creating a healthy market situation in which communities compete with one another for people and industry by offering the best services for the lowest tax price. Furthermore, the public choice view sees small units as more democratic and more responsive than larger units of government.

As we have seen, evidence to support the arguments of both sides of this debate is mixed. It is not always clear that bigger units are able to generate efficiencies by taking advantage of economies of scale. Small units may in some cases be more efficient. Some claim that small units are not only more efficient under some conditions but also more democratic. But there is some evidence that democratic participation in small governments is no greater than it is in the neighborhoods of large cities.

Whatever the strength of evidence on either side of the debate over the organization of metropolitan government, it seems clear that the impetus for reform solutions has diminished in recent years. The enthusiasm that spurred metropolitan reformers in the 1960s and 1970s and led to the consolidations in Indianapolis, Lexington, and several other smaller places has given way to the realization that suburban resistance is strong enough to block single-government solutions in most places. But if fragmentation is here to stay, this does not mean that chaos reigns unchecked in metropolitan America. In recent years state government action has begun to preempt local authority, particularly in the areas of low-income housing and environmental protection. In addition, if the St. Louis area is an indication, suburban communities are entering into various sorts of mutually beneficial agreements with one another to take advantage of economies of scale in everything from purchasing supplies to repairing police vehicles. People in metropolitan areas, therefore, have not made much progress in eliminating fragmentation, but they have learned to live with it and even on occasion to transcend it.

✦ KEY TERMS

annexation (p. 289)

city-county consolidation (p. 290)

fiscal disparities (p. 283)

Lakewood Plan (p. 293)

metropolitan areas (p. 279)

Mount Laurel I decision (p. 288)

Mount Laurel II decision (p. 288)

zoning laws (p. 286)

✦ FOR FURTHER READING

Michael Danielson and Jameson Doig, *New York: The Politics of Urban Regional Development* (Berkeley: University of California Press, 1982). A comprehensive analysis of the governance and problems of the New York metropolitan region.

Kenneth Jackson, *Crabgrass Frontier: The Suburbanization of the United States* (New York: Oxford University Press, 1985). A lively historical account of the development of suburban America.

David Rusk, *Cities Without Suburbs* (Washington, D.C.: Woodrow Wilson Center Press, 1993). An effort to revive support for metropolitan solutions to urban problems by the former mayor of Albuquerque.

✦ ENDNOTES

1. Kenneth Jackson, *Crabgrass Frontier: The Suburbanization of the United States* (New York: Oxford University Press, 1985), Chap. 13.

2. *Ibid.*, p. 50.

3. The story of Levitt and Levittown is told in Barbara Kelly, *Expanding the American Dream: Building and Rebuilding Levittown* (Albany: State University of New York Press, 1993).

4. Bradley Rice and Richard Bernard, "Introduction," in B. Rice and R. Bernard, eds., *Sunbelt Cities* (Austin: University of Texas Press, 1983), p. 10.

5. Nancy Burns, *The Formation of American Local Governments* (New York: Oxford University Press, 1994), p. 6.

6. To complicate matters, an MSA may have a population core of 50,000 even if the people are not all residents in a single city. Two adjacent (twin) cities with a total of 50,000 qualify the area as a metropolitan area, as long as its total population is 100,000. In New England, the total metropolitan population has to be only 75,000.

7. George Hemmens and Janet McBride, "Planning and Development Decision Making in the Chicago Region," in Donald Rothblatt and Andrew Sancton, eds., *Metropolitan Governance: American/Canadian Intergovernmental Perspectives* (Berkeley, Calif.: Institute of Governmental Studies Press, 1993), p. 117.

8. Eric Schmitt, "On Long Island, Many Governments Overlap to Form a Jurisdictional Jumble," *New York Times* (November 13, 1989).

9. Quoted in Jon Teaford, *City and Suburb* (Baltimore: Johns Hopkins Press, 1979), p. 2.

10. David Rusk, *Cities Without Suburbs* (Washington, D.C.: Woodrow Wilson Center Press, 1993), pp. xiii and 33.

11. Schmitt, "On Long Island."

12. Norton Long, *The Polity* (Chicago: Rand McNally, 1962), p. 157.

13. C. James Owen and York Willbern, *Governing Metropolitan Indianapolis: The Politics of Unigov* (Berkeley: University of California Press, 1985), p. 32.

14. *St. Petersburg Times* (October 18, 1973).

15. Stanley Scott and John Corzine, "Special Districts in the San Francisco Bay Area," in Michael Danielson, ed., *Metropolitan Politics* (Boston: Little, Brown, 1971), p. 203. See also Victor Jones and Donald Rothblatt, "Governance of the San Francisco Bay Area," in Rothblatt and Sancton, *Metropolitan Governance*.

16. National League of Cities, *City Distress, Metropolitan Disparities and Economic Growth* (Washington, D.C.: National League of Cities, 1992).

17. Roy Bahl, Jorge Martinez-Vazquez, and David Sjoquist, "Central City-Suburban Fiscal Disparities," *Public Finance Quarterly*, 20 (October 1992), 420–423.

18. National League of Cities, *City Distress*, p. 6.

19. U.S. Department of Housing and Urban Development, *Empowerment: A New Covenant with America's Communities*, President Clinton's National Urban Policy Report (Washington, D.C.: Government Printing Office, 1995), p. 16.

20. Quoted in Teaford, *City and Suburb*, p. 21.

21. Michael Danielson and Jameson Doig, *New York: The Politics of Urban Regional Development* (Berkeley: University of California Press, 1982), p. 77.

22. David Franklin and G. Alan Hickrod, *School Finance Equity: The Courts Intervene* (Elmhurst, Ill.: North Central Regional Educational Laboratory, 1992).

23. *New York Times* (October 3, 1989).

24. Mark Schneider, "Local Budgets and the Maximization of Local Property Wealth in the System of Suburban Government," *Journal of Politics*, 49 (November 1987), 1104–1116.

25. Vincent Ostrom, Charles Tiebout, and Robert Warren, "The Organization of Government in Metropolitan Areas: A Theoretical Inquiry," *American Political Science Review*, 55 (December 1961), 838.

26. Paul Teske, Mark Schneider, Michael Mintrom, and Samuel Best, "Establishing the Micro Foundations of a Macro Theory: Information, Movers, and the Competitive Local Market for Public Goods," *American Political Science Review*, 87 (September 1993), 702–713.

27. Elinor Ostrom and Gordon Whitaker, "Does Local Community Control of Police Make a Difference? Some Preliminary Findings," *American Journal of Political Science*, 17 (February 1973), 48.

28. Roger Parks and Ronald Oakerson, "St Louis: The ACIR Study," *Intergovernmental Perspective*, 15 (Winter 1989), 10.

29. W. E. Lyons and David Lowery, "Governmental Fragmentation Versus Consolidation: Five Public-Choice Myths About How to Create Informed, Involved, and Happy Citizens," *Public Administration Review*, 49 (November/December 1989), 533–543.

30. For a summary of these studies, see Elinor Ostrom, "Metropolitan Reform: Propositions Derived from Two Traditions," *Social Science Quarterly*, 53 (December 1972), 474–493.

31. *New York Times* (May 13, 1989).

32. Douglas Massey and Nancy Denton, *American Apartheid* (Cambridge, Mass.: Harvard University Press, 1993), p. 97.

33. City of Milwaukee, Office of the Controller, *Annual Review of Lending Practices of Financial Institutions*, December 1994, pp. 17–18.

34. Jackson, *Crabgrass Frontier*, p. 242. The court case in which zoning was upheld was *Euclid v. Amber.*

35. Massey and Denton, *American Apartheid*, p. 222.

36. Vincent Ostrom, *Water and Politics: A Study of Water Policies and Administration in the Development of Los Angeles* (Los Angeles: Haynes Foundation, 1963), p. 155.

37. Robert Thomas, "Urban Growth Decision Making in the Houston Area," in Rothblatt and Sancton, eds., *Metropolitan Governance*, pp. 283–328.

38. Joel Miller, "Municipal Annexation and Boundary Change," *The Municipal Yearbook, 1988* (Washington, D.C.: International City Management Association, 1988), p. 59.

39. Allan Wallis, "Inventing Regionalism: The First Two Waves," *National Civic Review,* 83 (Spring–Summer 1994), 166.

40. John Harrigan, *Political Change in the Metropolis* (New York: HarperCollins; Boston: Little, Brown, 1985), p. 318.

41. Owen and Willbern, *Governing Metropolitan Indianapolis*, p. 107.

42. J. Edwin Benton and Donald Menzel, "County Services: The Emergence of Full-Service Government," in David Berman, ed., *County Governments in an Era of Change* (Westport, Conn.: Greenwood, 1993), pp. 53–69.

43. Mark Schneider and Kee Ok Park, "Metropolitan Counties as Service Delivery Agents: The Still Forgotten Governments," *Public Administration Review,* 49 (July/August 1989), 347.

44. Lori Henderson, "Intergovernmental Service Arrangements and the Transfer of Functions," *Municipal Yearbook 1985* (Washington, D.C.: International City Management Association, 1985), pp. 195–198.

45. Henry Cisneros, *Regionalism: The New Geography of Opportunity* (Washington, D.C.: Department of Housing and Urban Development, 1995), p. 21.

46. Wallis, "Inventing Regionalism," p. 159.

47. Wood is a well-known political scientist and former HUD official. He is quoted in the *New York Times* (August 10, 1989).

48. Wallis, "Inventing Regionalism," pp. 168, 172.

49. Alan Ehrenhalt, "Cooperate or Die," *Governing,* 8 (September 1995), 31.

50. Advisory Commission on Intergovernmental Relations, *Metropolitan Organization: The St. Louis Case* (Washington, D.C.: Government Printing Office, 1988).

51. Parks and Oakerson, "St. Louis: The ACIR Study," p. 9.

52. *Ibid.,* p. 10.

53. Howard Chernick and Andrew Reschovsky, "Urban Fiscal Problems: Coordinating Actions Among Governments," *The La Follette Policy Report,* 6 (Fall 1995), 13.

PART FIVE

PUBLIC POLICY

THE POLITICS OF TAXING AND SPENDING IN STATES

axation is a contentious issue for citizens and state leaders. Few people like to pay taxes; most look with envy at places where taxes are low. States compete to minimize the tax burden on businesses and citizens because officials fear that high tax rates may drive firms and individuals away. Ratings of state business climate (such as the Grant Thornton annual survey) include taxes as a crucial component. Even for citizens who never intend to leave their home state, high taxes may incite them to "revolt." In 1978 California voters passed Proposition 13 in order to lower property taxes; many other states followed suit. Thus, the possibilities of exit and voice are ever present in discussions about taxes. Taxes, in turn, are necessitated by government expenditures. Expenditures provide public services that citizens value, reinforcing their loyalty to the state. Spending decisions, and the policy priorities they represent, are inevitably linked to taxation decisions. This chapter examines both.

✧ THE FISCAL POSITION OF STATE GOVERNMENTS

Each state makes its decisions about taxing and spending within the context of certain constraints. An important constraint is the national economy and its influence on state fiscal conditions. A poignant lesson occurred in 1981–1982, when the nation experienced a severe **recession** that rapidly created fiscal stress for states. Most states had to raise taxes in order to offset the recession-induced declines in their tax revenue. Again in 1990–1991 a recession occurred, felt most severely in California and the Northeast. Although about half of the states levied large tax increases, the states' response this time focused more on cutting spending growth. Macroeconomic performance—particularly the rate of economic growth, inflation, and recession—is a major determinant of states' economic health and fiscal performance.

A related macroeconomic factor is the ongoing regional shift of economic activity and population (described in Chapter 1). In the 1980s Nevada doubled in population while Arizona, Alaska, and Florida grew by a third. In the same decade the population decreased in Iowa, North Dakota, Wyoming, and West Virginia; population growth in Illinois was near zero. In the first half of the 1990s the West and the South continued to lead in population growth; the Northeast and the Midwest recorded only modest increases. Regional disparities in economic and population growth and decline present real problems for state governments. A shrinking economy and a shrinking population mean a smaller tax base, maybe even a poorer one if the wealthier and younger people leave. Addressing the problem of decline costs money, and the resulting tax bite may drive more businesses out.

Second, state fiscal decisions are significantly influenced by the amount of federal aid received. Indeed, federal aid is the largest source of state revenue, larger than any single tax. As federal aid goes, so go the states. Chapter 2 outlined the decline in federal aid during the 1980s. During the early 1980s, states had to contend with both a recession and

TABLE 12.1 STATES RANKED BY PER-CAPITA PERSONAL INCOME, 1994; TAX CAPACITY INDEX FOR 1991[a]   A state's per capita income is an important indicator of its wealth and ability to support public programs. But the tax capacity index measures taxable income more precisely because it includes a variety of sources besides personal income.

Rank	State	Per-Capita Income	Tax Capacity Index
1	Connecticut	$29,402	130
2	New Jersey	28,038	119
3	New York	25,999	103
4	Massachusetts	25,616	117
5	Maryland	24,933	106
6	Hawaii	24,057	146
7	Nevada	24,023	128
8	Alaska	23,788	178
9	Illinois	23,784	102
10	New Hampshire	23,434	110
11	Delaware	22,828	125
12	Washington	22,610	108
13	Virginia	22,594	103
14	California	22,493	115
15	Minnesota	22,453	101
16	Colorado	22,333	109
17	Michigan	22,333	94
18	Pennsylvania	22,324	96
19	Rhode Island	22,251	89
20	Florida	21,677	103
21	Wisconsin	21,019	90
22	Ohio	20,928	93
23	Kansas	20,896	93
24	Missouri	20,717	91
25	Nebraska	20,488	95
26	Wyoming	20,436	134

federal belt-tightening. But during the 1990–1991 recession, states benefitted from a loosening of the federal purse strings: The amount of federal aid gradually climbed in the first half of the 1990s. In 1996, state leaders braced for the consequences of the federal government's attempt to balance its budget, which inevitably will mean dramatic reductions in federal aid.

Like national economic trends, federal aid does not flow evenly across the United States. Rather, each federal program has its own allocation formula; the aggregate dollar sum favors some states over others. State leaders are constantly competing to attract federal dollars, just as they are constantly competing for new businesses. By and large the northern plains states and much of the South are the winners.

The third major component in a state's fiscal planning is its own economic base. In fact, one scholar has found that for the first time in the 1980s state economic effects

TABLE 12.1   (CONTINUED)

Rank	State	Per-Capita Income	Tax Capacity Index
27	Oregon	$20,419	100
28	Indiana	20,378	90
29	Iowa	20,265	93
30	Georgia	20,251	91
31	Vermont	20,224	105
32	Texas	19,857	97
33	North Carolina	19,669	93
34	Maine	19,663	95
35	South Dakota	19,577	86
36	Tennessee	19,482	82
37	Arizona	19,001	94
38	North Dakota	18,546	91
39	Idaho	18,231	82
40	Alabama	18,010	81
41	Montana	17,865	91
42	Kentucky	17,807	83
43	Oklahoma	17,744	87
44	South Carolina	17,695	83
45	Louisiana	17,651	89
46	West Virginia	17,208	77
47	New Mexico	17,106	87
48	Utah	17,043	82
49	Arkansas	16,898	78
50	Mississippi	15,838	68

[a] Tax capacity is the amount of revenue each state would raise if it applied a national average set of tax rates for 26 commonly used tax bases. The index listed is the per capita tax capacity divided by the per capita average for all states, with the index for the average set at 100.

Sources: U.S. Bureau of the Census, *Statistical Abstract of the United States: 1995* (Washington, D.C.: Government Printing Office, 1995), p. 161; Advisory Commission on Intergovernmental Relations, *Significant Features of Fiscal Federalism, 1994 Edition, Vol. II* (Washington, D.C.: Government Printing Office, 1994), pp. 198, 182.

became more important than national fluctuations.[1] State economic performance was more closely tied to the state's own economic base. States differ substantially in their fiscal capacities and in what there is to tax. A simple way to compare states' wealth is by looking at annual per capita personal income. Table 12.1 ranks the states on income per person in 1994. By this measure Mississippi is the poorest state: Its citizens average only $15,838 per year. The richest state is Connecticut, with an average income of $29,402. Its citizens have nearly twice as much income as the average Mississippian. This means that Connecticut can afford more government services than Mississippi. In a reversal of a historic trend, income gaps between the states widened during the 1980s.[2]

One drawback to the income measure is that it ignores tax exportation, the shifting of taxes to nonresidents. Nevada, for example, can tax tourists who come to gamble; Texas can impose a severance tax on oil paid for by customers in other states. The Advisory Commission on Intergovernmental Relations (ACIR) has developed an alternative measure of fiscal capacity. It includes a broad set of economic resources that can be taxed. Tax capacity is defined as the absolute amount of revenue each state would raise if it applied a nationally uniform set of tax rates to a common set of 26 tax bases.

The last column of Table 12.1 lists the ACIR's most recent calculation of the tax capacity index. Each state's tax capacity is indexed to the national average. All states above 100 have above-average capacities, and all states below 100 have below-average capacities. Some states exhibit especially high tax capacities due to their taxable natural resources; Alaska and Wyoming are examples. They can raise substantial tax revenues without taxing individual incomes. But states such as Connecticut have a high tax capacity due to citizens' income, and Hawaii is high due to the tourist industry. Mississippi still comes out at the bottom: Its tax capacity is only 68. Thus, it has neither personal income nor other resources to tax. Find your own state on the chart; how does its tax capacity compare to its personal income?

There is one other constraint within which states operate: the requirement of a balanced budget. Vermont is the only state that lacks this requirement. All other states require balance, although the stringency varies according to how large a deficit is allowed and how long the debt can be carried forward. In many states a deficit cannot be carried over at all. The result is that states often end the fiscal year with surpluses because they have to avoid deficits at all costs.

Each state begins its revenue planning with an assessment of the factors just discussed. What kinds of taxes can be applied to resources within the state to raise the most revenue? Will we drive away citizens and businesses if we adopt these taxes? What kinds of taxes can be applied that will shift the burden to residents of other states? State leaders also estimate the likely amount of federal aid coming in and the effect of national economic trends on the state economy. Federal budget-cutting or economic downturns may drastically reduce revenue flows.

✧ STATE REVENUE SYSTEMS

State officials must balance citizens' demands for services against the political costs of imposing taxes. In so doing, they pay attention to the public's views about taxes, economists' evaluations of taxes, and their own reelection prospects.

Perspectives on State Taxes

The ACIR regularly surveys the public about the best and worst taxes. Their results should be heartening to state officials. Americans dislike the federal income tax and the local property tax most. State sales and income taxes are the least disliked, according to a 1994 survey.[3]

Public finance experts also evaluate taxes but they use different criteria:

1. The tax system should be simple and comprehensible; that is, people must be able to understand how to fill out their tax forms and pay the proper amount.

2. The system's yield should be certain. Because taxes differ in their stability, diverse and multiple taxes should be used.

3. Tax revenue ought to be adequate: Sufficient revenues must come in to support the government.

4. **Elasticity** is preferred. An elastic tax changes as the economy changes. For example, the progressive income tax is elastic but the sales tax is less so. Elasticity is necessary so that government can grow as the economy grows.

5. Economy of administration is desirable. A tax should yield much more than it costs to collect it.

6. Equity is a goal: A tax should be fair in its impact on people. Equity has two dimensions: Horizontal equity means that people with the same income should pay the same tax. This is the basis for closing many of the loopholes in federal tax law (such as the three-martini lunch). Vertical equity means that those who earn more pay more. A pure **progressive income tax** achieves vertical equity.[4]

States have worked to improve their revenue systems in the past decade, particularly through revenue diversification. They are making more balanced use of the tax choices available so that state revenue systems are more stable during economic downturns. Since the tax revolt in the late 1970s, states have added user charges, lotteries, and other revenue-producing devices that do not involve a tax collector. State officials attempt where possible to export taxes. Finally, state officials have become more sensitive to the economic efficiency of taxes. Do taxes hinder economic growth? Do they change consumption patterns? If so, the tax may be inefficient; that is, it may actually hurt the economy more than it helps society.

Still, there is a general feeling that state tax systems are due for another overhaul.[5] The economy has changed greatly in the last 20 years so that today's tax systems do not collect enough revenue from new economic growth. The sales tax fits a manufacturing economy but not a service economy, for example. We discuss some of the possible reforms below.

Sources of State Revenue

At the beginning of the twentieth century, state governments relied heavily on the property tax. During the Great Depression, beleaguered local governments took over the property tax, whereas the federal government began to rely on the income tax. State officials saw that a general sales tax would be a stable source of revenue untapped by other governments. Mississippi in 1932 was the first state to adopt the sales tax; by the end of World War II the sales tax had become the number-one tax source for state governments.

The individual income tax spread more slowly: Several states, starting with Wisconsin, adopted the income tax before the Great Depression but it was not until after World War II that it became a significant source of state revenue. The tax on corporate income also started in Wisconsin, in 1911. Most states, when they first enacted income taxes, taxed both individuals and corporations.

Figure 12.1 shows the major sources of state revenue as of 1992. As suggested earlier, federal aid is a significant source, about 25 percent of state revenue. Of the taxes levied by states, the sales tax is the largest source. When combined with other gross receipts taxes, the retail sales tax produces almost 27 percent of state revenues. The tax on individual incomes yields 17 percent of state revenue, and the tax on corporate income yields nearly 4 percent. All other taxes amount to roughly 7 percent. The category of current charges is almost 9 percent and includes college tuition, highway tolls, and fees. The "other revenue" category includes revenue from insurance trust funds and other investments, and constitutes nearly 11 percent.

Sales Tax The sales tax most of us are familiar with is the general retail sales tax, which is levied at the cash register when you buy something. The fact that it is collected by merchants, not by state officials, means that costs of administration are low. The rate of the sales tax ranges from 3 percent in some states to 7 percent in others. It is often criticized for being a **regressive tax;** that is, it affects poor people more than rich people because the poor spend a greater part of their income on consumption. To cope with the problem of regressivity, many states exempt basic items such as prescription drugs, electricity, natural gas, and food. A few states allow people to deduct their sales tax from their income tax liability. In practice, then, the sales tax's regressivity is reduced.

In its pure form a sales tax has the advantage of stability: Its yield is certain because people have to eat and buy clothes in bad times as well as in good times. However, the exemptions for low-income people make the sales tax's yield less predictable. If a sales tax

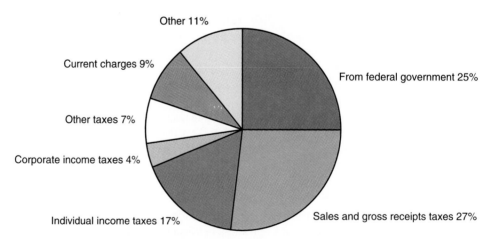

FIGURE 12.1 General Revenue of State Governments by Source, 1992. The sales tax is the number one source of state government revenue, followed closely by federal aid. A variety of other taxes make up the rest of the revenue stream.
Source: U.S. Bureau of the Census, *State Government Finances: 1992,* Series GF/92-3. Washington, D.C.: Government Printing Office, 1993, p. xiii.

is mostly levied on luxury goods, their consumption declines in bad economic times, and the tax's yield declines.

Perhaps because officials perceive the sales tax to be palatable to voters, most rate increases in the 1980s were in the sales tax, not the income tax.[6] In the 1990 postrecessionary period, tax increases were more evenly spread between the income tax and the sales tax. There was a tendency for states to make their tax systems more balanced: If a state relied heavily on the income tax, it raised the sales tax, and vice versa.[7] In an effort to broaden the sales tax's base, many states have extended it to cover services such as parking, dog grooming, dry cleaning, interior decorating, and lawnmower repair. The states that tax the most services include New Mexico and Hawaii, which tax 155 different services, and Washington, which taxes 152 services.[8] In 1987 Florida even extended its sales tax to advertising and business services, thereby hitting out-of-state firms doing business in the Sunshine State. But five months later the governor and legislature repealed the law due to public outrage. Massachusetts repeated this experience in 1990, passing a broad sales tax on business and professional services and repealing it the day after it first took effect, at the urging of new governor William Weld.

Nevertheless, most public finance experts believe that states will have to continue the practice of broadening the sales tax base. The sales tax was invented when manufactured goods were the mainstay of the economy; the tax was levied when someone bought a tangible good at the store. Today the economy's dominant sector is services: We eat out instead of buying groceries, and we rent videos instead of buying books. Unless such services are taxed, the public revenue system does not keep pace with growth in the economy.

Besides the general sales tax, selective taxes on sales are also important revenue sources. Selective sales (or excise) taxes are levied on services that provide particular benefits to individuals (such as a gasoline tax) or on items society frowns on (such as tobacco, liquor, and gambling). These rates vary by state; for example, the median tax on a pack of cigarettes is 25 cents. But in tobacco-growing states the situation is different: In Kentucky the tax is 3 cents, in North Carolina 5 cents, and in Virginia 2.5 cents.[9] In contrast, California assesses 35 cents per pack, and directs some of the proceeds to a television campaign to stop smoking.

The proceeds of selective sales taxes are often **earmarked,** or dedicated to a particular purpose (for example, the gasoline tax is often assigned to highway construction), but other revenues can be earmarked too. Although it reduces decisionmakers' flexibility, states use the practice extensively. Nearly one quarter of state tax revenues are earmarked, with Alabama using this practice most extensively at 89 percent.[10] Interest groups desiring to protect their programs are the major advocates of earmarking.

Individual Income Tax   The second largest source of state tax revenue, after the sales tax, is the individual income tax. This is a tax familiar to anyone who earns a wage. The rate varies from one state to another but nearly everywhere it has a progressive structure; that is, it taxes the upper income brackets at a higher rate than the lower brackets. The types of deductions and credits vary across states, although increasingly they conform to federal practices.

The income tax's advantages are its ease of administration, especially if linked to federal tax laws, and its progressivity. Because of its progressivity it is considered more equitable than the sales tax. However, a disadvantage is that its yield varies over the business cycle, declining in bad times and increasing in good times as people are pushed into higher tax brackets. Unless indexed, its yield increases with inflation. Because the income tax is highly visible, this "automatic" surplus may cause political problems; state governments found this out during the tax revolt of the 1970s. Problems also occur during recessions, when people are laid off from their jobs. It is difficult for state governments to help citizens weather a recession because income tax receipts fall.

In the late 1980s state officials became sensitive about raising income tax rates because they believed it to be bad for business. Business owners may prefer to locate in a state with a low personal income tax. But in the aftermath of the 1990s recession, states raised their income tax rates, especially those affecting the more affluent classes.

Corporate Income Tax   Nearly all states tax corporations as well as individuals. However, more states, use a flat rate on corporate income rather than a graduated rate. Like the individual income tax, the corporate tax is quite elastic: It responds to economic growth and inflation. Although the corporate tax furnishes less than 4 percent of the average state government's revenues, it is naturally the target of business opposition. Thus, states are reluctant to impose too heavy a burden on businesses they are trying to attract or retain. The income tax's impact on a corporation is quite complex to estimate, as it depends on the income base, the competitiveness of the market in which the corporation does business, and whether the corporation does business nationally or internationally.[11] States are finding that the corporate tax, like the sales tax, does not affect service businesses as much as it affects manufacturers. It is harder to determine in which state a service is performed than to say where an item is manufactured. For all these reasons, some states are considering a shift to an entirely different tax on corporations, one more like the European value-added tax (VAT).

Other Taxes   States also assess license taxes: You pay to own a car, to incorporate, or to go hunting, fishing, or cross-country skiing. Although these taxes amount to a small percentage of state revenue, like any other tax they can have political ramifications. An increase in the cost of a fishing or hunting license can provoke taxpayers' ire.

Most states also levy a **severance tax:** a tax on the extraction of nonrenewable natural resources such as oil, natural gas, coal, timber, or minerals. The severance tax is a significant revenue source in energy-rich states such as Alaska, Louisiana, Montana, New Mexico, North Dakota, and Wyoming. In these states the severance tax is a driving force behind state revenue choices. In 1992, 72 percent of Alaska's revenues and 39 percent of Wyoming's came from this source.[12] The severance tax constitutes at least 10 percent of the revenues in the other states listed.

The severance tax is advantageous for two reasons. First, it is a tax on people outside the producer states. Everyone consumes energy but only a few states produce it. Thus, the tax's bite is shifted to citizens in energy-poor states. Second, energy-rich states can avoid having to tax individual or corporate incomes. As a result, these states attract corporations looking for a favorable tax climate and citizens seeking low rates. The citizens of Alaska even get a bonus from their state's coffers. Oil prices have brought in so much money since the mid-1980s that rebate checks are mailed out: $950 per Alaskan in 1993.[13] However, when oil prices fall the energy-rich states discover the severance tax's disadvantage: Periodically they face huge budget deficits because revenues from the severance tax plummet. The perils of a nondiversified revenue system were clearly demonstrated in severe budget crises in Louisiana in the 1980s, and even in Alaska in the mid-1990s.

User Charges   Education is the source of about half of all user charges assessed. If you are paying tuition to your state college or university, you know that it can constitute a large amount per person although tuition is only about one-third of total educational costs. States also receive money from tolls on the use of roads and highways. If you have ever driven on the Pennsylvania or New Jersey turnpikes, you have paid such a fee. Finally, states get money from fees charged at state institutions such as hospitals and parks. Reliance on user fees is growing due to the pressure to find alternative revenue sources. User fees are based on the concept that those who benefit should pay; therefore, their effect is regressive.

Other Revenues This category includes a variety of things such as rents, royalties, fines, liquor store revenues (in the states that have government-run stores), utilities, and interest on various investments and trust funds. States must maintain trust funds for employee retirement, workers' compensation, and unemployment compensation. These funds amount to billions of dollars, so the earnings on these investments are substantial. Because this income must be directed toward meeting obligations to the entitled recipients, it is not available for general expenditure purposes.

A relatively new form of revenue raising is the lottery. Although it is not a tax, it is a method of generating revenue that may reduce the need for taxes. As of 1992, 37 states sponsored lotteries. Collectively they took in $19.7 billion in 1992 and provided almost $8 billion in net proceeds.[14] Lottery proceeds tend to be earmarked for specific purposes such as transportation, buildings, economic development, environment, senior citizens, and especially education, which received over half of the proceeds in 1993.[15]

The lottery raises a number of interesting questions. The cost of administration is very high compared to other taxes; roughly 60 percent of lottery sales are paid out in prizes and administration, leaving about 40 percent for the state. Some object to the lottery on moral grounds: It may lead to more gambling or attract organized crime. Others object because it is regressive: More low-income people play the lottery than high-income people. Box 12.1 explains some of the problems encountered. Still, the lottery generates state revenue that would not have been tapped otherwise (nearly 2 percent of state-generated revenues) and it seems to be popular with citizens after it gets started.

States' dependence on revenues raised from gambling goes far beyond the lottery. Forty-eight of the 50 states allow some form of legalized gambling which they then tax (Utah and South Carolina are the holdouts). Many states have for a long time allowed parimutuel wagering (on horse races and dog races, for example), but the revenues raised are not huge. Half of the states now allow casinos on riverboats, on Indian reservations, in Western theme towns, or anywhere else. Collectively, casinos yield about as much revenue as the lotteries do but most of the casino revenue is concentrated in Nevada and New Jersey. New Orleans recently had its new casino close due to insufficient business, which may be a harbinger for the future as the market gets saturated.

Patterns of State Taxation

So far we have described the separate sources of state revenue, but it is important to realize that a revenue system is a combination of taxes and other charges. State leaders face difficult choices in constructing their revenue systems: ensuring stability, achieving the desired amount of progressivity, creating incentives for business, and raising adequate revenues. All tax decisions involve weighing conflicting values. It makes sense for us to consider the patterns of tax reliance by states, paying particular attention to the systems' overall progressivity.

BOX 12.1 GAMING IN THE STATES: A LOSING BET?

An ever-increasing number of Americans are dropping coins into the slots or picking lottery numbers in the hopes of winning big. State governments are also hoping to win big by legalizing gambling. For many states, casino and lottery revenues seem to be the perfect alternative to raising taxes or cutting services; between 1990 and 1994, revenues from legal gambling grew by 50 percent, to $39.9 billion.[1] But in the past few years it has become clear that this revenue source is not as perfect as it seems. Casinos and lotteries come with social costs, and these costs may be greater than the money they generate. As these social costs mount, the gaming industry itself has become a powerful interest lobby in the United States.

In Minnesota, a state with a lottery and casinos, in less than a decade an estimated 38,000 residents have run into serious financial or family problems as a result of various gambling activities.[2] Many have piled up huge debts, and some have even attempted to take their own lives.

Most of the problem gamblers in that state are middle-class, although studies in other states indicate that poor people are the most likely to gamble. Certain forms of gambling cause more trouble than others. The majority of callers to the Minnesota Compulsive Gambling Hotline report problems with casino gambling. Calls about racing, lotteries, and bingo only make up a small percentage of the total.[3]

The high costs of gambling are even beginning to affect communities as a whole. For example, crime rates in some areas have skyrocketed as a result of casinos. Crime in rural Redwood County, Minnesota, jumped nearly 98 percent in the five years after a small bingo hall was transformed into a casino. This increase was five times greater than the average increase in crime in other Minnesota counties during the same time period.[4]

Minnesota is by no means unique in its gambling woes. In 1994 Florida's Office of Planning and Budgeting estimated the social and crime costs of proposed casino development in the state at $2.6 billion. The agency projected that proposed casino revenues would cover only 8–13 percent of the costs

Table 12.2 displays relevant data for 1992. First we have a calculation of the extent to which each state's overall tax system is progressive. A progressive tax system imposes a greater burden on those with high incomes; a regressive system burdens those with low incomes. This calculation was done by Richard Winters from data collected by the Citizens for Tax Justice in 1991.[16] He computed the ratio of the overall tax rates imposed on the top 5 percent of families as compared to the lowest 40 percent. The table shows that states such as Delaware and Vermont are the most progressive in taxation, and Texas and Florida are the least progressive (most regressive). If you have lived in states at the bottom and the top of this list, you would see a big difference in the "tax bite." Rich people have greater tax liability in states at the top and less in states at the bottom.

The third and fourth columns of Table 12.2 report the proportion of own-source revenues derived from the two major taxes, the individual income tax and the general sales tax. States high in tax progressivity tend to rely more on the individual income tax and place less emphasis on the sales tax. Oregon and Massachusetts are the heaviest users of the income tax; they rank 6th and 18th respectively in progressivity. The least progressive states (those at the bottom of the table) tend to rely on the sales tax and to avoid the income tax. Washington, for example, is the heaviest user of the sales tax and has no income tax. It ranks

associated with the casinos.[5] Wisconsin researchers estimated their state's social costs for casinos to be as much as $450 million.[6]

At the same time that the ills of casinos are coming to light, the lobbying arms of the gaming industry are growing. During the 1993–1994 election cycle the gaming industry contributed $2 million dollars to Congressional candidates. That level of spending put them in the same league as well-entrenched interest groups such as the United Auto Workers and the National Rifle Association. In Florida, progambling forces spent $16.5 million on an unsuccessful referendum on casinos in 1994, almost as much as was spent in the governor's race the same year. In Texas gambling interests hired 74 lobbyists for the 1995 legislative session; in Virginia, 48 lobbyists.[7] In Louisiana, gambling interests gave state legislators more than twice as much money as did the petrochemical industry, the state's leading industry. Only New Jersey prohibits political contributions from gambling interests.

These high campaign contributions do not mean that the gaming industries are growing unchecked. There is already some indication that the industry has saturated the market. In addition, voters in several states have recently rejected the expansion of gambling. These mixed costs and benefits of gaming mean that the verdict is still out on whether gambling will be a winning or losing bet for the states.

---

[1]Kevin Sack, "Gaming Lobby Gives Lavishly to Politicians," *New York Times* (December 18, 1995), A8.

[2]Chris Ison, "Dead Broke: How Gamblers Are Killing Themselves, Bankrupting Their Families and Costing Minnesota Millions," Minneapolis *Star Tribune* (December 3, 1995), A1.

[3]*Ibid.*, pp. A1, A18.

[4]Dennis J. McGrath and Chris Ison, "Gambling Spawns a New Breed of Criminal," Minneapolis *Star Tribune* (December 4, 1995), A1, A6.

[5]Stephen D. Gold, "Are Casinos a Windfall for State Budgets?," *State Fiscal Brief* (July 1995), 3.

[6]Ison, "Dead Broke," p. A18.

[7]Sack, "Gaming Lobby Gives Lavishly to Politicians," p. A8.

47th in progressivity. Washington's lowest-income families pay over 17 percent of their incomes for state taxes, whereas its wealthiest families pay around 3 percent.[17]

The states in the middle of the table follow a mixed strategy, relying on the sales tax and flat-rate income taxes. A few states—Alaska and Wyoming, for example—rely very little on either the income or sales tax. Remember that these states rely on the severance tax. Then there is tiny New Hampshire, which has no sales tax and almost no income tax. It relies instead on the property tax and doesn't spend much.

The choice between the two major taxes is not an either-or proposition. Thirty-nine states have both. Rather, the choice is the degree to which a state depends on one or the other. One trade-off is equity; the progressive income tax is considered more equitable than the sales tax. A second trade-off is revenue stability: In periods of economic growth, state leaders like the income tax's elasticity but this feature makes them more vulnerable to recessions. During recessions state officials may wish they had relied more on the sales tax. A third trade-off is efficiency: If a tax is so high that businesses go bankrupt or people move out of the state, then it defeats its purpose.

Several scholars have tried to explain state tax choices in terms of reliance on different taxes, progressivity, tax burden, and tax effort. The most important explanation

TABLE 12.2 STATES' RANK ON TAX PROGRESSIVITY, 1991; PERCENTAGE DISTRIBUTION OF STATE GOVERNMENT OWN-SOURCE REVENUE BY SOURCE, 1992   Vermont has the most progresive tax system in the country, and Texas the least progessive. Overall tax progressivity can be achieved in several ways but usually it is indicative of reliance on the income tax rather than the sales tax.

State	Rank on Progressivity	Individual Income Tax	Sales Tax
Vermont	1.5	16.0%	9.2%
Delaware	1.5	20.2	n.t.[a]
Hawaii	3	19.9	28.3
Montana	4	14.6	n.t.
Minnesota	5	24.3	17.7
Oregon	6	30.4	n.t.
Maine	7	17.9	17.3
Maryland	8.5	25.7	14.0
California	8.5	21.4	18.8
New York	10	24.7	9.9
South Carolina	11.5	17.9	18.5
North Carolina	11.5	23.9	14.5
Idaho	13	21.8	17.9
Ohio	14	19.2	16.3
West Virginia	15	13.4	17.5
Rhode Island	16	16.6	13.5
New Jersey	17	17.5	17.3
Massachusetts	18	29.3	10.9
New Mexico	19	9.4	20.7
Kentucky	20	18.2	14.8
Iowa	21	21.6	15.5
Wisconsin	22.5	25.0	16.9
Virginia	22.5	25.4	12.0
Arkansas	24	16.4	19.9
Oklahoma	25	17.8	14.2

is historical: States rely most on the taxes they adopted earliest.[18] Those that adopted the income tax first, such as Wisconsin, New York, and Massachusetts, continue to derive a larger proportion of revenue from this tax than states that adopted it later. Southern and midwestern states that adopted the sales tax early continue to rely on it heavily. The reason for this pattern is that it is politically harder to impose a new tax than to modify an old one.

Economic and political explanations have some validity. States with progressive tax systems tend to be wealthier and to have growing economies that are manufacturing-based.[19] They also tend to have competitive political parties, weak business interests, and are not traditionalistic in their political culture. Revenue systems reflect economic and political realities and are slow to change.

Because states extract revenues in diverse ways, it also makes sense for us to examine the total tax effort. Tax effort is the ratio of a state's tax collections to its tax capacity. Tax effort shows what use each state has made of its taxing potential. In Table 12.3 we have

TABLE 12.2   (CONTINUED)

Rank	Rank on Progressivity	Individual Income Tax	Sales Tax
Utah	26	19.2%	19.8%
Georgia	27	24.9	21.7
Colorado	28	23.0	13.0
Michigan	29	14.7	16.6
Arizona	30	15.6	26.2
Kansas	31	16.8	19.3
Mississippi	32	8.3	22.4
Nebraska	33	18.5	18.8
Alaska	34	n.t.	n.t.
North Dakota	35	6.6	14.2
Missouri	36	18.7	19.4
Indiana	37	18.0	22.7
Louisiana	38	8.4	12.2
Connecticut	39	18.4	20.6
Alabama	40	13.8	12.5
Illinois	41	19.8	18.4
Pennsylvania	42	15.7	15.1
New Hampshire	43	1.5	n.t.
Wyoming	44	n.t.	10.6
Tennessee	45	1.0	26.1
South Dakota	46	n.t.	19.1
Washington	47	n.t.	37.4
Nevada	48	n.t.	32.8
Florida	49	n.t.	35.1
Texas	50	n.t.	27.4

ª n.t. equals no tax.

Source: Rank on progressivity from Richard Winters, "The Politics of Taxing and Spending," in Virginia Gray and Herbert Jacob, eds., *Politics in the American States* (Washington, D.C.: CQ Press, 1996), Table 9.5. Individual income tax and sales tax from Advisory Commission on Intergovernmental Relations, *Significant Features of Fiscal Federalism, 1994 Edition, Vol. II* (Washington, D.C.: Government Printing Office, 1994), pp. 100–101.

ranked the states on tax effort in 1991. A typical high-effort state is New York, at 156. Because 100 is the average for all states, this figure means that New York's tax effort is 56 percent higher than that of the average state. Other high-effort states are Alaska, Wisconsin, and Rhode Island. Nevada is at the bottom with a score of 73, meaning that its tax effort is 73 percent of the average state. If you believe "that government is best which taxes least," then Nevada is the place for you. Or perhaps Montana.

The Past and Future of State Taxes

In 1978 the voters of California struck terror into the hearts of state officials when they approved an initiative to reduce the property tax. Rampant inflation, a strong housing market, and high property assessments meant that property tax bills increased rapidly. Eventually citizens noticed that they had a large tax burden while the state had a sub-

TABLE 12.3   STATES RANKED ON TAX EFFORT INDEX, 1991[a]   **Even if states all had the same tax capacity (and they don't), they would still differ in their tax effort. Those with scores above 100 tax more than average, and those below 100 tax less than average.**

Rank	State	Tax Effort
1	New York	156
2	Alaska	119
3	Wisconsin	118
4	Rhode Island	115
5	Minnesota	112
6	New Jersey	112
7	Michigan	107
8	Maryland	103
9	Arizona	103
10	Maine	102
11	West Virginia	102
12	Massachusetts	101
13	Illinois	100
14	Iowa	100
15	Kansas	100
16	Kentucky	100
17	Connecticut	99
18	Nebraska	99
19	Washington	99
20	Oregon	97
21	Vermont	97
22	New Mexico	96
23	Ohio	96
24	California	95
25	Georgia	95
26	Hawaii	95

stantial budgetary surplus. Long-time tax activist Howard Jarvis led a successful initiative to get Proposition 13 on the ballot, and it passed by a large margin. Proposition 13 reduced property taxes immediately by setting a maximum limit, limited the annual growth in property assessments, and required a two-thirds majority in the legislature for any new taxes. Numerous budget cuts and reductions in services ensued.

As it often is, California was a national leader: At least 22 other states passed some type of limitation on either taxes or expenditures, mostly between 1978 and 1980. Because nearly all state constitutions require a balanced budget, a limitation on either tax revenues or expenditures has the effect of reducing government programs. A few states, such as California, took aim at specific taxes; more states, however, adopted fiscal caps to hold growth in government to the rate of growth in the economy. Fiscal caps are supposed to keep the public sector from crowding out the private sector. For example, Tennessee

TABLE 12.3   (CONTINUED)

Rank	State	Tax Effort
27	Pennsylvania	95
28	Idaho	94
29	Utah	94
30	Indiana	93
31	Oklahoma	93
32	Mississippi	92
33	North Dakota	92
34	Virginia	91
35	South Carolina	90
36	Louisiana	89
37	North Carolina	87
38	Texas	87
39	Colorado	86
40	Florida	86
41	Missouri	85
42	New Hampshire	84
43	South Dakota	83
44	Arkansas	82
45	Tennessee	82
46	Alabama	81
47	Wyoming	81
48	Delaware	80
49	Montana	78
50	Nevada	73

[a] Tax effort is the ratio of a state's actual tax collections to its tax capacity.
The relative index of tax effort is created by dividing each state's tax
effort by the average for all states. The index for the U.S. average is 100.

Source: Advisory Commission on Intergovernmental Relations, *Significant
Features of Fiscal Federalism, 1994 Edition, Vol. II* (Washington, D.C.:
Government Printing Office, 1994), p. 183.

government said that growth in state tax revenues shall not exceed growth in state personal income.

The adoption of such limits signaled widespread voter resistance to high taxes. Proponents of tax and expenditure limitations predicted great results; opponents issued dire warnings about loss of government services. Although there were temporary disruptions of services in some states, a decade later few scholars are able to detect much effect of such caps.[20] The fiscal behavior of states with caps and states without caps is fairly similar, probably because the economies of most states expanded enough in the 1980s that the fiscal caps did not restrain much of anything. Also, state governments have enough flexibility that they can shift the impact onto others such as local governments. Finally, the anti-tax-and-spend mood was present in all states, not just those that adopted caps. Between 1978 and 1980 there were no new tax adoptions, 35 states decreased their income tax rates, and 19 states cut their sales taxes.[21] Thus, the fear of the tax revolt coming to their state may have restrained state leaders in their spending decisions.

Although the lessons of the tax revolt linger, the 1980s brought a different set of fiscal circumstances. In the early 1980s states experienced a recession, cutbacks in federal aid, and then fiscal stress as state revenues declined. By 1983, therefore, many states had to increase taxes, ending the tax revolt rather abruptly. In the mid-1980s state leaders began to focus on using government to stimulate the economy. This involves economic development programs (described in Chapter 14) and the effect of overall tax structure on business. In the interstate competition to attract business, there is an incentive for a state to hold down taxes, or at least not to levy the highest taxes in the region. As a result, there is some evidence of convergence in tax burdens among the states. States cannot afford to stand out.

The issue of the 1990s is expenditure pressure brought on by population growth; federal mandates; court rulings; growth in the number of welfare recipients, prisoners, and schoolchildren; and the anticipated loss of federal aid. California is one of the states feeling these strains. California's spending was limited by Proposition 13 and by the Gann Limit on annual spending adopted in 1979. However, it has to cope with huge increases in the number of school-age children, college-bound students, immigrants, and criminals, while its aging transportation system, air quality, and generous social services are besieged. The collapse of freeways in the San Francisco earthquake of 1989 was a vivid reminder of the necessity for maintaining public works. The cost of these repairs was a powerful prod for Californians' adopting a new proposition easing the tax limit and raising the gasoline tax in June 1990. By the summer of 1992 the Golden State's budget deficit was $14 billion; it was unable to pay its bills and had to issue IOUs to employees and vendors instead of cashable checks.[22] Since then, California has slowly reduced the magnitude of the budget problem by increasing taxes, reducing expenditures, and shifting responsibilities onto local government.[23] By the end of 1995 the economy had recovered, and California state government was actually in the black.

The states' overall response to the 1990s fiscal crisis has been mixed: A handful of states, including Colorado, Connecticut, Louisiana, and North Carolina, have enacted 1970s-style tax or expenditure limits but more than half the states instituted large tax increases; many states restrained the growth in real spending. Connecticut took all three actions; Box 12.2 describes its efforts. Overall, by the close of 1995 the states had rebounded from the crisis of the early 1990s and collectively had amassed a surplus, which will disappear when the federal government balances its budget.

✧ STATE BUDGETARY PROCESSES

Each state must formulate, enact, and follow a budget, usually drawn up on a biennial basis. Because in 49 of the states revenue and expenditures must balance, both taxes and spending require careful planning. If revenues are unexpectedly low or expenditures too high, the governor may use his or her power to reduce expenditures, or he or she may call a special legislative session to redraft the budget. Normally, the income and expenditure sides of the budget are handled separately within the legislature. Our consideration of the process begins with revenue policymaking.

BOX 12.2 CONNECTICUT'S RESPONSE TO FISCAL CRISIS

Like many other states in the early 1990s, Connecticut faced a profound fiscal crisis. Spending in Connecticut had significantly outpaced revenues; increased demand for services along with a 42 percent increase in spending for corrections and a 56 percent increase in spending for K–12 education ultimately added up to a cumulative deficit of $1 billion in fiscal year 1992.[1] These realities, coupled with decreased intergovernmental transfer from the federal government, a recession, court orders and consent decrees, and public attitudes made it necessary for the state to take drastic measures to return to fiscal solvency.

Before 1991 Connecticut was one of only a handful of states without an income tax. Aversion to the idea of a general income tax caused the state legislature to deal with the impending fiscal crisis by raising the state's sales tax to 8 percent in 1989, making its sales tax one of the highest in the nation. It soon became evident that this increase would not be sufficient to meet Connecticut's increasing needs.

After a campaign that centered around the state's fiscal crisis and how it should have been handled, Lowell Weicker, an independent candidate, was elected governor in 1990. Like all of the other candidates, Weicker had denied the possibility of the imposition of an income tax, but he had done so less vehemently than his competitors. A bombastic eccentric, Weicker centered much of his campaign on himself, deflecting inquiry into how he might handle Connecticut's finances.[2] In what was ultimately a feat of little surprise, Weicker proposed the income tax as part of his first budget package in February 1991.

A majority of voters in the state, along with many state legislators, opposed the income tax; however, many significant interest groups in the state advocated a switch from the relatively regressive sales tax to an income tax. Public employee unions, teachers, the media, and academics all supported the income tax, along with some members of the business community who saw it as an alternative to the 13.8 percent corporate profits tax. Politically, division over the income tax generally occurred along party lines, with Democrats favoring the tax and Republicans opposing it. During a special legislative session the income tax passed the state House in August 1991 by a vote of 75 to 73. An income tax of 4.5 percent was instituted, coupled with a decrease in the sales tax from 8 percent to 6 percent. Beyond this, revenues were affected by a reduced business tax, an increase in gambling revenues from a compact with the Mashantucket Pequot Native American tribe, and a change in deficit financing.[3]

Interestingly, the narrow majority on the income tax vote was achieved only by promises from the governor about what would be done with state spending. Weicker opposed a statutory cap on state spending, but signed one in order to sustain the majority on the income tax vote. This measure, along with a cap that was incorporated into the Connecticut constitution in 1992, ensures that general budget expenditures cannot increase more than the percentage increase in personal income or inflation, whichever is greater.

In addition to the spending cap, Connecticut has also enacted numerous spending cuts since 1991 to decrease the rate of growth in state spending. Cuts were made in K–12 education, state pension and retirement plans, aid to localities, corrections, aid to the poor, aid to the mentally ill and mentally retarded, and higher education. The result of these reductions in spending was a significant saving.

Although these measures to influence state revenues and expenditures have

Continued

addressed the fiscal crisis, citizens of Connecticut are not entirely pleased with the outcome. In 1992, when asked whether the state should keep the income tax as is, modify it, or repeal it, 43 percent said that they would prefer modification, with 33 percent saying they would repeal it and 22 percent saying they would leave it as is.[4] This is hardly a ringing endorsement of the income tax, but it does seem to indicate a disinclination toward repeal.

Today, various bond rating agencies have given Connecticut a clean bill of financial health, with *Financial World* ranking Connecticut near the midpoint of the states, whereas in 1991 they were ranked very low.[5] Current governor John Rowland reluctantly advocated a five-year plan for income tax repeal during his 1994 campaign. His initial budget was the first in three decades to reduce spending over the previous year's budget, but no definitive action on income

tax repeal was evident. Through a unique combination of factors, including budgetary discipline, a maverick governor, and an electorate with a relatively high average income, Connecticut was able to put itself back on solid financial footing.

[1]Carol W. Lewis, "Connecticut: Surviving Tax Reform," in Steven Gold, ed., *The Fiscal Crisis of the States: Lessons for the Future* (Washington, D.C.: Georgetown University Press, 1995), p. 142.

[2]Alan Ehrenhalt, "Lowell Weicker and the Charisma of Obnoxiousness," in Thad Beyle, ed., *State Government: CQ's Guide to Current Issues and Activities 1994-95* (Washington, D.C.: CQ Press, 1994), p. 115.

[3]Lewis, "Connecticut: Surviving Tax Reform," pp. 150-152.

[4]*Ibid.*, p. 150.

[5]*Ibid.*, p. 187.

Revenue Policymaking

Revenue policymaking is an integral part of the overall budgetary process. Indeed, formulation of the budget starts with a forecast of revenues and expenditures for the next biennium. On the revenue side this includes an estimate of federal aid to be received and user charges to be assessed, as well as the expected yield of various taxes. States employ economic experts to produce these forecasts, and they rely on the most sophisticated econometric models available. Nevertheless, the performance of a state's economy and tax system is hard to predict exactly. A recession can reduce the yield of the income tax and increase the unemployment rolls. Federal budget cuts can suddenly decrease grants-in-aid. A drop in oil prices can wreak havoc with the revenue picture for such states as Alaska and Montana. As a result, forecasting has a wide error margin, especially when the national economy is volatile. Hence, state leaders prefer taxes whose yield can be estimated reliably, diversified tax systems whose yield is stable in the aggregate, and economists who are accurate. Nearly all of the states have set aside "rainy day" funds to be called on in case the unexpected happens. These funds can be drawn on when the state is about to incur a deficit.

Forecasting is not only technically complex but also politically dangerous. In order to avoid the pain of raising taxes or cutting services, governors naturally prefer a rosy revenue estimate for the next biennium. They may pressure experts on their staff to produce optimistic predictions, or they may delay issuing pessimistic forecasts until their legislative program is enacted. Finance committees in the legislature may also have their own economic experts who estimate revenues. If the legislature is controlled by the opposition party, its experts may well produce a set of numbers quite different from those produced by the governor's staff. Often the first step in preparing a budget is a battle between experts over economic assumptions.

Selecting an economic forecast that turns out to be on the mark may be critical to the governor's reelection. A governor who runs up a big deficit may be accused of mismanagement. The special session to balance the budget is usually more painful than a regular session. If much of the fiscal year has elapsed, the legislature has no choice but to cut heavily into whatever funds are unspent. Producing a sizable surplus can be embarrassing too; the presence of big surpluses was one factor inciting California's tax revolt. When it is apparent that revenues will not be sufficient to meet projected expenditures, then new revenue strategies must be formulated. Susan Hansen has arranged the strategies in increasing order of political risk:[24]

1. Adjust existing taxes on an administrative basis (tighter enforcement of tax laws is an example) or use creative accounting techniques.

2. Increase user charges; raising tuition at the state university is an example. Usually increasing user charges produces less outcry than raising a tax that affects the whole population.

3. Increase the rate or broaden the base of an existing tax; a temporary income tax surcharge is illustrative, as is extending the sales tax to services.

4. Radically change an existing tax; for example, several states have considered a substitute for the corporate income tax.

5. Impose a brand-new tax; examples are hard to find because proposing a significant new tax is politically risky. Until Connecticut's adoption of an income tax in 1991, no state had adopted a new general sales tax or an income tax since the mid-1970s.[25] The lottery is the only new revenue-raising device but its popularity is due to the fact that it is not a mandatory tax.

Several scholars have studied the conditions that lead to the adoption of new taxes. Berry and Berry find that the chances of tax innovation are greatest when political and economic conditions converge to create a good political opportunity for adoption.[26] These conditions include a long time until the next election, the existence of a fiscal crisis, and the presence of neighboring states that have previously adopted the tax. These conditions create opportunities for politicians to shield themselves from the political costs of supporting a tax increase. In a follow-up study, Berry and Berry found that increases in existing taxes are explained by the same political opportunity model.[27]

Adoption of the lottery is a bit different. States turn to the lottery during election years, when they are under fiscal stress, and when party control is split between the two parties.[28] A lottery is something warring political parties, faced with a fiscal crisis, can agree on. New taxes are unlikely to be imposed in this situation.

Politicians' resistance to tax increases has certainly become greater because of the 1970s tax revolt. Many governors campaign with promises of no tax increases and then find themselves confronted with deficits. In this case they try to increase revenue in ways that will not be perceived as raising taxes. One way is the lottery. Another way is to engage in wholesale tax reform. If a state legislature adopts a comprehensive package that lowers some tax rates, raises some, and broadens the base of others, it is hard to characterize it as an increase. Because the political stakes are so high, tax policy tends to be relatively stable from one year to the next; major innovation is rare.

Tax policy is of general interest to the average citizen, but it is of intense interest to the groups and businesses likely to be most affected. Groups lobby vigorously against increases that affect their members and for tax changes that will shelter them. Legislators can curry favor with interest groups by inserting into the tax code seemingly innocuous loopholes that greatly benefit the members of the association. The tax code is sufficiently complex and arcane that often only the groups affected directly can understand the change. A particularly effective argument against the imposition of a tax is the threat of exit by the affected business. For example, in 1995 the Massachusetts legislature passed a $200 million tax cut largely designed to keep its largest employer, Raytheon Corporation, from moving to a low-tax state.[29] Most states also have a taxpayers' association or other umbrella business group that argues for low taxes in general. The cross-cutting pressure from organized interests is a major force keeping taxes stable from year to year.

Appropriations Policymaking

The budgetary process typically begins about a year in advance. Figure 12.2 displays the budget calendar in Minnesota. After the governor has received a preliminary estimate of expected revenues, each state agency is asked to submit a budget request. In good years, agencies might be allowed to request small percentage increases. In lean years, agencies might be told their funding level will be frozen or even cut. Agencies submit their requests to an executive fiscal agency, which reviews and scales down the requests, as they always exceed available funds.

After the governor receives the recommendations from the executive budget office, he or she reviews and revises them again, making sure that personal policy priorities are given sufficient resources. Interest groups approach the governor about their pet projects and so do legislators. By this point in the budget preparation cycle, there may be an updated revenue forecast that alters the spending projections. The governor may have to recommend tax increases or spending cuts if a balanced budget cannot be anticipated.

In most states the governor's budget is assigned to the appropriations committee in the lower house. Usually this committee is separate from the finance committee that authorizes revenues, although in some states a single committee handles both taxing and spending, or a joint (between the two houses) appropriations committee is used. The first stage of legislative review is typically conducted by fiscal analysts on the staff. They go over each financial item and prepare a recommendation for the appropriations committee. Legislators' own review begins in subcommittees of the appropriations committee. Subcommittees hold budget hearings at which the governor's budget advisors, agency heads, and interest groups appear. Subcommittee members then mark up and revise the bill in line with their own priorities, projected revenues, and their judgment about the agency's competence. Generally, the party leadership or caucus also plays an important role in determining the overall shape of the budget.

Once the appropriations bill (or bills) is reported out of committee, it goes to the floor of the house for debate and a vote. The budget debate is often contentious and an

May/June	Finance department sends budget guidelines to agencies.
October	Agency requests submitted to governor.
November/December	State economist issues revenue forecast.
November/December	Finance department holds agency hearings.
January	Governor's budget sent to legislature.
March/April	Revised revenue forecast issued.
May	Legislature adopts budget.
July 1	Fiscal year begins.

FIGURE 12.2 Minnesota's Budget Calendar The preparation of a state budget typically starts more than a year ahead of time. Shown here is the timetable in Minnesota.

occasion for a party line vote. Following the house vote, the entire process is repeated in the senate, although in fact budget deliberations may have begun weeks before. Throughout the deliberations, interest groups and private citizens are lobbying legislators to provide money for their favorite programs.

Many times significant differences between the two houses arise in the course of consideration. Then a **conference committee** irons out differences between the two houses. Usually the committee is in close contact with the governor as it deliberates in order to avoid a veto. Interest group scrutiny can be especially intense in this stage. Once the same budget bill is passed in both houses, the governor signs or vetoes it. As described in Chapter 6, most governors possess the item veto, meaning that they can delete specific items, and 11 governors can reduce the amount of an item. Item vetoes, like regular vetoes, can be overridden by the legislature. Most scholars have found that the item veto has little effect on holding down state spending. However, Berch did find that when governors had the power to reduce items (not just delete them), they reduced pork barrel spending.[30] But it makes little difference in overall spending patterns.

Of considerable interest to scholars and practitioners alike is the question of who wields the most power in the appropriations process. The general consensus is that the governor is the more powerful actor, although the legislature has grown more influential in recent years.[31] Like any generalization, there are exceptions: times and places when the legislature dominates. In general, tight revenues favor the governor at the expense of the legislature, so in the 1990s the trend has been toward the governor. California, Illinois, and Ohio are cited as strong executive states, whereas in Utah, Florida, Mississippi, and Texas the legislature maintains substantial influence over the budget.[32]

The governor's power derives from starting the process. The governor sets the initial targets for revenues and expenditures and puts the whole budget together into one document, setting the agenda for legislative debate and negotiation. The governor's staff monitors the budget's progress through the legislature. The governor engages in lobbying and "horse trading" when necessary to advance gubernatorial priorities. Ultimately the governor has the weapon of the item veto.

The legislature, in contrast, derives its power from the fact that it is the last group to shape the budget. Often last-minute decisions in conference committees are the most significant ones. Under the pressure of deadlines, stalemates are resolved. Also, legislative staff capacity has grown enormously in the last two decades so that they now can contest the executive's estimates and forecasts. The legislature's influence has increased accordingly.

Both branches of government must operate within fiscal constraints that limit their discretion. Revenue availability has already been mentioned as an important limit. Budgetary commitments or entitlements are another binding constraint. Health and welfare programs, aid to education, state employees' pay, and other major programs cannot suddenly be abandoned. A large proportion of state expenditures is relatively fixed from year to year. Only a small portion (usually 5 to 15 percent) is subject to gubernatorial and legislative control on an annual basis. This limits the number of new initiatives that can be undertaken.

Capital Budgets

The budgetary process we have described so far is the operating budget. States also have capital budgets, used for big purchases such as new buildings, highways, and bridges. Because these projects are so large and their life cycle so long, they are not included in the state's annual operating budget. Rather, the state borrows money to build them and then repays the loan, with interest, over a period of years. The interest shows up in the operating budget as an expense. This process is analogous to borrowing money in order to buy a car or a house and then making monthly payments on the loan.

Governments finance long-term debt through the sale of bonds of different types. General obligation bonds are secured by the full faith, credit, and taxing power of the government that issues them. Because the entire resources of the government are pledged, they carry the least risk for the investor, and hence have a low interest rate. Another type—revenue bonds—are secured only by the income expected from a specific project, such as a toll road. Hence, they are a riskier investment and have a higher interest rate.

States limit their long-term debt either constitutionally or statutorily. The bond market also effectively limits debt by making it expensive. If a government takes on too much debt in the eyes of investors, then its bond rating falls and the interest rate increases correspondingly. For example, in the 1992 budgetary crisis California's bond rating slipped from its usual AAA level. States also regulate the borrowing of their local governments. This is described in more detail in Chapter 13.

Collectively, the states owed $371.9 billion in 1992; nearly three-fourths of this was nonguaranteed debt, that is, payable from specific pledged sources.[33] This form of debt increased dramatically in the 1980s. States spend about 4 percent of their annual operating budgets to service this debt, but their borrowing is very modest when compared to the federal government's. The federal debt amounted to $16,006 per person in 1992, whereas the states' amounted to only $1,461.[34] (We note with alarm that these figures were $2,500 and $928.29, respectively, in the last edition of this book).

✦ STATE EXPENDITURE POLICY

Thus far in this chapter we have examined where the money comes from and how agencies compete for it. Now we turn briefly to the question of where the money goes and how much states spend overall. What are we getting for our money?

Total State and Local Expenditures

A summary measure for comparing state services is their total general expenditures per capita. This figure tells us how much states are spending per person or the amount of state services received by the average person. We use combined state and local expenditures because states vary so much in whether the state or the local government delivers the service. Looking at the state level alone would give a misleading picture of the services received by the average citizen.

Table 12.4 ranks the states on this measure for 1992. The states at the top of the scale, in the over-$4,000 category, include states with small populations such as Alaska, Hawaii, Wyoming, Rhode Island, Delaware, and Vermont. Their per capita expenditures are high because they cannot enjoy the economies of scale available to governments of larger states. Other states are at the top because they provide more services to their citizens: Connecticut, New York, New Jersey, Minnesota, Washington, California, and Massachusetts are examples of such high-service–high-expenditure states. At the bottom are states that spend less than $3,000: Missouri, Mississippi, and Arkansas. Government services are minimal in these states. Notice that the bottom tier tends to be southern or border states with traditionalistic political cultures. The most important determinant of state and local expenditures, however, is personal income: Wealthier states spend more than poorer states.[35]

The actual disparities in public service are even greater than what is shown in Table 12.4 because different states have different demands placed on them. Some have more school-age children, more poverty, and more need for highways. By this criterion, some lower-spending states such as Alabama and Mississippi have greater-than-average needs whereas high-spending states such as Connecticut and New Jersey have lower-than-average needs. Experts estimate that Mississippi would have to spend 22 percent more than the national average to provide an average level of service, given its high rate of poverty and its demographic makeup.[36]

State Expenditures by Function

As we made clear in the budgetary process discussion, state financial commitments do not vary much from year to year. When programs are aggregated into several broad categories, their distribution is relatively stable over time. Figure 12.3 shows the distribution of state-only expenditures in 1992. (Here we shift back to focusing solely on the state level; for

TABLE 12.4 STATES RANKED ON PER-CAPITA
DIRECT GENERAL EXPENDITURES OF STATE AND
LOCAL GOVERNMENTS, 1992 State and local
governments vary in the amounts they spend per
capita. Alaska has the highest spending, and Arkansas
the lowest.

Rank	State	Expenditures
1	Alaska	$10,047
2	New York	5,670
3	Wyoming	5,294
4	Hawaii	5,230
5	New Jersey	4,687
6	Connecticut	4,594
7	Minnesota	4,506
8	Rhode Island	4,408
9	California	4,289
10	Delaware	4,238
11	Washington	4,210
12	Massachusetts	4,145
13	Vermont	4,089
14	Wisconsin	3,997
15	Nevada	3,973
16	Oregon	3,966
17	North Dakota	3,910
18	Pennsylvania	3,793
19	New Mexico	3,785
20	Michigan	3,778
21	Maine	3,765
22	Colorado	3,707
23	Louisiana	3,688
24	New Hampshire	3,664

detail on local government expenditure, see Chapter 13.) Note that education is by far the number-one expenditure for states: 34 percent of their general expenditures go for this purpose. The second highest expenditure is public welfare: About 26 percent goes to welfare recipients. The third category is highways at 8 percent, closely followed by health and hospitals. Interest payments averages 4 percent, and corrections is over 3 percent.

A few points bear mention. Note that three of the top four priorities are for social purposes. Most state government activities are concentrated in the area of social policy, so it is no surprise that social expenditures consume over two-thirds of states' budgets. States also have important responsibilities in providing infrastructure for business. Highway expenditures reflect this emphasis. They may be on the increase soon, as many states have crumbling older roads and bridges. Other states with growing populations need many new roads. (Subsequent chapters describe these different program areas in more detail.)

We have already described states' ingenuity in finding new revenue sources, such as the lottery. States have been equally inventive in strategizing about the delivery of public

TABLE 12.4 (CONTINUED)

Rank	State	Expenditures
25	Maryland	$3,650
26	Iowa	3,606
27	Montana	3,561
28	Arizona	3,509
29	Florida	3,495
30	Illinois	3,472
31	Nebraska	3,456
32	Kansas	3,402
33	Ohio	3,401
34	Virginia	3,302
35	Georgia	3,300
36	South Carolina	3,235
37	West Virginia	3,218
38	Utah	3,207
39	Indiana	3,193
40	South Dakota	3,192
41	Kentucky	3,184
42	Texas	3,146
43	Oklahoma	3,144
44	North Carolina	3,111
45	Alabama	3,109
46	Idaho	3,064
47	Tennessee	3,006
48	Missouri	2,885
49	Mississippi	2,868
50	Arkansas	2,757

Source: Advisory Commission on Intergovernmental Relations, *Significant Features of Fiscal Federalism, 1994 Edition, Vol. II* (Washington, D.C.: Government Printing Office, 1994), pp. 124–125.

programs. One option is privatization, the private sector delivery of public services (described in Chapter 7). Its purpose is to save the government money by using private entrepreneurs. The primary form of privatization practiced so far is the contracting out of certain services. Privatization is most advanced at the local level, where garbage collection and fire protection have been farmed out to private vendors. At the state level, certain administrative services, toxic waste cleanup, and corrections have been contracted out.

⋄ **CONCLUSION**

This chapter has outlined the context of state fiscal policy, emphasizing the constraints on states' choices. The national economy, federal dollars, and state resources are among the important constraints. We described the major sources of state revenue in which the income and sales taxes loom large. They represent different choices: equity versus stability.

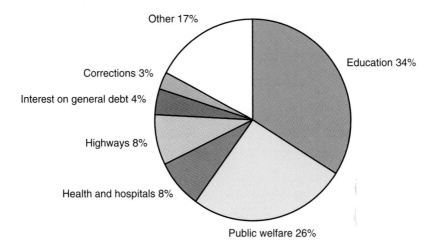

FIGURE 12.3 General Expenditure of State Governments by Function, 1992. Education spending consumes the largest chunk of most states' budgets, followed by public welfare, and a variety of other expenditure categories.
Source: U.S. Bureau of the Census, *State Government Finances, 1992,* Series GF/92-3. Washington, D.C.: Government Printing Office 1993, p. xiii.

The budgetary process involves both revenue and expenditure decisions. We looked at the different steps in the appropriations process and at both capital and operating budgets. Political and economic considerations play a part throughout the process. We reviewed the recent history of state taxation from the tax revolt in the late 1970s to the fiscal crisis of the 1990s. We particularly stressed interstate competition, which exerts a downward pressure on taxes as it exerts an upward pressure on government services. Obviously, governments cannot achieve both goals at the same time if they must rely on their own resources.

Accordingly, the states' competition is really over the balance between taxes and services. The balance preferred differs for different individuals and businesses. The impact of taxes on the economy was a hotly debated issue in the 1980s. What is the role of taxes in the relocation decision of a firm or a family? What is the overall effect of tax burden on economic growth? Businesses, of course, offer the theory that taxes matter a lot. Various rankings of "business climate" give heavy weight to state taxes, with states such as North and South Dakota ranking high on business climate.

Somewhat surprisingly, early research indicated that tax policy had no impact on growth. However, several more recent investigations have reported that taxes do matter. States with higher taxes grew at a slower rate in the late 1970s and 1980s. In a particularly useful study, Dye conducted an analysis within states to see what happened when tax burdens changed.[37] He found that increasing the tax burden retards economic growth. This relationship is strongest for high-tax states such as New York and Massachusetts. When they cut taxes in the late 1970s, their economies responded vigorously. However, Dye stressed that low-tax states such as Florida and Texas cannot expect to stimulate their economies by cutting taxes. Their economies might be more invigorated by spending on education or physical infrastructure.

At the same time, there is renewed interest in what services government can offer to enhance economic performance. State leaders have moved beyond a concern with the business climate and its emphasis on tax structure and location incentives. They are now more concerned with entrepreneurial climate and a broad range of policies to foster job creation and capital formation. These policies (described in Chapter 14 and subsequent chapters) range from investment in traditional infrastructure—highways and education—to innovative industrial policies. But government programs do cost money, which comes from tax revenues.

This brings us back to the balance between taxes and services. There is no shortage of demands on government to provide new programs and expand old ones. Even at the height of the tax revolt in the late 1970s, surveys showed that citizens wanted, indeed

The impact of taxes on business location decisions is hotly contested. Policymakers in Virginia obviously believe taxes make a difference; shown here is their ad pitching Virginia as a low-tax state. (*Source:* Produced by Siddall, Matus & Coughter Inc., Richmond, V.A. Art Director: Jessica Welton copywriter: Tommy Thompson)

demanded, government services. What they desired was more efficient provision of those services or, to put it more cynically, "something for nothing." There was little indication that the revolt was against government services per se.

Today states are coping with population growth, economic revitalization, and expensive problems such as AIDS. Each state is seeking to find the right mix of taxes and services that will enhance its economic position. Subsequent chapters explore the states' activities in the realms of economic and social policy.

✧ KEY TERMS

conference committee (p. 323)
earmarked (p. 309)
elasticity (p. 307)
progressive income tax (p. 307)

recession (p. 303)
regressive tax (p. 308)
severance tax (p. 310)

✧ FOR FURTHER READING

Advisory Commission on Intergovernmental Relations, *Significant Features of Fiscal Federalism, 1995 Edition* (Washington, D.C.: Government Printing Office, 1995). A valuable data resource published annually. Contains statistical information on revenues, expenditures, taxes, and other fiscal matters.

J. Richard Aronson and John L. Hilley, *Financing State and Local Governments* (Washington, D.C.: Brookings Institution, 1986). A classic textbook on public finance at the state and local levels for the nontechnical reader.

Thomas R. Dye, *American Federalism: Competition Among Governments* (Lexington, Mass.: Lexington Books, 1990). A political science analysis of state taxing and spending policies. Particularly strong in analyzing the effects of taxes on state economic growth.

Steven D. Gold, ed., *The Fiscal Crisis of the States: Lessons for the Future* (Washington, D.C.: Georgetown University Press, 1995). A recent analysis of the fiscal crisis of the early 1990s, with case studies of six states' responses to the crisis.

✧ NOTES

1. Paul Brace, *State Government & Economic Performance* (Baltimore: Johns Hopkins University Press, 1993), p. 81.

2. Steven D. Gold, "Legacy of the '80s: Richer Rich and Poorer Poor," *State Legislatures* (August 1990), 31–33.

3. "Statestats: Public Opinion of Taxes," *State Legislatures* (March 1995).

4. Advisory Commission on Intergovernmental Relations, *The Question of State Government Capability* (Washington, D.C.: Government Printing Office, 1985), pp. 204–205.

5. Ronald K. Snell, "Our Outmoded Tax Systems," *State Legislatures* (August 1994), 17–22.

6. Advisory Commission on Intergovernmental Relations, *Significant Features of Fiscal Federalism, 1985–86* (Washington, D.C.: Government Printing Office, 1986), p. 76.

7. Steven D. Gold, ed., *The Fiscal Crisis of the States: Lessons for the Future* (Washington, D.C.: Georgetown University Press, 1995), p. 21.

8. Advisory Commission on Intergovernmental Relations, *Significant Features of Fiscal Federalism: 1994, Vol. 1* (Washington, D.C.: Government Printing Office, 1994), p. 101.

9. *Ibid.*, p. 116.

10. Ronald K. Snell, "The Trouble with Earmarking," *State Legislatures* (February 1991), 35.

11. J. Richard Aronson and John L. Hilley, *Financing State and Local Governments*, 4th ed. (Washington, D.C.: Brookings Institution, 1986), p. 109.

12. Calculated from data in Bureau of the Census, *State Government Finances: 1992* (Washington, D.C.: Government Printing Office, 1993), pp. 10, 13.

13. Hugh Dellios, "Oil-Fueled Budget Crunch May Revive Alaska State Income Tax," St. Paul *Pioneer Press & Dispatch* (August 26, 1994), 4A.

14. Advisory Commission on Intergovernmental Relations, *Significant Features of Fiscal Federalism, 1994, Vol. 2* (Washington, D.C.: Government Printing Office, 1994), pp. 106, 108.

15. Bureau of the Census, *Statistical Abstract of the United States, 1994* (Washington, D.C.: Government Printing Office, 1994), p. 296.

16. Richard Winters, "The Politics of Taxing and Spending," in Virginia Gray and Herbert Jacob, eds., *Politics in the American States*, 6th ed. (Washington, D.C.: CQ Press, 1996), Table 9.5.

17. "In Taxation, Who's The Fairest of Them All?," *Governing* (July 1991), 18.

18. Susan B. Hansen, "The Politics of State Taxing and Spending," in Virginia Gray, Herbert Jacob, and Robert B. Albritton, eds., *Politics in the American States*, 5th ed. (Glenview, Ill.: Scott, Foresman/Little, Brown, 1990), p. 349.

19. David Lowery, "The Distribution of Tax Burdens in the American States: The Determinants of Fiscal Incidence," *Western Political Quarterly*, 40 (March 1987), 137–158; Neil Berch, "Explaining Changes in Tax Incidence in the States," *Political Research Quarterly*, 48 (September 1995): 629–641.

20. James Cox and David Lowery, "The Impact of the Tax Revolt Era State Fiscal Caps," *Social Science Quarterly*, 71 (September 1990), 492–509; Philip G. Joyce and Daniel R. Mullins, "The Changing Fiscal Structure of the State and Local Public Sector: The Impact of Tax and Expenditure Limitations," *Public Administration Review*, 51 (May/June 1991), 240–253. Also, caps do not seem to stop state governments from taking on more debt; see James C. Clingermayer and B. Dan Wood, "Disentangling Patterns of State Debt Financing," *American Political Science Review*, 89 (March 1995), 108–120.

21. Advisory Commission on Intergovernmental Relations, *Significant Features, 1985–86*, p. 76.

22. Paul E. Peterson, *The Price of Federalism* (Washington, D.C.: Brookings Institution, 1995), p. 2.

23. Jeffrey I. Chapman, "California: The Enduring Crisis," in Gold, ed., *The Fiscal Crisis of the States: Lessons for the Future*, p. 113.

24. Susan B. Hansen, "Extraction: The Politics of State Taxation," in Virginia Gray, Herbert Jacob, and Kenneth N. Vines, eds., *Politics in the American States: A Comparative Analysis*, 4th ed. (Boston: Little, Brown, 1983), p. 432.

25. Advisory Commission on Intergovernmental Relations, *Significant Features of Fiscal Federalism, 1994, Vol. 1*, pp. 34–35.

26. Frances Stokes Berry and William D. Berry, "Tax Innovation in the States: Capitalizing on Political Opportunity," *American Journal of Political Science*, 36 (August 1992), 715–742. They

also find, contrary to previous research, that unified party control has no effect on tax adoptions; however, Alt and Lowry find that unified governments react more quickly to eliminate budget deficits through a variety of fiscal policies, whereas divided governments adjust less easily; see James E. Alt and Robert C. Lowry, "Divided Government, Fiscal Institutions, and Budget Deficits: Evidence from the States," *American Political Science Review,* 88 (December 1994), 811–828.

27. Frances Stokes Berry and William D. Berry, "The Politics of Tax Increases in the States," *American Journal of Political Science,* 38 (August 1994), 855–859.

28. Frances Stokes Berry and William D. Berry, "State Lottery Adoptions and Policy Innovations: An Event History Analysis," *American Political Science Review,* 84 (June 1990), 395–415.

29. "Enjoy It—While It Lasts," *Business Week* (December 11, 1995), 34–36.

30. Neil Berch, "The Item Veto in the States: An Analysis of the Effects Over Time," *The Social Science Journal,* 29, no. 3 (1992), 335–346.

31. Alan Rosenthal, *Governors & Legislatures: Contending Powers* (Washington, D.C.: CQ Press, 1990), pp. 134–135; Glenn Abney and Thomas P. Lauth, *The Politics of State & City Administration* (Albany: State University of New York Press, 1986), p. 166; Sydney Duncome and Richard Kinney, "The Politics of State Appropriation Increases," *Journal of State Government,* 59 (September/October 1986), 114; Edward J. Clynch and Thomas P. Lauth, eds., *Governors, Legislatures, and Budgets* (New York: Greenwood Press, 1991), p. 149.

32. Clynch and Lauth, *Governors, Legislatures, and Budgets,* pp. 152, 154.

33. Advisory Commission on Intergovernmental Relations, *Significant Features of Fiscal Federalism, 1994, Vol. 2,* p. 164.

34. Bureau of the Census, *Statistical Abstract of the United States, 1994,* p. 297; Advisory Commission on Integovernmental Relations, *Significant Features of Fiscal Federalism, 1994, Vol. 2,* p. 170.

35. Thomas R. Dye, *American Federalism: Competition Among Governments* (Lexington, Mass.: Lexington Books, 1990), pp. 52–53.

36. Steven D. Gold, "A New Way to Compare States' Spending," *State Legislatures* (May/June 1989), 10–11. Gold describes the Representative Expenditure System developed by the Advisory Commission on International Relations.

37. Dye, *American Federalism.*

Taxing and Spending in Local Government

The context of local fiscal affairs has changed radically in the last quarter-century or so. As the national economy has traced patterns of boom and recession, local government fiscal fortunes have fluctuated. Global economic forces, too, now affect city economies: A recession in Japan or Europe may mean lower demand for export goods made in Seattle or Fort Worth or Kansas City, causing businesses in those cities to contract. Local tax bases and revenue receipts have also varied with shifting patterns of economic activity, changes in migration trends, and the transformation of the system of federal aid. At the same time, new problems and new responsibilities are continually being added to the urban agenda. All of these forces converge to place cities in a chronically precarious fiscal position.

There are no quick and easy answers. Cities cannot simply decide to raise taxes to meet their enlarged responsibilities or to hedge against hard times. Not only are they constrained by state constitutional and statutory limitations, but, as we have seen, taxing and spending policy bears to some extent on individual and business decisions to exercise their exit option. Let us look at the trends affecting local taxing and spending.

✧ THE CONTEXT OF MUNICIPAL FINANCES

Among all their other characteristics, cities are workplaces, economic subunits embedded in a set of larger economic and social systems. Because the city is an economic subunit, its prosperity is tied to the fortunes of these larger settings. In particular, its fiscal health—that is, its ability to raise sufficient revenues to meet its service obligations—is directly tied to larger economic and social forces at work in the metropolitan area, region, nation, and international marketplace. But a city's expenditures are also a function of the demands for services. Cities are expected to do more and more these days. Let us examine some of the forces at work that affect a city's taxing and spending capabilities and burdens.

Economic Boom and Bust

Domestic and international economic cycles have an impact on business firms, whose fortunes in turn affect the cities in which they are located. The recession of 1990–1991 threw some cities into bankruptcy, including Bridgeport, Connecticut, and it brought others, such as Philadelphia, to the brink. As the national economy recovered in the mid-1990s, however, most cities found that they were in better, though not good, fiscal shape.

Fluctuations in particular industries also affect certain cities. When the price of oil drops, Houston and New Orleans suffer. When the Pentagon stops buying combat aircraft, the economies of cities in Orange County, California, go into a steep decline. Conversely, lower interest rates, a sign of economic health, may spur a construction boom in cities such as Phoenix and Denver, adding jobs and augmenting the local tax base. As the national economy goes, so go local fiscal fortunes.

Economic Restructuring

As we saw in Chapter 10, the American economy has undergone a transformation from a heavy reliance on manufacturing work to service occupations. Manufacturing losses were especially heavy in the older industrial cities of the Northeast and the Midwest, as business firms moved their operations overseas or went out of business altogether. In the 1980s, for example, Milwaukee, a city of 630,000, lost over 33,000 factory jobs, and Chicago lost 150,000. New York City lost almost a half million jobs in this sector.

There has been new job growth in all these cities, but many, if not most, of the jobs tend to be in the low-paid service occupations. In Chicago, for example, the manufacturing losses were more than offset by growth in retail, clerical, restaurant, and janitorial jobs, but these tend to pay much less and have fewer benefits than factory work.

The concentration of low-paid service sector workers in the cities has implications for the tax base. Low-paid workers spend less on consumer goods, generate lower payroll taxes, and cannot pay high real estate taxes. They also rely more heavily on public services. For example, low-paid service workers are less likely to have health insurance and thus must rely on public hospitals.

Globalization

Since about 1970 the United States has been part of a rapidly expanding international marketplace. Some cities are well-positioned to take advantage of the export opportunities brought about by the economic growth of new markets abroad. For example, as the countries of Eastern Europe began to develop free-market economies, they began to import American construction and manufacturing equipment, greatly benefitting firms in cities such as Peoria and Racine.

But at the same time the emergence of a global marketplace has meant that other American businesses have greatly increased their investments abroad, creating jobs in other countries instead of the United States. Some of the manufacturing decline in the U.S. economy is a function of the movement of those jobs overseas. American multinational firms employ around 6 million workers in other countries.

The movement of investment capital is not unidirectional, however. Foreign investors have located plants and other facilities here in the United States, offsetting to

BOX 13.1 ECONOMIC TRANSFORMATION: WORKING FOR WAL-MART

One of the major transformations of the American economy is the rise of discount retailers such as Kmart, Target, Venture, and Home Depot as a major source of employment. However, none of these stores can compare to Wal-Mart's employment record. In the 30 months after the end of the 1990–1991 recession, Wal-Mart hired 153,000 new employees, or about 8 percent of the net increase in the 1.9 million jobs created in the entire United States during the economic recovery.

One of the reasons Wal-Mart and other discount retailers have become such a major source of employment is that they are adopting labor practices rejected elsewhere in corporate America. For most companies, increasing profits means downsizing and hiring more part-timers and getting more sales from fewer employees. In contrast, Wal-Mart has adopted the philosophy that increasing profits requires more full-time workers; thus, the company has increased the number of full-time workers from 50 percent of its workforce in 1988 to 70 percent by 1993. Wal-Mart concluded that cashiers and clerks were more enthusiastic toward customers if they worked full- rather than part-time. Similarly, Wal-Mart believes that neat shelves and short lines at checkout counters increase sales.

Wal-Mart and other discounters may be bucking national employment practices, but they have not adopted a similar policy of increasing wages. Very few hourly workers make more than $7 per hour in rural areas or $9 per hour in metropolitan areas. This low pay is compounded by the fact that "full-time" at most discount retailing jobs is usually only 28–30 hours per week compared to 35–40 hours in manufacturing. Discounters prefer such arrangements because it gives them the flexibility to increase workers' hours during busy periods without having to pay overtime rates, which start at 40 hours. As a result of these practices, the average discount employee earns about 40 percent of the average manufacturing wage.

Wal-Mart has attempted to sweeten the low pay by offering such benefits as limited health insurance and profit sharing. Unlike most service employers, which do not offer health insurance to their employees, Wal-Mart pays 70 percent of the cost of health insurance, though still less than the full coverage offered by most manufacturers with unions. A family policy for a Wal-Mart employee costs about $80 a month, a very large sum for a person only making $6 or $7 an hour. Thus, of Wal-Mart's 335,000 full-time employees, only 250,000 take the insurance. Wal-Mart also offers profit sharing in the form of an annual award of company stock equal to about 6 percent of a worker's pay. However, because of the high turnover of its employees, only 7,018 of Wal-Mart's employees have accumulated $50,000 or more worth of stock.

The growth of Wal-Mart and other discounters is playing an important role in providing jobs to the high-school-educated, who in the past worked in factories and trades. Moreover, their benefits package is considerably better than the nonexistent set offered by many other service sector jobs. At the same time, it is important to remember that these limited wages, benefits, and security are a pale shadow of those offered by manufacturing not long ago.

Source: Louis Uchitelle, "'Good' Jobs in Hard Times," *New York Times* (October 3, 1993), p. C1.

some degree the losses that come from the international investment of American capital. This capital in-migration affects the economic life of various cities. For example, in New York some 27,000 people are employed by the nearly 200 foreign banks that have located in the city.[1]

Concentration of Poverty

The migration to the suburbs of the middle class and the decline of good jobs for people with little education has led to a higher and higher concentration of poverty in the cities. Between 1970s and 1990 the number of people living in inner-city census tracts where over 40 percent of the residents are poor rose from 3.8 million to 10.4 million.[2] These high-poverty areas have unusually high rates of infant mortality, births out of wedlock, school dropout, and crime.

The concentration of poverty has two major impacts on city fiscal health. For one thing, it drives out businesses, eroding both the employment and tax base. In Los Angeles, a third of the supermarkets that existed in 1970 are gone; Boston has lost two-thirds of its food stores in that time.

Another impact is that it raises the cost of providing city services. The costs of providing municipal hospitals, public health, and various other welfare services are twice as high per capita in cities with high poverty concentrations as in cities with lower rates of poverty. Other public services, including police and fire protection, are more expensive in heavily poor cities than in cities where more people are economically better-off.[3]

Rising Labor Costs

Municipal employee wages and fringe benefits account for as much as 70 percent of city government expenditures. Since the mid-1960s, expenses in this area have tended to rise faster than the rate of inflation. The most rapid increase in wage rates came in the decade after 1966, a year in which the number of public employee strikes suddenly tripled. After the mid-1970s, wage increases leveled off for a brief time, but fringe benefit costs continued to skyrocket, driven especially by the cost of health care.[4] Extremely generous compensation packages over the years for Philadelphia's public employees were thought to be a major contributor to that city's dire fiscal condition in the early 1990s. When Ed Rendell became mayor there, he offered city workers a contract that froze wages for 33 months. The unions struck, but there was no public support for their cause. The public employees abandoned their strike and accepted the city's offer. The deal saved the city an estimated $374 million.[5]

New Expectations, New Problems

City expenditures are subject not only to economic and demographic pressures but also to the changing array of services and amenities that people want and to the emergence of new problems. Americans simply expect more from government. Take the area of recreation. With increasing affluence and more leisure time, the years between 1945 and 1986 saw the number of golfers in the United States rise by 500 percent; the number of adult softball teams went up by over 600 percent. All this was occurring in a period when the population was growing by only 50 percent. In response to growing interest in recreational sports, cities built municipal golf courses and softball diamonds (the number of both rose by 500 percent); urban park and recreation budgets went up in the postwar years by 700 percent in real terms.[6]

Cities have taken on a host of other obligations in these years. Some of these are recycling, leaf pickup, teen social services, public cable TV, economic development, day care, senior services, historic preservation, water pollution control, and convention centers. Not all cities provide each of these comparatively new functions and facilities, but many do.

Not only have cities taken on new responsibilities in response to public demand, but they are faced with new problems. AIDS, crack cocaine, and homelessness were all but unknown in 1980. City governments have also struggled, as they never did in the nineteenth century, with massive immigration. Social service agencies in Miami responded to the huge Cuban and Haitian immigrations of the 1980s, and New York City hired social workers and interpreters to help Russian Jews who flocked to the city in that decade.

✧ THE SOURCES OF LOCAL GOVERNMENT REVENUE

The fiscal health of cities and other local governments varies with macroeconomic and demographic changes because those fluctuations directly affect the sources of local tax revenues. Let us look at these sources and their sensitivity to these various fluctuations.

Local governments raise money for operating expenses from four basic sources: intergovernmental transfers, taxes, user charges, and a variety of miscellaneous charges, fees, assessments, and other income.

The degree to which each type of local government relies on these different sources varies (see Table 13.1). Counties, for example, are more heavily dependent on intergovernmental aid (mostly from the state) than are municipalities. Special districts rely more heavily on user charges (bridge tolls, for example, or in the case of mass transit authorities, fares) than other types of local governments. School districts, which get about half their revenues from the state, depend more heavily on the property tax for the remainder of their money than do municipalities or counties. To simplify our task, we will restrict the discussion of local finances and spending to municipalities.

Intergovernmental Transfers

We have already discussed in Chapter 2 municipalities' heavy reliance on aid from both the federal and the state government. This fiscal aid comes in various forms, but the most common is the categorical grant. Although the federal government no longer passes back revenues to communities for general purposes, most states have shared revenue programs.

TABLE 13.1 LOCAL GOVERNMENT REVENUE BY SOURCE AND LEVEL
OF GOVERNMENT, 1990–1991

	County	Municipal	Township	School[a]	Special
Federal aid	2.2%	3.6%	1.0%	0.7%	10.7%
State aid	31.3	16.6	19.0	51.1	4.8
Other local aid	1.6	1.8	2.0	1.7	5.5
Property tax	27.2	17.9	52.4	37.0	8.3
Sales tax	6.8	9.3	0.2	0.3	3.2
User charges	1.3	21.7	15.0	7.9	29.5
Miscellaneous	28.6	24.5	9.0	—	38.0
Income tax	1.0	4.6	1.4	0.3	—

[a] Column does not add up to 100% due to rounding.

The important point to understand about intergovernmental revenues is that they are declining as a proportion of local revenues, and federal assistance declined in the 1980s in absolute terms as well. Consider that in 1976 state aid to municipal governments amounted to 24.9 percent of all general revenues; by 1991 this figure had dropped to 16.6 percent. In the same period federal revenue fell as a proportion of city revenues from 13.4 percent to 3.6 percent.[7] In other words, in the space of 15 years combined intergovernmental aid from the federal and state governments dropped from over 38 percent of city budgets to about 20 percent.

Local Taxes

In fiscal year 1990–1991 cities and towns levied over $72 billion in taxes on their residents. The workhorse of the local tax system is the **property tax.** Levied mainly on real estate, it accounts for about half the tax dollars cities raise. It is expressed as a mill rate, or the dollars of tax per $1,000 of assessed value of a piece of property. Although states may set limits on how much local governments may increase the property tax in any one year, the mill rate is set annually within these limits by the city council. Municipal dependence on the property tax may be traced to the fact that other lucrative sources of tax revenues have already been claimed by other governments: The federal government taxes income heavily; the states tax sales. As we shall see, some cities also levy income and sales taxes, but these must defer to the claims made on these sources by superior governments.

Two trends in property taxation are important to note. One is that municipal reliance on property taxes is declining. As recently as 1976, property taxes accounted for a quarter of all municipal revenues. By 1991 the proportion had fallen to less than a fifth. Cities have greatly diversified their tax systems in recent years, reducing their need to raise money by means of this unpopular tax. The second trend is that the bulk of the burden of the property tax has been shifted over the last several decades from business firms to individual homeowners, a development that may be explained in part by city efforts to keep business firms in the community. State and local governments are aware, however, that poor people and people on fixed incomes are hit particularly hard by rising property taxes. Thus, at least 35 states have passed **circuit breaker laws,** that is, tax relief programs designed to protect homeowners from local property tax overload. When the property tax burden exceeds a certain percentage of a low-income household's earnings, then the state either refunds the additional tax directly to the household or gives them credit toward their state income tax.

Despite their importance to local governments, property taxes have many problems associated with them. They do not tax wealth held in forms other than real estate (such as bonds, stocks, jewelry, and automobiles). Property taxes also discourage absentee land-lords from improving their rental property because improvements might add to the value and thus the tax liability. Property tax delinquency rates are high, too, which means that cities are owed a significant amount of revenue that they do not collect in a timely way. Another problem is that a good deal of urban real estate is exempt from property taxation altogether. For example, churches, universities, charitable organizations, hospitals, foreign consulates, state and federal government facilities, and schools are all exempt from pay-ing property taxes. This can amount to as much as 40 percent of all real estate in a city.

Given some of the problems with the property tax, it is not surprising that cities have sought alternatives. In the midst of the Depression in the 1930s, New York City and then New Orleans adopted a tax on retail sales. Today 24 states, including California, New York, and Texas, permit some or all of their municipalities to levy sales taxes. Over 4,500 cities and towns take advantage of this, including 580 municipalities in Missouri and nearly 1,200 communities in Texas. However, because most states (45) also impose sales taxes, local governments cannot seriously impinge on that important source of state rev-enue. Thus, municipal sales tax rates tend to be a modest fraction of what the state levies. In Minneapolis, for example, the sales tax is 0.5 percent, whereas the state of Minnesota imposes a sales tax of 6 percent. Albuquerque gets along with a 0.4375 percent tax, but New Mexico levies 5 percent. Houston only collects 1 percent on sales, but the state of Texas collects 6 percent. Sales tax revenue makes up less than 10 percent of all monies collected by municipalities. One of its virtues is that people tend to believe that the sales tax is the least objectionable form of taxation. This attitude is no doubt due in part to its relative low visibility: People pay the sales tax a few pennies or dollars at a time. Another advantage from the city's point of view is that it permits tax exporting, or the shifting of part of the tax burden to nonresidents of the city who happen to make purchases in city stores. Tourists, commuters, and business travelers all help to share the cost of city ser-vices. Local merchants, however, tend to oppose municipal sales taxes: Customers often make it a point to travel to suburban malls or across state lines to make their major pur-chases, thus avoiding the municipal portion of the sales tax.

A less common local tax is the income or payroll tax. Pioneered by Philadelphia in 1939, it is permitted today in only ten states. Virtually every city, town, and village in Pennsylvania and Ohio levies an income tax, but elsewhere its use is limited. In New York state, only New York City and Yonkers levy such a tax; in Missouri, the tax is used only by St. Louis and Kansas City. In Delaware only Wilmington is allowed to levy a payroll tax.

These local income taxes are almost always limited to earned income, mainly salaries, wages, and commissions. Bank interest, capital gains, and other investment income is usu-ally exempt, although both the federal and state income taxes tap these sorts of income. Local income taxes, constrained by the fact that both the state and federal governments use this tax, take the form of low, flat-rate levies amounting to 1 or 2 percent of taxable income. One important advantage of the local income tax is that it is collected at the place of employment; thus, nonresident commuters must generally pay the tax too. A form of tax exporting, levying a payroll tax on commuters is justified by cities on the grounds that workers who come into the city use public services such as streets, police and fire protection, and parks, but would not contribute to their maintenance if they were not taxed in some way. Commuters get a break in some places, however: In Detroit, residents pay a 3 percent tax, but nonresidents pay only 1.5 percent. Both the local sales tax and the local income or payroll tax, it is important to point out, are regressive: Levied at flat percentage rates, both fall disproportionately on lower-income groups.

Cities levy countless other types of taxes besides these three main ones. Taxes may be found on hotel rooms, billboards, restaurant meals, stock transfers, parimutuel betting, automobile ownership, and vending machines. These do not account for much revenue, however. In the parlance of tax analysts, these are known as nuisance taxes.

Exit as a Constraint on Local Tax Systems   Cities (and states as well) are constrained from raising taxes too high by the fear that people and businesses may leave their jurisdiction. Businesses with a large investment in real property are not very likely to pick up and relocate, but occasionally they do. By contrast, we need only recall that roughly one out of every seven or eight Americans moves every year to realize that households are relatively mobile over the long term, seeking a new place to live as the size of the family, place of employment, or household income changes. Cities worry not only about keeping taxpayers from exiting, but also about attracting new ones. Households and businesses new to an area, public officials assume, will choose a community with lower property tax rates, all other things being equal.

A similar problem of taxpayer retention and attraction confronts cities that impose sales and income taxes. Consumers living in a city with a sales tax may simply choose to make their purchases, especially of big-ticket items, in neighboring towns that have no such tax. Not only are city tax collections hurt, but so are local businesses, which lose trade. If city officials worry that the presence of a sales tax will drive consumers across their borders, they also worry that an income tax will act as a disincentive to businesses seeking a new location. This is especially true of firms that operate in a very competitive labor market. Potential employees, choosing among employers, may prefer to work for a firm located in a community without an income tax.

Local officials believe that their community is in competition with other surrounding communities for tax-paying households and firms. Thus, to the extent possible, they try to impose taxes that resemble those of their neighbors both in kind and in rate. The principle in tax policy is to blend in, not stand out.

How much support is there for local officials' fears that taxes determine their ability to keep and attract firms and households? Evidence is certainly mixed. Roger Schmenner has shown, for example, that among firms that actually carried out short-distance moves within the same metropolitan area, the proportion that moved to lower-tax jurisdictions was exactly the same as the proportion that moved to higher-tax jurisdictions.[8] But Mark Schneider's work on competition among suburban municipalities concludes that "on the margin, both manufacturing and service firms avoid creating jobs in jurisdictions with higher taxes."[9]

The evidence is also mixed for households. Many analysts claim that home-seekers are not engaged in a single-minded search for the community with the lowest taxes, but rather hope to locate in the place where they get the most or best services for their tax dollars, even if that means they might pay more. However, in their analysis of the relationship between local tax and migration patterns in American cities, Terry Clark and Lorna Ferguson find that cities with high tax burdens generally lost population. In fact, they calculate that for every 10 percent increase in the tax burden, a city stood to lose one additional white person out of every 100 residents.[10]

User Fees and Miscellaneous Charges

Municipal swimming pools, museums, parking garages, bridges and tunnels, public hospitals, marinas, and bus and subway systems are among the services and amenities typically financed at least in part by user fees. Many cities own their water systems, and some own electric and gas utilities. The monthly utility bill for these is also a user charge. The idea behind user charges is to levy a price that reflects the cost of the service and to have those who use the service pay for it. People tend to think user fees are the fairest way for government to raise money: They like the idea that you pay for what you get. User charges, along with special assessments for new sidewalks and street paving, have been the fastest-rising source of municipal revenue since the late 1970s. Cities worried about the consequences of raising taxes and concerned about declining federal aid have seen user charges as a good alternative. Services that have traditionally been financed by the general tax levy, such as trash pickup and emergency ambulance services, are increasingly being viewed as candidates for user charges.

Municipal Borrowing

Cities generally spend their tax revenues, user fees, and some of their intergovernmental revenues for operating expenses, that is, for salaries, employee benefits, supplies, and equipment. To pay for land acquisition, large redevelopment and construction projects, and major capital or equipment purchases, however, cities borrow money. These things are so costly that no city could possibly afford to pay for them out of current revenues.

Cities borrow money by selling bonds. The bonds carry an interest rate that is slightly lower than that on private corporate bonds because purchasers are usually willing to trade a lower interest rate for the federal tax exemption available on municipal bonds. There are two main types of bonds. One is the **general obligation bond,** backed by the full faith and credit of the municipality or, in simpler language, by the taxpayers of the city. Thus, the city pledges to pay off the principal and interest when the bond matures. Normally, a city will use its tax revenues to do this. In the great fiscal crisis in New York City in the early 1970s, however, public officials sold short-term notes in order to pay off other short-term notes that had just come due, a practice that eventually had the city trying to sell $750 million in short-term notes every month.[11]

General obligation bonds are used to finance street construction, new sewers, land acquisition for redevelopment, a new jail or city hall, or the city's share of new buses.

The other general type of bond is the **revenue bond,** which is backed not by the taxpayers but by the revenues that the city anticipates will be generated by the project. Sports stadiums and toll bridges are the sorts of projects typically financed by revenue bonds. Income from tolls or admissions goes to pay off the principal and interest. In the 1970s cities also began to use revenue bonds extensively for economic development, issuing special industrial revenue bonds (IRBs) whose proceeds were then loaned at low rates to private companies to finance factory or office construction. Because the interest on IRBs is exempt from federal taxation (which means that the national government forgoes tax revenues it might otherwise have collected), Congress has limited the use of these financing instruments in recent years.

The purchasers of municipal bonds are mainly institutional investors—banks and insurance companies—but individuals may also be active in the bond market. It is important to understand that a city can borrow only as long as private lenders are willing to buy its bonds. In purchasing municipal bonds, investors evaluate the degree of risk to which they expose themselves. How likely is it, they ask, that the city will go bankrupt and be unable to pay off its bonds? New York City's fiscal crisis of 1974–1975 came to a head when investors decided not to buy any more city bonds out of fear that the city would not be able to repay them. The same thing happened in Philadelphia in 1993.

To help potential bond purchasers make a judgment about the creditworthiness of a particular bond issue various organizations rate every city's bonds. **Bond ratings** are not very scientific: The two best-known rating organizations, Standard & Poor's and Moody's, use not just fiscal data on a city but also what they call judgmental criteria, such as social, political, and demographic data, to establish a rating. A high rating means that the risk to the bond purchaser is presumably low; in return for low risk, therefore, the investor should be willing to take a slightly lower return. A city with a good bond rating—for example, Madison, Wisconsin, or Portland, Oregon—does not have to pay a high interest rate to borrow money. However, a city with a low rating, such as Newark, New Jersey, must pay a much higher interest rate to attract bond buyers. When a rating organization decides to lower a city's bond rating, there are serious fiscal consequences. The difference even between a AAA rating (the best) and a AA (the second best) could amount to $100,000 over the 20-year life of a $1 million bond.

Ironically, cities with a B credit rating (lacking the characteristics of desirable investment) are in fact no more likely to fail to pay off the bond when it comes due—that is, default—than are cities with a AAA rating. Indeed, defaults are fairly rare, and when they do occur, they usually do not involve a great deal of money. The Advisory Commission on Intergovernmental Relations estimates that between 1972 and 1983 there were approximately 85,000 bond issues by all types of local governments. Among these there were only 36 defaults, and 5 of these were "technical" defaults in which payments to investors were just delayed slightly. All but three of the total number of defaults—New York City, Cleveland, and the Washington Public Power Supply System—involved very small sums of money.[12] All in all, the record of municipalities in the bond market is a very good one.

✧ STATE CONSTRAINTS ON MUNICIPAL FISCAL POLICY

One reason cities rarely default on the bond obligations is that their borrowing activity is closely regulated by the state. The extreme reliance on short-term borrowing to pay off other short-term notes that helped to get New York City in such trouble in the mid-1970s was an aberration. Most states impose stringent borrowing limits on their municipalities and some states even require state review of bond issues before the bonds are sold. States have a legitimate interest in the creditworthiness of their municipalities: One community's poor credit rating affects the ratings not only of other communities but also of the state itself.

State restrictions on local debt take two forms. One type of restriction limits the total amount of indebtedness a city may incur, usually expressed as a percentage of the assessed value of all property in the jurisdiction. The other common type is a requirement that bond issues be approved in a local referendum. Along with these constraints, however, states in the 1980s adopted a number of measures designed to increase local government access to the credit markets. For example, several states now guarantee local bond issues, and more than half the states borrow money themselves and then relend the money to localities at a favorable interest rate.

In the wake of California's Proposition 13 limitation on property taxes (discussed in Chapter 12), a number of states also passed local taxing and spending limits. Although states had begun to limit local taxing authority in the last century, this practice did not become widespread until the tax revolt of the late 1970s. These limitations are designed mainly to establish a ceiling on the property tax. States may limit the amount of increase in property taxes in any given year or they may set a maximum amount of revenue that may be raised. In the mid-1980s at least 38 states had passed some sort of restriction on property taxes.

Sometimes, nothing that a state does can prevent a city from flirting with bankruptcy. Cities that have lost population and industry and have high numbers of poor people simply have few fiscal options. When New York City had its fiscal crisis in the mid-1970s, the state took the city's financial affairs out of local hands entirely. The governor of New York State appointed an Emergency Financial Control Board (EFCB), which had the power to approve or reject city budgets, contracts, and borrowing. Although the EFCB no longer exists, it can be resurrected any time up to the year 2008 if the city experiences an operating deficit of $100 million or more or fails to pay off its debts.

In a similar fashion, the state of Pennsylvania took over Philadelphia's finances in 1992: The governor appointed the Pennsylvania Intergovernmental Cooperation Authority to manage the city's budgeting, taxing, and borrowing, until Philadelphia had solved its fiscal difficulties.

In most such cases (and they are fairly rare), state stewardship of a city's finances imposes discipline, provides long-term financing, and enables the city to get out of some of its contractual obligations, such as wage and fringe benefit agreements with municipal employee unions. But in a few cases, all the state can do is provide what some analysts call artificial life support. This is the situation in East St. Louis, Illinois. The city has only about 200 public employees to serve a population of about 40,000. As Philip Dearborn and his colleagues observe, "Public services have been cut to levels that even in third-world cities would be considered bare bones, or less. For example, the city has provided no public trash collection since 1987."[13] The state of Illinois took over the city, creating the East St. Louis Advisory Authority in 1990 to provide loans to the city and help in other ways. Even so, the city in its present circumstances will be hard-pressed to pay off the loans or provide the normal array of urban services that Americans expect of their cities.

✧ MUNICIPAL SPENDING PATTERNS: WHAT DO CITIES DO?

Municipalities collectively spend more than $200 billion a year to provide services and amenities to their residents. Over a third of this sum goes for salaries and fringe benefits for city workers, and another third goes for other operating expenses—heating and electric bills, office supplies, computer time, equipment repairs, and the like. The remainder of city expenditures are devoted to construction, interest on debt, and equipment and land.

BOX 13.2 BANKRUPTCY IN ORANGE COUNTY

On December 7, 1994, Orange County—the nation's fifth-largest county in population and one of the wealthiest counties in the nation (its gross economic output of $77 billion is about the same as Greece's)—filed for bankruptcy with debts of $2 billion. It is by far the largest bankruptcy case involving a unit of government and the first involving a large American county.

Like many other California officials, Robert L. Citron, the Orange County treasurer for 24 years, was pressured to find new ways of generating revenues because of the strict limits on property taxes created by Proposition 13. Citron placed about two-thirds of a county-run investment fund in complex financial instruments known as derivatives. These bond-like securities are structured so that their value rises—and falls—much faster than ordinary bonds. In the spring of 1994, the Democratic treasurer was up for reelection, and he was criticized by his Republican opponent for the risky investments. However, the voters in the traditionally conservative county returned him enthusiastically by a 2-to-1 ratio. However, Citron had bet on lower interest rates, and instead they kept rising. By mid-November 1994, the county's $7.4 billion investment fund had suffered a $1.5 billion loss.[1]

Since filing for bankruptcy, Orange County has searched for ways to repay its $2 billion debt. The traditional method for large municipalities to avoid bankruptcy has been to increase sales taxes as Cleveland and New York did in the 1970s. However, Orange County's voters overwhelmingly rejected a half-cent increase in the sales tax by a 3-to-2 ratio even though the proposed sales tax increase of a half-cent per dollar would have cost the average resident only $50 a year while reaping $140 million in tax revenue, enough to procure a new loan to cover the county's financial obligations.[2] Instead, the county has followed a strategy of legal challenges and draconian austerity measures.

The county is challenging the basic underpinnings of municipal finance—the moral and legal obligation of a municipal borrower to pay its debts—by suing Merrill Lynch for more than $2 billion. The county contends that Merrill sold the county inappropriate securities and misled Citron. Unlike other major cities such as Cleveland and New York, which underwent considerable pain to protect their names, Orange County is treating its situation more like a high-stakes corporate bankruptcy than a bailout of a troubled government entity.

Because Orange County can no longer borrow money, it has been forced make sharp spending cuts of more than $180 million. This austerity drive has created the spectacle of one of America's most affluent counties slashing programs for the poor.

The county's Social Service Agency has borne the brunt of the budgetary cutbacks. In the food stamp program, employees' caseloads have surged to 216 recipients a month from 137. The county's probation department has had to shut down a program that allowed 110 low-risk prisoners to maintain jobs while living in halfway houses. Outreach programs for the 12,000 homeless people in the county were canceled. A program that trained and found jobs for 250 people with severe mental impairments has closed. One prenatal clinic for poor women closed and 15 monthly clinics for children were shut down. The number of workers monitoring child abuse was halved. Gang prevention and confinement programs eliminated.

"It's been the disadvantaged, the poor, the incarcerated who have felt what this bankruptcy is about," said Marian Bergeson, one of five county supervisors. "They have been the losers, and will continue to be."[3]

---

[1]James Sterngold, "Orange County Bankruptcy: The Poor Feel the Most Pain," *New York Times* (December 5, 1995), p. A1.

[2]Leslie Wayne, "Tax Defeat Makes Orange County's Fate More Perilous," *New York Times* (June 29, 1995), p. D1.

[3]Sterngold, p. A1.

Every city performs a slightly different mix of responsibilities. New York City, for example, is responsible for education, public welfare, and hospitals, but Los Angeles does none of these. In California, these are either school district or county functions, not municipal responsibilities. On the other hand, Oakland, California, spends about $30 million a year for its airport, but New York City does not spend a cent for LaGuardia and Kennedy airports. These latter facilities are the responsibility of a special district, the Port Authority of New York and New Jersey. Chicago is not responsible for jails (they are a Cook County function), but the city of Dallas must spend nearly $75 million a year on corrections costs. Residents of American cities usually enjoy access to a similar range of services, but the type of local government that provides the service differs from one place to another.

Nearly all municipalities provide certain common functions. These are listed in Table 13.2. Note that public safety responsibilities—police and fire combined—account for the largest portion of the common functions budget. Infrastructure—sewer systems and treatment facilities, streets and highways—accounts for the second largest bite out of city budgets.

Although it is common to speak of these functions, not all cities are responsible for all of them. Scottsdale, Arizona, uses a private fire department, and a number of cities use private garbage pickup services. Parks and sewers are often managed not by cities but by special districts.

TABLE 13.2   MUNICIPAL EXPENDITURES, FISCAL YEAR 1990–1991 (IN BILLIONS)   Public safety responsibilities—police and fire, combined—account for the largest portion of the common functions budget.

Common Functions	
Police	$19.1
Highways, streets	12.6
Sewer	10.8
Fire	10.0
Parks and recreation	8.4
Solid waste	6.2
Financial administration	3.9
Judicial system	2.3
Inspection and regulation	1.6
Other Functions	
Education	$18.3
Housing and development	8.2
Public welfare	7.7
Hospitals	6.9
Airports	3.0
Corrections	2.2
Libraries	2.1
Parking	.6

Source: U.S. Bureau of the Census, *Government Finances, 1992* (Washington, D.C.: Government Printing Office, 1992), Table 6.

Other functions are even less common. Take education: Most schools are administered by separate school districts, but a few systems are part of municipal government. This is the case in New York City, Boston, Baltimore, Memphis, Hartford, and Norfolk, among others. Public welfare is a county function in most communities, but in New York City it is a city responsibility, commanding 15 percent of the municipal budget. Transportation functions—mass transit, parking, and air and port terminals—are the responsibility of special districts in many places, as is the administration of public housing programs.

There is an important lesson to be learned from looking at the range of municipal functions: Cities are responsible for a wide range of public services that have a powerful bearing on the quality of daily life. Imagine living in a city without a sewer system or without paved streets or street lighting or without a police department. Consider what life would be like without parks to provide relief from the built-up cityscape or fire departments to save property or public health departments to contain infectious diseases. Neither state nor the federal government activities have so direct and intimate a bearing on the conditions of daily life.

✧ BUDGET POLITICS: WHO MAKES TAXING AND SPENDING DECISIONS?

Budgeting is the process of deciding how to allocate fiscal resources to various uses. Although it is a very technical activity, it is deeply political in the sense that it involves making crucial choices and setting priorities that have consequences for all the various interests in the city. In a lean year, should the police department get its budget request while the municipal parks and swimming pool get less than they requested? Should the city hire more office workers or should it purchase enough electronic office equipment to permit it to lay off some workers? Can the city afford to fund a new experimental program in waste recycling or should it go on disposing of garbage in the old way? Should downtown streets get priority for repaving while neighborhood streets have to wait another year?

Many cities have begun to develop long-term strategic plans to inform their budget deliberations. These plans, developed usually in a budget office but in consultation with agency heads and even the city council, represent a vision of where the city ought to be in the future. Strategic plans first provide an audit of the city's assets—its economic base, its population demographics, and its growth prospects—and then an assessment of the forces, both internal and external, that affect the city's fiscal and social well-being. Then strategic plans set goals: smaller government, a lower crime rate, better housing, and so on. The plans are not rigid, nor do they have the force of law; rather, they function as guidelines for the budget-makers.

In city manager and strong mayor systems, developing a city budget each year is an executive responsibility. The typical process is as follows: Several months before the final budget must be in place, the chief executive asks each city department to work up its budget request for the next fiscal year. The budget process is highly ritualized. Department heads are almost always told that the city faces a lean year and that they must emphasize efficiency and cost cutting in order to hold the line on taxes. (Few observers of city politics ever recall a mayor sending out a call for the budget with a covering letter that says how flush the city is financially and that department heads should feel free to ask for whatever they think necessary!)

The department heads know, however, that their current budget is rarely likely to be cut, except in the most dire fiscal emergency. Thus, they try to develop a budget request not only somewhat larger than their current allocation but also larger than what they think they really need, for they know that they will probably not get all of the increase they request.

Once all of the departments—streets, parks, fire, police, public health, and so on—have submitted their budget requests to the mayor or manager, he or she puts together a comprehensive document to submit to the city council. This involves more than stapling all of the separate requests together: The chief executive reviews each request, cutting or eliminating some, adding here and there, or forcing modifications in priorities. In the public debate over the budget that ensues when the document is considered in the city council (and in the press), it is known as the mayor's (or manager's) budget. In many weak mayor cities, the departments submit their budget requests directly to the budget committee of the city council, which undertakes a similar process of modification.

The final stage of the budget process is the responsibility of the city council. Here the budget is debated and finally passed. City councils are not mere rubber stamps; however, their influence on the final document is generally modest. Many councils make token cuts, just to show that they must be reckoned with. Most councils, however, do not have the staff or independent sources of information to make well-informed budget modifications.

If the budget process is political in the sense that it involves making choices among interests, to what degree do various groups—downtown business, small neighborhood business, minorities, public employee unions, neighborhood associations, developers, environmental organizations, and so on—take part in and influence the pattern of resource allocation? In order to answer this question, it is important to understand first that budgeting is a technical process involving internal negotiation among municipal bureaucrats, executive branch officials, and city council representatives. Furthermore, budgeting tends to be an incremental process; that is, each year's budget allocations are based first and foremost on last year's allocations. What a department or agency got last year is the starting point; as such, it is a given, not really subject to close scrutiny. Growth in the budget typically occurs at the margins in the form of small additions to existing departments and programs. Only occasionally do cities add large new programs or whole new agencies.

That the budget process is a highly technical matter involving internal bargaining means that opportunities for outside groups to influence resource allocation are not numerous. In addition, an incremental budget process means that contending groups are struggling over marginal changes in the overall budget, not the structure of the budget itself. The result is that extensive participation by external interest groups in city budget politics is not very common.

✧ THE POLITICS OF SERVICE DELIVERY

The politics of budgeting mainly concerns two matters: How much should the city spend? On what should the city spend it? The latter is a substantive question in the sense that it poses choices among particular uses, or in concrete terms, among departments and programs. However, budgeting is only one aspect of the larger category of spending policy. There are at least two other important questions. One asks where the money is spent in the city, an equity question; the other asks how efficiently the city performs its various responsibilities.

Equity

The question of where cities deliver services is important because what appears to be a simple matter of geography really turns out to have critical social implications. Cities are spatially divided by class, race, and ethnic lines. This is most obvious where African Americans are concerned: They are the most residentially segregated group in American society, more so than Asians, Hispanics, or any white ethnic group. But spatial divisions also follow social class lines, so that cities are roughly divided into poor, working-class, middle-class, and upper-class areas. Thus, where the city provides services or amenities has implications for how equitably the city serves different social groups.

The point is easily understood if we consider that because resources are limited, city governments must decide which streets to resurface each summer, where to place a new municipal swimming pool, where to build a new fire station, where to open the next branch library, how many times a week to pick up garbage in each neighborhood, where to locate police precinct stationhouses, in what areas to plant trees along the median strip of the boulevard, and where to route the new urban rail mass transit system. Who gets easy access to these services and who does not?

Urban residents, as well as urban analysts, have wondered whether there is bias in the patterns of service and amenity distribution. It is widely assumed that poorer, blacker parts of the city receive fewer (and poorer) services than upper-income, white areas. Social scientists have sought to explore patterns of service distribution by investigating several possible hypotheses. They have focused on four different possible explanations for how services are distributed.

The Underclass Hypothesis

The underclass hypothesis suggests that there is deliberate bias against blacks in particular and the poor more generally. This is intuitively appealing for anyone who has ever been in an inner-city ghetto. Support for this hypothesis was provided by the findings of a federal court case, *Hawkins v. Shaw* (1971), in which the court found the municipality of Shaw, Mississippi, guilty of systematically favoring white neighborhoods in the provision of street paving, street lighting, sewer lines, and fire hydrants. Black sections of town had dirt streets, inadequate sewerage, and no street lighting.

But surprisingly, perhaps, a great deal of careful research has subsequently found little evidence that racial bias is commonly at work in the distribution of urban services. Robert Lineberry's study of the distribution of parks, police services, fire protection, and libraries in San Antonio found that the percentage poor and minority in a neighborhood was not associated with access to or quality of these services.[14] In fact, for example, the mean distance of poor people's houses from the nearest fire station was shorter (and thus the fire department's response time was quicker) than the mean distance of middle-class homes. Across the different services Lineberry found that not all parts of the city were served equally, but the patterns of inequality could not be explained by the racial makeup of the different neighborhoods.

A study of the distribution of expenditures for seven different services in New York City reaches the same conclusion: There is no support for the notion that service expenditures in black or poor areas are systematically lower. In fact, expenditures for health, education, and social services were higher in low-income neighborhoods, suggesting that service distribution is responsive to needs.[15]

The Per-Capita Equality Hypothesis

The per-capita equality explanation suggests that different areas receive equal services, regardless of differences in need. Thus, a poor neighborhood with no access to private pools and tennis clubs would receive exactly the same per-capita recreation facility expenditures as a wealthy neighborhood, many of whose residents belong to private sports clubs. Although a study of recreation expenditures in Philadelphia found exactly this pattern,[16] no other investigations have found that per capita equality is a common way for cities to distribute services.

The Contributory Hypothesis   Some analysts have suspected that neighborhoods that produce political support for the incumbent mayor or that generate the greatest tax revenues receive the best and the most services. Kenneth Mladenka investigated the first possibility in the case of Chicago. He found, however, that wards that tended to vote for Mayor Richard J. Daley and the Democratic machine candidates did not receive proportionately more or better services than Republican-voting areas. He concluded that "distributional decision making is routinized and largely devoid of explicit political content."[17]

The Compensatory Hypothesis   Some inequalities in the distribution of services are a function of the different needs of different neighborhoods. Thus, a city may spend more in poor areas to meet the greater need. Inequalities are redistributive in favor of the poor. Levy, Meltsner, and Wildavsky found a similar pattern for school expenditures in Oakland, California.[18] The concentration of police resources and firefighting equipment in poor areas, both common patterns, are simply rational bureaucratic decisions to respond to the fact that crime and fires are more likely to occur in such neighborhoods than elsewhere.

Clearly, the determinants of service distribution vary from city to city. No single hypothesis accounts for all patterns. Efforts by city agencies to respond rationally to needs seem to account better for many allocation decisions than the underclass hypothesis, simple per-capita equality, or contributory factors. Other factors also determine the pattern of services in cities. Bureaucratic decision rules that have nothing to do with need may have an impact. For example, street maintenance departments may have a repaving schedule that begins at the northern edge of the city and works south. Other factors have to do with idiosyncratic historical phenomena. Fire stations in older parts of Chicago are close together, for example, because they were built in a period during which horses were used to pull firefighting equipment.

Efficiency

When Stephen Goldsmith became mayor of Indianapolis in 1992, he instituted a management program called Competition and Costing. Its object is to introduce competition into the provision of public services. If potential service providers have the opportunity to compete to offer a service, then the idea is that they will be as efficient, lean, and cheap as possible while still meeting service standards. What makes the program particularly interesting in Indianapolis is that private companies as well as the traditional city departments may submit bids to offer a particular service. One recent winner was the city Street Department, which submitted a successful bid to repair streets. To develop the winning bid, the city employees eliminated excess middle-management positions, resulting in street repairs at 25 percent less than they had cost before. Other city departments have also won in competitive bidding against private companies, including the right to pick up trash and maintain the city's fleet of trucks and police cars. The result so far of this competitive bidding system has been a 2 percent overall reduction in the city's annual operating expenses and a reduction in the size of the workforce.[19]

Most cities these days are under pressure to reduce the cost of government and at the same time to improve the quality of services. It was thought for a long time that the answer lay in privatizing public services, that is, in contracting out such responsibilities as garbage collection, park maintenance, and halfway houses for drug offenders to private companies. The assumption behind privatization is that the public sector is inherently inefficient and likely to be unresponsive to citizen desires to boot.

There are a number of reasons for this assumption. For example, civil servants have life tenure in the job; it is more difficult to fire a public employee who is not doing the job in the most effective way than it is to get rid of an inefficient worker in the private sector. Municipal employee unions are also seen by some urban officials as barriers to efficiency. A recent proposal in Wisconsin to hire part-time teachers to teach specialized high school classes just a few hours a week in, say, Japanese or engineering, ran aground on the objections of the teachers' union, although proponents contended that this would be an efficient way to add more variety to the curriculum. Rates of unionization in the private sector tend to be lower than in municipal government. (In 1993 about 38 percent of government workers were members of unions, compared to only 11.2 percent of private sector workers.[20])

Another problem with municipal agencies in the eyes of critics is that they are typically monopoly operations. In many cities the municipal sanitation department is the only provider of garbage and trash pickup service. Monopolies need not be careful about letting costs rise (there are no competing providers to offer the service at a lower cost), and they may not be very responsive to the people they serve. Like the phone company in the famous comedy routine, they don't have to care.

Competitive bidding programs, where city and private firms compete, such as the program in Indianapolis and similar ones in Phoenix (which began in 1980), Wichita, and Minneapolis, suggest that the indictment of the public sector is too simple. Public employees can be just as or even more efficient than private company workers if they are put in a competitive situation. Allowing city agencies and departments to enter into competitive bidding can be complicated, however. What does the city do with the workers if the city agency does not win the bid one year? A more common solution for many cities is to contract out the service to private businesses. Philadelphia is an example of a city vigorously privatizing responsibilities that once belonged exclusively to the city: janitorial work in City Hall, museum guards, maintenance of a local expressway, and trash hauling have all been privatized under Mayor Ed Rendell.

Privatization in municipal government began in earnest in the 1980s, although the federal government has long used private companies to build weapons and construct military installations.[21] Today, all sorts of city services that were once municipal are provided by private companies on a contract basis. The most common is probably residential solid waste collection. Between 14 and 21 percent of cities contract out some or all of their garbage pickup.

Besides garbage and refuse pickup, cities contract with private firms for everything from firefighting (17 private companies in the United States offer such services to cities) to jails to tax collecting to ambulance services. One national survey found that 80 percent of city and county governments that replied to the questionnaire had contracted out for at least one service. The most common services that cities ask private firms to provide are housekeeping and physical maintenance tasks.

Interest in privatization was stimulated partly by the tax revolts in the late 1970s. A survey of local officials found that of all the factors that heightened their cities' interest in privatization, the two most important were the growing demand for services and taxpayer resistance to tax increases.[22] Cost savings and the ability to avoid having to deal with municipal unions were the two most important perceived advantages of contracting out reported in this national survey.

To what extent is privatizing a public service the cheaper alternative? Most studies indicate that private companies perform garbage pickup more cheaply than city sanitation departments.[23] Consider other findings:

- ◇ A study in 20 cities found that contract street sweeping was 43 percent cheaper than municipal sweeping.
- ◇ An analysis comparing municipal water supply in 88 cities and private water supply in 24 cities found the former to be a third more costly than the latter.
- ◇ Municipal tree maintenance is 37 percent more expensive than the private service.[24]

The reasons for these cost savings often have to do with the use of nonunion labor, more careful equipment maintenance, fewer worker absences, and higher labor productivity. Some of these elements are a function of the profit motives of private firms, as they seek to maximize their returns while still charging the lowest rates to the city.

Studies of private provision of social services, such as day care and education, and protective services, such as police and fire protection, are less conclusive about the relative costs. The private provision of social services, many of which serve primarily the needy, raises issues of equity (would everyone who has a need have access to the service if the provider were a profit-seeking private firm?) and standards (would the private provider maintain high standards, even if they are costly?).

It is important in evaluating privatization as an alternative mode of service delivery to understand that the private sector has no monopoly on efficiency or on dedicated employees, as the case of the Indianapolis street department makes clear. Many public agencies achieve high levels of cost effectiveness, and many civil servants are hard-working and conscientious. Conversely, private firms fail all the time from inefficient management, despite the profit motive, and many are plagued by worker absenteeism and poor performance. Thus, it would be a mistake to assume that private provision of public services is always the preferable alternative. Finally, Hirsch warns that the cost savings from privatizing might be greatly overstated: He points out that Los Angeles County worked hard for decade to privatize as many services as possible. At the end of the period it had managed to contract out only 1.5 percent of its budget, reducing expenditures only by one half of one percent.[25]

Turning public services over to private firms is not the only alternative mode of service delivery cities have employed. Another involves either transferring responsibility to another government or even contracting with another government to perform the task. Some cities have transferred services or facilities to higher-level governments in order to take advantage of a larger tax base. Detroit, for example, handed over control of the city art museum to Wayne County. Madison, Wisconsin, turned over the municipal airport to the county.

The best-known example of contracting with another government to perform a local service is the Lakewood Plan in Los Angeles County. Since 1954, towns and cities, beginning with the community of Lakewood, have contracted with the county for everything from emergency ambulance services to law enforcement to animal control. Cities realize cost savings because they can share county facilities—such as a police dispatcher service—rather than having to purchase or develop their own.

◆ CONCLUSION

The fiscal situation of American cities has changed radically since the 1970s. From a period in which city officials assumed that the federal government would always be there to help them out, the nation's localities now find that they must plan for fiscal self-sufficiency. These days, the city leaders who earn accolades as America's boldest mayors are those helping their cities to live within their means by instituting strategic planning and experimenting with management reforms such as competitive bidding for service contracts.[26] In the process, cities are learning to wean themselves from federal dollars, pare down their city governments, improve productivity of their workers, and hold the line on taxes. Mayor John Norquist of Milwaukee is a prime example of the new breed of mayors: He never lost an opportunity to point out that he cut the property tax rate every year he was in office while still maintaining high quality services.

Another way for cities to survive fiscally in the new "postfederal" environment is to enlarge their tax base. This strategy has led to the rise of economic development on local agendas. The effort to attract new business, retain existing firms, and stimulate the formation of new businesses within city borders has become a major preoccupation of local officials. Job creation and business development rank near the top of the urban political agenda.

All in all, the cities' fiscal world is far different now from what it was in the heady days of the Great Society in the 1960s, when Washington supplied an ever-increasing flow of dollars and America's boldest mayors were social reformers rather than management experts.

◆ KEY TERMS

bond ratings (p. 342)	property tax (p. 338)
circuit breaker laws (p. 338)	revenue bond (p. 341)
general obligation bond (p. 341)	user charges (p. 341)

◆ FOR FURTHER READING

Helen Ladd and John Yinger, *America's Ailing Cities: Fiscal Health and the Design of Urban Policy* (Baltimore: Johns Hopkins Press, 1989). A study of the underlying factors that determine cities' fiscal strength.

Martin Shefter, *Political Crisis/Fiscal Crisis: The Collapse and Revival of New York City* (New York: Basic Books, 1987). The best scholarly analysis of the famous fiscal crisis of the 1970s in New York.

✧ NOTES

1. Matthew Drennan, "The Decline and Rise of the New York Economy," in John Mollenkopf and Manuel Castells, eds., *Dual City* (New York: Russell Sage, 1991), p. 37.

2. U.S. Department of Housing and Urban Development, *Empowerment: A New Covenant with America's Communities*, President Clinton's National Urban Policy Report (Washington, D.C.: July 1995), p. 14.

3. *Ibid.*, p. 16

4. Helen Ladd, "Big City Finances," in George Peterson, ed., *Big-City Politics, Governance, and Fiscal Constraints* (Washington, D.C.: Urban Institute Press, 1994), p. 204; and Philip Dearborn, George Peterson, and Richard Kirk, "City Finances in the 1990s" (Washington, D.C.: The Urban Institute, September 1992).

5. Ben Yagoda, "Mayor on a Roll: Ed Rendell," *New York Times Magazine* (May 22, 1994), 26–29.

6. Lawrence Herson and John Bolland, *The Urban Web* (Chicago: Nelson-Hall, 1990) 360–361.

7. U.S. Bureau of the Census, *Government Finances, 1990–91* (Washington, D.C.: Government Printing Office, 1993), p. 7.

8. Roger Schmenner, *Making Business Location Decisions* (Englewood Cliffs, N.J.: Prentice-Hall, 1982), p. 48.

9. Mark Schneider, *The Competitive City* (Pittsburgh: University of Pittsburgh Press, 1989), p. 162.

10. Terry Clark and Lorna Ferguson, *City Money* (New York: Columbia University Press, 1983), pp. 207–209.

11. Martin Shefter, *Political Crisis/Fiscal Crisis: The Collapse and Revival of New York City* (New York: Basic Books, 1987), p. 106.

12. Advisory Commission on Intergovernmental Relations, *Bankruptcies, Defaults, and Other Local Government Financial Emergencies* (Washington, D.C.: Government Printing Office, 1985), pp. 20–22.

13. Dearborn, Peterson, and Kirk, "City Finances in the 1990s," pp. 7–8.

14. Robert Lineberry, *Equality and Urban Policy* (Beverly Hills, Calif.: Sage, 1977).

15. John Boyle and David Jacobs, "The Intracity Distribution of Services: A Multivariate Analysis," *American Political Science Review*, 76 (June 1982), 371–379.

16. Cited in Lineberry, *Equality and Urban Policy*, pp. 108–109.

17. Kenneth Mladenka, "The Urban Bureaucracy and the Chicago Political Machine: A Multivariate Analysis," *American Political Science Review*, 74 (December 1980), 996.

18. Frank Levy, Arnold Meltsner, and Aaron Wildavsky, *Urban Outcomes: Schools, Streets, and Libraries* (Berkeley: University of California Press, 1974).

19. Charles Mahtesian, "Opening Up the Bidding," *Governing*, 9 (November 1995), 39–40.

20. U.S. Bureau of the Census, *Statistical Abstract of the United States, 1994* (Washington, D.C.: Government Printing Office, 1994), p. 438.

21. Werner Z. Hirsch, *Privatizing Government Services* (Los Angeles: Institute of Industrial Relations, UCLA, 1991), p. 33.

22. Touche Ross and Co., *Privatization in America* (Washington, D.C.: Touche Ross, 1987), p. 4.

23. Werner Z. Hirsch, "Contracting Out by Urban Governments," *Urban Affairs Review,* 30 (January 1995), 467.

24. These examples all come from E. S. Savas, *Privatization: The Key to Better Government* (Chatham, N.J.: Chatham House, 1987), pp. 131, 148, 159.

25. Hirsch, "Contracting Out by Urban Governments," p. 470.

26. William Eggers, "City Lights: America's Boldest Mayors," *Policy Review* (Summer 1993), 67–74.

14

GOVERNMENT
IN THE ECONOMY

Although Americans like to imagine that they maintain a free-market economy, the fact is that state and local governments are major economic actors. Indeed, their efforts to promote economic growth within their borders are often so energetic that some scholars call them "growth machines." In prior chapters we have shown how interstate competition for economic resources—firms, taxpayers, and investment—forces governors and legislatures to respond. In this chapter we explore more specifically the economic policies through which state and local governments try to facilitate and promote economic growth.

In the economic arena, states and their cities face problems different from those at the national level. The government in Washington, D.C., deals with a national economy, which it attempts to steer through the use of its fiscal and monetary policy instruments. Congress can pass job-creation legislation and other spending bills to stimulate the economy, sometimes running up a massive deficit in the process. The Federal Reserve Bank can regulate the money supply and influence interest rates, thereby controlling inflation and economic growth. State and local governments have few of these tools: They do not print their own currency or manipulate interest rates, they cannot borrow money to "prime the pump", and they cannot regulate interstate commerce. Often state and local economies are heavily at the mercy of the national economy. Thus, as Paul Peterson argues, cities, and by implication states, are limited in what they can do.[1] These limits are significant constraints on what subnational governments can do to affect the economy.

Although their policy choices are fewer than the national government's, cities and states make many decisions that have important economic consequences. If natural resources such as coal and oil are squandered, then a resource is depleted forever and that source of state income is not available. If pollution or crime is so bad that tourists stay away, then the city loses needed revenues. If roads, schools, and other basic services are deficient, then high-tech industries will not stay. Given these pressures, states and cities try to make policy decisions that enhance their economic positions, not hurt them.

Subnational governments have three factors of production to work with: land, labor, and capital.[2] Land area is a fixed factor but also the factor over which governments have the most control. The land (and what is underneath it) determines whether a state has an agricultural base, mining industries, or beautiful vistas that draw tourists. Access to waterways and land routes historically has determined which cities flourished economically and which did not. Cities exercise control over land through their zoning power and influence economic development through construction of public works. States control land use preserving agricultural land and requiring environmental reviews before industrial development may go forward.

Labor, as we have emphasized, is increasingly mobile. Each government jurisdiction tries to adopt policies that attract skilled labor and professionals while deterring less-skilled and unemployable people. For cities this generally means providing an adequate housing stock, parks and recreational amenities, and good schools at the lowest possible cost. The particular mix of benefits and costs is crucial because at the local level people can rather easily "vote with their feet." They can move to the suburbs if they find city taxes too high and city schools poor. For states, policies to attract labor involve efforts to improve the quality of the workforce through education, training, and retraining. Also they regulate conditions in the workplace, including health and safety, workers' compensation, and unemployment insurance.

Capital is the other factor of production that is mobile. Cities try to attract capital by offering low-cost loans, land, and low taxes and by minimal regulation of industrial pollution. States traditionally have attracted capital by lowering the cost of doing business through low income taxes, minimal regulations, and **right-to-work laws.** In the last couple of decades some states experimented with **venture capital** funds to promote capital formation.

Today states and cities are engaged in an intense competition to maximize their economic positions. The competition is most intense over capital but also includes battles over land and labor. Cities and states do everything they can to improve their economic standing. Often the competition appears to be a **zero-sum game,** one in which one state loses a firm to another state or a central city loses educated workers to a neighboring suburb. Although in the 1980s states and cities began to concentrate more on nurturing indigenous businesses (a sort of "grow your own" strategy that would produce **positive-sum** gains, that is, an increase that does not come at another's expense), there is still concern that too much money is going into "stealing" business from other places. For example, in 1994 St. Louis persuaded the Los Angeles Rams professional football team to abandon southern California and move to Missouri. The cost to Missouri and St. Louis taxpayers was estimated at $720 million. Amarillo, Texas, was also in the industrial raiding business that year, but it took a novel approach: The city sent a check for $8 million to 1,300 different companies around the United States, which a company could cash if it committed to creating 700 new jobs in Amarillo.[3]

Today's economic policies are a far cry from government's hands-off policy toward the economy through much of our history. The classic statement about government's role was provided in 1776 by Adam Smith in *Wealth of Nations*.[4] Smith argued that the free market was the best mechanism for promoting economic performance and that government intervention or interference impedes performance. He saw only three duties for government: protecting the society from the violence and invasion of other independent societies, protecting every member of the society from injustice and oppression, and erecting and maintaining certain public works and public institutions. In other words, Smith allowed for government to provide selected **public goods** (national defense, parks, roads) and to regulate business and society in certain cases (for example, to stop criminal behavior and to enforce contracts). Any other government activity was deemed an intrusion into the free workings of the economy.

Of course, the economy has changed a lot since 1776; although some conservative economists stick with Smith's three principles, most people see a broader role for government to play. State and local governments are involved in their economies in three major ways: they regulate private business, they promote economic growth and development, and they provide physical infrastructure for business and society. In this chapter we examine selected instances of state and local activity in the first two of these areas; we reserve treatment of infrastructure for the next chapter. Throughout the discussion we pay attention to the costs and benefits of such policies. Which particular mix of economic policies will maximize the economic interests of the city and the state? Who is advantaged by such policies and who is disadvantaged?

◆ STATE AND LOCAL REGULATORY POLICIES

Nobody likes regulation, it seems. Both Jimmy Carter and Ronald Reagan rose from the governor's office to the presidency by railing against government regulation. Indeed, both worked hard at reducing federal regulation. Bill Clinton put Vice President Al Gore in charge of the National Performance Review, an effort to root out senseless rules and red tape in the federal government. The Republican leadership of Congress called for deregulation in its Contract with America. Yet much more regulating is done by state and local governments than by federal officials in Washington, D.C. States and localities today regulate countless products and services. Much of their regulation is autonomous and independent of the national government. Much of the newer federal legislation, however, depends on state-level enforcement. Therefore, there is considerable intergovernmental regulatory activity as well.

Government steps in to regulate when the market fails in some way. There are three major reasons for government intervention into the marketplace: to maintain **efficiency,** to ensure **equity,** and to redress **externalities.**[5] Let us explore these justifications and some of the policies states and localities pursue in each category.

Regulation for Efficiency

One kind of market failure is inefficient competition, that is, when monopolies develop or when key industries must be stimulated to develop. Regulation to restore competition is well-established and provokes less controversy than the other two types of regulation.

Public Utilities One of the foremost examples of efficiency regulation is state regulation of public utilities: electricity, gas, and water transmission. Private business depends on having good utility services. Because a single utility supplier is generally a natural monopoly, it could easily disrupt the flow of electricity or gas or water service to consumers.

All 50 states have public utility or public service commissions that intensively regulate public utilities. Such services were privately owned and competitive from colonial times until the early twentieth century. In the 1800s larger cities often granted several electric franchises to different companies but the quality of service was low, and eventually a single monopolistic company would emerge. States saw dangerous monopolies developing and realized the need for government action, including public ownership of utilities. The electricity industry feared government takeover and in order to forestall it, they advocated government regulation of privately owned utility companies.[6] In 1907 New York and Wisconsin became the first states to regulate public utilities. Other states quickly followed suit.

The electrical utility industry concentrated its efforts on retaining as much autonomy as possible and on shaping the regulatory laws to its benefit. Electrical utility regulation was relatively tranquil for the next half-century. Indeed, it tended to fit the **capture theory** of regulation; that is, the regulation generally benefitted the regulated industry more than the consumers.[7]

In the 1970s, however, the Arab oil embargo set off dramatic price increases in electricity, and the politics of utility regulation suddenly became visible and conflictual. Public participation in rate-setting proceedings increased, consumer advocacy groups gained representation, commission staffs became more professionalized, commission budgets increased, and governors and legislators became involved. The result is that the electrical utility industry no longer dominates the regulatory process.

Scholars who studied public utility commissions at the end of the 1970s found that several conditions operated against the operation of capture theory. William Berry discovered that where the regulatory issues were highly salient to the consumer (for instance, where the electricity rate structure hurt the small consumer), the degree of industry capture was less.[8] Also, where the state commissions had greater resources and more professionalism, the degree of capture was less.

William Gormley's research echoed these findings; he found that the degree of agency capture depended on the state's political culture, the process of selecting commissioners, the extent of public advocacy, and the level of commission professionalism.[9] In Mississippi, North Dakota, and Wyoming, low electricity rates and elected commissions discouraged public intervention in commission proceedings; also, their commissions had small staffs with small budgets. Thus, it would be difficult for them to challenge the utility companies; not surprisingly, none of these states had adopted reforms such as lifeline rates. In contrast, in Massachusetts, Michigan, and New York, relatively high rates and appointed commissions encouraged public intervention by grass-roots and proxy advocates. These states also have very professional commissions. Not surprisingly, they have adopted reform measures such as time-of-day rates.

Cable Television   Like natural gas and electrical utilities, cable TV was once thought to be a natural monopoly. Cities sought to regulate cable TV by granting franchises, but the development of cable technology and the emergence of satellite TV has led to competition among cable companies. Nevertheless, cities still license cable operations, requiring that they maintain public access channels, universal service, and state-of-the-art systems.

Regulation for Equity

A second reason for regulation is to ensure equity, especially between buyer and seller. To the extent that such regulation is simply enforcing a fair contract, it would have even Adam Smith's approval. Equity regulation has a long history at the state and local level. In 1877 the U.S. Supreme Court, in *Munn v. Illinois*, upheld the state's right to regulate prices, saying the state of Illinois could regulate prices charged by grain warehouses because warehousing was a business "affected with a public interest." Equity regulation today is controversial because the concept of equity has been broadened.

Municipal regulations to ensure fair business practices predate even those of the states. Teaford's study of local government in America from 1650 to 1825 shows that most early municipal ordinances were regulations that barred monopolies, prohibited cheating, and fixed prices on essential commodities.[10] Today, city inspectors still make their rounds of retail merchants, checking on the honesty of scales, gas pump gauges, taxi meters, and other weighing and measuring devices. Cities may also check the accuracy of weights on package labels. The smooth operation of the market depends on the perception that buyers get fair value for their money.

Insurance   Perhaps the most significant area of equity regulation is the states' purview over the insurance industry, including life, property, auto, casualty, and medical malpractice insurance. State agencies oversee the financial soundness of companies, the rates charged for insurance, and the fairness of company practices. Insurance companies, which number about 6,000, constitute a significant sector of the economy, and they are very mobile because any insurance company could be located almost anywhere. Hence, their threat of exit from a state is very potent. States began to regulate life insurance early in the nineteenth century; by the 1860s life insurance trade associations began to rebel against strict state controls and eventually pressed for federal regulation.[11] But Congress passed the McCarran-Ferguson Act in 1945, which kept regulatory authority at the state level.

Studies of the effectiveness of state regulation of the insurance industry do not provide much comfort for the consumer. The companies' requests for rate increases are routinely approved, consumer complaints are not acted upon, and in general insurance regulators behave like the classic captured agency.[12] The insurance industry's ability to capture the regulators derives from its potency as a lobbying force, the technical nature of actuarial information, the small size of state agency budgets, and the lack of organized consumer opposition.

In response to this perceived lack of rigorous enforcement, in the 1990s some members of Congress threatened to take over insurance regulation. At the same time, the National Association of Insurance Commissioners (a group composed of the state regulators) tried to pressure states into adopting tougher and more uniform laws. They did this by denying accreditation to some states whose legislatures failed to adopt the group's model laws, which naturally annoyed the legislators.[13]

At various times consumers have revolted against the insurance companies and achieved some results. For example, in California in 1988 voters passed an initiative that forced a substantial rollback of auto insurance rates and made the insurance commissioner an elected official rather than appointed. Although companies threatened to leave the state, because the California market is so large, few have done so.

Another area marked by consumer revolt is medical malpractice. For several years both the number of malpractice lawsuits and the jury awards in those suits have increased, driving up the costs of malpractice premiums for doctors and increasing the costs of health care for consumers and employers. Legislatures in several states have responded by enacting measures to cap damages. In isolated instances, insurance companies have announced that they will no longer issue coverage in states enacting such reforms but relatively few such boycotts have occurred, sometimes because state legislatures later modified their strict regulations.

Rent Control   Approximately 200 communities since 1970 have adopted some sort of rent control on residential apartments, including Boston, Washington, D.C., Los Angeles, and San Francisco.[14] Such regulations were used historically when scarcity of housing drove rents up, as happened during World War II, placing severe hardship on people with low and fixed incomes. Today, rent controls are imposed to insulate low-income people from inflation in the housing market. Rent controls establish maximum allowable rents on certain portions of the housing stock, and they limit permissible increases. Approximately 15–20 percent of the U.S. housing stock in the rental market is subject to rent control.[15]

Proponents of rent control argue that it prevents the imposition of unfair rents; opponents claim that controls discourage investment in new rental housing and deprive landlords of the income necessary to maintain their properties in good condition.

Occupational Licensing   Another kind of equity regulation is intended to redress the disparity in information between buyer and seller. The licensing of occupations is an example: At least 1,100 different occupations are regulated by some state.[16] Every state regulates accountants, architects, attorneys, real estate agents, doctors, nurses, dentists, teachers, and barbers. A handful of states also regulate aerial crop dusters, tree surgeons, chauffeurs, tattoo artists, and elevator inspectors. Cities license plumbers and building contractors. The rationale for government intervention is that consumers do not possess enough information to evaluate the service performed. Consumers, it is thought, need government to protect them from incompetent providers. In fact, occupations have often sought government regulation in order to weed out quacks and protect competent practitioners.

The politics of occupational regulation often tends toward the capture model described previously. State commissions regulating occupations are usually small, and in many cases are composed of people from the regulated occupation. Doctors and dentists have been particularly successful in controlling the selection of their commission members. Occupational regulation is rarely a visible issue for the general public, which further increases practitioner influence. The issues are usually highly technical and specialized, not easily understood by outsiders.

Occupational regulation is not always in the interests of the regulated, however. Kenneth Meier has found that states that have active consumer groups generally have more severe regulation, as do states with competitive party systems.[17] Party and consumer group activity provide issue visibility, and they counter producer interests. To help consumer interests, 35 states have established a central agency for all licensed boards, but often it is responsible only for administrative details, with the individual boards retaining disciplinary authority. A few states, including Florida and California, have consolidated all licensing functions into one large agency; this appears to result in a more proconsumer stance because no single regulated industry can control the agency and because bureaucratic professionals make the decisions.

Labor Policies   States also regulate many aspects of the relations between workers and bosses because workers are likely to be in an inferior bargaining position. Both the federal government and the states regulate labor-management relations: The federal government sets the minimum wage, governs important aspects of union activity, and, since the Occupational Safety and Health Act of 1970, regulates workplace safety and health. The states, on the other hand, can outlaw **union shops,** have a key administrative role in Occupational Safety and Health Administration (OSHA), and operate workers' compensation programs. Let us examine each of these regulatory programs briefly.

The issue of whether a particular workplace or shop is open to any worker or only to those paying union dues (if the employees have chosen to unionize) is a critical one in the success of unions. A union shop means that labor and management can enter into a contract requiring that all workers join a union or pay its dues; obviously most potential employees will join the union in order to get a job. An open shop means that anyone can work there, in which case there is little reason to join a union. The labor movement obviously wants union shops; in 29 states they have succeeded. Management obviously prefers open shops; they have succeeded in the 21 states that have right-to-work laws. States with right-to-work laws are located primarily in the South and West. These states have lower levels of unionization than the rest of the country.

Right-to-work laws are regarded by their proponents as a way of keeping labor costs down and a way of maintaining more flexible labor-management relations. Nonunionized labor tends to earn less than union workers, even in the same industries. Because wages and fringe benefits account for the bulk of the costs that business bears, states with low labor costs are thought to be more attractive to industries looking for places to locate.

About half the states operate their own OSHA programs. The federal OSHA law allows this if the state program is at least as effective as the federal program; the federal government then provides half of the operating costs of the state agency. There is some evidence that the state-run programs are less stringent than the federal one, presumably because the threat of industry exit keeps safety regulations lax.[18] However, the federal government's own program has varied in its stringency over time, standards being especially relaxed in the Reagan administration, and states vary in their effectiveness, so a blanket comparison is hard to make.

Workers' compensation programs are entirely state-controlled and thus vary a great deal in cost and benefit levels. Before the turn of the century, employers were perceived to have little legal responsibility for injuries suffered by their employees. As industrialization proceeded, the number of industrial accidents increased dramatically and juries began to award damages to workers. Business groups reluctantly began to support a common compensation plan as a way of avoiding expensive and unpredictable court settlements.

By the end of the first decade of the twentieth century, trade unions also adopted the principle of uniform compensation as they saw laborers' settlements consumed by the cost of litigation. With the unusual support of both labor and management, compensation legislation passed rapidly through state legislatures. The first state to adopt was Montana; by 1916, 32 states had adopted, with the rest following in the late 1940s.[19] Pavalko found that the speed of adoption of these regulations was strongly influenced by the overall relationship between capital and labor and possible threats to it posed by the work-accident problem.[20] States with more manufacturing industries, with higher rates of productivity, and with more court cases from workers adopted earlier than others.

As a result of these laws employers are required to obtain insurance either privately or from the state; the insurance then pays for any awards the state makes to injured workers. The politics of workers' compensation is quite different from that of occupational regulation or utility regulation. The history of workers' compensation has been a continuous struggle between organized labor and business; the struggle's outcome depends on the balance of power between labor and business in each state. Most research confirms that the power of business lobbyists (described in Chapter 3) and the degree of unionization influence the level of benefits received.[21]

In the second half of the 1980s, workers' compensation costs doubled due to rising medical costs and litigiousness.[22] The increasing financial pressure has caused many state legislatures and governors to scrutinize the cost incurred by business. For example, in the early 1990s the governors of California and Maine brought the legislative budget process to a halt while they battled legislators over cost containment in the workers' compensation program. These costs are one of the factors included in business climate rankings. A generous workers' compensation program is presumed to drive away business and is therefore treated as a negative factor in measuring a state's business climate. Fear of having a climate hostile to business operates to reduce workers' benefits.

Tenants' Rights   Like workers vis-à-vis employers, tenants in rental housing may also be in an inferior bargaining position in relation to their landlords. Landlords may refuse to make needed repairs, they may not return rental deposits when tenants move, or they may try to evict their tenants without notice. Thus, many states and cities regulate tenant-landlord relationships. Some cities, for example, require landlords to hold rental deposits in an interest-bearing escrow account; others permit renters to withhold rent when landlords refuse to make repairs; some cities permit a tenant to back out of a lease if the property is not fit to inhabit.

Consumer Protection   As a result of the nationwide consumer movement in the 1960s inspired by Ralph Nader, consumer protection statutes and regulations exist in all states and most communities. These regulations are aimed at preventing a wide variety of offenses in the selling of products, such as auto dealers tampering with automobile odometers or selling cars that are "lemons," salespeople pushing pyramid investment schemes or time-share investments in nonexistent properties, or salespeople pressuring consumers into purchases over the phone or in their homes. A three-day "cooling off" period is now standard for in-home sales in many states. Recent legislation has been directed at high-tech sales developments such as computerized calling, junk fax, scams on the Internet, and so forth. Another active area is the labeling of food products: Some states require organic labeling, warnings about cancer-causing chemicals, nutrition information, produce dating, and maple syrup grading (in Vermont).[23]

Sigelman and Smith found that consumer protection legislation is more likely to be adopted in affluent states in moralistic political cultures with highly professional legislatures.[24] They found that California, Florida, and Hawaii had adopted the most consumer legislation and Arkansas the least. The effect of such legislation depends ultimately on the actions of attorney generals, many of whom have achieved popularity with the voters by making vigorous enforcement a hallmark of their administrations.

Regulation to Address Externalities

Many of the early economic regulations are relatively well-accepted because they keep the marketplace running smoothly or because they make contracts valid. In either case, they were perceived as useful for business. During this century, however, states and cities have moved into regulatory activities that raise more controversy. Many of these activities relate to the third purpose of regulation: to redress externalities.

Externalities are negative byproducts imposed on others as a result of someone's activities. Some examples of negative externalities are the noise your "boom box" makes at the beach, toxic and hazardous waste produced by industries, and acid rain from other states. Pollution regulations are especially controversial because they impose costs on industry. If an industry is mobile, state officials worry that it may relocate to escape strict enforcement. Thus, the decision to regulate always involves trade-offs between the costs to a small group (business) and the benefits for the whole society. Given the mobility of business, state governments do not enter the regulatory arena lightly.

Pollution Regulation Environmental legislation is a prime example of the regulation of externalities. States were the first to regulate the environment, but their policies varied widely in effectiveness and strictness due to fear of business exit. Beginning in 1970, the federal government got into the act, so much pollution legislation now is intergovernmental. Nearly every federal act has an important role for the states; states can take over the responsibility of environmental protection from the federal government if they meet certain standards. Moreover, states can usually go beyond federal minimal standards if they so choose.

Originally, states housed environmental protection programs within public health agencies; 11 states still use this structure.[25] After the establishment of the federal Environmental Protection Agency (EPA) in 1970, many states created their own "mini EPAs" that consolidate the administration of pollution control programs into a separate agency; 19 states use this method. Sixteen states administer pollution control programs through a "superagency" that combines the pollution control function with fish and wildlife management, energy and natural resources, and other functions. A few states use idiosyncratic structures. Overall, states spend less than the federal government on pollution control (about $4 billion in 1992) but their expenditures have been holding steady or slightly increasing while the federal government's have been decreasing since the Reagan years.[26] Each pollution problem is governed by different legislation so we will discuss each separately.

The problem of water pollution occurs due to discharges from both point sources—factories and cities—and nonpoint sources such as the runoff from farms, forests, and mines. Water pollution is dealt with principally by the 1972 Water Pollution Control Act Amendments and the Water Quality Act of 1987. The 1972 legislation established a national goal of fishable and swimmable waters by 1983, which has not yet been achieved. States are responsible for designating the purpose of each body of water, specifying the level of water quality for each designation, establishing plans to meet federal goals, and implementing these plans by the granting of waste discharge permits. These permits allow industrial sites and municipalities to emit waste into waterways; thus they control point sources only. The newer legislation directs states to act on nonpoint or diffuse sources of pollution using the best practices available. The 1972 act's implementation has been less controversial than other pollution laws, in part because the act also contains a big spending program for local governments. In fact, the $24 billion authorized for construction of waste treatment plants was one of the largest public works projects ever passed by Congress.[27]

The problem of air pollution involves stationary sources—factories and utilities—and mobile sources such as automobiles and trucks. Air pollution was attacked by the Clean Air Act of 1970 and its extensions in 1977 and 1990. The Clean Air Act also involves states in its implementation but is considerably more controversial than water pollution legislation. For stationary pollution, the federal government set air quality standards, established specific emissions standards for new sources of pollution, and left it up to states to draw up plans (subject to federal approval) and take action to meet those standards. Many state environmental agencies were hesitant to regulate plant emissions aggressively because they feared that firms might move to another state or close. Air pollution has an interstate dimension because acid rain from "dirty" states, principally those burning high-sulfur coal, drifts over into "clean" states and into Canada. Also controversial were the standards imposed on automobile emissions because automobile manufacturers had to meet a rigid timetable for developing new technology. But smog is a serious problem in many cities, so when federal law finally permitted it in 1990, 11 northeastern states joined California in establishing stricter standards than the federal government's.

One of the most serious environmental issues is the safe disposal of hazardous waste. Most waste that is hazardous or toxic is produced by the chemical industry. In the past, the generators of such waste disposed of it by dumping it in concealed locations. Two federal acts now regulate the disposal of hazardous waste. The first was the Resource Conservation and Recovery Act of 1976, amended in 1984, which set federal standards for the transportation and disposal of waste (the cradle-to-the-grave approach). It allowed states to develop specific plans and administer them, with the EPA's approval; 42 states have done this.

The second piece of federal legislation was the so-called Superfund bill of 1980, amended in 1986, which covers cleanup of existing sites, especially if the owners cannot be located. States are responsible for identifying the hazardous sites and for providing matching funds for cleanup. Over half the states offer incentives to reduce or recycle hazardous wastes, and most states have their own superfund statutes covering contaminated sites too small for federal designation.[28] The implementation of these statutes falters when a storage or treatment site is needed because communities react with the response "Not in My Backyard" (or the NIMBY problem).

In the last few years scholars have attempted to understand the politics of state environmental policy, usually explaining the strength or severity of state regulation. Many studies find that the balance of interest group forces—the regulated industries versus consumers—determines the severity of regulations. Evan Ringquist ranked states on the strength of their water pollution control programs and then predicted which states had strong versus weak cleanup programs.[29] He found that the single most important factor was the strength of the mining industry: States with strong mining industries develop weaker water pollution programs. However, this effect could be mitigated by the strength of agricultural interests, which worked to strengthen the cleanup programs.

Ringquist also investigated the causal factors behind state air pollution control programs. Here he found that wealthier states and those with professional legislatures have stronger control programs. Interest group effects were also significant: States with stronger polluting industries enact stronger legislation (maybe they need it more) but states heavily dependent on fossil fuels enact weaker legislation.[30]

Hazardous waste programs have been the object of research by Bruce Williams and Albert Matheny, who illuminated the pressures against strict state regulation.[31] As their dependent variable they used expenditure data, and found that state spending on regulation is lower where the polluting industries are a significant part of the state's economy. The state is unwilling to impose costs on such industries because it fears that a critical component of the economy will migrate. However, more regulatory spending occurs where proenvironment groups are strong. Thus, effective group pressure can shield lawmakers from industries' pressure.

The question of the effect of state regulations can be assessed now that pollution control programs have been in effect for more than 20 years. Air pollution abatement has worked: Air quality has improved, and it has improved most in states with strong pollution control programs.[32] Water pollution is a different matter: State regulation has not appreciably improved water quality, due to the lack of control over nonpoint sources, but at least water quality has not gotten worse.[33] Hazardous waste regulations have only been in effect for about 10 years, so less definitive assessment can be made. One study by Templet asserts that spending on pollution control results in reduction of toxic emissions.[34] Box 14.1 gives examples of several states that have effective pollution control programs.

Most people would agree that pollution control spending and enforcement have improved the environment, but many still question whether that benefit has been achieved at a very high cost to industry, a cost that might drive industries to relocate to states with laxer regulations. Empirical studies vary from those finding that environmental regulations have a small negative economic effect (reviewed in Ringquist)[35] to those finding a positive effect on a state's economy. Templet, for example, shows that high pollution levels in states are associated with lower per-capita incomes, more unemployment, and worse economic indicators.[36] He argues that cleaning up the environment is as important for business success as is maintaining the highway infrastructure.

The politics of environmental regulation, like that of workers' compensation, depends on the balance between organized groups. In the environmental arena the struggle is between groups representing business and proenvironment or public interest groups. The latter are very difficult to organize and maintain because, unlike labor unions, which have a clear stake in the workers' compensation outcome, the general public has less to gain. The benefits from joining a group to preserve a public good—clean air or water, for example—are often intangible. Thus, the effectiveness of environmental regulations is likely to erode over time unless proenvironmentalists are constantly mobilizing. It is easier for industrial interests to organize and to maintain their effectiveness. Also, the intense competition to attract mobile capital means that state officials will pay attention to essential industries. Pollution regulation at the state level is not likely to be overly harsh.

Zoning and Housing Codes   Cities also have a prime role in regulating externalities. The basis of their actions is their inherent **police power,** that is, the power to regulate private activities in order to protect the public health, safety, welfare, and morals. We have already encountered one of the most important municipal police powers, namely the power to zone land.

Zoning grew out of the English **nuisance laws,** in existence as early as Elizabethan times. City governments were allowed to ban the construction of wooden buildings (they constituted a fire hazard) and to limit the location of noxious businesses (stables and tanneries, for example). From this power it was but a short way to regulating other uses of urban land in densely populated areas, a practice that developed in Germany and England in the nineteenth century. American cities, as we have seen, adopted zoning ordinances shortly after World War I.

Zoning is clearly meant to protect the public from negative externalities that come from various sorts of private activities. Certain kinds of industry produce noxious smells or fire hazards; certain sorts of commerce bring dense traffic. Zoning laws attempt to isolate geographically activities that impose burdens on others. Thus, cities zone space for

BOX 14.1 EFFECTIVE ENVIRONMENTAL REGULATION IN THE STATES

Although stories of environmental horrors in the states have long been covered by journalists, stories of successful state efforts to remedy environmental problems often go untold. The experiences of several states that had profound environmental crises reveal that states can and do implement environmental policies that work. New Jersey, Louisiana, Iowa, and California have all confronted serious threats to their environments and show signs of effectively managing their problems.

New Jersey's environmental woes are well-known. As recently as 1988, the extent of New Jersey's environmental problem became evident when a malfunctioning sewage treatment plant necessitated the closing of several New Jersey beaches due to water contamination. Between 1980 and 1988 half of all of the federal government's funds for superfund site cleanup went to the state of New Jersey. In fact, when the federal superfund program ran out of funds in 1986, New Jersey lent the EPA money to run the federal program until it was reauthorized by Congress.[1] New Jersey's record with the superfund program speaks to the nature of its hazardous waste problem. In 1983 the state legislature passed the Environmental Responsibility Clean-Up Act, which mandated that in order for property to be sold, transferred, or closed, the site could not be toxically contaminated. By 1991, 300 such

cleanups had occurred and 475 more were in progress. Included among the cleanups conducted was a $4 million effort by the Ford Motor Company.[2] Although some have questioned this law's impact on urban revitalization, efforts by the courts to limit enforcement of the law seem to have balanced the needs of the inner city with the need to clean up toxic sites.

Along Louisiana's "Cancer Alley," state regulations have not only improved the environment but have had a positive economic effect. Between 1988 and 1992 emissions by manufacturers declined by 50 percent, and manufacturers implemented a sixfold increase in their capital outlays on pollution control.[3] These enhanced efforts at controlling toxic emissions resulted in an economic boom from Baton Rouge to New Orleans. First, the pollution control business created 14,000 new jobs directly, with another 64,000 related jobs due to increased pollution control spending.[4] In addition, investment in Louisiana increased two and one-half times between 1988 and 1992.[5] Environmental regulation in Louisiana has enhanced the quality of life along this notorious stretch of the Mississippi River by improving the environment and the economy.

In Iowa, water pollution from agricultural sources—sediment, fertilizers, herbicides, and pesticides—has been acknowledged by

industrial use, residential use, or commercial use. In many cities, for example, one may not start a business in one's home—say a beauty salon or a child-care center—without violating zoning laws.

Increasingly, the externalities produced by development affect people beyond the boundaries of the city; accordingly, several states have strengthened their role in land-use planning and growth management. Hawaii was the first state to enact a statewide land-use control law in the 1960s; in the early 1970s several states (New York, California, Oregon, Florida, and Vermont) imposed land-use controls to protect rural or scenic areas from development.[37]

environmentalists, farmers, and government officials alike. A spirit of reform has surrounded the state's efforts at environmental regulation since 1972, when the first regulations governing animal feeding operations were instituted.[6] A combination of regulation and voluntary compliance has created a situation where environmentalists have actually urged federal compliance with Iowa's higher standards.[7] Regulations on fertilizer and pesticide dealers and farmers and the creation of soil preservation districts all reflect the belief of one Iowa farmer that when it comes to the need for some regulation, "there's something to it."[8]

California has long had a problem with smog. The combination of pollution produced in cities such as Los Angeles coupled with climactic and geological features created the need for air pollution control as early as 1947, when the first air pollution district was created.[9] Air pollution in California is largely due to the 24 million vehicles that operate in the state. Since 1984, however, vigorously enforced tailpipe emissions testing has resulted in a 17 percent reduction in emissions.[10] In the Southern California Air Quality Management District, regulations on such diverse sources of emissions as oil refineries, lawnmowers, utilities, and backyard barbecues have been enacted since 1989, with positive results. Plans to reduce emissions further through such programs as commuter fees ensure that innovative policy-making in California will continue.[11]

In these four states environmental regulation has addressed serious threats to the continued vitality of the state. Although the problems and solutions in the states differ, attempts at environmental regulation have all begun to produce the desired effect. These states show that through careful public policy creation, tough but practical enforcement, and consensus over the magnitude of the problem, environmental regulation can protect natural resources.

[1]Barbara G. Salmore and Stephen A. Salmore, *New Jersey Politics and Government: Suburban Politics Comes of Age* (Lincoln: University of Nebraska Press, 1993), p. 282.

[2]*Ibid.*, p. 282.

[3]Paul H. Templet, "The Positive Relationship Between Jobs, Environment and the Economy: An Empirical Analysis and Review," *Spectrum*, 68 (Spring 1995), 43.

[4]*Ibid.*, p. 44.

[5]*Ibid.*, p. 43.

[6]William R. Lowry, *The Dimensions of Federalism: State Governments and Pollution Control Policies*, (Durham, N.C.: Duke University Press, 1992), p. 117.

[7]*Ibid.*, p. 116.

[8]*Ibid.*, p. 117.

[9]*Ibid.*, p. 92.

[10]*Ibid.*, p. 92.

[11]*Ibid.*, pp. 92–93.

A second wave of reform followed in the late 1980s and early 1990s, with Maine, Rhode Island, Delaware, New Jersey, and Maryland joining the ranks of states with broader regulations. This set of states was motivated more by the sheer magnitude of suburban growth, traffic congestion, and urban sprawl than by aesthetic concerns.[38] In most cases the state's entry into land-use planning set off a serious tussle with local officials who understandably want to retain their control over land decisions.

Closely related to zoning laws are building and housing codes. These codes are sets of standards concerning construction materials and methods, the placement of buildings on land, and the safety, health, and comfort of housing. Such regulations are designed to promote public health and safety. Building codes specify such details as the sort of pipes that may be used in residential plumbing, the nature of the wiring systems, the method of pouring cement for foundations, and the amount of space that must be left on a lot between the building and the lot line.

Housing codes regulate residential dwellings. Municipal enforcement usually focuses on rental housing. New York state's Tenement House Act of 1867 is regarded as the precursor of modern housing codes. The act called for adequate ventilation in bedrooms, banisters on staircases, one toilet for every 20 residents, and other health and safety features. Various cities used this act as a model to write their own local housing codes. Later codes focused on safety by requiring fire exits and establishing maximum occupancy standards in public places. The federal Housing Act of 1954 made funds available to cities to support the development of housing codes, and in the 1960s federal grants underwrote local code enforcement. Today building inspectors monitor everything from dilapidated front porches to lead-based paint in dwellings to radon in basements.

One of the latest trends is the effort by a number of communities, supported by the insurance industry, to impose more stringent codes to strengthen dwellings sufficiently to withstand hurricane, earthquake, and hailstorm damage. Home builders are generally opposed to these tougher codes, arguing that they will increase the cost of new housing. But local officials point out that taxpayers will save in the long run: If buildings sustain less damage in violent storms or earthquakes, the federal government will have to pay out less in disaster relief.[39]

Summary

We have outlined some of the major state and local regulatory programs aimed at maintaining efficiency in the marketplace, ensuring equity between buyers and sellers, and redressing externalities. These include programs such as electrical utility regulation, occupational licensing, consumer protection, insurance regulation, labor legislation, and environmental protection. These programs are often politically controversial because regulation involves imposing costs on some groups so that other groups (including the general public) may benefit. The small group bearing the cost (usually industry) has more incentive to organize through PACs and lobbying groups than does the general public. Consequently, enacting legislation and enforcing regulations is a battle. The desire of states to maximize their economic position relative to competitors also means that regulation is limited. In many instances, especially in the environmental area, federal regulation is necessary if problems are to be dealt with effectively.

✦ THE PROMOTION OF ECONOMIC GROWTH

A second important role for government in the economy is to promote economic development. Economic development policy can be defined as state and local government efforts to encourage new business investment in particular locales in the hopes of creating jobs and enhancing the tax base.[40] Shortly after the American Revolution, the young state governments were vigorous interveners in the private economy, providing selected infant industries with various tax breaks and subsidies to help get them going.[41] States also promoted their economies' growth through building harbors, canals, and later railroads and highways to get goods to markets. New York built the Erie Canal at a cost of $7 million; the state of Pennsylvania spent $18 million on various canals.[42] States gave the railroad companies over a quarter of the nearly 180 million acres of public lands allocated for railroad development.[43] But for most of the nineteenth century, the dominant pattern was for subnational government to play only a peripheral role in the market.

In the 1920s states began to intervene in new ways, engaging in "smokestack chasing," a mix of programs to entice major manufacturing firms to move into their state. Mississippi was one of the first to do this with its Balance Agriculture with Industry program, which lured northern industry by offering tax incentives.[44] This development spread in the 1950s so that most states had offices of economic development, which offered modest financial incentives to businesses interested in relocation.

As traditional heavy industries (such as auto and steel manufacturing) declined in the United States, the economy began to shift toward a service economy and high technology became more important. Although many states continued to seek such prizes as the huge Japanese auto plants now scattered through Tennessee, Indiana, Illinois, and Ohio, they also began to chase companies that are technologically advanced (the "chip-chasing" strategy). High-tech companies that make electronic components or do biotechnology research offer the advantage of employing white-collar workers and being competitive in the international marketplace. States have also become heavily involved in encouraging new business formation and expansion by assisting local entrepreneurs in starting their own businesses and helping them to find markets abroad for their products. This "grow your own business" strategy now coexists with industrial recruitment efforts.

Contemporary economic development policy can be divided into two main types: supply-side and demand-side policies, with the supply-side policies generally coinciding with the older industrial recruitment programs and the demand-side policies mostly coinciding with the newer development programs.[45] Increasingly, states are putting some of their development resources into a third type of policy approach, which some call third-wave strategies. This involves using state resources to build the capacity of individuals, firms, and governments to compete in the global marketplace through education and job training, industrial modernization, and planning.[46] Third-wave policies coexist with the other two.

The basic assumption behind supply-side policies is that economic growth is promoted by lowering the costs of factors in production, that is, lowering the costs of land, labor, and capital. States can subsidize a company's costs by tax breaks, location incentives, training of workers, and so forth. A company will then move to the area where its production costs are lowest.

Demand-side policies, in contrast, rest on the assumption that innovation, rather than production costs, is critical to economic growth, so the emphasis is on discovering new products, new markets, and new industries. State governments can help private enterprise by subsidizing innovation, taking on risk, reducing regulatory burdens, and supporting research, development, and education. Often the demand-side policies expand the economic pie whereas the supply-side policies work by one state raiding another. Thus, the supply-side policies have a zero-sum character to them whereas the demand-side programs have a positive-sum quality. Also, demand-side policies imply a more active intervention by government, often entailing creating new and more flexible public/private organizations to do the work, giving rise to the term *entrepreneurial state*.[47]

BOX 14.2 THE BRIDGEPORT ENTERPRISE ZONES

In July 1981, Democratic Governor William O'Neill of Connecticut signed legislation creating the first urban enterprise zones in the United States. The measure attempted to revive declining economic prospects of inner-city areas by exempting companies that relocated there from certain state taxes and regulations. Eligibility criteria for zone designation was strict. The proposed zone had to consist of two contiguous census tracts in which 25 percent of the population was below the poverty level or 25 percent or more of the population was on welfare or the unemployment rate was at least twice that of the state. Although 16 cities qualified, only 6 were chosen. The designated areas received an 80 percent local property tax abatement for 5 years, $500 or $1,000 job grants, a 50 percent state corporate tax credit for 10 years, a rate reduction for state industrial loans and industrial mortgage guarantees, and a state sales tax exemption on replacement parts. Commercial and residential properties were also eligible for a 7-year graduated tax deferral on improvements to property. Finally, all businesses could get access to job training benefits and a special venture capital loan fund.[1]

If there was ever a ideal candidate for the program, it was Bridgeport, Connecticut, which had suffered years of industrial decline. The Bridgeport Urban Enterprise office has the largest staff of any of the Connecticut zones, with three full-time employees and an annual budget of more than $150,000. Borders of the zone feature a "Welcome to the Bridgeport Enterprise Zone" street sign. Since the implementation of the two enterprise zones in Bridgeport, the city has been widely admired and studied by other states and cities as the model city for the effectiveness of enterprise zones.

Proponents of the Bridgeport enterprise zone boast that it attracted $33 million in new investments during its first 5 years.[2] More importantly, the zone is the most successful of the six zones in Connecticut in terms of creating jobs for its residents. Unemployment has fallen by 31 percent in one tract and 35 percent in the other, the greatest decline of any zone in the state. A

By the 1990s the role of the states in promoting economic growth had changed enormously from what it had been just 20 years before. The total amount of state financial assistance to business has increased dramatically and the types of government aid have expanded. We will look first at three supply-side strategies by which governments have assisted businesses and then turn to some of the newer demand-side programs. Most local economic development efforts mirror states' efforts: Many have separate departments of economic development, and they offer an array of incentives and assistance that reinforces state programs.

Supply-Side Policies

These policies are aimed at improving a state or city's ability to compete with other locations for industry by lowering the costs of doing business. They range from vague goals such as creating a "good business climate" to specific financial incentives, including tax breaks, location incentives, and debt financing. Labor policy, such as right-to-work laws and workers' compensation rates, and regulatory policy, especially pollution control, can also be policy tools in the supply-side arsenal; they were discussed earlier in the chapter.

1984 report by the New York State Legislative Commission estimated that 80 percent of the new jobs had gone to zone residents.[3]

Le Font Electronic, a telecommunications parts manufacturer, is an example of the zone's impact on Bridgeport. The company initially refurbished about 18,500 square feet in the former Singer Sewing Machine building, doubled its size a year later, and 3 years after that built a second facility, also within the zone. Le Font Electronics now employs about 120 people, most of whom live within the zone. The owner of the company, who grew up in the eastern part of Bridgeport where the zone is located, stated, "The enterprise zone was one of the things that got us to move into this site."[4]

However, not all estimates of the effectiveness of the program are as optimistic. The head of the Bridgeport program admits that at least 60 percent of the development would probably have taken place without the zone, although he credits the zone with helping to target resources more effectively and increasing confidence in the area among investors and property owners. Other studies have been even more critical. In a comparison of a zoned area with a similar but unzoned area of Bridgeport, University of Illinois professor Earl Jones found no difference in investments and rehab activity during the first two years of the program.[5] A 1986 Housing and Urban Development case study found that not one businessperson who had received zone benefits said that the benefits were "the principal motivating factor in making a particular investment decision."[6]

---

[1]William H. Miller, "Industrial Development in the Snowbelt Gets Hot," *Industry Week* (August 24, 1981), 61.

[2]David Osborne, "The Kemp Cure-All: Why Enterprise Zones Don't Work," *The New Republic*, 200, no. 14 (April 3, 1989), 22.

[3]Murphy Cait, "Connecticut; EZ Does It," *Policy Review* (Spring 1986), 68.

[4]*Ibid.*, p. 67.

[5]Osborne, "The Kemp Cure-All," p. 23.

[6]*Ibid.*, p. 23.

Tax Breaks   In Chapters 12 and 13 we outlined the major taxes states and local governments use to raise revenue and noted that businesses seek a low tax environment: low or no corporate tax, low personal income tax, and so forth. In this section we consider more specific breaks given to business. For example, states may grant an exemption for pollution-control equipment. This lowers the cost of complying with the state's pollution regulations. Exemptions for research and development or for raw materials used in manufacturing are also common. Localities may exempt a new company from the local property tax for an initial period. The latter exemption is called a tax abatement. A moratorium on taxing machinery or equipment, goods in transit, or inventories is another common option.

Location Incentives   States and localities have also traditionally offered financial assistance to businesses that will move to particular locations in their state. The simplest efforts involve a government buying a site and preparing it for industrial or commercial use. This involves the physical preparation of the site, construction of streets, installation of water and electricity lines, and even landscaping. But state and local governments also use selective incentives to entice businesses to locate in distressed areas in the hope that new businesses will spur growth in that community.

Two particular geographically targeted efforts bear special mention: enterprise zones and incubators. An enterprise zone is a defined geographic area, usually a depressed rural or urban area. Governments offer financial incentives and tax breaks in order to get industries to locate there (see Box 14.2). Thirty-seven states offer such programs.[48] The incubator is a related concept: States or local governments set up buildings in which new companies can enjoy inexpensive office and laboratory space, shared secretarial and support services, and low taxes. Once the company is up and running, it moves to its own location. At least 18 states and countless cities have these programs.

Some location incentives focus more on the labor force than on the physical site. Most states have programs that fund industrial training or retraining; some offer special tax breaks to companies that offer jobs or training for minorities. Another popular approach is to offer financial incentives, such as tax credits, to companies that create new jobs.

In the 1980s and 1990s, location incentives rocketed upward; no longer were site preparation and a few tax breaks enough to attract companies. For example, the Intel Corporation in 1992 issued a 104-item wish list to prospective bidders for its computer chip factory, including such demands as immediate resident status for its employees and their dependents (so they could receive in-state college tuition), discounts on moving expenses and mortgage costs, and other assorted goodies.[49] This new "war between the states" featured numerous attempts to attract foreign manufacturers, especially automobile manufacturers, to locate in particular states. States improved roads and sewer systems, purchased land, and provided worker training, grants, loans, and tax breaks in an effort to lure foreign investment. Sometimes the winning state's bids contained unusual elements: To land a Toyota plant, the state of Kentucky promised to provide school on Saturdays to children of Toyota employees. (In Japan children go to school six days a week, and Japanese parents did not want their children to fall behind their peers at home).

Box 14.3 describes the recent interstate competition for a Mercedes Benz plant. Experts have analyzed the costs of such competitions for the winning states and noted the dramatic escalation of costs.[50] Figure 14.1 combines several studies' results: A 1980 contest cost Tennessee $11,000 per new employee, a 1985 contest cost Kentucky $49,900 per employee, a 1992 contest cost South Carolina $68,000 per employee, and a 1993 contest cost Alabama $166,000 per job.[51] Clearly industrial recruitment became much more expensive over time, as more states vied for new foreign investment.

Interestingly enough, a study of Japanese investment decisions in the United States found that Japanese companies do not focus as much on low production costs as do domestic firms; rather, they emphasize a loyal and flexible workforce and a government that is easy to work with.[52] Thus, the cost escalation in the "car wars" may have been unnecessary. Some states have perhaps begun to realize this: Indiana won a Toyota plant in 1995 at a cost in state incentives of only about $23,000 per job.[53]

Cities were also active in business recruitment, participating in states' bids for companies and in their own efforts. One of the most striking examples of public assistance for private business occurs these days in the competition for professional sports teams. Cities (and states) put up massive sums of money to keep or lure baseball and football teams.

BOX 14.3 **MERCEDES-BENZ IN THE HEART OF DIXIE**

Alabama won the 5-month, 35-state, 100-site bidding war for the first Mercedes-Benz plant to be built in the United States with a record incentives package estimated at $250 to $300 million. The plant will produce a new four-wheel-drive sports utility vehicle and directly employ 1,500 workers as well as creating thousands of other jobs in related industries. The plant, which is scheduled to begin production in 1997, will be built on 1,000 hilly acres of pine forest about 11 miles east of Tuscaloosa.

In the beginning, the German Mercedes executives, accustomed to the strict European limits on the incentives localities can offer relocating firms, told inquiring state officials their location decision would not be affected by a bidding war. But as states started offering tax incentives, Mercedes willingly played auctioneer, playing states off one another to get the best possible deal. In the end, Alabama's incentive package was a bit richer than North and South Carolina's, although Mercedes officials said long-term operating costs in all three locations were roughly equal. "Whether you get $10 million more or less in one state doesn't make any difference," said one official. The deciding factor to locate in Alabama was Alabama's zeal. "We sensed a much higher dedication to our project," said the managing director.[1]

There was no denying the zeal shown by Alabama's government and citizens. Visiting Mercedes officials were wooed with the use of private airplanes and helicopters, as well as tours of the University of Alabama in Tuscaloosa and a concert on the university's $1 million organ.[2] The local government offered to provide a special Saturday school to keep German students up to back-home standards in science and math, paid for by state and local taxpayers and run by the university. The state legislature offered to rename a section of Interstate 20/59 the Mercedes-Benz Autobahn.[3] The University of Alabama even placed the Mercedes-Benz insignia on the top of the scoreboard during a Crimson Tide game.[4]

More importantly, Alabama offered an extraordinary array of financial incentives. They included $77.5 million to improve water, sewer, gas, and electrical services; $92.2 million to improve and develop the factory site; and $60 million to train Mercedes employees, suppliers, and workers in related industries.[5] Alabama also committed to building a $5 million welcome center for visitors to the plant, purchasing a fleet of the new Mercedes vehicles for state use, and paying workers' wages while they are in training.[6]

Many critics of the deal suggest that Alabama's deal is the latest and most egregious example of out-of-control competition for industry by state governments. In 1980, Tennessee offered incentive packages totaling $11,000 per job to induce a Nissan automobile manufacturing plant to locate in Tennessee. Not to be outdone, in 1985 Kentucky offered financial incentives worth about $50,000 per job to lure a Toyota plant to Kentucky. However, Alabama's 1993 deal with Mercedes-Benz broke all records by offering approximately $166,000 in state subsidies for each of the 1,500 expected jobs.[7]

At this price, the question arises whether the state will come out ahead. Moreover, skeptics suggest that these huge corporate subsidies are particularly perilous for a state such as Alabama, which has an educational system so deficient the state's Supreme Court ruled that it failed to provide students with the minimally adequate education guaranteed by the state constitution.

However, Alabama Governor Jim Folsom argued that the Mercedes deal was a unique opportunity to break through old stereotypes and announce to the corporate world that Alabama is open for business. Historically, Alabama has been second to last among southern states in attracting foreign business. Since the Mercedes deal, David Hutchinson, project manager at the Alabama Development Office, says he's been busier than ever. "Our activity has increased tremendously. The fact that

Continued

Mercedes located here makes some companies say, 'Hey, if they looked at them, let's look at them, too.'"[8] Many citizens apparently agree. As one local resident put it, "We probably gave away half the state, but it's probably worth it."[9]

[1]David Woodruff and John Templeman, "Why Mercedes Is Alabama Bound," *Business Week* (October 11, 1993), 138.

[2]"Mercedes in Alabama; The Invaders Are Welcome," *The Economist* (January 8, 1994), 42.

[3]Woodruff and Templeman, "Why Mercedes Is Alabama Bound," p. 138.

[4]Charles Mahtesian, "Romancing the Smokestack," *Governing* (November 1994).

[5]Peter Applebome, "South Raises Stakes in Fight for Jobs," *New York Times* (October 4, 1993), A12.

[6]Mahtesian, "Romancing the Smokestack," p.

[7]*Ibid.,* p.

[8]"Jobs at Any Price: Alabama Raises the Ante in Recruitment; Incentives Lure Businesses to Alabama," *Georgia Trend* (May, 1994), 19.

[9]"Mercedes in Alabama," p. 42.

Coors Stadium in Denver, where the Colorado Rockies play, was financed entirely by $139 million in municipal bonds. Jacobs Field in Cleveland was financed in a similar way. The baseball owners are responsible for paying off only a small part of the debt: In both those cities a county sales tax surcharge was imposed to generate revenue to cover the interest expenses.

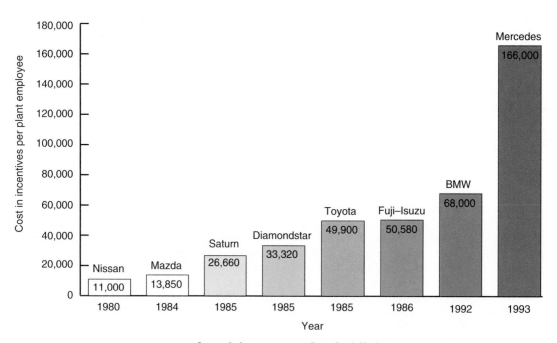

FIGURE 14.1 **The Rising Cost of Subsidizing Automotive Manufacturing Jobs.** The cost of incentives to lure automobile manufacturers has risen drastically, so that some say we have a new war between the states.

Source: H. Brinton Milward and Heidi Newman, "State Incentive Packages and the Industrial Location Decision, *Economic Development Quarterly,* 3 (August 1989), 240; and the authors' own calculations. The cost per worker of the Mercedes incentive package is based on the low estimate of $250 million in public assistance.

Governors do many things to promote economic development, such as attracting amateur and professional sporting events to the state. Here, Governor Arne Carlson, Minnesota's number-one Gopher fan, leads a rally aimed at retaining the University of Minnesota's athletic director. The effort was successful.

Debt Financing   Traditionally states have assisted business through direct low-interest loans from the state, business development corporations that make loans, loan guarantees to private lenders, or the issuance of industrial revenue bonds (IRBs). IRBs, used extensively in the early 1980s, were sold to investors and the proceeds were then lent to private firms to build new facilities or purchase new equipment. The interest on bonds issued in the name of local or state government is free of federal taxes. Because investors enjoy this tax break, they are willing to take a lower interest rate on the bonds than if the proceeds were subject to taxation. The lower interest rate translates into a lower charge for the loans to the private businesses the government is trying to help. The cost of IRBs has been borne mostly by the federal government in forgone taxes.

Local governments have also provided financial assistance to private business in the form of low-interest loans, using federal Community Development Block Grant entitlement funds. When the money is paid back, the city lends it out again to help finance other economic development projects. These revolving loan funds provide cities with a significant say in development projects.

Another common device used at the local level to help pay for local development is **tax increment financing** (TIF). This arrangement permits cities to issue bonds to help pay for a development project in the expectation that the new development will generate enough increased property tax revenue to pay off the bonds. TIF bonds may be used to finance land acquisition and clearance for a project (say, a downtown hotel and convention center) and the necessary infrastructure, such as sidewalks, new sewers, parking, and even landscaping.

Because the individual economic development programs are so small and so varied, most analysts believe that one must look at a state's overall strategy toward economic development rather than at single policies. Toward this end, Susan Clarke and Martin Saiz have computed an index for what they call locational incentives, or what we label supply-side policies.[54] As shown in Table 14.1, in 1991 the heaviest users of supply-side policies were Arizona, New Hampshire, and Tennessee. Others at the top of the scale tend to be less populated, less urbanized, and southern states that have relied on supply-side

TABLE 14.1 LOCATIONAL ECONOMIC DEVELOPMENT POLICY INDEXES Some states rely heavily on the old style, supply-side strategies to attract companies. Arizona is the most reliant on these techniques for economic development.

Rank	State	Locational Index 1991
1	Arizona	3.67
2	New Hampshire	3.60
3	Tennessee	3.30
4	Idaho	3.14
5	South Carolina	2.89
6	Rhode Island	2.85
7	Alabama	2.77
8	South Dakota	2.75
9	Kentucky	2.73
10	Oklahoma	2.70
11	New Mexico	2.67
12	Maine	2.62
13	West Virginia	2.53
14	Colorado	2.50
15	Wyoming	2.50
16	Washington	2.50
17	Virginia	2.50
18	Mississippi	2.46
19	Hawaii	2.43
20	Texas	2.42
21	Nebraska	2.36
22	Delaware	2.31
23	Vermont	2.29
24	Indiana	2.26
25	Nevada	2.25

policies in the past. Otherwise, there is little regional pattern to the use of these policies. After 1985 so many states had adopted so many of the supply-side policies that their relative effectiveness was in doubt.[55] Hence, the states began to emphasize the newer demand-side policies.

Demand-Side Policies

Beginning around 1985, states turned to developing new growth opportunities for local entrepreneurs and businesses. States made more planned and targeted interventions into the economy; they sought to expand the economic pie by enticing foreign investment and touting exports to foreign markets. In short, states became entrepreneurs. Three areas are particularly significant: high-tech development, venture capitalism, and international trade.

TABLE 14.1 (CONTINUED)

Rank	State	Locational Index 1991
26	Michigan	2.21
27	Louisiana	2.21
28	Utah	2.11
29	Connecticut	2.10
30	Iowa	2.06
31	Massachusetts	2.05
32	New Jersey	2.05
33	Illinois	2.00
34	North Dakota	2.00
35	Maryland	2.00
36	California	2.00
37	Florida	1.95
38	Pennsylvania	1.95
39	Montana	1.95
40	Alaska	1.93
41	Ohio	1.92
42	Kansas	1.92
43	North Carolina	1.90
44	Wisconsin	1.87
45	Missouri	1.80
46	Arkansas	1.75
47	Oregon	1.73
48	Georgia	1.65
49	New York	1.65
50	Minnesota	1.52

Source: Susan E. Clarke and Martin R. Saiz, "Economic Development and Infrastructure Policy," in Virginia Gray and Herbert Jacob, eds., *Politics in the American States,* 6th ed. (Washington, D.C.: CQ Press, 1996), p. 533; *Directory of Incentives for Business Investment and Development in the United States* (Washington, D.C.: The Urban Institute, 1983, 1986, 1991).

High-Tech Development State interest in attracting high-tech companies and encouraging the formation of new ones is founded on the belief that high-tech industries provide a desirable economic base, one that may replace dying traditional industries. Those that concentrate on research and development (R&D) especially tend to generate high payrolls and attract government research dollars to the area. The success of the Route 128 corridor around Boston, Silicon Valley in California, and the Research Triangle in North Carolina has inspired other states to emulate them. Because such industries are not tied to any fixed location (as, say, mining is), they are quite mobile. Therefore, states compete to attract and keep them. States have spent hundreds of millions of dollars in the last decade on high-tech programs. In 1988 alone, 43 states allocated $550 million for research centers, research grants, and venture capital for new high-tech companies and incubators.[56]

Because high-tech companies are knowledge-intensive, a key element in attracting high-tech industries is the presence of good universities that train top-flight scientists and engineers. It is the combination of scientific research in university labs and high-tech applications in the workplace that transforms the economy. Thus, a state's brainpower has become a significant factor in interstate economic competition. One result may be an increase in state funding for some kinds of university-based research. The Utah legislature, for example, appropriated $5 million in 1989 to support cold fusion research (the nuclear reaction in a jar), even though the commercial significance of this controversial development had not yet been demonstrated.[57] At least 30 states have established biotechnology research centers, usually at universities, whose average annual budget is around $2.5 million.[58]

One of the best examples of a state betting its future on high technology is Pennsylvania, which spent almost $50 million on science and technology efforts in 1988.[59] Its Ben Franklin Partnership is a collaborative arrangement among universities, private firms, economic development groups, and state government; it is administered through four advanced technology centers located in different regions of the state. The partnership provides funds for business incubators, a venture capital fund, small-business seed grants, grants to engineering schools, and a R&D program. Their emphasis is on enhancing the competitiveness of existing firms and encouraging the development of new firms rather than "chip chasing."

Entrepreneurial activity in high-tech areas is inherently risky and takes a long time because many of the processes are just being invented. Thus, their commercial application is unknown, as is their profitability. It is definitely investment in the future.

Venture Capitalism The latest innovation in debt financing is the state-sponsored venture capital program. *Venture capital* refers to making an equity investment in high-risk companies in the early stage of the business life cycle. Many such firms are high-tech businesses or small businesses that find it hard to obtain capital from standard banking sources. The argument for state intervention is that the new firms promise to tap or create expanding markets, thus justifying state assistance. The potential downside is that the state takes on considerable financial risk if the fledgling company does not survive. In 1991, 17 states had a total of 23 programs of one sort or another to invest public funds (for example, legislative appropriations or bond proceeds) in new businesses; the investment totaled about $180 million.[60] In addition, 21 states had invested their public employee pension funds in venture capital funds; these investments are larger, perhaps close to $1 billion.[61] States that have vigorously pursed venture capital programs include Michigan, Massachusetts, and Connecticut.

International Trade and Investment In an effort to expand the economic pie, state and local governments have turned their attention outside the United States, both to lure foreign investment here and to stimulate export trade. Attracting foreign investors was described earlier; on the export front state governments are involved in arranging or offering financing, targeting specific industries for export promotion assistance, doing market feasibility studies for interested companies, and reducing the complexities for businesses seeking to sell their products abroad. This assistance is particularly critical in emerging markets such as Eastern Europe and the former Soviet Union.

Efforts to foster export to new overseas markets and to attract trade and investment from outside a state's boundaries increased dramatically in the 1980s, with the focus shifting to export promotion after 1985.[62] Some of this money goes to support 112 state trade offices maintained by 41 states in locations that range from Tokyo and Hong Kong to Frankfurt and Brussels to Lagos and Mexico City.[63] These state "embassies" advertise goods made in their states, seek out potential buyers, and promote their states as places in which foreign companies might wish to invest and as places tourists might like to visit.

State overseas trade offices are not the only way that states try to promote local products for the export market and attract foreign companies. Every year more than half the nation's governors lead trade delegations abroad. Governors have become the chief salespeople for their states' firms, touting everything from costume jewelry (from Rhode Island) to porcelain bathroom fixtures (from Wisconsin). Governors and mayors are also major recruiters of foreign companies looking for locations in the United States.

Local governments are nearly as active as the states in the international arena. Over 80 percent of all cities over 150,000 in population are engaged in economic development programs that have an overseas component. One analyst found in a survey that 25 percent of these cities have their own overseas trade offices, 34 percent have participated in foreign trade missions or trade fairs, and 30 percent include foreign investment or trade as part of their economic development plan.[64] The city of San Jose provides a typical example: It established a Center for International Trade and Development in 1988 with an appropriation of $350,000 from the city treasury. Its purpose is to promote foreign investment in San Jose, develop export possibilities for local firms, and promote marketing and licensing arrangements between San Jose firms and firms overseas.[65]

States' reliance on entrepreneurship can best be seen by a summary measure rather than a listing of single policies. In Table 14.2 is a ranking of the states' use of demand-side policies in 1991 (called entrepreneurial orientation by the authors Clarke and Saiz). Minnesota, New York, and North Carolina place the greatest emphasis on this newer approach, whereas Arizona has no entrepreneurial programs. Overall, the states increased their reliance on demand-side approaches, with the index increasing by 34 percent between 1986 and 1991.[66] There is no seeming regional pattern to the use of the newer strategies. Many states overlay the two approaches, adding demand-side policies to their policy arsenal rather than getting rid of supply-side policies.

In making economic policy decisions, states often rely on a strategic plan for the state economy in which planners establish economic goals, evaluate a state's economic strengths and weaknesses, and target particular industries for special assistance. The plan is an attempt to establish a **comparative advantage** in national and international markets by building on the state's particular economic strengths. Thus, for example, the state of Pennsylvania targeted nine advanced technologies and pledged to "give young, small advanced technology industries special consideration in all state technical and financial assistance programs."[67] Other states target everything from forest products (Wisconsin) to telemarketing (Nebraska) to furniture manufacture (California) to tourism (Hawaii). By 1989, 37 states had written strategic plans.

TABLE 14.2 ENTREPRENEURIAL ECONOMIC DEVELOPMENT POLICY INDEXES   Some states rely heavily on the new style, demand-side strategies to attract investment. Minnesota is the leader in using this style of economic development.

Rank	State	Entrepreneurial Index 1991
1	Minnesota	2.57
2	New York	2.51
3	North Carolina	2.50
4	Arkansas	2.38
5	Pennsylvania	2.36
6	Georgia	2.29
7	Massachusetts	2.29
8	Oregon	2.27
9	Missouri	2.17
10	New Jersey	2.14
11	North Dakota	2.00
12	Florida	1.95
13	Alaska	1.93
14	Ohio	1.92
15	Montana	1.80
16	Kansas	1.79
17	Wisconsin	1.73
18	Michigan	1.71
19	Vermont	1.71
20	Illinois	1.69
21	Maryland	1.67
22	Connecticut	1.65
23	Utah	1.56
24	Delaware	1.54
25	Iowa	1.50
26	Nevada	1.50

The Politics of State Economic Development Policy

Political scientists have been interested in explaining the policy choices states make in the economic development policy area. Because location incentives and other supply-side strategies have diffused rather widely across the states, most analytic attention has focused on why states adopt demand-side or entrepreneurial strategies. A study by Virginia Gray and David Lowery found that states adopting more entrepreneurial policies in the mid-1980s shared certain political, governmental, and economic characteristics.[68] They were states that had experienced economic stress in the early 1980s, states with more balanced interest group systems (where business does not dominate), with competitive political parties, and strong governmental capacity. These states (Michigan and Indiana, for example) had both the political will and the governmental means to attack their economic problems. Other scholars have found that political culture makes a difference as well.[69]

TABLE 14.2 (CONTINUED)

Rank	State	Entrepreneurial Index 1991
27	Nebraska	1.45
28	Indiana	1.42
29	Louisiana	1.37
30	West Virginia	1.35
31	Maine	1.31
32	Virginia	1.30
33	Washington	1.20
34	Kentucky	1.18
35	California	1.17
36	Mississippi	1.15
37	Hawaii	1.14
38	Wyoming	1.00
39	Rhode Island	1.00
40	South Carolina	1.00
41	Texas	0.92
42	Alabama	0.92
43	Colorado	0.92
44	Oklahoma	0.80
45	South Dakota	0.75
46	New Mexico	0.67
47	Tennessee	0.50
48	Idaho	0.43
49	New Hampshire	0.40
50	Arizona	0.00

Source: Susan E. Clarke and Martin R. Saiz, "Economic Development and Infrastructure Policy," in Virginia Gray and Herbert Jacobs, eds., *Politics in the American States*, 6th ed. (Washington, D.C.: CQ Press, 1996), p. 535. Computed from program descriptions in Urban Institute et al., *Directory of Incentives for Business Investment and Development in the United States* (Washington, D.C.: The Urban Institute, 1983, 1986, 1991).

The Effects of Economic Development Policies

Clearly a lot of money has been spent in efforts to improve states' economies. It would be helpful to know whether economic performance has improved as a result. That question is very difficult to answer because it involves careful measurement of the costs of a variety of programs and the actual economic outcome of those programs: the jobs created, the new firms started, the additional business attracted. It is not surprising that different studies come up with varying estimates of the impact of development policies. Early studies evaluated the effects of traditional supply-side policies (location incentives and so forth) and concluded that they are often ineffective. But Bartik's careful review of a large number of studies concludes that "state and local policies can have significant effects on local growth." Specifically, reducing state and local taxes by 10 percent increases business activity, all things being equal, by about 2.5 percent. But for this equation to hold, public services must remain as good as they were before the tax cut.[70]

More recent studies focus on newer demand-side policies that try to generate new investment and demand. For example, Paul Brace finds that state policies have a modest effect on economic growth, particularly policies put in place after the mid-1980s, the time when states began to adopt entrepreneurial programs.[71] Brace's careful empirical work lends support to Eisinger's argument that these newer policies do work on a modest scale, stimulating new investment that leads in most cases to new jobs.[72]

It is essential to understand that public economic development efforts are very small relative to private investment and thus the effects are tiny.[73] For example, in 1989 the amount of private venture capital was 170 times the amount of public venture capital.[74] Thus, publicly financed development efforts have only a marginal effect on economic growth. Economic development policy can best be understood as indicative of a general commitment on state government's part to a probusiness climate. Such commitment can then give private investors the confidence to expend their capital.

In addition to the economic costs and benefits of development policies, the political benefits and costs can be significant as well. Economic conditions of the early 1980s placed enormous pressure on state officials, particularly governors, to do something about the economy. Therefore, the appearance of activity by governors is necessary, whether or not it is successful. If a governor lands a new plant, it may well help at the polls next time. If a state loses a competition, there is pressure on the governor and legislature to change policies before the next race: to lower taxes, to improve the educational system, or to increase the incentive package. There is understandably a tendency for the governor to up the ante, leading to the escalation in the cost of incentive packages reflected in Figure 14.1.

Many people feel that the states collectively have overinvested in economic development programs because of the potential political payoff. Some of this feeling derives from the sheer magnitude of the incentive packages in an era of limited finances; as a result, in the 1990s many states are reducing their budgets of their economic development offices, and some programs have been terminated.[75] The governors have agreed among themselves to stop the escalation of bidding; in 1993 the National Governors' Association declared a truce in the bidding wars. It remains to be seen whether that works.

Some of the criticism leveled at economic development efforts derives from the fact that plants recently lured at great expense sometimes fail to live up to their promises or even go out of business entirely. For example, the Anchor-Hocking Glass Company received a range of location incentives to locate in Clarkesburg, West Virginia. It was taken over by another corporation, which decided to close the plant. In 1987 the state of West Virginia sued and won an out-of-court settlement giving the state the right to sell the plant.[76] In 1992 the state of Minnesota agreed to a mammoth package of loans, grants, and tax breaks so that its local airline, Northwest Airlines, would site a maintenance facility on the depressed Iron Range. Then on the verge of bankruptcy, the airline took the money but did not build the center; now financially healthy, it finally built the facility in mid-1996.

States have fought back by enacting a variety of protective laws, including "clawbacks" (which require a publicly subsidized firm not achieving its employment targets to pay back some of the subsidy), plant-closing laws, right-to-know laws (which evaluate the potential costs and benefits of a plant), and public participation laws. But these laws are hard to enforce, and ultimately there is little a state can do to make a company be profitable; for instance, Minnesota is reluctant to move against its only major airline.

Now some have turned to Congress to stop the bidding for business. Economists Burstein and Rolnick have called for Congress to invoke the Commerce Clause against states and cities that engage in bidding, prohibiting them from using subsidies and preferential taxes to compete with one another.[77] Others point out that international agreements such as GATT (General Agreement on Tariffs and Trade) and especially NAFTA (North American Free Trade Agreement) will also restrict export promotion programs, state tax policy, and environmental regulations.[78] Overall, it seems that economic development policy has reached a contentious phase in which no one is satisfied.

✧ CONCLUSION

States and cities have become increasingly involved in shaping their economies. Many subnational governments face real constraints: scarce water, a harsh climate, a remote location, an unproductive labor force, and so forth. Whatever its liabilities, each government faces an imperative to develop its economy to its fullest potential, to be a "smart" state or city. The competition among states became intense as the national and worldwide economies deteriorated in the early 1980s.

A traditional role for states and cities was to regulate the economy in cases of market failure: when monopolies threaten efficiency, when marketplace transactions are inequitable, or when industrial byproducts harm public goods such as clean air and water. The politics of regulation is often fierce because it involves the imposition of costs on some person or firm. Because capital is mobile, there is always the fear that businesses will move out of state to escape severe regulation. Thus, states find it hard to enforce strict regulations.

A second role for government in the economy is a promotional and developmental one. We discussed traditional supply-side programs such as tax breaks, location inducements, and various means of debt financing. We also described newer demand-side programs such as high-tech development, venture capitalism, and international trade. It is this role that has changed the most. States have become more activist and entrepreneurial. A more activist posture has been politically beneficial for governors, making economic development popular among politicians, and has yielded some economic benefits as well.

✧ KEY TERMS

capture theory (p. 358)   positive-sum (p. 356)
comparative advantage (p. 380)   public goods (p. 357)
efficiency (p. 357)   right-to-work laws (p. 356)
equity (p. 357)   tax increment financing (p. 375)
externalities (p. 357)   union shops (p. 360)
nuisance laws (p. 365)   venture capital (p. 356)
police power (p. 365)   zero-sum game (p. 356)

✧ FOR FURTHER READING

Paul Brace, *State Government & Economic Performance* (Baltimore: John Hopkins University Press, 1993). Reports on a statistical analysis of the impact of state policy on economic growth; also presents four case studies of selected state interventions.

Peter K. Eisinger, *The Rise of the Entrepreneurial State* (Madison: University of Wisconsin Press, 1988). A comprehensive examination of state and local development policy. Contrasts traditional supply-side policies with newer demand-oriented efforts. Shows how government involvement in the economy has changed.

R. Scott Fosler, ed., *The New Economic Role of American States: Strategies in a Competitive World Economy* (New York: Oxford University Press, 1988). Describes states' new activist role in economic development and industrial policy. Focuses on selected states that have successfully improved their economies.

Kenneth J. Meier and E. Thomas Garman, *Regulation and Consumer Protection,* 2nd ed. (Houston: Dame Publications, 1995). An introduction to regulatory policies in seven key areas, covering both federal and state activities.

Evan J. Ringquist, *Environmental Protection at the State Level* (Armonk, N.Y.: M.E. Sharpe, 1993). A statistical analysis of the politics of air and water pollution regulation by state governments and of the outcomes of such regulation.

✧ NOTES

1. Paul Peterson, *City Limits* (Chicago: University of Chicago Press, 1981).

2. *Ibid.*, p. 24.

3. Melvin Burstein and Arthur Rolnick, "Congress Should End the Economic War Among the States," *Federal Reserve Bank of Minneapolis, 1994 Report* (Minneapolis: Federal Reserve Bank, 1994), p. 3.

4. Adam Smith, *An Inquiry into the Nature and Causes of the Wealth of Nations, Vol. II* (London: W. Strahan & T. Cadell, 1776).

5. Alan Stone, *Regulation and Its Alternatives* (Washington, D.C.: Congressional Quarterly Press, 1982).

6. Bruce Williams, "Bounding Behavior: Economic Regulation in the American States," in Virginia Gray, Herbert Jacob, and Kenneth Vines, eds., *Politics in the American States: A Comparative Analysis*, 4th ed. (Boston: Little, Brown, 1983), p. 350.

7. *Ibid.*

8. William Berry, "Utility Regulation in the States: The Policy Effects of Professionalism and Salience to the Consumer," *American Journal of Political Science*, 23 (May 1979), 263–277.

9. William T. Gormley, Jr., *The Politics of Public Utility Regulation* (Pittsburgh: University of Pittsburgh Press, 1983).

10. Jon Teaford, *The Municipal Revolution in America* (Chicago: University of Chicago Press, 1975), Ch. 2.

11. Bruce Williams, "Economic Regulation and Environmental Protection," in Virginia Gray and Herbert Jacob, eds., *Politics in the American States*, 6th ed. (Washington, D.C.: CQ Press, 1996), p. 496.

12. *Ibid.*, p. 497.

13. Michael Quint, "A Battle Over Regulating Insurers," *New York Times* (July 29, 1994), D1, D5.

14. Anthony Downs, *Residential Rent Controls: An Evaluation* (Washington, D.C.: Urban Land Institute, 1988), p. 1.

15. Robert Arnott, "Time for Revisionism on Rent Control?," *Journal of Economic Perspectives*, 9 (Winter 1995), 99–120.

16. Pamela L. Brinegar and Kara L. Schmitt, "State Occupational and Professional Licensure," in *Book of the States, 1992–93, Vol. 29* (Lexington, Ky.: Council of State Governments, 1992), pp. 567–572.

17. Kenneth J. Meier, *Regulation* (New York: St. Martin's Press, 1985), pp. 193–194; see also Kenneth J. Meier and E. Thomas Garman, *Regulation and Consumer Protection*, 2nd ed. (Houston: Dame Publications, 1995), Ch. 3.

18. Meier and Garman, *Regulation and Consumer Protection*, Ch. 8.

19. Eliza K. Pavalko, "State Timing of Policy Adoption: Workmen's Compensation in the United States, 1909–1929," *American Journal of Sociology*, 95 (November 1989), 593–594.

20. *Ibid.*, p. 607.

21. Williams, "Bounding Behavior."

22. Jeffrey L. Katz, "Workers' Comp: Ready for Prime Time," *Governing* (September 1991), 25.

23. W. John Moore, "Stopping the States," *National Journal* (July 21, 1990), 1758–1762.

24. Lee Sigelman and Roland E. Smith, "Consumer Legislation in the American States: An Attempt at Explanation," *Social Science Quarterly*, 61 (June 1980), 58–70.

25. Evan J. Ringquist, *Environmental Protection at the State Level* (Armonk, N.Y.: M. E. Sharpe, 1993).

26. *Ibid.*, p. 20.

27. William R. Lowry, *The Dimensions of Federalism: State Governments and Pollution Control Policies* (Durham, N.C.: Duke University Press, 1992), p. 59.

28. *Ibid.*, p. 129; Charles E. Davis, *The Politics of Hazardous Waste* (Englewood Cliffs, N.J.: Prentice-Hall, 1993), p. 99.

29. Ringquist, *Environmental Protection at the State Level*.

30. *Ibid.*

31. Bruce A. Williams and Albert R. Matheny, "Testing Theories of Social Regulation: Hazardous Waste Regulation in the American States," *Journal of Politics*, 46 (1984), 428–458.

32. Ringquist, *Environmental Protection at the State Level*, p. 150.

33. *Ibid.*, p. 191.

34. Paul H. Templet, "The Positive Relationship Between Jobs, Environment and the Economy: An Empirical Analysis and Review," *Spectrum*, 68 (Spring 1995), 37–49.

35. Ringquist, *Environmental Protection at the State Level*, p. 25.

36. Templet, "The Positive Relationship Between Jobs, Environment and the Economy," p. 41.

37. William Fulton, "In Land-Use Planning, A Second Revolution Shifts Control to the States," *Governing* (March 1989), 40–45.

38. Robert Guskind and Neal R. Peirce, "Jammed in Jersey," *National Journal* (April 23, 1988), 1072–1074.

39. Michael Quint, "Storm Over Housing Codes," *New York Times* (December 1, 1995).

40. Peter Eisinger, *The Rise of the Entrepreneurial State: State and Local Economic Development Policy in the United States* (Madison: University of Wisconsin Press, 1988), pp. 3–4.

41. Oscar Handlin and Mary Handlin, *Commonwealth: A Study of the Role of Government in the American Economy: Massachusetts, 1774–1861*, rev. ed. (Cambridge, Mass.: The Belknap Press of Harvard University Press, 1969).

42. Paul Brace, *State Government and Economic Performance* (Baltimore: Johns Hopkins Press, 1993), p. 19.

43. Susan Clarke and Martin Saiz, "Economic Development and Infrastructure Policy," in Virginia Gray and Herbert Jacob, eds., *Politics in the American States*, 6th ed. (Washington, D.C.: CQ Press, 1996), p. 522.

44. Brace, *State Government and Economic Performance*, p. 25.

45. Eisinger, *The Rise of the Entrepreneurial State*.

46. Peter Eisinger, "State Economic Development in the 1990s: Politics and Policy Learning," *Economic Development Quarterly*, 9 (May 1995), 146–158.

47. Eisinger, *The Rise of the Entrepreneurial State*, uses this term.

48. Robert Guskind, "Zeal for the Zones," *National Journal* (June 3, 1989), 1358.

49. Charles Mahtesian, "Romancing the Smokestack," *Governing* (November 1994), 37.

50. H. Brinton Milward and Heidi Hosbach Newman, "State Incentive Packages and the Industrial Location Decision," *Economic Development Quarterly*, 3 (August 1989), 203–222.

51. Charles J. Spindler, "Winners and Losers in Industrial Recruitment: Mercedes-Benz and Alabama," *State and Local Government Review*, 26 (Fall 1994), 202.

52. Peter B. Doeringer and David G. Terkla, "Japanese Direct Investment and Economic Development Policy," *Economic Development Quarterly*, 6 (August 1992), 255–272.

53. *New York Times* (November 30, 1995).

54. Susan E. Clarke and Martin R. Saiz, "Economic Development and Infrastructure Policy," in Virginia Gray and Herbert Jacob, eds., *Politics in the American States*, 6th ed. (Washington, D.C.: CQ Press, 1996), p. 533.

55. Don Sherman Grant II, Michael Wallace, and William D. Pitney, "Measuring State-Level Economic Development Programs, 1970–1992," *Economic Development Quarterly*, 9 (May 1995), 134–145.

56. Minnesota Office of Science and Technology, *State Technology Programs in the United States, 1988* (Minneapolis: Minnesota Office of Science and Technology, 1988), p. 2.

57. William Schmidt, "Utah, Thinking of Fusion, Dreams of Gold," *New York Times* (April 21, 1989), p. A1, A18.

58. Ann Pelham, "States Scurry to Cash In on Biotech Bonanza," *Governing*, 2 (October 1988), 68–79.

59. Dianne Rahm and Thomas F. Luce, Jr., "Issues in the Design of State Science-and-Technology-Based Economic Development Programs: The Case of Pennsylvania's Ben Franklin Partnership," *Economic Development Quarterly*, 6 (February 1992), 41.

60. Peter Eisinger, "State Venture Capitalism, State Politics, and the World of High-Risk Investment," *Economic Development Quarterly*, 7 (May 1993), 131–139.

61. Peter Eisinger, "The State of State Venture Capitalism," *Economic Development Quarterly*, 5 (February 1991), 70.

62. Renee J. Johnson, "Government Influence on Economic Development: The Case of State Export Promotion Programs," paper presented at the annual meeting of the Midwest Political Science Association, Chicago, April 1995, p. 1

63. National Association of State Development Agencies, *State Export Program Database* (Washington, D.C.: NASDA, 1988), p. 35.

64. Robert Maffin, "Local Government in the International Arena: The Federal System in a Global Economy," report prepared for the Advisory Commission on Intergovernmental Relations, Washington, D.C., October 1989.

65. *Ibid.*, p. 19.

66. Clarke and Saiz, "Economic Development and Infrastructure Policy," p. 536.

67. Quoted in Peter Eisinger, "Do the American States Do Industrial Policy?," *British Journal of Political Science*, 20 (October 1990), 517.

68. Their term was *industrial policy*, which is equivalent to our usage here of *demand-side* or *entrepreneurial policy*; see Virginia Gray and David Lowery, "The Corporatist Foundations of State Industrial Policy," *Social Science Quarterly*, 71 (March 1990), 3–24.

69. Russell L. Hanson, "Political Cultural Variations in State Economic Development Policy," *Publius*, 21 (Spring 1991), 63–81.

70. Tim Bartik, *Who Benefits from State and Local Economic Development Policies?* (Kalamazoo, Mich.: Upjohn Institute, 1991), p. 205.

71. Brace, *State Government and Economic Performance*, p. 111.

72. Eisinger, *The Rise of the Entrepreneurial State*, pp. 338–339. But a recent analysis of entrepreneurial/industrial policy indicates that the economic growth gains may be short-lived; see David Lowery and Virginia Gray, "The Compensatory Impact of State Industrial Policy: An Empirical Assessment of Midterm Effects," *Social Science Quarterly*, 76 (June 1995), 438–446.

73. The findings cited above pertain only to the specific development policies already discussed; the general effect of state fiscal and taxation policies on state economic growth is well-established in the literature; see Bartik, *Who Benefits from State and Local Economic Development Policies?* Brace, *State Government and Economic Performance*.

74. Eisinger, "The State of State Venture Capitalism," p. 68.

75. Eisinger, "State Economic Development in the 1990s," pp. 146–158.

76. Alan H. Peters, "Clawbacks and the Administration of Economic Development Policy in the Midwest," *Economic Development Quarterly*, 7 (November 1993), 328–340.

77. Burstein and Rolnick, "Congress Should End the Economic War Among the States," pp. 3–20.

78. Benjamin J. Jones, "The Effects of Free Trade Agreements on State Sovereignty," *The Book of the States 1994–95* (Lexington, Ky.: Council of State Governments, 1994), pp. 616–621.

15

PUBLIC WORKS, INFRASTRUCTURE, AND HOUSING POLICY

Periodically, major lapses in the maintenance of physical infrastructure make front-page news: In 1992 the people of Chicago were deluged by 250 million gallons of river water that entered through a break in the tunnel system, causing $1 billion in property damage and shutting down the city core for several days. All of this happened because city crews failed to do a $10,000 patch-up job.[1] In California in 1989 an earthquake crumbled bridges and buckled roads, disrupting the travel patterns of an estimated 1 million drivers for nearly a year.[2] The transportation repairs alone cost $300 million. At least some of the massive damage was attributed to California's neglect of its infrastructure since the imposition of tax limits in the 1970s.

Providing and maintaining the public works infrastructure that makes modern economic and social life possible is a major responsibility of government. Public works infrastructure is the various physical installations that support community development and commerce and enhance health and safety.[3] The provision of public infrastructure, including highways and roads, water and sewer systems, ports and airports, mass transit, convention centers, and libraries is a shared government function in the United States.

Federal, state, and local governments build the highways and roads that connect marketplaces, they finance and manage wastewater treatment facilities and provide clean water essential to health, and they share responsibility for airports and mass transit systems that move people and goods around the country. Although *infrastructure* has traditionally meant physical facilities, today the term also encompasses technological infrastructure involved in communication systems, computer networks, and the Information Superhighway.

Governments also play a role in regulating the private housing market and in providing housing subsidies for the middle class and the poor. The housing stock is a key part of the physical setting of economic and social transactions, and the health of the housing market is crucial to the health of the national economy.

Transportation facilities have long been accepted government responsibilities, but housing as a public function is a comparatively new idea in the United States. Although Americans have been accustomed to debating the public role in infrastructure development at least since the Gallatin report of 1808, which recommended the creation of a federally financed national road network, the public provision of housing dates only to the 1930s. Even today, the overwhelming preponderance of housing in the United States has been built and financed by the private sector.

The politics of infrastructure and housing often revolves around the distribution and location of facilities and who should pay for them: Where should the highway be located? Who should pay for the bus system or the sewage treatment plant? Should housing for the poor be a federal or local responsibility, or one left entirely to the private sector? We begin with transportation systems, the most visible and expensive form of infrastructure.

✧ TRANSPORTATION

Transportation is literally the means by which people exercise their exit options, but it is more than this. The means of transportation and the infrastructure to support it shape the urban space we live in and influence our national and regional economic growth patterns and prospects.

History of Transportation

Transportation in the United States has evolved as technology has changed. The earliest forms of interstate and interurban transportation were labor-intensive and relied on human or animal power. Turnpikes, canals, and riverboats were the major forms of transit in the first half of the nineteenth century. We noted in Chapter 14 that the development and costs of these early transportation systems were shared among private investors and all levels of government. Federal aid came through the land-grant mechanism and assistance from the Army Corps of Engineers. Cities grew at key transfer points along rivers and canals.

Transportation within cities in the early part of the republic was also by foot or animal. To move from home to work on foot or horseback in an efficient way required a fairly compact settlement pattern. Historians refer to these young urban communities as walking cities. The first mass-transit system (defined as transportation along a fixed route according to a fixed schedule at a fixed fare and open to the public)[4] appeared in 1827 with the introduction of a horse-drawn omnibus operating on Broadway in New York.

By the middle of the nineteenth century, the introduction of the railroad helped cities and metropolitan areas to expand in size and helped isolated rural regions to grow. Within cities, horse-drawn street railways, beginning in 1832, displaced the slower and much bumpier omnibuses that rolled over granite and stone pavement. This was the beginning of urban mass transit. Intercity rail developed at rapid rate in the years around the Civil War: In 1850 there were only about 9,000 miles of track in the United States. By 1870 this had increased to 52,922, and by 1900 the figure had risen to 258,784.[5] Long-distance railroads created new cities and drew traffic away from riverfront locations.

Historians believe, for example, that Chicago's vigorous efforts to attract railroads permitted it to surpass other midwestern cities, such as St. Louis and Cincinnati, that still relied primarily on river transport.

Commuter railroads also developed in this period, enabling the wealthy to live outside the cities in new suburban communities and still travel on a daily basis into town. Towns along the Philadelphia Main Line and along Lake Michigan north of Chicago were literally created by the railroads, ensuring a steady customer base of commuters.

In the early twentieth century the invention of the automobile marked a third major change. Very substantial capital outlays were required to build roads. Again the new forms of transit changed the positions of cities: The construction of highways that led from the countryside to downtown allowed car owners to live outside the city but commute easily to work, thus stimulating the beginning of mass suburbanization. Perhaps the biggest stimulus to suburban settlement came with the Highway Act of 1956, which authorized the construction of the interstate highway system. Nearly one-fifth of the nearly 43,000-mile highway network consists of ring roads or arterial freeways into the city centers. Although mayors and traffic planners supported the construction of these bypasses and freeways to ease traffic congestion, they did not anticipate that people would exercise their exit option, fleeing the cities for the suburbs beyond. It is no coincidence that many of the older cities of the Northeast and Midwest reached their population peaks in 1950. By the 1960 census the flight from the cities, facilitated by the interstate highways, was well under way.

The interstate highway system literally reshaped America. No understanding of American migration and settlement patterns is complete without acknowledging the impact of this highway network. Not only did it facilitate suburbanization, but it opened up regions of the country that were previously remote and inaccessible. Interstate highways opened remote parts of the South to truck traffic, facilitating the industrialization of that part of the country. The mass migration in the postwar years of job-seekers and retirees to Arizona, Texas, and Florida is, according to some historians, inconceivable without the interstates.[6]

By mid-century the growth of the commercial aviation industry further changed the means of transit. The ability to travel coast-to-coast in a few hours has contributed greatly to the nationalization of the economy, the reduction in regional cultural and economic differences, and the willingness of industry to shift locations and to spread branch plants across the land.

Highways

The introduction of each new form of transportation has required some degree of government subsidy, with highways probably receiving the most. Our discussion of transportation concentrates on the highway system because it continues to be an important responsibility of state and local governments, constituting about 70 percent of all public transportation expenditures.[7] A highway system consists of interstate highways, primary roads (which connect urban centers), secondary roads (which carry farmers' products to market), and tertiary roads in urban areas (that is, city streets).

Creating a network of smooth, durable roads through the forests and across the plains, deserts, mountains, and rivers of America was a monumental undertaking. The first comprehensive federal survey of roads in the United States, which took place in 1904, found slightly over 2.1 million miles of road, but all but about 150,000 miles were simply dirt (or mud) paths through the countryside. The remaining "improved" roads were surfaced with gravel, shells, or wooden planks. The first cement highway was not constructed until 1908.[8] Political pressure to build good roads swelled as more and more Americans bought automobiles. In 1905 some 78,000 cars were registered; in just two decades the figure rose to 23 million.[9]

Most financing for highways came from state and local funds. In 1891 New Jersey became the first state to appropriate money from general revenues for highway construction. Just after World War I, however, states began to enact gasoline taxes to pay for the new roads, and by 1929 every state depended on such a levy. The first major federal contribution to road building came with the 1916 Federal Highway Act. Widely known as the get-the-farmer-out-of-the-mud act, the law provided federal grants to build farm-to-market roads in rural areas. On the eve of the Great Depression, federal highway grants under this program constituted by the far the largest share of all federal intergovernmental grants.

Federal highway spending took a huge jump with the passage of the Federal Highway Act of 1956, which authorized construction of the interstate system. Washington provided 90 percent of the cost of this huge project, drawing mainly on a trust fund derived from a tax on gasoline and tires. States paid the remaining 10 percent. But state highway responsibilities are far greater than their share of interstate construction and maintenance. They finance most primary roads (state highways) and allocate money to counties for their roads.

State expenditures for highways and roads are sizable: It is the third largest item in the state budget, after education and welfare, and tied with health and hospitals. In 1992 state highway spending averaged 8 percent of the budget. Some states spend more than others, of course. Mountainous states and states with sparse populations spend a lot just to maintain their extensive highway systems. Highways are crucial to linking the widely spread populations of these thinly populated states. Generally, rural states are big spenders on highways and urban states are low spenders because of these physical differences and because urban states have to spend more on education and welfare (see Table 15.1). Highways, therefore, tend to be a lower priority in urban states. Thus, Alaska, Wyoming, and New Mexico were at the top in highway expenditures per capita in 1992, and more densely populated, urbanized states such as California, Wisconsin, and Michigan were at the bottom.[10]

State highway funds come primarily from a special tax on gasoline and secondarily from license fees, with trucks and buses being charged more on the theory they do more damage to road surfaces. The proceeds from these sources are usually earmarked for highway and road construction only. The rate of the gasoline tax varies quite a lot: In 1994 Connecticut had the highest at 32 cents per gallon and Florida had the lowest gas tax at 4 cents per gallon.[11] The earmarking practice provides a stable base for highway funding, protecting it from the ebbs and flows in the rest of the state budget. State officials, aided by powerful construction interests, try to protect the highway budget from other competing priorities, although in recent years some states have allowed diversion of highway funds to other uses, primarily to mass transit.

TABLE 15.1 STATE PER-CAPITA HIGHWAY
EXPENDITURES, 1992   States vary widely in what
they spend on highways; the small, sparsely populated
states spend the most per capita.

Rank	State	Expenditure
1	Alaska	$874
2	Wyoming	618
3	New Mexico	367
4	Delaware	331
5	Montana	328
6	Hawaii	311
7	North Dakota	293
8	West Virginia	282
9	South Dakota	276
10	Vermont	271
11	Iowa	244
12	Connecticut	242
13	New Jersey	235
14	Kentucky	225
15	Virginia	214
16	Kansas	213
17	Nebraska	208
18	Maine	205
19	Idaho	202
20	Oklahoma	200
21	Louisiana	196
22	North Carolina	192
23	Arkansas	190
24	Nevada	190
25	Rhode Island	181

Despite the earmarking and powerful political protection of highway funds, it is generally acknowledged that the building and especially the maintenance of highways, bridges, and roads is not keeping pace with development. The deterioration is partly due to the fact that until recently federal money went for new construction, not maintenance and improvement. Highways and bridges are literally crumbling away in many states. About 40 percent of the nation's 600,000 bridges are rated as deficient (120 collapse every year) and 60 percent of the nation's nearly 3.9 million miles of highways need repair.[12] Florida leads the states in the percentage of highways rated as deficient, and New York leads in the percentage of deficient bridges.[13] These abysmal standings seem to be the direct result of low spending: Florida and New York rank relatively low among the states in per-capita spending on highways, and they have among the lowest excise taxes on gasoline.

Poor roads and bridges are thought to hurt business. For example, U.S. Steel claims that a lowered weight limit on a poorly maintained bridge in Pittsburgh cost the company $5 million per year in additional transportation costs.[14] Most states and cities are engaged in massive efforts to rebuild their deteriorating transportation systems as part of

TABLE 15.1 (CONTINUED)

Rank	State	Expenditure
26	Tennessee	$176
27	Mississippi	175
28	Illinois	174
29	Washington	168
30	Arizona	165
31	Minnesota	161
32	Pennsylvania	157
33	New Hampshire	154
34	Massachusetts	153
35	Missouri	152
36	Utah	152
37	Florida	149
38	South Carolina	147
39	Maryland	140
40	Texas	139
41	Ohio	138
42	Colorado	134
43	Alabama	132
44	New York	132
45	Indiana	130
46	Oregon	129
47	Georgia	128
48	California	103
49	Wisconsin	98
50	Michigan	80

Source: Advisory Commission on Intergovernmental Relations, *Significant Features of Fiscal Federalism, 1994 Edition, Vol. II* (Washington, D.C.: Government Printing Office, 1994), p. 136.

their economic development strategy. The task is immense: It is estimated that the nation will have to spend between $3 and $5 trillion to repair its infrastructure, a terrible strain on all governments.[15]

Most analysts believe that investment in public infrastructure increases private sector productivity. Good roads reduce time spent commuting and help to speed the delivery of goods. Good public water and sewer systems open up parts of the country for industrial development that may be close to raw materials or labor markets. One study calculates that every dollar spent on public infrastructure generates a $4 increase in the Gross National Product.[16] Others believe that such a high ratio is an exaggeration. The case seems clear, however, that the efficient functioning of a modern economy requires a good system of well-maintained public works.

In 1991 Congress passed the **Intermodal Surface Transportation Efficiency Act (ISTEA)** which channels money to states for maintenance and improvement of high-use highways. It gives significant authority to state officials to decide where and how to spend the money. The act also encourages state officials to allocate money to alternative modes of transportation, such as mass transit and bikeways, that will curb congestion and reduce environmental degradation. It remains to be seen whether this more flexible approach works.

Some financial support for highways and bridges comes from user fees or tolls: The Pennsylvania Turnpike and the New Jersey Turnpike are well-known examples of toll roads. Toll road authorities exist in several states to construct, operate, and maintain roads on which people pay to drive. Additional states apply the toll concept to bridges, such as those in New York City. User charges such as these may be part of the solution to upgrading our transportation infrastructure.

As part of the general move to privatization and user charges, recently some states have tried congestion pricing. For example, in 1996 California permitted a private firm to build a tollway in the Los Angeles metropolitan area; the firm guarantees that drivers will be able to drive at 65 miles per hour or get their money back. To maintain this guarantee, the company raises tolls as more drivers choose to use the road. This differential pricing scheme, which varies tolls hour by hour, uses market forces to keep traffic manageable.

Mass Transit

There are roughly 1,800 public mass transit systems in the United States. Most of them are administered not by city governments but by special transportation authorities. Many of these are metropolitan or regional in scope, such as San Francisco's Bay Area Rapid Transit Authority and the Southeastern Michigan Transportation Authority, which serves Detroit.

Fares are a major source of revenue for these systems, but few manage to cover even their operating costs from the fare box. Most must rely on state and federal aid. More than half the states provide money to their cities for mass transit systems, with the more urbanized states being the larger spenders.

If state transportation policy is concerned mainly with expanding, refurbishing, and maintaining a good road system, cities are torn between accommodating automobiles and providing mass transit. Consider the problems New York City faces: On the average day, close to 3.5 million people enter downtown Manhattan. About half come by subway and another 15 percent come by bus and commuter railroad. But that leaves well over a third who come by private car or taxi.[17] What is the city to do? It must provide good streets for its automobile and truck travelers, but it must also provide an efficient mass transit system of gargantuan proportions. Although the problem is greater in New York than elsewhere, other cities face the same need to provide for different modes of transportation.

Before the 1960s, urban transportation policy focused on highways to meet growing automobile use. But in many cities there still existed a significant demand for public transportation. This was true in the congested cities of the Northeast and Midwest, but it was also true in the newer cities of the Sun Belt, which had grown up with the automobile. Frustrated automobile commuters, the poor, the very young, and the elderly are the mass transit users in every city. The question for cities, therefore, was what sort of mass transit system to develop for the latter part of the twentieth century.

When the federal government passed the **Urban Mass Transportation Act** in 1964, which provided subsidies equal to 80 percent of the cost of capital equipment and construction, many cities began to plan rapid rail systems. Washington, D.C., began building its 70-mile Metro subway system. It was joined by Atlanta, with its 32-mile network of subway and above-

Where will all the smart roads and smart cars get their intelligence?

By the early 21st century, your car will be equipped with an electronic map that will navigate you through traffic. A computerized voice will direct you as you drive. Electronic road signs will warn you of traffic congestion and suggest alternate routes. Traffic signals will automatically adjust to the ebb and flow of cars.

This is no passing fancy. The technology is already here. And much of it is coming from companies located in Fairfax County.

The network of satellites, sensors, onboard computers and guidance systems that will make intelligent highways and vehicles work are by-products of technologies that these companies developed for the national defense.

Further, the policies that will be used to deploy this technology are being developed at Fairfax County's George Mason University.

Smart ideas like smart cars and smart roads are why smart companies move to Fairfax County.

If you want to compete in the 21st century, it's the best route you can take.

Fairfax County, Virginia. The 21st Century Is Here.

States providing infrastructure such as "smart roads" have a competitive advantage in luring business to their state. Fairfax County, Virginia, shown here, is a site for the development of intelligent highways. (*Source:* Courtesy of the Fairfax County Economic Development Authority)

ground trains, and a host of other cities, including Baltimore, Detroit, Miami, and San Diego. Eleven entirely new systems have opened since the mid-1970s.[18] In the mid-1990s at least 30 cities were considering light-rail systems, including Denver, Orlando, and Minneapolis.

A few of these new systems are regarded as successes: Portland, Oregon, and San Diego have trolley lines that serve more people than projected and that cover the majority of their costs from the fare box. But for most cities, there are significant problems with rail transport. They are extremely expensive, particularly compared to bus systems. For example, the money spent for capital assistance to urban transit systems under the National Mass Transportation Assistance Act of 1974 supports rail facilities on which about a million people ride each day. The same amount of money could have been used to develop bus systems serving about 65 million people per day.[19] The Los Angeles system, which opened in 1990, carries only about 40 riders a day per million dollars spent on construction, a smaller ratio than in virtually any other city.[20] Cities cannot count on federal grants to support operations, as they once did. Although the ISTEA legislation set aside $31 billion in federal funds for public transportation capital construction and equipment through 1997, the Clinton administration and Congress at the same time were cutting operating subsidies.

Rail systems are not only expensive but they are also inflexible; they cannot be moved or extended easily to accommodate unexpected population growth. Buffalo, New York, built a light-rail system of a little over 6 miles in length. Unfortunately, it is too short to reach the booming suburbs around the city, but there are no funds to extend it. Then, too, metropolitan areas made largely of single-family housing, as most American cities are, do not acheive sufficient housing densities in the rail corridors to provide a large enough rider pool. It should not be surprising, then, that few urban rail systems have attracted their projected ridership. The 21-mile Miami system, projected to serve 200,000 riders every day, only carries 36,000. Baltimore's light-rail system, 22 miles long, was supposed to serve 33,000 riders a day, but so far no more than 13,000 ride it.[21] One final problem with the light rail systems built in the 1980s: They are all designed to bring people from the edge of the city downtown to work, but the workplaces in American cities are increasingly located in suburban communities. Workers must often commute *between* suburbs, not from suburb to city. Light rail has not been designed to do this. (See Table 15.2).

Most cities are not willing to give up the idea of a rail system, however, for such transportation has become a state-of-the-art symbol of modern urbanity. The issue for the coming century, therefore, is to integrate more flexible bus and paratransit (shared rider arrangements of various sorts) systems with urban rail transportation.

Ports and Airports

Nearly all of the 200 domestic ports, including all of the larger ones, and about half of the largest airports are governed by special authorities. Airports stick generally to handling passenger and freight air traffic, deriving the major portion of their revenues from airline use agreements. These fees, paid by the major air carriers, are used to back the bonds issued by the airport authority for construction and maintenance. Airports may also receive revenues from federal and state grants.

Port authorities manage seaports and river ports, but they also engage in a host of economic development activities. The best-known of these **multifunctional port authorities** is the Port Authority of New York and New Jersey, which administers the New York Bus

TABLE 15.2 URBAN LIGHT RAIL SYSTEMS OPENED IN THE 1980s AND 1990s

City	Length (Miles)	Year Opened	Average Weekday Trips	Cost (Millions)	Percentage Federal Funding	Percentage of Operating Costs Covered by Fares
Baltimore	22.5	1992	13,000	$364	0%	25.0%
Buffalo	6.2	1985	29,900	536	79	32.5
Los Angeles	21.6	1990	40,000	877	0	15.6
Pittsburgh	22.6	1987	32,500	539	80	27.8
Portland (OR)	15.1	1986	24,500	214	82	47.1
Sacramento	18.3	1987	23,400	176	56	30.9
San Diego	36.0	1981	45,000	308	17	69.0
San Jose	21.0	1987	21,000	500	50	11.0
St. Louis	18.0	1993	22,000	351	98	27.7

Source: Reprinted with permission, *Governing* magazine, copyright 1994.

Terminal, various bridges and tunnels, and airports, as well as owning and developing some commercial and industrial property. The Port Authority once owned the World Trade Center twin towers, for example. Port districts derive their revenues from operations, including docking and loading fees and terminal rentals.[22]

✧ OTHER PUBLIC WORKS

Water and Sewer Systems

Water and sewer systems were among the first great public works projects in most American cities. Milwaukee's original waterworks is a good example. After the Wisconsin state legislature authorized the city to issue bonds to finance the project in 1871, the city government constructed a system that pumped water from Lake Michigan to a reservoir that held 21.5 million gallons of water, enough to serve half a million people, or five times the size of the city's population. The waterworks was the first major construction financed by the citizens of the city themselves.[23]

Milwaukee's system was modest by New York standards, however. In the 1830s New York City began construction of the 30-mile Croton Aqueduct from the Catskill mountains. It was so ambitious a project that contemporary observers called it the biggest water engineering undertaking since the Roman Empire. The Croton Aqueduct was supplemented in the 1890s by a second enormous system. Together this aqueduct and pipe network provided New York reservoirs with 42 billion gallons of water.[24]

Projects such as these were replicated in other cities in the late nineteenth century, bringing American city dwellers more abundant clean water and more extensive sanitary facilities than Europeans enjoyed at this time. By the end of the century, flush toilets and bathtubs were standard equipment in middle-class and even tenement housing in American cities; such amenities were still rarities in European capitals.[25]

Today, of course, access to water and sewer systems is virtually universal in urban areas. Americans are served by approximately 16,000 wastewater treatment systems and

BOX 15.1 DENVER INTERNATIONAL AIRPORT: SOMETHING FOR NOTHING?

In 1989, Denver voters were faced with a unique opportunity to have a new billion-dollar airport built entirely with private investment and federal funding using no Denver taxpayer dollars. As Denver's air traffic had decreased along with the regional economy, the new airport offered a way to create thousands of jobs and lure new businesses to Denver. To no one's surprise, voters approved the referendum to build the Denver International Airport (DIA), the first major new airport to be opened in the United States since Dallas/Fort Worth International in 1974. However, when the airport finally opened on February 28, 1995, 16 months late and $3 billion over budget, the airport's luster and voters' enthusiasm had waned considerably.

Almost no one disagreed about the need for a new airport facility. The existing Denver airport, the 65-year-old Stapleton International Airport, was the nation's sixth busiest airport. However, it had the third worst record of delays because of its inability to handle the bad weather endemic to its location in the Rocky Mountains.[1] Moreover, Denver had agreed to close Stapleton by the year 2000 as part of a settlement over a noise level suit.

To finance the construction of the new airport, Denver sold $3.2 billion in revenue bonds to private investors. The bondholders hoped to recoup the cost of their investment over 30 years based on the projected revenues from landing and user fees charged to airlines as well as concessions, parking, and building rentals. The federal government also chipped in $685 million from the Airport and Airway Trust Fund toward the new airport. Of this, about $223.6 million went for new air traffic control hardware such as radars, weather sensors, instrument landing systems, and approach lighting.[2]

Critics of the new airport charge that Denver's lack of financial accountability for the project has encouraged frivolous and wasteful spending. The cost of the airport has ballooned from $1.3 billion in 1985 to $4.2 billion in 1994. The city, eager to impress visitors to Denver, has saddled the new airport with such expensive luxuries as Italian marble floors, $7.2 million in art, a tentlike roof

180,000 water systems. Unfortunately, many of these facilities are deteriorating, and demand for entirely new systems in growing parts of the country is high. Urban water systems, many still essentially unchanged from when they were put in place in the nineteenth century, have high leakage rates, costly in terms of waste. Leaky city water systems are also vulnerable to groundwater contamination, as Milwaukee discovered in the early 1990s when thousands of residents fell ill from cryptosporidium toxins that leached into the system from farm runoff.

A key policy issue today is the cost and the source of refurbishing these systems. Capital financing for wastewater treatment facilities, once shared by all levels of government, is now exclusively a state and local responsibility. The federal government no longer provides grants for their construction. The need for repair and new construction, however, far outstrips state and local fiscal capacity. The Environmental Protection Agency estimates that it will cost more than $84 billion for new and refurbished wastewater treatment facilities to bring communities into compliance with the federal Clean Water Act; in addition, local governments will have to increase their capital investment in water systems by 50 percent to achieve the standards set by the federal Safe Drinking

designed to imitate the nearby Rocky Mountains, and a state-of-the-art $193-million computer-operated baggage system.[3] This system, in its first year of operation, displayed an unfortunate tendency to devour luggage rather than deliver it to the passenger. Moreover, critics point out that the new airport is more than twice as far from downtown Denver as the old Stapleton airport.

To help pay for the new facility, the 19 airlines using the airport had to raise fares. Continental Airlines and United Airlines announced that passengers flying into or out of Denver will pay up to $40 a ticket extra to defray the airport's costs, more than two or three times the surcharge at Stapleton Airport.[4] DIA's facility charges, at almost twice the national average, are now the highest in the nation. At these prices, cost-conscious airlines are increasingly unwilling to use DIA, which has important ramifications for the financial viability of the project. If passenger traffic falls 20–25 percent lower than the estimate of 18.3 million passengers by the year 2000, then there is a significant risk of default.[5]

Although Denver's mayors have told taxpayers that they would not be financially responsible for the airport, Denver residents are increasingly uncertain about the prospects of their taxes being used to fund the project. A telephone survey found that 59 percent of respondents said they would vote against the project if given the opportunity again.[6] Perhaps Denver voters can find consolation in noting that in 1929 critics of the "new" Stapleton airport said it was too costly and too far from the city to ever be financially viable.

---

[1]Adam Bryant, "Denver's New Airport Still a 'Field of Dreams,'" *New York Times* (May 11, 1994), A23.

[2]Edward Phillips, "GAO Says DIA Can Pay Its Way," *Aviation Week and Space Technology* (October 24, 1994), 60.

[3]Bryant, "Denver's New Airport," p. A23.

[4]Stephen Hedges, Brian Duffy, and Ancel Martinez, "A Taj Mahal in the Rockies," *U.S. News and World Report* (February 13, 1995), 48.

[5]Phillips, "GAO Says DIA Can Pay Its Way," p. 60.

[6]Bryant, "Denver's New Airport," p. A23.

Water Act. Current annual state and local expenditures are only a small fraction of the sums required.[26]

Convention Centers and Stadiums

Despite the evident need for investment in the basic infrastructure of roads, bridges, and water and sewer systems, cities are spending an increasing amount of their public works budgets for facilities such as convention centers and sports stadiums. Annual state and local government spending for such facilities rose from just under $700 million in the mid-1970s to about $2 billion in the 1990s, nearly half of what these governments were spending on highways and streets.[27] The rationale is that such amenities position a city to compete for tourist and convention dollars and provide jobs in construction and the hospitality industry.

Conventions—meetings of professional, interest, sales, and trade groups—are big business. Convention-goers usually spend $200–300 per day on food, lodging, taxis, and entertainment. A two- or three-day convention attended by 5,000 people represents a substantial stimulus to a city's economy. In the mid-1970s, American cities hosted about

30,000 such meetings a year. The annual total today is in the six-figure range, fueling private sector construction of hotels, restaurants, and shopping facilities and public construction of convention centers.[28]

In 1970 only 15 cities could handle a trade show for 20,000 people. By 1985, 150 cities had built convention facilities of that size.[29] City governments financed these centers by a variety of means. Some, such as Chicago, issued general obligation bonds and serviced the debt with proceeds from a state cigarette tax; other cities, such as San Francisco and Madison, Wisconsin, used hotel room taxes. Ironically, convention centers themselves almost always lose money. But the point is not to make a profit on the facilities themselves, say convention center administrators. Rather, the object is to bring high-spending conventioneers into the city.

City officials have similar objectives in spending public funds for sports stadiums, but additionally, they are convinced that big-league teams give a city a major-league aura that can translate into economic growth. A dozen stadiums were built in the 1970s and 1980s, including domed stadiums in Pontiac, New Orleans, Seattle, Minneapolis, and Indianapolis. The most expensive of these was the New Orleans Superdome, financed with a $163-million bond issue by a special authority, the Louisiana Stadium and Expo District. The pace of stadium construction accelerated considerably in the 1990s. As many stadiums were built or scheduled for completion in the first 5 years of the decade as had been finished in the previous 20 years, including Camden Yards in Baltimore and Jacobs Field in Cleveland. A number of these new ballparks and football fields were financed with new local sales taxes, hotel taxes, and revenue bonds. Box 15.2 describes a recent bidding war over the Cleveland Browns.

Most studies show that the economic impact of major-league sports is much smaller than city officials claim when they argue for public subsidies for stadium construction. Many cities must cover big operating deficits for stadiums, and few find that fans spend enough outside the stadiums in restaurants, bars, and retail establishments to make a huge economic splash. The notion that "major-league status" attracts business and thus justifies stadium spending is apparently without empirical basis. In general, cities with professional sports teams appear to grow no faster than cities without them.[30] Stadiums are probably better justified as public works amenities that provide pleasure rather than major elements of the economic development infrastructure.

Libraries

Municipal public libraries have been known for more than a century as major institutions for popular education. Unlike their European counterparts, which were designed to serve scholars, municipal libraries in the United States were free and open to the people. In the nineteenth century, American public libraries pioneered the modern card catalogue, open stacks, children's collections, and the traveling library.[31]

Library construction seems to follow roughly 50-year cycles. Although Boston and Cincinnati established the first public libraries in major American cities in the 1850s, most municipal library construction was completed in the last decade of the nineteenth century. Many of these grand neoclassical buildings, such as the Boston and New York libraries, are still in use today. A second round began in the 1950s, with the construction of functional, boxy, officelike buildings. In the mid-1990s, American cities are overseeing

BOX 15.2 THREE CHEERS (AND A PUBLICLY FINANCED STADIUM) FOR THE HOME TEAM

The Browns football team called Cleveland home for half a century. In 1996 the team decided to move to Baltimore, Maryland. Cleveland tried desperately to hang on to the Browns whose stadium was located near other tourist attractions such as the Rock and Roll Hall of Fame.[1] Fans attended rallies, and the city initiated a lawsuit in an attempt to force the Browns to stay for three more years. Cleveland eventually dropped the suit in order not to kill the chance of getting a new team.[2]

In the end, money dictated where the Browns went. The state of Maryland offered team owner Art Modell a very sweet deal. Maryland promised to build the team a $200 million stadium *and* to allow the team to keep all revenues generated from the stadium including ticket sales, concessions, parking, and bill-board advertising.[3] The new stadium will include 108 luxury boxes usually bought by corporations and 7,500 club seats where affluent fans pay sky-high prices. To top it all off, Modell will collect a management fee and fifty percent of the profits when the stadium is used for college football or other events.[4]

The Browns' move is part of a larger trend in the politics between sports teams and local and state governments. Cities across the nation are fighting it out for major league sports teams. Increasingly, these battles come with a huge price tag for taxpayers.

States and cities have not always subsidized their sports teams. Forty years ago, professional team owners also owned the buildings in which their teams played. More recently, governments entered into partnerships in which the public sector provided the capital for facilities, and the team provided money for stadium operating costs and capital improvements. But now many sport teams are demanding direct public subsidies. In the last 15 years, almost all professional sports franchises have threatened to move in order to secure certain benefits.[5]

State and local governments have responded to these threats by issuing half a billion dollars worth of bonds to build stadiums and arenas in 1995. At the same time that public financing of major league sports is increasing, the cost of building new facilities is also soaring. All this means that the public sector is paying more and receiving less from major league sports.

The teams and their supporters claim that major league teams generate enthusiasm, tax revenue, and jobs for their home cities. But the actual impact of the teams is not as great as the teams say. Stadiums generate jobs, but the majority of the jobs are temporary, seasonal, and low-paying.

These trends have prompted some to ask why governments should subsidize successful private enterprises that pay their employees millions of dollars. Cleveland city council member Pat O'Malley noted that none of the Browns players lived in the city of Cleveland and said, "All this money doesn't do anything for Cleveland's rank and file ... Public schools are closing and other city needs are not being taken care of."[6]

---

[1]Joseph Spiers, "Are Pro Sports Teams Worth It," *Fortune* (January 15, 1996), 29–30.

[2]Richard Sandomir, "Compromise Got Cleveland a Stadium," *New York Times* (February 12, 1996), B9.

[3]Spiers, "Are Pro Sports Teams Worth It," pp. 29–30.

[4]George F. Will, "Modell Sacks Maryland," *Newsweek* (January 22, 1996), 70.

[5]Charles C. Euchner, *Playing the Field: Why Sports Teams Move and Cities Fight to Keep Them*, (Baltimore: Johns Hopkins Press, 1993), p. 5.

[6]Spiers, "Are Pro Sports Teams Worth It," pp. 29–30.

an explosive third round of library construction. This new building wave has been spurred both by the vast increase in published materials (collections have tended to double every couple of decades, quickly outgrowing existing shelf space) and the inability of older buildings to accommodate the wiring requirements of high-tech library operations that use on-line catalogues, CD-ROM players, and microcomputers.

Many of these new buildings are stunning pieces of urban public architecture, causing comment, attracting visitors, and serving as community gathering places. Examples include Chicago's Harold Washington Library, the bright red San Antonio library, and new buildings in Denver, San Francisco, Phoenix, and a dozen other cities. Interestingly, although this construction boom has occurred in a period of great public distrust of government, voters approved more than 90 percent of all library bond referenda in the 1980s and more than 75 percent in recent years.[32]

Summary

State and local governments can advance the economy by providing physical infrastructure. Indeed, the conduct of business depends on transportation and on public facilities for sewage and water. History shows how profoundly transportation systems shape economic development and growth. Cities are also involved in providing meeting and exhibition space for trade associations and conventions, a function related to their historic obligation, dating from early colonial times, of providing public markets. Cities also provide public works amenities that may not be related directly to economic development, such as libraries, but that nevertheless enhance the quality of life that public officials are convinced creates a favorable climate for growth.

Expenditures for highways continue to be a primary way state governments provide infrastructure and shape the economy. Highway expenditures are the third largest expenditure of state governments. Urbanized states struggle to provide public transportation so that workers can get to their jobs.

The politics of transportation revolves around who benefits and who pays. Should users or the general public pay? Can any transportation needs be privately supported? Should developers pay for roads and sewers in new developments? As need for new highways and urban railways increases, the controversies will intensify. Increased resources for transportation depends on convincing policymakers that there will be an economic payoff. Powerful interest groups representing the construction industry stand ready to do just that.

✦ HOUSING

Government participation in the housing market is regarded as an element of both economic and social welfare policy. By world standards, most Americans are housed very well. Our housing is relatively new (the median year of construction is 1965; only about 18 percent of all units were built before World War II), spacious (the average home has only 2.5 people), and well-equipped (99 percent have complete indoor plumbing facilities).[33] Yet some analysts argue that a significant housing problem still exists.[34] Indeed, after years of steady growth, the rate of home ownership in the United States has fallen slightly since the early 1980s, as the cost of housing has outstripped wages and earnings. The burden of housing costs for the poorest among us has increased, and the problem of homelessness appears to have grown.

Most of our housing is built and financed by the private sector and owned by private individuals. The federal government plays an important role by insuring the mortgages on about a fifth of all single-family homes, most of them for middle- and working-class families, through the Federal Housing Administration (FHA) program, but it is not an important supplier of housing. Public housing for the poor, for example, accounts only for 1.4 million units, that is, just over 1 percent of the more than 106 million housing units in the United States.

Housing policy may be defined in part as government expenditures, loans, and loan guarantees for investment in residential structures. Government has intervened in the housing market for many different reasons: to increase the supply of available housing for particular income groups, to decrease the cost of housing for particular income groups, to prevent or reverse deterioration of existing housing stock, to stimulate employment in the construction and real estate industries, and to promote community economic and social development, among others. Not all housing programs are aimed at the poor. Several programs that originated during the depression were designed to bring home ownership within reach of the middle class and to stabilize the home mortgage industry.

Federal Housing Policy

In the United States most housing policy originated with efforts by Washington to revive the housing market and provide shelter for the poor during the Depression. Federal programs dominated housing policy for the next half century. When federal housing programs were cut drastically during the Reagan presidency (new commitments of federal housing assistance fell from $30 billion per year in 1981 to $7.5 billion per year in 1989), state and local governments began to pick up the slack.[35] The story of housing policy innovation and action in the 1980s and 1990s has a distinct subnational focus.

Federal housing policy from 1934 to the present is characterized by an enormous mix of different programs. Each era, however, has been marked by distinctive approaches and goals. In the 1930s, Congress established two programs that survive today: the Federal Housing Administration mortgage guarantees, which enabled moderate-income working people to purchase houses (1934), and public housing (1937). The main housing goal of both programs was to increase the supply of available housing, although the programs also aimed to stimulate employment in the hard-hit construction industry, where new housing starts had fallen from as many as 700,000 per year in the 1920s to only 93,000 in 1933.[36] The FHA program guaranteed mortgages made by private banks and savings and loans. This guarantee meant that lenders could take higher risks and charge lower interest rates, thus opening home ownership to a broader range of purchasers than ever before. The 1937 Housing Act established the public housing program. The federal government provided grants to local housing authorities to pay off the principal and interest of bonds sold to finance public housing construction. Maintenance costs were paid with rental income.

In the 1950s and 1960s much federal housing policy was tied to urban redevelopment, or urban renewal, as it came to be called. The key pieces of federal legislation here were the 1949 and 1954 Housing Acts. The first authorized the construction of more public housing, promising in its famous preamble "a decent home and suitable living environment for every American." It also provided federal grants to cover two-thirds of the cost of acquiring and clearing dilapidated neighborhoods to prepare them for development projects. The second act provided federal subsidies for housing rehabilitation and neighborhood revitalization.

Instead of emphasizing an increase in the supply of the nation's low-income housing stock, however, these urban renewal programs were used more often to redevelop aging downtown commercial areas. Developers and local officials preferred to build office towers, parking structures, and new public buildings on urban renewal land, rather than less-lucrative low-income housing. Many poor people—perhaps as many as one million—were displaced from their homes during the urban renewal program, most of them members of minority groups. In the end, the 1949 Housing Act produced no net gain in the low-income housing stock of the United States.

The 1959 Housing Act marked a major shift in the approach of federal housing policy: It authorized direct federal loans at below-market interest rates to nonprofit organizations (often associated with churches or labor unions) to build low-income housing. The emphasis was still on increasing the supply of housing, just as the Depression-era programs had aimed to do. But the agent for accomplishing this had shifted from the federal government and local housing authorities to private nonprofit organizations. As one scholar notes, "This approach became the mechanism of choice in the explosion of housing programs in the 1960s."[37]

Housing legislation in 1961 and 1962 created federal loan programs for nonprofit organizations to build rental housing for the elderly in urban and rural areas. Then in the 1968 Housing Act, Congress provided low-interest loans directly to low-income households to purchase or rent housing. This shift from a focus on the supply side to the demand side (that is, from an approach that sought to increase the pool of housing units to one that attempted to strengthen housing consumers) has been the preferred approach in federal housing policy ever since.

In 1973 President Nixon suspended all new construction of public housing for the poor, claiming that the program had made the federal government the largest slumlord in history. In its place, Congress passed the Housing and Community Development Act of 1974, which contained several provisions that addressed housing for low- and moderate-income people. Section 8 of the 1974 act provides rent supplements in the form of vouchers or certificates for low-income tenants who rent on the private market. These supplements, which go to approximately 2.5 million households, are worth the difference between locally established "fair market rents" for moderate- and low-income units and 30 percent of the tenant's income. Although standards for the program are set by the Department of Housing and Urban Development (HUD), which also supplies funding, it is implemented by local housing authorities, who inspect dwellings to see whether they meet federal standards, select qualifying tenants, and approve leases. Clinton administration housing initiatives in the 1990s expanded this tenant-based assistance, providing subsidies to people rather than to projects.[38]

Despite the federal cutback in housing assistance in the 1980s, Congress passed a number of new housing programs in that decade. Most of them were never funded beyond the demonstration stage, including a program to encourage the sale of public housing units to tenants, another program to subsidize low-income home ownership, and Housing Development Action Grants to local governments. But one program is still important: the 1987 Stewart McKinney Homeless Assistance Act, named after a member of Congress who died of AIDS. The program provides grants to localities for the construction or rehabilitation of homeless shelters. Homelessness is a major urban problem, though there is little agreement on its dimensions. Estimates range between 360,000 and 3 million. What is known is that the homeless population now contains more young people, more families, and more minorities compared with a few decades ago, when the homeless were mainly white, single, older males.[39] The McKinney Act also provides funds for emergency food, health, education, and job-training programs for the homeless.

State and Local Housing Programs

Local governments have a long history of regulation of housing that can be traced to the early tenement codes of the nineteenth century and to the zoning restrictions to protect residential neighborhoods that emerged in the 1920s. Later, city governments became involved in housing through the implementation of building codes, rent controls, and tax abatements designed to encourage multifamily housing investment. Since the 1930s, local governments have been partners with the federal government in public housing and other forms of assisted housing for low-income and other targeted population groups. In recent years the city government role in housing has expanded, as federal programs have been cut back. Big cities now spend about 5 percent of their budgets on housing and related functions.

Innovative local programs in housing include the establishment of housing trust funds to finance new and rehabilitated housing. Cities generate monies for these funds by a variety of means, including so-called linkage fees levied on downtown developers in exchange for permission to build commercial projects. Boston and San Francisco pioneered the use of linkage fees for housing development.

More widespread than linkage fee financing of housing are community development partnerships for housing and neighborhood economic development. Community development corporations (CDCs) are private, nonprofit organizations that raise money from banks, business corporations, charitable foundations, religious institutions, and the federal and state government to develop housing and make loans to local small businesses. Data on the total housing production of these CDCs is not available, but it is possible to determine their responsibility in the cases in which they use federal housing subsidies to finance the housing projects. Between 1960 and 1990, community development corporations were responsible for producing 14 percent of all housing built under the various federal programs, or about 750,000 units.[40] Many additional housing projects have been initiated by CDCs without federal funds.

State involvement in housing activities is more recent, dating mainly from the 1960s, when states began to establish home financing agencies. These lending institutions, which exist in at least 40 states, provide low-interest construction loans to developers of single-family homes for low-income buyers. The number and variety of state housing programs increased sharply in the 1980s, again in response to federal cuts in housing programs. These include funds to invest in partnerships with local CDCs, homeless assistance programs, and state fair-share housing requirements. The latter, pioneered in New Jersey, require communities to commit to building or financing a certain number of low-income housing units. The state provides developers with low-interest loans and grants to accomplish the task. State housing programs are still very small, however: States spend on average less than 1 percent of their budgets on housing and related community development activities.

Summary

There are several conclusions we can draw with regard to housing policy. First, most programs seek to rehabilitate or make affordable existing, privately owned housing stock.

BOX 15.3 WHO ARE THE HOMELESS?

Much of the debate over what to do about homelessness has focused on the characteristics of homeless people themselves. Many advocates for expanded programs for the homeless have argued that changing economic conditions such as layoffs, plant closings, and unemployment have created a new homeless class consisting of families and people with stable work histories and no personal problems.

In the first national study of the urban homeless in 1987, the Urban Institute randomly sampled 1,704 homeless people in soup kitchens and shelters in 20 representative cities across the United States. By extrapolating from the sample, the total U.S. homeless population on any given night in March 1987 was estimated to be between 500,000 and 600,000, of whom approximately 15 percent were children. Because examining the characteristics of the homeless population as a whole obscures the differences among distinctive subgroups, it is best to examine the two largest demographic blocs that account for over 80 percent of homeless households: single men and single women with children.

Single men are by far the largest single homeless group, constituting 73 percent of the adult urban homeless population. Demographically, they are relatively diverse, 40 percent black and 48 percent white, with an average age of 39. About half of the single men have been homeless for a year or less, but there is a sizeable group of long-term homeless, 34 percent, who have been homeless for 2 years or more. Only 9 percent have been jobless for 3 months or less; 47 percent have been jobless for 2 years or more. Homeless single men are also very likely to have experienced some form of institutionalization; 40 percent have either had mental hospitalization or inpatient chemical dependency treatment and 60 percent have been in jail. Only 26 percent of homeless single men have never been in prison, a mental hospital, or a chemical treatment program.

The next largest demographic subgroup of the homeless is single women with children, who make up 9 percent of urban homeless families. This group is overwhelmingly minority, 56 percent black and 22 percent Hispanic, and young—the average age is 30. In comparison with single men, single women with children have been homeless for a shorter period of time, with 70 percent being homeless for less than a year and only 15 percent being homeless for 2 years or more. Single women with children were also much less likely than single men to have ever been in prison, mental hospitals, or chemical treatment programs. About 80 percent of the women surveyed reported never having been institutionalized. These women also had a wide range of job histories. Of those interviewed, 10 percent were currently working at a steady job and another 25 percent had never worked at a steady job.

If we want to know what percentage of the homeless are "just like you and me"—defined as a short period of homelessness, stable work history, high school diploma, and an intact marriage—this accounts for only 3 percent of homeless households, which are not representative of the homeless population in general. Knowing who the homeless are has important political and policy implications about who deserves aid and what types of aid should be provided. The numbers provided by the Urban League study suggest that any search for what causes homelessness and what can be done about it should start with single men and then focus on female-headed families.

Source: Martha Burt, *Over the Edge: The Growth of Homelessness in the 1980s* (New York: Russell Sage Foundation, 1992), Ch. 2.

Little new public housing construction has occurred since the early 1970s. Whatever new construction has occurred has generally been done by CDCs, using a mix of public and private funds. Second, the housing market is not providing affordable housing for the extremely poor. Nor has government intervention filled the gap. Homelessness became a major problem in the 1980s. Finally, there are some variations from place to place in participation and funding. For example, because Community Development Block Grant (CDBG) funding is allocated by formula to local jurisdictions on the basis of age of housing stock and poverty, it is a redistributive program that serves the needs of the most needy cities. The federal government calculated that the 10 percent of the most distressed cities receive about 3.7 times more per capita in CDBG monies than the 10 percent least distressed.[41]

✧ CONCLUSION

The infrastructure debates of the next century are likely to revolve around the **Information Superhighway** rather than the asphalt highway. Channels that carry voice, video, data, and imaging can now be linked together in integrated telecommunications networks, either locally or worldwide. The Internet is the communications network most people are likely to be familiar with but others are being developed. The development of these high-speed communication networks is critical for the private sector, much as railroads were critical in the nineteenth century and interstate highways were essential in the twentieth century. The possibilities are endless: Telemedicine can be practiced via fiberoptic cables, videoconferencing can replace expensive airline trips, and telecommuting can replace driving long distances to get to work.

Integrated communication networks are equally essential for the conduct of state government and the provision of distance education and library services. Government benefits can be dispensed electronically via a "smart card," at a kiosk or on the home computer citizens can register to vote or get their driver's license or birth certificate without standing in line, and unemployed people can send in a résumé and search for job listings via computer. Computers can store vast amounts of records and information, freeing up file cabinets in government offices, and can process a variety of routine reports, saving the time of government bureaucrats to deal with clients with unusual problems. Video conferencing capability allows courts to conduct oral arguments and arraign prisoners over long distances. Some people believe that government's use of information technology—and the resulting service improvement—is the key to restoring public confidence in government.

Although the private sector has funded most of the Information Superhighway thus far, several governance issues have arisen. Who will regulate access to these networks—national or state governments? Even after significant deregulation, all three levels of government are still involved in some aspect of telecommunications regulation, with the cities focusing on cable TV and state governments on telephone companies. Which level should regulate the new integrated telecommunications companies that combine video, phone, and computers? Or should the federal government build the Information Superhighway by itself as a tool of economic development? A single source could ensure compatibility of equipment and integration of networks and provide equal access to all parts of the country. The Clinton Administration has supported this major capital investment, estimated at $200 billion.[42]

In the meantime, several states have developed their own information networks. Iowa, for example, is financing and building its own fiberoptic network to ensure universal service and access in rural areas; it hopes to lease it to private firms and thereby recoup some of the capital cost.[43] The Iowa Communications Network is a 2,800-mile highway of fiberoptic cable connecting more than 100 points throughout the state, costing more than $100 million so far.[44] Initially, it was designed for education, government, and health care uses.

North Carolina took a different approach, forming a public-private partnership with telephone firms to develop a statewide network. The state share was nearly $100 million.[45] State officials expect that the existence of a statewide computer network will attract firms to North Carolina because it lowers their cost of doing business. Its uses include distance learning, telemedicine, and video arraignments of prisoners.

New Jersey—the home of Bell Labs and AT&T—took a different approach still: It encouraged private industry to build the telecommunications network. The state deregulated telephone rates in exchange for a promise to have 56 million miles of fiberoptic cable in place by 2010.[46] So each state is struggling in a different way to provide an information network and to regulate its use. How these struggles get resolved is a significant development in infrastructure policy.

✧ KEY TERMS

Information Superhighway (p. 407)
infrastructure (p. 388)
Intermodal Surface Transportation Efficiency Act (p. 393)

multifunctional port authorities (p. 396)
Urban Mass Transportation Act (p. 394)

✧ FOR FURTHER READING

Robert A. Caro, *The Power Broker: Robert Moses and the Fall of New York* (New York: Random House, 1974). A Pulitzer-prize winning account of how America's greatest builder, Robert Moses, shaped New York City's physical structure, its politics, and its subsequent urban problems.

Charles C. Euchner, *Playing the Field: Why Sports Teams Move and Cities Fight to Keep Them* (Baltimore: Johns Hopkins Press, 1993). The author examines why cities are so vulnerable to the relocation threats of sports teams. Includes case studies of Los Angeles, Baltimore, and Chicago.

David C. Perry, ed., *Building the Public City* (Thousand Oaks, Calif.: Sage, 1995). A collection of essays on the role of infrastructure in economic development at the city level. Includes both historical and contemporary articles.

Peter H. Rossi, *Down and Out in America: The Origins of Homelessness* (Chicago: University of Chicago Press, 1989). Based upon a survey of the homeless population in Chicago, the author shows the changes in the composition of this group and proposes policies to change the situation.

Jon Teaford, *The Unheralded Triumph* (Baltimore: Johns Hopkins Press, 1984). An interesting book by an urban historian showing how changes in city government structure made it possible for leaders to build the infrastructure needed for the modern city.

✧ NOTES

1. David C. Perry, "Building the Public City: An Introduction," in David C. Perry, ed., *Building the Public City* (Thousand Oaks, Calif.: Sage, 1995), p. 2.

2. Leigh Stoner, "Managing the Work," *Governing* (July 1995), 70.

3. Claire Felbinger, "Conditions of Confusion and Conflict: Rethinking the Infrastructure-Economic Development Linkage," in Perry, ed., *Building the Public City*, p. 104.

4. Kenneth Jackson, *Crabgrass Frontier* (New York: Oxford, 1985), p. 33.

5. Dennis Judd, *The Politics of American Cities* (Glenview, Ill.: Scott, Foresman/Little, Brown, 1988), p. 24.

6. Louis Jacobson, "The Roads that Reshaped America," *National Journal* (May 13, 1995), 1200.

7. Robert S. Friedman, "The Politics of Transportation," in Virginia Gray, Herbert Jacob, and Robert Albritton, eds., *Politics in the American States*, 5th ed. (Glenview, Ill: Scott, Foresman/Little, Brown, 1990), p. 536.

8. John Butler, *First Highways of America* (Iola, Wisc.: Krause Publishing, 1994), p. 33.

9. Mark Rose, *Interstate: Express Highway Politics, 1939–1989* (Knoxville: University of Tennessee Press, 1990), p. 2.

10. Advisory Commission on Intergovernmental Relations, *Significant Features of Fiscal Federalism, 1994 Edition, Vol. II* (Washington, D.C.: Government Printing Office, 1994), p. 193.

11. Advisory Commission on Intergovernmental Relations, *Significant Features of Fiscal Federalism, 1995, Vol. I* (Washington, D.C.: Government Printing Office, 1995), Table 29.

12. Perry, "Building the Public City," p. 3.

13. Victoria Van Son, *CQ's State Fact Finder* (Washington, D.C.: Congressional Quarterly, 1993), pp. 336–337.

14. Elaine B. Sharp, *Urban Politics and Administration* (New York: Longman, 1990), p. 185.

15. Felix Rohatyn, "To Repair Our Nation," *New York Times* (December 17, 1989).

16. Felbinger, "Conditions of Confusion and Conflict," p. 123. The study cited is by David Ashauer.

17. Richard Levine, "Car Madness in Manhattan: Cure Sought," *New York Times* (October 11, 1987).

18. Peter Applebome, "Moving Cities' People by Rail: Systems Spread Doubt," *New York Times*, (July 23, 1988).

19. Wilfred Owen, *Transportation for Cities: The Role of Federal Policy* (Washington, D.C.: Brookings Institution, 1976), p. 20.

20. Eliza Newlin Carney, "A Desire Named Streetcar," *Governing* (February 1994), 36.

21. Applebome, "Moving Cities' People"; and Carney, "A Desire Named Streetcar."

22. James Leigland, "Public Infrastructure and Special Purpose Governments: Who Pays and How?," in Perry, *Building the Public City*, pp. 150–151.

23. Anthony Orum, *City-Building in America* (Boulder, Colo.: Westview, 1995), p. 63.

24. Jon Teaford, *The Unheralded Triumph* (Baltimore: Johns Hopkins Press, 1984), p. 223.

25. *Ibid.*, pp. 219–221.

26. Felbinger, "Conditions of Confusion and Conflict," pp. 117–118.

27. Heywood Sanders, "Public Works and Public Dollars: Federal Infrastructure Aid and Local Investment Policy," in Perry, *Building the Public City*, p. 183.

28. Dennis Judd and Todd Swanstrom, *City Politics* (New York: HarperCollins, 1994), p. 351.

29. Bernard Frieden and Lynne Sagalyn, *Downtown, Inc.* (Cambridge, Mass.: MIT Press, 1989), p. 270.

30. Charles Euchner, *Playing the Field* (Baltimore: Johns Hopkins University Press 1993), p. 73.

31. Teaford, *The Unheralded Triumph*, p. 258.

32. Anne Jordan, "Library Renaissance," *Governing*, 9 (January 1996), 20–25.

33. U.S. Bureau of the Census, *Statistical Abstract of the United States, 1995* (Washington, D.C.: Government Printing Office, 1995), p. 734.

34. Some argue that homelessness is not primarily a problem of lack of housing. They point out that many of the homeless are disabled in some sense: 33 percent are alcoholics, 25 percent are drug abusers, and 34 percent are mentally ill. Such people cannot enter the labor force and earn enough to rent or buy shelter. See Irving Welfeld, "The State of the Nation's Housing Problem" unpublished paper, U.S. Department of Housing and Urban Development, April 1990.

35. Mary Nenno, "State and Local Governments: New Initiatives in Low-Income Housing Preservation," *Housing Policy Debate*, Vol. 2, Issue 2, 1991, p. 470.

36. Kerry Vandell, "FHA Restructuring Proposals: Alternatives and Implications," *Housing Policy Debate*, 6, no. 2 (1995), 301.

37. David Listokin, "Federal Housing Policy and Preservation: Historical Evolution, Patterns, and Implications," *Housing Policy Debate*, 2, no. 2 (1991), 157.

38. U.S. Department of Housing and Urban Development, *Empowerment: A New Covenant with America's Communities* (Washington, D.C.: Government Printing Office, 1995), p. 42.

39. Peter H. Rossi, *Down and Out in America: The Origins of Homelessness* (Chicago: University of Chicago Press, 1989), Ch. 2.

40. Christopher Walker, "Nonprofit Housing Development: Status, Trends, and Prospects," *Housing Policy Debate*, 4, no. 3 (1993), p. 373.

41. Peter Eisinger, *The Rise of the Entrepreneurial State* (Madison: University of Wisconsin Press, 1988), p. 107.

42. William Fulton and Morris Newman, "Who Will Wire America?," *Governing* (October 1993), 28.

43. Susan E. Clarke and Martin R. Saiz, "Economic Development and Infrastructure Policy," in Virginia Gray and Herbert Jacob, eds., *Politics in the American States* (Washington, D.C.: CQ Press, 1996), p. 530.

44. Fulton and Newman, "Who Will Wire America?," p. 26.

45. M.J. Richter, "A Guide to the Information Highway," *Governing* (September 1994), 68.

46. Fulton and Newman, "Who Will Wire America?," p. 30.

CHAPTER 16

PUBLIC ORDER POLICIES

I t would probably come as a surprise to most Americans today that crime and other offenses against public order have actually declined since the nineteenth century. Although good historical statistics on crime are hard to come by, the best evidence is that rates of violent crime, property crime, and public drunkenness and disorder have all gone down, even though there are short-term fluctuations at various different periods.[1] Even if crime rates have decreased, however, it is hard for the ordinary citizen on the street to see the trendlines. It takes only one assault or burglary hitting near home or a particularly horrendous murder on the late evening local news to instill a healthy fear of crime.

The protection of public safety and public order is one of the most important functions of local government. Unless people can move freely and safely about the city, commerce is hindered, the social trust necessary for active civic and political participation is destroyed, and the daily quality of life is grim. High crime rates raise insurance costs and frighten workers, driving businesses out of the central city. Shops cannot stay open after dark and people do not want to commute to work at night. In high-crime areas, people are less likely to take part in parent-teacher organizations or other organizations. People who live in high-poverty, high-crime neighborhoods are less likely to belong to a church, attend meetings about community problems, or join civic organizations, even when social class is controlled.[2] When people fear for their safety, they cannot socialize in the evenings on the front stoop or allow their children to play outdoors untended. How well city government protects its citizens and relieves their fears, then, is a key indicator of its effectiveness.

The challenge for city government—and for other levels of government, for that matter—is a huge one. For one thing, crime is not easy to control. And although crime has not risen appreciably in recent decades (contrary to popular belief), fear of crime is nevertheless fairly high. The Gallup Poll has been asking samples of Americans a question about their fear of crime for a number of years. Respondents in these national surveys are asked if there are any areas near where they live that they would be afraid to walk alone in at night. In 1972, 42 percent of the Gallup sample said yes; in 1993 the figure had risen to 43 percent. Fear of criminal victimization has been fairly constant over time, but it is widely felt.[3]

If fear of crime has not increased significantly, there is evidence that it has become more important in relation to other issues. Whereas economic concerns, such as unemployment and declining wages, typically tended to dominate most surveys in which people were asked what the most important issues facing the nation or state or city are, such worries have receded in recent years. Because fear of crime has remained steady, it is now one of the most important issues people are concerned about.[4]

Americans are afraid not only that their homes will be burglarized or that they will be raped, but that they will encounter less violent but nevertheless unpleasant and threatening forms of public disorder. In surveys in Seattle and Dallas, for example, people expressed fear not just of violent crime but also of having a group of juveniles disturbing the peace near their home, being panhandled by beggars, and receiving obscene phone calls.[5] In city politics, it is common for city councils to come under pressure to deal with homeless people, who live and toilet in public places. These various behaviors are all symptoms of a fraying public order, just as much as crime is.

To add to the sense that American society is less orderly than it once was, we are deeply divided on various moral issues such as abortion, standards of sexual behavior, and the role of religion in public life. The intensity of the debate on these matters has convinced many Americans, on both the Left and the Right, that we have forgotten basic rules of civility in public discourse. Asking state and local government to maintain and foster community by fighting crime and obnoxious behavior and establishing moral standards not only is difficult but risks treading on certain freedoms of belief and behavior.

✧ CRIMINAL JUSTICE

The Crime Problem

Just how serious is crime today? What are the recent trendlines? In 1993 just over 14 million crimes were reported to the police.[6] In absolute terms, this is much higher than a decade before: In 1983 the figure was 12.1 million. But the interesting trend in those 10 years is that the crime rate—the number of offenses per 100,000 people—rose to a peak in 1991 and has fallen since. In fact, the big crime story of the mid-1990s was the declining murder rate in the nation, particularly in many of its most dangerous cities.

Homicide rates fell in New York between 1994 and the first six months of 1995 by 31.8 percent, reaching a 25-year low. They fell in Houston by 32 percent and in Atlanta by 18.4 percent. Other cities with violent reputations also experienced big declines: Detroit, Chicago, Los Angeles, New Orleans, and Washington, D.C., all experienced dropping murder rates.

Officials and sociologists are not sure why murder rates in these cities went down in these years. City leaders like to credit more police and better policing. Houston, for example, added 1,000 police officers to its force, bringing the total to 4,900. Houston also began to assign more police to work out of storefront offices in the city's worst crime locations. In Houston, Kansas City, and Indianapolis police have begun programs designed to find people carrying guns.[7] Many cities have begun community policing programs.

Other explanations for the decline in the murder rate have to do with the declining number of teenage males (the most crime-prone group) and the decline in the use of crack cocaine, which makes users more violent and impulsive, in favor of heroin, a depressant. Longer prison sentences and more prison cells have also kept many repeat offenders behind bars.

None of this is to suggest that the United States is suddenly a peaceful nation. Drug use is rampant and is associated with crime. More than two-thirds of all arrestees in a sample of 24 big cities tested positive for drug use, most often cocaine. There are still about 25,000 murders per year in the United States (nearly three-quarters by gunshot), as well as more than 105,000 reported rapes. Because the number of rapes reported to the police is only about half of what people report in victimization surveys, the actual number is much higher. The gap between crimes reported and crimes experienced holds also for assaults, robberies, and burglaries. Furthermore, it seems clear that youth gang violence increased during the 1980s, much of it tied to drug trafficking and the easy availability of high-powered weapons.[8]

Different demographic groups perpetrate and experience crime to different degrees. Crime has a racial dimension: "African Americans are disproportionately represented at every step in the criminal justice process, from arrest to imprisonment," according to Wesley Skogan.[9] Blacks commit relatively more crimes and more violent crimes (mostly against other blacks) than do whites and are arrested and imprisoned in disproportionate numbers. Homicide rates per 100,000 people, for example, are higher for black men (67.5) than for white men (9.1) and higher for black women (13.1) than for white women (2.8). Blacks make up about 12.5 percent of the U.S. population, but they account for more than 30 percent of those arrested for all crimes. (It is important to keep in mind that these arrest rates do not necessarily mean that blacks account for more than 30 percent of all crimes. It is possible, for example, that blacks are simply arrested in disproportionate numbers.)

The incidence of crime also varies around the country, as noted in Table 16.1, but one trend that is apparent is crime's association with population growth. The incidence of property crime, but not violent crime, is strongly associated with population growth. Florida and Arizona were among the top four states in population growth rates in the 1980s and are in the top three of the total crime index and the property crime index. Crime is more common in urban areas than in rural places. North and South Dakota and West Virginia are good bets if one wants to minimize the chances of being a crime victim. States with more disadvantaged people have higher rates of both violent crime and property crime.[10] This factor accounts for the relatively high crime rate, especially of violent crime, in states with high poverty rates such as New Mexico, Louisiana, and New York (which has the urbanization dimension as well).

Criminal Justice Structure and Expenditures

Crime is a problem dealt with primarily by state and local governments. The federal government plays only a minor role, the 1994 Violent Crime Control & Law Enforcement Act notwithstanding. Local agencies of the criminal justice system include the police and sheriffs, criminal courts, prosecutors, defenders, and jails. State responsibilities include the state police, state courts, prisons, parole, and probation.

These agencies collectively are referred to as the criminal justice system. The system has three major components: police, judicial (including prosecution, defense, and courts), and corrections. Table 16.2 lists these functions by government level and cost in 1990. Slightly over half the criminal justice expenditures are made by local governments. By far the largest category of local expenditure is the police. Over one-third of

TABLE 16.1   CRIME RATES IN THE STATES RANKED BY TOTAL CRIME INDEX, 1993   The total crime index is composed of violent crimes and property crimes relative to the size of the population. States whose populations are growing fastest tend to have high total crime rates.

Rank	State	Total Crime Index	Violent Crime Index	Property Crime Index
1	Florida	8,351	1,206	7,145
2	Arizona	7,432	715	6,717
3	Louisiana	6,847	1,062	5,785
4	California	6,457	1,078	5,379
5	New Mexico	6,266	930	5,336
6	Texas	6,439	762	5,677
7	Hawaii	6,277	261	6,016
8	Georgia	6,193	723	5,470
9	Nevada	6,180	875	5,305
10	Maryland	6,107	998	5,109
11	Washington	5,952	515	5,438
12	South Carolina	5,903	1,023	4,880
13	Oregon	5,766	503	5,263
14	North Carolina	5,652	679	4,973
15	Illinois	5,618	960	4,658
16	Alaska	5,568	761	4,807
17	New York	5,551	1,074	4,478
18	Colorado	5,527	567	4,960
19	Michigan	5,453	792	4,661
20	Oklahoma	5,294	635	4,659
21	Tennessee	5,240	766	4,474
22	Utah	5,237	301	4,936
23	Missouri	5,095	744	4,351
24	Kansas	4,975	496	4,479
25	Massachusetts	4,894	805	4,089

total criminal justice expenditures come from state governments. Their largest category is corrections. The federal government spends the least, and most of that is on police (the Federal Bureau of Investigation). The state share of criminal justice expenditures has been growing primarily due to the cost of constructing and operating prisons. We will examine police and corrections as examples of local and state criminal justice responsibilities, respectively.

Local Governments, Crime, and Policy

Local government is certainly on the front lines in the fight against crime: Policing is a predominantly local function. Yet as Herbert Jacob has pointed out, crime is the product of large national forces over which local police have little control. Crime rates have risen with the increase in the number of young underemployed and unemployed males, the rampant use of drugs, the growing availability in people's homes of easily portable electronic equipment, and the fact that many homes are unguarded now because so many

TABLE 16.1 (CONTINUED)

Rank	State	Total Crime Index	Violent Crime Index	Property Crime Index
26	Alabama	4,879	780	4,098
27	Delaware	4,872	686	4,186
28	Arkansas	4,811	593	4,218
29	New Jersey	4,801	627	4,174
30	Montana	4,790	178	4,613
31	Connecticut	4,560	456	4,194
32	Rhode Island	4,499	402	4,097
33	Ohio	4,485	504	3,981
34	Indiana	4,465	489	3,976
35	Mississippi	4,418	434	3,984
36	Minnesota	4,386	327	4,059
37	Wyoming	4,163	286	3,877
38	Nebraska	4,117	339	3,778
39	Virginia	4,116	372	3,743
40	Wisconsin	4,054	264	3,790
41	Vermont	3,972	114	3,858
42	Iowa	3,846	326	3,521
43	Idaho	3,845	282	3,563
44	Pennsylvania	3,271	418	2,854
45	Kentucky	3,260	463	2,797
46	Maine	3,154	126	3,028
47	South Dakota	2,958	208	2,750
48	New Hampshire	2,905	138	2,767
49	North Dakota	2,820	82	2,738
50	West Virginia	2,533	208	2,324

Source: U.S. Bureau of the Census, *Statistical Abstract of the United States: 1995* (Washington, D.C.: Government Printing Office, 1995), p. 200.

women have joined the workforce.[11] The crime rate reflects larger social problems and trends. It is perhaps unrealistic under those circumstances to expect the police to prevent crime.

For a long time, prevailing social science wisdom held that the police were fairly powerless, whatever they did. If they put officers on every subway car, the criminals moved up to the streets. If the police saturated high-crime areas, the criminals plied their trade in other neighborhoods. A famous experiment in Kansas City encouraged the view that nothing the police did made a big difference. Over the course of one year (1972–1973), Kansas City police divided their patrol beats into three groups, each group similar in terms of crime history, income, racial and ethnic composition, and population stability. In one group the police eliminated preventive patrols altogether. In the second group patrolling was increased by two or three times the normal intensity. In the third group, the police patrolled at the normal rate. The results were surprising: There were no differences among the three groups in the levels of reported crime, victimization levels, citizen fear of crime, and police response time.[12]

TABLE 16.2 CRIMINAL JUSTICE EXPENDITURES, 1990 (IN MILLIONS) Criminal justice is one policy area in which federal spending is dwarfed by state and local spending. The three levels of government also emphasize different functions within the criminal justice system.

All Governments	$74,249[a]
Federal Government	10,058
Police	4,020
Judicial	3,477
Corrections	1,597
Other	964
State Governments	28,005
Police	5,197
Judicial	5,533
Corrections	16,693
Other	582
Local Governments	39,667
Police	23,081
Judicial	8,109
Corrections	8,244
Other	233

[a] Total adjusted to exclude duplication of intergovernmental expenditures.

Source: U.S. Census Bureau, *Statistical Abstract of the United States: 1994* (Washington, D.C.: Government Printing Office, 1994), p. 209.

Since the Kansas City experiment, however, many cities have embraced the concept of **community policing.** Proponents claim that it has made a big difference. In a community policing system, officers become intimately involved in the areas they police. Some cities emphasize foot patrols; others emphasize storefront police stations. The point is to get to know the community, to listen to its residents, and to come to understand its problems. The officer seeks to gain the trust of residents and to become a problem-solver, not simply a law enforcer. In community policing, officers function as social workers, youth workers, and mediators, and they are accorded more discretion in how they do their jobs of maintaining public order than are officers in traditional police departments. Communities such as St. Petersburg, Florida, believe that community policing has reduced crime and citizens' fear of crime (see Box 16.1).

Although a number of big cities have embraced community policing, including Chicago, not every city is enamored of this approach. An alternative approach is simply aggressive policing backed up by high-tech information processing capabilities designed to pinpoint high-crime areas and concentrate police resources. New York police officials track crime statistics daily with computerized maps, sending additional officers into "hot spots." In addition, police have cracked down on quality-of-life offenses such as public drinking and graffiti. In Houston, which tried community policing and gave it up, the department has concentrated on aggressive patrolling, faster response times, arresting parole violators, and saturation of high-crime areas with a visible police presence.[13]

BOX 16.1 COMMUNITY POLICING IN ST. PETERSBURG

St. Petersburg, Florida, has had considerable success since implementing community policing in 1990. The city designated 48 community policing areas and identified one officer to get to know each neighborhood very well. So far, it appears to be working. Both the crime rate and residents' fear of crime are dropping, and public support for the police has increased. Some neighborhoods have even bought bicycles for their community police when department budgets ran short. At the heart of community policing is the expectation that police officers should become roving problem solvers instead of just walking a beat.

In the racially mixed Coquina Key neighborhood, Officer Terrell Skinner observed that the activities of a few unruly teenagers while their single parents were working were leading neighbors to put their houses up for sale. The neighborhood was gradually losing control. Skinner met with the parents and got blanket trespass warnings to limit visitors while the parents were away working, allowing Skinner to crack down. The evidence of success was obvious: The 'For Sale' signs went away.

In the middle-class northern part of town, Officer Mark Blackwood has made an effort to get to know the youngsters of the neighborhood by going to local sports events and buying lemonade from their stands. These efforts to cultivate trust paid off when two kids threw a stink bomb into an elderly lady's mail slot and set her rug on fire. Within a day, he identified the culprits and brought them to the woman's house the next day to discuss how to make amends.

In both instances, the job of Officers Skinner and Blackwood went beyond simple law enforcement to act as social workers and civic ombudsmen. This expanded conception of the role of police beyond the job of catching criminals to the larger task of promoting community is at the heart of community policing.

Source: Rob Gurwitt, "Cops and Community," *Governing* (May 1995), pp. 16–24.

To some extent, the growth of community policing simply represents a formal recognition that a good deal of police work has always involved helping people and solving problems rather than fighting crime. Various studies have shown that most police work—in some cities as many as 90 percent of all calls to the police—involve matters other than crimes. The police function is the only 24-hour source of help in the society. Thus, people call them when there are traffic accidents, lost children, intoxicated or mentally ill people behaving strangely in public, and pregnant women needing quick transportation to the hospital. People call the police to help maintain order: When fights break out in a tavern, when domestic quarrels lead to violence, or even when a huge crowd gathers for a rock concert, it is the job of the police to help.

Community policing also represents an effort to reduce or eliminate the historic suspicion that tends to plague the relationship between minority communities and the police. Tensions between African Americans and the largely white police forces sparked many of the urban riots that occurred in the long hot summers of the 1960s. The police were often regarded as an occupying army from outside the community. Community policing is an effort to make the police integral parts of the neighborhoods they patrol.

Of course, police departments have changed a good deal since the 1960s. For one thing, police academies provide much more training in community relations and civil rights today than they once did. For another, there are many more minorities and women in urban police departments, many of them in positions of authority. A generation ago cities such as Detroit and Chicago had very small numbers of minority officers. In 1995, fully 25 percent of Chicago's police force was black; in Detroit the figure was 58 percent. Cities with large Hispanic populations have also made strides: 27 percent of the Los Angeles police force was Hispanic in 1995, as was 15 percent of Houston's. Women made up nearly one-fifth of the officers in those cities.[14]

Community policing, new modes of training, and diversity in hiring are all designed to adapt policing to the realities and expectations of modern urban America. Of course, these various efforts have not eliminated racism or racial tensions in police forces. Americans were shocked, but perhaps not surprised, at the racist views of a key police witness in the O.J. Simpson trial in Los Angeles in 1995, and there continue to be episodes in which black suspects mysteriously die or are beaten while in police custody. Furthermore, white officers occasionally believe that affirmative action efforts have denied them promotion opportunities.[15] But despite these obvious problems, police practices and police-community relations on the whole represent a marked improvement over earlier times.

State Governments and Corrections

State legislators write their states' criminal codes, defining what is crime and what is justice. Their decisions have been very expensive: Correctional expenses were the fastest growing part of most states' budgets throughout the 1980s. From 1985 to 1990 state corrections expenditures increased by 90 percent, although the rate of increase did moderate in the first half of the 1990s.[16] Several developments led to the explosion in prison costs.

Sentencing Reform   For most of this century states used **indeterminate sentencing** in which judges could render sentences of widely varying length and state parole boards decided how long criminals actually remained in prison, depending on their progress in rehabilitation. During the 1970s, the consensus on this correctional philosophy disappeared. Academic studies seemingly proved that rehabilitation does not work. Conservatives demanded that states get tough with criminals instead of coddling them in rehabilitative programs. Liberals objected to racial and class differences in sentencing patterns. People from a variety of perspectives were dissatisfied with the discretion exercised by judges in sentencing criminals and by parole boards in releasing them. At the same time, the nation's crime rate soared, making it imperative that new correctional alternatives be tried.

In the 1980s, most states revolutionized their penal codes. The most significant part of the revolution was the move to **determinate sentencing,** or presumptive sentence lengths for each crime. This strategy constrains judges in levying sentences and limits parole boards in releasing prisoners. Thus, it makes both conservatives and liberals happy, conservatives because the prison time served is longer than before and liberals because the time served is the same for different classes of people. Other related get-tough reforms include the reappearance of the death penalty in 37 states, the abolition of parole for good behavior, and mandatory sentences for certain crimes. Also, some states targeted career criminals, an effort to reduce crime by getting those who commit the most crimes off the streets.

Overcrowding   The consequences of these sentencing reforms have been enormous. By 1993 the number of people in state prisons had increased by 183 percent since 1980, mostly because of the longer sentences mandated by determinate sentencing and related reforms.[17] More people are coming into prison, and they are staying longer. For example, in 1994 Illinois legislators proposed that felons serve at least 85 percent of their sentences; this change would require 28 new prisons and a doubling of the state's prison capacity over the next decade.[18]

The obvious consequence of more prisoners staying longer is that prisons became overcrowded. In 1992, 37 states exceeded the capacity of their prisons, with California being the most crowded at 191 percent of capacity.[19] State correctional budgets have shot up as a result but still they are not keeping pace with demand. It was estimated in 1992 that 1,100 new beds were required each week to keep up with new admissions.[20]

Overcrowding effectively increases the harshness of the sentence, a trend that has brought increased scrutiny from federal judges. Since the 1970s many lawsuits have been brought against the unsanitary and dangerous conditions of prison life, arguing that they constitute cruel and unusual punishment, forbidden by the Eighth Amendment. Federal judges have responded by issuing court orders or entering into consent decrees specifying how prison life is to be conducted. In 1992, for example, the entire prison systems of 11 states were operating under court order; 26 other states had at least one prison operating under such orders.[21] Often judicial orders require that state legislatures spend more money on existing prisons or build new ones. Judicial intervention has had a significant effect on prison life, especially in southern states.

Solutions to Overcrowding   The solutions to prison overcrowding take several forms. One is to build new prisons, which many states have done. But at $75,000 per bed in a high-security prison, building enough new prisons is not a popular option. States have found they can rarely keep up with the demand, so they pack prisoners into existing prisons or sometimes into local jails. For example, in 1991 Louisiana had a quarter of its prisoners in local jails to reduce overcrowding.[22] Jails are not suited for long-term incarceration, so again the degree of punishment is effectively increased.

Another response is to let prisoners out early, before their terms are served. Many states with overcrowded prisons routinely use emergency release for minor offenders; California, for example, freed 37,000 prisoners early in 1986.[23] Prison officials release less violent offenders and those near the end of their sentences. But as one Florida official said, "955 prisoners coming in the front door pretty much means 955 prisoners going out the back door. And some of those we must release are not very nice folks."[24] The average time served in Florida is about one-third of the original sentence.

Still another response is to search for low-cost alternatives to state-run prisons. One option is privatization of prisons, whereby the state contracts with private industry to house its prisoners. Private prisons can yield a modest savings because they typically hire nonunion guards. Private management of prisons has progressed slowly, totaling about 49,000 prisoners in 1994, all in minimum-security prisons.[25] The practice is most advanced in Texas and has been hailed as successful in Tennessee (see Box 16.2).

Nonviolent offenders are increasingly put into **diversion programs,** which divert them from traditional prison settings. Some diversion options include residential care facilities, at-home detention, intensive probation supervision, and community service. Residential care facilities are halfway houses located in the community; they involve supervision of work and living arrangements, but cost less than traditional penal institutions, about $11,000 per year versus $18,300 in a minimum-security prison.[26] At-home detention has become more popular since the invention of low-cost electronic monitoring

BOX 16.2 CUTTING THE COST OF INCARCERATION

Burgeoning inmate populations and court orders to relieve overcrowding in state prisons have caused huge increases in the cost of prison system administration in many states. In order to control these costs, states have had to make hard choices and confront tough realities about crime and society. Three states, North Carolina, Arizona, and Tennessee, have enacted bold policy programs for coping with the high price of incarceration.

In 1994 North Carolina's legislature passed "structured sentencing" legislation. Structured sentencing works on the assumption that there are two categories of criminals: people whom society is afraid of and people whom society is angry at.[1] Recognizing these two different groups, North Carolina has opted to treat them differently to free up prison space and to cut the costs of punishing less-dangerous offenders. Violent offenders get a full sentence under structured sentencing, but those convicted of less violent felonies or misdemeanors can be sentenced to a wide variety of community-based penalties including probation, halfway houses, supervised community service, day reporting centers, drug and alcohol treatment, bootcamp, electronic anklet monitoring, and fines. Sentences are administered according to a sentencing grid established by the North Carolina legislature. In addition to these structured sentences, every bill proposed in the state legislature that affects prison space must include a cost estimate. Analysts in North Carolina have argued that assured sentences and realistic cost calculations have slowed the growth of costs and have increased the chances of rehabilitation.[2]

Arizona judges, through the use of alternative sentencing, have reduced the daily cost per inmate from \$38–44 to \$12.[3] By using measures such as supervised house arrest, Arizona has realized significant savings over the costs involved with incarceration. Alternative sentencing differs from structured sentencing in that judges are not bound by a grid imposed by the state legislature, but rather have fairly broad latitude in applying sentences that seem appropriate given the crime.

Critics have argued that giving judges this discretion does not reduce the number of inmates, but rather has the effect of increasing the punishment given to those who would have otherwise received only probation as a sentence.[4] Others have suggested that the cost savings incurred under alternative sentencing are illusory, as the marginal cost for one more prisoner is not as high as the \$38–44 figure cited by alternative sentencing advocates.

In an attempt to meet these criticisms, under the Community Punishment Program the state devoted \$2.5 million in 1990 to divert offenders from prison in the first year.[5] The diversions substituted intensive probation and treatment programs for prison sentences. Most offenders in the program are

devices such as ankle bracelets; this costs about \$3,500 per year.[27] More than 30 states are experimenting with some version of intensive supervision probation in which probationers are heavily monitored; this costs about \$2,700 per year.[28] Finally, a few states—Minnesota for example—sentence offenders to perform community service in lieu of jail time or require them to pay restitution to victims. Box 16.2 describes how diversion programs work in Arizona.

These diversion alternatives work only for nonviolent offenders, first-time offenders, and for those whose main problem is alcohol or drug abuse rather than crime. They are not meant for hardened criminals. The overall thrust of these solutions is to link either drunk drivers or chemical dependents who must undergo mandatory treatment in lieu of a serving a sentence in prison. In its first year of operation a total of 479 diversions were made.[6] Although critics still see problems with alternative sentencing, Arizona has witnessed positive preliminary results.

Tennessee has taken a different path to cost containment in its prison system. Through a comparison of a prison in the state run by the Corrections Corporation of America and two public prisons, Tennessee has attempted to demonstrate the logic of privatized prisons. South Central Correctional Center in Clifton, Tennessee, is run by the Corrections Corporation of America, and according to a study conducted by the Tennessee legislature, it is providing a cheaper and safer correctional alternative.[7]

When compared with two similar small, minimum security facilities, South Central appears to be administering justice efficiently. South Central had no escapes during the period considered, whereas the other two prisons had one and two escapes respectively. In addition, 80 assaults on guards occurred at South Central; the other two institutions had 69 and 165. Costs at South Central were $35.18 per day, compared with a state average of $35.76. Prisoners in South Central also offered kudos to the institution, with one inmate suggesting that "all penitentiaries should be privately run."[8]

Critics of privatizing prisons argue that philosophically the privatization of state police functions seem unjust. Furthermore, the cost savings may be realized due to the use of nonunionized labor and less attractive pension systems which may impact the ability of private prisons to maintain employees. Still, even the harshest critics admit that the evidence thus far from Tennessee's experiment is impressive.[9]

Structured sentencing, alternative sentencing, and privatizing prisons are all attempts by states to save money under conditions of increasing demand for prison space. Although the preliminary evidence of the success of these programs is mixed, enough positive response has been garnered to ensure continued experimentation. Scholars of the criminal justice system can look to the states for innovative ways to contain the cost of state prison systems.

[1]Neal R. Peirce, "Seeing Prisons Through New Prisms," *National Journal* (December 17, 1994), 2988.

[2]*Ibid.*

[3]Penelope Lemov, "The Next Best Thing to Prison," *Governing* (December 1991), 34.

[4]*Ibid.*, p. 39.

[5]*Ibid.*, p. 38.

[6]*Ibid.*, p. 39.

[7]Fox Butterfield, "Private Tennessee Prison Is Praised in State Studies," *New York Times* (August 19, 1995), 6Y.

[8]*Ibid.*

[9]*Ibid.*

sentencing policy to prison capacity. "We can't afford to have shoplifters in prison," one official said. North Carolina is one of the leaders in taking a rational approach to prison capacity (see Box 16.2), matching sentences with available prison capacity and diverting less serious offenders to other settings.

New Pressures to Get Tough   At the same time that states are struggling to cope with the dramatic increases in corrections costs and with inventing alternative punishments, there are new pressures to send even more people to prison. The slogan of the mid-1990s was "three strikes and you're out!" New federal and state legislation embraced this

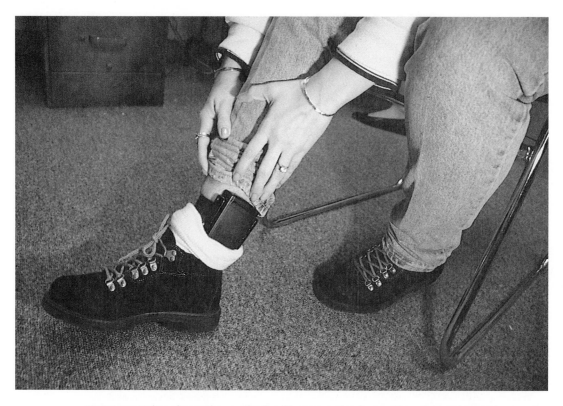

States are trying alternative methods of incarceration in an attempt to reduce prison costs. Here is an ankle bracelet used to monitor people serving their sentences outside of prison. (*Source:* © James Nubile/JB Pictures)

philosophy, in which a felon with two previous convictions receives an especially harsh sentence. California's 1994 tougher sentencing act says, among other things, that a criminal with "three strikes" must receive a prison sentence of at least 25 years. Recall that California already had the most overcrowded prison system in the country. According to experts, this law increases the expected prison population by one-third and means the construction of 15 new prisons at a cost of $4.5 billion, just to stay at the current overcrowded capacity level.[29]

Another source of pressure to send more people to prison comes from changes in the criminal code (new definitions of crime or cracking down on existing crime). The most obvious example is the seriousness with which states now treat drunk driving. In the past the police were lenient toward offenders but since the mid-1980s more than half the states have adopted more stringent penalties for driving while intoxicated (DWI), including mandatory jail time. Even though such time is usually served on the weekends, DWI offenders do tie up valuable jail cells and contribute to overcrowding. Another example is that drug use is now taken more seriously, partly because of the link between drug use and other crimes. As of 1992, 30 percent of new inmates in state prisons were there solely for drug offenses, more than were incarcerated for violent offenses, again contributing to overcrowding.[30]

Still another pressure to "get tough on crime" can be seen in the application of the death penalty. Since the U.S. Supreme Court cleared the way in *Gregg v. Georgia* (1976), 37 states have enacted the death penalty. As shown in Figure 16.1, outside of the Midwest and the Northeast, nearly every state has the death penalty on the books. By 1996, over 3000 people were on death row awaiting execution but only 318 people had been executed since 1976.[31] Due to a complicated appeals process and the natural interest of prisoners in fighting their sentences, at the present rate of implementation, "more of these criminals will die from old age than from gas, electricity or lethal injection", says one author.[32] The states vary widely in the number of people on death row and in the number of executions actually carried out. Over half the death row inmates are in the South; with over 300 each, Texas, California, and Florida have the most people on death row. Texas and Florida have actually executed the most; California has executed only two people since 1976. Within states, the propensity to seek the death penalty varies: Houston, Texas, for example, has contributed 28 percent of those on the Texas death row and 40 percent of those already executed.[33] Houston's district attorney is said to be a strong supporter of the death penalty.

Summary

The politics of criminal justice fits many of our characterizations of social policy in the next chapter. Crime is a political hot potato, and its solutions are very politicized.

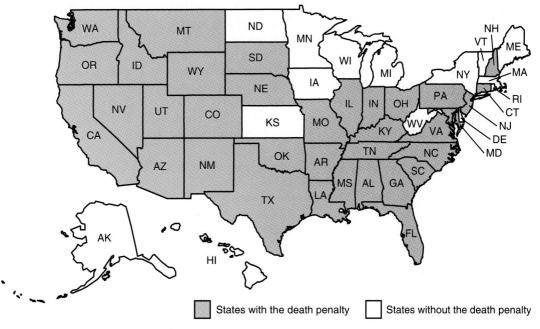

States with the death penalty   States without the death penalty

FIGURE 16.1 States with the Death Penalty.   Since the early 1970s most states have reinstituted the death penalty, although its use has not occurred very often.
Source: Sourcebook of Criminal Justice Statistics, 1993.

Politicians cannot afford to be soft on crime, nor can local governments be complacent about criminal activity: People will not stay in high-crime areas. At least some of the migration of poor people is as much to get away from big-city crime as it is to get the higher welfare benefits in more generous states. But doing something about crime is a difficult and expensive proposition. The growth in corrections expenditures soaks up money from other government programs. Finally, some aspects of criminal justice have moral overtones that spark controversy. For example, capital punishment is a moral dilemma for many people. For all these reasons crime continues to be a problem that ranks high on the political agenda.

Recently many states have adopted a costless method of dealing with crime that is popular with the gun lobby: allowing citizens to arm themselves. In 28 states with the least restrictive laws citizens are issued permits to carry concealed weapons unless there is a specific reason to disqualify them.[34] In 14 other states the law is more restrictive, giving the police discretion to issue such permits if the circumstances warrant it. The "right to carry" was a lively issue in many state legislatures in 1995 and 1996.

✧ MORALITY POLICY

Moral issues are some of the most divisive issues in American politics, and they are the province of state and local governments. States have traditionally exercised police powers, regulated familial and sexual relations, and safeguarded public health and safety. Local communities have set standards for obscenity, regulated gambling, and controlled liquor sales. In addition, state and local governments implement federal laws. Thus, they can affect the degree of compliance with federal directives on school prayer, free speech, and similar issues.

Among the salient moral issues today are abortion, pornography, school prayer, homosexuality, gun control, and AIDS. Moral issues of earlier times and places included liquor, prostitution, the Equal Rights Amendment (ERA), racial segregation, and slavery. Moral issues generate intense heat, sometimes tearing communities, countries, and families apart.

Morality policy is the exercise of legal authority to enforce, modify, or replace community values, moral practices, and norms of interpersonal conduct.[35] This use of government authority to regulate social relationships reflects beliefs about how far government ought to go in controlling the lives of individuals.

Another feature of morality legislation is that it demonstrates the values of society through the private practices government upholds. Government puts the stamp of disapproval (or approval) on various behaviors when it outlaws (or fails to outlaw) them. For instance, legalizing marijuana, gambling, or flag burning can be perceived as saying that it is permissible to smoke dope, gamble, or burn the flag. Others see legalization as allowing individual choice, as the government staying out of people's business. Herein lie many of the controversies.

In addition, morality policies often have a "zero-sum" character about them. If one group's moral code is enacted, they win and the other group loses. Decisions on slavery, prohibition, or abortion cannot be compromised as easily as budgetary decisions can. Thus, decisions about morality policy can be very controversial. Morality policy tends to be very salient because threats to one's values motivate people to pay attention.

State Morality Policy

State governments have long attempted to regulate public morality. Regulations on birth control, abortion, and homosexuality affect sexual practices of individuals. Regulation of divorce and the failure to pass the ERA affect gender roles and family life. Laws on gambling and liquor influence recreational and social life.

Morality regulations vary in the degree of their restrictiveness, that is, in the extent to which the state tries to prevent acts such as abortion, drinking alcohol, and gambling. One study found that religious variables were the best explanation for overall state differences in morality policy.[36] States with large Protestant populations, especially fundamentalist Protestant, restrict liquor and gambling opportunities, whereas states with large Catholic populations restrict divorce and birth control practices. Similarly, another study found that religious fundamentalism was a major explanation for the failure of the ERA.[37] States with many fundamentalists and traditionalistic political cultures did not ratify the ERA.

Abortion We begin with perhaps the most controversial moral issue today: abortion. The states regulated abortion from the 1860s until **Roe v. Wade** in 1973. States prohibited abortion in this time period, whereas before the Civil War abortion was generally permitted, especially before "quickening" (before the fourth month). By the late 1960s, 14 states had reformed their prohibitive regulations so as to permit exceptions in specific circumstances, and in 1970 New York, Hawaii, Alaska, and Washington repealed their prohibitions, allowing abortion for any reason during the first trimester. The remaining 32 states had highly restrictive statutes, permitting abortion only to save the mother's life.

The Supreme Court's decision in 1973 to void the abortion laws of 46 states surprised everyone. Invoking the constitutional right to privacy set forth in *Griswold v. Connecticut* (1965), the majority said that a woman's right to privacy was paramount in the first trimester of pregnancy. In the second trimester, the state's interest in protecting "potential" life becomes larger, and it becomes compelling in the last three months, when the state may even proscribe abortion except where the life or health of the mother is at stake. The decision's import was that states could not regulate abortion at all in the first three months and could do so only to protect maternal health in the second three months.

Following *Roe*, there was a jump in the number of abortions performed, approaching one-third of all pregnancies. New political organizations sprang up on both the pro-choice and anti-abortion sides, and a flurry of lawmaking activity took place in state legislatures. From 1973 to 1989, states adopted various regulations to reduce the number of abortions—requiring parental consent and restricting public funding of abortions, for example—but almost all such laws were overturned when they reached the U.S. Supreme Court. Thus, effectively *Roe v. Wade* greatly reduced the states' ability to regulate abortion.

In 1989, however, in **Webster v. Reproductive Health Services,** the Supreme Court upheld Missouri's significant restrictions on abortion such as fetal viability tests before abortions could be performed, a ban on public funds to counsel women about abortions, and a prohibition on use of public facilities to perform abortions. This decision sent a clear signal that the Court was rethinking *Roe*'s trimester formula. In the 12 months immediately following the *Webster* decision, 351 bills were introduced in state legislatures, some in special sessions called for that purpose.[38] Abortion became an issue in several gubernatorial elections.

In 1992 in ***Planned Parenthood of Southeastern Pennsylvania v. Casey,*** the Court said that the right to an abortion is no longer a fundamental right. Abortion can be restricted by states as long as those restrictions do not constitute an "undue burden." By this logic, the Court upheld Pennsylvania's requirement of parental consent for minors and a 24-hour waiting period, although it struck down spousal notification. Continuing the line of thinking in *Webster*, the Court replaced *Roe*'s trimester framework with a "viability" test: A woman has a right to an abortion before the fetus is viable outside the womb; after viability, the state has the power to restrict abortion, except in life- or health-threatening pregnancies.

The net effect of these two Court decisions is that abortion is again regulated in important ways by the states, and abortions are harder to obtain than in the mid-1970s. State legislatures in the 1990s again saw a flurry of activity as abortion opponents tried to pass new laws in an effort to test the bounds of the Court's rulings. Help in predicting the outcomes in the 1990s comes from studies of policymaking in the post-*Roe* period, that is from 1973 to 1989. Glen Halva-Neubauer found that the policy response of the states to the *Roe* ruling depended on the strength of organized interests on both sides of the abortion issue, the position of legislative leaders and the governor, and the presence of a legislative champion.[39] When key legislative leaders or the governor opposes further abortion restrictions, anti-abortion measures fail. But well-organized anti-abortion groups or strong legislative champions increase significantly the chances for restricting abortion.

Thus far, the legislative response of the states to the *Webster* and *Casey* rulings appears to follow the same pattern. State legislatures that had challenged the *Roe* ruling have seen more restrictive legislation introduced since the subsequent decisions allowed them leeway. Other states without a history of anti-abortion activism have remained quiescent since *Webster* and *Casey*. Box 16.3 describes efforts to restrict or ensure access to abortion in four states.

Other researchers have found additional factors to be important explanations of legislative action in the post-*Webster* era. Strickland and Whicker found that per-capita income and the conservatism of the state's Congressional delegation were most significant: States with low per-capita incomes and conservative congresspeople were more likely to adopt restrictive legislation.[40] Cohen and Barrilleaux examined public opinion on abortion; they found that most states have a pro-choice majority but that public opinion must be consensual to prevail over interest groups' role in regulating abortion.[41] States with more Catholics have more restrictive abortion laws.[42] Finally, the number of female legislators is a factor: Where there are more women serving in the legislatures, abortion access is preserved.[43]

The effect of abortion restrictions on the number of abortions is an interesting question, as Figure 16.2 makes apparent. Although abortion opponents obviously intend to stop the legal performance of abortion, few researchers find a strong link between the stringency of abortion restrictions and the number of abortions performed.[44] Abortion rates tend to be stable over time; interestingly, abortion rates are lowest in moralistic political cultures even though they have the most liberal abortion policies. Getting an abortion seems to be governed more by long-standing cultural norms than by laws. As the four cells of the figure illustrate, states are quite dispersed.

BOX 16.3 POST-WEBSTER ABORTION POLICY IN FOUR STATES

In 1989 the Supreme Court decided a landmark abortion case, *Webster v. Reproductive Health Services of Missouri,* in which it ruled that states could exercise considerably more latitude in regulating access to abortion. Following this decision, many states made changes to their abortion laws. The politics surrounding the enactment of abortion laws following *Webster* in four states—Louisiana, Maryland, Pennsylvania, and Washington—reveal the volatile nature of abortion policymaking. Each of these states enacted new laws in the early 1990s, but none of them departed significantly from their previous position on abortion.

In Louisiana, restrictions on abortion were old news. Before the Supreme Court's 1973 *Roe v. Wade* decision, Louisiana had a total ban on abortions that had been in effect since 1855.[1] A combination of strong Roman Catholicism and evangelical Protestant religious affiliations and rural political conservatism created a political climate in which abortion restrictions were supported more than in other parts of the country. In 1991 the state legislature passed a bill in which abortion was criminalized with no exception for rape or incest unless a police report had been filed before the woman discovered she was pregnant. The legislature overrode a veto by then-governor Buddy Roemer, but ultimately the law was struck down in the federal courts. Although abortion has been a less salient issue of late, Louisiana remains a state in which few abortions occur, as clinics operate only in New Orleans and Shreveport.[2]

Despite a similarly activist Roman Catholic church, Maryland reached a radically different political outcome in the debates that followed the *Webster* decision. In 1991 Maryland voters upheld through referendum a bill passed by the state legislature that essentially codified the 1973 *Roe* decision.[3] After a 3-year legislative battle marked by bitter disputes and an 8-day filibuster in the

state senate, the bill passed, largely due to the switched vote of senate president Mike Miller, a Roman Catholic. Within three weeks of passage, anti-abortion forces had gathered three times the number of signatures necessary to force a referendum on the bill. Ultimately the pro-choice bill was upheld through the referendum by a margin of 62 percent to 38 percent, an outcome that reflects the general level of acquiescence to abortion rights in the state. Maryland continues to demonstrate general support for abortion rights, as witnessed by its 1993 health care bill, which included coverage for abortion services.[4]

Despite a far more restrictive climate with regard to abortion, in Pennsylvania the political system has stymied implementation of the law. After the *Webster* decision, the Pennsylvania legislature passed the Pennsylvania Abortion Control Act, which contained provisions for parental consent for minors, a state-mandated patient information statement to be read by a doctor, a moratorium on abortions past the twenty-fourth week of pregnancy, a 24-hour waiting period, meticulous reporting requirements for clinics, and spousal notification.[5] In 1992 the Supreme Court upheld all provisions of this bill, except for the spousal notification requirement, in *Planned Parenthood of Southeastern Pennsylvania v. Casey.* Despite the apparent legality of the bill, an injunction effectively blocked implementation for 2 years. With a staunchly anti-abortion governor in office, abortion rights groups are mobilizing to circumvent the effects of the bill through such measures as an "overground railroad," sending women to neighboring states where abortion is less restricted. In a state where the majority of the population still supports access to abortion, the political value of rhetoric appears to be of greater

Continued

importance, in some respects, than the implementation of restrictive abortion policy.[6]

Washington state has long provided relatively easy access to abortion services. In 1970, three years before the *Roe* decision, the state passed a statute making abortions legal through the fourth month.[7] After the *Webster* decision, Washington faced a vote on referenda dealing with euthanasia, abortion, and term limits that was characterized by one commentator as a vote on the "end to life, pregnancy and the pursuit of politics."[8] The abortion referendum was a radical measure, including public funding for abortions and no timetable for fetal viability, and still it passed. In this progressive state with low church involvement and a relatively young electorate, no efforts have been made to overturn the state law; in fact, the state went further in 1992 to prohibit interference with clinic access. Washington has not surprisingly been rated by NARAL as among the states at lowest risk of repealing *Roe* if it is overturned by the Supreme Court.[9]

The stories of these four states show that given more latitude, the states will adopt very different policies with regard to abortion access. State political cultures, the religious affiliations of state electorates, and the impact of organized political interests all contribute to distinctly different outcomes in post-*Webster* abortion politics.

[1]Christine L. Day, "Religious Politics and the Pro-Life Cause," in Mary C. Segers and Timothy A. Byrnes, eds., *Abortion Politics in the American States* (Armonk, N.Y.: M.E. Sharpe, 1995), p. 70.

[2]*Ibid.*

[3]Eliza Newman Carney, "Maryland: A Law Codifying *Roe v. Wade*," in Segers and Byrnes, eds., *Abortion Politics in the American States*, p. 52.

[4]*Ibid.*, p. 65.

[5]Susan B. Hansen, "What Didn't Happen: The Implementation of the *Casey* Abortion Decision in Pennsylvania," in Thad Beyle, ed., *State Government: CQ's Guide to Current Issues and Activities* (Washington, D.C.: Congressional Quarterly, 1994) p. 199.

[6]*Ibid.*, pp. 202–203.

[7]Mary T. Hanna, "Washington: Abortion Policymaking Through Initiative," in Segers and Byrnes, eds., *Abortion Politics in the American States*, p. 155.

[8]*Ibid.*, pp. 152–153.

[9]*Ibid.*, p. 154.

[10]*Ibid.*, p. 152.

The states in the lower left cell have few legal restrictions but low abortion rates relative to the number of births; Mississippi and Alabama are examples, suggesting that cultural norms are operating. Above them are states with few restrictions but high abortion rates such as New York and California. On the right side at the bottom are states with many restrictions and few abortions; Utah and North Dakota are illustrative. At the upper right are those with many restrictions and many abortions, such as Massachusetts, indicating the ineffectiveness of laws. There is some fragmentary evidence that decreased access to abortion services is lowering abortion rates. The number of abortion providers has dropped and the incidence of clinic violence has increased, making access more problematic.[45]

Homosexuality   Just as abortion has tremendous moral significance to many people, so does homosexuality. From some religious points of view, sexual relations between people of the same sex is against the word of God and therefore should not be sanctioned in secular law. Advocates of gay and lesbian rights believe organized religion and state law should not

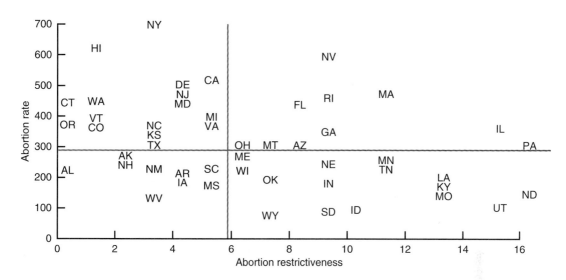

FIGURE 16.2 Abortion Rate, 1992, by Abortion Restrictiveness, **1994.** States vary in their restrictions on abortion but these restrictions do not affect the actual abortion rate very much.

Sources: U.S. Bureau of the Census, *Statistical Abstract of the United States: 1994,* Washington, D.C.: Government Printing Office, 1994. p. 86; Glen A. Halva-Neubauer, "The States After Roe: 'No Paper Tigers,'" in Malcolm L. Goggin, ed., *Understanding the New Politics of Abortion,* Newbury Park, Calif.: Sage Publications, 1993, pp. 195-196. The index has been subsequently updated to reflect laws and resolutions enacted between 1989 and 1994, by personal communication from the author.

interfere with their practices; to this end, they have been working to deregulate sexual behavior.

States for a long time outlawed same-sex relations between consenting adults, but now those laws have been repealed in about half of the states. States with such prohibitions tend to be conservative as measured by the presence of a conservative Democratic party, a Baptist population, and a traditionalistic political culture.[46] Such prohibitions were upheld by the U.S. Supreme Court in 1986 in *Bowers v. Hardwick,* in which the majority said that the constitutional right to privacy does not extend to homosexual relations.

Gay and lesbian couples have campaigned for a variety of rights heterosexual couples have in regard to marriage and the family. There are currently no states that recognize gay marriages, but seven states—California, Michigan, New Jersey, Oregon, Virginia, West Virginia, and Wisconsin—allow nontraditional families to register as nonprofit associations. State sanctioning of gay marriages may come first in the state of Hawaii, because in 1993 its Supreme Court ruled that denial of a marriage license to gay and lesbian couples amounted to sex discrimination; they returned the case to a lower court for rehearing.[47] If Hawaii eventually recognizes such marriages, then the courts will be asked whether other states have to recognize marriages conducted in Hawaii.

Divorce   Divorce also has moral significance to many people, although it is much more prevalent than abortion and homosexual relationships. Divorce rates have increased greatly over this century, and state divorce laws have changed dramatically in the last 30 years. But in contrast to our other examples of morality legislation, divorce reform did not provoke political controversy.

Traditionally, divorces were granted only after marital misbehavior (such as adultery) was proven; today all states have some provision for no-fault divorce, in which "irretrievable breakdown" of the marriage is the criterion for dissolution. Related changes are equally dramatic: Traditionally mothers were presumed to be the better guardian for the children after divorce; now mothers and fathers have more equal footing in gaining child custody. Similarly, property and other financial assets no longer go to the person who earned them; alimony is not automatic, it depends on the circumstances.

These dramatic changes in divorce law have been called the silent revolution by scholar Herbert Jacob. He writes,

> *Most of these laws were enacted after 1965. No party platform or social protest spurred legislators to accept them. Neither national politicians nor Congress played a part in their adoption. No bureaucracy or national interest group promoted them. Little political conflict accompanied them. While controversy raged about civil rights, Vietnam, Watergate, state taxation, abortion, the Equal Rights Amendment, Iranian hostages, and the withdrawal of government involvement from the private sector by the Reagan administration, state legislators quietly adopted the radically new rules for divorce.*[48]

New York was the first state to adopt the no-fault doctrine in 1966, followed by California in 1969. No-fault divorce spread rapidly: By 1974, 45 states had a no-fault provision, and in 1985 South Dakota became the last state to adopt these grounds for divorce.[49] The time was ripe for such an innovation in the context of other social change, and bureaucrats, lawyers, experts, and other policy entrepreneurs skillfully and quietly guided the reform through state legislatures around the country.

Although no-fault divorce laws definitely make divorce easier to obtain, experts are divided over whether the reform itself contributes to the increase in divorce rates. One unanticipated consequence of the divorce reform, according to some but not all scholars, has been that women are on average financially worse off under no-fault laws than under traditional laws.[50] This is because men are no longer obligated to pay alimony, so in essence they are better off after divorce.

Right-to-Die Legislation   Our final example of state morality regulation has to do with a person's right to die. Traditionally doctors have stopped medical treatment in hopeless cases and withdrawn life-sustaining treatment. However, in recent years lawsuits and court intervention have made this practice less routine. State legislation and court decisions have helped to define the parameters of these decisions, especially when the patient has previously established a living will. So far more active interventions, such as assisted suicide as practiced by Dr. Jack Kevorkian, are illegal in all states. The right to die issue raises many of the same concerns as does abortion except at the opposite end of the life cycle. Many religious people see advocacy of the right to die as infringing on the power of God to control life; others see it as involving government in something that ought to be a private matter between doctor and patient.

Following some well-publicized court cases, in the mid-1970s state legislatures began to consider **living will** legislation. A living will allows people to specify in advance their preferences regarding life sustaining medical treatment in case of a terminal illness or permanent vegetative state (only a few states have this latter provision). California in 1965 was the first state to adopt such legislation, and it was rapidly followed by several western states.[51] Then activity slowed down until 1984 and 1985, when there was another flurry of activity, partly because the Catholic Church ended its active opposition to the measure; by 1991, 45 states had joined the pack. As more states adopted living wills, the laws became more facilitative; that is, they made it easier for patients or their families to control final medical treatment.[52] Henry Glick's analysis of the dates of adoption of living will laws shows that earlier adopters had smaller Catholic populations, more media attention to the issue, and more court decisions.[53]

Summary   State morality legislation has been illustrated by reference to policies in four areas: abortion, homosexual relations, divorce, and the right to die. States vary considerably in their approach to these issues but everywhere they are salient and controversial topics. In contrast to other policy areas, economic variables have little to do with state variations in morality policy. Rather the explanatory factors tend to be religious, cultural, and ideological ones. General public opinion liberalism or conservatism matters, as do long-standing political cultural differences and the power of organized groups.

Local Morality Policy

City government also plays a role in promoting and enforcing certain moral values. Municipal morality policy mostly has to do with the regulation of sin and sex; occasionally it also involves the promotion of particular religious values.

Different communities clearly have different levels of tolerance for unconventional behavior and deviance from the norm. What in one place is cause for alarm and formal sanction is in another place either ignored or dealt with informally. James Q. Wilson's classic study of police behavior found that styles of policing varied from city to city.[54] In cities dominated by a partisan, working-class, ethnic political culture, Wilson discovered that the police were likely to treat public drunkenness, disorderly conduct, gambling, and even prostitution as problems calling for informal resolution. As long as these breaches of order or morality did not impinge on others, the police in these cities rarely resorted to formal arrest. Drunks were driven home or to the police station to sober up, prostitutes were shooed off the main streets, gambling went undisturbed as long as it was done in private.

In contrast, in cities governed by nonpartisan reform-style administrations with largely middle-class populations, the police tended to respond to the same range of problems in a legalistic way. As one police chief interviewed for the study remarked, "Laws are on the books to be enforced."[55] Arrest rates in cities in which police practices were characterized as "legalistic" were much higher for the same offenses than they were in the more relaxed environment in which informal responses were the norm.

Differences in police styles are in part responses to differences in community standards. Whereas people in one community might be offended by the presence of backroom card games in the corner tavern, people in other places tolerate not only card games but the numbers game on the streets and bookies in the barbershops. Differences in standards bear not only on enforcement, but also on sanctions. In some college towns in the Midwest, for example, the possession of marijuana for personal use is treated as a misdemeanor, whereas in other cities the same amount of dope exposes the smoker to arrest.

City governments are also involved in efforts to regulate and even ban pornography. Some places, such as Boston, have tried through their zoning powers to contain pornography shops and adult movies in one part of town (the Boston area was dubbed the Combat Zone) where a concentrated police presence could maintain order. Other cities, under pressure from an alliance of women's rights groups and religious organizations, have sought to ban pornography altogether.[56] Arguing that pornography oppresses and discriminates against women—and thus denies them civil rights—proponents of a pornography ban succeeded in persuading the Minneapolis city council to pass a restrictive ordinance in 1983. The mayor vetoed the law on the grounds that it violated First Amendment free speech guarantees. A similar ban was later passed in Indianapolis, but it was struck down in the federal courts on similar grounds. In other cities the effort to eliminate or restrict pornography is more oblique: New York City, for example, has begun a massive redevelopment effort in Times Square, designed both to bring respectable tourism back to the area and at the same time drive out pornography shops by driving up property values and thus rents.

City politics is also a major setting in which debate over the expansion of homosexual rights is taking place. In this sphere the impact of municipal action in some places, particularly university towns, has been to promote or at least accept a broader sexual moral code. Madison, Wisconsin, for example, prohibits housing discrimination on the basis of sexual preference. Perhaps the key issue in gay rights at the local government level is whether notions of the family ought to be expanded to include gay couples. Several California cities, led by West Hollywood in 1984, have passed local ordinances that give gay municipal employees with partners the same rights granted to married couples with regard to hospital and jail visitation, bereavement leave, and family health insurance coverage.

These laws are controversial. When San Francisco passed such an ordinance in 1989, conservative religious groups barred its implementation by successfully petitioning to place the measure on the ballot that November. In the ensuing election, the law was narrowly defeated.[57] In 1993 two cities and four counties in Oregon passed referenda barring gay rights laws, and Lewiston, Maine, voters defeated a proposed nondiscrimination ordinance. In 1994 Austin, Texas, voters repealed a law providing health insurance benefits for gay partners of city employees.[58] Gay rights proponents clearly have not managed in many places to win equal rights guarantees from local governments.

Municipal government has been involved not only in the regulation of sexual behavior and morals but also in religious matters. Many cities use their zoning powers to make sure that establishments with liquor licenses are not located near schools and churches, a response particularly to Protestant denominations that frown on drinking. Municipal activities that seem to favor or promote religion or some particular church run up against the First Amendment prohibition against the establishment of religion. Many local controversies involve the display of religious symbols—nativity scenes, menorahs, and crosses—on city property at holiday time. In *Lynch v. Donnelly* (1984) the U.S. Supreme Court upheld the display of a crèche on city property in Pawtucket, Rhode Island.

Because the crèche was part of a display that contained nonreligious symbols such as Santa Claus, the court held that the city was not trying to aid religion in general or any particular faith. However, in *Allegheny v. ACLU* (1989) the Supreme Court said that the display of a solitary nativity scene at a Pittsburgh courthouse, a place "closely associated with a core government function," violated the establishment clause of the First Amendment.

Summary

Moral issues are among the most controversial issues governments handle. Morality legislation is perceived to uphold the values of one group and trample the values of another. The abortion conflict is the major moral dilemma facing state governments since 1989 and 1992 Supreme Court rulings opened the door for more state restrictions. Homosexual rights and the right to die are also pressing issues of morality; divorce law has seemingly been settled. Local governments are involved in regulating pornography, rights of homosexuals, and religious practices. Religious, cultural, and political values of states and communities shape government responses to these moral issues.

✧ CONCLUSION

Maintaining public order is essential to the preservation of community. Economic activity, social life, and civic and political involvement all require a basic level of order, safety, and public trust. State and local governments place a high priority on maintaining and fostering public order. Public order is a complex idea, however. Various forms of criminal behavior represent one sort of threat to public order. There is widespread agreement on the need for protection from thugs and predators; the criminal challenge to public order is a clear threat to personal safety and personal property. The role of government in policing and corrections is relatively clear here, although there are arguments about how far the police and legislatures may go in trying to combat crime.

But public order also has a normative dimension. Whose values are to prevail? Should state and local governments take a position on normative issues? What is acceptable behavior to some—drinking, abortion, homosexuality, or gambling—may be an affront to the public moral order for others. Many believe that public order cannot exist if people embrace different lifestyles and different beliefs. Here the role of state and local government in the maintenance of public order is more controversial. Unlike the case of crime, Americans do not agree on the proper role of government when issues of morality are at stake.

✦ KEY TERMS

community policing (p. 416)
determinate sentencing (p. 418)
diversion programs (p. 419)
indeterminate sentencing (p. 418)
living will (p. 431)
morality policy (p. 424)

Planned Parenthood of Southeastern Pennsylvania v. Casey (p. 426)
Roe v. Wade (p. 425)
Webster v. Reproductive Health Services (p. 425)

✧ FOR FURTHER READING

John J. DiIulio, Jr., *Governing Prisons: A Comparative Study of Correctional Management* (New York: Free Press, 1987). The author compares prison management in Texas, California, and Michigan and traces the differences to contrasting philosophies of government in each state.

Donald Alexander Downs, *The New Politics of Pornography* (Chicago: University of Chicago Press, 1989). Exploration of the antipornography movement (focusing upon landmark cases in Minneapolis and Indianapolis) and its impact on free speech.

Henry R. Glick, *The Right to Die: Policy Innovation and Its Consequences* (New York: Columbia University Press, 1992). The author traces the diffusion of right to die legislation and judicial doctrines from state to state.

Herbert Jacob, *Silent Revolution: The Transformation of Divorce Law in the United States* (Chicago: University of Chicago Press, 1988). An analysis of how a revolutionary change in divorce law was achieved in the states with little controversy.

Mary C. Segers and Timothy A. Byrnes, eds., *Abortion Politics in American States* (Armonk, N.Y.: M.E. Sharpe, 1995). A collection of case studies in ten states, analyzing the diversity and complexities of abortion politics.

✧ NOTES

1. Eric Monkkonen, *American Becomes Urban* (Berkeley: University of California Press, 1988), pp. 225–226.

2. Cathy Cohen and Michael Dawson, "Neighborhood Poverty and African American Politics," *American Political Science Review*, 87 (June 1993), 286–302.

3. Mark Warr, "Public Opinion on Crime and Punishment," *Public Opinion Quarterly*, 59 (Summer 1995), 297.

4. Richard Berke, "Fears of Crime Rival Concern over Economy," *New York Times* (January 23, 1994), 1 (Section 1).

5. *Ibid.*, p. 299.

6. U.S. Bureau of the Census, *Statistical Abstract of the United States, 1995* (Washington, D.C.: Government Printing Office, 1995), p. 199. This is the source of all crime statistics discussed below, except where noted.

7. Fox Butterfield, "Many Cities in U.S. Show Sharp Drop in Homicide Rate," *New York Times* (August 13, 1995).

8. Scott Cummings and Daniel Monti, eds., *Gangs: The Origin and Impact of Contemporary Youth Gangs in the United States* (Albany: State University of New York Press, 1994).

9. Wesley Skogan, "Crime and Punishment," in Virginia Gray and Herbert Jacob, eds., *Politics in the American States*, 6th ed. (Washington, D.C.: CQ Press, 1996), p. 394.

10. *Ibid.*, p. 364.

11. Herbert Jacob, *The Frustration of Policy: Responses to Crime in American Cities* (Boston: Little, Brown, 1984), p. 55.

12. Jeffrey Henig, *Public Policy and Federalism* (New York: St. Martin's Press, 1985), pp. 278–279.

13. John Tierney, "The Holy Terror," *New York Times Magazine* (December 3, 1995), 82; Rob Gurwitt, "Cops and Community," *Governing*, 8 (May 1995), 21.

14. Charles Mahtesian, "The Big Blue Hiring Spree," *Governing,* 9 (January 1996), 30–31.

15. *Ibid.*

16. Bureau of Justice Statistics, *Sourcebook of Criminal Justice Statistics, 1993* (Washington, D.C.: Government Printing Office, 1994), p. 3.

17. U.S. Bureau of the Census, *Statistical Abstract of the United States, 1995,* p. 217.

18. Skogan, "Crime and Punishment," p. 384.

19. *Ibid.,* pp. 384–385.

20. *Ibid.,* p. 384.

21. *Ibid.,* p. 380.

22. Bureau of Justice Statistics, *Sourcebook of Criminal Justice Statistics, 1993,* p. 597.

23. Skogan, "Crime and Punishment," p. 387.

24. Andrew H. Malcolm, "Florida's Jammed Prisons: More in Means More Out," *New York Times* (July 3, 1989), 1.

25. Fox Butterfield, "Private Tennessee Prison Is Praised in State Studies," *New York Times* (August 19, 1995), A6.

26. Skogan, "Crime and Punishment," p. 371.

27. *Ibid.,* p. 371.

28. *Ibid.,* p. 371.

29. Penelope Lemov, "Roboprison," *Governing* (March 1995), 25; Fox Butterfield, "Prison-Building Binge in California Casts Shadow on Higher Education," *New York Times* (April 12, 1995), A11.

30. W. John Moore, "Locked In," *National Journal* (July 30, 1994), 1788.

31. Penelope Lemov, "Long Life on Death Row," *Governing* (March 1996), 34.

32. *Ibid.,* p. 30.

33. Tamar Lewin, "Who Decides Who Will Die? Even Within States, It Varies," *New York Times* (February 23, 1995), A1, A13.

34. Ellen Perlman, "Living With Concealed Weapons," *Governing* (February 1996), 33.

35. Raymond Tatalovich and Byron W. Daynes, eds., *Social Regulatory Policy* (Boulder, Colo.: Westview Press, 1988), p. 1.

36. J. David Fairbanks, "Politics, Economics, and the Public Morality: Why Some States Are More Moral than Others," in Thomas R. Dye and Virginia Gray, eds., *The Determinants of Public Policy* (Lexington, Mass.: Lexington Books, 1980), pp. 95–106.

37. Pamela Johnston Conover and Virginia Gray, *Feminism and the New Right: Conflict over the American Family* (New York: Praeger, 1983).

38. Mary C. Segers and Timothy A. Byrnes, "Introduction: Abortion Politics in American States," in Mary C. Segers and Timothy A. Byrnes, eds., *Abortion Politics in American States* (Armonk, N.Y.: M.E. Sharpe, 1995), p. 8.

39. Glen Halva-Neubauer, "Abortion Policy in the Post-*Webster* Age," *Publius,* 20 (Summer 1990), 27–44.

40. Ruth Ann Strickland and Marcia Lynn Whicker, "Political and Socioeconomic Indicators of State Restrictiveness Toward Abortion," *Policy Studies Journal,* 20 (Winter 1992), 598–617.

41. Jeffrey E. Cohen and Charles Barrilleaux, "Public Opinion, Interest Groups, and Public Policy

Making: Abortion Policy in the American States," in Malcolm L. Goggin, ed., *Understanding the New Politics of Abortion* (Newbury Park, Calif.: Sage, 1993), pp. 203–221. An even stronger effect of public opinion was found by Wetstein; see Matthew E. Wetstein, *Abortion Rates in the United States* (Albany: State University of New York Press, 1996).

42. Robert E. O'Connor and Michael B. Berkman, "Religious Determinants of State Abortion Policy," *Social Science Quarterly*, 76 (June 1995), 447–459.

43. Susan B. Hansen, "Differences in Public Policies Toward Abortion: Electoral and Policy Context," in Goggin, ed., *Understanding the New Politics of Abortion* pp. 222–248; Michael Berkman and Robert E. O'Connor, "Do Women Legislators Matter? Female Legislators and State Abortion Policy," *American Politics Quarterly*, 21 (January 1993), 102–124.

44. Susan Welch, Sue Thomas, and Margery M. Ambrosius, "The Politics of Family Policy," in Virginia Gray and Herbert Jacob, eds., *Politics in the American States*, 6th ed. (Washington, D.C.: CQ Press, 1996), pp. 566; Hansen, "Differences in Public Policies Toward Abortion." The simple correlation in Figure 16.2 is −.35, without controlling for other causes.

45. Welch, Thomas, and Ambrosius, "The Politics of Family Policy," p. 567; Glen A. Halva-Neubauer, Raymond Tatalovich, and Byron W. Daynes, "Locating Abortion Clinics: Aggregate Data and Case Study Approaches to the Implementation Process," presented at the annual meeting of the American Political Science Association, Washington, D.C., September 1993.

46. David C. Nice, *Policy Innovation in State Government* (Ames: Iowa State University Press, 1994), Ch. 9.

47. Bettina Boxall, "Hawaii May Let Gays Tie the Knot," *Minneapolis Star Tribune* (April 4, 1995), 4A.

48. Herbert Jacob, *Silent Revolution: The Transformation of Divorce Law in the United States* (Chicago: University of Chicago Press, 1988), p. 3.

49. Note that only 15 states eliminated all fault provisions; 35 states simply added some form of no-fault to existing fault grounds for divorce.

50. Lenore Weitzman, *The Divorce Revolution: The Unexpected Social and Economic Consequences for Women and Children in America* (New York: Free Press, 1985).

51. Henry R. Glick and Scott P. Hays, "Innovation and Reinvention in State Policymaking: Theory and the Evolution of Living Will Laws," *Journal of Politics*, 53 (August 1991), 839.

52. *Ibid.*, p. 842.

53. Henry R. Glick, *The Right to Die: Policy Innovation and Its Consequences* (New York: Columbia University Press, 1992), p. 177.

54. James Q. Wilson, *Varieties of Policy Behavior* (Cambridge, Mass.: Harvard University Press, 1968).

55. *Ibid.*, p. 177.

56. Donald Downs, *The New Politics of Pornography* (Chicago: University of Chicago Press, 1989).

57. G. M. Bush, "Domestic Partner Is New Addition to 'Family,'" *Los Angeles Daily Journal* (July 11, 1989); Rex Bossert, "Proponents of S.F. Domestic Partnership Law to Renew Efforts," *Los Angeles Daily Journal* (November 9, 1989).

58. *New York Times* (May 9, 1994).

SOCIAL POLICY

The provision of social services was historically the responsibility of state and local governments. Public poorhouses and orphanages, public elementary schools, homes for the deaf, and rudimentary facilities for the mentally ill pretty much defined the limits of the nineteenth-century welfare state in America. Today these traditional responsibilities have been vastly augmented, and responsibility is shared with the federal government. Not only do we have a much broader notion about the appropriate scope of government responsibility, but new problems arise all the time. Thus, the arrival of refugees from Haiti and Southeast Asia, the spread of AIDS, the surge in teen pregnancy, the emergence of crack addiction, and the increase in homelessness are all problems that appeared in the late twentieth century that must be dealt with by state and local governments.

Among the many social problems states and localities handle, three broad ones stand out. First is the problem of poverty. States help to fund and administer welfare programs that try to ameliorate poverty. Second is health care, traditionally offered alongside welfare programs. Today states are being challenged to cover people other than welfare recipients. A third important social policy area is education, often the means for preventing and solving social problems. Historically local school boards have controlled the public schools, but in the 1980s the states became the dominant partner in their funding. In this chapter we examine policies aimed at addressing these social problems.

✧ THE POLITICS OF SOCIAL POLICY

Although there are many programmatic differences among various social policies, there are some crucial similarities in their politics. First, choices in social programs are often controversial because they involve fundamental questions about the role of government in society. Should welfare recipients be allowed to stay home with their children or should they be required to work outside the home? Should mentally ill people walk and sleep on the streets freely or should government restrain them? Each of us answers these questions differently depending on our political ideology. For many people the questions are moral ones as well, and there is a "moral" answer and an "immoral" answer. Thus, social issues provoke more personal and more intense responses than do the economic issues considered in Chapter 14.

Second, social policies often involve **redistribution,** the transfer of wealth from the rich to the poor. Sometimes the intent is explicitly redistributive: Welfare programs focus solely on people below the poverty line. Other times the program's effect is redistributive: Public education may benefit the lower class more than it benefits the upper class. Whenever a policy is perceived to be redistributive, whether by design or by practice, its politics are likely to be contentious, involving conflicts between the haves and the have-nots.

Third, redistributive choices are more complicated in a federal system under which people can move freely. Taking their own self-interest into account, upper-income people may prefer to live in states and communities in which minimal redistribution occurs, that is, where taxes are low and social programs are modest. Lower-income people, if they are the beneficiaries of social programs, will rationally prefer to live where maximum redistribution occurs. State and local policymakers are constrained in their policy choices by the possibility that higher taxes and generous social benefits will drive away upper-income people and attract less desirable residents in turn. They fear that too much redistribution will have negative economic effects on their community or state.

For all these reasons the redistributive politics surrounding social policymaking is very different from the developmental politics described in Chapter 14. Redistribution pits groups against each other—situations in which someone wins and someone loses (a zero-sum game). Losers can "vote with their feet"; that is, they can move to another community, one whose residents have similar ideas about the value of redistribution. In addition, winners and losers often portray each other in moral terms, thus rendering social policymaking intensely political.

✧ WELFARE POLICY

The Poverty Problem

In 1994, 38 million people in this country were poor, down slightly from the year before; they constituted 14.5 percent of the nation's population. The number of poor people and the poverty rate increased in the early 1990s. Poverty is measured in the United States by the number of people who fall below a money income threshold established by the federal government. The threshold varies by family size and composition. In 1993 the poverty threshold for a family of four was $14,763.[1] (Note that a person who works full-time over the course of an entire year at the prevailing minimum wage would still earn an income substantially below the poverty line.)

Among the significant factors associated with poverty are race, sex, age, and region. In 1993, 33.1 percent of blacks and 30.6 percent of Hispanics were poor, compared to only 12.2 percent of whites. Among types of families, 38.7 percent of all families headed by single women were poor (as compared to 13.6 percent of all families). Fully half of all black and Hispanic families headed by single women fell below the poverty line. The high incidence of poverty among female-headed households is described as the **feminization of poverty.**

Poverty is also linked to age. In fact, about half the nation's poor in 1993 were either under 18 or over 65 years of age. The poverty rate also varies by region of the country (the South had the highest rate of 17.1 percent, the West had the next highest rate at 15.6 percent, the Northeast and Midwest the lowest rates at 13.3 and 13.4 percent, respectively) and by place of residence. The nation's central cities generally contain the highest concentration of poor people.

Table 17.1 ranks the states according to the percentage of poor people in 1993. Poverty is obviously unequally distributed: A quarter of Louisiana's and Mississippi's population lives in poverty, whereas less than 9 percent of the citizens in Hawaii, Delaware, and Connecticut are poor. The redistributive effort required to eliminate poverty in Louisiana and Mississippi is much greater than the effort required in Hawaii, Delaware, and Connecticut. On the other hand, states such as Connecticut and Delaware may exercise restraint for fear of becoming a welfare magnet, attracting poor people from other states. Hawaii has less to worry about because its location away from the mainland protects it from immigration.

Poverty is not an isolated social problem; it is associated with other problems. Poor people often have more serious health problems than wealthier people; they often lack a good education and job skills. The need for health care, education, and training programs is greater in states with large poverty populations. Poverty is usually correlated with crime, especially in urban areas. The criminal justice system, therefore, is more burdened in poorer states. Because many other social problems are intertwined with poverty, welfare policy is the centerpiece of social policy.

The Structure of Welfare Policy

Welfare is defined as "government provision of cash and in-kind assistance in relief of poverty."[2] Welfare is a redistributive policy because wealth is taxed away from citizens in order to fund assistance to the poor. Its politics are often controversial because many people believe that poverty is the fault of those who are poor. Welfare policy has long been an intergovernmental maze of national, state, and local programs, sometimes working together and sometimes working at cross-purposes. One former cabinet official once pointed out that our welfare system is overseen and administered by 9 federal executive departments, 21 congressional committees, 54 state-level welfare agencies, and over 3,000 local welfare agencies.[3]

Few people defend our welfare system, and reform has been part of the political agenda in both the Congress and the White House in recent years. In 1996, Congress gave the states more control over the array of welfare programs and helped them to finance these programs with block grants. No recipient will be entitled to a benefit; eligibility and level of benefits depend on the state. Understanding the system that originated in the Great Depression and prevailed for more than half a century is essential to understanding the reform enacted in the Clinton years.

The **Social Security Act of 1935** and its subsequent amendments set the basic framework for welfare policy. This act contained several different programs based on two major principles. One is the **social insurance principle,** according to which the government underwrites a nationwide insurance pool for workers and their families. The Old Age, Survivors, Disability, and Health Insurance program (OASDHI), commonly known as Social Security, covers workers who are no longer employable due to old age or disability and provides benefits to the families of workers who die. Social Security is an entitlement program: Its benefits go to anyone, regardless of income, who has paid the Social Security tax. Because it covers so many people, it is very expensive. Medical assistance

TABLE 17.1 PERCENTAGE OF PEOPLE IN POVERTY BY STATE, 1993 The percentage of people living in poverty varies widely among the states, with Louisiana having the most poor people and Hawaii the least.

Rank	State	Percentage
1	Louisiana	26.4%
2	Mississippi	24.7
3	West Virginia	22.2
4	Kentucky	20.4
5	Arkansas	20.0
6	Oklahoma	19.9
7	Tennessee	19.6
8	South Carolina	18.7
9	California	18.2
10	Florida	17.8
11	Alabama	17.4
12	Texas	17.4
13	New Mexico	17.4
14	New York	16.4
15	Missouri	16.1
16	Maine	15.4
17	Michigan	15.4
18	Arizona	15.4
19	Montana	14.9
20	North Carolina	14.4
21	South Dakota	14.2
22	Illinois	13.6
23	Georgia	13.5
24	Wyoming	13.3

through the Medicare program is an additional benefit available to Social Security recipients. Social Security and Medicare are federal programs with no state component.

Another social insurance program contained in the 1935 act is unemployment compensation. It is designed to prevent poverty among workers who are temporarily unemployed (that is, laid off). Unemployment compensation is financed jointly by the national government, the states, and employers, but is administered by the states.

The 1935 act also contained programs based on a second principle: the **public charity principle.** These programs require a means test, that is, proof that the person is poor. The act (as later amended) provided assistance to poor people who are aged and not covered by Social Security, blind, permanently and totally disabled, and to families with dependent children. In 1972 the first three categories of recipients were combined into a single program, called Supplemental Security Income (SSI). The SSI program is administered by the federal government and provides a uniform national benefit. States can supplement this benefit; accordingly, there is variation in the benefits recipients get in different states.

TABLE 17.1 (CONTINUED)

Rank	State	Percentage
25	Pennsylvania	13.2%
26	Idaho	13.1
27	Kansas	13.1
28	Ohio	13.0
29	Wisconsin	12.6
30	Indiana	12.2
31	Washington	12.1
32	Oregon	11.8
33	Minnesota	11.6
34	North Dakota	11.2
35	Rhode Island	11.2
36	New Jersey	10.9
37	Utah	10.7
38	Massachusetts	10.7
39	Nebraska	10.3
40	Iowa	10.3
41	Vermont	10.0
42	New Hampshire	9.9
43	Colorado	9.9
44	Nevada	9.8
45	Maryland	9.7
46	Virginia	9.7
47	Alaska	9.1
48	Connecticut	8.5
49	Delaware	8.5
50	Hawaii	8.0

Source: U.S. Bureau of the Census CD-ROM, *Income and Poverty: 1993.*

The fourth category—children—remain in a separate program, Aid to Families with Dependent Children (AFDC), until 1997. It is a joint federal-state program, funded by both levels of government and administered by the states. Because the states determine eligibility and benefit levels, there is wide variation in access and benefits received in different states. The program was originally designed to support orphaned children but has in fact supported more children born out-of-wedlock. Medical assistance is provided to SSI and AFDC recipients and other poor people through the Medicaid program, also a joint federal-state program.

Table 17.2 contains information on the costs of these welfare programs expressed as expenditures on benefit payments in 1992 or 1993, depending on data availability. Social Security expenditures dwarf all other programs, amounting to $302.4 billion in 1993. The Medicare program is also quite expensive for the federal government, totaling $93.5 billion in 1993. For states, Medicaid is the biggest expenditure, its benefits constituting $50.2 billion in 1992; this is in addition to the federal contribution of $67.8 billion. Unemployment compensation was second, totaling 21.8 billion paid out in benefits in 1993. The AFDC

TABLE 17.2 SOCIAL WELFARE BENEFIT PAYMENTS, 1992 AND 1993 (IN BILLIONS) The largest social welfare programs— Social Security and Medicare—are run by the national government. The state and local welfare programs tend to be smaller, except for Medicaid which is a substantial expenditure at both governmental levels.

	Federal Dollars	*State/Local Dollars*
Social Insurance Programs		
Social Security, 1993	$302.4	none
Unemployment Compensation, 1993	0.8	$21.8
Medicare, 1993	93.5	none
Means-Tested Programs		
SSI, 1993	20.7	3.9
AFDC, 1992	12.1	9.8
General Assistance, 1992	none	3.3
Medicaid, 1992	67.8	50.2
General Assistance: Medical, 1992	none	4.8
Food Stamps, 1993	22.8	none

Sources: 1992 data from U.S. Bureau of the Census, *Statistical Abstract of the United States: 1994* (Washington, D.C.: Government Printing Office, 1994), p. 373; 1993 data from Social Security Administration, *Annual Statistical Supplement to the Social Security Bulletin, 1994,* pp. 13–15.

program is more modest in cost, amounting to 9.8 billion for the states in 1992; in addition, the federal government contributed $12.1 billion. Thus, the degree of public controversy over welfare programs is not necessarily tied to their cost. Rather, the controversy reflects underlying attitudes toward the poor and society's obligation to them.

Several differences between the social insurance principle and the charity principle are important to note. Because recipients of Social Security, Medicare, and unemployment benefits have paid into the system, they are entitled to draw benefits, regardless of their income level. This, in turn, means that these programs have a sense of legitimacy; recipients do not have the stigma of being "on the dole." The means-tested programs, on the other hand, have great stigma attached to them. Recipients are not entitled to support in the same sense as are Social Security recipients. Financial support is at the discretion of the government. One result of this difference is financial: Social Security stipends have been indexed so that they increase with the cost of living. Public officials have allowed the value of AFDC payments to be eroded by inflation.

Among the means-tested programs, public sentiment is more favorable toward SSI recipients than toward AFDC recipients. The aged, disabled, and blind are considered to be among the "deserving poor," those worthy of public assistance. Their benefits cost the federal government $20.7 billion in 1993 and the states $3.9 billion. AFDC recipients, on the other hand, are more often regarded as "undeserving poor," people who have contributed to their misfortune through laziness, promiscuity, and lack of character. (A Los Angeles Times poll found that 61 percent of the people it surveyed agreed with the statement that "poor young women often have babies so they can collect welfare."[4]) The stereotypical welfare recipients are the minority single mother and her large family.

In fact, however, the AFDC rolls are almost evenly split between whites and blacks, with whites being in a slight majority. Furthermore, most welfare families are small: In 1992, 42.5 percent of welfare families consist of mothers with only one child, and another 30.2 percent had only two children.[5] Most welfare recipients could not work if they wished: Two-thirds of them are children. Most of the adult women on welfare would prefer to work than to receive the meager dole from the welfare office. But stereotypes die hard. It is no wonder that advocates for means-tested welfare programs are at a significant disadvantage in lobbying for additional funding as compared to lobbyists for Social Security funding.

Outside the structure of the Social Security Act are two additional welfare programs. These are the only programs available to the poor who are not in one of the above categories. One program, Food Stamps, is totally federally funded but is administered jointly with state and county welfare departments. Food stamps help about one out of every eight or nine American families with their grocery costs and cost $22.8 billion in 1993. Welfare recipients are automatically eligible for food stamps; some of the working poor also qualify for food stamps.

Another program is General Assistance (GA), a generic term applied to the short-term relief programs operated by about two-thirds of the states. In these states the able-bodied poor, mostly single men, can collect limited cash benefits. The modest benefit levels reflect the public's attitude that the able-bodied are not deserving of public assistance. Nearly a dozen states, led by Michigan in 1991, have abolished General Assistance altogether. As Table 17.2 makes clear, General Assistance expenditures—$3.3 billion in 1992—are dwarfed by Food Stamps. Medical assistance for these beneficiaries cost the states an additional $4.8 billion in 1992.

State Variations in Welfare Policy

Individual states have considerable discretion over welfare policy under the SSI, AFDC, and Medicaid programs and total discretion in General Assistance. The result is substantial variation in benefits awarded to the needy in different states. The SSI program's benefits are the most uniform across states because the federal minimum floor—$446 per month for an individual in 1994—reduces variation.[6] SSI is also the most generous of the welfare programs, averaging about twice the AFDC payment level. States can supplement the federal minimum; all but seven states do so, often at a modest level.

AFDC benefits, in contrast, vary widely across states because the individual states determine many aspects of the program. To begin with, each state sets a need standard, a minimal level of income. In 1993 the need standard for a family of four ranged from $385 per month in Indiana to $1,988 in New Hampshire.[7] In nearly all states the need standard was below the federal poverty level. Then state legislatures decide how much of the "need" will be met by AFDC monthly payments. Only 13 states meet their own need standards; New Hampshire, for example, pays the typical family only $575. States make decisions about eligibility, such as whether to assist pregnant women, set the monthly benefit level for households of varying sizes, and decide how to count other sources of income. However, state discretion is significantly limited by federal rules; for example, since 1990 the federal government has required that states offer the AFDC-UP option so that two-parent poor households (with an unemployed parent) could receive benefits.

Table 17.3 displays the average monthly AFDC benefit per family in 1992. The payments ranged from $750 in Alaska and $639 in Hawaii to a mere $122 in Mississippi and $144 in Alabama per month. Because these families generally receive food stamps, their AFDC stipend must cover all other needs (housing, electricity, clothes, and so forth). Even taking into account differential costs of living around the country, it is clear that Mississippi and Alabama recipients are much worse off than are Alaska and Hawaii recipients. Remember though that Hawaii had the lowest proportion of its residents living in poverty (Table 17.1) and Alaska ranked very low as well. So they can afford to be more generous than Mississippi, which ranked second in poverty population, and Alabama, which ranked eleventh.

The greatest variation among the states lies in the General Assistance programs, which are entirely the province of the states. The average GA grant is much smaller than that from either SSI or AFDC, and the number of recipients is smaller. General Assistance recipients are often perceived as people who are not truly needy. During the budget crises of the early 1990s a number of states eliminated their programs, reduced the size of benefit checks, or eliminated categories of eligibility, affecting about one-third of

TABLE 17.3   AVERAGE MONTHLY AFDC PAYMENTS PER FAMILY BY STATE, 1993

Families on AFDC get different amounts of money to live on each month, depending on the state. Alaska is the most generous to its recipients, and Mississippi the least generous.

Rank	State	Payment
1	Alaska	$748
2	Hawaii	654
3	California	568
4	Connecticut	560
5	Massachusetts	549
6	New York	546
7	Vermont	543
8	Rhode Island	506
9	Minnesota	501
10	Washington	498
11	Wisconsin	460
12	Michigan	438
13	New Hampshire	433
14	Maine	404
15	Oregon	395
16	Pennsylvania	371
17	Iowa	370
18	North Dakota	365
19	New Jersey	356
20	Utah	354
21	Kansas	346
22	Wyoming	332
23	Montana	331
24	Nebraska	325

recipients nationwide.[8] For example, when Michigan ended General Assistance in 1991, 82,000 recipients were left to fend for themselves. Another 20,000 beneficiaries were shifted to an emergency assistance program.[9]

The Politics of Welfare Policy

Differences among the states in their generosity toward welfare clients can be traced to several factors. Scholars have established these patterns most clearly for the AFDC program; the SSI program varies less among states for the reasons explained above; few data are available for the GA program because it is entirely state-run. The most important determinant of generosity is the wealth of the state: Richer states pay higher benefits than poorer states. Mark Rom has calculated that for every $1,000 increase in median state income, the AFDC benefit rises $280 per year.[10] Other determinants are political: Politically competitive states tend to have higher AFDC benefits, as do states with moralistic political cultures and states with liberal ideologies. However, most scholars find that the state's wealth is the most important factor in determining generosity.[11]

TABLE 17.3   (CONTINUED)

Rank	State	Payment
25	New Mexico	$324
26	Illinois	324
27	Maryland	319
28	Colorado	319
29	Arizona	318
30	Ohio	317
31	Idaho	307
32	South Dakota	291
33	Delaware	291
34	Nevada	282
35	Florida	275
36	Virginia	262
37	Missouri	261
38	Georgia	255
39	West Virginia	246
40	Indiana	235
41	North Carolina	227
42	Kentucky	211
43	Oklahoma	197
44	Arkansas	186
45	South Carolina	184
46	Tennessee	168
47	Louisiana	164
48	Texas	159
49	Alabama	154
50	Mississippi	120

Source: U.S. Bureau of the Census, *Statistical Abstract of the United States: 1995* (Washington, D.C.: Government Printing Office, 1995), p. 388.

State policymakers also keep an eye on the level of welfare benefits in other states, especially neighboring ones. Unlike economic development, in pursuit of which states vie to give more than the next state, on welfare programs states often vie to give less. Being too generous to the poor can become a negative symbol, much like a high tax rate. For example, the governor of Wisconsin, Republican Tommy Thompson, feared that his state was becoming a "welfare magnet" for residents of Illinois. Box 17.1 discusses the reforms Thompson engineered in Wisconsin.

The scholarly research on the "welfare magnet" proposition is quite mixed. Using aggregate data, Paul Peterson and Mark Rom find evidence in support of the proposition.[12] They find that poor people move in part because states have higher welfare

---

BOX 17.1 WISCONSIN: A WELFARE POLICY LABORATORY

Under the leadership of Republican governor Tommy Thompson, the state of Wisconsin has experimented with a variety of welfare reforms, intended to prevent Wisconsin from becoming a "welfare magnet." Between 1986 and 1989 21,000 new families moved into Wisconsin and collected AFDC benefits. One-third of these families moved to Wisconsin from Illinois, with 30 percent settling in Milwaukee and the southeast corner of the state.[1] Complaints about strains on the schools, housing, and the criminal justice system caused Governor Thompson to embark on a bold series of reforms that are part of what Thompson calls "a rebirth of [state power]."[2]

Thompson's reforms are, in part, responsible for renewed interest in the states as "laboratories for democracy" in the area of welfare policy. As a response to innovations such as those in Wisconsin, Congress has considered and approved, with presidential agreement, significant changes in the way the AFDC program is administered. The most profound change involves giving block grants to the states for their welfare programs, giving the states broader latitude for experimentation. Thompson welcomes the greater flexibility, saying, "I'm totally comfortable with the states' ability to handle it."[3]

Wisconsin's experiments have emphasized the role of school and work in welfare programs, penalized childbearing, and altered the administration of child support payments. In 1989 Thompson gained approval for changes to Wisconsin's AFDC program that reduced benefits for newcomers by 25 percent and imposed a 60-day waiting period before applicants could become eligible for benefits.[4] Although this reform was struck down by the state's intermediate appellate court, in 1992 the Wisconsin Supreme Court upheld the 60-day waiting period.[5]

Two recent reforms limit eligibility for benefits under the AFDC program. The Work Not Welfare program, approved in November 1993, put time limits on AFDC eligibility. Under this program, eligibility for AFDC is limited to 2 out of 4 years, and once benefit eligibility has been exhausted, people are banned from eligibility for 3 years. In addition this program administers child support payments to custodial parents.[6] Caps on benefits for AFDC recipients were instituted under the "ABC" (AFDC Benefit Cap) program in 1994. This reform denies additional benefits to AFDC recipients for children born more than 10 months after the parent begins receiving benefits.[7]

Wisconsin's latest reform program, Pay for Performance, emphasizes the role of work in welfare. AFDC applicants have a mandatory meeting with a financial planning

benefits, although job opportunities are even more important determinants. The poor are exercising their exit option, looking for greener pastures elsewhere. The authors conclude that state policymakers adjust benefit levels with this prospect in mind. States with minimal benefits exert a downward pressure on benefits in generous states. The result is that less redistribution occurs than would occur if welfare were a national policy.

On the other hand, Russell Hanson and John Hartman, using survey data, find no evidence that poor women are attracted to states with high welfare benefits.[13] They conclude that state policymakers are unnecessarily restricting access to welfare benefits because they fear the magnetic effect.

specialist to investigate alternatives to welfare. After this meeting and before receiving benefits, applicants must engage in job training, education, and employment activities. After this, if applicants become eligible, they must continue to participate in job-related activities, and their pay is docked for non-participation.[8] Thompson's goal is cut all direct payments to able-bodied recipients by 1997.[9]

The results of Thompson's experiments are not clear. Although the welfare rolls have been reduced by 26 percent since 1987, the extent to which people have been moved off of AFDC permanently is not known, as an estimated 30 to 40 percent of applicants each year have been on AFDC before.[10] Anecdotal evidence suggests that the "welfare magnet" effect persists.[11] Furthermore, the extent to which Wisconsin should be viewed as a policy laboratory has been criticized by a number of commentators due to Wisconsin's exceptionally low unemployment rate and generally strong economy.

Still, certain lessons may be drawn from Wisconsin's experience, including the importance of training case workers and providing certain supportive services. Scholars also suggest the importance of continual experimentation with different strategies for welfare reform.[12] Such evidence, although not conclusive, fueled efforts to increase the

flexibility given to the states for AFDC administration. Through the end of the century, at least, the rest of the nation can look to Wisconsin for ways to reform welfare.

[1]James N. Baker, "Welfare Migrants Getting Cold Shoulder in Wisconsin," *Newsweek* (August 14, 1989), 23.

[2]Kevin Kelly, "Power to the States," *Business Week* (August 7, 1995), 51.

[3]*Ibid.*, 51.

[4]Dirk Johnson, "Wisconsin Weighs 2 Tier Benefit to Keep Poor from Moving In," *New York Times* (March 15, 1989), A1.

[5]"60 Day Wait for Welfare is Upheld in Wisconsin," *Chicago Tribune* (June 20, 1992), 15.

[6]Department of Health and Human Services Press Release (November 1, 1993).

[7]Department of Health and Human Services Press Release (June 24, 1994).

[8]Department of Health and Human Services Press Release (August 14, 1995).

[9]Kelly, "Power to the States," p. 53.

[10]Richard A. Melcher, "Another Dose of Tommy Thompson's Tough Love," *Business Week* (August 7, 1995), 52.

[11]Dirk Johnson, "Larger Benefits and Safer Streets Attract Chicagoans to Wisconsin," *New York Times* (May 8, 1995), A1, A8.

[12]Melcher, "Another Dose of Tommy Thompson's Tough Love," p. 52.

Welfare Reforms

In the 1980s criticism of welfare programs mounted, and by the mid-1990s a national consensus was reached that welfare programs have to change. Its critics charge that welfare, by which they mostly mean AFDC, creates dependency, promotes out-of-wedlock births, and reduces the work ethic. They assert that there is a "culture of poverty," which is learned. The norms of this culture include indifference, apathy, irresponsibility, family instability, and immediate gratification, so that when welfare recipients get money, they do not use it wisely,[14] nor do they try to get off the welfare rolls. In short, the welfare program creates more problems than it solves.

During the 1980s a number of states experimented, with federal approval, with a variety of welfare reforms that generally tried to emphasize marriage, work, and responsibility. A few states, including Wisconsin and Ohio, tried "learnfare" programs in which AFDC benefits depend on children's school attendance; benefits are cut if children miss school. Others, including New Jersey and Virginia, implemented family caps so that benefits do not increase as the family grows larger. Still others, including Illinois, Michigan, and New Jersey, instituted "workfare" programs under which benefits depend on finding work or participating in education. Finally, some states, including Wisconsin and Vermont, have placed limits on the number of years a person can receive welfare benefits. Some of these programs are experimental, several are limited to a few counties, and some have been challenged in court. Welfare reform is a dynamic area as other states are rushing to follow the lead of these pioneering states.

The first round of state welfare experiments greatly influenced subsequent federal innovation. In 1988 the National Governors' Association drafted a welfare reform proposal and presented it to the U.S. Congress. Somewhat surprisingly, the governors' ideas for reducing welfare dependency were accepted by Congress and the president in short order. While offering more extensive services (child care and transportation, for example) to AFDC recipients, the Family Support Act does require more of recipients enrolled in the JOBS program. Importantly, mothers of children over 3 are now expected to work (in a job or in community service) or to be in work training.

After a second round of state reforms in the early 1990s, the nation was poised to take yet another step. The Republican House majority proposed as part of "Contract with America" a radical redesign of welfare policy. The proposal sought to end AFDC (and numerous other programs) as entitlement programs. Instead the federal government would make block grants available to states for welfare purposes; the states would then determine, within federal rules, who would get welfare benefits.[15]

The House bill, moderated a bit by the more liberal Senate, was twice vetoed by President Clinton. But finally in August of 1996 Clinton, mindful of the upcoming presidential election and his pledge during the 1992 campaign to "end welfare as we know it," decided to sign the bill eliminating AFDC as of July 1997. The new law is expected to save $55 billion over six years primarily by restricting the number of recipients.[16] Noncitizens can no longer receive welfare benefits (including food stamps and SSI), unmarried teen mothers can receive benefits only if they stay in school and live with an adult, most adults must go to work within two years, and each family has a lifetime limit of five years on welfare. In the future, fewer people will be supported by federal welfare benefits.

Viewed from the states' perspective, the end of AFDC is a mixed blessing, though on the whole the nation's governors supported its demise. The states will have more flexibility and authority in deciding how to use federal block grant funds, and they can continue their own innovative welfare programs already in place. But they will receive less federal welfare money overall (the federal food stamp program was also cut by $27 billion and SSI eligibility was tightened), and the maintenance of these funds is contingent on the state's being able to meet ambitious federal employment goals for recipients. Those states with large number of legal and illegal immigrants will be hit hard because federal funds will be denied to noncitizens. States, in most instances, can decide if they want to replace the lost federal benefits, but then they run the risk of being "welfare magnets."

From the recipients' perspective, they will have to accept more personal responsibility because they will have to find jobs (or perform community service), and their benefits will be strictly time-limited. But these principles should sound familiar as they are the ones the states had already applied in their various reforms. We can expect more policy divergence among the states in the future as they experiment with implementing the new block grant welfare program.

Summary

The paramount social problem is poverty, a problem affecting some states more than others. Programs to combat poverty are based on either the social insurance principle or the public charity principle. Social insurance programs have better benefits and more legitimacy. State governments are more heavily involved in the means-tested programs such as AFDC, SSI, Medicaid, and GA. Benefits in these programs vary by state, depending on political and economic conditions in the state. Policymakers' fear of making their state a "welfare magnet" holds down welfare spending.

✧ HEALTH CARE POLICY

Americans commonly think of their health care system as a private system apart from the government, yet about 42 percent of the nation's health care expenditures are provided by government, primarily through the Medicare or Medicaid programs.[17] Medicare is the program that provides medical assistance to people receiving Social Security benefits. It is funded entirely by the federal government. Medicaid is the program that provides medical assistance to people on AFDC and SSI and to some of the working poor, under specified conditions. Medicaid is a joint federal and state program. Both were created during the 1960s as part of the Great Society effort.

Governments' expenditures on health care, in turn, are a significant portion of the total social welfare bill. Referring to the data in Table 17.2, the reader can deduce that the federal government spends 31 percent of its welfare dollars on the provision of health care to welfare recipients; for states, the fraction spent on furnishing health care is even higher, 58.6 percent. This fraction is high primarily because of the Medicaid program: It is the largest single welfare expenditure of state governments (see Table 17.2). Thus, health care policy is intimately tied to welfare policy.

State governments focus on many of the same problems in health care as does the federal government. One is the problem of access to health care. Typically access has involved providing health care to the poor: Even with the Medicaid program, only about 42 percent of the poor are covered.[18] But today access also means helping the uninsured, whether poor or not, obtain health insurance: 43.4 million are uninsured.[19] This constitutes about 18.7 percent of the population under 65. The proportion of uninsured varies by state: In 1993 Oklahoma and Louisiana were the highest, with 27.4 and 27.0 percent, respectively.[20] The smallest percentage is in Wisconsin, with 10.0 percent uninsured. Some states have tried to address the access problem through comprehensive reforms or through subsidizing coverage for low-income people.

The second problem is cost, which makes the problem of access more difficult: Since 1980 health care spending has grown annually by 10.5 percent, well above inflation in the rest of the economy.[21] State governments have attacked this problem through regulation. Third is the problem of quality of life, which includes both prevention of disease and quality of medical care when we get sick. State governments have long been involved in prevention through their public health programs, and some have begun new efforts such as attacking smoking. In addition, state governments affect the quality of medical care through regulation.

We consider three topics below: state governments' involvement in providing health care to individuals, the regulation of health care providers and insurers, and public health and prevention programs.

Medicaid

Medicaid is a federal-state entitlement program in which the federal government establishes certain guidelines for coverage and eligibility, and the state governments design and administer the program. The two levels of governments split the cost based on the federal matching formula; the federal share ranges from 50 percent to 83 percent, depending on state per-capita income. The significance of the entitlement nature of the program is that every eligible recipient is entitled to the range of medical services previously agreed-to. This means that governments cannot predict precisely how much they will have to spend on Medicaid each year, nor can they cut off recipients or reduce services in a budget crunch. Medicaid patients select their own doctors and hospitals and use their services, and then the provider applies for reimbursement. Therefore, total Medicaid expenditures depend heavily on the fees charged by doctors and hospitals in the private sector as well as on the number of recipients and how sick they are.

Originally Medicaid was for people on the welfare rolls; states must include people on the AFDC and SSI rolls in their Medicaid program. But Congress has steadily directed the states to add other low-income groups, especially poor children and pregnant women. These requirements are a prime example of the unfunded mandates governors are so irked about. In addition, states have the option of adding "medically needy" people to the Medicaid rolls. This category includes people who would be poor if they paid their medical bills. A prominent example is senior citizens who have exhausted their Medicare benefits and who can't pay their medical bills. The federal matching formula applies to both sets of clients—mandated and optional—so that the state has an incentive to expand eligibility so as to capture federal dollars.

The federal government also requires states to offer recipients a certain set of basic benefits, which are broader than those offered under Medicare (they include prescription drugs and home health care, for example) and which the states can supplement. The states decide on the rate of reimbursement to hospitals and physicians, although some federal guidelines affect that rate.[22] The federal matching formula again applies to both the mandated and the optional services states provide, so states find it cheaper to participate in the Medicaid program than to go it alone.

Medicaid expenditures, as noted in Table 17.2, dwarf both SSI and AFDC; moreover, medical expenditures have been growing at a faster rate than other kinds of state expenditures, increasing 16.7 percent in 1991 and 19.6 percent in 1992.[23] The explosive rate of growth leads some to call Medicaid the "Pac Man" of state government because it gobbles up everything in its path.[24] In 1994 Medicaid accounted for 19.4 percent of total state spending.[25] The types of recipients using Medicaid services are part of the explanation for growth: In 1992, 37 percent of Medicaid payments went to the blind and disabled, 32 percent to the elderly, and only 27 percent to AFDC recipients.[26] The disabled portion of the caseload has been growing, the elderly portion exists because of the inadequacies of Medicare, and the AFDC share has been relatively stable. In addition, federal mandates and the recession of the early 1990s enlarged the Medicaid-eligible population, and inflation in the health care industry added to the bill.

Just as states vary in their cash welfare benefits, they also vary in their Medicaid benefit levels and coverage generosity. For example, Connecticut spent an average of $21,494 per elderly enrollee whereas New Mexico spent only $4,588 per elderly recipient.[27] A handful of scholars have analyzed these differences and found that both political and economic factors influence states' Medicaid generosity. Among the significant political factors are the strength of interest groups (particularly provider groups such as those representing hospitals and nursing homes), political culture (with moralistic cultures being the most generous), political party control, and the race of the recipients (as the proportion of whites increases, generosity increases).[28] State per-capita income also positively affects Medicaid payments.

General Assistance Medical

Associated with their General Assistance welfare programs, many states also offer medical assistance to indigents who do not qualify for SSI or AFDC. Looking back at Table 17.2, we see that states spent more on GA medical assistance than on its cash benefits, $4.8 billion in 1992. At least 35 states provide some type of medical assistance to this population; four more states have programs restricted to indigent children.[29] Very little study has been done of these programs.

Health Care Reform

Given these cost pressures, governors and legislators, and now the U.S. Congress, have been interested in reforming Medicaid in order to reduce its costs. States have focused their efforts on managed care and rationing of benefits. At least nine states have received approval from the federal government to steer significant numbers of Medicaid patients into managed care organizations such as HMOs and preferred provider networks. Thus far, these experiments appear to save 5–10 percent over using fee-for-service doctors. Perhaps as important, capitated or managed care provides states some predictability in budgeting, which traditional reimbursement for services rendered does not provide. Tennessee, Michigan, Hawaii, Kentucky, Arizona, Minnesota, and Florida are among the leading states trying this approach.

Oregon has taken another tack, rationing benefits to Medicaid recipients. It ranked 709 medical procedures in order of importance and effectiveness and can afford to reimburse the top 587 of them. Among the conditions not covered are the common cold, diaper rash, food allergies, and conditions with low survival rates such as end-stage HIV disease and extremely low birth weight.[30] With the money saved, the state can expand its Medicaid program to cover everyone below the poverty line regardless of welfare eligibility. Initially the Bush administration rejected this proposal but the Clinton administration later approved it.

The federal government may speed up Medicaid cost-containment efforts if a pending proposal passes Congress. The plan is similar to that for AFDC: Convert Medicaid into a block grant and cut the total funds by over $180 billion between 1995 and 2002. Although governors would welcome a loosening of federal mandates in the current program, the loss of funds would be difficult to deal with. Also depending on how Congress sets up the funding formula, some states would lose more than others.

Discouraged by their progress on Medicaid and growing numbers of uninsured, in the 1990s states turned to more fundamental reforms of their health care systems. By 1994, 49 of the 50 states (excepting Nevada) had established an access commission, task force, or

---

BOX 17.2 HEALTH CARE HAWAIIAN STYLE

As the first state to enact universal health care coverage, Hawaii stands out among the 50 states as a health care innovator. Because Hawaii enacted this program before passage of federal ERISA law, Hawaii has had more latitude in the construction of its health care plan, particularly regarding the use of employer mandates. Hawaii's health care initiatives have been successful and have come at relatively small cost. The number of uninsured Hawaiians has declined from nearly 12 percent in 1971 to under 4 percent in 1993.[1] Despite this reduction in the ranks of the uninsured, small business has not been adversely affected, even though nearly 97 percent of employers in Hawaii have fewer than 100 employees.[2] Some have attributed the relative ease of achieving universal coverage in the state to the general overall longevity and good health of its residents, the high physician-to-population ratio, and the fact that the state's top three employers—tourism, government, and agriculture—are not generally as injurious to health as other industries.[3] Still, the record of continuous improvements to the provision of universal health in Hawaii makes it worthy of careful attention.

At the core of Hawaii's health care system is its 1974 Prepaid Health Care Act. This legislation mandated that employers and employees equally share financing of a health care system that relies on the state's two largest health care providers for coverage. Under this law, employers must provide coverage for full-time employees (defined as those working 20 or more hours per week), but cost is shared with employees until the point where the employee's contribution exceeds 1.5 percent of his or her total wages. Only state and local governments, the self-employed, workers on commission, and seasonal workers were exempted from the provisions of this law.[4]

Intriguingly, state legislators saw this innovation as enacting what was about to become a requirement at the national level. Based on the passage of Medicaid and Medicare in 1965, and repeated federal efforts to enact universal health care coverage, Hawaii legislators tried to create a program that would put them ahead of the national agenda.[5] In actuality, Hawaii preempted not only federal, but most state efforts at health care reform by nearly 20 years.

In 1989, under the governorship of John Waihee, Hawaii created the State Health Insurance Program (SHIP). This further innovation provides subsidized insurance coverage to Hawaiians not covered by their employers' policies. SHIP attempts to insure a "gap group" who are not insured by public or private insurers, but whose incomes are

study group to contemplate health care access and cost. Florida, Hawaii, Massachusetts, Minnesota, Oregon, and Washington enacted universal health coverage, mostly during the early 1990s. But for various reasons only the Hawaii plan, which has been in effect for 20 years, is now fully operational.[31] In other states the political climate changed as new governors and legislators were elected who were unsympathetic. At the same time federal health care reform collapsed. Most states ran into financial difficulties, met strong opposition from the health care community, or failed to get relief from the federal Employment Retirement Income Security Act (ERISA) that prevents states from regulating significant areas of employee benefits. These experiences have been a sobering lesson for state health care reform and for health care reform in general. Still, the beacon of Hawaii shines; Box 17.2 describes this program, and what lessons might be learned.

low enough that they cannot afford coverage.[6] This addition to the coverage provided under the Prepaid Health Care Act emphasizes primary and preventive care in order to remain cost-effective.[7] Like the Prepaid Health Care Act, SHIP relies on Hawaii's two major health care providers, Kaiser and the Hawaiian Medical Services Association.

Hawaii has continued to enact innovative health care policy into the 1990s. In 1993 the state received a federal waiver for a program called Project Quest, which combines the state's Medicaid grant, SHIP funds, and General Assistance into one program. QUEST is, in effect, an insurance purchasing pool for Medicaid and SHIP recipients, allowing the state to obtain similarly low group rates for recipients of publicly sponsored or subsidized health insurance.[8] This program provides a standard benefits package for Medicaid and SHIP recipients and incorporates a set of modest copayments for coverage, rather than the open-ended payment scheme used under Medicaid.[9] Some commentators see Hawaii's efforts to create managed competition as an attempt to preempt the Clinton administration's efforts at reform, just as they attempted to preempt the Nixon administration in the early 1970s.[10]

When compared with the nation as a whole, Hawaii is clearly among the vanguard of health policy innovators, as evidenced by the fact that the state spends only 7.8 percent of its state product on health care, compared to a national average of 13–14 percent.[11] Given its geographical isolation and unique demographics, perhaps Hawaii's experience is not easily transferrable to other states. Still, the impact of Hawaii's effort to reform health care suggests that carefully constructed health care policy can have impressive results.

[1]"Hawaii Health Care Is Called a Model for U.S.," *New York Times* (May 19, 1993), A13.

[2]*Ibid.*

[3]Deane Neubauer, "Hawaii: The Health State," in Howard M. Leichter, ed., *Health Policy Reform in America* (Armonk, N.Y.: M.E. Sharpe, 1992), pp. 147–172.

[4]Elizabeth Buerger, "State Health-Care Reform Initiatives," *The Book of the States* (Lexington, Ky.: Council of State Governments, 1994), p. 565.

[5]Neubauer, "Hawaii: The Health State," p. 156.

[6]*Ibid.*, p. 158.

[7]*Ibid.*

[8]Deane Neubauer, "Hawaii: A Pioneer in Health System Reform," in Daniel M. Fox and John K. Iglehart, eds., *Five States That Could Not Wait: Lessons for Health Reform from Florida, Hawaii, Minnesota, Oregon and Vermont* (Cambridge: Blackwell Publishers, 1994), p. 82.

[9]*Ibid.*

[10]*Ibid.*

[11]*Ibid.*, p. 81.

Regulation of Health Care

States are significant regulators of health care: They license and regulate suppliers such as doctors, nurses, pharmacists, technicians, hospitals, and nursing homes. For example, some require that the identity of disciplined physicians be made public; others do not allow providers to refer patients to medical facilities in which they have a financial interest.

Beginning with New York in 1964, most states regulate the construction of new health facilities through the certificate-of-need process, in which a proposed hospital must prove that additional beds are needed before it can be built. This procedure is designed to prevent unnecessary construction, thereby holding down the cost of health care. States also regulate the rate structure of hospitals so as to control costs. New York, Massachusetts, California, New Jersey, and Maryland have the most extensive programs of rate-setting.[32] Most states have legislation that encourages the substitution of generic drugs, which are cheaper.

States also regulate the insurers of medical care in terms of benefits offered; for example, both New Jersey and Minnesota have mandated that insurance companies offer bone marrow transplants to victims of breast cancer; a handful of states have mandated that mental health problems be covered to the same extent as physical health problems. States regulate insurers to improve access. For example, fifteen states require some form of community rating; that is, insurers must charge policyholders the same rate for premiums regardless of a person's health status, 29 mandate portability (people must be allowed to move from one employer's plan to another without a waiting period), and half offer a risk pool to people who ordinarily can't get coverage.[33]

Public Health and Prevention

Historically, state and local governments have been responsible for public health: immunization and communicable disease control, safety of drinking water and food, public sanitation, waste disposal, environmental health, school health programs, public health nursing, mental health services, disaster relief, medical care for prisoners, and so forth. Massachusetts was the first state to establish a board (later department) of health in 1869, followed by California; by the beginning of the twentieth century the rest of the states joined them.[34] Today the health agency may be a separate department or may be lodged in an umbrella agency with several health and welfare organizations.

Cities established public health departments in the 1860s and 1870s, led by New York and Boston. Most inspected water, meat, and milk, but some offered free vaccinations for smallpox and other diseases. A few functioned as major medical research laboratories: Public health departments in Providence, Rhode Island, and New York City conducted important research on drinking water contamination and diphtheria, respectively, helping in both cases to establish the new science of bacteriology.[35] By World War II local health departments had succeeded through vigorous immunization programs in eliminating most of the infectious diseases that plagued American cities in the nineteenth century. Today, municipal public health departments are on the front lines against diseases such as tuberculosis and AIDS, and they are important in sponsoring programs of prenatal care for poor women and infant vaccination. Local health departments, however, command only about 1 percent (or roughly $8 billion in 1993) of all dollars spent on health care in the United States.[36]

State spending on health and hospitals in 1992 was $48.1 billion.[37] This function is the fourth largest expenditure of state governments, ranking slightly behind highways. Nearly half of the health expenditures are directed at maternal and child health and nutrition programs. In addition, state health departments collect vital statistics, issue birth and death certificates, do epidemiological studies, conduct research, operate laboratories, engage in public education, and screen the population for various diseases. They also get involved in the areas of environmental policy and occupational health and safety. Some health departments venture into alcohol and drug abuse, tobacco use, violence, and other societal problems that cause injury and death.

States and especially localities operate a number of public hospitals that serve the poor who have no other way to receive care. These community hospitals handle the bulk of the uncompensated care. Moreover, state universities have hospitals that also carry some of the burden of indigent care. Finally, states also operate mental institutions, though fewer since the deinstitutionalization movement began. Since the 1970s many states have moved mental patients out of institutions and asylums into community settings. Some of these patients then became homeless in the 1980s.

State governments have been particularly active in meeting the number one public health challenge: The AIDS crisis, which began in 1981. Their activities include allocating money for treatment, educating people about the disease, and regulating treatment of people with AIDS. For example, states have passed laws to find and identify those who are infected, laws to protect the privacy of those who are infected, and laws to provide treatment for those who are ill. Testing for the HIV virus, preventing discrimination against AIDS victims, doing research, and providing medical care to the victims are all state functions. The Medicaid program bears much of the brunt of the care. California and New York have been particularly innovative in their approach to the AIDS crisis.[38] They, along with Florida, have the highest rates of AIDS cases in the nation.[39]

In recent years states have become more involved in trying to prevent sickness and premature death through passing mandatory seat belt and minimum drinking age laws and restricting the sale of tobacco and alcohol. We will take tobacco use as an example of this trend because it is the largest threat to public health, estimated to be responsible for 400,000 deaths per year.[40] All but four states have some sort of restrictions on smoking in public places. Vermont and California have the most ambitious controls on smoking; California's extensive advertising campaign against smoking is funded by a tax on cigarettes. Fifteen states, including Mississippi, West Virginia, Massachusetts, Florida, and Minnesota, have filed suit against tobacco manufacturers, seeking to recover the money the state spends on the medical bills of residents with tobacco-related ailments.

Summary

State governments, along with local governments, are active in trying to provide access to health care, keep its cost affordable, and maintain high-quality services. A major focus of their efforts is the Medicaid program, which gives the poor access to medical care. But Medicaid costs have risen much faster than anyone ever predicted, leading many states to rein in expenses. A few states tried innovative comprehensive reforms but most seem doomed to fail. States continue their historic function of regulation; some are trying to achieve access and low cost through this route. At the same time states and localities continue their historic function of watching out for the public health and safety.

✦ EDUCATION

Goals in Education

Education is not like crime or even welfare, where one can look at a single data series—such as the crime rate or the poverty rate—and grasp the nature of the problem. We have by and large accomplished the goal of providing free education to the masses. Two important goals remain, however. One is the goal of ensuring equality of educational opportunity, which concerned us particularly in the 1970s. In the 1980s and 1990s we were preoccupied with a second goal: achieving quality in the classroom.

Inequality has plagued our education system. Historically, low-income people went to schools that had worse facilities and fewer educational resources, blacks went to schools that were separate and inherently unequal, the disabled did not receive education appropriate to their needs, and non–English speakers did not receive bilingual education. In other words, our school systems through the 1950s denied equal opportunities to various disadvantaged groups.

Substantial progress, often spurred by the federal government, was made in equality reforms in the 1960s and 1970s. The U.S. Congress in 1965 passed its first significant aid to education bill, the Elementary and Secondary Education Act. It provided federal money to local school districts to meet the special needs of educationally deprived children. A decade later, Congress mandated that disabled children receive free education and be mainstreamed to the greatest extent possible. The U.S. Supreme Court was equally active, rendering landmark decisions in school desegregation cases, beginning with **Brown v. Board of Education of Topeka** in 1954. The Court also changed the nature of bilingual instruction through its 1974 ruling in *Lau v. Nichols*.

In addition, state courts prodded their legislatures into actions that helped to equalize educational access. During the 1970s more than half the states reformed their school finance systems to provide more aid to low-income districts. Another spurt of school finance reform began in 1989.

In the 1980s and 1990s the goal of achieving quality in the public schools preoccupied education policymakers. Scores on nationwide standardized tests, reports of national study commissions, the views of employers, comparisons with Japan, and public opinion all indicated that the public schools were not performing adequately. The widespread perception was that students were not learning enough. In response, a nationwide educational reform movement began, with state governments leading the way.

The Local Role in Public Education

Public schools are administered in some 14,000 school districts across the nation. The number used to be much greater: At the end of World War II there were 101,000 school districts, many of which ran one-room rural schoolhouses. In the half-century since the war, tens of thousands of rural districts have been consolidated, with rural elementary schools feeding into regional high schools. Most school districts are independent units of local government supervised by elected school boards. One responsibility of these boards is to hire a school superintendent to administer the system. In a few states—New York, Maryland, Virginia, and Massachusetts, for example—the school system is an agency of municipal government rather than a separate government unit.

Although certain aspects of local education are controlled by state education departments, as we see in the next section, the tradition of local autonomy is a strong one. Thus, local boards in most states determine the choice of textbooks, the salaries of teachers, the range of extracurricular activities offered, and curricular issues such as when to start foreign language instruction and how many years of math to offer in high school.

School politics can be extremely intense. Consider the range of issues that may arise in a typical school system: The role of parent influence in school policymaking, racial balance and desegregation, the choice of curricular materials, the unionization of teachers, state-church issues such as prayer in schools, crime and drug use in the schools, and sex and AIDS education are just some of the problems that galvanize parent and teacher groups. Busing to achieve racial balance and the question of whether a school teaches Darwinian evolution exclusively or includes instruction on religious creationism are specific examples of school issues that are likely to engage a community's passions far more profoundly than most other sorts of local political conflicts.

Parent Influence   One thread that runs through much of school politics is the question of the degree of parent influence. As teachers have increasingly become unionized and as school administration has become increasingly responsive to state and federal mandates, many parents feel that they have no role in the education of their children. School professionals often believe they know how best to teach a diverse student population, carefully maintaining a value-neutral environment. Many parents, on the other hand, worry that teachers are not interested in average students or minority students and that they teach values incompatible with those taught at home or in church.

Most school districts handle these conflicts between professional school officials and amateur parents through parent-teacher associations and at meetings of the school board. Of course, election campaigns for school board members also offer an occasion for voters to hold school officials accountable. A very few school districts have tried more radical reforms. In 1969 the New York state legislature passed a law decentralizing the New York City school system into 32 neighborhood school districts, each with a locally elected school board. Although these boards are able to adapt school programs to local conditions, most authority over budgets, personnel, and programs is still retained by the central school bureaucracy. Critics argue that New York City's decentralization plan hardly increased parent influence: The boards are dominated by members and supporters of the major teachers' union.

Chicago is the setting for a more radical decentralization reform, passed by the Illinois legislature in 1989. Under this plan each of the 540 schools in the system is governed by an elected board, a majority of whose members are parents with children in the school. These boards have the authority to hire, fire, and evaluate a principal, develop a school improvement plan, work out the budget for the school using a lump sum allocated by the central Board of Education, and advise the principal on attendance and disciplinary policies. Elections to the local boards were first held October 1989.

School decentralization is no longer seen as the most effective way to increase parent influence in the schools. Some reformers look to **charter schools** to accomplish this.

Parents and teachers who are dissatisfied for some reason with the public school system may seek a charter from the local school board or the state board of education to form their own school. These charter schools are public schools that receive public tax dollars, but they are not controlled by the local school board. They must be open to all students, and they may not teach religion. But their curriculum is custom-designed by a board of teachers and parents, which also runs the charter school. A charter school may also specialize in a particular learning method, in children of a particular age, or even in a particular field, such as science and mathematics. For example, schools with Afrocentric curricula, "back-to-the basics" approaches, schools for dropouts, and Montessori schools are examples of possible charter schools. The first state to permit charter schools was Minnesota in 1991. By 1995 sixteen more states had followed Minnesota's lead.[41]

Another reform designed to increase parent influence is school choice. The idea is to give parents the right to choose their child's school rather than being assigned to a neighborhood school (or in the case of busing, a nonneighborhood school). The principle, articulated by John Chubb and Terry Moe in their influential book *Politics, Markets, and America's Schools,* is that of competition: If schools are forced to compete for students,

Many public school systems are experimenting with alternative schools that offer a distinctive choice. Some, such as the Boston school pictured here, use an Afrocentric curriculum in an effort to reach young black males. (*Source:* Akos Szilvasi/Stock, Boston)

they will work harder at being excellent.[42] Teachers will work at being more effective, curricula will be more carefully designed to encourage learning, and children will, as a result, do better.

In 1988 Minnesota was the first state to adopt statewide open enrollment in public schools (where the result would not be adverse to racial balance) and it was quickly joined by 17 other states.[43] Wisconsin is the only state to have enacted a true voucher system in which students can choose either public or nonsectarian private schools. The program is limited to low-income children in Milwaukee, and the number is capped at no more than 1.5 percent of the children in the city's public school system. The state sought to expand the program to permit children to use the vouchers in parochial schools as well, but in August 1995 the Wisconsin Supreme Court issued an injunction barring this modification on the grounds that it might violate church-state separation.

Although proponents of choice argued that children would do better if their parents were able to choose their school, the results of a four-year study of choice participants show no differences in scholastic achievement compared to public school students, controlling for class, race, and other demographic variables. However, the study does show that parents of choice participants are much more satisfied with the schools than parents whose children go to public schools.[44]

School Integration   If parent involvement in the schools is one major theme in the politics of public education, a second major theme is race. Desegregating the schools has remained one of the thorniest social problems in this century. Although progress was made for a long time, the dream of a fully integrated school system is far from reality, and it may be more distant now than it has been for many years.

From the late 1960s to the late 1980s, schools throughout the nation made steady gains toward integration. It is true that in the mid-1980s about one-third of black students still went to schools that were nearly all-black. About two-thirds of black children still attended schools that were more than half black.[45] But this was a vast improvement over earlier times. Then at some point in the late 1980s, progress toward integration stopped, and many urban school systems in particular experienced resegregation. Gary Orfield, who has tracked school desegregation trends, found that by 1993 segregation levels in American public schools were as high as they had been at any time since 1968. Two-thirds of black children were in schools that were more than half black.[46]

Several factors account for increasing segregation levels. One is that the white middle class continues to migrate out of the central cities to suburban communities. There are simply fewer and fewer white children left in the cities, even in cities that are still predominantly white. For example, although the city of Milwaukee is over 60 percent white, white children make up only 30 percent of the public school enrollment.

Another factor is the judicial retreat from busing as a means for desegregation. Urban school systems had long been barred by the U.S. Supreme Court in *Milliken v. Bradley* (1974) from seeking compulsory desegregation solutions that involved busing between the city and the surrounding autonomous suburban school districts. A number of cities nevertheless worked out voluntary busing arrangements that took white suburban students into central city **magnet schools** and bused minority children from the city to suburban schools. St. Louis, Hartford, and Milwaukee are three examples of cities that have had active cross-district busing.

Prohibited from busing children from one school district to another, many school districts in the 1970s also began intradistrict busing programs to achieve integration. In many cases these busing arrangements were ordered and supervised by the federal courts. Many of these achieved a high degree of success. Buffalo, New York, is a case in point. Under a federal court order to desegregate swiftly, the city established 22 magnet schools with special programs and extra resources. Then it announced that 30,000 students would have to be bused in order to achieve desegregation. The magnet schools were so attractive that over 25,000 students volunteered to participate in the busing program. Buffalo officials reported that test scores have risen, that several hundred children were leaving private and parochial schools each year to enroll in the public schools, and that there was no evidence of an increase in white flight.[47]

Charlotte, North Carolina is another example of a city that achieved integration through busing. In Charlotte, as in many places in the South, the school district is organized on a countywide rather than municipal basis, making it easier to involve predominantly white suburbs. This is exactly what Charlotte did, the first urban school system ordered by the federal courts to desegregate by busing. By all accounts the program was a substantial success. When President Reagan went to Charlotte in 1984 and announced that busing was a failed "social experiment that nobody wants," the local newspaper replied on its editorial page the next day, "You Were Wrong, Mr. President."[48]

By the 1990s, however, as the proportion of minority children in many urban school systems schools began to rise again, a number of cities sought to end busing. A series of decisions by the U.S. Supreme Court between 1990 and 1994, involving school desegregation in Oklahoma City, DeKalb County (Georgia), and Kansas City have made it easier for local governments to be released from desegregation orders. Despite the fact that the federal government has been a party to more than 500 court orders compelling school integration, lower federal courts have begun to back away. In Denver, for example, a federal judge ruled that the school district had made a 25-year good faith effort to desegregate but could no longer make any progress. The court released the schools from federal supervision and allowed the district to end busing.[49] Efforts to end intradistrict busing also occurred in Minneapolis, Cleveland, Pittsburgh, Seattle, Indianapolis, and Wilmington N.C., among other places.

Opponents of busing argue that returning to neighborhood schools will end white flight and even attract suburban whites back to the city, although there is no evidence that this would actually occur. Support for busing has begun to wane even within the black community. Arguing that the bulk of the burden of busing is borne by black children, some black leaders (though by no means all) are calling for resources to be put into improving the quality of the schools that black children attend rather than into the busing effort. To the degree to which efforts to achieve racial balance in the schools must rely only on intracity solutions, it seems clear that busing black children to attend schools with the few remaining white students will not be effective. Any solution will require including the predominantly white suburban schools in the metropolitan area, and voters, state legislatures, and the federal courts were not inclined at the end of the 1990s to take such steps.

State Role in Education

Financing   The state's role in education has changed dramatically. States are now the dominant financial partner and play a much larger role in shaping and overseeing educational policy than in the past. Table 17.4 displays expenditure data that reflect these changes. The state share of total public education financing increased from 34.6 percent in 1970 to 43.3 percent in 1980; 1990 brought only a slight additional increase. The local share declined in that same time period, from 47.5 percent in 1970 to 40.7 percent in 1990. The federal percentage varied over time, starting at 7.4 percent, spiking up in 1980, and then declining to its lowest level in 1990. Other private sources of funding are slightly higher than the federal contribution, especially in 1990, when they amounted to 10.1 percent.

Centralization in financing at the state level came about as a direct result of the equality reforms of the 1970s. In order to achieve redistribution from rich to poor districts, state governments had to get more involved. Also, the taxpayer revolt of the mid-1970s led to pressure to hold down local spending as did competition between the two political parties.[50] But as state spending on education increased, state policymakers' interest in controlling education also increased. Thus, the changes of the 1970s set the stage for far-reaching changes in the 1980s.

Although the states' financial share has increased over time, it still varies widely among states. In Hawaii, the state assumes all the costs of education; in New Hampshire the local districts shoulder most of the burden. The degree of state financial support is linked to state decisions about equalization among local school districts, to overall state wealth, and to long traditions of overall centralization of state services.

Control over the substance and content of education varies as well, with some states exercising very extensive control over education policies and other states leaving many areas to local discretion. Research by Fred Wirt found that state control was highest in the South, lowest in the Northeast, and intermediate in the West and Midwest.[51] He concluded that states with traditionalistic political cultures have high state control of schools whereas moralistic states have less state control (or more local autonomy).

Even more important to students is total spending per pupil by both levels of government. One notable feature is the distance between the top-spending states and the others, as displayed in Table 17.5. The states at the top (New Jersey at $9,712 and Alaska at $9,290) spent more than twice as much in 1993 as the states at the bottom (Mississippi at $3,390 and Utah at $3,218). Although money does not necessarily guarantee a good education, the absence of financial support makes it hard to offer a variety of educational programs. Various measures of educational quality may be related to spending; for

TABLE 17.4 GOVERNMENT EXPENDITURES ON ELEMENTARY AND SECONDARY EDUCATION IN CONSTANT DOLLARS
State governments are the senior partner in education spending; local governments also contribute a substantial share, and the federal government furnishes a small portion.

	1970	*1980*	*1990*
Total Expenditures (billions)	$162.0	$177.9	$242.9
Percentage federal	7.4%	9.1%	5.7%
Percentage state	34.6	43.3	43.6
Percentage local	47.5	40.3	40.7
All other	10.5	7.3	10.1

Source: U.S. Bureau of the Census, *Statistical Abstract of the United States: 1994* (Washington, D.C.: Government Printing Office, 1994), p. 154.

example, the proportion of high school graduates is correlated with the states' expenditure rankings. Indeed, as we shall see in the following, states at the bottom of the expenditure scale, particularly the southern ones, have worked hard at educational reform in an effort to improve their standing.

Perhaps as important as the interstate disparities in school expenditures are the intrastate disparities. These come about because school districts vary in taxable wealth and in tax effort; hence, students get different educations depending on whether they live in a poor district or a rich district. For example, in 1990 the state of Alaska had the greatest funding gap between districts ($13,040), followed by Massachusetts ($7,118), and New York ($6,286).[52] State courts first addressed this problem in the early 1970s, and they are still addressing it. In the landmark case *Serrano v. Priest* (1971) the California Supreme Court ruled that its school financing system discriminates against the poor. The New Jersey Supreme Court in *Robinson v. Cahill* (1973) announced another important and similar ruling. Because of lawsuits or the threat of them, about half of the states reformed their school financing systems between 1971 and 1983 so as to reduce the disparities between school districts.[53]

TABLE 17.5   PUBLIC ELEMENTARY AND SECONDARY SCHOOL EXPENDITURES BY STATE, 1993   The amount of education spending per pupil varies widely among the states, with the top state spending about three times as much as the bottom state. But spending also varies by school district within a single state.

Rank	State	Amount
1	New Jersey	$9,712
2	Alaska	9,290
3	New York	8,525
4	Connecticut	8,188
5	Pennsylvania	7,748
6	Vermont	7,172
7	Rhode Island	6,649
8	Massachusetts	6,505
9	Wisconsin	6,500
10	Maryland	6,447
11	Delaware	6,420
12	Michigan	6,402
13	Oregon	6,240
14	Maine	6,162
15	Ohio	5,963
16	Wyoming	5,932
17	Hawaii	5,806
18	West Virginia	5,689
19	Indiana	5,641
20	New Hampshire	5,619
21	Minnesota	5,572
22	Washington	5,528
23	Virginia	5,517

Unfortunately, funding inequalities between districts did not change substantially, so by the late 1980s states were again subject to lawsuits over the same issue. Since 1989 the courts in Massachusetts, Montana, Texas, New Jersey, Kentucky, and Alabama have ruled that their states' systems of school finance are unconstitutional (although some other state courts have upheld the constitutionality of their systems). As was explained in Chapter 8, state supreme courts base their interpretations on sections of their state constitutions that require education to be "efficient" or of "quality." The implementation of these rulings has been difficult, particularly in Texas where the legislature presented several funding formulae before the court finally approved the spending allocation.

The state of Michigan took a different approach in 1994 to eliminating fiscal disparities among districts; its legislature and governor eliminated the property tax as the financing mechanism. Faced with the prospect of no money to finance schools, Michigan voters agreed to raise their sales tax and devote it all to schools. This solution will necessarily

TABLE 17.5   (CONTINUED)

Rank	State	Amount
24	Kansas	$5,459
25	Montana	5,348
26	Florida	5,303
27	Iowa	5,297
28	Illinois	5,191
29	Nevada	4,976
30	Colorado	4,969
31	Nebraska	4,950
32	Kentucky	4,942
33	Texas	4,933
34	North Carolina	4,810
35	New Mexico	4,643
36	California	4,608
37	South Carolina	4,573
38	Georgia	4,544
39	Missouri	4,487
40	North Dakota	4,404
41	South Dakota	4,359
42	Louisiana	4,352
43	Arizona	4,140
44	Oklahoma	4,085
45	Tennessee	4,033
46	Idaho	4,025
47	Arkansas	3,838
48	Alabama	3,779
49	Mississippi	3,390
50	Utah	3,218

Source: U.S. Bureau of the Census, *Statistical Abstract of the United States: 1994* (Washington, D.C.: Government Printing Office, 1994), p. 168.

erase fiscal disparities because every district will get the same amount of state aid, and local districts' ability to add onto that base will be restricted.

The courts in Alabama and Kentucky have taken a still different approach; instead of focusing on intrastate disparities, they have concentrated on the adequacy of the educational outcome. They determined that poor funding produces an outcome so inferior that it violates the state constitution. They have ordered the state to set achievement standards, increase per-pupil spending, and so forth. Box 17.3 describes the outcome in Kentucky.

Litigation over the equity of school financing seems likely to go on for awhile. The battles over aid and who will finance it will be fierce because they are redistributive in nature: Taking money from richer school districts to give to poorer districts is bound to raise ire. But in the 1990s, raising expenditures across the board is also contentious because it means raising someone's taxes. When courts get involved in determining the adequacy of educational outcomes, the judgments just get more difficult.

Politics   The big news in the 1980s was the increased role of the state legislature and governor in educational policymaking. A six-state study found that individual legislators on education committees were ranked first in importance, followed by the state legislature as a whole.[54] The educational establishment—school boards, state departments of education, superintendents, principals, and teachers' organizations—is no longer the dominant player in most states. The fact that education is the largest item in states' budgets (34.6 percent) and the perception that the schools are not doing the job has attracted the interest of state legislators.

Governors, particularly those interested in economic development, saw education as the first step toward economic progress. Governors such as Lamar Alexander of Tennessee and Bill Clinton of Arkansas gained national prominence based on their championing of reform. The National Governors' Association made educational reform its top priority in the mid-1980s. Its report *A Time for Results* (1986) was influential in stimulating state reform focused on changing schools. Legislators and governors extended their interest into many different areas of educational policy as they found the general public and the business community strongly supportive of their efforts. Business groups are credited with many of the reforms of the 1980s; for example, Ross Perot played a key role in Texas school reform. In addition, the state judiciary, as already noted, plays a sporadic but important role in education policy. As some say, "Education has become too important to be left to the educators."[55]

Improving the Quality of Public Education   Perhaps the best demonstration of the shift in power from educational specialists to elected generalists is the **quality reforms** adopted by many states in the mid-1980s. These reforms were spurred in part by the 1983 report *A Nation at Risk: The Imperative for Education Reform*. This, and other studies, showed that American students do not perform as well as do students in many other countries or as well as American students of the past. The generation of students in the 1980s does not possess the competitive educational edge necessary to sustain economic leadership in the future, according to various reports.

In the mid-1980s, state legislatures adopted a series of measures designed to strengthen the educational experience. One set was aimed at students. For example, 45 states increased the number of courses required for graduation; half the states instituted minimum

BOX 17.3 OVERHAULING PUBLIC EDUCATION IN KENTUCKY

In 1989, many rural Kentucky schools were barely functioning. While schools in the Louisville area provided high-tech computer facilities for students, schools in two rural counties used maps from the 1950s and 1960s.[1] Nepotism also ran high in rural districts where school systems were often the largest employers. Some administrators hired their friends and relatives and drove away teachers who spoke out on school issues. Tax assessors underassessed or failed to assess the property needed to generate tax revenues.[2]

These problems prompted the Kentucky Supreme Court to set the stage for sweeping reform. In 1990, the court declared the overwhelming financial disparities between rich and poor school districts unconstitutional and invalidated the state's system of financing public schools. The justices also confirmed a lower court's claim that Kentucky's children were suffering from "educational malnutrition." They set a deadline for the state to formulate a plan to reform the school system.[3]

With the court's decision, Kentucky embarked upon one of the most comprehensive reforms of public education in this country's history. The overhaul emphasized both equity between schools and excellence within them. The state and local governments increased per-pupil spending by 40 percent between the 1989–90 and 1993–94 school years, from $3,079 per student to $4,291 per student. Kentucky spent over $100 million on computers and technology. Pre-schools for low-income students were opened across the state, and after-school tutoring programs were established in 800 schools.[4]

The state bureaucracy was directed to outline broad educational goals and to leave decisions about particulars such as how many minutes a student must spend in class up to the school districts.[5] In addition, the state developed a performance test to reward school districts with increased performance and punish those with decreasing performance.[6]

Results from the Kentucky reform are starting to come in and, so far, they have been mixed. Many schools now have the money to buy necessary teaching resources. The Kentucky performance tests—tests which many claim are flawed—show an increase in achievement at different grade levels. However, there has been no improvement in national test scores among high school seniors. When students in Louisville took the national Comprehensive Test of Basic Skills, test scores actually declined after the reforms.

It may still be too early to label the Kentucky project either a success or a failure. Education reform will not yield instantaneous results. As the executive director of the Prichard Committee for Academic Excellence which supports the state's reforms said, "We can't claim we've worked miracles, but we're moving forward . . . Still there's no way around the basic point that this could take twenty years to get everything in place."[7]

---

[1]Rochelle L. Stanfield, "Equity and Excellence," *National Journal* (November 23, 1991), 2860.

[2]Neal R. Peirce, "School Finance Cases May Presage Big Reforms," *National Journal* (January 13, 1990), 84.

[3]*Ibid* p. 84.

[4]Peter Applebome, "Revamped Kentucky Schools Are a Study in Pros and Cons," *New York Times* (March 24, 1996), A1.

[5]Jonathon Walters, "The Most Radical Idea in Education: Let the Schools Run It," *Governing* (January 1991), 42.

[6]Mark J. Fenster, "An Assessment of High Stakes Education Accountability: The Case of Kentucky," paper prepared for Annual Meeting of the American Political Science Association, Chicago, September 1995.

[7]Applebome, "Revamped Kentucky Schools Are a Study in Pros and Cons," pp. A1, A6.

competency tests for high school graduation; most states established minimum grade-point averages for participation in sports.[56] Texas's "no pass, no play" rule is a notable example because sports are taken very seriously in that state.

A second set of reforms was directed at teachers. Thirty-five states now require standardized tests for people entering the teaching profession, nearly half adopted some type of merit-pay incentive, and nearly all raised teachers' salaries. Merit pay is a major change in the reward structure for teachers and is often opposed by their unions. Interestingly enough, the southern states were the most active in embracing these reforms.[57] The educational quality movement was spearheaded by state policymakers—governors and legislators. The educational establishment and the local school boards had little input; indeed, sometimes they were defined as part of the problem. Thus, the transfer of power from the local to the state level that began in the 1970s had solidified by the end of the 1980s.

Finally, it must be remembered that charter schools and school choice are not simply efforts to increase parental influence in the schools but also attempts to improve quality by forcing the public schools to compete with one another and with private schools for students. The notion is that the public schools that do not improve the quality of their curriculums and teaching methods will not survive in a system in which they must compete for students and therefore tax dollars.

Summary

Achieving the goal of equality was the focus of education policy in the 1970s; achieving quality was the centerpiece of the 1980s and 1990s. As goals changed, financial and political control shifted; the states became the dominant financial partner, and governors and legislators became more interested in the substance of education policy. The most recent reforms—local and statewide school choice efforts and statewide quality measures—wrest control from professional educators and put it in the hands of parents or the market.

✧ CONCLUSION

This chapter has provided an overview of state and local policy with respect to welfare, health, and education. We can offer several broad observations about social policy. One is that the scope of state and local government policy, once fairly limited, is now extremely broad. Subnational governments play some sort of role, sometimes as the major player and sometimes as part of the supporting cast, in policies that touch everything from welfare to education to health care.

At the same time, it is striking that this broad reach of government activity is not often accompanied by great generosity. Welfare payments, for example, even in states that provide the highest support, still take recipients only part way to the poverty line income.

A third observation is that states and localities do not have the resources to deal generously with social problems, and they are inhibited in their efforts to increase spending. For one thing, there is little political support to increase spending for programs addressing poverty. Eight out of ten Americans polled say that welfare is in need of fundamental reform.[58] Efforts by subnational governments to increase spending on poverty run the risk of inducing exit to other, less generous places by middle- and upper-class taxpayers. States and localities cannot count on the federal government in the 1990s to provide any new funding as long as federal deficit reduction remains a priority.

The conclusion, then, is that the state and local welfare state in America, ranging from poverty programs to health to education, is likely to remain funded at a level short of the optimum.

✦ KEY TERMS

Brown v. Board of Education of Topeka (p. 456)
charter schools (p. 457)
feminization of poverty (p. 438)
magnet schools (p. 459)

public charity principle (p. 440)
quality reforms (p. 464)
redistribution (p. 438)
social insurance principle (p. 439)
Social Security Act of 1935 (p. 439)

✦ FOR FURTHER READING

John E. Chubb and Terry M. Moe, *Politics, Markets, and America's Schools* (Washington, D.C.: Brookings Institution, 1990). Provocative book that argues that the democratic control of schools is the cause of poor school performance. Advocates market control instead.

Howard M. Leichter, ed., *Health Policy Reform in America: Innovations from the States* (Armonk, N.Y.: M.E. Sharpe, 1992). A collection of essays about states' attempts to reform their health care systems, including Hawaii and Oregon.

Paul E. Peterson and Mark C. Rom, *Welfare Magnets: A New Case for a National Standard* (Washington, D.C.: Brookings Institution, 1990). The authors use statistical analysis and a case study of Wisconsin to show that poor people move in part because of higher welfare benefits and that state policymakers refrain from offering higher benefits due to fear of becoming magnet states.

Kevin B. Smith and Kenneth J. Meier, *The Case Against School Choice: Politics, Markets, and Fools* (Armonk, N.Y.: M.E. Sharpe, 1995). As the title makes apparent, this book attacks Chubb and Moe's advocacy of school choice.

✦ NOTES

1. U.S. Bureau of the Census CD-ROM, *Income and Poverty: 1993*. All data in this section were taken from this source.

2. Robert Albritton, "Social Services: Welfare and Health," in Virginia Gray, Herbert Jacob, and Robert Albritton, eds., *Politics in the American States*, 5th ed. (Glenview, Ill.: Scott, Foresman/Little, Brown, 1990), p. 411.

3. Jeffrey Henig, *Public Policy and Federalism* (New York: St. Martin's Press, 1985), p. 89.

4. Reported in I. A. Lewis and William Schneider, "Hard Times: The Public on Poverty," *Public Opinion*, 8 (June–July 1985), 6.

5. Committee on Ways and Means, U.S. House of Representatives, *The Green Book, 1994* (Washington, D.C.: Government Printing Office, 1994), Tables 10-26, 10-27; CD-ROM.

6. Mark Rom, "Health and Welfare in the American States: Politics and Policies," in Virginia Gray and Herbert Jacob, eds., *Politics in the American States*, 6th ed. (Washington, D.C.: CQ Press, 1996), p. 404.

7. Department of Health and Human Services, *Overview of the AFDC Program* (Washington, D.C.: Government Printing Office, 1994), CD-ROM. All data in this paragraph come from the same source.

8. Kathleen Sylvester, "The War Against the 'Able-Bodied' Poor," *Governing* (February 1992), 24.

9. William P. Browne and Kenneth VerBurg, *Michigan Politics and Government* (Lincoln: University of Nebraska Press, 1995), p. 13.

10. Rom, "Health and Welfare in the American States," p. 415.

11. The literature is voluminous but a few are classics: Richard Dawson and James Robinson, "Inter-Party Competition, Economic Variables, and Welfare Policies in the American States," *Journal of Politics* (May 1963), 265–289; Thomas R. Dye, *Politics, Economics, and the Public* (Chicago: Rand McNally, 1966); Robert D. Plotnick and Richard F. Winters, "A Politico-Economic Theory of Income Redistribution," *American Political Science Review*, 79 (June 1985), 458–473.

12. Paul E. Peterson and Mark C. Rom, *Welfare Magnets* (Washington, D.C.: Brookings Institution, 1990).

13. Russell L. Hanson and John T. Hartman, "Do Welfare Magnets Attract?" (Madison: Institute for Research on Poverty Discussion Paper, 1994), p. 26.

14. Charles Murray, *Losing Ground: American Social Policy, 1950–1980* (New York: Basic Books, 1984).

15. "Most 'Contract' Bills Progress," *Congressional Quarterly Weekly Reports* April 8, 1995, 994.

16. Robert Pear, "Clinton to Sign Welfare Bill That Ends U.S. Aid Guarantee and Gives States Broad Power," *New York Times* (August 1, 1996), A1.

17. Calculated from data in U.S. Bureau of the Census, *Statistical Abstract of the United States, 1994* (Washington, D.C.: Government Printing Office, 1994), 109.

18. Colleen M. Grogan, "Federalism and Health Care Reform," *American Behavioral Scientist*, 36 (July 1993), 745.

19. Keith Bradsher, "As 1 Million Leave Ranks of Insured, Debate Heats Up," *New York Times* (August 27, 1995), A1, A10.

20. Milt Freudenheim, "States Shelving Ambitious Plans on Health Care," *New York Times* (July 1, 1995), A14.

21. Katharine R. Levit, Helen C. Latzenby, Cathy A. Cowan, and Suzanne W. Letsch, "Health Spending by State: New Estimates for Policy Making," *Health Affairs* (Fall 1993), 9.

22. In addition, in several states the courts have forced legislatures to increase the reimbursement rates.

23. These are general fund expenditures; the increase in all fund expenditures was even steeper. Steven Gold, ed., *The Fiscal Crisis of the States* (Washington, D.C.: Georgetown University Press), p. 7.

24. Carol Weissert, "Medicaid in the 1990s: Trends, Innovations, and the Future of the 'PAC-Man' of State Budgets," *Publius*, 22, no. 3 (1992), 93–110.

25. Colette Fraley, "States Guard Their Borders as Medicaid Talks Begin," *Congressional Quarterly Weekly Reports* (June 10, 1995), 1637.

26. Calculated from data in U.S. Bureau of the Census, *Statistical Abstract, 1994*, p. 116.

27. Fraley, "States Guard Their Borders," p. 1640.

28. These findings are from Colleen Grogan, *A Political Theory to Explain the Variation in State Medicaid Policies*, Ph.D. dissertation, University of Minnesota, 1991; also see Colleen M. Grogan, "Political-Economic Factors Influencing State Medicaid Policy," *Political Research*

Quarterly, 47 (September 1994), 589–622; Charles J. Barrilleaux and Mark E. Miller, "The Political Economy of State Medicaid Policy," *American Political Science Review,* 82 (December 1988), 1089–1107; Russell L. Hanson, "Medicaid and the Politics of Redistribution," *American Journal of Political Science,* 28 (May 1984), 313–339; Robert J. Buchanan, Joseph C. Cappelleri, and Robert L. Ohsfeldt, "The Social Environment and Medicaid Expenditures: Factors Influencing the Level of State Medicaid Spending," *Public Administration Review,* 51, no. 1, (January/February 1991), 67–73.

29. Calculated from Intergovernmental Health Policy Project, *State Profiles: Health Care Reform* (Washington, D.C.: George Washington University, 1994).

30. Penelope Lemov, "Climbing Out of the Medicaid Trap," *Governing* (October 1991), 50.

31. The Minnesota plan, MinnesotaCare, is partially operational in that poor children are covered, although the expansion to adults has been put on hold.

32. Kenneth E. Thorpe, "American States and Canadian Provinces: A Comparative Analysis of Health Care Spending," in James A. Morone and Gary S. Belkin, eds., *The Politics of Health Care Reform* (Durham, N.C.: Duke University Press, 1994), pp. 405–417.

33. Colleen M. Grogan, "The Politics of Interstate Health Policy Competition and Intergovernmental Health Financing," paper presented at the annual meeting of the American Political Science Association, New York, September 1994.

34. George Pickett and John J. Hanlon, *Public Health: Administration and Practice,* 9th ed. (St. Louis: Times Mirror, 1990), p. 33.

35. Jon Teaford, *The Unheralded Triumph* (Baltimore: Johns Hopkins University Press, 1984), pp. 247–248.

36. Brenda Wilson, "Cities and Contagion," *Governing,* 6 (June 1993), 30.

37. Council of State Governments, *The Book of the States, 1994–95 Edition, Vol. 30* (Lexington, Ky.: Council of State Governments, 1994), p. 352.

38. Daniel M. Fox, "The Once and Future Payers of Last Resort: The States and AIDS," in Howard M. Leichter, ed., *Health Policy Reform in America* (Armonk, N.Y.: M.E. Sharpe, 1992), pp. 24–48.

39. U.S. Bureau of the Census, *Statistical Abstract, 1994,* p. 139.

40. Rom, "Health and Welfare in the American States," p. 427.

41. Jennifer Preston, "Trenton Senate Votes to Subsidize Charter Schools," *New York Times* (December 22, 1995), p. A1.

42. John E. Chubb and Terry M. Moe, *Politics, Markets, and America's Schools* (Washington, D.C.: Brookings Institution, 1990). Their point of view has been vigorously contested by Kevin B. Smith and Kenneth J. Meier in *The Case Against School Choice: Politics, Markets, and Fools* (Armonk, N.Y.: M.E. Sharpe, 1995).

43. Michael Mintrom, "Policy Innovation Diffusion: Exploring the State-Local Nexus," paper delivered at the annual meeting of the Midwest Political Science Association, Chicago, April 1995, p. 11. Three other states have local-level school choice experiments, the first of which was in the Alum Rock School District, near San Jose, California, in the early 1970s.

44. John Witte, Christopher Thorn, Kim Pritchard, and Michelle Claibourn, *Fourth Year Report Milwaukee Parental Choice Program* (Madison: La Follette Institute of Public Affairs, 1994).

45. Gary Orfield and Franklin Montfort, "Change in the Racial Composition and Segregation of Large School Districts, 1967–1986," a report to National School Boards Association, June 1988, p. 27.

46. Peter Applebome, "A Wave of Suits Seeks a Reversal of School Busing," *New York Times* (December 15, 1993).

47. Michael Winerip, "School Integration in Buffalo Is Hailed as a Model for U.S.," *New York Times* (May 13, 1985).

48. Tom Wicker, "Fighting the Last War," *New York Times* (June 7, 1985).

49. "Court Oversight of Denver Schools Is Ended," *New York Times* (September 13, 1995).

50. Kenneth K. Wong, "Fiscal Support for Education in American States: The 'Parity-to-Dominance' View Examined," *American Journal of Education*, 97 (August 1989), 329–357.

51. Frederick M. Wirt, "Institutionalization: Prison and School Policies," in Virginia Gray, Herbert Jacob, and Kenneth Vines, eds., *Politics in the American States*, 4th ed. (Boston: Little, Brown, 1983), pp. 306–308.

52. Dan A. Lewis and Shadd Maruna, "Education," in Virginia Gray and Herbert Jacob, eds., *Politics in the American States*, 6th ed. (Washington, D.C.: CQ Press, 1996), p. 453.

53. *Ibid.*, p. 455.

54. Douglas Mitchell, Catherine Marshall, and Frederick Wirt, "The Context of State-Level Policy Formation," *Educational Evaluation and Policy Analysis*, 8, no. 4 (1986), 351.

55. Ellen Hoffman, "The 'Education Deficit,'" *National Journal* (March 14, 1987), 621.

56. Frederick Wirt and Samuel Gove, "Education," in Gray, Jacob and Albritton, eds., *Politics in the American States*, 5th ed. 447–478.

57. Doh C. Shinn and Jack R. Van Der Slik, "The Plurality of Factors Influencing Policymaking: School Reform Legislation in the American States, 1982–84," *Policy Studies Review*, 7 (Spring 1988), 537–562.

58. See poll results reported in B. Guy Peters, *American Public Policy*, 4th ed. (Chatham, N.J.: Chatham House, 1996), p. 296.

PART SIX

THE FUTURE

STATE AND LOCAL GOVERNMENTS IN THE TWENTY-FIRST CENTURY

The genius of the American form of government lies perhaps in its capacity for measured change and adaptation. Over the course of two centuries American politics has generally been marked by a pragmatic search within the broad framework of a democratic faith and a constitutional order for the most effective institutional arrangements and relationships for governing. When the allocation of responsibilities among institutions or the division of powers between the branches of government has not worked the way we wished, we have not hesitated to make adjustments. Nowhere is this pattern more evident than in the transformation of the role and capacity of state and local government in the federal system. If the twentieth century was the story of the rise and then retrenchment of the federal government in domestic politics, then the twenty-first will surely begin as the story of the growing strength of states and cities.

Our argument in this book starts with the observation that state and local governments these days have become hotbeds of policy innovation and initiative. But not only is state activity the main engine of domestic policy invention, subnational government is also increasingly the locus of responsibility for solving a growing range of problems. Fortunately, state and local governments are much stronger, more capable, and more professional than they were a couple of decades ago. But the sheer capacity for policy invention and competent administration is not enough; states and localities must also raise the revenues to fund and administer new policies. However, states and their local governments can no longer count on steadily increasing federal aid, and therefore they are finding that they must generate their own resources.

Their capacity to raise revenues is largely a function of the health of state economies. If local industries are growing, developing new products, and finding new markets, then the resulting job growth and capital investment will generate tax revenues. Growing areas also attract ambitious and energetic migrants in search of job opportunities, thus augmenting the tax-paying population. Conversely, a declining economy means lost jobs, out-migration of workers, failing retail and service businesses, and higher burdens on state and local governments, which must help those left behind. In short, states and localities find themselves in a highly competitive world in which the prizes are people, investment, businesses, jobs, and markets.

How, then, can states and localities best manage to maximize their resources? We have suggested throughout that an important task of state and local government in this competitive environment can be understood in general terms as preventing the exit of its most productive citizens and firms (and conversely, attracting productive newcomers) and encouraging participation, or voice, both as the source of new ideas and policy innovations and as the means by which polities generate commitment or loyalty.

Granted, a good deal of the movement of individuals and capital is not affected by the different patterns of taxation and public services from state to state or city to city. Patterns of mobility are often rooted in personal needs, or they are responsive to large economic forces beyond the control of states and cities. But public officials in state and local government believe nevertheless that they can minimize the exit of productive people (and even increase their productivity), maximize the appeal of their state or community to newcomers, and at the same time develop loyalty by offering an optimally attractive package of public services and tax burdens. For most states and cities, this means achieving some sort of balancing act: After all, a strategy that opted for very low taxes might attract some people, but most would be driven away by the lack of a good road system, first-rate universities and public schools, a well-staffed police department, and adequate sewer and water facilities. Very high taxes, on the other hand, might also drive people away, even if they provided the resources for excellent services and amenities.

Our analysis in this book has proceeded by reference to this framework. We have explored the institutional components and characteristics of state and local government, and we have shown how these governments have assumed a steadily more important role in the federal system. We have also examined the fiscal resources available to subnational governments, both those provided by the federal government and those raised at home. Finally, we have explored some policy problems and solutions in which subnational governments play a major role. In all of this we have been aware that state and local politics occurs in an environment marked by the high mobility of people, firms, and capital. Thus, we have conceived state and local governance in part as a problem of competition for mobile resources.

✧ CHANGE IN STATE AND LOCAL GOVERNMENT

At the same time that we have stressed the competitive environment in which state and local governments must operate, we have also pursued the theme of change. Let us review some ways in which government and politics at the subnational level have changed in the last couple of decades.

The Changing Shape of Federalism

As the United States begins a new century, it is clear that states in particular will be playing a more active role in the business of government than at any time in their history. The process of **devolution**—that is, turning over program responsibilities of the federal government to the states—began in earnest in the Reagan presidency, but it continued in the 1990s. Congress and the presidents of both parties worked hard to shift the burdens of everything from welfare to health care to environmental protection from Washington to the states.

Take the issue of who pays for the construction of wastewater treatment plants. Beginning in 1970 grants for this purpose by the Environmental Protection Agency grew to become one of the largest federal intergovernmental aid programs in existence. With the passage of the Water Quality Act of 1987, however, the EPA began to phase out construction aid to municipalities and to phase in one-time capitalization grants to states for the purpose of establishing revolving loan funds to finance wastewater treatment facilities. Today, states completely control the financing of local treatment plants by lending money from the revolving funds to local governments for construction. The funds are replenished as localities repay the loans. This example capsulizes a growing pattern of federal disengagement from subnational affairs.

Several factors account for the shift from a Washington focus to a state focus in the federal system. The shift in the burden of responsibilities is propelled first by an ideological commitment to smaller government. President Reagan came into office declaring that "big government" was part of the problem and that solutions to America's problems lay at the grass roots. This belief was also central to the Republican "revolution" of the 1990s. When Newt Gingrich, the Republican congressperson from Georgia, led his party to victory in Congress in the 1994 elections, he did so behind the "Contract with America," an agenda to wipe away the last vestiges of the New Deal and the Great Society and to balance the federal budget.

The deficit is a related reason for the federal cutback and the reallocation of responsibility to the states. Reagan's presidency began with a combination of tax cuts and rapid increases in defense spending, producing the highest deficits in peacetime history. These deficits will continue to plague Washington into the next century. The result of spending more every year than the government takes in has been, as David Walker observes, "to dampen the ardor of policy activists in Washington [and] to curb program growth."[1] There simply isn't any money with which to build a new Great Society agenda.

Americans are more confident today that the states can handle their new responsibilities because state governments have modernized in the last quarter century. This is a development we have discussed throughout the book. It refers to the development of professional managerial and technical skills, diverse and productive fiscal tools, and strong political institutions at the state and local level of government.

A fourth factor in the rise of subnational government in the federal system stems from the effects of the U.S. Supreme Court decision in *Baker v. Carr* (1962). This was the first of the famous **reapportionment** cases in which the Court enunciated what it called the "one man, one vote" principle. The effect of the ruling was to force states to reapportion legislative districts, greatly increasing urban and suburban representation at the expense of rural strength in the state legislatures. The shift in the urban-rural balance of power, according to Richard Nathan, brought greater public pressure and support for a larger state government role in dealing with problems of urbanization.[2]

To summarize, the role of the states and their local governments in the federal arrangement has grown considerably in recent years. The focus of domestic policy initiation and invention is not the nation's capital, as it was from the Great Depression to the

Great Society, but in the 50 statehouses and the many city halls. When Americans gather in the twenty-first century to solve their collective domestic problems, it is less likely to be in Washington than in their local communities and state capitals.

Increased Functional Responsibilities and Institutional Capacity

Cities and states are simply responsible for more things these days than they used to be. Senator Dianne Feinstein (D-Cal.) reflected back on the days when she was mayor of San Francisco and how the job had changed:

> *Mayors who once worried about clean streets now have to worry about clean air, toxic wastes, controlling development, job training, teenage pregnancy, narcotics, labor relations, and of course, the economic viability of their cities.[3]*

These new concerns translate into new job titles in city government, and a cluster of new job titles often means a whole new agency or department. The tendency of subnational government to take on an increasing number of new or expanded responsibilities is much the same at the state level. The following example illustrates these increased responsibilities.

In 1980 AIDS was a little-known, exotic disease. In the space of just 15 years, however, according to the U.S. Center for Disease Control, over half a million Americans had developed AIDS and 311,381 had died of the disease.[4] Many AIDS victims are poor people; many others exhaust their medical insurance; most in the end cannot live on their own. The burden of caring for these people and educating the general public has fallen heavily on the shoulders of state and local governments, a whole new area of concern that appeared in less than the space of a decade.

By the early 1990s every state legislature had mandated the formation of some sort of AIDS advisory task force. Most states had mandated education programs in the public schools to prevent AIDS (although in 1996 there were efforts in at least a dozen states by conservative religious interest groups to eliminate such programs). Many states had actually established separate state AIDS offices. For example, New York State created a state AIDS Institute in 1983. Wisconsin began a formal state AIDS bureau in 1985. California has an Office of AIDS, and Maryland has an AIDS Administration. Some local governments have also responded: The South Florida AIDS Network, for example, is a two-county organization that contracts with community agencies to provide services to people with AIDS.

As these new agencies have been established and as their caseloads have increased, public spending on AIDS has grown. In 1986, the first year for which there are data on state spending on AIDS, the states spent a total of $27.5 million of their own money on all AIDS-related programs. Within just a few years state spending had increased to $251.8 million.[5]

The task of AIDS treatment tends to overwhelm municipal public hospitals, so many cities have been experimenting with alternative care facilities. New York City runs eight homes for homeless people with the disease, accommodating over 800 patients. Other cities support hospice facilities, contract with neighborhood clinics for treatment of people in the early stages of the disease, and manage a network of foster homes for children with AIDS.

Care and treatment are not the only concerns of state government. State legislatures have passed a multitude of AIDS-related laws, concerning confidentiality issues, job and housing discrimination, testing procedures and counseling, blood donations, AIDS in correctional facilities, criminal penalties for deliberate transmission, public education, school attendance by students with AIDS, and spousal notification.

Other examples abound of recently emerging responsibilities to which states and cities have responded. One that we have already examined is economic development. Although several states in the South established bureaus in the 1920s to attract industrial development, almost all of these poorly funded, poorly staffed agencies were abolished in the 1940s.

Today, however, all 50 states have substantial departments of economic development. Nearly half of these have been established since 1970. Most cities also created such departments only recently: Minneapolis, New Haven, and Chicago, for example, all established economic development offices in the early 1980s.

Another example of a new responsibility is environmental protection. States, which used to do little more about the environment than establish state parks and fish hatcheries and manage the state's game population, have taken the lead in addressing acid rain (New York and New Hampshire have sought to cut sulfur dioxide emissions within their borders) and passed tough hazardous waste cleanup laws. Cities have gotten into the act too: Many have implemented recycling programs and several have banned non-biodegradable containers. (Portland, Oregon, at one point had a full-time city employee to enforce the city's prohibition against styrofoam food containers in fast-food establishments. Local residents dubbed him Styro-Cop.)[6]

As the range and complexity of state and local functional responsibilities have expanded, government institutional capacities have grown and strengthened. Consider some of the recent changes at the state level: At least 40 states have written new constitutions or significantly amended their old ones since the 1960s; professionals have replaced elected officials in such positions as attorney general, state school superintendent, and secretary of state; and the office of governor has been strengthened with longer terms, the ability to serve more than one term, and the development of cabinets.

State legislatures have also become more capable and more efficient. In 1960 not one single state provided standing committees in the legislature with professional staff; by 1994, 47 states staffed legislative committees with professionals.[7] In 1960 most state legislatures met only once every two years, and most of these sessions lasted less than 2 months. Today, all but a handful of legislatures meet annually and for much longer sessions. State bureaucracies have changed also. They exhibit a greater range of specialized agencies and more professionalism among their employees.

Municipal governments, too, are more capable than they used to be. A number of cities have rewritten their charters (New York is an example) and many have increased the education and training requirements of their public employees. Compared to 20 years ago, city governments manage a wider range of technical functions, and the specialized agencies are staffed with more professionals than ever before. Perhaps the most striking indication of the increased capacity of local governments is their enthusiastic embrace of management reforms in the 1990s such as Total Quality Management (TQM). Cities that have instituted TQM believe that their agencies run more efficiently, that they are more sensitive to the citizens they serve, that city agencies are able to measure more precisely their effectiveness, and that city employees are more committed to their work and more involved as problem solvers.[8]

The Changed Demographics of Subnational Politics

It was hardly unusual that the new governor of Virginia should wish to associate himself with the distinguished roster of former governors of his state, including Thomas Jefferson and Patrick Henry, by proclaiming in his inaugural speech that "I am a son of Virginia." What was unusual, however, was that this new governor was a black man. Douglas Wilder, who assumed office in the capital of the old Confederacy in 1990, the first black to be elected to a governorship, is the grandson of slaves. His election breached one of the last remaining barriers to black political achievement and symbolizes how far the face of state and local politics has changed in a few short decades.

Politics at the state and local level in the next century will involve a greater variety of racial and ethnic groups than at any time in the twentieth century—and perhaps than at any time in our history. New arrivals from Asia, the Middle East, Eastern Europe, Central America, the Caribbean, and the old Soviet Union have swollen the immigration rolls. Many of these groups have settled in our cities: Hmong from the hills of Cambodia, Filipinos, Koreans, Cubans, Russians, Poles, mainland Chinese, and Palestinians. Any consideration of urban and state politics in the coming decades will have to factor in the influence of these groups. The new immigrant groups join minorities long present in American society but who are comparatively new participants in politics.

Many cities these days are dominated by black mayors and their electoral coalitions. The presence of black mayors in our major cities is hardly remarkable now, but a short time ago it was hard to imagine, as we saw in Chapter 11. Despite the emergence of the civil rights movement at the end of the 1950s, black political activity in the cities in those days was still heavily shaped by and subordinate to white political needs. As Hanes Walton wrote in his study of black politics:

> Each white machine had its black "submachine." A black boss was picked to secure black votes to support the white machine. The black electorate was in every instance subordinate to and manipulated by the white machine.[9]

Whether or not cities were dominated by a white political machine, black political influence, where it existed, was generally restricted exclusively to the black community and was almost never brought to bear on white interests. Blacks were even less visible in state politics than they were in their auxiliary role in urban machines. There were certainly very few black elected officials at any level of government at that time: In 1965 one count found only 280 blacks nationwide serving in state or local political office.[10]

The combined effects of the mass mobilization and leadership development that came out of the civil rights movement and the programs of the War on Poverty, the surge in black voter registration under the **Voting Rights Act of 1965,** and the rising black middle class produced minority political gains in city after city beginning in the 1970s. Today, black control of city hall and black representation in state legislatures is commonplace (see Table 18.1).

TABLE 18.1 MINORITY OFFICE-HOLDERS
Black control of city hall and black representation in
state legislatures is commonplace.

	1970	1993
Black		
U.S. and state legislators	179	561
City and county offices	715	4,819
Law enforcement and judges	213	922
Education	362	1,682
	1985	**1994**
Hispanic		
U.S. and state legislators	129	182
City and county offices	1,316	2,023
Law enforcement and judges	517	651
Education	1,185	2,412

Source: U.S. Bureau of the Census, *Statistical Abstract of the United States: 1995* (Washington, D.C.: Government Printing Office, 1995), p. 287.

Gains by other racial and ethnic minorities in state and local politics have not been as great as those made by blacks. Hispanic mayors appeared on the scene in San Antonio, Miami, and Denver in the 1980s, and Asians made their first appearance in state and local politics in Hawaii and California. One reason for the slower political development of these groups is that both are composed of many different peoples who do not necessarily find it easy to coalesce with one another for political purposes. Third- or fourth-generation Japanese Americans may feel little in common with newly arrived Southeast Asians, nor do prosperous Cuban expatriates in south Florida necessarily have much natural affinity with poor Mexican American barrio dwellers in south Texas. Another reason for the slow political emergence of these groups is that a high proportion of their members are not American citizens, many having immigrated only recently. Nevertheless, the politics of states and cities, particularly on the three coasts, will certainly be increasingly affected in the new century by the concerns of these groups as well as those of blacks and whites.

✧ AN AGENDA FOR THE TWENTY-FIRST CENTURY

It does not take much imagination to construct a domestic policy agenda as we approach the next century. Although the problems American society faces cover an enormous range, from environmental pollution to rising health care costs to rural decline to creating a fair and effective welfare system, the problems that most trouble people are either those that are all too visible on the nightly television news and in our streets or those that threaten our economic well-being.

Interestingly, both conservatives and liberals (and probably most people in between) agree on what many of the problems are. Some of the most pressing stem from the predicament of those who live in a chronic state of dire poverty and who have little hope or opportunity of ever rising. Most analysts agree that there is a circle of pathology whose elements of poverty and family disintegration interact with devastating effect. The dimensions of the challenge become concrete when one considers that in New York City alone 14,000 teenage girls bear children every year, four out of every ten children live in poverty, and more than half of all minority families are headed by single women. Nationally, fewer than half of all teenage mothers ever graduate from high school, and 70 percent of them have a second child within two years of the first. Since the advent of the American welfare system in the 1930s, responsibility for these social problems has been shared among all levels of government. In the new century, however, the major responsibility falls on states and local governments for the crime, drug use, teen pregnancy, and poor employment prospects among the very poor. Whether these subnational governments will allocate the resources necessary to attack these problems is still an open question.

Most people also agree that our education system has failed to prepare us adequately to meet the challenges of international economic competition, all the while shutting out the poorest among us from the possibility of leading productive lives. Manufacturing jobs, the route to social mobility for generations of Americans, have declined as a proportion of all jobs. They have been replaced by jobs in the service sector. Many of these are low-paying, minimum wage positions behind the counter of fast-food restaurants. Although these offer employment for the unskilled, they do not hold out the prospect of upward mobility. Other service sector jobs in the American economy, such as those in health care, finance, law, real estate, and banking, require levels of learning beyond secondary school, yet many young people from poor backgrounds never make it through high school.

Not all of the critical domestic problems involve the plight of poor people. It is also generally acknowledged that much of our infrastructure—the network of urban and state roads, sewers, highways, dams, transit systems, and water mains—must be modernized or replaced. For example, over 600 urban water systems in the United States were built before 1880 and are now past the average life expectancy of about 100 years. The result is that a city such as Boston loses half of its fresh water every day to leaky pipes. Similarly, most of the interstate highway system was built in the 1950s and 1960s; the lifetime of highway pavement is about 20 years. These water and highway systems must be replaced, and the costs are enormous. Without a modern, efficient infrastructure, the possibilities for economic growth are limited.

Not only do people across the political spectrum seem to agree on what the major problems are, but there also seems to be something of a convergence among liberals and conservatives on what certain of the solutions should be. The era of big government is over, as both President Clinton and Newt Gingrich declared. Deficit reduction poses a major barrier to the expansion of the federal government along the lines of the New Deal or the Great Society. People must take personal responsibility for their lives, although liberals and conservatives disagree somewhat about how much government ought to help them accomplish this. People on both ends of the political spectrum agree that work is preferable to welfare. Strengthening neighborhoods by encouraging community-based organizations to develop housing and businesses is another idea embraced by Republicans and Democrats alike. Although the tone of political rhetoric seems to many to be particularly harsh at the century's end, the gap between the parties on how to address the social problems concentrated in cities seems closer than at any time since the Great Depression.

We do not wish to exaggerate the degree of consensus among Democrats, Republicans, and independents. Differences remain: Should drug users be punished severely or treated in rehabilitation centers? Should day care be subsidized by government or left entirely in private hands? Are we better off putting more resources into public education or should we provide subsidies to families who wish to send their children to private schools?

Addressing these various problems at the end of twentieth century and into the next is a massive job. It is likely that most programs will be an amalgam of conservative and liberal preferences, enlisting the resources and energies of all levels of government and the private sector as well. It would be foolhardy to predict that Americans will ever completely eliminate poverty, drug abuse, street crime, or urban decay, for it is clear that we have neither the political will nor the resources to do those things. We may not even have the social technology, the know-how, to solve certain of our problems. But Americans are fortunate at least in having better state and local governments today than they did only a few decades ago. As we go about the task of trying to ameliorate the problems of life in the United States at the dawn of the new century, it is no small comfort to know that our subnational governments are more democratic, more competent, more professional, more innovative, more energetic, and even more fiscally sound than at perhaps any other time in our history.

✧ KEY TERMS

devolution (p. 474)

reapportionment (p. 475)

Voting Rights Act of 1965 (p. 478)

✧ SUGGESTED READINGS

Alan Ehrenhalt, *The Lost City: Discovering the Forgotten Virtues of Community in the Chicago of the 1950s* (New York: Basic Books, 1995). The author explores the factors that made for a sense of community half a century ago and wonders whether it can ever be recaptured.

Witold Rybczinski, *City Life* (New York: Scribner, 1995). An essay about the good and bad qualities of American cities that distinguish them from European cities.

Carl E. Van Horn, ed., *The State of the States*, 3rd ed. (Washington, D.C.: CQ Press, 1996). A collection of essays by leading observers of state politics. Highlights the profound changes that state governments have undergone.

✧ NOTES

1. David Walker, *The Rebirth of Federalism* (Chatham, N.J.: Chatham House, 1995), p. 154.

2. Richard Nathan, "The Role of the States in American Federalism," in Carl Van Horn, ed., *The State of the States* (Washington, D.C.: CQ Press, 1989).

3. Quoted in David Morgan and Robert England, *Managing Urban America*, 4th ed. (Chatham, N.J.: Chatham House, 1996), p. 379.

4. Timothy Egan, "A Surprise from a State Official: AIDS from Artificial Insemination," *New York Times*, (January 17, 1996).

5. Mona Rowe and Rita Keintz, "National Survey of State Funding for AIDS," *Intergovernmental AIDS Reports*, 2 (September–October, 1989), a publication of the George Washington University Intergovernmental Health Policy Project.

6. Timothy Egan, "A New Law Enforcer Pursues Plastic Foam," *New York Times* (May 9, 1990).

7. Council of State Governments, *Book of the States, 1994–95* (Lexington, KY: Council of State Governments, 1994), p. 155.

8. Jonathan Walters, "The Cult of Total Quality," *Governing*, 5 (May 1992), 38–44.

9. Hanes Walton, *Black Politics* (Philadelphia: Lippincott, 1972), pp. 57–58.

10. Thomas Cavanagh, "Black Political Participation," in Gerald David Jaynes and Robin Williams, Jr., eds., *A Common Destiny: Blacks and American Society* (Washington, D.C.: National Academy Press, 1989).

INDEX